A BOOK OF MIDDLE ENGLISH

A BOOK OF MIDDLE ENGLISH

SECOND EDITION

J. A. Burrow
and
Thorlac Turville-Petre

BLACKWELL
Publishers

First published 1992
Reprinted 1992, 1994, 1995
Second edition published 1996
Reprinted 1996, 1997, 1999

Blackwell Publishers Ltd
108 Cowley Road
Oxford OX4 1JF, UK

Blackwell Publishers Inc
350 Main Street
Malden, Massachusetts 02148, USA

British Library Cataloguing in Publication Data
A CIP catalogue record for this book is available from the British Library

Library of Congress Cataloging in Publication Data
Burrow, J. A. (John Anthony)
A book of Middle English/J. A. Burrow and Thorlac Turville-Petre
—2nd ed.
p. cm.
Originally published: 1992.
Includes bibliographical references
ISBN 0–631–19352–9 — ISBN 0–631–19353–7 (pbk)
1. English language – Middle English, 1100–1500 – Grammar.
2. English language – Middle English, 1100–1500 – Readers
I. Turville-Petre, Thorlac. II. Title
PE.535.B87 1996 95-22664
427'.02 – dc20 CIP

Typeset in 10 on 12pt Ehrhardt
by Joshua Associates Ltd, Oxford
Printed and bound in T. J. International Limited, Padstow, Cornwall

This book is printed on acid-free paper

Contents

PART TWO: PROSE AND VERSE TEXTS

List of Illustrations

Clerkes knoweþ wel ynow þat no synfol man doþ so wel þat he ne
myȝte do betre, noþer makeþ so good a translacyon þat
he ne myȝte make a betre.

Trevisa

Preface to the Second Edition

This book is a companion to Mitchell and Robinson's *Guide to Old English*. It contains representative pieces of English writing from the period *c.* 1150–*c.* 1400. We have included examples of romance, battle poetry, chronicle, biblical narrative, debate, dialogue, dream vision, religious and mystical prose, miracle story, fabliau, lyric poetry and drama. Although the choice of pieces has been determined by literary considerations, the general introduction concentrates on matters of language. We have attempted, in this introduction, to give readers only such information about the language as we consider essential for the proper understanding and appreciation of the texts. Since these texts exhibit many varieties of Middle English, from different periods and regions, our account is inevitably selective and somewhat simplified. For further reading on the language, and also on the history and literature of the period, the reader is referred to the Bibliography.

The headnote to each text provides a brief introduction, together with a short reading list. Annotations and Glossary are both quite full; but, for reasons of space, explanations given in notes at the foot of the page are not duplicated in the Glossary.

The new edition has been revised throughout, and includes as texts 15 and 16 a selection of poems by Chaucer. As a consequence, the Glossary has been considerably expanded, and furthermore we now provide brief etymologies there.

Our debts to earlier editors will be evident throughout. We are particularly grateful to Ronald Waldron for allowing us to use his work on the Trevisa (text 11). Hanneke Wirtjes kindly read Part One and suggested improvements. We received advice from the Custodian of Berkeley Castle, Richard Beadle, Alison McHardy, Jeremy Smith, Michael Smith, Myra Stokes, and Anthony Tuck. For help with the etymological entries in the Glossary we owe a great debt to David A. H. Evans. We are also grateful to the libraries which granted us access to their manuscripts, to Aberdeen University Press for permission to reproduce the maps on p. 17, to the many colleagues who responded to the questionnaire originally sent out by the publishers, and to several reviewers of the First Edition and to correspondents who suggested improvements. We are indebted also to Margaret Aherne for her meticulous work on the Second Edition.

J.A.B., T.T.-P.

Abbreviations

AV	Authorized Version of the Bible
Bede, *History*	*Bede's Ecclesiastical History of the English People*, ed. Bertram Colgrave and R. A. B. Mynors (Oxford, 1969)
Chaucer	References are to *The Riverside Chaucer*, ed. Larry D. Benson (Boston, 1987; Oxford, 1988)
EETS	Early English Text Society (e.s. = extra series)
Guide to Old English	Bruce Mitchell and Fred C. Robinson, *A Guide to Old English* (5th edn, Oxford, 1992)
Linguistic Atlas	A. McIntosh, M. L. Samuels and M. Benskin, *A Linguistic Atlas of Late Mediaeval English* (Aberdeen, 1986)
ME	Middle English
MED	*Middle English Dictionary*
OE	Old English
OED	*Oxford English Dictionary*
ON	Old Norse
PL	*Patrologia Latina*, ed. J.-P. Migne
Trevisa, *Properties*	*On the Properties of Things. John Trevisa's Translation of Bartholomæus Anglicus De Proprietatibus Rerum* (Oxford, 1975)
Vulgate	References are to the Douai translation of the Latin Vulgate Bible (see 11/92n.)
Whiting	B. J. Whiting and H. W. Whiting, *Proverbs, Sentences, and Proverbial Phrases from English Writings Mainly Before 1500* (Cambridge, Mass., 1968)

Abbreviations of grammatical terms are listed in the Headnote to the Glossary.

Part One

1

Introducing Middle English

1.1 THE PERIOD

The term 'Middle English' has its origins in nineteenth-century studies of the history of the English language. German philologists then divided the history into three main periods: Old (*alt-*), Middle (*mittel-*), and New or Modern (*neu-*). Middle English is commonly held to begin about 1100–50 and end about 1450–1500. Unlike periods in political history, many of which can be dated quite precisely if need be (by a change of monarch or dynasty or regime), linguistic periods can be defined only loosely. Languages change all the time in all their aspects – vocabulary, pronunciation, grammatical forms, syntax, etc. – and it is impossible to decide exactly when such changes add up to something worth calling a new period. Yet, for all this lack of precision, it seems clear that the language of a mid-twelfth-century writing such as our extract from the *Peterborough Chronicle* (text 1) differs sufficiently from Old English to count as belonging to a new period.

1.1.1 From Old to Middle English

The Old English described in our companion volume, Mitchell and Robinson's *Guide to Old English*, is based on the language of the West-Saxon kingdom as it was written in the days of King Alfred of Wessex (d. 899). It was the English of this part of the country which, in the last century before the Norman Conquest in 1066, came to be accepted as the standard written form of English. People went on talking in their own various dialects; but most of the English writings set down at this time (including most Old English poetry and prose known to us) conform to this Late West-Saxon standard language. As is usually the case with such standards, this written English owed its predominance to a political fact: the predominance of Wessex itself under King Alfred and his successors over the other old kingdoms of Anglo-Saxon England. But after 1066, Wessex became no more than one, rather remote, part of a French-speaking king's realm; and the language of Wessex accordingly lost its special status too, ending up eventually as just another form of written Middle English: 'South-Western'. This development goes a long way to explain why most writings of the twelfth century present such a different appearance from those of the tenth or eleventh. The language as spoken had, of course, changed in the interval, but the nature of our written evidence for it changed more drastically. Twelfth-century scribes, unlike their Anglo-Saxon predecessors, customarily employed whichever form of English they or their authors happened to use. Hence they represent in their writings changes which had already occurred in the spoken language of late Old English, but which had left no more than occasional traces in the writings of that period. For it is the nature of standard forms of language to be fixed and therefore conservative in the face of linguistic change.

Three features particularly distinguish Middle from Old English:

(i) A much simpler system of inflexions, especially in nouns and adjectives. A major cause of this simplification was the tendency to blur the distinction between vowel-sounds in the unstressed syllables of words, reducing most of them to /ə/, the sound heard in the unstressed, second syllable of the modern word 'China'. Since inflexional endings were regularly unstressed, this tendency obliterated many distinctions between them, e.g. between Old English *stānes* (genitive singular of the masculine noun *stān*, 'stone') and *stānas* (nominative and accusative plural). An associated change was the eventual loss in all Middle English dialects of 'grammatical gender' in nouns and adjectives, since the division of these into masculine, feminine and neuter in Old English had depended upon inflexional distinctions most of which failed to survive. (On inflexions generally, see chapter 4 below.)

(ii) Increased reliance upon word-order and prepositions to mark the relationships of words in a sentence. This change also goes along with the simplification of inflexions. In many singular nouns, for instance, Old English had distinguished the nominative (subject) form from the accusative (object) form. Where that distinction was lost, as in Middle English generally, it was only word-order that could distinguish the subject of a verb from its object. (On Middle English syntax, see chapter 5 below.)

(iii) An increasingly more 'mixed' vocabulary. English is in its origin a Germanic language. The vocabulary of Old English had relatively few words from other sources (though there were significant borrowings from the Latin of the Church). By contrast, Middle English draws heavily on French and Latin, and also on the languages of the Scandinavian settlers who had populated large areas of England (but not Wessex) in the later Anglo-Saxon period. (On Middle English vocabulary, see chapter 3 below.)

1.1.2 From Middle to Modern English

Our anthology of prose and verse is mainly confined, for purely practical reasons, to writings before 1400; but historians of the language commonly hold the Middle English period to have extended for as much as a century after that date, placing its end at about 1450–1500. This dating evidently owes a good deal to non-linguistic considerations (the coming of the Tudors in 1485, or even 'the waning of the Middle Ages'), and it is not easy to justify from a strictly linguistic point of view. But two factors may be singled out:

(i) The Great Vowel Shift. This complex set of changes in the pronunciation of English long vowels serves more than anything else to explain the differences between Chaucer's pronunciation and our own (see below, 2.2.1). Yet these changes occurred over a long period of time and were by no means complete by 1500.

(ii) The rise of Modern Standard English. The history of this familiar form of the written (not spoken) language properly begins about 1430, with the so-called 'Chancery Standard' employed by bureaucrats in Westminster and elsewhere. The advent of printing in 1473 or 1474, when William Caxton first printed a book in English, eventually served to confirm the national standing of that form of English. The Middle English period may therefore be said to have ended with the establishment of a new national written standard, just as it may be said to have begun with the disestablishment of an old one (1.1.1 above).

1.2 VARIETIES OF MIDDLE ENGLISH

The absence of a nationally recognized standard of written English in the period unfortunately presents readers of Middle English literature with problems of linguistic diversity much greater than those encountered in the reading of post-medieval texts – or indeed Old English ones. Geoffrey Chaucer complained of the 'gret diversité / In Englissh and in writyng of oure tonge' (*Troilus* 5.1793–4). This complaint makes a necessary distinction, between 'Englissh' and the 'writyng' of it. Any language spoken by many people for any length of time will naturally exhibit 'gret diversité': usage will vary from place to place, time to time, occupation to occupation, individual to individual. The function of a fixed written standard is to mask such variations in so far as they interfere with communication across barriers of place, time, etc. It is the absence of such a generally accepted standard in Middle English which leads to the 'gret diversité in *writyng* of oure tonge' observed by Chaucer.

1.2.1 Regional Dialects

The main source of diversity in written Middle English is regional and local variation. Spoken English has always been diversified in this way and still is today; but literary texts outside the Middle English period rarely exhibit any regional forms other than those represented in the written standards observed by authors, scribes or printers. By contrast, authors in the twelfth, thirteenth and fourteenth centuries generally wrote the English that they spoke – whether in London, Hereford, Peterborough, or York – and the scribes who copied their work either preserved that language or else more or less consistently substituted their own, equally local, forms.

There are several different ways of classifying the many regional varieties of Middle English. The simplest is to distinguish, as John Trevisa did in the fourteenth century, between 'Southeron, Northeron, and Myddel speche'. Modern scholars commonly make further distinctions, at least for the Southern and Midland areas, which are more fully represented in surviving texts than the Northern. Thus, in our own map (p. 7), we distinguish South-Eastern from South-Western, and West Midland from East Midland. Further refinements are of course possible; but even these bear only a rough-and-ready relation to realities. To describe a regional dialect is to specify certain features which are held to be characteristic of its vocabulary, idiom, spelling, grammatical forms, sounds, etc. But if you take such features and map them individually according to their occurrence in localizable texts, as has been done for many in the *Linguistic Atlas of Late Mediaeval English* (see Bibliography, 8.2, and map p. 17 here), two awkward facts emerge. First, an individual dialect feature – say, a locally characteristic word – will not normally be separated off from its neighbouring alternatives by a clear boundary. Second, such boundaries as can be drawn, albeit roughly, for individual features – the so-called 'isoglosses' – will not commonly coincide or bundle together with one another in such a way as to define a single firm and satisfactory dialect boundary. Rather, what one finds is a 'complex of overlapping distributions' (*Linguistic Atlas* I 4).

Something of the range of dialect variation in Middle English may be gathered from text 16a, the Reeve's Tale. Here Chaucer, himself a Londoner, imitates the speech of two students from 'fer in the north' – probably Northumberland, and therefore well north of the northernmost of our texts (no. 14). He notices three main types of feature:

Phonological: especially the Northern preservation of Old English (and Scandinavian) /a:/ in words where London English had an 'open *o*', /ɔ:/ (see 2.2.1 below). Thus: *bathe*, *twa*, *wha*, when Chaucer normally has *bothe*, *two*, *who*.

Inflexional: especially the -(*e*)*s* ending for the third person present indicative of verbs (see 4.5.2 below). Thus: *he fyndes*, *he brynges*. This Northern and North Midland form later spread south and superseded Southern *-eth*, which was Chaucer's usual form. Hence it is the students' form, not Chaucer's, which will in this case appear 'normal' to the modern reader.

Lexical: words and meanings alien to London English. Thus: the words *heythen*, 'hence', and *ille*, 'bad'; and *hope* in the sense 'expect'. Many of these are of Scandinavian origin (see 3.2 below).

The dialect areas of Middle English cannot be at all precisely mapped, as one can map a county. It remains possible, of course, to describe this or that feature as broadly characteristic of this or that area; and later sections of this introduction will touch on some regional variations in inflexions and

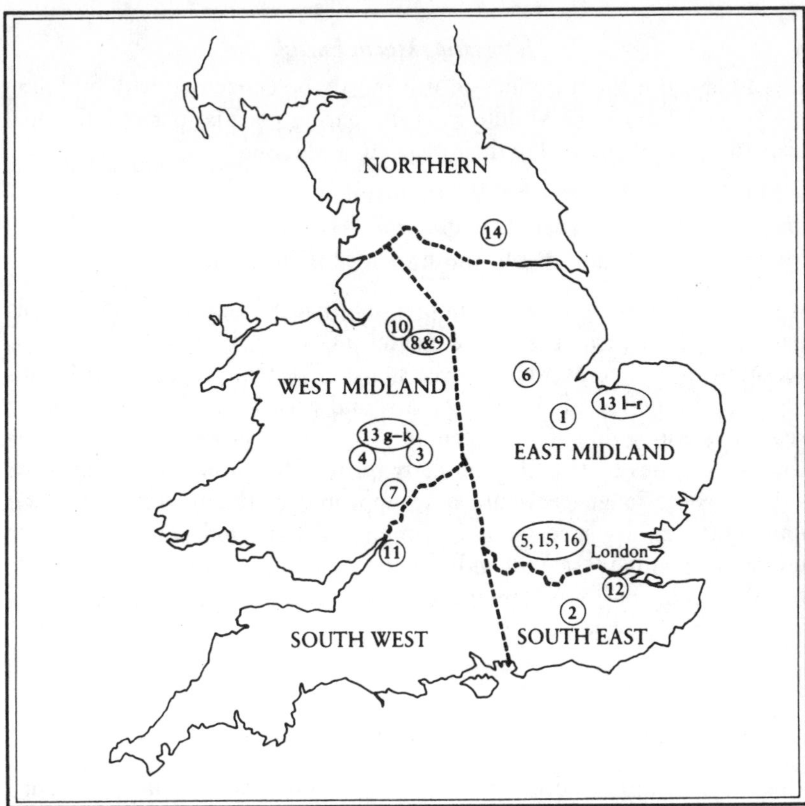

1 *The Peterborough Chronicle*
2 *The Owl and the Nightingale*
3 Laȝamon's *Brut*
4 *Ancrene Wisse*
5 *Sir Orfeo*
6 *The Cloud of Unknowing*
7 Langland: *Piers Plowman*
8 *Patience*
9 *Sir Gawain and the Green Knight*
10 *St Erkenwald*
11 Trevisa: *Dialogue between a Lord and a Clerk*
12 Gower: *Confessio Amantis*
13 Lyrics
14 The York Play of the Crucifixion
15 Chaucer: *The Parliament of Fowls*
16 Chaucer: *The Canterbury Tales*

The dialects of Middle English. The mappings of the texts are approximate. They represent the dialects of the texts as printed here from scribal copies, which may differ from the author's own regional form of English. For further details see the individual headnotes, and for comments on 'dialect boundaries' see 1.2.1.

vocabulary. But the introduction will mostly be concerned with outlining the general features of Middle English, leaving peculiarities of individual texts to be briefly treated in their respective headnotes.

1.2.2 Early and Late Middle English

It would be wrong to leave the impression that the 'gret diversité' of written Middle English is solely a matter of regional variation. There is variation over time as well as over space. The texts represented in this book span a period of about 250 years, and even in the Middle Ages 250 years was a long time. Our selection opens with a group of Early Middle English writings by twelfth- and early thirteenth-century poets and prose writers whose language would have appeared distinctly archaic to their fourteenth-century successors. Laȝamon and Langland both belonged to the same South-West Midland dialect area; but Langland would have found much that was strange in the vocabulary and inflexions of Laȝamon's *Brut*, had he known it.

1.2.3 Spelling

One further source of diversity remains to be mentioned. The absence of a national written standard means that, even where differences of spoken form are not in question, the same word may be spelled in a variety of different ways. The writing of Middle English was by no means an uncontrolled or anarchic activity; and in some cases the usage of a scribe can be shown to be quite strictly determined by a local school of practice, such as that in which the writer of *Ancrene Wisse* (text no. 4 here) was evidently trained. But the usage of such 'schools' prevailed only in specific areas and for limited periods of time; and in general one has to be prepared for a good deal of inconsistency in scribal spellings. The evidence for this may be found in our Glossary, where we have frequently had to cross-refer from one form of a word to another.

2

Pronouncing Middle English

2.1 INTRODUCTION

Although the scribes who copied our texts wrote Middle English in a variety of differing forms, their spelling generally keeps closer to the sounds of words than does that of Modern English. Modern English spelling, largely fixed by the usage of early printers, has in many words preserved letters which no longer correspond to anything in the changed spoken language – as in 'knight', for instance. Middle English spelling, being more fluid, was better able to adapt to changes in pronunciation as they occurred. None of the spelling systems represented in this book can be called 'phonetic', in the sense of having one and only one written symbol for each sound; but there are relatively few words in which a letter (like *k* in modern 'knight') has no corresponding sound in the spoken form.

It is always desirable to have some idea of how poetry should sound; but in the case of Middle English writings – prose as well as verse – there are particular reasons for trying to hear as well as see them. In an age when written copies were still relatively scarce, texts were often transmitted by reading them aloud to a listener or group: in his *Troilus*, Chaucer describes Criseyde sitting with two other ladies in her parlour listening to a maiden reading aloud from a book (*Troilus* 2.81–4). Even solitary readers commonly murmured as they read. The kind of speed-reading which leaps straight from the printed form of a word to its meaning was rarely possible in an age of manuscript, where handwritings and spellings varied from copy to copy. Hence medieval texts make bold use of effects designed to strike the ear – rhymes, alliterations, rhythmical parallels, and the like.

What follows is no more than a rough guide, to enable readers to produce or imagine approximately the right sounds. These are indicated between slashes (/ /). Where modern equivalents are given, these are drawn from standard British English (RP, 'Received Pronunciation'). For fuller accounts of Middle English phonology, see Blake (1992) and Jordan in Bibliography 8.2 below.

2.2 VOWELS

2.2.1 The Long Vowels

The main system of long vowel sounds in Middle English was as follows (a colon indicates length):

/a:/ as in modern 'father'
/ɛ:/ as in French 'bête' ('open *e*', roughly as in modern 'there')
/e:/ as in French 'thé' ('close *e*', roughly as in modern 'say')
/i:/ as in modern 'see'
/ɔ:/ roughly as in modern 'broad' ('open *o*')
/o:/ as in French 'eau' ('close *o*', roughly as in modern 'go')
/u:/ as in modern 'do'

The following Middle English words illustrate typical ways of representing these sounds:

save and *caas* (modern 'case') have /a:/
lene, *heeth* and *death* commonly have /ɛ:/
nede and *sweete* have /e:/
fine and *shyne* have /i:/
holy and *oon* (modern 'one') have /ɔ:/
foot and *mone* (modern 'moon') have /o:/
hous and *lowde* have /u:/

Three observations may be added. The long open *e*, /ɛ:/, was unstable: words such as *lene* commonly have variants with the long close vowel, /e:/. Secondly, neither the distinction between open and close long *e* nor that between open and close long *o* is regularly marked by Middle English spelling. Modern spellings are a better guide, in cases where the word survives. Thus *-ee-* and *-oo-* in modern words (e.g. 'feet', 'moon') frequently indicate a close vowel in the Middle English word. Similary, *-ea-* and *-oa-* in modern words (e.g. 'heath', 'boat') frequently indicate earlier open vowels. Finally, it should be noted that two of our early texts, nos 1 and 3, employ the Old English vowel symbol *æ* (known as 'ash'), most often for /ɛ:/, but also for /a:/.

It will be seen that in Middle English spellings the letters *a*, *e*, *i*, *o*, and *u*, when they represent long vowels, have values very different from those in Modern English. But it is Modern English which is out of line here. Middle English scribes followed Latin usage (going back to the time when Anglo-Saxon was first written in the Latin alphabet) and also, to a lesser extent, French. This is the usage which still prevails in the writing of French and other continental languages. English is now 'out of line' as a result of a series of changes which affected all the English sounds in question during the fifteenth, sixteenth and seventeenth centuries: the so-called Great Vowel Shift. Thus, Middle English /a:/ shifted to /e:/; but the words in which it occurred ('case', 'name' etc.) preserved their old *a* spelling. Similar changes affected the sounds but not the spellings of the other Middle English long vowels. So, by the eighteenth century:

/a:/ became /e:/ and later the diphthong /ei/ (modern 'name')
/ɛ:/ became either /e:/ (modern 'break') or more often /i:/ (modern 'heath')
/e:/ became /i:/ (modern 'see')
/i:/ became the diphthong /ai/ (modern 'time')
/ɔ:/ became /o:/ (modern 'boat')
/o:/ became /u:/ (modern 'moon')
/u:/ became the diphthong /au/ (modern 'house')

2.2.2 The Short Vowels

The letters *e* and *i* or *y*, where they represent short vowels in words such as Middle English *hell*, *pit* or *synne*, are to be pronounced as in Modern English. The letter *a* is always to be pronounced /a/ as in French 'patte', not as in the modern 'cat' (in Received Pronunciation). The letter *æ* (in Nos 1 and 3 only), where it represents a short vowel, signifies either /a/ or /e/. The letter *u* is always to be pronounced /u/ as in modern 'put', even in words whose modern descendants have the sound of 'cut'; but where the modern descendant has an *e* or *i* (as in 'merry' for the Western Middle English *murie*, or 'kin' for Western *kunne*), the *u* is to be pronounced as in French 'du'. The letter *o* is normally much as in Modern English 'God'; but it also acts as a spelling for /u/ in words such as *yong* or *love* (where modern usage commonly offers a guide).

2.2.3 Unstressed Final -e

In the spelling of modern words such as 'name', 'fine' and 'nice', the final letter *-e* serves to define the sound of the previous vowel and often also that of the intervening consonant. In Middle English spelling, however, it had a more straightforward function: to indicate a final *e* sound. Sometimes it represents the sound /e:/, in which case it is distinguished in this book by an acute accent (*pité*, pronounced /pite:/). But its main function was to represent the unstressed final /ə/, as in the second syllable of modern 'China'. Thus, in the poetry of Gower, a word such as *name* will have two syllables, /na:mə/, except where the final vowel is lost before a following word which begins with a vowel or some kinds of *h*- (see 6.2 below). There was, however, a tendency for /ə/ to be lost in such unstressed positions, especially in more northerly dialects. Hence the rhymes of the *Gawain*-poet indicate a northerly usage varying between pronounced and silent final *-e*: compare the rhymes in 9/176, 178 and 9/413, 415 here.

2.2.4 The Diphthongs

One may start with the assumption that, in Middle English spelling, combinations of vowel-letters such as *ai* or *au* represent (as they rarely do in modern spelling) sequences which begin with the sound indicated by the first letter and end with the sound indicated by the second. Thus, Middle English *day* was pronounced with /a/ + /i/, as a single syllable, much like modern 'die'; and Middle English *cause* has the diphthong of modern 'cow', /a/ + /u/. Similarly, *eu* or *ew* represent an *e* sound followed by /u/, which is also as it should be. But note the following:

(i) *ei* originally represented /e/ + /i/; but this diphthong developed into /a/ + /i/ in the thirteenth century. So *alwey* rhymes with *may* thereafter.

(ii) *oi* commonly represented /o/ + /i/, but also sometimes /u/ + /i/. The two diphthongs occur as alternatives in certain words, e.g. *boy*.

(iii) *ou* or *ow* represented /o/ + /u/ in such words as *foughten*; but in words now pronounced with /au/, like 'house', they represented /u:/. (See 2.2.1 above.)

(iv) *ea* and *eo* spellings do not represent diphthongs in Middle English, though they had done so in Old English. In each case, the Old English diphthong has become a single vowel sound in Middle English, while retaining the two-letter spelling. So Middle English *ea* represents /ɛ:/; and *eo* represents /e/ when short, and /e:/ when long. In Early Middle English writings of Western origin such as Laȝamon's *Brut* or *Ancrene Wisse* (texts 3 and 4 here), however, *eo* is to be pronounced like the vowel in French 'peuple' (short or long).

2.3 CONSONANTS

We have already seen how, in the post-medieval period, the spelling of vowels failed to keep pace with changes in the sounds themselves (2.2.1 above). The spoken language went on changing, but the written or printed language assumed a standardized, and therefore largely unchanging, set of forms. The result, so far as consonants are concerned, is that modern spelling persists in recording sounds which have long since ceased to be pronounced at all. Examples are the initial letters in modern 'gnaw', 'knot' and 'wring'; the final letters in 'damn' and 'comb'; and the medial letters of 'would' and (in most pronunciations) 'night'. It can safely be assumed that letters such as these are to be pronounced whenever they occur in medieval spellings. Thus, Middle English *gnawen* begins with /g/ – as one might, after all, expect.

Middle English scribes, as represented in this book, employed three consonant symbols unfamiliar to the modern reader. These are: *ð* (known as 'eth'), *þ* ('thorn'), and *ȝ* ('yogh'). Of these, the first two both represent what would now be called '*th* sounds', without distinguishing in either case between the initial sounds of 'thin' and 'this'. 'Eth' is the Latin *d* with a cross-stroke, hence *Đ* in its capital form. This went out of fashion earlier than 'thorn', a letter borrowed by Anglo-Saxon scribes from the runic alphabet. In some areas the letter *þ* became indistinguishable from *y*: hence the use of *y* for *th* in 'Ye Olde Teashoppe'. This confusion no doubt contributed to the general adoption of the two-letter spelling *th* after 1400. 'Yogh' (*ȝ*) is simply the descendant of the Anglo-Saxon letter-form for *g*, which Middle English scribes retained alongside the ancestor of the modern form of *g*. They tended to use modern *g* for the stop consonant as in 'good', reserving *ȝ* for other purposes. It corresponds to modern consonantal *y* in words such as *ȝong*, 'young', and to modern *gh* in words such as *riȝt*, 'right'. In the latter case, *ȝ* represents sounds heard in Scots 'licht' and 'loch'.

The adoption of *th* for *þ* and of *gh* for *ȝ* in later Middle English contributed to the establishment of a set of modern two-letter spellings for single consonant sounds, where *h* is regularly the second, differentiating letter. Thus: *ch*, *gh*, *sh*, *th*. This pattern not being yet established in Middle English, 'child' may be spelt *cild*, 'shall' may be *schal.*

2.4 STRESS

The main rule governing word-stress in Middle English is to place the primary stress on a word's first syllable unless that syllable is an unstressable prefix. Thus: *wíldernes*, *kíngdom*; but *uncoúþ*, *bihýnden.* Since this is also modern English practice, the reader will encounter no difficulty with most words.

Stressing on the first syllable was a general rule in Germanic languages, which therefore governed Scandinavian borrowings in Middle English as well as native words. The rule in medieval French, however, was almost the exact opposite: to stress a word on the heavy syllable closest to the *end* of the word (so not, for example, on an unstressable final /ə/). English has borrowed many words from French, and in most cases these now conform to the Germanic rule; but in Middle English such words commonly vary between French and native stressing – thus, *natúre* beside *náture.* Mossé, in his *Handbook of Middle English*, illustrates this with a line of Chaucer's: 'In dívers art and in divérse figures'.

Middle English words of two or more syllables have, more frequently than in Modern English, a secondary as well as a primary stress. Thus Gower can rhyme *lye* with *avánterìe* (12/39, 40) and *springe* with *knówlechìnge* (12/15, 16).

3
Vocabulary

3.1 INTRODUCTION

The vocabulary of Middle English is considerably more varied in its origins than that of Old English (see above, 1.1.1 (iii)). This variety has two main causes: the influence of Scandinavian languages, and the combined influences of Latin and its vernacular derivative, French. These influences operated in different ways. French or Latin words might be adopted or 'borrowed' wherever English people used those languages, which could be anywhere in the country; but Scandinavian loan-words appeared at first only in those northern and eastern regions where Danish or Norwegian was spoken. Although many such borrowings from Scandinavia eventually came into general use, they had, to begin with, a distinctively regional distribution.

3.2 SCANDINAVIAN

Scandinavian or 'Viking' raids on Anglo-Saxon England led to settlements whose southern and western limit was defined roughly by a line drawn from London to Chester in a treaty of about 886. To the north and east of this line lay the Danelaw. Large parts of this area were settled by the immigrants, as is still shown by place-names with Scandinavian elements such as '-by' and '-thorpe' (Grimsby in Lincolnshire, Milnthorpe in Cumbria). In these circumstances, Scandinavian words naturally found their way into the speech of the native English who came into contact with the settlers, and also into the speech of the settlers themselves as they came to abandon their own Danish or Norwegian and speak the language of their adopted country – a process evidently complete by the twelfth century.

Many such Scandinavian loan-words have continued throughout their career in English to be regional or 'dialect' words. Thus the borrowing from Danish, *kay* meaning 'left' (*Sir Gawain*, 9/422 here), survived as a Cheshire dialect word into modern times, but never achieved general currency. Chaucer attributes several such words to the two Northumbrian students in his Reeve's Tale (text 16a here), as part of a humorous imitation of their Northern speech: e.g. *lathe* for 'barn' (Old Norse *hlaða*). It should be remembered, however, that local users of such words, in Cheshire or

Northumberland, would not have regarded them as 'dialectal', still less have used them with any special intention of local colour – in the absence, that is, of any recognized national standard vocabulary with which they might be contrasted.

But Scandinavian influence upon English vocabulary is by no means confined to areas of the Danelaw. By a process of secondary, internal borrowing, many loan-words came to be used in other, and often in all, parts of the country. In this way such very common words as 'die', 'knife', 'law', 'skin' and 'take' early established themselves in the mainstream of English, and so formed part of the normal vocabulary of Southern writers such as Gower or Chaucer. This process of adoption continued throughout the Middle English period. Thus the word 'ill', from Old Norse *illr*, used in *Sir Gawain* (9/346), had not yet penetrated to London by 1400: Chaucer attributes it to his Northern students. The most remarkable case is that of the pronouns of the third person plural, modern 'they, their, them'. It is rare for a language to borrow pronouns from another; but in the course of the Middle English period, these Scandinavian forms in 'th-' gradually replaced native forms beginning with 'h-' (Old English *hie*, *hiera*, *him*). The first to be replaced were the nominative forms derived from Old English *hie*, which had become easily confused with the third person singular forms such as *he* or *hi*. By 1400, the Scandinavian 'they' had been adopted practically everywhere; but 'their' and 'them' are found only sporadically south of a line from the Wash to the Severn. Thus Chaucer and Gower have a mixed set: *they*, *here*, *hem*. (See map, p. 17.)

Since Scandinavian languages were a branch of that same Germanic family to which English also belonged, many of the settlers' words were similar in form and meaning to kindred ('cognate') native words. So in Middle English we find Scandinavian forms such as *kyrk* (Old Norse *kirkja*) and *gyfe* (Old Norse *gefa*) in more northerly texts (e.g. *St Erkenwald*, 10/16, 276), where southerly writers will use the equivalent native forms *chirche* (Old English *cirice*) and *yive* (Old English *giefan*).

3.3 ENGLISH, FRENCH AND LATIN

Neither English literature nor the English language, as they developed in the years 1150–1400, can be understood without appreciating that there were in England throughout this period not one but three languages in active use: English, French and Latin. Latin was especially the second (or third) language of the scholar or 'clerk', who learned it in the Grammar course which formed the first part and foundation of the common medieval school syllabus (the Seven Liberal Arts). It was spoken – since women more rarely had the opportunity of learning Latin – mostly by men: monks preaching, diplomats negotiating, philosophers disputing. It was also the common

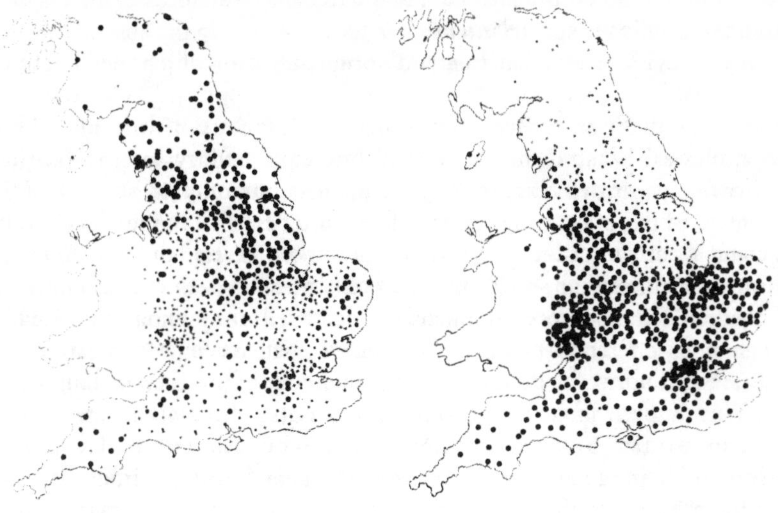

THEM: 'th-' type, all variants. THEM: 'h-' type, all forms.

These two maps, reproduced with permission from *A Linguistic Atlas of Late Mediaeval English* (see Bibliography 8.2), show the distribution of words for 'them' beginning with 'th-' (e.g. *them*, *tham*) and 'h-' (e.g. *hem*, *ham*) respectively. The grey dots mark the locality of the texts used as evidence by the *Atlas*. The black dots indicate the frequency of the forms in question in those texts where they occur: thus, the largest black dot indicates that the forms are either unrivalled or dominant there. These particular maps show that, in the period 1350–1450 covered by the *Atlas*, 'h-' forms deriving from Old English were largely confined south of a line from the Mersey to the Wash, while the Northern 'th-' forms, from Old Norse, were spreading south into that area: see 3.2 and 4.3.5.

written language of official documents, chronicles, the liturgy of the Church, theological treatises, and the like. Many native poets, too, wrote their verses in Latin. French and English were both in more general use. Norman French had been the first, maternal language of the Norman conquerors. For how long French continued to be the first language of the aristocracy and royalty of England is a matter of considerable dispute. King Henry IV (b. 1366) is said to have been the first post-Conquest English monarch whose maternal language was English. Many other English people, especially among the gentry, spoke and wrote French; but for them it was generally a second, acquired language, more or less familiar but increasingly recognized as foreign. It remained, however, an acknowledged medium of administrative, legal and polite discourse, used and understood throughout the country – though not, usually, by the common people, whose sole language was most often English. This was the language which, according to one mid-fourteenth-century writer, everyone knew, learned and ignorant alike: 'Boþe lered and lewed, olde and ȝonge, / Alle understonden English tonge' (*Speculum Vitae*).

Nowadays 'literature-in-England' forms only a small part of 'literature-in-English'; but in the period 1150–1400 the opposite was the case. Literature-in-English was only a part of literature-in-England. Three examples will illustrate this. The early thirteenth-century *Ancrene Wisse* (text 4 here) was written first in English for a community of anchoresses in Herefordshire; but it was soon translated into French and into Latin for the benefit of other readers – perhaps more noble in the one case and more learned in the other – who had devoted themselves to the religious life. Laȝamon's *Brut* (also early thirteenth-century, text 3 here) is an English version of a French poem by the Jersey poet Wace, who wrote, or so Laȝamon reports, for Eleanor of Aquitaine, wife of the English king Henry II. Wace's *Brut*, in turn, is a version of a Latin chronicle of the kings of Britain written by another subject of the English crown, Geoffrey of Monmouth, in the 1130s. John Gower's *Confessio Amantis*, written in the late fourteenth century (text 12 here), is, for all its Latin title, a poem in English; but Gower also wrote a long poem in Latin, the *Vox Clamantis*, and another in French, the *Mirour de l'Omme* – though this last effectively marked the end of Anglo-Norman literature.

Given the co-existence of these three languages, it is natural that words and idioms should have been carried over from one to another by bilingual users. Thus, French borrowed learned terms from Latin, and Latin drew on both French and English for various contemporary terms of technology, law, and the like. But English was the chief 'borrower', partly because it was for long the language of least prestige, and partly because, as it came to share and eventually take over the functions of French and later of Latin, it took over their vocabulary for the purpose.

3.4 LATIN LOAN-WORDS

Old English had already borrowed words from Latin, and in Middle English direct borrowing from Latin continued, but still on a fairly modest scale. Even such an evidently clerical work as *St Erkenwald* (text 10 here) has only four clear cases of post-Conquest Latin borrowing: the administrative terms *commit* (201) and *deputate* (227), and the ecclesiastical *martilage* ('martyrology', 154) and *pontificals* (130). In the whole of the more popular romance *Sir Orfeo* (text 5) there are none at all. Direct borrowing from the Latin becomes more extensive in the work of fourteenth-century translators of learned Latin treatises, such as John Trevisa (text 11 here); but these translators mark only the beginnings of the long process by which English was to supersede Latin as the language of learning and adopt much of its specialized terminology accordingly.

3.5 FRENCH LOAN-WORDS

Like all Romance languages, French derives from the spoken language of the Roman Empire; but medieval French also borrowed direct, in both England and France, from the Latin known to and used by the scholars of the time. Thus, the medieval French word *processioun* did not come down in the vernacular from Roman antiquity: it was borrowed from the medieval Latin *processio(nem)*. The Middle English *processioun* (5/587 here) reflects the form of the French word; but it is difficult – and unnecessary, so far as stylistic values are concerned – to distinguish between Latin and French sources in such a case. Perhaps it would be better to say that *-ion* and *-ation* words and many other similar are 'Latin-French'.

But French influence upon Middle English vocabulary was by no means confined to such rather bookish-sounding Latinate words. Consider the opening lines of *Sir Gawain and the Green Knight*:

> Siþen þe sege and þe assaut watz sesed at Troye,
> þe borȝ brittened and brent to brondez and askez . . .

All the words in the second line are of Germanic (Old English or Scandinavian) origin; but the first line turns on three French words alliterating together. *Sese* ('cease', Old French *cesser*, Latin *cessare*) is an example of a French word expressing a common idea with, in English, a certain extra politesse. *Sege* and *assaut* both belong to the language of post-Conquest warfare: a castle (French *castel*) is first besieged and then assaulted. Yet there is no strong sense of stylistic contrast between the two lines: taken together, they illustrate rather the intimate blending of the two languages. It has been calculated that, of a total of 2,650 words in this particular poem, as many as 750 are of French origin.

4

Inflexions

4.1 INTRODUCTION

4.1.1 The Inflexional System

The inflexions of a word are its changes in form to express grammatical function and meaning. Some classes of word have preserved their system of inflexion better than others in Modern English; verbs, for example, distinguish *tense*, past from present, and third *person* (e.g. 'goes') from other persons; nouns distinguish *number*, singular from plural. The inflexional system to distinguish *case* has for the most part been greatly simplified. In Modern English, distinct case-forms survive best in personal pronouns: e.g. *he*, *his*, *him*; where *he* is the subject ('nominative') form, *his* the possessive ('genitive') form, and *him* the object form, used for the direct object of verbs, the object of prepositions (as in 'with *him*'), and the indirect object of verbs (as in 'I gave *him* the book'). Old and Early Middle English pronouns commonly distinguish two object forms: the 'accusative' for the direct object of verbs (as in *hine bilæfde*, 'left him', 3/3); the 'dative' for the indirect object (as in *him is loþ*, 'is hateful to him', 2/194), and for the object of many prepositions. The distinction between accusative and dative forms is generally lost early in the Middle English period so that a single object case remains, as in Modern English.

4.1.2 Loss of Inflexional Endings

By comparison with Modern English, Old English was highly inflected. In Late Old English there was a gradual loss of distinctiveness in inflexional endings and short vowels in unstressed syllables were progressively simplified, until by the eleventh century in most dialects they had all been reduced to one, usually written *e*, and sounded as /ə/ (the final sound of Modern English 'China'). In addition, the dative ending *-um* had in Late Old English become /ən/, which in Middle English was written as *-en*. These early sound-changes had profound consequences for the system of inflexions as well as for the distinctions in grammatical gender that depended upon that system.

Two rather later sound-changes that had further effects upon inflexions were the loss in unstressed syllables of final *-n* after *-e*, and then the loss of final *-e* itself. To take as an example the infinitive of a verb: *drincan* in Old English became *drinken* in Early Middle English (as in 4/68), then *drinke*, and finally *drink*. This last stage was reached during the thirteenth century in parts of the North, and had probably extended to the whole country by the beginning of the fifteenth century, although the situation is obscured by the tendency of later scribes to add final *-e* when it was not sounded.

The process of change and simplification advanced at very different rates in the various dialects of Middle English. The earliest Middle English texts of the North and East already have a system of inflexions radically different from that of standard written Old English, while the dialects of the South and West were much less innovative, no doubt partly because they were less sharply brought up against the language of the Scandinavian settlers. These variations in the pace of development are strikingly illustrated by a comparison of the earliest of our texts, the mid-twelfth-century *Peterborough Chronicle* from the North-East Midlands (text 1), with three late twelfth- and early thirteenth-century texts from the South and from the South-West Midlands, *The Owl and the Nightingale*, Laȝamon's *Brut* and the *Ancrene Wisse* (texts 2–4). In very many respects the language of these latter works is much more conservative than that of *The Peterborough Chronicle*, and represents a transitional system undergoing a process of simplification and loss that was already well advanced in the North and East.

4.2 NOUNS

4.2.1 Introduction

The blurring of vowels in unstressed syllables had consequences that may clearly be seen in the noun inflexions. The system in Old English was complex, with differentiation possible between gender, case, and strong and weak classes. So the nominative plural of nouns might be marked by *-as*, *-u*, *-a*, *-e*, *-an* or no ending at all, and other endings distinguished one case from another. With the falling together of unstressed vowels, the whole variety of inflexional endings was reduced to *-e*, *-es*, *-en* and *-ene*. In practice only those forms ending in a consonant, *-es* and *-en*, were sharply distinctive, and therefore they were useful as grammatical markers, to indicate possession and to distinguish the plural. The ending *-es* was the marker of the genitive singular of the Old English strong masculine nouns; it was the most distinctive of all the endings in the singular, and in Middle English it became generalized to serve as the ending for the genitive of the great majority of nouns, and indeed the only singular inflexion that regularly survived. Similarly the ending *-as*, the nominative and accusative plural ending of Old English strong masculine nouns, developed into *-es* in Middle English, and in many dialects became the usual way of marking the plural. Southern dialects, on the other hand, preferred the *-en* ending of the plural, derived from the Old English weak plural ending *-an*, and extended this ending to nouns that historically had other endings, as in *shon*, 'shoes' (OE plural *scōs*), and *sunnen*, 'sins' (OE plural *synna*). These endings, either *-es* or *-en*, were then extended throughout the plural, until there was no distinction of case there.

In this way the modern system of noun inflexions was reached, with distinctions in form only between singular and plural, and between the genitive singular and the other cases of the singular. (The use of an apostrophe to mark the genitive singular and genitive plural is a written convention regularized in the eighteenth century.) The concept of grammatical 'case' had thus been all but eliminated in the nouns, and grammatical function in Middle English is instead indicated by relatively fixed word-order and the greatly increased use and variety of prepositions. A further consequence of the reduction of distinctive noun inflexions is that there is no longer any indication of grammatical gender except sometimes in the accompanying articles and pronouns. In Early Middle English grammatical gender survives to a limited extent (see 5.1 below); soon, however, natural gender takes its place; that is, the gender of pronouns and the like is determined not by the grammatical gender-class of the nouns to which they refer, but by the natural distinction between human male, human female, and non-human.

4.2.2 Noun Inflexions: Early Southern Texts

The system of noun inflexions is one of considerable variety during the Early Middle English period, particularly in the dialects of the South and the South-West Midlands (texts 2, 3 and 4 in this book). Two basic patterns may be disentangled, principally derived from (a) OE strong masculine nouns (e.g. *engel*), and (b) OE weak nouns (e.g. *nama*). The first pattern has no ending in the nominative and accusative singular, *-es* in the genitive and usually *-e* in the dative; the plural is marked by *-es*, often throughout, although the genitive plural sometimes ends in *-e* or *-ene*, and the dative plural sometimes in *-e*. The second pattern has *-e* throughout the singular, and generally *-en* throughout the plural. Note that in neither pattern is the accusative distinguished from the nominative. As typical paradigms we may set out *engel*, 'angel', as an example of the first pattern, and *nome*, 'name', as an example of the second:

		(a)	(b)
sg.	*nom./acc.*	engel	nome
	gen.	engles	nome
	dat.	engle	nome
pl.	*nom./acc.*	engles	nomen
	gen.	engles *or* engle *or* englene	nomen
	dat.	engles *or* engle	nomen

Some examples from texts 2, 3 and 4 in this book will better illustrate the wide diversity of noun-endings in these early texts:

gen. sg.	*havekes*, 'hawk's', 2/271; *Drihtenes*, 'God's', 3/23; *helle*, 'of hell', 4/34.
dat. sg.	*from þe liȝte*, 'from the light', 2/198; *to Arðure*, 'to Arthur', 3/1; *on his steden*, 'on his horse', 3/25; *in helle*, 'in hell', 4/42; but *wið ȝelp*, 'with boasting', 4/2.
nom./acc. pl.	*tide*, 'hours', 2/26 (OE pl. *tīda*); *crowe*, 'crows', 2/304 (OE *crāwan*); *wepnen*, 'weapons', 3/52 (OE *wǣpen*); *hundes*, 'dogs', 3/115 (OE *hundas*); *deoflen*, 'devils', 4/32 (OE *dēoflas*).
gen. pl.	*wise*, 'of ways', 2/20; *kingen*, 'of kings', 3/113; *Ancrene Wisse*, 'Anchoresses' Guide', 4/*title* (uninflected form *Ancre*).
dat. pl.	*mid þine clivres*, 'with your talons', 2/84; *wit his bridde*, 'with his chicks', 2/111; *smale foȝle*, 'to small birds', 2/277; *mid sweordes*, 'with swords', 3/69, and yet *mid sweoreden*, 3/143.

4.2.3 Developments in Noun Inflexions

This diversity of forms was simplified from an early date in northern and eastern parts of the country. In the mid-twelfth century *The Peterborough Chronicle* (text 1) has what is essentially the modern paradigm:

sg.	*nom./acc.*	tun
	gen.	tunes
	dat.	tun *or* tune
pl.	(*all cases*)	tunes

After prepositions the noun in the singular sometimes has the dative *-e*, but is as often uninflected, and in later texts the inflexion is dropped altogether except in a few phrases such as *of his live* (rhyming with *bilive*), 5/583, *for soþe* (rhyming with *to þe*), 9/415. The *-es* ending, often reduced to *-s*, becomes the general marker for the plural with few exceptions; the poems of the *Gawain* manuscript (represented by texts 8 and 9) have *yȝen*, 'eyes', and *oxen*. A second plural *-en* was sometimes added to *yȝen*, giving *yȝnen* (*ehnen*, 4/13); and similarly with *child*, the plural *childer* 8/388 (OE *cildru*), usual in the North, has in the South the 'double plural' form *children*, 7a/65. The genitive plural -(*e*)*ne* still occasionally appears in forms such as *lollarne*, 'of idlers', 7a/31.

4.2.4 Genitive Singular Without Ending

The genitive singular ending *-e* survives until the end of the period in nouns that were formerly of the feminine or weak declensions, as in *fole hoves*, 'hooves of the horse', 9/459, but it becomes increasingly rare. Gower has such genitive forms as *herte*, *ladi*, *soule*. The final *-e* is often dropped by later writers.

Nouns of relation ending in *-er*, such as *doughter* and *moder*, are quite commonly without ending in the genitive, as they were in Old English; examples are *fader bone*, 'father's murderer', 10/243, *fader brain*, 12/170. Proper names in Northern texts often have no genitive inflection, as in *Hengyst dawes*, 'Hengest's days', 10/8, *Adam kynde*, 'Adam's kindred', 14/62; and note *God hert*, 16a/233.

4.2.5 Unchanged Plurals

A few nouns have plurals without ending. Some are survivals of Old English neuter nouns that were unchanged in the nominative and accusative plural, such as *þing*, 5/4, *word*, 2/139, *wunder*, 1/11, and also *hors*, 5/304 and other words for animals, as *deore*, 3/117; compare the Modern English plural 'deer'. Others are terms of measure following a numeral: *þre mile*, 5/350, *fyfty syþe*, 'fifty times', 13j/46, on which see also 5.2. The plural *dede*, 'deeds', 15/82, is a late survival of the OE feminine plural *dǣda*; compare *dædes* already in the *Peterborough Chronicle*, 1/53. Words already ending in *-s* in the singular may be unchanged in the plural: *kindenes*, 'kindnesses', 6/209.

4.2.6 Mutated Plurals

Many of the Old English mutated plurals (with change of stem vowel) survive, as indeed they do in Modern English. In *The Owl and the Nightingale* the following forms are found for *man*:

sg.	*nom./acc.*	mon, man
	gen.	monnes
	dat.	men, manne
pl.	*nom./acc.*	men
	gen.	monne
	dat.	monne, manne, men

Here the mutated form *men* may be dative singular as well as plural. This survival of the Old English pattern is exceptional, and other texts have the mutated form only in the plural. The genitive plural is elsewhere usually *men(ne)s*, but note *men hacches*, 'men's kitchen-doors', 7a/29, and *bondemen barnes*, 'villeins' children', 7a/70.

Other nouns of this type are:

singular	*plural*
fot, 'foot'	fet
gos, 'goose'	ges
mous, 'mouse'	mys (mus 2/87)
toþ, 'tooth'	teþ

Broþer had the plural *breþer*, 9/39, but in the South an additional *-en* plural was often added, as in *bretherne*, 7b/217, whence Modern English 'brethren'.

4.3 PRONOUNS AND ARTICLES

4.3.1 Forms of the Personal Pronouns

The personal pronouns of *The Owl and the Nightingale* (Southern English of *c.* 1200) represent the forms derived from Old English. They are:

	singular			*plural*
	first person: 'I' and 'we'			
nom.	ich, I			we
acc.	me			us
gen.	min, mi			ure
dat.	me			us
	second person: 'thou' and 'you'			
nom.	þu			ȝe
acc.	þe			ow
gen.	þin			ower
dat.	þe			ow
	third person: 'he', 'it', 'she', 'they'			
	singular			*plural*
	masc.	*neut.*	*fem.*	
nom.	he	hit	ho, he(o), hi	hi, ho, heo
acc.	hine	hit	hi, heo	hi
gen.	his	his	hire, hore	hore, heore
dat.	him	him	hire	hom, heom

4.3.2 First and Second Person Pronouns

Forms of the first and second person pronouns survived throughout the Middle English period with little change. From an early date *ich* is often reduced to *I*, as in *I ne can ne I ne mai*, 1/33, and in some dialects *ich* is attached to a verb beginning with a vowel or *h* or *w*, as in *ichil*, 'I will', 5/132, *ichot* (*ich* + *wot*), 'I know', 13g/10. Similarly *þou* is sometimes attached to the verb it follows, in which case its consonant is assimilated into the preceding /t/ of the verb-ending: *artow* (for *art þow*), 5/421; *neltu*, 'will you not' (*ne* + *wult* + *þu*), 2/150. *Min* and *þin* are often reduced to *mi* and *þi*, but the full forms are retained before vowels and *h*: *þi reson . . . þin affeccion*, 6/24–5. The second person plural forms show only few variations in spelling in our texts (e.g. *ȝe* and *ye*, *ow* and *ȝou*, *ower* and *ȝour*). The general use of *you* as a nominative form is a development of Early Modern English, and in Middle English the distinction between the nominative *ȝe* and the accusative/dative *ow* or *ȝou* is generally well preserved. (On the usage of *þou* and *ȝe* see 5.4.1.)

The Old English 'dual' pronouns (meaning 'we two' and 'you two') survived for a short while; e.g. nominative *wit*, 'we two', 3/151, genitive *unker*, 'of us two', 2/151.

4.3.3 Third Person Pronouns: Masculine and Neuter Singular

There were minor changes in the masculine and neuter pronouns. The masculine had an unstressed nominative form *a*, 'he', as in 7b/201. The accusative *hine* was rapidly superseded by the dative form *him*; *The Peterborough Chronicle* already uses *him* as direct object, and it is universal by the fourteenth century.

In the neuter, genitive *his* was occasionally replaced by *hit* (e.g. 8/12, 10/309); the modern form *its* does not appear until the end of the sixteenth century. The dative neuter form *him* was also sometimes replaced by *hit*, but more commonly a periphrasis with 'there-' was used to avoid it altogether; e.g. *þarmid þu clackes*, 'you clack with it (your bill)', 2/81; *leyd þeron*, 'applied to it (harping)', 5/30.

4.3.4 Third Person Pronouns: Feminine Singular

The changes affecting the feminine and plural pronouns over the period were far-reaching. The forms were not sufficiently distinctive, particularly with the blurring of the quality of the vowel, and in any case varied greatly from dialect to dialect as the result of regular sound-changes. The chaotic results are illustrated above from *The Owl and the Nightingale*, where *he* may represent either 'he' or 'she', *hi* may be feminine or plural, nominative or accusative.

The distinctive nominative feminine form *she*, the origin of which is disputed, was adopted at very different times in different parts of the country. In the spelling *scæ*, it first appears in the final section of *The Peterborough Chronicle* in the mid-twelfth century, but two hundred years later the form *ho* is regularly used in the *Gawain* manuscript, side by side with occasional instances of *scho*. By the early fourteenth century, the old accusative form *hi* had been supplanted by the dative *hire*, a development that had already taken place in *The Peterborough Chronicle*, where *hire* is used as a direct object.

4.3.5 Third Person Pronouns: Plural

The forms of the plural pronoun also show major regional differences in their development. The oblique (non-subject) forms derived from Old English survived particularly well, so that Chaucer and Gower at the end of the fourteenth century use *hem*, 'them', and *here*, 'their', but *they* for the nominative. The modern plural forms are Scandinavian in origin (cf. ON *þeir*, *þeira*, *þeim*), and they are all recorded from the beginning of the thirteenth century in the East Midlands where Scandinavian influence was strong. (See map on p. 17.)

In later texts the genitive adds *-s* when it stands alone: *for hores is þe heven-ryche*, 'for theirs is the kingdom of heaven', 8/28.

The forms of the feminine and plural pronouns as they appear in the *Gawain* manuscript are set out for comparison with those of *The Owl and the Nightingale* above:

	fem. sing.	*plural* (*all genders*)
nom.	ho *or* scho	þay
acc. & dat.	hir *or* her	hem, hom *or* him
gen.	hir *or* her	hor, her *or* þayr

4.3.6 The Definite Article

The definite article 'the' had in Old English no fewer than ten different forms depending on gender, case and number, but these distinctions could not survive the decay of the system of noun inflexions, with the result that there remained only the indeclinable form *þe* (or in some dialects *te* following *-d/-t*, as in *and te*, *at te*). *Þe* is the invariable form in all texts in this book except in two early works from the South and South-West Midlands (texts 2 and 3). Forms there for the singular definite article are:

masculine:		
nom.	þe	(*þe riche mon*, 3/47)
acc.	þane, þene	(*þene hul*, 'the hill', 3/96)
gen.	þas	(*þas monnes*, 2/338)
dat.	þan, þon	(*to þan hulle*, 'to the hill', 3/87)
feminine:		
nom./acc.	þo, þa, þæ	(*þo ule*, 'the owl', 2/26)
gen./dat.	þere, þare	(*þare hule*, 'of the owl', 2/28)

The nominative and accusative neuter form is *þat*, still used as the definite article as well as the demonstrative: *þat alre worste*, 'the worst of all', 2/10.

Plural forms are:

nom./acc.	þa	(*þa Bruttes*, 3/128)
dat.	þan	(*to þan hulles*, 3/94)

In later texts there are occasional fossilized remains of an inflected form, as in the phrases *after þan*, 'after that', 5/597, and *for þe nones*, 'indeed', 5/53, 10/38, from the earlier *for þan anes.*

4.3.7 Demonstratives

As *þe* became the invariable form of the definite article, *þat*, originally its neuter form, became restricted to demonstrative use for all genders, though in early texts it is used only with singular inanimate nouns, as in *al ðat iren*, 'all that iron', 1/32–3. At first its plural is naturally that of the definite article, *þa/þo*, 'those', used for all genders: *þa men*, 'those men', 1/16–17, *of þat stering or of þoo sterynges*, 6/50.

The plural demonstrative 'these', *þās* or *þǣs* in Old English, has a range of forms in Early Middle English, as in *þos word*, 'these words', 2/139, *þeose bemeres*, 'these trumpeters', 4/8–9, *þes rikeneres*, 'these auditors', 4/46–7. In addition, a new plural *þise* was coined on the basis of the singular *þis*. Eventually two sets of forms were distinguished in sense, so that *þese* and *þise* became the forms for 'these', as in *þise gentyle kniȝtes*, 'these noble knights', 9/42, while *þase* and *þose* became the forms for 'those', as in *þose traytoures*, 8/77, and so displaced the earlier *þa/þo* as the plural of *þat*. In Northern texts only, the word for 'these' is *thir/ther* (14/145), of obscure origin.

The singular *þis* is generally undeclined, though some inflexional forms remain in Early Middle English: for example dative masculine *þissen*, 3/111, nominative feminine *þos*, 2/41.

4.3.8 The Indefinite Article

The indefinite article 'a' is an unstressed form of the Old English numeral *ān*, 'one'. In early texts its spellings are very variable, as is illustrated within the one line *An hule and one niȝtingale*, 'an owl and a nightingale', 2/4. There are also some inflected forms, such as (in text 3) masculine accusative *ænne*, dative *ane*; (in text 2) dative feminine *ore*. Even in these early texts the form is often reduced to *a* before a consonant: *a word*, 2/45.

4.4 ADJECTIVES AND ADVERBS

4.4.1 Definite and Indefinite Inflexions

Adjectives of one syllable ending in a consonant, e.g. *old*, add *-e* in the plural, and also in the singular in certain circumstances: when used with the definite article *þe*, a demonstrative adjective *þis* or *þat*, a possessive pronoun such as *hir* or *our*, or a name or other term of address. In other circumstances the adjective has no ending. This survival of the Old English definite (or 'weak') declension contrasting with the indefinite (or 'strong') declension may be observed up to the end of our period in the metre of careful writers of the South, such as Gower and Chaucer. Some examples are:

	singular		*plural*
	indefinite (without *þe*, demonstrative or possessive)	*definite* (with *þe*, *þis*, *þat*, *hire* etc.)	
Text			
1:	god man (72)	þe ilce pining (76)	gode men (73)
4:	lud dream (3)	his wide þrote (68)	sharpe word (30–1)
5:	a gret ost (290)	þe selve way (341)	wide wones (365)
12:	a chambre derk (205)	þis proude vice (11)	suche wiles (190)
16a:	a whit thyng (447)	this white top (15)	wilde mares (211)

The signs are that the inflexion of adjectives was maintained in written English long after it was effectively dead in the spoken language. Though it had a metrical and rhythmic function, it could not survive the general silencing of final *-e*, and increasingly throughout the fourteenth century scribal disregard for final *-e* played havoc with the poets' rhythms. So in *Sir Orfeo*, written down in about 1340, there are forms with unhistorical *-e*, such as *it bled wete* rhyming with *fet* (5/79–80), and forms that lack *-e*, such as *þis ich quen* (5/63), where the metre would be improved with an extra syllable.

Adjectives of more than one syllable are usually inflected in earlier texts, though less regularly in later ones: so *manifældlice miracles*, 'numerous miracles', 1/81, *þe muchele angoise*, 'the great anguish', 4/25, *diverse kinges*, 12/65, *oþre þinges*, 12/66.

Adjectives that etymologically end in *-e* in their uninflected form, such as *fre*, *grene*, *swete* (OE *frēo*, *grēne*, *swēte*), remain unchanged throughout.

4.4.2 Inflexions for Case

Though this distinction between definite and indefinite adjectival inflexions survived for a considerable time, the Old English adjectival case system was dismantled much more rapidly. In Old English the adjective agreed with its noun in case, gender and number. Only in Southern and South-Western texts do the case-inflexions survive to a limited extent.

In Laȝamon's *Brut* (text 3) there are, in addition to the ending *-e* (or *-en*) for adjectives of the definite declension, the following inflexions for indefinite adjectives:

singular		
masc.	*nom.*	no ending: god (137)
	acc.	-ne: nenne (28), stærcne (59), bradne (115)
	gen.	-es
	dat.	-en: aðelen (11)
fem.	*dat.*	-ere: ludere (30), hæhȝere (126)
plural	*gen.*	-(e)re: alre (33), wihtere (125)

In *The Owl and the Nightingale* (text 2), adjectives add *-e* for all cases in the definite declension, and all in the indefinite declension except the nominative singular of all genders and the accusative singular masculine and neuter. So when qualifying a noun that is subject the adjective has no ending, as the three here: *þat plait was stif and starc and strong* (l. 5); with a feminine noun that is object, the adjective has *-e* as in *grete tale*, 'a great debate' (l. 3).

4.4.3 Comparison of Adjectives

Comparatives and superlatives are formed, as today, by the addition of *-er*, previously *-(e)re*, and *-est* to the positive form: *wis*, *wiser*, *wisest*; *laþ*, 'hateful', *laþre*, *laþest*. Where the vowel is long, it is often shortened in the comparative and superlative, with the final consonant doubled, as *greet*, 'great', 16a/133; *grettest*, 16a/200. *Cortays*, 'courteous', has superlative *curtest* (10/249). Adjectives ending in *-ly* or *-lich* have, beside *-lier* and *-liest*, alternative endings *-loker* and *-lokest*: *semloker*, 'more seemly', 9/83; *semlokest*, 13g/6.

A few adjectives change their stem vowel: *long*, *lenger*; *old* or *ald*, *eldest*; *strong*, *strengest*.

Irregular forms are mostly familiar from Modern English; for example, in text 9: *god*, *better*, *best*; *littel*, *lasse*, *lest*; *muche*, *more*, *most*; in text 1: *yvel*, *werse*.

4.4.4 Comparison of Adverbs

Adverbs have the same comparative and superlative forms as adjectives; e.g. *sone*, 'quickly', *soner*, *sonest*; *wisely*, comparative *wiselier*, 14/38; *swote*, 'sweetly', superlative (dropping the final *-t*) *swotes*, 13a/3. *Longe*, 'for a long time', has comparative *leng* or *lenger*: in the same text there is *no leng abide*, 'stay no longer', 5/84, and *no lenger abide*, 5/330. *Neh*, 'nearly', has comparative *ner*, and superlative *next*, although its comparative form is increasingly used simply to mean 'nearly': *dispayred wel nere*, 8/169. *Wel* has comparative *bet* and superlative *best*: *ho wel wiste*, 'she knew well', 2/147, *on joustep wel, anoþer bet*, 12/116.

4.5 VERBS

4.5.1 Introduction

In Middle English, as in Old and Modern English, the verb has just two tense-forms, present and past. The way in which the past tense is formed divides the regular verbs into two classes, weak and strong. The great majority of verbs are weak and their numbers steadily increased, since most newly formed or introduced verbs were weak; also there was a tendency for verbs that were strong in Old English to become weak in Middle English. Many of the commonest verbs, however, are strong. The distinction between the two classes is that weak verbs form their past tense and past participle with 'a dental suffix', that is, an ending containing a *d* or *t* (e.g. in modern English *kill*, *laugh*, *learn*, *bend*), whereas strong verbs form their past tense and past participle by changing their stem vowel in accordance with an ancient rule that goes right back to the remote ancestor of English, the 'Indo-European mother-tongue'. Examples of strong verbs in modern English are *drive*, *sing*, *bear*, *choose*. However, a few verbs both have a dental suffix and change their stem vowel (e.g. in modern English *seek*, *buy*, *bring*, *think*); these are weak verbs, the change in their stem vowel not being ancient but having taken place in early Old English. See *Guide to Old English*, paragraphs 122–3.

The verb has three moods: indicative, subjunctive and imperative. The distinction between indicative and subjunctive is explained later (5.6.6); broadly, it is that the subjunctive is a non-factual mood, used to express a doubt, hypothesis, conjecture, wish or the like. The imperative is used for orders and requests.

In the indicative mood, verbs may distinguish in form between the first, second and third persons of the singular, but all verbs have just one form throughout the plural (for *we*, *ȝe* and *hi/þei*). The subjunctive has just one form throughout the singular, to which it adds *-n* throughout the plural.

There are two participles or adjectival forms of the verb: the present participle (in Modern English the '*-ing* participle'), and the past participle (used to form verb-tenses with 'have' and 'be', and also as an adjective).

4.5.2 Present Tense

The endings of the present tense are the same for weak and strong verbs, but there are considerable variations according to dialect. Differences may be illustrated by setting out the forms in the language of the *Ancrene Wisse* (early thirteenth century, South-West Midlands) side by side with those in the language of the *Gawain* manuscript (late fourteenth century, North-West Midlands), taking the verb *here(n)*, 'to hear', as the example:

	Ancrene Wisse		*Gawain*	
infinitive		heren		here
indicative				
sg. 1	ich	here	I	here
2	þu	herest	þou	heres
3	he	hereð	he	heres
pl.	we, ʒe, ha	hereð	we, ʒe, þay	here(n), heres
subjunctive				
sg.	ich, þu, he	here	I, þou, he	here
pl.	we, ʒe, ha	heren	we, ʒe, þay	here(n)
imperative				
sg.		her		her(e)
pl.		hereð		heres
present participle		herinde		herande

Wherever it occurs, the *-en* ending is gradually lost, leaving *-e* or no ending. The result of this development, in some dialects, is that only the indicative second and third persons singular and the present participle have distinctive endings. In Northern texts the verb ending is generally lost when the plural pronoun immediately precedes the verb: *we tyne*, 14/300.

The dialectal variations, affecting chiefly the endings of the present indicative third person singular and the plural, and the present participle, are as follows:

Third person singular

(i) *-es* is Northern and North Midland (in texts 8–10, and predominantly in 14, with a few *-eth/-ith* forms; also in the speech of the Northern students in 16a).

(ii) *-eth* is Southern and South Midland (to the south of Cheshire, Derbyshire and Lincolnshire).

(In Southern dialects the ending *-eth* is reduced to *-th*, which is assimilated into a stem ending in *d* or *t*, so that *he findeth* becomes *he fint*, 'he finds' (5/239); similarly *fyght*, 'fights' (15/103), *last*, 'lasts', *sit*, 'sits', *stant*, 'stands', *went* (from *wenden*), 'goes'.)

Plural

(i) *-eth* is Southern and South-West Midland (to the south of Shropshire, Warwickshire, Cambridge and Norfolk). It is the form in texts 2–5 and 11.

(ii) *-e(n)/-on* is North-West Midland, East Midland, and from there spread to London (in texts 1, 6, 8–10, 12, 15 and 16).

(iii) *-es* is Northern (Lancashire, Yorkshire, Lincolnshire and further north), as in text 14 and occasionally 8 and 9; also in the speech of the Northern students in 16a.

Present participle

(i) *-ing* is the general Southern and Midland form (in texts 5–7 and 11).

(ii) *-and* is the Northern form, which is also found elsewhere, particularly around London (texts 8–10, 14, and twice in 5).

(iii) *-inde* is found in the South-West Midlands (texts 2, 3 and 4).

(iv) *-ende* is used in the East (texts 1 and 12).

(Note that in many dialects the present participle, which is an adjective, is distinguishable from the verbal noun or gerund which ends in *-ing* in all dialects. Compare the participle in *þe stif kyng hisselven / Talkkande*, 9/107–8, with *Dere dyn upon day, daunsyng on nyȝtes*, 9/47, where *daunsyng* is a noun parallel to *dyn.*)

In Southern dialects, including the South-West Midlands, some verbs have infinitives in *-i(e)n* or *-i(e)*; e.g. *makien*, *lokin*, *luvie.* These descend from Old English Class 2 weak verbs, ending *-ian* (see *Guide to Old English*, §124). These verbs retain the *-i-* in all parts of the present except the second and third persons singular of the indicative and the imperative singular. Hence in *Ancrene Wisse*, *makien*, infinitive (4/13), *makeð*, third person singular (4/46), *makieð*, plural (4/3); in *Piers Plowman*, the infinitives *wedy*, 'weed', 7b/66, and *gladyen*, 'gladden', 7b/126. Some French and Scandinavian loans were conjugated according to this pattern; e.g. *servið*, '(they) serve', 4/14, *proferi* (infinitive), 'offer', 5/434.

4.5.3 Past Tense and Past Participle

In some dialects the verb in the past tense has distinctions in form for the indicative and subjunctive in the singular, though the subjunctive plural is always the same as the indicative plural. The third person singular of the indicative has the same form as the first person singular.

In the South and South-West Midlands the past participle has the prefix *i-* or *y-*, derived from Old English *ge-*, unless there is some other prefix already present: so *isiȝen*, 'come', 3/111, *ybuld*, 'built', 11/1; but *bigrowe*, 'overgrown', 2/27, already has the prefix *bi-*. Langland uses this *y-* prefix sometimes – compare *ycrouned*, 7a/59, with *crouned*, 7a/63 – but Gower rarely has it.

4.5.4 Past of Weak Verbs

Weak verbs form their past tense by adding *-ed(e)*, *-d(e)* or *-t(e)*, and their past participle by adding *ed*, *-d* or *-t*; thus *heren*, 'to hear', past tense *herde*, past participle *iherd*; *luvien*, 'to love', past tense *luvede*, past participle *iluvet*; *slepen*, 'to sleep', past tense *slepte*.

The past tense of *heren*, 'to hear', in the language of the *Ancrene Wisse*:

indicative		
sg. 1	ich	herde
2	þu	herdest
3	he	herde
pl.	we, ȝe, ha	herden
subjunctive		
sg.	ich, þu, he	herde
pl.	we, ȝe, ha	herden
past participle		iherd

With the loss of *-en* and then of *-e*, the past tense is often unchanged throughout except for the *-est* of the second person singular of the indicative. In the North and the North Midlands the second person singular ends *-es/-ez*, as in *sendez*, 8/415, or has *-e* or no ending so that there is one form throughout the past; e.g. second person singular *þou me herde*, 8/306, past participle (with 'unhistorical' *-e*) *I haf herde*, 9/26.

A few common verbs historically classed as weak not only add *-t*(*e*) in the past tense but also modify the stem itself. Most have survived into Modern English. Examples taken from the *Gawain* poems are:

infinitive	*pa. and pp.*
bryng, 'bring'	broȝt
seche, 'seek'	soȝt
þenk, 'think'	þoȝt
þynk, 'seem'	þuȝt
worch, 'work'	wroȝt

4.5.5 The Verbs 'Have' and 'Say'

Two very common weak verbs show a great variety of dialectal forms. They are *habben/haven*, 'have', and *seggen/sayen*, 'say'. Here for comparison are the forms in the language of the *Ancrene Wisse* and *Gawain*:

	Anc. W.	*Gawain*	*Anc. W.*	*Gawain*
infin.	habben	have	seggen	say
pres. indic.				
sg. 1	habbe	haf, have	segge	saye
2	havest	habbes, hatz	seist	seggez, says
3	haveð	habbes, hatz	seið	says, sayez
pl.	habbeð	haf, haven, han, hatz	seggeð	sayn
imp. sg.	have	haf	sei	say

past indic.				
sg. 1	hefde	had(e)	seide	sayd(e)
2	hefdest	hadez	seidest	—
3	hefde	had(e)	seide	sayd(e)
pl.	hefden	hade(n)	seiden	sayden
past ppl.	ihaved, -et	hade	iseid	sayd

4.5.6 Past of Strong Verbs

Strong verbs form their past tense by changing the stem vowel. In early texts a verb may exhibit as many as four different stem vowels: one in the infinitive and present tense, a second in the first and third persons singular of the past tense indicative, a third in the other forms of the past tense, and a fourth in the past participle. For example, in the language of the *Ancrene Wisse*, *scheoten*, 'to shoot':

infin.	*pa. 1 & 3 sg.*	*pa. pl.*	*pp.*
scheoten	scheat	schuten	ischoten

Gradually the two vowels of the past tense were reduced to one, sometimes settling on the stem vowel of the singular, sometimes on that of the plural; but this took place quite unsystematically, leaving doublet forms even in the same text: e.g. in *Gawain* there are the past tense plural forms *ran* and *runnen*. (Compare *sunk* and *sank* as alternative past tense forms in Modern English.)

The past tense of *driven*, 'to drive', in the language of the *Ancrene Wisse*:

indicative		
sg. 1	ich	draf
2	þu	drive
3	he	draf
pl.	we, ȝe, ha	driven
subjunctive		
sg.	ich, þu, he	drive
pl.	we, ȝe, ha	driven
past participle		idriven

Note that in the indicative the forms of the first and third persons singular are identical, and the form of the plural is that of the second person singular with the addition of *-n.* In the subjunctive the singular and plural forms are the same as the second person singular and the plural of the indicative respectively. These observations apply to all regular strong verbs.

In the same 'class' as *driven* – that is to say, with the same series of vowel changes – are *riden*, *writen*, *biden*, 'to wait', *risen* and others. In this class, the vowel of the infinitive stem is long, /i:/, while the vowel of the past tense plural and past participle is short, /i/; compare Modern English *drive–driven*, *ride–ridden*, etc.

In Old English seven classes of strong verbs may be distinguished. During the Middle English period these began to be affected by so many dialectal changes and alterations by analogy with other verbs that it is no longer helpful to classify strong verbs in this way. Forms in the texts in this book may be followed up in the Glossary, and for a fuller display the *Oxford English Dictionary* and the *Middle English Dictionary* may be consulted.

Forms of the past tense were progressively simplified, first in Northern texts, so that in the language of the *Gawain* manuscript the past tense often has the same form throughout the singular and plural, indicative and subjunctive. Thus *drof* is both the singular and the plural form of 'drove', as in *stremes... drof hem*, 8/234–5; whereas in Chaucer's Prioress's Tale the past tense plural form of *risen*, a verb in the same class, is *they ryse*, 'they rose', 16b/227.

The past participle of strong verbs retained its *-en* longest in the North, but the ending was earlier lost in the South and in the Midlands. In *Sir Orfeo* are the forms *ynome*, 'taken' (from *nimen*), 5/182, *ycore*, 'chosen', hence 'excellent' (from *chesen*), 5/105, and *ydrawe*, 'drawn', 5/295; but also *yborn* (from *beren*), 5/174, and both *totore* and *totorn*, 'torn apart', 5/171–3. Gower has *write*, 'written', 12/60, and *ȝove*, 'given', 12/127, together with *spoken* in the same line, while the *Gawain* manuscript usually keeps the *-en*, as in *nomen*, 8/360, *bounden*, 9/192. From such variants arise modern doublets such as the alternative British and American forms *got* and *gotten*.

4.5.7 Irregular Verbs

So-called 'Preterite-Present' verbs have a present tense that was in origin a past tense, and have formed a new past tense. The commonest are *cunnen*, 'to know how to' (modern 'can'), *mahen*, 'to be able, have the ability, may', *moten*, 'to be allowed to, compelled to' (its past tense gives modern 'must'), *schulen*, 'to have to, shall', and *witen*, 'to know'. In the language of the *Ancrene Wisse* they have these forms:

present indicative					
sg. 1	can	mei	mot	schal	wat
2	canst	maht	most	schalt	wast
3	can	mei	mot	schal	wat
pl.	cunnen	mahen	moten	schule(n)	witen
subjunctive					
sg.	cunne	mahe	mote	schule	wite
past indicative					
sg. 1, 3	cuðe	mahte	moste	schulde	wiste

(conjugation continues as for weak verbs: 4.5.4)

The verb *willen*, 'to want, wish, will', has the following forms in the language of the *Ancrene Wisse* and *Gawain*:

	Ancrene Wisse	*Gawain*
present indicative		
sg. 1	wulle	wyl(le), wol
2	wult	wyl(t)
3	wule	wyl
pl.	wulleð	wyl
subjunctive		
sg.	wulle	wyl
pl.	wullen	wyl
past indicative		
sg. 1, 3	walde	wolde

There are negative forms for all parts of the verb, illustrated by *wolle thow, nulle thow*, 'whether you wish it or not' (subjunctive), 7b/153. The verb may be run together with a personal pronoun, particularly in Southern texts (see 4.3.2).

4.5.8 The Verb 'To Be'

This is particularly irregular, and has wide variation in form in different regions. Some parts of the present indicative have two forms from different stems; where there are alternatives the *b-* forms are often used in a future sense, as in *swa þe bið alre laððest*, 'as shall be most hateful to you', 3/152.

To illustrate the variety, here are the forms of the verb 'to be' in the language of the *Ancrene Wisse* and *Gawain*:

	Ancrene Wisse	*Gawain*
infinitive	beon	be, bene
present indicative		
sg. 1	am, beo	am
2	art, bist	art
3	is, bið	is, betz
pl.	beoð	ar(n), ben
present subjunctive		
sg.	beo	be
pl.	beon	be(n)
past indicative		
sg. 1	wes	watz, was
2	were	watz, were
3	wes	watz, was
pl.	weren	wer(en)

past subjunctive		
sg.	were	wer(e)
pl.	weren	wer(e), wern
past participle	ibeon	ben(e)

Chaucer gives his Northern students *is* throughout the singular as extreme Northernisms.

Negative forms may be illustrated from *Sir Orfeo*: present *nam*, *nis*; past *nas*, *nere*.

5
Syntax

5.1 GENDER

In Early Middle English, as in Old English, noun, adjective and pronoun agree in gender, as well as in case and number. The decay of the system of inflexions in nouns and adjectives and the simplification of the forms of the definite article, however, left nouns with progressively fewer indications of gender. In Old English *se stān* (nominative singular) is clearly masculine, and *þǣre tale* (genitive singular) clearly feminine, but the corresponding *þe ston* and *þe tales* in Middle English have no indications of gender. With such developments the notion of grammatical gender could not long survive, and it was replaced by the present distinction between human male, human female, and non-human: 'natural gender'. Nouns in Early Middle English still commonly retain grammatical gender, as indicated by forms of the article, or by pronouns or adjectival inflexion; e.g. (with the nominative feminine of the definite article) *þo ule*, 'the owl', 2/26, *he* referring to *halm*, 'helmet', 3/19, *scaft stærcne* (with the *-ne* masculine accusative inflexion of the adjective), 3/59.

In later texts examples of references to inanimate objects as 'he' or 'she' are generally to be explained as personifications rather than as survivals of grammatical gender: *ho*, 'she', referring to *suffraunce*, 8/4, *Zeferus . . . he*, *þe cler sunne . . . ho*, 8/470–2.

5.2 NUMBER

There is variation in the treatment of collective nouns, such as 'court', 'folk', 'world', just as there is today: *al þe tunscipe* (sg.) *flugæn* (pl.), 1/49; *al watz* (sg.) *þis fayre folk in her* (pl.) *first age*, 9/54. In 8/157, *bale*, 'packages', is treated as a singular noun with plural sense.

A co-ordinated group of nouns may be regarded as a single entity: *þe sege and þe assaut watz sesed*, 9/1.

After numerals nouns sometimes have no plural ending. Some (e.g. *ȝer*, 'years') may be explained as survivals of Old English nouns with unchanged plurals, and others (e.g. *siþe*, 'times') represent former genitive plurals after numerals (see 5.3.2 below). Examples are: *xix wintre*, 1/55, *foure and twenty ȝere*, 6/104, *fyfty syþe*, 13j/46. 'Many' is often accompanied by the singular: *wes moni ȝimston*, 3/17, *mony luflych lorde*, 9/38.

As in Old English, the neuter pronoun 'it' may be used with the verb *are/were* to refer to a plural subject: *hit are my blody bretherne*, 7b/217, *hit arne refetyd*, 'they are fed', 10/304.

5.3 USE OF CASES

5.3.1 Nominative and Accusative

The nominative case is used for the subject, the accusative for the object, but the distinctions in form are rapidly lost from all except pronouns. In early texts the distinctions can still sometimes be observed in articles and adjectives: see 4.3.6 and 4.4.2.

The accusative is used after some prepositions in early texts, where it is still distinct from the dative: *over bradne wæld*, 3/115.

5.3.2 Genitive

The genitive indicates possession: *þe kinges halle*, 5/410, *þas monnes earen*, 'the ears of the man', 2/338; or definition: *Ancrene Wisse*, 'Guide for Anchoresses' (with genitive pl. ending *-ene*).

Occasionally the genitive is without ending (4.2.4), though often the relationship between the nouns is not clearly distinguishable from that of a noun-compound where two nouns are in parallel. So while *Uryn son*, 'Urien's son', 9/113, has an endingless genitive proper name, *sister sunes*, 'nephews', 9/111, might be analysed as 'sister's sons' or sister-sons'. More clearly compounds are *munster dor*, 8/268, and *sumere dale*, 2/1.

The use of the *of*-phrase as an alternative way of indicating possession or definition becomes increasingly common. Compare the early *Stephnes kinges time*, 1/74–5, with the later expressions *þe face of frelych dryȝtyn*, 8/214, *þe termes of Judé*, 8/61.

In a few texts, mainly from the South-West Midlands, the genitive inflexion is replaced by *his*. In this book it is found only in Trevisa: *God hys heste*, 'God's commandment', 11/167; *Seint Gregore hys bokes Dialoges*, 'St Gregory's books "The Dialogues"', 11/121–2. The construction becomes common for a time in Early Modern English.

Two or more genitive nouns may be in parallel: *He wes Uðeres þas aðelen kinges*, 'It had been the noble king Uther's', 3/18. If the noun that governs the genitive expression is also present, the genitive group often splits around it, and only the first element is inflected, as in this example where *love* governs both *lordes* and *Sir Orfeo*, but the name is not inflected: *mi lordes love Sir Orfeo*, 'my lord Sir Orfeo's love', 5/518. With the same word-order is *for the Lordes love of hevene*, 'for the love of the Lord of heaven', 7b/16.

The genitive is used with superlative adjectives: *læðest alre þinge*, 'most hateful of all things', 3/33 (OE genitive pl. *þinga*); *aðelest kinge*, 'noblest of kings', 3/53. Later *of* becomes standard: *þe fairest of every kinne*, 13a/7.

Adverbial uses of the genitive are most common in expressions of time: *þu fliȝst niȝtes* (genitive sg.), 'you fly at night', 2/238 (compare *flo bi niȝte*, 2/390). In *be nihtes and be dæies*, 1/17–18, the writer reinforces the adverbial genitive with a preposition. Other adverbial uses are *hire þonkes*, 'willingly', 2/70, *wintres and sumeres*, 'in the winter and in the summer', i.e. 'all the time', 3/170, *nanes weis*, 'in no way, not at all', 4/16.

After numbers the 'partitive genitive' is found, especially in early texts: *fif and twenti þusend / Wihtere monnen*, '25,000 (of) bold men', 3/124–5. By contrast, the genitive is often not used with nouns such as *score*, *maner*, *kin*: *such manere argement*, 'such kind of argument', 11/88, *alle kyn craftes*, 'all kinds of trades', 7b/58.

In early texts the genitive is occasionally used after some adjectives, such as *ful*, 'full', and *unilic*: *ælchen oðere unilic*, 'unlike all others', 3/19.

5.3.3 Dative

The most common use of the dative case is with prepositions such as *to*, *mid* and *bi*. Compare *þi song* (nominative) with *bi mine songe* (dative), 2/220 and 46. After the dative singular *-e* ending was lost from nouns (see 4.2.3), the dative became indistinguishable from other cases without inflexion.

The dative was used for the indirect object: *hi hadden him manred maked*, 'they had done him homage', 1/11. Without a distinct form for the dative, however, the indirect object had to be distinguished from the direct object by word-order or the use of *to*, as it is in Modern English: *seist me boþe tone and schame*, 'say to me both insult and shame', 2/50; *ȝeve hem benes*, 'give them beans', 7b/177.

Some adjectives, such as *loþ* and *lef*, have a dative object: *loþ smale foȝle*, 'hateful to small birds', 2/277; *lof him were niȝtingale*, 'nightingales were dear to him', 2/203.

The Old English use of a dative pronoun to indicate possession is still found, particularly in early texts: *him bræcon alle þe limes*, 'all his limbs broke', 1/28; *freshe hym þe face*, 'his face unblemished', 10/89.

The adverbial dative of the type *ludere stæfne*, 'with a loud voice', 3/30, is rare even in early texts, and is superseded entirely by prepositional phrases; so *mid fulle dreme and lude stefne*, 2/314.

A pleonastic dative pronoun *me*, the 'ethic dative', is a characteristic feature of the *Gawain* poems: *he swenges me þys swete schip*, 'it turns this fine ship', 8/108; also *made me þane unto þis tree*, 'fastened then to this tree', 14/42. This kind of dative expresses the speaker's interest in the fact stated.

For other uses of the dative with verbs, see 5.4.5 (reflexive pronouns), 5.6.8 (impersonal verbs) and 5.6.9 (verbs of motion).

5.4 PRONOUNS AND ARTICLES

5.4.1 Þou and Ȝe

The use of *ȝe* as a polite form of address to one person is found from the late thirteenth century, and is modelled on French practice. Usage varies from text to text, and even within a text, but the distinction is broadly that *þou* is used between equals and to inferiors, whereas *ȝe* is used in representations of polite speech in address to a superior. In the selection from *Gawain* the usage is quite consistent: Arthur uses *þou* both to Gawain and to the Green Knight, but *yow* to Guenevere (9/470); Gawain uses *þou* to the Green Knight but *ȝe* to the King (9/343–61); the Green Knight, as a hostile challenger, always uses *þou*, even to the King – his *ȝe* in l. 265 is addressed to the court in general. In Trevisa's *Dialogue* (text 11) the Clerk addresses the Lord as *ȝe* and the Lord replies with *þou*, while in *Sir Orfeo þou* is general, but the polite *ȝe* is used at a moment of solemn formality (5/582). In addressing God or the Virgin Mary, however, the singular form is customarily used, as by Chaucer's Prioress (16b/1).

5.4.2 Non-expression of Personal Pronouns

Quite regularly a personal pronoun, either subject or object, is not expressed in Middle English. As indeed in Modern English, the subject pronoun does not need to be expressed in a series of co-ordinate clauses: *þe niȝtingale hi iseȝ / And hi bihold and overseȝ*, 'the nightingale saw her, and beheld and watched her', 2/29–30. There are other situations, however, where the subject pronoun would normally be expressed in Modern English but does not need to be in Middle English. A sentence may begin: *Kimeð* . . ., '(He) comes . . .', 4/59, where the subject is understood from the previous sentence. The subject of the subordinate clause may be understood from the main clause, as in *he watz sokored . . . þaȝ were wanlez of wele*, 'he was protected . . . though (he) was without hope of well-being', 8/262. When the subordinate clause precedes, the subject of the following main clause may be understood from it: *Hwen ha ihereð þet god, skleatteð þe earen adun*, 'When they hear anything good, (they) flap their ears down', 4/18–19. In other cases the unexpressed subject is clear from verb-endings and other grammatical features, as in *Or beggest thy bylyve*, 'Or (you) beg for your food', 7a/29; *and diden an scærp iren abuton þa mannes throte*, 'and (they/people) put a sharp iron band round the man's throat', 1/31. The grammatical subject 'it' may be unexpressed: *þagh had bene my fader bone, I bede hym no wranges*, 'though (it) had been my father's murderer, I gave him no wrong decisions', 10/243. Non-expression of subject 'it' is especially common in impersonal expressions; see 5.6.8.

Similarly the object pronoun may be understood from the context. A straightforward example is *lacche water / And cast upon þi faire cors*, 'fetch some water and cast (it) on your fair body', 10/316–17. So also: *þa þe castles waren maked, þa fylden hi mid deovles*, 'When the castles were made, they filled (them) with devils' (*hi* is subject), 1/15–16.

5.4.3 Man

The indefinite pronoun *man* causes difficulties on several counts. Firstly it varies in form: *man*, *mon*, *men*, and often the unstressed form *me*, which in context can sometimes be mistaken for the first person pronoun. Secondly there is no exact equivalent for *man* in Modern English, for we select from a range of indefinite pronouns to suit the occasion – one, anyone, they, people, we, you – or a passive construction is used instead. All these possibilities must be considered when translating Middle English *man*; e.g.: *me ne chide wit þe gidie*, 'one should not quarrel with fools' (a proverbial expression), 2/291; *riȝt so me grulde schille harpe*, 'just as if a shrill harp were being twanged', or 'someone were twanging . . .', 2/142; *ne isæh nævere na man selere cniht*, 'a better knight was never seen', 3/28; *me hi halt*, 'she is held', or 'people think her', 2/32.

5.4.4 Self

In Modern English a reflexive pronoun is distinguished by the addition of *-self*: 'the man hurt himself'. In Middle English, on the other hand, *self* serves to reinforce the pronoun, so that *Ywan, Uryn son, ette with hymselven*, 9/113, means 'ate with him', not 'ate by himself', and *syre, now þouself jugge*, 8/413, is 'now, sir, *you* judge', not 'judge yourself'. Particularly in early texts, *self* is simply added to the personal pronoun, as in *þouself* above, where it is subject. Later *self* is treated as a noun and accompanies the genitive pronoun, as in *myselfe and my soule*, 10/300, and *þiself arte clensid*, 6/15, though in the third person the masculine form remains *himself* and the plural *hemselven*: *himself he lerned for to harp*, 'he himself learnt to harp', 5/29.

Self is used in the same way to reinforce nouns: *þe sulve mose*, 'the titmouse itself', 2/69, and (with the noun in the genitive) *under Krystes selven*, 'under Christ himself', 9/51.

5.4.5 Reflexive Pronouns

There is no distinctive reflexive pronoun in Middle English. The ordinary personal pronoun is used: *ȝif ich me loki*, 'if I guard myself', 2/56; *þe byschop hym shope*, 'the bishop got (himself) ready', 10/129. There is reciprocal use in *we custe us*, 'we kissed one another', 13j/46. The pronoun may be reinforced by the addition of *self*: *if any so hardy . . . holdez hymselven*, 'if anyone thinks himself so brave', 9/285.

Some verbs expressing fear, anger and the like, and many verbs of motion, are accompanied by a reflexive pronoun: *thenne gan Wastor to wrath hym*, 'then

Waster began to get angry', 7b/149; *he gooth hym*, 16a/208. Even the verb 'be' may occasionally take a reflexive pronoun in Laȝamon: *þene him wes Arður*, 'than Arthur was', 3/29. On verbs of motion see 5.6.9.

5.4.6 Relative Pronouns

Over most of the Middle English period the most common relative pronoun corresponding to Modern English 'who', 'which' and 'that' is *þat*, used to refer to both personal and non-personal antecedents, singular and plural: *King Pluto and . . . King Juno . . . þat sumtime were as godes yhold*, 'who were once regarded as gods', 5/43–5.

In early texts *þe* and *þa* are also used. In Laȝamon's *Brut*, *þe* tends to be used with reference to masculine singular antecedents, *þa* for plural and for feminine singular, and *þat* for inanimate or neuter singular: thus *Hengest þe cnihten wes faȝerest*, 'Hengest who was most gracious of knights', 3/168. Yet the distinction in usage is not clear-cut; here *þa* is used to refer to a neuter noun: *his spere . . . þa Ron wes ihaten*, 'his spear that was named Ron', 3/24.

þat is regularly used as a relative without the antecedent noun or pronoun, when it is equivalent to modern 'what' or 'he who', 'anyone who' etc.: *now þat London is nevenyd*, 'what is now called London', 10/25; *betere therby þat byleve the fynden*, 'benefit thereby those who provide you with food', 7a/21; *þe devel have þat reche*, 'the devil take anyone who bothers', 7b/127. In the following example the reader may easily misinterpret *þat*, wrongly supposing that it is *þe water* that wants to escape: *scopen out þe scaþel water þat fayn scape wolde*, 'those who were keen to escape scooped out the dangerous water', 8/155.

In order to indicate case, *þat* is combined with a personal pronoun, so *þat . . . his* means 'whose': *þat merkid is in oure martilage his mynde*, 'whose memory is set down in our burial-register', 10/154. *þat* may refer back to a genitive pronoun rather than its noun, in this instance *his* rather than *bour*: *þer watz bylded his bour þat wyl no bale suffer*, 'there was built the bower of the man who will suffer no harm', 8/276.

In later Middle English *which* becomes increasingly common as an alternative to *þat*, for both persons and things: *sche which kepþ þe blinde whel*, 12/92. *Which*, 'who', is accompanied by *þat* as a conjunction in *This abbot, which þat*, 16b/190. The combination *þe which* was favoured by some writers: *o principal worching miȝt þe whiche is clepid a knowable miȝt*, 6/63–4.

There is sometimes no relative pronoun at all. The 'zero' relative pronoun is used in Modern English as the object of the clause: 'the woman (whom) I saw'. In Middle English it is also used when it is subject: *fro bale has broȝt us*, 'who has brought us from anguish', 10/340; *for hym þe boght*, 'for him who redeemed you', 14/101.

5.4.7 The Articles

Usage of the definite article is variable when proper names are accompanied by a noun. Expressions such as *þe king Stephne*, 1/1, are commoner in early use, and later it is *Kyng Charles*, 11/114; similarly *Seint Jerom*, 11/92, and even *segge Jonas*, 'the man Jonah', 8/409. When the noun follows the name there need be no article, especially in early texts: *Martin abbot*, 1/56, but *Arðure þan kinge*, 3/1, and *Peres þe plouhman*, 7b/124.

Both the definite and indefinite articles may be absent where Modern English would use them: *which bar corone*, 'who was king', 12/63; *have an horn and be hayward*, 7a/16; *wæs god munec and god man*, 1/72.

The adjectives *ech* and *every* may be followed by *a*: *everich·a grot*, 'every detail', 5/490.

5.5 ADJECTIVES AND ADVERBS

5.5.1 Position

Attributive adjectives most commonly precede the noun: *not by soche a devoute and a meek blynde stering of love, bot by a proude, coryous and an ymaginatiif witte*, 6/145–7. In verse they may follow the noun: *sceld deore*, 'beloved shield', 3/20; *burn rych*, 'noble man', 9/20. Two or more adjectives may be grouped around the noun: *pore folke syke*, 7b/147; *wylde werbles and wyȝt*, 'wild and loud trillings', 9/119; *he milde man was and softe and god*, 1/9–10. In Laȝamon's *Brut* the adjective sometimes precedes the article or possessive pronoun: *balde mine beornes*, 'my bold knights', 3/133, *mid aðelen his crafte*, 'with his excellent skill', 3/11. Compare Shakespeare's *dear my lord.*

5.5.2 Comparatives and Superlatives

Comparative and superlative adjectives and adverbs are formed by adding the endings *-er* and *-est*; see 4.4.3–4. The use of *more* and *most* is not so common and, in contrast to modern usage, is found chiefly with short adjectives: *most kyd*, 9/51. Even with an adverb such as *wiseli*, the comparative is *wiselier*, 14/38. Double comparison, with both *more* and the suffix *-er*, is seen in *more wighter*, 'stronger', 14/201.

Superlatives may be intensified in various ways: by adding the prefix *alder-* (from OE *alra*, 'of all'): *alder-grattyst*, 'greatest of all', 10/5; by a following phrase such as *of all oþer*; or by the expression *one þe* before the superlative: *on þe most*, 'the very biggest', 9/137; *one þe unhapnest hathel*, 'quite the most unfortunate man', 10/198. This last construction may easily be wrongly identified with the modern 'one of the most . . .'.

5.5.3 Adjectives as Nouns

Adjectives may be used as nouns more freely than in Modern English, with or without an article, in both the singular and the plural. This usage is particularly characteristic of alliterative verse. So *wise and snepe*, 'wise and foolish people', 2/225; *þe schene*, 'the bright sun', 8/440; *busy*, 'busy activity', 8/157; *ronk*, 'determination', 8/298; *the seke*, 'the sick man', 15/104.

5.6 VERBS

5.6.1 Use of Present Tense

English has only two tense-forms, present and past. The present tense expresses habitual action and general truths: *þu chaterest so doþ on Irish prost*, 'you chatter like an Irish priest', 2/322; *wel fiȝt þat wel fliȝt*, 'well fights that well flees' (proverbial), 2/176. In Middle English the simple present is also used where Modern English has the progressive 'am' + '-ing', to express an action that is in progress over a limited period: *al dares for drede*, 'they are all cowering for fear', 9/315.

As in Old English, the present tense is frequently used to refer to the future: *þay ta me bylyve*, 'they will seize me at once', 8/78. Nearly always the context makes it quite clear that the action is in the future, for example with an expression of time: *we foure rayse it noȝt right to-yere*, 'the four of us will not raise it upright this year', 14/164. Compare 'I go to London tomorrow' in Modern English.

The historic present, not found in Old English, becomes common in the later fourteenth century, particularly in narrative of past events in order to place reader and writer in the middle of the action: *þer hales in at þe halle dor an aghlich mayster*, 'there comes in at the hall door a fearsome knight', 9/136. In relating a series of such events, the writer may switch quite freely between past tense and historic present; see for example the description of Jonah entering the whale's mouth, 8/246–53.

5.6.2 Use of Past Tense

The past tense is similarly used to express both simple and progressive aspects; see the translation of the verbs *sete* and *underȝete* here: *þo al þo þat þerin sete / þat it was King Orfeo underȝete*, 'then all those who were sitting there understood that it was King Orfeo', 5/575–6. Especially in early texts, the past tense can be used for the perfective, where Modern English uses 'have' or 'had': *ne isæh nævere na man selere cniht nenne*, 'no one had ever seen a better knight', 3/28.

5.6.3 Auxiliaries of the Past

The perfective, bringing past action up to the present ('have done', etc.) or to some point in the more recent past ('had done', etc.), is regularly used in Middle English: *þy bone þat þou boden habbes*, 'the request that you have asked for', 9/327; *uche lede as he loved and layde had his hert*, 'each man in the way he loved and had set his heart', 8/168. To form the perfective of intransitive verbs involving change of state, and particularly verbs of motion, the auxiliary *be* is generally used: *he is nu suþe acoled*, 'he has now cooled off considerably', 2/205; *he watz flowen*, 'he had fled', 8/183; *when he was in þe roche ygo*, 'when he had gone into the rock', 5/349. *Be* is also used with verbs meaning 'become' which have a noun as complement: *he is bicumen hunte*, 'he has become a huntsman', 3/114; *my bapteme is worthyn*, 'has become my baptism', 10/330.

In narrative style the perfective can be used to suggest that the consequences of an action are still developing: *so long he haþ þe way ynome / To Winchester he is ycome*, 'so long has he taken the way that he has arrived at Winchester', 5/477–8; *anon þe wylde loves rage . . . haþ mad him . . .*, 12/222–4. As a feature of narrative style it may alternate with the simple past tense: *he mette Massynysse / That hym for joy in armes hath ynome*, '. . . who took him in his arms', 15/37–8. So narrative of past events can be told with the simple past tense, the historic present, or the perfective.

The verb *ginnen* (also *anginnen*, *onginnen*) originally meant 'begin'. Its past tense *gan/gune* (and related forms *can/con*) was also frequently used with an infinitive as an equivalent of a past tense. Context generally determines which sense is appropriate; so *seþþen þat ich here regni gan*, 5/425, is 'ever since I began to reign here', whereas *boþe breþes con blowe*, 8/138, may be translated with a simple past tense, 'both winds blew'. In other cases the uncertainty may be a feature of the style, creating an expectant sense of events to be recounted: *þa riden agon Arður*, 'then Arthur rode' or 'began to ride' (when something happened), 3/47. Considerations of metre and rhyme no doubt also play a part in this example: *as sone as sche gan awake / Sche crid and loþli bere gan make*, 'as soon as she woke up she cried and made/began to make a horrible noise', 5/77–8.

5.6.4 Auxiliaries of the Future: *shall* and *will*

The original function of *shall* was to express obligation or necessity, and of *will* to express wish or intention, and this distinction is still often present when they are used as auxiliaries to refer to the future. Compare *it schal be so!*, 5/226, with *ich wille bon of þe awreke*, 'I intend to get even with you', 2/262; or the two verbs here: *þu clumbe . . . swulc þu woldest to hævene; nu þu scalt to hælle*, 'You climbed as if you wished (to get) to heaven; now you shall (get) to hell', 3/165–6. So *shall* often expresses the notion of what is bound to happen quite independent of what anyone wants: *nu we scullen riden*, 'now we are going to ride', 3/44; in the Beatitudes 'Blessed are . . .' *for þay schal* . . ., 8/16, 18, 20 etc. *Shall* becomes the general auxiliary of the future, whereas *will* still generally implies volition: *wo schal us seme / þat kunne and wille riȝt us deme*, 'who is going to reconcile us, who is able and willing to judge us justly?', 2/187–8; *he wile gon a riȝte weie*, 'he intends to follow a right path', 2/214; *if þou be so bold . . . þou wyl grant me*, 9/272–3. As this last instance shows, the sense of volition, though present, may be faint, and sometimes the two verbs occur simply as alternative auxiliaries without any apparent distinction in meaning: *I wyl me sum oþer waye, . . . I schal tee into Tarce*, 'I'll go some other way, . . . I'll travel into Tarshish', 8/86–7.

A common construction contrasts *will* in a subordinate clause with *shall* in the main clause: *if ȝe wyl lysten . . . I schal telle hit as tit*, 'if you are willing to listen . . . I'll tell it at once', 9/30–1; *ȝif þou wilte besily travayle . . . þou schalt come þerto*, 'if you will work assiduously . . . you'll get there', 6/29–30.

For the use of *will/wolde* as a 'modal auxiliary' in hypothetical statements and the like, see 5.6.6.

5.6.5 The Infinitive

The infinitive form is used on its own, with *to* or with *for to*. The practice of using the plain infinitive or the infinitive with *to* is for the most part the same as in Modern English, though there are some differences in detail. The plain infinitive is used directly after auxiliary verbs such as *shall*, *will*, *can*, *may*, *mot*, and others such as *dare* and *let* etc.: *ich nolde don*, 'I would not do', 2/159; *his hors he lette irnen*, 'he let his horse run', 3/60. With some other verbs such as *gin*, *go*, *here*, *þink*, etc., where Modern English has the infinitive with *to*, Middle English may have a plain infinitive: *cleopien agon*, 'began to call', 3/132; *þohte forð siðen and over sæ liðen*, 'intended to go forth and (to) travel over the sea', 3/85; *þee byhoveþ . . . riȝt so put*, 'it will be necessary for you . . . just so to put', 6/181–2. With a pair of infinitives, the first may be without and the second with *to*, and this is different from modern usage: *lovede wel fare / And no dede to do*, 'loved to live well and do nothing', 7a/8–9; *here schulde wight men worschippe wynne / And noght with gaudis al day to gone*, 'here should bold men win honour and not go . . .', 14/199–200.

The infinitive may have a passive sense: *avantarie is to despise*, 'boasting is to be despised', 12/58; *nas no coumfort to kever*, 'there was no comfort to be obtained', 8/223; *ha beoð þe leasse to meanen*, 'they are the less to be pitied', 4/25–6. Verbs of commanding and the like may be followed by an infinitive with passive sense: *bede unlouke þe lidde*, 'ordered the lid to be released', 10/67; *he let ordeine*, 'he caused orders to be given', 12/106; *late bere*, 'cause to be carried', hence 'carry!', 14/178; *do dryve out a decré*, 'have a decree issued', 8/386; *the Jewes leet he bynde*, 'he had the Jews bound', 16b/168.

The verb *come* can be followed by the infinitive of another verb of motion defining the manner or direction in which the coming takes place: *þenne comeð þe wulf wilde touward hire winden*, 'then the wild wolf comes moving towards her', 3/98.

The construction with the infinitive as a complement is commoner than in Modern English, and is used where we might use the '-ing' form: *Arður isæh Colgrim climben*, 'Arthur saw Colgrim climb(ing)', 3/86; *iherde ich holde grete tale / An hule and one niȝtingale*, 'I heard an owl and a nightingale conducting a great argument', 2/3–4.

After an auxiliary verb, the infinitive *be* is occasionally omitted: *oþir trowid ever shulde*, 'or was believed ever likely (to be)', 10/255. On the much commoner omission of infinitive verbs of motion, see 5.6.9.

The infinitive with *for to* originally expressed purpose, as in: *com to him for to here*, 'came in order to hear him', 5/440. Increasingly it became used as an equivalent of the *to* infinitive, sometimes for reasons of metre and rhythm: *ne wonde / þis aventure for to frayn*, 'do not hesitate to attempt this adventure', 9/488–9; *he may noȝt hure speche vor to lurne*, 'he is unable to learn their speech', 11/5.

5.6.6 The Subjunctive

The subjunctive mood of the verb indicates a particular attitude in the writer's or speaker's mind towards the event or action described. Its use is restricted in Modern English to a few contexts: in *if* clauses where the event is highly improbable or impossible, 'if I were you'; in clauses dependent upon verbs of wishing, demanding, requesting etc. (more common in American than British English), 'I wish I were dead', 'He recommends that she sell the book'; and in a handful of fixed phrases, expressing wishes such as 'God bless!', or a hypothesis in 'as it were', or a condition in 'be they good or bad'. The subjunctive form is distinct from the indicative in Modern English only in the third person singular of the present ('sell' above), first and third person singular 'were', and present tense 'be'.

As described in 4.5, the subjunctive has distinct forms in many Middle English dialects for the whole of the present tense except the first person singular, for the second person singular of the past tense of weak verbs, and for the first and third persons singular of the past tense of strong verbs and the verb 'to be'. It is used more widely in Middle English than today, though the basic idea is the same, in that it is a *non-factual* mood, concerned with events not as actually happening, but as possibilities to be desired, envisaged or conjectured. Hence most of the following categories express such notions as wishes, commands and hypotheses.

In main clauses the present tense of the subjunctive is used for wishes and commands, as *Drihten us fulsten*, 'may God help us!', 3/46; *fo we on*, 'let us proceed', 2/179. Wishes are often introduced by *so*, *as* or *þer*: *so hit bitide þat ich mote*, 'may it happen that I can', 2/52; *as help me . . . he þat on hyȝe syttes*, 'so help me he who sits on high', 9/256; *þer Ragnel . . . hym rere*, 'may Ragnel wake him', 8/188. The past tense of the subjunctive is used where Modern English uses 'would' to express something that is unlikely to happen: *that were a long lettyng*, 'that would be a long delay', 7b/5; *hit were now gret nye to neven / So hardy a here*, 'it would today be very difficult to name so bold a company', 9/58–9; *alle were þe better*, '(to have) all would be better', 8/34; *a sory couple of ȝou it were*, 'you would make a sorry couple', 5/458. The same writer uses the idiom *þat nouȝt nere* with the past subjunctive, 'that would not be possible', 5/457, and *þat nouȝt nis*, 'that is not possible', 5/131, with the present indicative. These hypothetical sentences often include an *if* or *though* clause: *nere ich never no þe betere / þeȝ . . .*, 'I should not be at all better off, even though . . .', 2/283–4.

In subordinate clauses the subjunctive is most commonly used for a condition or hypothesis. Such clauses are often introduced by *if* or sometimes *so*: *ȝif ich were Orfeo þe king*, 5/558; *if þou crave batayl*, 9/277; *þu starest so þu wille abiten*, 'you are staring as if you wish to bite', 2/77. There are also conditional clauses with no conjunction where the word-order of subject and verb is reversed (see 5.9.1 (iii)): *be Hunger went*, 'once Hunger has gone', 7b/211; *wolle thow, nulle thow*, 'whether you wish it or not', 7b/153; *wer I as hastif as þou*, 'if I were as hasty as you', 8/520.

The verb is in the subjunctive in subordinate clauses of concession, introduced by *though*, *never so* and the like: *þaȝ hit displese ofte*, 'even though it may often displease', 8/1; *ne bo þe song never so murie*, 'however delightful the song may be', 2/345; or introduced by *al*, in which case the verb precedes the subject: *al were his bodi sturne*, 'although his body was/may have been forbidding', 9/143. The subjunctive is also often used in clauses of purpose or result, introduced by *þat*, *lest*, etc.: *that þou betere therby*, 'so that you may thereby benefit', 7a/21.

In subordinate clauses of time that look forward to an anticipated event, introduced by conjunctions such as *er* or *til*, the subjunctive is usual with the present tense: *er þou glyde hens*, 'before you go from here', 8/204; *tyl þou fele lyst*, 'until you feel desire', 6/19. It is quite common when the point of view is in the past: *or he wer tille þe booryngis brought*, 'before he was brought to the nail-holes', 14/146.

With reference to place, the subjunctive is used for subordinate clauses introduced by *where* to express uncertainty with the indefinite meaning 'wherever': *where he in court were*, 'wherever he may have been at court', 9/100.

The subjunctive is very often found after verbs of thinking, seeming or saying, for indirect statements and questions, since these are not facts but reports or opinions: *and weneþ it be Glodeside*, 'and believes it to be Glodeside' (it isn't), 12/209; *I hope þat he were*, 'I believe he was', 9/140; *bet þuȝte þe dreim þat he were / Of harpe*, 'the music seemed rather to come from a harp', 2/21–2; *y preye the . . . what beste be to done*, 'I ask you what it is best to do', 7b/209–10. Verbs of knowing, on the other hand, normally take the indicative if no uncertainty is involved. So compare the confident indicative in *ich wot he is nu suþe acoled*, 'I know he has now cooled off considerably', 2/205, with the subjunctive where there is a stronger element of opinion: *uch wyȝe may wel wit no wont þat þer were*, 'each person may well know that there was no shortage', 9/131.

As the distinctions between the subjunctive and the indicative forms – always only partial – were reduced, the subjunctive mood came more and more to be expressed by other means, in particular by the use of the modal auxiliaries such as *shall* and *sholde*, *may* and *miȝt*, *will* and *wolde*. Modern English has, of course, developed further along the same lines. In Middle English the modal auxiliaries are quite often found as equivalents to the subjunctive, e.g. in an indirect question: *to spyr uschon oþir / Quat body hit myȝt be*, 'each one to ask the other what body it might be', 10/93–4.

5.6.7 The Imperative

The imperative generally has distinct forms for singular (addressed to one person) and plural; see 4.5.2. It can also be expressed by *do* with another imperative, as in *do gyf glory to þy godde*, 8/204. Another common way of giving an order is with imperative *look* followed by the subjunctive: *loke þou drynke*, 7b/277; *loke þee loþe*, 'make sure that you find it hateful', 6/4 (see note there).

5.6.8 Impersonal Verbs

Some verbs which have a personal subject in Modern English, such as 'I like', are impersonal in Middle English, with *it* as subject and *me* etc. as dative object: *it likes me*. Quite regularly the dative object precedes the verb and the subject *it* is not expressed: *me lykes / þat I schal fange*, 'it is pleasing to me/I'm glad that I shall receive', 9/390–1. Another common impersonal verb with the same meaning is *list*; such constructions may need to be paraphrased rather than translated word for word: *me luste bet speten*, 'it pleases me better to spit', so 'I'd rather spit', 2/39; *ne lust him nu to none unrede / Nu him ne lust na more pleie*, 'nor is he attracted now to any evil counsel, nor does he like fooling around any more', 2/212–13. *Hunger*, 'be hungry', *fall*, 'happen', *need*, 'be necessary', and *reche*, 'care', are some other common verbs that may be used impersonally: *ow* (dative) *schal eaver hungrin*, 'you'll always go hungry', 4/64; *hym neded no gyde*, 'no guide was necessary to him', 16a/166; *me no reche*, 'I don't care', 5/342.

The verb *think* is derived from two Old English verbs, *þencan*, 'to think', and *þyncan*, 'to seem'. The two are still distinguished as *þenk* and *þynk* in the *Gawain* manuscript: *þenk wel, Sir Gawan*, 9/487; *what maystery þe þynkez*, 'what accomplishment does it seem to you', 8/482. In the line *þenne byþenk þe, mon, if þe forþynk sore*, 8/495, the first verb (OE *biþencan*) means 'consider' and has a reflexive pronoun *þe*; the second has an impersonal construction (and is subjunctive after *if*), 'if it upsets you'. In *me thynkes / Hom burde*, 'it seems to me they ought to', 10/259–60, there are two impersonal verbs together.

Some adjectives governing the dative have similar impersonal constructions: *lever me were*, 'I should rather', 5/177; *me is þe wurs*, 'it is the worse for me', 2/34; *þe is bettere*, 13j/23; *wel is me*, 13q/17; *hou wo þe beet*, 'how great is your grief', 13p/18.

5.6.9 Verbs of Motion

Intransitive verbs expressing movement, *fare*, *go*, *turn* and the like, are often accompanied by a reflexive pronoun: *Jonas hym ȝede*, 'Jonah went', 8/355; *Childric . . . gon him to charren / And beh him over Avene*, 'Childric . . . turned back and made his way over the Avon', 3/78–9. The infinitive verb of motion is often not expressed after an auxiliary verb: *and wold up and owy*, 'and wanted (to get) up and (to go) away', 5/96; *þider ichil* (the pronoun *ich* run together with the verb *wil*), 'I'll (go) there', 5/316; *I wyl me sum oþer waye*, 'I'll go some other way', 8/86 (where the reflexive pronoun remains). In *Ticius to Tuskan*, 9/11, the verb of motion has to be understood from the context even without an auxiliary verb.

5.6.10 The Passive

The passive is most often expressed by the verb *be*: *he . . . wæs wæl underfangen fram þe pape Eugenie*, 'he was well received by Pope Eugenius', 1/63. Until the end of the fourteenth century it was also expressed by *worthe*, 'to be, come to be', particularly in a future sense: *blessid þou worth*, 'may you be blessed', 10/340; *þou worst wiþ ous yborn*, 'you shall be carried off with us', 5/174.

Only one verb, *hoten*, has a passive form, *hat*(*te*), 'is called' or 'was called': *as hit now hat*, 'as it is now called', 9/10. Increasingly *hiȝte*, in origin the active past tense, was used in a passive sense: *his sone hihte*, 'his son was called', 7b/82.

The indefinite pronoun *man* was frequently used where Modern English uses a passive construction; see 5.4.3.

5.7 NEGATION

In earlier texts the usual way of negating a verb was to place *ne* (or *no/na*) immediately in front of it, and indeed this practice continued throughout the period: *I ne can ne I ne mai*, 'I do not know how to nor am I able to', 1/33; *ne wonde / þis aventure for to frayn*, 'don't hesitate to attempt this adventure', 9/488–9. *Ne* was run together with *have*, *wil* and parts of *be* beginning with a vowel or *w*-: e.g. *nadde*, *nil*, *nis*, *nere* (4.5.7–8).

Ne could be reinforced by another negative word elsewhere in the sentence. The commonest was *nouȝt*, originally a noun meaning 'nought' or 'nothing', which developed into the adverb *not*: *he no schuld nouȝt fram hem go*, 'he would not go from them', 5/225; with the subject following the verb: *ne reche ich noȝt*, 'I don't care', 2/58; with *noȝt* modifying another adverb, *wel*: *his nest noȝt wel he ne bihedde*, 'he did not guard his nest well', 2/102.

From the fourteenth century it became common to negate the verb with *not* alone, usually following the verb: *I know not þe*, 'I don't know you', 9/400; *Arthure wolde not ete*, 9/85. In verse, where word-order is more flexible, bringing *noȝt* forward gives it additional emphasis: *þat noȝt hit yow falles*, 'that it is not fitting for you', 9/358. The modern construction with auxiliary 'do not' was not fully established until the seventeenth century.

The notions that multiple negation, as in 'he ain't been nowhere', is sub-standard, and that 'two negatives make a positive', have no historical basis. In Middle English piling up of negatives is very common, and its purpose is to reinforce the negative. Notable examples are: *never him nas wers for noþing*, 'he was never more distressed about anything', 5/98; *ne isæh nævere na man selere cniht nenne*, 'no-one had ever seen a better knight', 3/28.

5.8 QUESTIONS

In direct questions the subject follows the verb, whether or not an interrogative word such as 'why' or 'what' is used: *how schal I do?*, 6/102; *can thow serven?*, 7a/12; *whi seist þou so?*, 13j/25. The modern use of *do* as an auxiliary in questions is unusual even at the end of the period; compare quotation with translation here: *wenst þu þat ich ne cunne singe?*, 'do you think that I can't sing?', 2/47.

As in Modern English, the 'declarative question', in which the word-order is that of a statement, is also possible. Here the context, and in this particular case the addition of the adverbial clause, make it clear that this is a question: *thow art broke, so may be?*, 'you are injured, maybe?', 7a/33.

A negative question has verb–subject word-order with *ne* before the verb: *why ne dyȝttez þou me to diȝe?*, 'why don't you condemn me to die?', 8/488; *nas I a paynym?*, 'was I not a pagan?', 10/285.

The word *whether* may be used to introduce a question, especially if there is doubt between two alternatives: *wheþer ys ȝow levere have* . . ., 'would you rather have' (where the choice is between rhyme or prose), 11/145.

5.9 WORD-ORDER

5.9.1 Inversion

As in Old English and in Modern English, the usual word-order of a statement in Middle English was subject–verb–object. Because Middle English has fewer inflexions to mark the function of words in a sentence, there is less variation of standard patterns than in Old English, though writers of verse had more freedom than prose writers to alter the word-order for stylistic or metrical effects, provided the relationship between the words was clear from grammatical form or context. Most instances cited here to show standard patterns are therefore taken from the prose texts.

Inversion, where the subject follows the verb, is found particularly in the following circumstances, some of which have been discussed already:

(i) In questions (see 5.8).

(ii) In commands and wishes: *construe þou cleerly*, 6/126; *see who bi grace see may*, 6/74. (See 5.6.6.)

(iii) In conditional or concessive clauses introduced by *al*, 'although', or without a conjunction (see 5.6.6), including hypothetical sentences containing *never so*: *be þeo neode never so gret*, 'however great the need is', 11/9.

(iv) Often after an adverb or phrase of place, time, manner etc.: *here liþ counforte*, 'here lies comfort', 6/125; *for ever schal he do it, and never schal he seese for to do it*, 6/73–4; *riȝt wel hast þou seide*, 6/113; *and so þarynne ys noble and gret informacion and lore*, 11/27–8; *on al þis yvele time heold Martin abbot his abbotrice*, 1/56. In a correlative construction, most frequent in Early Middle English, the inverted word-order is used in the main clause. Common correlatives are *þa . . . þa*, 'when . . . then', or *so . . . so*: *þa þe king Stephne to Englaland com, þa macod he his gadering*, 'when King Stephen came to England, (then) he held his council', 1/5–6; *þa he hafden al his iweden, þa leop he on his steden*, 'when he had all his gear, (then) he leapt on his steed', 3/25. The inversion in the main clause is a useful indication that *þa* is an adverb, 'then', not a conjunction, 'when'.

(v) After an adverbial phrase that has been fronted for emphasis: *by love may he be getyn*, 'he may be reached by love', 6/222.

(vi) In negative statements with *ne*, particularly in early verse: *ne kep ich noȝt*, 'I don't care', 2/154; *ne schaltu nevre*, 2/209 (see 5.7).

(vii) After *there*, where *there* is used as a dummy subject: *þer ys moche Latyn in þeus bokes*, 11/47. Earlier *it* was used in place of *there*: *it nis no bot*, 'there is no remedy', 5/552. Sometimes, especially in early texts, there is no dummy subject: *wes nævre gæt mare wreccehed on land*, 'there was never before more misery in the land', 1/43.

5.9.2 The Object

A pronoun object often precedes the verb, its inflected form determining its relationship: *þe biscopes and lered men heom cursede ævre*, 1/50–1. The same order is possible with a noun object, and even a noun object with a relative clause, as *lordes* here: *that sche þe lordes ate feste / That were obeissant to his heste / Mai know*, 'so that at the feast she may get to know the lords who were subject to him', 12/103–5.

5.9.3 Prepositions

In verse, and particularly in alliterative verse, prepositions may follow the noun or pronoun: *þe peple biforne*, 'in front of the people', 9/123; *him barones besyde*, 'barons beside him', 10/142. Deferred prepositions at the end of relative or infinitive clauses, of the type *þe prik þat he schoteþ to*, 6/199–200, can be brought forward, especially in verse: *þe werst piler on to biholde*, 'the worst pillar to look at', 5/367; *this present to plese with Honger*, 'this present to please Hunger with', 7b/318.

5.9.4 Relative Clauses

A relative *þat*-clause is quite often separated from the antecedent to which it refers, and this can cause difficulty since it is not possible in Modern English. In *he shal have my soule þat alle soules made*, 7b/96, it is obvious enough that the antecedent of the *þat*-clause is *he* and not *my soule*, 'he who made all souls shall have my soul'. Less obviously, *al studied þat þer stod*, 9/237, is 'all those who were standing there looked intently', not 'all looked intently at the one who stood there', though it is only the context that determines it; and *þe man marred on þe molde þat moȝt hym not hyde*, 8/479, makes better sense as 'the man who could not shelter himself suffered on the bare earth', than as 'the man suffered on the bare earth that could not shelter him'.

5.9.5 Adverbial Phrases

The position of adverbial phrases is very flexible, and they may even be placed outside the clause to which they belong: *in worlde quat weghe þou was*, 'what man you were in the world', 10/186. This is especially characteristic of Gower: *wiþ al his herte and most it hateþ*, 'and most hates it with all his heart', 12/56; *wiþinne his herte and tok a pride*, 'and grew proud in his heart', 12/135.

5.9.6 Verb in Final Position

A common word-order is for the verb to come at the end of a subordinate clause, particularly in verse: *Ne schaltu nevre so him queme / þat he for þe fals dom deme*, 2/209–10; *þis watz kynges countenaunce where he in court were*, 9/100.

5.10 RECAPITULATION AND ANTICIPATION

A pronoun may recapitulate or anticipate a clause or a noun phrase. There are some good examples of this in *Piers Plowman*. In *prestes and oþer peple towarde Peres they drowe*, 7b/190, *they* stands for the noun phrase which is separated from its verb. In *meschef hit maketh they ben so meke*, 7b/212, *hit* anticipates the clause that follows. In *ho-so beste wrouhte / He sholde be huyred*, 7b/120–1, *He* sums up the preceding clause 'whoever did best', and the same structure is seen in *þat was bake for Bayard hit may be here bote*, 'what was baked for Bayard, (it) may be their salvation', 7b/178. In *alle þat grat in thy gate for Godes love aftur fode / Part with hem of thy payne*, 7b/284–5, the inflected form *hem* both sums up the clause of l. 284 and establishes its dependence on *Part with*. The same structure, again with an imperative verb, is illustrated from the York Play: *this traitoure here teynted of treasoune / Gose faste and fette hym*, 14/77–8.

6
Metre

6.1 INTRODUCTION

Two distinct metrical traditions are represented in this book: rhymed verse and alliterative verse. The verse of French and Anglo-Norman poets was the chief model for the former; the history of alliterative verse is less clear, but it is a verse-form native to Germanic peoples and used by the Anglo-Saxons. English rhymed verse is based on the regular alternation of stressed and unstressed syllables; alliterative verse is based on stress and is syllabically variable.

6.2 RHYMED VERSE

Throughout the period the standard form of rhymed verse was the couplet of eight or nine syllables, with four beats or stresses. This is seen at its most controlled in Gower's *Confessio Amantis*, in which the author's metrical precision has been faithfully transmitted by a scribe no less attentive to the syllabic regularity of the metre.

Almost invariably Gower has an iambic line of eight syllables:

> Som góodly wórd þat þée was tóld (12/24)

or nine syllables if the last is unstressed:

> Wiþ ál his hérte and móst it háteþ (12/56)

The reader may begin with the expectation that word-endings containing a vowel, such as *-e*, *-ed*, *-es*, are to be pronounced as a syllable. So in the first line:

> The více cléped Ávantánce (12/1)

both *vice* and *cleped* have two syllables, and *Avantance* has four. Similarly, *dukes*, *helpe* and *soghte* are all disyllabic in:

> Wher þei þe dukes helpe soghte (12/241)

The chief exception to this is that a final vowel is elided before another vowel, and before *h-* when it is silent or in an unstressed syllable. So while the *-e* of *make* is sounded in *make myn avant* (12/37), it is lost in *make avanterie*

(12/40), and by the same principle the word 'token' has one syllable in *tokne or lettre* (12/25). Because the *h-* of *hond* is aspirated, the final *-e* of the adjective 'own' is sounded in *his oghne hond* (12/81). The *-e* of *scholde* is sounded before *have* in 12/144 because *have* is stressed, but that same *-e* is elided in 12/41, *scholde have do*, where *have* is unstressed. Despite its spelling, *hire* is generally a monosyllable, whatever sound follows, as the examples of it in 12/86–8 demonstrate. Words such as *evere* and *nevere* are disyllabic, *nev're*, with the second *-e-* elided (e.g. 12/32), so that with the final *-e* lost before a vowel they become monosyllabic, as in *For évere I schál* (12/220).

These rules sound complicated when listed in this way, but – such is the meticulousness of both poet and scribe – reading Gower aloud with attention to the metre will at once bring out the regularity of the rhythm. Variations upon the iambic pattern are occasional and therefore often very striking, as in *Drink wiþ þi fáder, dáme* (12/153), where the inversion of the first foot gives dramatic emphasis at this crucial point in the tale (see the note there). Inversion within the line is rarer still, but it can, for example, convey the speech-rhythm of a colloquial phrase in *téll and sei hów* (12/20).

The same four-stress verse-form is used some two centuries earlier for *The Owl and the Nightingale.* Perhaps because of the stronger influence of the native line upon the early poet, there is much greater freedom in rhythmic patterns than Gower permits, but even so, greater freedom does not generally mean less control. A straightforwardly regular line is:

> þarmíd þu cláckes óft and lónge (2/81)

Final *-e* needs to be sounded in:

> And áfter þáre lónge tále (2/140)

but within the line *-e* is elided in:

> Ich hábbe on bréde and ék on léngþe (2/174)

There is striking inversion of the first foot in:

> Wái þat he nís þaróf biréved (2/120)

and shifting of stress within the line brings to prominence the alliteration and rhyme of a colloquial phrase:

> Wel fíȝt þat wel flíȝt séiþ þe wíse (2/176)

In

> þu cháterest so dóþ on Írish próst (2/322)

the chatter of the extra syllable of *chat'rest so* might be regarded as artful, but it is as well to remember that this poet's scribes were not especially faithful to his intentions, and that metrical variation may sometimes be a sign of scribal carelessness.

The text of *Sir Orfeo* (from about 1330) presents a rougher form of the four-stress couplet. It is evident that at least some of the metrical irregularities were contributed by a scribe or a series of scribes, yet it is unlikely that the poet himself wrote a formal iambic line. Whatever the practices of individual poets, strict regularity of syllables was not fundamental to English verse as it was to French, and modulations of the standard pattern are often effectively used. In *Sir Orfeo* it may be that the marked irregularity of the passage describing the horror of the undead in the Fairy World (5/391–400) is designed as a jolt to the reader; on the other hand the restoration of earlier inflected forms (not attempted in this book) would often give a smoother line:

And súm[e] láy[en] wóde ybóunde (5/394)

So, too, the irregularity of

And whén ȝe understónd þat ý be spént (5/215)

would be improved by the substitution of the synonymous verb *wite*, which is actually used in the parallel line in another manuscript.

Chaucer employed short couplets in some early works, but later preferred a longer line of ten or eleven syllables, either in rhyming couplets (e.g. the Reeve's Tale, text 16a) or in stanzaic form. Both *The Parliament of Fowls* (text 15) and the Prioress's Tale (text 16b) are composed in 'rhyme-royal' stanzas of seven lines rhyming *ababbcc*. Like Gower, Chaucer was concerned with achieving the correct number of syllables in his longer line, and observed the same rules of elision; but, in the *Parliament* especially, the manuscripts are less faithful to his original intentions.

Rhymes in these poems are generally true, though later sound changes may have obscured this. 'Boards' and 'words' would now be half-rhymes, but in Gower *bordes* and *wordes* (12/131–2) are true rhymes, as are *dale* and *smale* in *Sir Orfeo* (5/537–8). Identical rhymes are quite common, but only when they involve different parts of speech, as *clawe*, noun and verb, in 2/153–4, or a simple word with a compound, as *soghte* and *besoghte* in 12/241–2. For remarks on rhyme and word-stress see 2.4 above.

Writers of lyrics chose a wide range of stanza-forms, from the very simple patterns of the Rawlinson Lyrics (13a–f), which are perhaps for singing, to the more complex schemes of the Harley Lyrics (13g–k). A burden or refrain accompanies one of the simplest (13b), as well as one of the most elaborate (13g). The models for lyric stanzas will again often have been French or Anglo-Norman, though Latin hymns were also a strong and direct influence upon writers such as John of Grimestone (13l–r).

Rhymed verse frequently uses alliteration as an ornament of style; sometimes that alliteration is very heavy, as in the York Play (text 14), which is written in twelve-line stanzas of regularly iambic lines.

6.3 ALLITERATIVE VERSE

In the later fourteenth century alliterative poetry flourished in the hands of some remarkable poets of the West and North-West Midlands. They are represented in this book by William Langland, the *Gawain*-poet, and the author of *St Erkenwald* (texts 7–10).

The alliterative line is based on principles quite different from those of rhymed verse, but they are essentially easy to understand. Each line is divided into half-lines bound together by alliteration. Each half-line normally has two stressed syllables; the two stresses of the first half-line alliterate with the first stress of the second half-line, while the last stress does not alliterate. So, with *a* standing for 'alliteration', the standard alliterative pattern is denoted *aa/ax*:

> þe **t**úlk þat þe **t**rámmes . of **t**résoun þer wróȝt
> Watz **t**ríed for his **t**rícherie . þe **t**réwest on érthe
> Hit watz **É**nnias þe **á**thel . and his **h**íghe kýnde (9/3–5)

In the practice of these poets, any vowel may alliterate with any other vowel and with *h*-, as in the last line quoted.

This structural alliteration normally falls on stressed syllables. As already described in 2.4, the way a word is stressed in Modern English is generally a good guide to its Middle English stress-pattern, although there are some variations, particularly in French loan-words. So 'deserved' alliterates and is stressed on the first syllable in

> Such a **d**únt as þou hatz **d**ált . **d**ísserved þou hábbez (9/452)

'Important' words (nouns, adjectives, adverbs and verbs) are normally stressed in preference to 'little' words (prepositions, articles and conjunctions). When an adjective accompanies a noun, either may be stressed, as the following line illustrates:

> Of **b**rýȝt golde upon silk **b**órdes . **b**árred ful rýche (9/159)

Sometimes there are three alliterating syllables in the first half-line. It may be appropriate to subordinate one of these, so that in the following the first word, *siþen*, is presumably unstressed, though alliterating:

> **S**iþen þe **s**ege and þe a**s**saut . watz **s**esed at Troye (9/1)

Yet it is more difficult to subordinate the noun *borȝ* in the next line:

> þe **b**orȝ **b**rittened and **b**rent . to **b**rondez and askez (9/2)

Non-standard alliterative patterns, such as *ax/ax* or *aa/xx*, are also found, but many of them are perhaps the result of scribal error. An obvious example of such corruption is:

Wolde ȝe **w**orþilych lorde . quoþ Gawan to þe kyng (9/343)

where we have adopted the simple emendation to *Wawan*, a form of Gawain's name used elsewhere by the poet, to restore the standard alliterative pattern.

A stressed syllable is called a *lift*, a group of unstressed syllables a *dip*. The dips vary in length, and this determines the rhythmic structure of the half-line. In the following two lines, the first has a four-syllable dip before the first stress, while the next has no dip at all between the stresses of the second half:

þat siþen de**p**réced **p**róvinces . and **p**átrounes bicóme
Wélneȝe of al þe **w**éle . in þe **w**ést íles (9/6–7)

In *Sir Gawain and the Green Knight*, from which all these examples have been taken, a varying number of alliterative lines is rounded off by a rhyming 'bob and wheel' of five lines, the 'bob' of one stress and the four lines of the 'wheel' of three stresses.

The basic description of the alliterative line applies also to the verse of *Piers Plowman*, but the variations in Langland's line are considerably greater than those in the *Gawain*-poet and the other writers of the North-West. One very characteristic feature of Langland's verse is the alliteration of an unstressed syllable before a non-alliterating stressed syllable. So in this second half-line, *fro* alliterates but *morw-* is stressed:

And **fl**ápton on with **fl**áles . **f**ro mórwen til éven (7b/180)

Variant alliterative patterns, in particular *aaa/xx* and *aa/xa*, are found quite frequently in *Piers Plowman* and are perhaps authentic, but scribal intervention in this text is a major problem, and many of the metrical anomalies may be a result of corruption.

6.4 LAȜAMON'S *BRUT*

Laȝamon, writing in about 1200, used both rhyme and alliteration, sometimes as alternatives, sometimes together. He seems to have relied on two distinct models: the stress-based alliterative line of Germanic tradition, and the rhyming couplets of Romance verse. The alliterative line was inherited from Old English, but perhaps not directly; there are examples even from before the Conquest of a much looser alliterative line with sporadic internal rhyme. On this model Laȝamon superimposed a metre learnt from Anglo-Norman and Latin poets writing rhyming couplets. In Laȝamon's *Brut* the half-lines are of varying length, predominantly of two stresses, and are linked to one another sometimes by rhyme or half-rhyme, sometimes by alliteration, sometimes by both. With rhyme but not alliteration is:

Hí3enliche swíðe . fórð he gon líðe (3/4)

The next line has alliteration but not rhyme:

þat he **b**íhalves **B**áðe . **b**éh to ane vélde (3/5)

Two lines further on, the word *burnen* both alliterates and rhymes with the second half-line:

And ón mid heore **b**úrnen . **b**éornes stúrne (3/7)

In his work La3amon was recreating a heroic British past for an Anglo-Norman present, and his metrical form, like other features of his style, recalls pre-Conquest traditions. Yet his *Brut* does not attempt to reproduce an Anglo-Saxon verse form, but instead develops English verse by assimilating Continental traditions.

7
From Manuscript to Printed Text

The following is a passage from one of our texts (10), *St Erkenwald* lines 257–64: first, as it appears in the one surviving manuscript copy; then, as it would appear in a 'diplomatic' or letter-by-letter transcription; and finally, as it appears in our edited version.

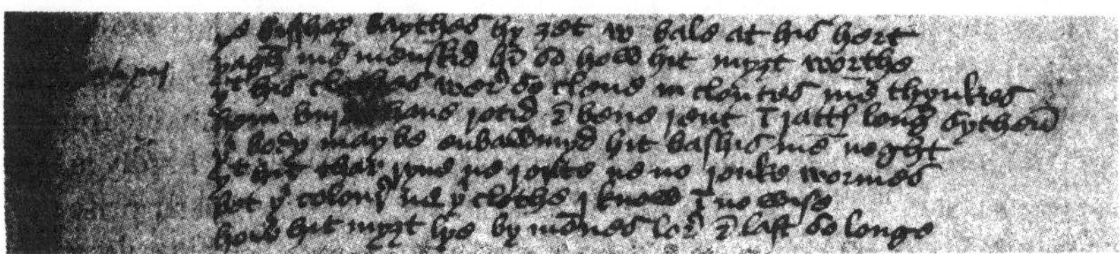

Lines from *St Erkenwald* (MS Harley 2250). Reproduced by permission of the British Library.

be, co to paſ

y^{e} bisshop baythes hȳ ȝet w^{t} bale at his hert
yagh me̅ menskid hī so how hit myȝt worthe
y^{t} his clothes wer so clene in cloutes me thynkes
hom burde haue rotid & bene rent ī ratt long sythen
y^{i} body may be enbawmyd hit bashis me noght
y^{t} hit thar ryne ne ro~~u~~te ne no ronke wormes
bot y^{i} colour ne y^{i} clothe I know ī no wise
how hit myȝt lye by mōnes lor & last so longe

þe bisshop baythes hym ȝet with bale at his hert,
þagh men menskid him so, how hit myȝt worthe
þat his clothes were so clene. 'In cloutes, me thynkes,
Hom burde have rotid and bene rent in rattes long sythen.
þi body may be enbawmyd, hit bashis me noght
þat hit thar ryne no rote ne no ronke wormes;
Bot þi coloure ne þi clothe – I know in no wise
How hit myȝt lye by monnes lore and last so longe.'

We ignore the early-modern hand which has marked *worthe* and *rattes* with underlining, and glossed the former (correctly) 'be, com to pas', although such annotations have their own interest as testifying to post-medieval study of Middle English texts. The original is written in a late fifteenth-century hand. As was common at the time, the scribe uses a *y* shape for both *y* and *þ*, but we distinguish them: *þe* for *ye* (257), but *myȝt* (258). He also writes *u* for modern *v* in the middle of words (*haue* 260), but our practice is to 'normalize' this. We expand the abbreviation for *and*. The line over vowels indicates either *m* or *n*, and has been represented accordingly: *hym* (257), *men* (258), *in* (260, 263), *monnes* (264); but that over *þagh* (258) has been ignored, though it might be expanded, as by other editors, to (unetymological) *-e*. The *-es* abbreviation has been expanded in *rattes* (260), as have the customary short forms of *with* (257) and *þat* (259, 262). A final upward curl is taken to represent *-e* after *r* (*were* 259, *coloure* 263, *lore* 264), but not after other letters (*long sythen* 260). Editors differ in their practice on this point.

Line 262 presents editorial problems of a fairly typical kind. The scribe himself went wrong, correcting *route* to *rote*. Earlier in the line, some editors read *ryue*, that is, *ryve*, 'tear asunder'; but, *u* being indistinguishable from *n*, we prefer to read *ryne*, 'touch'. In either case, anyway, the line hardly makes sense as it stands: '[Your body may be embalmed, so it does not surprise me] that it need not touch/tear nor rot nor any foul worms'. We have therefore emended the first *ne* to *no*, assuming an error easily made by the scribe. This emendation turns *rote* into the noun 'rot' and makes it the subject of *ryne* – which is accordingly more appropriate than *ryve*, since rot can touch but hardly tear. So the line, in our version, means: 'that no rot need touch it, nor any foul worms'. The word-order object–verb–subject is common in Middle English verse.

The passage also illustrates the difficulties and responsibilities that face editors as they punctuate their texts. Most Middle English verse is not punctuated at all, as in the case of *St Erkenwald*, or has nothing but metrical punctuation such as marks the half-lines in alliterative poems. So all punctuation in modern editions should be treated with scepticism, as representing nothing more authoritative than an editor's judgement of the syntax and meaning of the original. Modern habits of punctuation, furthermore, are in many respects ill-suited to the fluid and often colloquial structure of medieval sentences. Thus, the enclosing of the first half of line 258 between commas tends to disguise the fact that it belongs inside the clause that follows: 'The bishop asks him further with anguish in his heart how it could be that, even though people had honoured him so, his clothes were so perfectly preserved'. Again, line 259 should slip into direct speech more easily than it does in our text, where modern punctuation has required a heavy stop, an inverted comma, and a capital letter. The comma after *enbawmyd* (261) is a deliberate underpointing, designed to keep the line and the sentence moving; but the awkwardly overemphatic dash in line 263 seems the only way of representing a usage hardly permissible in modern written English: *coloure* and *clothe* announce the subject of *myȝt lye* in the next line, to be recapitulated there by the pronoun *hit* (see 5.10).

Elsewhere in our texts, editorial punctuating involves more far-reaching decisions about meaning. An extreme example, and one where the present editors have not been able to agree a solution, is presented by the opening lines of *Sir Gawain and the Green Knight* (text 9 here). These appear as follows, without any punctuation, in the sole manuscript:

Siþen þe sege and þe assaut watz sesed at Troye
þe borȝ brittened and brent to brondez and askez
þe tulk þat þe trammes of tresoun þer wroȝt
Watz tried for his tricherie þe trewest on erthe
Hit watz Ennias þe athel and his highe kynde
þat siþen depreced provinces and patrounes bicome
Welneȝe of al þe wele in þe west iles

The question of interpretation at its most basic is: who is the *tulk* of line 3? Two answers have been proposed.

(i) The *tulk* is Antenor who, according to well-known accounts of the fall of Troy, betrayed the city to the Greeks. The opening sentence is built round a correlative pair of *siþens*, at lines 1 and 6: '*After* the siege and the assault of Troy were over, the city destroyed and burned to brands and ashes, . . . it was the noble Aeneas and his great descendants who *afterwards* subjugated nations . . .'. On this reading, the *Hit watz* of line 5 points forward to what follows. Lines 3–4 are left as a parenthesis; and they should accordingly be set off by dashes: '– the man [Antenor] who carried out the treasonable schemes was famous for his treachery, the most notable on earth –'.

(ii) The *tulk* is Aeneas. Aeneas, according to the Troy story, at first conspired with Antenor to betray the city; but then he rescued the Trojan princess Polyxena from the clutches of the victorious Greeks. This further act of treachery, this time to the new masters of the city, was revealed to the Greeks who then exiled Aeneas from Troy. On this reading, the *Hit watz* of line 5 refers back to the *tulk*, identifying him as Aeneas, and so is best preceded by a colon at the end of line 4. Line 3 refers to the treason of Aeneas in betraying Troy; line 4 to his noble treachery in rescuing Polyxena: Aeneas 'was exposed for his treachery, the most honourable on earth'.

Since the two present editors do not agree on this matter, and since in any case the issues would not have been as clear-cut for a medieval reader or listener, we have adopted in our text a light and non-committal punctuation.

8

Select Bibliography

8.1 BIBLIOGRAPHIES AND INDEXES

General bibliographies of Middle English studies may be found in Watson and Severs and Hartung. The volumes of the latter, still appearing, treat works in detail, according to genre (e.g. Vol. 1 Romance, Vol. 5 Drama). The standard indexes are Brown and Robbins and its supplement Robbins and Cutler for verse, and Edwards for prose – the latter still in progress.

Brown, Carleton and Robbins, Rossell Hope, *The Index of Middle English Verse* (New York, 1943)

Edwards, A. S. G., ed., *The Index of Middle English Prose* (Cambridge, 1984–)

Laing, Margaret, *Catalogue of Sources for a Linguistic Atlas of Early Medieval English* (Cambridge, 1993)

Rice, Joanne A., *Middle English Romance: An Annotated Bibliography, 1955–1985* (New York, 1987)

Robbins, Rossell Hope and Cutler, John L., *Supplement to the Index of Middle English Verse* (Lexington, 1965)

Severs, J. Burke and Hartung, Albert E., eds, *A Manual of the Writings in Middle English, 1050–1500* (New Haven, 1967–)

Stratman, Carl J., *Bibliography of Medieval Drama*, 2nd edn revised, 2 vols (New York, 1972)

Watson, George, ed., *The New Cambridge Bibliography of English Literature, Vol. I 600–1660* (Cambridge, 1974).

8.2 LANGUAGE STUDIES

Short accounts of Middle English may be found in two general histories of English, Baugh and Cable, and Strang. The latter reverses chronological order and starts in the present day, with interesting results. Crystal provides a simple guide to English grammar and to the terminology used in this book. The first 130 pages of Mossé treat Middle English sounds, grammar and syntax quite comprehensively. On sounds, see also Blake (1992), Brunner and Jordan. The grammar of individual texts is best studied in editions such as the Tolkien–Gordon–Davis *Sir Gawain and the Green Knight* (see text 9). The standard treatment of syntax is Mustanoja, but the second volume (on word-order and sentence structure) has not appeared. McIntosh *et al.* is by far the most detailed study yet of Middle English dialects, covering the period 1350–1450, with many maps. The *Middle English Dictionary* (passing through T at the time of writing) is invaluable, but does not in all respects supersede the *Oxford English Dictionary*. Among glossaries, that by Norman Davis in Bennett and Smithers is outstanding. Whiting is a dictionary of proverbs, alphabetically arranged.

Baugh, A. C. and Cable, T., *A History of the English Language*, 3rd edn (London, 1978)

Bennett, J. A. W. and Smithers, G. V., with a Glossary by N. Davis, *Early Middle English Verse and Prose*, 2nd edn (Oxford, 1968)

Blake, Norman, *The English Language in Medieval Literature* (London, 1977)

Blake, Norman, ed., *The Cambridge History of the English Language, Vol. II 1066–1476* (Cambridge, 1992)

Brunner, Karl, *An Outline of Middle English Grammar*, trans. Grahame Johnston (Oxford, 1963)

Burnley, J. D., *The Language of Chaucer* (London, 1989)

Crystal, David, *Rediscover Grammar* (Harlow, 1988)

Elliott, Ralph W. V., *Chaucer's English* (London, 1974)

Greenbaum, Sidney, *et al.*, *A Student's Grammar of the English Language* (London, 1990)

Jordan, R., *Handbook of Middle English Grammar: Phonology*, trans. and revised E. J. Crook (The Hague, 1974)

McIntosh, Angus, Samuels, M. L. and Benskin, Michael, *A Linguistic Atlas of Late Mediaeval English*, 4 vols (Aberdeen, 1986)

Middle English Dictionary, ed. H. Kurath et al. (Ann Arbor, 1952–)

Mossé, Fernand, *A Handbook of Middle English*, trans. James A. Walker (Baltimore, 1952)

Mustanoja, Tauno F., *A Middle English Syntax, Part I: Parts of Speech* (Helsinki, 1960)

Serjeantson, Mary S., *A History of Foreign Words in English* (London, 1935)

Sheard, J. A., *The Words We Use* (London, 1954)

Strang, Barbara M. H., *A History of English* (London, 1970)

Whiting, Bartlett Jere and Whiting, Helen Wescott, *Proverbs, Sentences, and Proverbial Phrases from English Writings Mainly Before 1500* (Cambridge, Mass., 1968)

Wright, J. and E. M., *An Elementary Middle English Grammar*, 2nd edn (Oxford, 1928).

8.3 GENERAL STUDIES OF THE LITERATURE

The longest-running series of editions is that of the Early English Text Society (1864–). The failure of many texts to survive – see Wilson (1970) –

creates difficulties for literary history. Baugh and Malone is a useful reference work, and Pearsall is excellent on the poetry in its context. For a variety of general critical approaches, see Burrow (1982), Patterson, Spearing (1972) and Speirs. Lewis (1964) gives a vivid account of a 'world picture'. Bennett, Bolton, Everett, Ford, Spearing (1987) and Woolf all have good essays on particular authors and texts. For the earlier Middle English period, Salter (1988) is specially valuable. Studies of fourteenth-century writing are more numerous: Aers, Burrow (1971), Coleman, Muscatine and Salter (1983). On alliterative poetry, see Lawton and Turville-Petre. For prose, see Edwards. Three older studies of particular topics remain valuable: Chaytor, Lewis (1936) and Owst. On medieval literary theory and criticism, consult Minnis and (with an anthology of translated texts) Minnis and Scott. Curtius is the classic study of Latin tradition in the Middle Ages. The standard work on Anglo-Norman literature is Legge.

Aers, David, *Community, Gender, and Individual Identity: English Writing 1360–1430* (London, 1988)

Baugh, Albert C. and Malone, Kemp, *The Middle Ages*, 2nd edn (New York, 1967)

Bennett, J. A. W., *Middle English Literature*, ed. Douglas Gray (Oxford, 1986)

Bloomfield, Morton W., *The Seven Deadly Sins* (Michigan, 1952)

Bolton, W. F., ed., *The Middle Ages* (Sphere History of Literature, Vol. I), 2nd edn revised (London, 1986)

Burrow, J. A., *Ricardian Poetry: Chaucer, Gower, Langland and the 'Gawain' Poet* (London, 1971)

Burrow, J. A. *Medieval Writers and Their Work: Middle English Literature and its Background, 1100–1500* (Oxford, 1982)

Burrow, J. A., *Essays on Medieval Literature* (Oxford, 1984)

Chaytor, H. J., *From Script to Print: An Introduction to Medieval Literature* (Cambridge, 1945)

Coleman, Janet, *English Literature in History, 1350–1400: Medieval Readers and Writers* (London, 1981)

Curtius, Ernst Robert, *European Literature and the Latin Middle Ages*, trans. Willard R. Trask (London, 1953)

Edwards, A. S. G., ed., *Middle English Prose: A Critical Guide to Major Authors and Genres* (New Brunswick, 1984)

Everett, Dorothy, *Essays on Middle English Literature*, ed. Patricia Kean (Oxford, 1955)

Ford, Boris, ed., *Medieval Literature: Chaucer and the Alliterative Tradition* (The New Pelican Guide to English Literature, Vol. I Part One) (Harmondsworth, 1982)

Lawton, David, ed., *Middle English Alliterative Poetry and its Literary Background: Seven Essays* (Cambridge, 1982)

Legge, M. Dominica, *Anglo-Norman Literature and its Background* (Oxford, 1963)

Lewis, C. S., *The Allegory of Love* (Oxford, 1936)

Lewis, C. S., *The Discarded Image: An Introduction to Medieval and Renaissance Literature* (Cambridge, 1964)

Meale, Carol M., ed., *Women and Literature in Britain, 1150–1500* (Cambridge, 1993)

Minnis, A. J., *Medieval Theory of Authorship: Scholastic Literary Attitudes in the Later Middle Ages* (London, 1984)

Minnis, A. J. and Scott, A. B., *Medieval Literary Theory and Criticism c.1100–c.1375: The Commentary-Tradition* (Oxford, 1988)

Muscatine, Charles, *Poetry and Crisis in the Age of Chaucer* (Notre Dame, 1972)

Owst, G. R., *Literature and Pulpit in Medieval England*, 2nd edn (Oxford, 1961)

Patterson, Lee, *Negotiating the Past: The Historical Understanding of Medieval Literature* (Madison, 1987)

Pearsall, Derek, *Old English and Middle English Poetry* (London, 1977)

Rigg, A. G., *A History of Anglo-Latin Literature, 1066–1422* (Cambridge, 1992)

Salter, Elizabeth, *Fourteenth-Century English Poetry: Contexts and Readings* (Oxford, 1983)

Salter, Elizabeth, *English and International: Studies in the Literature, Art and Patronage of Medieval England*, ed. Derek Pearsall and Nicolette Zeeman (Cambridge, 1988)

Spearing, A. C., *Criticism and Medieval Poetry*, 2nd edn (London, 1972)

Spearing, A. C., *Readings in Medieval Poetry* (Cambridge, 1987)

Speirs, John, *Medieval English Poetry: The Non-Chaucerian Tradition* (London, 1957)

Turville-Petre, Thorlac, *The Alliterative Revival* (Cambridge, 1977)

Wilson, R. M., *Early Middle English Literature*, 2nd edn (London, 1951)

Wilson, R. M., *The Lost Literature of Medieval England*, 2nd edn (London, 1970)

Woolf, Rosemary, *Art and Doctrine: Essays on Medieval Literature*, ed. Heather O'Donoghue (London, 1986).

8.4 STUDIES OF PARTICULAR GENRES

Boitani and Mehl are useful studies of narrative poetry. For Arthurian romance, the standard work of reference is Loomis (with chapters on Laȝamon's *Brut*, *Sir Gawain and the Green Knight*, etc.). On the mystery plays, consult Woolf (1972) and Kolve. Excellent books on the religious lyric are Woolf (1968) and Gray. There is no comparable study of secular lyric; but Part Two of Stevens (1979) is very good on the lyric of 'courtly love'.

Beadle, Richard, ed., *The Cambridge Companion to Medieval English Theatre* (Cambridge, 1994)

Boitani, Piero, *English Medieval Narrative in the Thirteenth and Fourteenth Centuries*, trans. J. K. Hall (Cambridge, 1982)

Gray, Douglas, *Themes and Images in the Medieval English Religious Lyric* (London, 1972)

Kolve, V. A., *The Play Called Corpus Christi* (Stanford, 1966)

Kruger, Steven F., *Dreaming in the Middle Ages* (Cambridge, 1992)

Loomis, Roger Sherman, ed., *Arthurian Literature in the Middle Ages: A Collaborative History* (Oxford, 1959)

Mehl, Dieter, *The Middle English Romances of the Thirteenth and Fourteenth Centuries* (London, 1968)

Reed, Thomas L., *Middle English Debate Poetry and the Aesthetics of Irresolution* (Columbia, 1990)

Riehle, Wolfgang, *The Middle English Mystics*, trans. Bernard Standring (London, 1981)

Spearing, A. C., *Medieval Dream-Poetry* (Cambridge, 1976)

Stevens, John, *Medieval Romance: Themes and Approaches* (London, 1973)

Stevens, John, *Music and Poetry in the Early Tudor Court*, 2nd edn (Cambridge, 1979)

Woolf, Rosemary, *The English Religious Lyric in the Middle Ages* (Oxford, 1968)

Woolf, Rosemary, *The English Mystery Plays* (London, 1972).

8.5 HISTORICAL AND SOCIAL STUDIES

On the development of medieval society Southern (1953) is excellent. Also helpful are Morris and Clanchy (1993), the latter on the growth of literacy. The standard Oxford Histories of the whole period are Poole, Powicke and McKisack. For less detailed accounts, see the Fontana Histories, Clanchy (1983) and Tuck. The standard discussion of feudal society is Bloch. On the peasantry, H. S. Bennett, Hilton and Homans offer a variety of approaches (conservative, radical and sociological, respectively). Keen (1984) gives an excellent account of chivalry. For other aspects of aristocratic life, see Given-Wilson, McFarlane and (on 'court culture') Mathew and Scattergood/Sherborne. Hamilton and Southern (1970) give general surveys of the medieval church. Leclercq on monastic culture and Pantin on the later medieval English church are both specially recommended. On medieval learning, Piltz may be supplemented by Orme (on education) and Courtenay. Smalley is the indispensable guide to medieval readings of the Bible. On the merchant class, see especially Thrupp. Recent studies in the history of particular regions are well represented by M. J. Bennett.

Bennett, H. S., *Life on the English Manor: A Study of Peasant Conditions, 1150–1400*, 3rd edn (Cambridge, 1948)

Bennett, Michael J., *Community, Class and Careerism: Cheshire and Lancashire Society in the Age of 'Sir Gawain and the Green Knight'* (Cambridge, 1983)

Bloch, Marc, *Feudal Society*, trans. L. A. Manyon (London, 1961)

Chibnall, Marjorie, *Anglo-Norman England 1066–1166* (Oxford, 1987)

Clanchy, M. T., *England and Its Rulers, 1066–1272* (London, 1983)

Clanchy, M. T., *From Memory to Written Record: England 1066–1307*, 2nd edn (Oxford, 1993)

Courtenay, William J., *Schools and Scholars in Fourteenth-Century England* (Princeton, 1987)

Given-Wilson, C., *The English Nobility in the Late Middle Ages* (London, 1987)

Hamilton, Bernard, *Religion in the Medieval West* (London, 1986)

Heath, Peter, *Church and Realm, 1272–1461* (London, 1988)

Hilton, R. H., *Bond Men Made Free: Medieval Peasant Movements and the English Rising of 1381* (London, 1973)

Hilton, R. H., *The English Peasantry in the Later Middle Ages* (Oxford, 1975)

Homans, George Caspar, *English Villagers of the Thirteenth Century* (Boston, 1941)

Keen, Maurice, *England in the Later Middle Ages: A Political History* (London, 1973)

Keen, Maurice, *Chivalry* (London, 1984)

Keen, Maurice, *English Society in the Later Middle Ages, 1348–1500* (London, 1990)

Leclercq, Jean, *The Love of Learning and the Desire for God: A Study of Monastic Culture*, trans. Catharine Misrahi (New York, 1961)

McFarlane, K. B., *The Nobility of Later Medieval England* (Oxford, 1973)

McKisack, May, *The Fourteenth Century, 1307–1399* (Oxford, 1959)

Mathew, Gervase, *The Court of Richard II* (London, 1968)

Miller, E. and Hatcher, J., *Medieval England: Rural Society and Economic Change, 1086–1348* (London, 1978)

Morris, C., *The Discovery of the Individual, 1050–1200* (London, 1972)

Orme, N., *English Schools in the Middle Ages* (London, 1973)

Pantin, W. A., *The English Church in the Fourteenth Century* (Cambridge, 1955)

Piltz, Anders, *The World of Medieval Learning*, revised edn, trans. David Jones (Totowa, N.J., 1981)

Poole, Austin Lane, *From Domesday Book to Magna Carta, 1087–* 1216, 2nd edn (Oxford, 1955)

Powicke, F. M., *The Thirteenth Century, 1216–1307*, 2nd edn (Oxford, 1962)

Robertson, D. W., Jr, *Chaucer's London* (New York, 1968)

Scattergood, V. J. and Sherborne, J. W., eds, *English Court Culture in the Later Middle Ages* (London, 1983)

Smalley, Beryl, *The Study of the Bible in the Middle Ages*, 2nd edn (Oxford, 1952)

Southern, R. W., *The Making of the Middle Ages* (London, 1953)

Southern, R. W., *Western Society and the Church in the Middle Ages* (Harmondsworth, 1970)
Thrupp, Sylvia L., *The Merchant Class of Medieval London (1300–1500)* (Ann Arbor, 1948)
Tuck, Anthony, *Crown and Nobility 1272–1461: Political Conflict in Late Medieval England* (London, 1985)
Ziegler, Philip, *The Black Death* (London, 1969).

Part Two
Prose and Verse Texts

Treatment of Texts

Texts have been freshly prepared from the manuscripts. Departures from the base manuscript are recorded in the Textual Notes, pp. 316–21. Word-division, capitalization and punctuation are editorial. On punctuation, see Part One, chapter 7. Scribal abbreviations are silently expanded. The spelling of the manuscripts is preserved, including their use of the letters *æ*, *ȝ*, *þ* and *ð*; but the distributions of *u/v* and *i/j* have been changed to bring them into line with modern practice (e.g. *have* for *haue*). Where early texts (texts 1–4 and 13) represent *w* by the corresponding Old English runic letter or by *u*, *uu* or *v*, the modern letter has been substituted. An accent has been added to *e* in words such as *diversité* and *destyné*.

I

The Peterborough Chronicle 1137

At some date after 1121, the Benedictine monks of Peterborough Abbey copied out a version of the *Anglo-Saxon Chronicle* (see *A Guide to Old English*, text 7). The manuscript is now Bodleian Library MS Laud Misc. 636. Over the following decade, entries for the years 1122 to 1131 were added. Finally, probably in about 1155, some of the events of the intervening years were recorded, ostensibly still in the form of annals, but now with much more emphasis given to thematic relationship than to chronological order. So in the entry for 1137, given here, the writer surveys the nineteen terrible years of Stephen's reign (1135–54), the successes of Abbot Martin who died in 1155, and the martyrdom of St William of Norwich in 1144. The cruelties in the country at large, so barbarous that men concluded that Christ was asleep (54), are set beside the account of the abbot's achievements in rebuilding the abbey church and peacefully establishing financial stability. Lastly comes the demonstration that Christ is indeed not asleep, as the child William re-enacts the Crucifixion and 'through our Lord performed many wonderful miracles' (74–82). The account of the miseries of Stephen's reign may be read in the light of the assessment of a modern historian, R. H. C. Davis, *King Stephen* (London, 1967).

Since the text can be closely dated and located, it is particularly important for a study of the language at a crucial period in its development. There is a considerable Scandinavian element in the vocabulary, to be expected in an East Midland text; e.g. *carlmen*, 'men' (18), *bryniges*, 'coats of mail' (22), *hærnes*, 'brains' (24), *brendon*, 'burned' (38). Even at this early date there are several Romance loans, such as *tresor* (3), *carited* (58), *privilegies* (64), *miracles* (81). The grammar of the *Chronicle* is significantly more advanced than the later texts from further south and west, *The Owl and the Nightingale* and Laȝamon's *Brut.* Nouns have already lost all indication of grammatical gender. In the singular the ending *-e* after prepositions survives only sporadically: compare *in tune* (39–40) with *in the hus* (58–9); in the plural the ending is generally *-s*, though *wunder* (11, 34) is an example of an unchanged plural. Adjective inflexions are greatly simplified: definite adjectives generally end in

-e (or *-æ*) whatever their case, singular and plural, while indefinite adjectives have *-e* in the plural, though sometimes even this is lost in adjectives of more than one syllable; compare *scærpe stanes* (27) and *mid... yvele men* (16) with *hethen men* (44) and *cnotted strenges* (22–3). The definite article is indeclinable *þe*, though earlier sections of the *Chronicle* show some variation. The present plural ending of verbs is *-en*: *lien* (65), *willen* (74). In the past tense of weak verbs the singular ending *-e* is sometimes dropped and the plural ending *-en* (or *-an*, *-æn*, *-on*) dropped or reduced to *-e*, particularly before vowels or *h*; e.g. singular *macod he* (6), plural *cursede ævre* (51), *pined heom* (18–19) – compare *pineden him* (76). The third person plural pronouns are *hi*, 'they' (in l. 12 *he*), and *heom*, 'them'. The syntax is at an interesting stage of development, retaining many of the constructions and patterns of word-order characteristic of Old English prose despite the losses in the inflexional system.

Edition

Cecily Clark, *The Peterborough Chronicle 1070–1154*, 2nd edn (Oxford, 1970)

Facsimile

D. Whitelock, *The Peterborough Chronicle* (Copenhagen, 1954)

Study

Bruce Mitchell, 'Syntax and Word-Order in *The Peterborough Chronicle* 1122–1154', *Neuphilologische Mitteilungen*, 65 (1964), 113–44

1137. Ðis gære for þe king Stephne ofer sæ to Normandi, and ther wes underfangen forþi ðat hi wenden ðat he sculde ben alswic alse the eom wes and for he hadde get his tresor – ac he todeld it and scatered sotlice. Micel hadde Henri king gadered gold and sylver, and na god ne dide me for his saule tharof. Þa þe king Stephne to

1–4 During the summer of 1137, Stephen conducted an unsuccessful campaign to establish order in Normandy after the death there of his uncle, Henry I.

1 **for** 'went', past tense of *faren*.

3 **get** 'still'.

5 **me** the indefinite pronoun (see 5.4.3); so 'it was not used for the benefit of his soul'. On his deathbed Henry had 'made his arrangements for almsgiving' (*The Historia Novella*, trans. K. R. Potter (London, 1955), pp. 13–14).

5–9 Roger, bishop of Salisbury, the old king's chief justiciar, remained in control, together with his nephews, the bishops of Lincoln and Ely and the chancellor Roger le Poer (actually his illegitimate son, according to some accounts). At

Englaland com, þa macod he his gadering æt Oxeneford, and þar he nam þe biscop Roger of Serebyri, and Alexander biscop of Lincol and te canceler Roger, hise neves, and dide ælle in prisun til hi iafen up here castles. þa the swikes undergæton ðat he milde man was and softe and god and na justise ne dide, þa diden hi alle wunder. Hi hadden him manred maked and athes sworen, ac hi nan treuthe ne heolden. Alle he wæron forsworen and here treothes forloren, for ævric rice man his castles makede and agænes him heolden, and fylden þe land ful of castles. Hi swencten swyðe þe wrecce men of þe land mid castel-weorces. þa þe castles waren maked, þa fylden hi mid deovles and yvele men. þa namen hi þa men þe hi wenden ðat ani god hefden, bathe be nihtes and be dæies, carlmen and wimmen, and diden heom in prisun and pined heom efter gold and sylver untellendlice pining, for ne wæren nævre nan martyrs swa pined alse hi wæron. Me henged up bi the fet and smoked heom mid ful smoke. Me henged bi the þumbes other bi the hefed and hengen bryniges on her fet. Me dide cnotted strenges abuton here hæved and wrythen it ðat it gæde to þe hærnes. Hi diden heom in quarterne þar nadres and snakes and pades wæron inne, and drapen heom swa. Sume hi diden in 'crucethur' – ðat is, in an ceste þat was scort and narew and undep –

his Council at Oxford in June 1139, Stephen ordered them all to surrender their offices and their castles.

8 **te** a form of *þe* after *d*.

9 The *swikes* are the nobles who supported Henry I's daughter Matilda.

10 **na justise ne dide** 'did not inflict punishment'.

11 **wunder** plural, 'atrocities'.

11ff. In 1143 Stephen dispossessed Geoffrey de Mandeville, who retreated to the fenlands not far from Peterborough, where for a year he terrorized the surrounding countryside. In response the king's supporters built castles in an attempt to contain the revolt. The Peterborough monks therefore had first-hand knowledge of the turmoil. Accounts from other parts of the country are very similar; for example: 'There were many castles all over England, each defending its own district or, to be more truthful, plundering it. . . . Even bishops or monks could not safely pass from village to village' (*Historia Novella*, pp. 40–1). An even more dramatic account is given in *Gesta Stephani*, ed. and trans. by K. R. Potter (2nd edn, Oxford, 1976), pp. 153–7.

16 **þa fylden hi** After *þa* in the main clause, the subject (*hi*) follows the verb; see 5.9.1 (iv). The object is understood from *castles* in the previous clause.

17–18 **be nihtes and be dæies** adverbial genitive (singular); see 5.3.2.

20 **Me henged** 'they were hung'; see 5n. With *and hengen* . . . in l. 22, the construction changes in mid-sentence, with a personal subject 'they' understood. The two past-tense forms *henged* and *hengen* are respectively weak and strong, the former related to ON *hengja*, the latter from OE *hōn*, pa. pl. *hēngon*.

23 There is inconsistency in number: *here hæved*, 'their head'; *it* referring formally to *strenges*.

25 **pades** 'toads', which were thought to be poisonous and to devour flesh; cf. Shakespeare's 'venom toads' (*King Henry VI, Part Three*, II ii 138).

26 **crucethur** evidently a box in which victims were crushed; probably from Latin *cruciator*, 'torturer'.

and dide scærpe stanes þerinne, and þrengde þe man þærinne ðat him bræcon alle þe limes. In mani of þe castles wæron lof and grin – ðat wæron rachenteges ðat twa oþer thre men hadden onoh to bæron onne. þat was swa maced ðat is fæstned to an beom; and diden an scærp iren abuton þa mannes throte and his hals ðat he ne myhte nowiderwardes – ne sitten, ne lien, ne slepen – oc bæron al ðat iren. Mani þusen hi drapen mid hungær. I ne can ne I ne mai tellen alle þe wunder ne alle þe pines ðat hi diden wrecce men on þis land; and ðat lastede þa xix wintre wile Stephne was king, and ævre it was werse and werse. Hi læiden gæildes on the tunes ævre umwile and clepeden it 'tenserie'. þa þe wrecce men ne hadden nammore to gyven, þa ræveden hi and brendon alle the tunes, ðat wel þu myhtes faren al a dæis fare, sculdest thu nevre finden man in tune sittende, ne land tiled. þa was corn dære, and flec and cæse and butere, for nan ne wæs o þe land. Wrecce men sturven of hungær; sume ieden on ælmes þe waren sumwile rice men, sume flugen ut of lande. Wes nævre gæt mare wreccehed on land, ne nævre hethen men werse ne diden þan hi diden; for oversithon ne forbaren hi nouther circe ne cyrceiærd, oc namen al þe god ðat þarinne was and brenden sythen þe cyrce and al tegædere. Ne hi ne forbaren biscopes land ne abbotes ne preostes, ac ræveden munekes and clerekes, and ævric man other þe overmyhte. Gif twa men oþer iii coman ridend to an tun, al þe tunscipe flugæn for heom; wenden ðat hi wæron ræveres. þe biscopes and lered men heom cursede ævre, oc was heom naht þarof, for hi weron al forcursæd and forsworen and forloren. Warsæ me tilede, þe erthe ne bar nan corn, for þe land was al fordon mid swilce dædes; and hi

28 **him bræcon alle þe limes** 'all his limbs broke'. On the possessive dative *him*, see 5.3.3.

lof and grin heavy shackles whose use is described in the next lines. A *lof* is a fetter for the neck, and a *grin* is a noose.

29–30 **ðat twa . . . onne** 'such that two or three men could only just manage to carry one of them'; *onne*, 'one', has the masculine accusative ending *-ne* (OE *ānne*).

31 **diden** 'they put'; see 5.4.2.

31–2 **ne myhte** 'could not (turn)'; see 5.6.9.

32 **bæron** infinitive: 'but (he had to) bear'.

35 **xix wintre** 'nineteen years'.

36–7 **ævre umwile** 'repeatedly'.

37 **tenserie** 'protection money'; a French word.

44 **hethen men** perhaps a reference to the Viking invasions described earlier in the *Chronicle*; see *A Guide to Old English*, text 7.

47 The genitives *abbotes* and *preostes* are parallel to *biscopes*.

48 **ævric . . . overmyhte** The verb *ræveden* is understood: 'every man who had greater power (robbed) the other'.

51 **cursede** 'excommunicated'; so too *forcursæd* in l. 52.

was heom naht þarof 'that meant nothing to them'.

sæden openlice ðat Crist slep, and his halechen. Swilc and mare þanne we cunnen sæin we þoleden xix wintre for ure sinnes.

On al þis yvele time heold Martin abbot his abbotrice xx wintre and half gær and viii dæis mid micel swinc, and fand þe munekes and te gestes al þat heom behoved, and heold mycel carited in the hus; and þoþwethere wrohte on þe circe, and sette þarto landes and rentes, and goded it swythe and læt it refen, and brohte heom into þe newæ mynstre on St Petres mæsse dæi mid micel wurtscipe; ðat was *anno ab incarnatione Domini mcxl, a combustione loci xxiii.* And he for to Rome and þær wæs wæl underfangen fram þe pape Eugenie, and begæt thare privilegies, an of alle þe landes of þ'abbotrice, and anoþer of þe landes þe lien to þe circewican; and, gif he leng moste liven, alse he mint to don of þe horderwycan. And he begæt in landes þat rice men hefden mid strengthe. Of Willelm Malduit þe heold Rogingham þæ castel he wan Cotingham and Estun, and of Hugo of Waltervile he wan Hyrtlingbyri and Stanewig and lx *solidos* of Aldewingle ælc gær. And he makede manie munekes, and plantede winiærd, and makede mani weorkes, and wende þe tun betere þan it ær wæs, and wæs god munec and god man, and forþi him luveden God and gode men.

Nu we willen sægen sumdel wat belamp on Stephnes kinges

55 Such disasters, both natural and man-made, were commonly interpreted as punishment for sin.

56 Martin of Bec was abbot of Peterborough from 1132.

58 **gestes** monasteries were used as staging posts by nobles and ecclesiastics.

59–60 **sette . . . rentes** 'devoted to it income from lands and other revenues'.

60 **læt it refen** 'had a roof put on it'; see 5.6.5.

61 **St Petres mæsse dæi** the feast-day of Saints Peter and Paul, 29 June.

62 'In the year 1140 after the birth of the Lord, 23 after the burning of the building.' The old church had burnt to the ground in 1116.

63–6 Eugenius III became pope in 1145. The texts of the *privilegies*, dated 1146, are given in full in the Latin chronicle of the Peterborough monk Hugh Candidus. They are special papal grants to protect the abbey's lands and their revenues from expropriation by the king or the nobles. Lands were allocated to specific offices of the abbey, as here that of the sacrist and the cellarer, both for administrative convenience and to prevent the Exchequer from claiming the revenues during a period when the abbacy was vacant.

65 **circewican** the office of the sacrist, who took care of the vestments and sacred vessels.

65–6 **gif he leng moste liven** 'if he had been spared to live longer'.

66 **horderwycan** the office of steward or cellarer, in charge of buying food and clothes.

67–70 William Mauduit was constable of Rockingham Castle, Northamptonshire. In the same county are Cottingham, Irthlingborough, Stanwick and Aldwinkle, with Great Easton in Leicestershire.

69 **lx solidos** 'sixty shillings'.

74–82 This is the earliest of the stories, which later became widespread, of the ritual murder of Christian children. Chaucer's Prioress's Tale (text 16b/232) refers to another supposed case, that of Hugh of Lincoln. The report of the martyrdom of the boy William caused a great stir in Norwich in 1144. According to *The Life and*

time. On his time þe Judeus of Norwic bohton an Cristen cild beforen Estren and pineden him alle þe ilce pining ðat ure Drihten was pined, and on Lang Fridæi him on rode hengen for ure Drihtines luve, and sythen byrieden him; wenden ðat it sculde ben forholen. Oc ure Dryhtin atywede ðat he was hali martyr, and to munekes him namen and bebyried him heglice in þe minstre, and he maket þurh ure Drihtin wunderlice and manifældlice miracles. And hatte he St Willelm.

Miracles of St William of Norwich (ed. A. Jessopp and M. R. James, Cambridge, 1896), the boy's mother was given three shillings to allow him to go and work in the arch-deacon's kitchen. Instead he was taken to the house of a Jew, where he was tortured and crucified, and his body was then hidden in a wood, where it was revealed by a light in the sky.

77 **Lang Fridæi** Good Friday.

79 **to** 'the'; see 8n.

2

The Owl and the Nightingale

The Owl and the Nightingale is a poem of 1794 lines, only the first 390 of which are printed here. Since it refers (1091–2) to a 'King Henri' as dead, it must have been written after the death of Henry II in 1189, and also probably (though not certainly) before the accession of Henry III in 1216. Though very English in setting and language (with rather few French words), the poem has its chief roots in the Latin and French literatures of twelfth-century England and France. Its metrical form, the short or 'octosyllabic' couplet, was evolved by twelfth-century French poets as their chief medium of narrative; and its genre, the debate or *altercatio*, was much favoured by Latin poets of the time, who evidently enjoyed mustering arguments *pro* and *contra*. The altercation between the Owl and the Nightingale involves a wealth of fact and fable about the birds themselves; but it also raises a variety of human issues, especially in that part of the poem not represented here (552–1652) where the birds argue about their usefulness to mankind. Gravity is set against gaiety, permanence against transience, religious chant against love-songs, etc. By associating such rival views with species in God-created nature, the poet (like Chaucer in *The Parliament of Fowls*, text 15 here) seems to imply that human beings also, for all their love of winning arguments, will naturally and inevitably differ in their attitudes to life. Thus, people may be inclined to favour nightingales in youth and owls in age, like that 'Maister Nichole of Guldeforde' whom both birds are ready to accept as judge between them (187–214). It is likely that Nicholas of Guildford, who here receives such handsome testimonials to his broad-minded wisdom from both adversaries, himself wrote the poem. At the end of the debate, when the birds are preparing to fly off to receive his judgement (which is not reported), Nicholas is described as a country priest living in a Dorset village, Portesham, and shamefully neglected there by bishops who ought to know better than to let such wisdom go to waste in an obscure parish (1751–78). It is the poem's last sally of wit: an amusingly devious plea for preferment.

The poem survives in two manuscripts, both of the second half of the thirteenth century: British Library MS Cotton Caligula A IX

(C), upon which the present text is based, and Jesus College, Oxford, MS 29 (J). The language of Cotton represents the poet's own South-Eastern English (perhaps that of Guildford in Surrey) overlaid with other Southern features. Voicing of /f/ to /v/ at the beginning of words is common (*vor* 'for', *vaire* 'fair'). Confusingly, Old English words with *ēo*, which commonly have *ee* where they survive today, are written with an *o*, representing the vowel of French 'peuple' (see 2.2.4). So, *flo* and *so* (33–4) correspond to Old English *flēo* and *sēo*, and to Modern English *flee* and *see*. Similarly, *bo* (e.g. 315) is 'be'.

Adjectives most often end in unstressed *-e*, the inflexional ending for all plurals and for most singular forms: see 4.4.1, 4.4.2. In nouns, inflexional *-e* has two main functions: after prepositions (compare *mid riȝte* 184 with *riȝt* 229), and in certain plural forms such as *tide*, 'hours' (26), *bridde*, 'young birds' (111), and *monne*, 'of men' (289). Nouns commonly still have grammatical gender: see 5.1. The definite article declines in agreement with its noun, as in Old English. Thus, in the masculine singular, *þe* nominative, *þane* accusative (249–50), *þas* genitive (*þas monnes* 338), *þan* dative (*þon* at 135); and in the feminine singular, *þo* nominative (*þo ule* 26), *þare* genitive and dative (28, 31). The indefinite article also declines: see 1n. and 17n. Similarly the demonstrative: *þes dai* (masculine noun), but *þos hule* (feminine). Among personal pronouns, note particularly the following forms: feminine singular *ho*, 'she' (less often *he* or *hi*) and accusative *hi*, 'her' (29, 30, 32); third person plurals *hi*, 'they' (less often *ho*), *hore*, 'their', and *hom*, 'them'. The indefinite pronoun *me*, 'one' (*man* without stress) is common and easily mistaken for *me*, 'me' (e.g. 32, 142). In verbs, the present plural indicative ending is always *-eþ* (sometimes in the form *-et*), and past participles commonly have the prefix *i-*. Old English weak verbs of the *-ian* type still preserve *i* in many endings (*ich wundri* 228).

Editions and Facsimile

J. W. H. Atkins, *The Owl and the Nightingale* (Cambridge, 1922)

N. R. Ker, *The Owl and the Nightingale: Facsimile of the Jesus and Cotton Manuscripts*, EETS 251 (1963)

Eric Stanley, *The Owl and the Nightingale*, Nelson's Medieval and Renaissance Library (London and Edinburgh, 1960)

Studies

Kathryn Hume, *The Owl and the Nightingale: The Poem and its Critics* (Toronto, 1975)

Derek Pearsall, *Old English and Middle English Poetry* (London, 1977), pp. 91–4

Thomas L. Reed, *Middle English Debate Poetry and the Aesthetics of Irresolution* (Columbia, 1990)

Elizabeth Salter, *English and International: Studies in the Literature, Art and Patronage of Medieval England* (Cambridge, 1988), chapter 2

R. M. Wilson, *Early Middle English Literature* (London, 1951), Chapter VII

Ich was in one sumere dale,
In one suþe diȝele hale,
Iherde ich holde grete tale
An hule and one niȝtingale.
Þat plait was stif and starc and strong,
Sumwile softe and lud among,
An aiþer aȝen oþer swal
And let þat uvole mod ut al,
And eiþer seide of oþeres custe
Þat alre worste þat hi wuste.
And hure and hure of oþeres songe
Hi holde plaiding suþe stronge.
Þe niȝtingale bigon þe speche
In one hurne of one breche,
And sat up one vaire boȝe
Þar were abute blosme inoȝe,
In ore vaste þicke hegge
Imeind mid spire and grene segge.
Ho was þe gladur vor þe rise
And song a vele cunne wise.
Bet þuȝte þe dreim þat he were
Of harpe and pipe þan he nere;
Bet þuȝte þat he were ishote

1. **one** an inflected form of the indefinite article, most often after prepositions (cf. 14–15): 'in a summer valley'.

5 **plait** a legal term, 'plea', applied here to a debate conducted at times like a lawsuit. Cf. *plaiding* (12) and 217–52n.

7 **An** an unstressed form of *and.*

10 **þat alre worste** 'the worst of all', 'the very worst'; OE *ealra*, genitive plural of *eall.*

17 'In an impenetrable thick hedge'. *Ore* is the dative singular feminine of the indefinite article (OE *anre*), agreeing with the feminine noun *hegge. Vaste* (the reading of J) represents *fast*, 'secure', with *v* for initial *f*: see Headnote.

19 **Ho** 'she'. Both birds are female.

20 **a vele cunne wise** 'in many kinds of ways'. *A* is an unstressed form of *on*, 'in'.

21–2 'The music seemed rather to come from harp and pipe than otherwise.'

Of harpe and pipe þan of þrote.
þo stod on old stoc þarbiside
þar þo ule song hire tide,
And was mid ivi al bigrowe:
Hit was þare hule eardingstowe.
þe niȝtingale hi iseȝ
And hi bihold and overseȝ,
And þuȝte wel vul of þare hule,
For me hi halt lodlich and fule.
'Unwiȝt,' ho sede, 'awei þu flo.
Me is þe wurs þat ich þe so.
Iwis for þine vule lete
Wel oft ich mine song forlete.
Min horte atfliþ and falt mi tonge
Wonne þu art to me iþrunge.
Me luste bet speten þane singe
Of þine fule ȝoȝelinge.'
þos hule abod fort hit was eve:
Ho ne miȝte no leng bileve,
Vor hire horte was so gret
þat welneȝ hire fnast atschet,
And warp a word þarafter longe:
'Hu þincþe nu bi mine songe?
Wenst þu þat ich ne cunne singe
þeȝ ich ne cunne of writelinge?
Ilome þu dest me grame
And seist me boþe tone and schame.
Ȝif ich þe holde on mine vote –
So hit bitide þat ich mote –
And þu were ut of þine rise,
þu sholdest singe an oþer wise!'
þe niȝtingale ȝaf answare:
'Ȝif ich me loki wit þe bare

26 **hire tide** 'her hours'. The Owl's solemn song is compared to the chanting of the daily services by priests, monks and nuns. Cf. 322–30n.

27 **ivi** The Owl's evergreen ivy contrasts symbolically with the Nightingale's spring blossom.

31 Literally: 'And it seemed (to her) quite disgusting with regard to the Owl'.

32 **me hi halt** 'one holds her', 'she is held'. *Me* is the unstressed form of impersonal *man*, as often.

38 'When you are forced upon me'.

41 Whereas nightingales sing by day as well as by night (cf. 336), owls sing only at night.

46 **þincþe** 'does it seem to you': *þincþ þe* run together.

51 **holde** 'held' (past subjunctive, OE *hēolde*).

56 'As long as I keep clear of (literally, 'guard myself against') the open.'

And me schilde wit þe blete,
Ne reche ich noȝt of þine þrete;
Ȝif ich me holde in mine hegge,
Ne recche ich never what þu segge.
Ich wot þat þu art unmilde
Wiþ hom þat ne muȝe from þe schilde,
And þu tukest wroþe and uvele,
Whar þu miȝt, over smale fuȝele.
Vorþi þu art loþ al fuelkunne,
And alle ho þe driveþ honne
And þe bischricheþ and bigredet
And wel narewe þe biledet;
And ek forþe þe sulve mose
Hire þonkes wolde þe totose.
þu art lodlich to biholde
And þu art loþ in monie volde:
þi bodi is short, þi swore is smal,
Grettere is þin heved þan þu al,
þin eȝene boþ colblake and brode
Riȝt swo ho weren ipeint mid wode.
þu starest so þu wille abiten
Al þat þu mist mid clivre smiten.
þi bile is stif and scharp and hoked
Riȝt so an owel þat is croked;
þarmid þu clackes oft and longe,
And þat is on of þine songe.
Ac þu þretest to mine fleshe,
Mid þine clivres woldest me meshe.
þe were icundur to one frogge
þat sit at mulne under cogge;
Snailes, mus and fule wiȝte
Boþ þine cunde and þine riȝte.

63–4 'And you rough up (*tukest*... *over*) small birds cruelly and wickedly wherever you can.'

65–70 The lines refer to the mobbing of owls by other birds.

70 **Hire þonkes** 'if she had her way'.

72 **in monie volde** 'in many ways'.

74 **þu al** 'the whole of the rest of you'.

77 **so** 'as if'.

80 **owel** 'hook'.

82 The sense is uncertain. Perhaps: 'And that is all there is of your singing', taking *on*, 'one, only', as meaning 'all there is'.

85 'You would have more natural liking for a frog.' Literally: 'It would be more natural to you in respect of a frog'. There is a similarly unusual use of impersonal *icunde* at 114.

88 'Are natural and proper (food) for you.' Owls deserve to eat only such foul creatures.

þu sittest adai and fliȝst aniȝt,
þu cuþest þat þu art on unwiȝt.
þu art lodlich and unclene –
Bi þine neste ich hit mene
An ek bi þine fule brode;
þu fedest on hom a wel ful fode.
Wel wostu þat hi doþ þarinne,
Hi fuleþ hit up to þe chinne;
Ho sitteþ þar so hi bo bisne.
þarbi men segget a vorbisne:
"Dahet habbe þat ilke best
þat fuleþ his owe nest."
þat oþer ȝer a faukun bredde;
His nest noȝt wel he ne bihedde.
þarto þu stele in o dai
And leidest þaron þi fule ey.
þo hit bicom þat he haȝte
And of his eyre briddes wraȝte,
Ho broȝte his briddes mete,
Bihold his nest, iseȝ hi ete.
He iseȝ bi one halve
His nest ifuled uthalve.
The faucun was wroþ wit his bridde
And lude ȝal and sterne chidde:
"Segget me, wo havet þis ido?
Ou nas never icunde þarto.
Hit was idon ou a loþe custe;
Segget me, ȝif ȝe hit wiste."
þo quaþ þat on and quað þat oþer:
"Iwis hit was ure oȝe broþer,
þe ȝond þat haveð þat grete heved.
Wai þat he nis þarof bireved!
Worp hit ut mid þe alre vurste

92 'I am referring to your nest.'

94 'You are bringing up in them a very filthy family.'

99 'A curse on that creature.' This proverb (*vorbisne*) is common in ME (Whiting B306) and other languages.

101–38 The fable of the falcon and the owl (or buzzard) is employed from the twelfth century in French and Latin writings (printed by Atkins, pp. 196–9) to demonstrate that nature – and especially a bad nature – is stronger than nurture. So here, 129–38.

105–6 'Then it came about that she hatched and made birds from her eggs.' The mother falcon is variously referred to by feminine pronouns (*he*, 'she') and by neuter (*his*, 'its').

114 'It was never natural for you to do that.' See 85n.

115 'You have been treated in (*a*, 'in') a loathsome fashion.'

121 **mid þe alre vurste** 'among the first of all', i.e. 'at once'. On *alre*, see 10n.

þat his necke him toberste."
þe faucun ilefde his bridde
And nom þat fule brid amidde
And warp hit of þan wilde bowe
þar pie and crowe hit todrowe.
Herbi men segget a bispel,
þeȝ hit ne bo fuliche spel:
Also hit is bi þan ungode
þat is icumen of fule brode
And is meind wit fro monne,
Ever he cuþ þat he com þonne,
þat he com of þan adel eye
þeȝ he a fro nest leie.
þeȝ appel trendli fron þon trowe
þar he and oþer mid growe,
þeȝ he bo þarfrom bicume,
He cuþ wel whonene he is icume.'
  þos word aȝaf þe niȝtingale,
And after þare longe tale
He song so lude and so scharpe
Riȝt so me grulde schille harpe.
þos hule luste þiderward
And hold hire eȝe noþerward,
And sat toswolle and ibolwe
Also ho hadde one frogge iswolȝe;
For ho wel wiste and was iwar
þat ho song hire a bisemar.
And noþeles ho ȝaf andsware:
'Whi neltu flon into þe bare
And sewi hwaþer unker bo
Of briȝter howe, of vairur blo?'
'No, þu havest wel scharpe clawe;
Ne kep ich noȝt þat þu me clawe.
þu havest clivers suþe stronge;
þu twengst þarmid so doþ a tonge.

128 'Though it is not completely a fable', i.e. although the story is used as a parable (*bispel*), such things do happen – or so the Nightingale claims. Cf. the use of *spelle* at 264.

131 **wit fro monne** 'with freemen'.

135–8 This proverb (Whiting A169) is associated with the fable of the falcon and the owl by other authors, e.g. Nicole Bozon: 'Trendle the appel nevere so fer, he conyes (makes known) fro what tree he cam'.

148 'That she sang in mockery of her.'

151 'And find out which of us two is . . .' *Unker* is genitive: OE *uncer* from *wit*, 'we two'.

154 **Ne kep ich noȝt** 'I have no wish'.

þu þoȝtest, so doþ þine ilike,
Mid faire worde me biswike.
Ich nolde don þat þu me raddest:
Ich wiste wel þat þu me misraddest.
Schamie þe for þin unrede!
Unwroȝen is þi swikelhede.
Schild þine swikeldom vram þe liȝte,
And hud þat woȝe among þe riȝte.
þane þu wilt þin unriȝt spene
Loke þat hit ne bo isene;
Vor swikedom haveð schome and hete
Ȝif hit is ope and underȝete.
Ne speddestu noȝt mid þine unwrenche,
For ich am war and can wel blenche.
Ne helpþ noȝt þat þu bo to þriste:
Ich wolde viȝte bet mid liste
þan þu mid al þine strengþe.
Ich habbe on brede and ek on lengþe
Castel god on mine rise.
"Wel fiȝt þat wel fliȝt," seiþ þe wise.
  Ac lete we awei þos cheste,
Vor swiche wordes boþ unwreste,
And fo we on mid riȝte dome,
Mid faire worde and mid ysome.
þeȝ we ne bo at one acorde,
We muȝe bet mid fayre worde,
Witute cheste and bute fiȝte,
Plaidi mid foȝe and mid riȝte;
And mai ur eiþer wat hi wile
Mid riȝte segge and mid sckile.'
  þo quaþ þe hule, 'Wo schal us seme
þat kunne and wille riȝt us deme?'
'Ich wot wel,' quaþ þe niȝtingale,
'Ne þaref þarof bo no tale:
Maister Nichole of Guldeforde.

157 **so doþ þine ilike** 'as your sort do'.

165 **þane** 'when'.

172 **liste** 'cunning, skill'. The opposition between *liste* and *strengþe* (173) was proverbial: Whiting L381. Compare 6/227 here.

176 Proverbial: 'Well fights that well flees', Whiting F141.

180 **ysome** 'peaceable', qualifying *worde*.

185–6 'And each of us can say justly and reasonably whatever she wishes.'

190 'There need be no argument about that.'

191 At the end of the poem, the birds fly off to receive the judgement of Master Nicholas at Portesham in Dorset, where he lives in undeserved obscurity as a parish priest. See Headnote.

He is wis an war of worde;
He is of dome suþe glew,
And him is loþ evrich unþew.
He wot insiȝt in eche songe,
Wo singet wel, wo singet wronge;
And he can schede vrom þe riȝte
þat woȝe, þat þuster from þe liȝte.'
þo hule one wile hi biþoȝte,
And after þan þis word upbroȝte:
'Ich granti wel þat he us deme;
Vor þeȝ he were wile breme
And lof him were niȝtingale
And oþer wiȝte gente and smale,
Ich wot he is nu suþe acoled.
Nis he vor þe noȝt afoled
þat he for þine olde luve
Me adun legge and þe buve.
Ne schaltu nevre so him queme
þat he for þe fals dom deme.
He is nu ripe and fastrede,
Ne lust him nu to none unrede;
Nu him ne lust na more pleie,
He wile gon a riȝte weie.'
þe niȝtingale was al ȝare;
Ho hadde ilorned wel aiware.
'Hule,' ho sede, 'seie me soþ,
Wi dostu þat unwiȝtis doþ?
þu singist aniȝt and noȝt adai,
And al þi song is wailawai.
þu miȝt mid þine songe afere
Alle þat ihereþ þine ibere.
þu schrichest and ȝollest to þine fere

199 **hi biþoȝte** 'bethought herself', i.e. 'considered'.

204 **gente and smale** 'gracious and slender', epithets commonly applied in ME to young women, e.g. Alisoun in Chaucer's Miller's Tale: 'As any wezele hir body gent and smal', *Canterbury Tales* I 3234.

205 **acoled** 'cooled off'. Ageing was regarded as a process of physiological cooling. After a naturally hot youth in days gone by (*wile* 202), Nicholas is now naturally coolheaded and sober. So, according to the Owl, he will favour her cause.

206 'He is not one to be taken in by you.'

207 **þine olde luve** 'his longstanding affection for you'.

210 **þe** 'thee'.

212 'Nor is he attracted now to any evil counsel.'

217–52 In this speech the Nightingale brings three distinct charges against the Owl, each of which is answered separately in the Owl's long reply: that the Owl hides in the daytime (answered in 265–308); that her song is ugly and depressing (answered in 309–62); and that she cannot see in daylight (answered in 363–90).

þat hit is grislich to ihere:
Hit þincheþ boþe wise and snepe
Noȝt þat þu singe, ac þat þu wepe.
þu fliȝst aniȝt and noȝt adai,
þarof ich wundri and wel mai.
Vor evrich þing þat schuniet riȝt
Hit luveþ þuster and hatiet liȝt,
And evrich þing þat is lof misdede
Hit luveþ þuster to his dede.
A wis word, þeȝ hit bo unclene,
Is fele manne a muþe imene,
For Alvred king hit seide and wrot:
"He schunet þat hine vul wot."
Ich wene þat þu dost also,
Vor þu fliȝst niȝtes ever mo.
An oþer þing me is a wene:
þu havest aniȝt wel briȝte sene,
Bi daie þu art stareblind
þat þu ne sihst ne bow ne rind.
Adai þu art blind oþer bisne.
þarbi men segget a vorbisne:
Riȝt so hit farþ bi þan ungode
þat noȝt ne suþ to none gode,
And is so ful of uvele wrenche
þat him ne mai no man atprenche,
And can wel þane þustre wai
And þane briȝte lat awai;
So doþ þat boþ of þine cunde,
Of liȝte nabbeþ hi none imunde.'
   þos hule luste suþe longe
And was oftoned suþe stronge.
Ho quaþ, 'þu hattest niȝtingale;

225 'It seems to all and sundry.'
snepe 'foolish'.

231 'And every creature to which wrongdoing is dear.'

234 **a** 'in': 'is common in the mouths of many men'.

235 **Alvred** King Alfred of Wessex (d. 899) was commonly named as the authority for proverbial utterances, as in the so-called *Proverbs of Alfred* (found along with *The Owl* in the Jesus Manuscript).

236 'He who knows himself to be filthy keeps out of the way': Whiting S290. The Nightingale alludes again to the toilet-training of owls.

239 **me is a wene** 'comes into my mind' (*a* unstressed for *on*).

242 **ne bow ne rind** 'neither bough nor bark'. This phrase, evidently representing the world as seen through a bird's eyes, puzzled the scribes: see Textual Notes.

251 'That is what those of your sort do.'

þu mi3test bet hoten galegale,
Vor þu havest to monie tale.
Lat þine tunge habbe spale.
þu wenest þat þes dai bo þin o3e;
Lat me nu habbe mine þro3e.
Bo nu stille and lat me speke,
Ich wille bon of þe awreke;
And lust hu ich con me bitelle
Mid ri3te soþe witute spelle.
   þu seist þat ich me hude adai:
þarto ne segge ich nich ne nai;
And lust, ich telle þe þarevore
Al wi hit is and warevore.
Ich habbe bile stif and stronge,
And gode clivers scharp and longe,
So hit bicumeþ to havekes cunne.
Hit is min hi3te, hit is mi wunne
þat ich me dra3e to mine kende;
Ne mai me no man þarevore schende.
On me hit is wel isene,
Vor ri3te cunde ich am so kene.
Vorþi ich am loþ smale fo3le
þat floþ bi grunde an bi þuvele:
Hi me bichermet and bigredeþ
And hore flockes to me ledeþ.
Me is lof to habbe reste
And sitte stille in mine neste;
Vor nere ich never no þe betere
þe3 ich mid chauling and mid chatere
Hom schende and mid fule worde,
So herdes doþ, oþer mid schitworde.
Ne lust me wit þe screwen chide,
Forþi ich wende from hom wide.

256 **galegale** a made-up word, reduplicating the second element of *nightingale*, which derives from OE *galan*, 'sing' (ME *gale*), and implying monotonous repetition: 'sing-sing'.

259 **bo þin o3e** 'is yours'.

266 'To that I will not say either "not I" or "nay"', i.e. 'I will not deny that'. The Owl admits the first of the Nightingale's three charges (217–52n.), but goes on to justify her behaviour.

267 **þarevore** 'where that is concerned'.

272–3 'It is my delight and my joy to be true to my nature.' The Owl is not ashamed to be a bird of prey (*havekes cunne* 271).

277–80 Another reference to the mobbing of owls: cf. 65–70.

283 'For I would not be at all better off.'

Hit is a wise monne dome,
And hi hit segget wel ilome,
þat me ne chide wit þe gidie,
Ne wit þan ofne me ne ȝonie.
At sume siþe herde I telle
Hu Alvred sede on his spelle:
"Loke þat þu ne bo þare
þar chauling boþ and cheste ȝare;
Lat sottes chide and vorþ þu go."
And ich am wis and do also.
And ȝet Alvred seide an oþer side
A word þat is isprunge wide:
"þat wit þe fule haveþ imene,
Ne cumeþ he never from him cleine."
Wenestu þat haveck bo þe werse
þoȝ crowe bigrede him bi þe mershe
And goþ to him mid hore chirme
Riȝt so hi wille wit him schirme?
þe havec folȝeþ gode rede
And fliȝt his wei and lat hi grede.
  ȝet þu me seist of oþer þinge,
And telst þat ich ne can noȝt singe,
Ac al mi rorde is woning
And to ihire grislich þing.
þat nis noȝt soþ; ich singe efne
Mid fulle dreme and lude stefne.
þu wenist þat ech song bo grislich
þat þine pipinge nis ilich.
Mi stefne is bold and noȝt unorne;
Ho is ilich one grete horne,

289 'It is in accord with the judgement of wise men.' *Dome* has the dative *-e* ending, following the preposition *a* (unstressed for *on*).

291–2 'One should not quarrel with fools, nor try to outgape an oven', i.e. fools will always get the better of an exchange of insults, just as an oven door will always be wider than an open mouth. Proverbial: Whiting O59.

295–7 A somewhat similar saying is attributed to Alfred in *The Proverbs of Alfred* (see 235n.): Whiting S91.

296 'Where scolding and strife are ready to hand.'

299 'And furthermore Alfred said on another occasion.' *Side* is probably a form of *siþe*, 'occasion'.

301 'One who has dealings with the foul.' Proverbial: Whiting F558.

304 **crowe** 'crows'.

306 **wille** subjunctive plural: 'Just as if they were wanting to fight with him'. On the hostility of crows to birds of prey, see Trevisa, *Properties*, 620–1.

309 The Owl turns to the second of the Nightingale's charges (217–52n.).

312 'And a dreadful thing to hear.'

316 'That is not like your piping.'

And þin is ilich one pipe
Of one smale wode unripe.
Ich singe bet þan þu dest:
þu chaterest so doþ on Irish prost;
Ich singe an eve a riȝte time,
And soþþe won hit is bedtime,
þe þridde siþe a middelniȝte,
And so ich mine song adiȝte.
Wone ich iso arise vorre
Oþer dairim oþer daisterre,
Ich do god mid mine þrote
And warni men to hore note.
Ac þu singest alle longe niȝt
From eve fort hit is dailiȝt,
And evre leist þin o song
So longe so þe niȝt is long,
And evre croweþ þi wrecche crei
þat he ne swikeþ niȝt ne dai.
Mid þine pipinge þu adunest
þas monnes earen þar þu wunest
And makest þine song so unwurþ
þat me ne telþ of þar noȝt wurþ.
Evrich murȝþe mai so longe ileste
þat ho shal liki wel unwreste,
Vor harpe and pipe and fuȝeles song
Mislikeþ ȝif hit is to long.
Ne bo þe song never so murie
þat he ne shal þinche wel unmurie
Ȝef he ilesteþ ure unwille.
So þu miȝt þine song aspille;
Vor hit is soþ, Alvred hit seide

320 **wode** 'plant' ('weed', not 'wood').

322–30 Whereas the Nightingale chatters away night and day (cf. 336), like a voluble Irish priest, the Owl claims to sing at fixed intervals of the night only, as if she were a monk singing the night hours (cf. 26n.). These are: Vespers (*eve* 323), Compline (*bedtime* 324), Matins (*middelniȝte* 325), and Prime (*dairim* 328).

327 'When I see arising far off.' The Owl does not sing Prime, which was begun in full daylight.

335 **crei** 'throat' (not *cry*, which would not rhyme): cf. 329.

338 'The ears of the man where you live', i.e. the master of the house near which the Nightingale lives.

340 **of þar** 'thereof'. So: 'That people don't think much of it.'

345–6 The logic of these lines requires their expansion: 'However delightful the song may be, (it will never be so delightful) that it will not seem very tiresome.'

347 **ure unwille** 'against our will', i.e. after we no longer wish to hear it (OE *urum unwillum*). But the reading of both manuscripts, *over unwille*, could mean 'despite displeasure'.

And me hit mai ine boke rede:
"Evrich þing mai losen his godhede
Mid unmeþe and mid overdede."
Mid este þu þe miȝt overquatie,
And overfulle makeþ wlatie;
An evrich mureȝþe mai agon
Ȝif me hit halt evre forþ in on,
Bute one, þat is Godes riche
þat evre is swete and evre iliche.
þeȝ þu nime evere of þan lepe
Hit is evre ful bi hepe.
Wunder hit is of Godes riche
þat evre spenþ and ever is iliche.
  Ȝut þu me seist on oþer shome,
þat ich am on mine eȝen lome,
An seist, for þat ich flo bi niȝte,
þat ich ne mai iso bi liȝte.
þu liest! On me hit is isene
þat ich habbe gode sene,
Vor nis non so dim þusternesse
þat ich ever iso þe lesse.
þu wenest þat ich ne miȝte iso
Vor ich bi daie noȝt ne flo.
þe hare luteþ al dai,
Ac noþeles iso he mai.
Ȝif hundes urneþ to himward
He gencheþ swiþe aweyward
And hokeþ paþes swiþe narewe,
And haveþ mid him his blenches ȝarewe,
And hupþ and stard suþe cove,
And secheþ paþes to þe grove;
Ne sholde he vor boþe his eȝe
So don, ȝif he þe bet niseȝe.
Ich mai ison so wel so on hare,
þeȝ ich bi daie sitte an dare.

351–2 Proverbial: Whiting E168. Proverbs commonly warn against immoderation (*unmeþe*). The following lines continue in proverbial style.

354 **overfulle makeþ wlatie** 'surfeit causes disgust'.

356 'If one keeps on with it continuously without a break.'

363 The Owl answers the third charge (217–52n.).

376–7 'He dodges away rapidly and follows very narrow zig-zag paths.'

378 'And has all his tricks ready about him.'

381–2 'But he would not do so, to save his life, if he were not able to see the better.' Cf. 10/194n. *Niseye* represents *ne* + *iseye*.

þar aȝte men boþ in worre,
An fareþ boþe ner an forre
An overvareþ fele þode,
An doþ bi niȝte gode node,
Ich folȝi þan aȝte manne
An flo bi niȝte in hore banne.'

385 'Where valiant men are at war.' The Owl's claim that, as a bird of prey, she joins warrior-bands in their night expeditions concludes her present speech on a heroic note.

389 **þan aȝte manne** 'the valiant men', dative plural after *folȝi*. For the form of the noun see 4.2.6.

3
Laȝamon: *Brut*

Geoffrey of Monmouth's Latin *History of the Kings of Britain* (*Historia Regum Britanniae*, first issued *c.* 1136) tells the story of the kings of Britain from their legendary founder Brutus, great-grandson of Aeneas of Troy (cf. text 9 here, lines 1–19), to the last of the line, Cadwallader, who finally abandoned Britain to the Saxons. The greatest of them is King Arthur, the hero of the book. In 1155 the Norman poet Wace completed his rendering of Geoffrey's Latin into French octosyllabic couplets; and it was this, the *Roman de Brut*, that Laȝamon adapted into English, expanding and reshaping its episodes with considerable freedom. Laȝamon's *Historia Brutonum* ('History of the British', now known as *Brut*) was probably composed some time in the first half of the thirteenth century – certainly after the death of Henry II in 1189, but not later than the second half of the thirteenth century, when the two surviving copies were made. These are British Library MS Cotton Caligula A IX (C) – which also contains *The Owl and the Nightingale* – and British Library MS Cotton Otho C XIII (O).

Laȝamon identifies himself in his opening lines as a parish priest:

An preost wes on leoden, Laȝamon wes ihoten;
He wes Leovenaðes sone – liðe him beo Drihten.
He wonede at Ernleȝe at æðelen are chirechen,
Uppen Sevarne staþe, sel þar him þuhte,
Onfest Radestone, þer he bock radde.

[There was a priest among the people called Laȝamon; he was the son of Leovenað – may God be gracious to him. He lived at Ernleȝe at a noble church, on the banks of the Severn, and good it seemed to him there, near Radestone, where he read books.]

'Ernleȝe' is Areley Kings, Worcestershire, in that part of England, the West Midlands, where native literary traditions were still strong at the time (cf. *Ancrene Wisse*, text 4 here, probably written about twenty-five miles further west). By comparison with Wace, Laȝamon appears both archaic and also very un-French. In MS C especially, there are strikingly few French loan-words (only one in 173 lines here: *liun* 80). In the following extract, references to Wygar and Witeȝe (11–12n.) and expressions such as *fæiesið makeden* (144n.) look directly back to Anglo-Saxon poetry and legend. On the other hand, the elaborate similes (see 76–7n.) probably testify to Laȝamon's reading of Latin heroic poets such as Virgil or the twelfth-century Joseph of Exeter. Together with the set speeches, the similes contribute to an elevated epic style which, although its language is thoroughly English, belongs in a general European tradition of heroic verse (Salter).

The structure of Laȝamon's verse is similarly eclectic. Its main affinities are with native alliterative verse. All lines are divided into half-lines of variable rhythm and length (marked off in the manuscripts), most often with two stressed syllables in each half-line. In most cases (126 out of 173 lines here) half-lines are coupled by alliteration, thus: 'þat his **h**alm and his **h**æfd . **h**alden to grunde' (139). But rhyme and half-rhyme also play a part in the coupling, either with or without alliteration (in 53 lines here). Thus: 'Nu we scullen *riden* . and over lond *gliden*' (44), or (with alliteration also) 'And uppen Colgrime *smiten* . mid swiðe smærte *biten*' (127). Rhyme is rare in surviving Old English alliterative verse, and its use here reflects Laȝamon's reading of rhymed poetry in either French (e.g. Wace) or Latin or both.

The language of the Caligula Manuscript, the source of the present text, represents the poet's own Worcestershire English overlaid with other Southern features. Voicing of /f/ to /v/ at the beginning of words is irregular and probably scribal: it may obscure the alliteration (compare lines 8, 27 and 40). But a probably genuine authorial feature is 'nunnation' – the frequent addition of /n/ after final vowels (e.g. *hafden* 25 and *weoren* 80, both verbs with singular subject). Nunnation complicates the inflexion of nouns, where *-en* is anyway the proper ending of some dative singulars (others have *-e*) and of many plurals such as *sconken* 13 (accusative), *leoden* 73 (genitive) and *burnen* 7 (dative). Nouns generally preserve grammatical gender (see 5.1), and adjectives decline accordingly: examples are the masculine *bradne* 115 (accusative singular) and *aðelen* 11 (dative singular), and the feminine *ludere* 30 (dative singular). Main forms of the definite article 'the' are: in the masculine singular, *þe* nominative, *þene* accusative (27), *þas* genitive (18, 138) and *þan* dative (1); in the feminine singular, *þa* or *þæ* nominative (60, 63, 65) and *þere* genitive and dative (96n., 156); and in the neuter singular, *þat* (84, 158, meaning 'the', not 'that'). The plural of the definite article is *þa* nominative and accusative (73, 128) and *þan* dative (137). The indefinite article also declines: *ænne* accusative (20), *ane* dative (5). So does the demonstrative: *to þissen londe* dative singular masculine (111). Among personal pronouns, note particularly the third person plural forms *heo*, 'they', *heore*, 'their', and *hom* or *heom*, 'them'; also *hine* accusative singular masculine (3). Relative pronouns *þe* (11, 12) and *þa* (24, 26) co-exist with *þat*. In verbs, the present plural indicative ends in *-eð*, and the present participle in *-inde* (3).

The following extract corresponds to lines 10534–10706 in the complete text edited by Brook and Leslie.

Editions

Rosamund Allen, trans., *Lawman: 'Brut'* (London, 1992)

I. D. O. Arnold and M. M. Pelan, *La Partie Arthurienne du Roman de Brut* (Paris, 1962) [Arthurian section of Wace]

G. L. Brook, with Preface by C. S. Lewis, *Selections from Laȝamon's 'Brut'*, 2nd edn, revised J. Levitt (Exeter, 1983)

G. L. Brook and R. F. Leslie, *Laȝamon: 'Brut'*, EETS, Vol. I, 250 (1963), Vol. II, 277 (1978) [complete text of both manuscripts]

Joseph Hall, *Layamon's 'Brut': Selections* (Oxford, 1924)

Lewis Thorpe, trans., *Geoffrey of Monmouth: The History of the Kings of Britain* (Harmondsworth, 1966)

S. C. Weinberg and W. R. J. Barron, ed. and trans., *Laȝamon's Arthur: The Arthurian Section of Laȝamon's 'Brut'* (Harlow, 1989)

Studies

H. S. Davies, 'Laȝamon's Similes', *Review of English Studies*, n.s. 11 (1960), 129–42

Dorothy Everett, *Essays on Middle English Literature* (Oxford, 1955), Chapter II

C. S. Lewis, *Studies in Medieval and Renaissance Literature* (Cambridge, 1966), pp. 18–33

R. S. Loomis, ed., *Arthurian Literature in the Middle Ages* (Oxford, 1959) [Chapter 8 'Geoffrey of Monmouth', Chapter 9 'Wace', Chapter 10 'Layamon's *Brut*']

Derek Pearsall, *Old English and Middle English Poetry* (London, 1977), pp. 108–13

Elizabeth Salter, *English and International: Studies in the Literature, Art and Patronage of Medieval England* (Cambridge, 1988), pp. 48–70

Françoise Le Saux, *Laȝamon's 'Brut': The Poem and Its Sources* (Cambridge, 1989)

E. G. Stanley, 'Laȝamon's Antiquarian Sentiments', *Medium Ævum*, 38 (1969), 23–37

J. S. P. Tatlock, *The Legendary History of Britain* (Berkeley and Los Angeles, 1950)

þa comen tydinge to Arðure þan kinge
þat seoc wes Howel his mæi – þerfore he wes sari –
I Clud ligginde, and þer he hine bilæfde.
Hiȝenliche swiðe forð he gon liðe
þat he bihalves Baðe beh to ane velde.
þer he alihte and his cnihtes alle,
And on mid heore burnen beornes sturne,
And he a fif dæle dælde his ferde.
þa he hafde al iset and al hit isemed,
þa dude he on his burne ibroide of stele
þe makede on alvisc smið mid aðelen his crafte:
Heo wes ihaten Wygar, þe Witeȝe wurhte.
His sconken he helede mid hosen of stele.
Calibeorne his sweord he sweinde bi his side:
Hit wes iworht in Avalun mid wiȝelefulle craften.
Halm he set on hafde, hæh of stele,
þeron wes moni ȝimston, al mid golde bigon:
He wes Uðeres þas aðelen kinges,

1–5 The young King Arthur, with the help of his kinsman Howel of Brittany, has defeated the pagan Germanic invaders under their 'kaiser' Childric and the brothers Colgrim and Baldulf, forcing them to leave Britain under oath; but while the king is campaigning in Scotland, he learns of the invaders' treacherous return. They have landed again at Dartmouth on the south coast, and are besieging Bath.

3 **Clud** Dumbarton, Scotland.

5 'Until he came to a plain close by Bath.' Bath, on the river Avon in Somerset, was identified by Geoffrey of Monmouth with the 'Mons Badonis' or Mount Badon where, according to early and possibly historical tradition, Arthur inflicted his decisive defeat on the Saxon invaders.

7 'And resolute warriors put on their corslets.' *On mid* 'on with': the verb is implied, as in 'On with the motley'.

8 **a** 'into' (unstressed form of *on*).

9 **isemed** 'organized' (*MED semen* v. (1) (c)).

10–24 The Arming of Arthur. The arming of the hero is a common theme in epic and romance: e.g. in England, *Beowulf* 1441–72, *Sir Gawain and the Green Knight* 566–89. Laȝamon here follows Wace (9274–300), with some interesting additions.

10 **dude he on** 'he donned'.

11–12 'Which an elvish smith made with his noble skill: it was called Wygar, which Witeȝe wrought.' An addition to Wace. *Wygar* perhaps goes back to Old English *wigheard*, 'battle-hard'. The scribe writes *Witeȝe* with a small *w*, presumably taking it for the common noun meaning 'wise man'; but the absence of an article suggests a proper name. This Witeȝe is probably to be identified with the Old English Widia, a son of the legendary smith Weland. The corslet worn by Beowulf was made by Weland himself (*Beowulf* 455). But see Le Saux, pp. 196–9.

14 **Calibeorne** This name, like *Pridwen* (21) and *Ron* (24), is given by Wace, following Geoffrey. Geoffrey names Arthur's sword *Caliburnus* (from a Welsh source) and says that it was 'forged in the Isle of Avalon'. The more familiar form of the name, *Excalibur*, derives from later French romances.

15 **mid wiȝelefulle craften** 'with magical arts'. Laȝamon's addition.

17 **bigon** 'encircled', referring to the gold circlet round the helm ('E d'or li cercles envirun', Wace 9285).

18 'It had been the noble king Uther's.' Uther Pendragon was Arthur's father.

He wes ihaten Goswhit, ælchen oðere unilic.
He heng an his sweore ænne sceld deore:
His nome wes on Bruttisc Pridwen ihaten;
þer wes innen igraven mid rede golde staven
An onlicnes deore of Drihtenes moder.
His spere he nom an honde, þa Ron wes ihaten.
  þa he hafden al his iweden, þa leop he on his steden.
þa heo mihte bihalden þa bihalves stoden
þene væireste cniht þe verde scolde leden;
Ne isæh nævere na man selere cniht nenne
þene him wes Arður, aðelest cunnes.
þa cleopede Arður ludere stæfne:
'Lou war her biforen us heðene hundes,
þe slo3en ure alderen mid luðere heore craften,
And heo us beoð on londe læðest alre þinge.
Nu fusen we hom to and stærcliche heom leggen on,
And wræken wunderliche ure cun and ure riche,
And wreken þene muchele scome þat heo us iscend habbeoð
þat heo over uðen comen to Dertemuðen;
And alle heo beoð forsworene and alle heo beoð forlorene –
Heo beoð fordemed alle mid Drihttenes fulste.
Fuse we nu forðward vaste tosomne
Æfne alswa softe swa we nan ufel ne þohten;
And þenne we heom cumeð to, miseolf ic wullen onfon,
An alre freomeste þat fiht ich wulle biginnen.
Nu we scullen riden and over lond gliden,
And na man bi his live lude ne wurchen,

19 **Goswhit** 'Goosewhite', a name for the shining helm, not recorded elsewhere.

ælchen oðere unilic 'unlike all others': see 5.3.2.

21 **Pridwen** The name in Welsh (*Bruttisc*) means 'blessed form', and perhaps refers to the image of the Virgin engraved on the inner side of the shield.

24 **Ron** from Welsh *ron* 'spear'.

25 In Wace Arthur mounts, as a knight should, before receiving shield and spear – a detail missed by the priestly translator.

26 'Then those who stood nearby could observe.'

31–46 Arthur's speech is loosely derived from Wace 9317–36.

31 'See here the heathen dogs before us.'

32 **mid luðere heore craften** 'with their wicked tricks': cf. 11, 94, 133 here, and 5.5.1.

33 **alre þinge** 'of all things', genitive plural (OE *ealra þinga*).

36 'And avenge the very shameful way in which they have injured us.' Arthur refers to his enemies' treacherous return to Dartmouth (see 1–5n.). The repetition of *wreken* 'avenge' in ll. 35–6 corresponds to a sevenfold repetition of *venger* by Wace's Arthur.

41 'Just as quietly as if we intended no harm.'

43 **An alre freomeste** 'alone foremost of all'.

45 **lude ne wurchen** 'make any noise'.

Ah faren fæstliche. Drihten us fulsten!'
  þa riden agon Arður þe riche mon,
Beh over wælde and Baðe wolde isechen.
þa tidende com to Childriche þan strongen and þan riche
þat Arður mid ferde com, al ȝaru to fihte,
Childric and his ohte men leopen heom to horsen,
Igripen heore wepnen; heo wusten heom ifæied.
þis isæh Arður, aðelest kinge,
Isæh he ænne hæðene eorl hælden him toȝeines
Mid seoven hundred cnihten al ȝærewe to fihten.
þe orl himseolf ferde biforen al his genge,
And Arður himseolf arnde bivoren al his ferde.
Arður þe ræie Ron nom an honde,
He stræhte scaft stærcne, stiðimoden king,
His hors he lette irnen þat þa eorðe dunede,
Sceld he braid on breosten – þe king wes abolȝen.
He smat Borel þene eorl þurhut þa breosten
þat þæ heorte tochan, and þe king cleopede anan:
'þe formeste is fæie! Nu fulsten us Drihte
And þa hefenliche quene þa Drihten akende.'
þa cleopede Arður, aðelest kinge:
'Nu heom to! Nu heom to! þat formest is wel idon!'
Bruttes hom leiden on, swa me scal a luðere don:
Heo bittere swipen ȝefven mid axes and mid sweordes.
þer feolle Cheldriches men fulle twa þusend,
Swa nevere Arður ne les nævere ænne of his.
þer weoren Sæxisce men folken alre ærmest,
And þa Alemainisce men ȝeomerest alre leoden.
Arður mid his sweorde fæiescipe wurhte;
Al þat he smat to, hit wes sone fordo.

47–83 The battle with Childric before Bath and his flight across the river Avon is added by Laȝamon. In Wace, the enemy all withdraw at once to the hills, as Colgrim and Baldulf do later here (86ff.).

52 **heo wusten heom ifæied** 'they knew themselves to be the enemy' (*MED feied* ppl.).

53 The line is repeated almost exactly at ll. 91 and 130.

aðelest kinge 'noblest of kings'. See 5.3.2.

57 **ferde** 'host', a term regularly used of friendly troops, as in OE. The enemy has a *genge* (56), here a disrespectful term.

67 'Now up and at them! We've made a good start.' *þat formest* is neuter, 'the first thing' (as against *þe formeste* 64, which is masculine).

68 **swa me scal a luðere don** 'as one should do with the wicked'.

72–3 Laȝamon recognizes a distinction between the Saxons, led by Colgrim and Baldulf, and the Germans (*Alemainisce*) under their 'kaiser' Childric.

72 **folken alre ærmest** 'the most wretched of all peoples'. A common second half-line pattern: cf. 73, 95, 105, 113.

Al wæs þe king abolȝen swa bið þe wilde bar
þenne he i þan mæste monie swyn imeteð.
  þis isæh Childric and gon him to charren
And beh him over Avene to burȝen himseolven;
And Arður him læc to, swa hit a liun weoren,
And fusde heom to flode; monie þer weoren fæie.
þer sunken to þan grunde fif and twenti hundred,
þat al wes Avene stram mid stele ibrugged.
Cheldric over þat water flæh mid fiftene hundred cnihten,
þohte forð siðen and over sæ liðen.
  Arður isæh Colgrim climben to munten,
Buȝen to þan hulle þa over Baðen stondeð,
And Baldulf beh him after mid seove þusend cnihtes.
Heo þohten i þan hulle hæhliche atstonden,
Weorien heom mid wepnen and Arður awæmmen.
þa isæh Arður, aðelest kingen,
Whar Colgrim atstod and æc stal wrohte,
þa clupede þe king kenliche lude:
'Balde mine þeines, buhȝeð to þan hulles!
For ȝerstendæi wes Colgrim monnen alre kennest;
Nu him is alswa þere gat, þer he þene hul wat;
Hæh uppen hulle fehteð mid hornen,
þenne comeð þe wulf wilde touward hire winden.
þeh þe wulf beon ane, buten ælc imane,
And þer weoren in ane loken fif hundred gaten,
þe wulf heom to iwiteð and alle heom abiteð.

76–7 Arthur is compared to a wild boar angered by the presence in his forest of a herd of swine eating the acorns. Elaborate similes (cf. 96–101, 107–10, 114–17 here) occur especially often in that section of the *Brut* which concerns Arthur's wars with the Saxons (Davies). Laȝamon probably draws hereabouts upon some source in addition to Wace, perhaps a Latin poem: see Salter (1988).

81 'And drove them into the water . . .' There is no river in Wace. Laȝamon uses his own knowledge of local topography to good effect, vividly imagining the Saxons' death in the Avon (cf. 106–10).

82 **grunde** 'bottom of the river'.

84 Childric escapes to his ships also in Wace (9359–62), but not across a bridge of steel.

92 'Where Colgrim stopped and also made a stand.'

93–119 In these triumphant speeches, invented by Laȝamon, Arthur takes each of the three enemy leaders in turn and contrasts his present plight, represented by humiliating comparisons, with his brave past. In each case 'yesterday' is followed by 'now': 95–6 (Colgrim), 105–6 (Baldulf), 113–14 (Childric).

96 'Now as he defends the hill, he is like the goat'; literally, 'it is for him as for the goat'. *Gat* 'goat' is a feminine noun (whence the feminine article *þere*) and refers to the female animal, as usually in early English. But MS O reads *him* for *hire* at l. 98.

99 **buten ælc imane** 'without any companion'.

100 **loken** 'enclosure' (cf. OE *gāta loc*, 'an enclosure for goats').

101 **heom to iwiteð** 'approaches them'.

Swa ic wulle nu todæi Colgrim al fordemen.
Ich am wulf and he is gat; þe gume scal beon fæie.'
Þa ȝet cleopede Arður, aðelest kingen:
'Ȝurstendæi wes Baldulf cnihten alre baldest;
Nu he stant on hulle and Avene bihaldeð,
Hu ligeð i þan stræme stelene fisces;
Mid sweorde bigeorede, heore sund is awemmed;
Heore scalen wleoteð swulc goldfaȝe sceldes,
Þer fleoteð heore spiten swulc hit spæren weoren.
Þis beoð seolcuðe þing isiȝen to þissen londe:
Swulche deor an hulle, swulche fisces in wælle.
Ȝurstendæi wes þe kaisere kennest alre kingen;
Nu he is bicumen hunte and hornes him fulieð,
Flihð over bradne wæld, beorkeð his hundes.
He hafeð bihalves Baðen his huntinge bilæfved,
Freom his deore he flicð; and we hit scullen fallen
And his balde ibeot to nohte ibringen,
And swa we scullen bruken rihte biȝæten.'
Efne þan worde þa þe king seide
He bræid hæȝe his sceld forn to his breosten,
He igrap his spere longe, his hors he gon spurie.
Neh alswa swiðe swa þe fuȝel fliȝeð
Fuleden þan kinge fif and twenti þusend
Wihtere monnen, wode under wepnen;
Hælden to hulle mid hæhȝere strengðe
And uppen Colgrime smiten mid swiðe smærte biten;
And Grim heom þer hente and feolde þa Bruttes to grunde,
I þan vormeste ræse fulle fif hundred.
Þat isæh Arður, aðelest kingen,

107–10 A remarkable reversed comparison. The dead warriors in the river are seen as steel fishes, whose scales and fin-spines (*spiten*) are then compared to gleaming shields and floating spears.

108 'Equipped as they are with swords, their swimming is impeded.'

113 **þe kaisere** Childric, Emperor of the Germans.

114–17 Childric is first reduced from *kaisere* to huntsman (*hunte*), and then mockingly said to flee from the very animals he has been hunting.

117 **and we hit scullen fallen** 'and we must put a stop to it' (*MED fallen* v. 18 (b)).

119 'And so we shall enjoy what is rightfully ours.'

121–2 Wace 9351–2: 'L'escu levé, l'espee traite, / Ad cuntremunt sa veie faite' ('With shield raised and sword drawn, he made his way up the hill').

125 **wode under wepnen** 'furious with their weapons'. Descriptions of the form 'adjective *under* noun' are common in alliterative verse: cf. 'stifest under stelgere' (No. 9 here, l. 260).

128 **Grim** See Textual Notes. *Grim* is evidently an abbreviated form of 'Colgrim', serving to shorten a long line, strengthen its alliteration, and accentuate the man's ferocity.

And wrað him iwræððed wunder ane swiðe;
And þus cleopien agon Arður þe hæhȝe man:
'War beo ȝe, Bruttes, balde mine beornes?
Her stondeð us bivoren ure ifan alle icoren;
Go we mid isunde and legge we heom to grunde.'
Arður igrap his sweord riht and he smat ænne Sexise cniht
þat þat sweord þat wes swa god æt þan toþen atstod;
And he smat enne oðer, þat wes þas cnihtes broðer,
þat his halm and his hæfd halden to grunde;
þene þridde dunt he sone ȝaf and enne cniht atwa clæf.
þa weoren Bruttes swiðe ibalded,
And leiden o þan Sæxen læȝen swiðe stronge
Mid heore speren longe and mid sweoreden swiðe stronge.
Sexes þer vullen and fæiesið makeden,
Bi hundred bi hundred hælden to þan grunde,
Bi þusund and bi þusend þer feollen ævere in þene grund.
   þa iseh Colgrim wær Arður com touward him;
Ne mihte Colgrim for þan wæle fleon a nare side,
þer fæht Baldulf bisiden his broðer.
þa cleopede Arður ludere stefne:
'Her ic cume, Colgrim! To cuððen wit scullen ræchen;
Nu wit scullen þis lond dalen swa þe bið alre laððest.'
Æfne þan worde þa þe king sæide
His brode swærd he up ahof and hærdliche adun sloh,
And smat Colgrimes hælm þat he amidde toclæf
And þere burne hod, þat hit at þe breoste atstod;

131 'And became wondrously enraged.' *Wrað* is metathesized from *warð*, 'became'. *Him* is reflexive: see 5.4.5, and compare 7b/149.

134 **icoren** 'excellent, worthy' (literally 'chosen, picked out').

135 **mid isunde** 'in security, safe and sound', i.e. without receiving any damage to ourselves. See Textual Notes.

142 **læȝen** 'blows' (so *MED lau* n.). The verb *leiden* suggests a pun on *læȝen*, 'laws'. 'And imposed very strict laws on the Saxons' would give an ironical metaphor of a sort common in battle-poetry.

144 **Sexes** 'Saxons'.

fæiesið makeden 'made a death-doomed journey', i.e. died.

147–73 Expanding a single line of Wace: 'Mort fu Baldulf, morz fu Colgrin' (9358).

148 'Colgrim could not escape in any direction because of the corpses.' *Nare* is dative singular feminine of *nan*, 'no'.

151 **To cuððen wit scullen ræchen** 'We two must vie for the kingdom'. But the exact sense of *ræchen to* is not certain. *Wit*, here and in the following line, is the dual pronoun 'we two'.

152 'Now we two must divide up this land in the way most hateful of all to you (*þe*)' (leaving Colgrim only enough land for a grave).

156 **þere burne hod** Arthur's blow splits not only the helmet but also the mail hood of the corslet (*þere burne*, feminine genitive) under it.

And he sweinde touward Baldulfe mid his swiðren honde
And swipte þat hæfved of, forð mid þan helme.
þa loh Arður, þe aðele king,
And þus ȝeddien agon mid gomenfulle worden:
'Lien nu þere, Colgrim! þu were iclumben to haȝe!
And Baldulf þi broðer lið bi þire side.
Nu ich al þis kinelond sette an eower ahȝere hond,
Dales and dunes and al mi drihtliche volc.
þu clumbe a þissen hulle wunder ane hæȝe
Swulc þu woldest to hævene; nu þu scalt to hælle
þer þu miht kenne muche of þine cunne.
And gret þu þer Hengest, þe cnihten wes faȝerest,
Ebissa, Octa and Ossa and of þine cunne ma,
And bide heom þer wunie wintres and sumeres;
And we scullen on londe libben in blisse,
Bidden for eower saulen þat sel ne wurðen heom navære;
And scullen her æuwer ban biside Baðe ligen.'

157 **swiðren** 'right'. The horizontal stroke which beheads Baldulf requires only one hand, as against the two-handed vertical blow to Colgrim. Cf. the sequence of blows at 136–9.

160 **gomenfulle** 'merry'. The savage and exultant humour plays on associations of high ground with ambition (161) and heaven (166).

163–4 An ironical act of submission to the two dead enemies.

166 Verbs of motion are omitted: see 5.6.9.

168–9 Hengest (of Hengest and Horsa) first led the Saxons to Britain. His son Octa succeeded him as leader. He was killed by Uther Pendragon's men, along with his companions Ebissa and Ossa (*Brut* 9760), and was succeeded as leader by Colgrim.

172 'Pray for your souls, that good may never befall them.'

4
Ancrene Wisse

The *Ancrene Wisse*, 'The Guide (or Rule) for Anchoresses', was composed in the early thirteenth century, probably not long after 1215, originally for three sisters 'of one father and of one mother in the blossom of your youth', who had adopted the life of recluses. The manuscript from which this extract is taken, Corpus Christi College, Cambridge, MS 402, was copied around 1230, and is apparently a fair copy of the author's revised text. This manuscript was donated before 1300 to the Augustinian abbey of Wigmore in north Herefordshire.

The author sets out to direct the recluses on how they should regulate their lives, and in doing so gives many indications of the routine and the difficulties of the enclosed life. The work is divided into eight parts, dealing in turn with prayers, the control of the senses, the regulation of the feelings, temptations, confession, penance, love, and the 'outer rule' on practical matters. The extract here is from the fourth part on temptation, where the author discusses the nature and purpose of temptation and ways of overcoming it, and then portrays the Seven Deadly Sins as beasts – the lion of pride, the bear of sloth, the scorpion of lechery and so forth – together with their progeny, that is, the sins that result from them. There follows the present extract, in which those under the influence of the beasts are described as courtiers of the devil, performing at his court for his amusement. This is a version of the motif of the 'Infernal Pageants', found also in a contemporary Latin account of Thurkill's vision of Hell, where he is allowed to glimpse sinners performing before the devil.

The passage is a good representative of the stylistic features of *Ancrene Wisse*, with its extensive use of allegory and imagery of all sorts, and its assured control of rhythm and rhetorical devices. The author was widely read in the theological works of medieval Europe, and his style owes as much to Latin techniques of biblical exposition as to an English prose tradition reaching back to the Anglo-Saxon models of Ælfric and others.

The work is named *Ancrene Wisse* only in the Corpus manuscript. Editors have adopted the name *Ancrene Riwle* for other versions preserved in four other thirteenth-century manuscripts. There are also later texts and adaptations, and translations into both French and Latin.

The language of the Corpus manuscript of *Ancrene Wisse* and of a group of saints' lives in MS Bodley 34 (the '*Katherine*-group') is a highly consistent form of a South-West Midland dialect, and represents an early example of a literary standard, to which local scribes must have been trained to conform. Forms of the plural personal pronouns here are: for 'you', *ȝe* (nominative), *ower* (genitive), *ow* (dative); for 'they', *ha* (nominative), *ham* (accusative and dative), *hare* (genitive). In the present tense of verbs, the third person singular ending is -(*e*)*ð* as in *wrencheð* (20), except in verbs whose stem ends in *-d* or *-t* where the inflexion is simplified, as in *bihalt*, 'beholds' (48) and *blent*, 'blinds' (46). In the present plural the ending is also -(*e*)*ð*, as in *draheð* (1) and *doð* (2). The endings derived from Old English *-ian* verbs are well preserved, as in present plural *makieð* (3); verbs of this class with a long or disyllabic stem have infinitive *-in* and present plural *-ið*: *lokin* (16), *rikenin* (47), *winkið* (16), *leornið* (26). Many plural nouns end in *-en*, including those that were originally strong masculine or feminine: *bemen* (4), *deoflen* (23), *pinen* (35), *ehnen* (13). The genitive plural ending *-ene* is seen in *englene*, 'of angels' (4), and in the title itself *Ancrene*, 'of Anchoresses'. In marked contrast to Laȝamon's *Brut*, there is a significantly high proportion of French words; first recorded here in English are *augrim* (46), *cuvertur* (54), *temptatiuns* (92), and *manciple* (57) which is not otherwise found until the late fourteenth century.

Editions

Joseph Hall, *Selections from Early Middle English* (Oxford, 1920), No. IX

Geoffrey Shepherd, *Ancrene Wisse Parts Six and Seven* (London, 1959)

J. R. R. Tolkien, *Ancrene Wisse Edited from MS. Corpus Christi College Cambridge 402*, EETS 249 (1962)

Translations

M. B. Salu, *The Ancrene Riwle* (London, 1955)

Hugh White, *Ancrene Wisse: Guide for Anchoresses* (London, 1993)

Studies

Morton W. Bloomfield, *The Seven Deadly Sins* (Michigan, 1952)

Roger Dahood, '*Ancrene Wisse*, the Katherine Group, and the *Wohunge* Group', in A. S. G. Edwards, ed., *Middle English Prose: A Critical Guide to Major Authors and Genres* (New Brunswick, 1984), pp. 1–33 [with bibliography]

E. J. Dobson, *The Origins of Ancrene Wisse* (Oxford, 1976)

Bella Millett, 'The Origins of *Ancrene Wisse*: New Answers, New Questions', *Medium Ævum*, 61 (1992), 206–28

J. R. R. Tolkien, '*Ancrene Wisse* and *Hali Meiðhad*', *Essays and Studies*, 14 (1929), 104–26

þe prude beoð his bemeres, draheð wind inward wið worltlich hereword ant eft wið idel ȝelp puffeð hit utward as þe bemeres doð, makieð noise ant lud dream to schawin hare orhel. Ah ȝef ha wel þohten of Godes bemeres, of þe englene bemen þe schulen o fowr half þe world bivore þe grurefule dom grisliche blawen, 'Ariseð, deade, ariseð! Cumeð to Drihtines dom forte beon idemet, þear na prud bemere ne schal beon iborhen!' – ȝef ha þohten þis wel, ha walden inohreaðe i þe deofles servise dimluker bemin. Of þeose bemeres seið Jeremie: *Onager solitarius in desiderio anime sue attraxit ventum amoris sui* – of þe wind drahinde in for luve of hereword, seið as ich seide.

Summe juglurs beoð þe ne cunnen servin of nan oþer gleo bute makien cheres, wrenche þe muð mis, schulen wið ehnen. Of þis meoster servið þe unseli ontfule i þe deofles curt, to bringen o lahtre hare ondfule laverd. Ȝef ei seið wel oðer deð wel, ne mahen ha nanes weis lokin þider wið riht ehe of god heorte, ah winkið o þet half ant bihaldeð o luft ȝef þer is eawt to edwiten, oðer ladliche þiderward schuleð mið eiðer. Hwen ha ihereð þet god, skleatteð þe earen adun; ah þe luft aȝein þet uvel is eaver wid open. Þenne he

1 **his** the Devil's. The writer has been enumerating the Seven Deadly Sins and explaining that the sinful serve in the Devil's court.

4–5 **o fowr half þe world** 'in the four quarters of the world'. The source is the Apocalypse (Revelation) 7.1: 'four angels standing on the four corners of the earth'. Compare Donne's sonnet, 'At the round earths imagin'd corners, blow / Your trumpets, Angells, and arise, arise / From death'.

9–10 'A wild ass accustomed to the wilderness in the desire of his heart snuffed up the wind of his love' (Jeremiah 2.24, alluding to the defection of Israel).

10–11 'He says what I have just said about air being snuffed up for love of praise.'

14–15 **to bringen o lahtre** 'to make laugh'. The envious (*ontfule*) distort their eyes (16–18), their ears (18–19) and their mouths (19–21).

15 **ondfule** here 'malicious': St Augustine's notion of envy includes not merely sorrow at others' happiness, but also happiness at others' sorrow.

16 **ehe** the Latin verb *invidere*, 'to envy', meaning literally 'to look evilly', lies behind this image of the 'heart's eye'. Much bolder is the image of the *heortes nease*, 'nose of the heart', in l. 90.

16–17 **winkið o þet half** 'close their eyes on that (right) side'. The play on the two senses of *riht* reinforces the traditional associations of the left side (*luft*) with wickedness.

18 **þet god** 'anything good'.

19 **ah . . . open** 'but the left (ear) is always open wide towards what is evil'.

wrencheð þe muð hwen he turneð god to uvel, ant ȝef hit is sumdel uvel, þurh mare lastunge wrencheð hit to wurse. þeos beoð forecwidderes, hare ahne prophetes; þeos bodieð bivoren hu þe eateliche deoflen schulen ȝet ageasten ham wið hare grennunge, ant hu ha schulen hamseolf grennin ant nivelin ant makien sur semblant for þe muchele angoise i þe pine of helle. Ah forþi ha beoð þe leasse to meanen þet ha bivorenhond leornið hare meoster to makien grim chere.

þe wreaðfule bivore þe feond skirmeð mid cnives ant is his cnif-warpere, ant pleieð mid sweordes, bereð ham bi þe scharp ord up on his tunge. Sweord ant cnif eiðer beoð scharpe ant keorvinde word þet he warpeð from him ant skirmeð toward oþre; ant he bodeð hu þe deoflen schulen pleien wið him mid hare scharpe eawles, skirmi wið him abuten ant dusten ase pilche clut euch toward oðer, ant wið helle sweordes asneasen him þurhut, þet beoð kene ant eateliche ant keorvinde pinen.

þe slawe lið ant slepeð o þe deofles bearm as his deore deorling, ant te deovel leið his tutel dun to his eare ant tuteleð him al þet he wule. For swa hit is sikerliche to hwam se is idel of god: meaðeleð þe feond ȝeorne ant te idele underveð luveliche his lare. Idel ant ȝemeles is þes deofles bearnes slep, ah he schal o Domesdei grimliche abreiden wið þe dredfule dream of þe englene bemen ant in helle wontreaðe echeliche wakien. *'Surgite!' aiunt, 'mortui, surgite et venite ad judicium salvatoris!'*

þe ȝiscere is his eskibah, feareð abuten esken ant bisiliche stureð him to rukelin togederes muchele ant monie ruken, blaweð þrin ant

21–2 'These are forecasters, prophets of their own doom.'

23 **ȝet** 'in the future'.

26 **to meanen** 'to be pitied'; passive infinitive, 5.6.5.

þet 'in as much as'.

30 **eiðer beoð** 'both represent'.

33 **pilche clut** 'a bit of old fur', a clout or remnant of clothing made of skin or fur.

34–5 The *þet*-clause defines *helle sweordes.*

37 **te** after *d* and *t*, *þe* becomes *te* and *þis* becomes *tis* (e.g. l. 48).

tutel 'mouth'. The word is found only in *Ancrene Wisse*; it is related to a Dutch word referring to something that protrudes, a spout etc.

38 **to hwam se is idel of god** 'for anyone who is devoid of virtue'. *Idel* also carries the sense of 'lazy', which is exploited in the next lines.

41 **dream** not 'dream', a sense derived from ON *draumr*, but rather 'sound' (OE *drēam*), as in l. 3.

42–3 '"Arise", they say, "arise, you dead, and come to the judgement of the Saviour".' This is translated in 5–6 above.

44 **eskibah** literally 'ash-fool'. Compare the Scottish and Irish word *ashiepattle*, 'a dirty child that lounges about the hearth' (*English Dialect Dictionary*). The etymology is discussed by Joan Turville-Petre, *Studia Neophilologica*, 41 (1969), 156–8.

blent himseolf, peaðereð ant makeð þrin figures of augrim as þes rikeneres doð þe habbeð muche to rikenin. þis is al þe canges blisse, ant te feond bihalt tis gomen ant laheð þet he bersteð. Wel understont euch wis mon þet gold ba ant seolver ant euch eorðlich ahte nis bute eorðe ant esken þe ablendeð euch mon þe ham in blaweð, þet is, þe bolheð him þurh ham in heorte prude. Ant al þet he rukeleð ant gedereð togederes ant ethalt of ei þing þet nis bute esken, mare þen hit neodeð, schal in helle wurðen him tadden ant neddren; ant ba, as Ysaie seið, schulen beon of wurmes his cuvertur ant his hwitel, þe nalde þerwið neodfule feden ne schruden. *Subter te sternetur tinea et operimentum tuum vermis.*

þe ȝivere glutun is þe feondes manciple, ah he stikeð eaver i celer oðer i cuchene; his heorte is i þe dissches, his þoht al i þe neppes, his lif i þe tunne, his sawle i þe crohhe. Kimeð bivoren his laverd bismuddet ant bismulret, a disch in his an hond, a scale in his oðer, meaðeleð mis wordes, wigleð as fordrunke mon þe haveð imunt to fallen. Bihalt his greate wombe, ant te deovel lahheð. þeose þreatið þus Godd þurh Ysaie: *Servi mei comedent et vos esurietis et cetera.* 'Mine men schulen eoten ant ow schal eaver hungrin', ant ȝe schule beon feondes fode world buten ende. *Quantum glorificavit se et in deliciis fuit, tantum date illi tormentum et luctum. In Apocalipsi. Contra unum poculum quod miscuit miscete ei duo.* Ȝef þe kealche-cuppe wallinde bres to drinken. Ȝeot in his wide þrote þet he swelte inwið. Aȝein an ȝef him twa. þullich is Godes dom aȝein ȝivere ant druncwile i þe Apocalipse.

þe lecchurs i þe deofles curt habbeð riht hare ahne nome, for i þes muchele curz þeo me cleopeð lecchurs þe habbeð swa forlore

46 **figures of augrim** 'arithmetical figures'. Nicholas, the student in Chaucer's Miller's Tale, has *augrym stones*, counters with Arabic numerals, to make his calculations (*Canterbury Tales* I 3210).

49 **gold ba ant seolver** 'gold and silver too'.

51 **þe bolheð . . . prude** 'who puffs himself up in pride of heart as a consequence of them'.

53 **mare þen hit neodeð** 'over and above what is essential'.

54 **ba** 'both', referring forward to *cuvertur* and *hwitel.*

55 **þe** 'who', refers back to *his*; see 5.4.6.

55–6 'Under thee shall the moth be strewed, and worms shall be your covering' (Isaiah 14.11).

57 The manciple buys provisions for the household.

61–2 **haveð imunt to** 'is about to' (*minten*, 'intend').

62 **Bihalt** 'he [the devil?] looks at'; cf. l. 48.

63–4 'My servants shall eat, and you shall be hungry, etc.' (Isaiah 65.13).

64 **ow** dative; see 5.6.8.

65–7 'As much as she hath glorified herself and lived in delicacies, so much torment and sorrow give ye to her. In the Apocalypse. In return for one cup wherein she hath mingled, mingle ye double unto her.' Adapted from the curses on Babylon in the Apocalypse (Revelation) 18.6–7.

72 **þeo me cleopeð** 'those are called'. 'Lecher' was also a general term of abuse for those intent on *vilainie.*

scheome þet heom nis nawiht of scheome, ah secheð hu ha mahen meast vilainie wurchen. Þe lecchur i þe deofles curt bifuleð himseolven fulliche ant his feolahes alle, stinkeð of þet fulðe, ant paieð wel his laverd wið þet stinkinde breað betere þen he schulde wið eani swote rechles. Hu he stinke to Godd i *Vitas Patrum* þe engel hit schawde, þe heold his nease þa þer com þe prude lecchur ridinde, ant nawt for þet rotede lich þet he healp þe hali earmite to biburien. Of alle oþre þenne habbeð þeos þe fuleste meoster i þe feondes curt þe swa bidoð hamseolven; ant he schal bidon ham, pinin ham wið eche stench i þe put of helle.

Nu ȝe habbeð ane dale iherd, mine leove sustren, of þeo þe me cleopeð þe seove moder-sunnen ant of hare teames, ant of hwucche meosters þes ilke men servið i þe feondes curt þe habbeð iwivet o þeose seoven haggen, ant hwi ha beoð swiðe to heatien ant to schunien. Ȝe beoð ful feor from ham, ure Laverd beo iþoncket; ah þet fule breað of þis leaste unþeaw, þet is, of leccherie, stinkeð se swiðe feor, for þe feond hit saweð ant toblaweð over al, þet ich am sumdel ofdred leste hit leape sum chearre into ower heortes nease. Stench stiheð uppart, ant ȝe beoð hehe iclumben þer þe wind is muchel of stronge temptatiuns. Ure Laverd ȝeove ow strengðe wel to wiðstonden!

73 **nawiht of scheome** 'nothing that is shameful'.

secheð 'they seek'. The subject is understood from the previous dative pronoun *heom*; see 5.4.2.

76 **paieð** 'gratifies'.

77 **stinke** subjunctive in an indirect question; see 5.6.6.

78 **hit** recapitulates the *hu*-clause (5.10). The source cited here, the Latin *Lives of the Fathers* (*PL* 73.1014), gives a rather different version of the story of the angel, the hermit and the corpse. Much closer is the version in the *Exempla* of Jacques de Vitry (*c.* 1180–1240), ed. T. F. Crane (London, 1890), No. CIV, and the story is later widely disseminated.

82 **eche** 'eternal'.

86–7 **to heatien ant to schunien** passive infinitives; see 5.6.5.

88 **leaste** 'last'.

90 **heortes nease** see note to l. 16.

91–2 In his opening remarks on temptations the author had used this same image to show the greater perils to the good who have climbed high: 'As the hill is higher, so the wind is greater on it'.

5
Sir Orfeo

Sir Orfeo was composed in the late thirteenth or early fourteenth century in the South Midlands, perhaps London. There are three texts, the earliest (1330–40) in the Auchinleck manuscript, National Library of Scotland MS Advocates 19.2.1, one of the most important English manuscripts of the period, apparently produced in London, and containing a large collection of romances and religious poems. Later and rather corrupt copies of the poem are in two fifteenth-century manuscripts. The text here is based on the Auchinleck manuscript (see also 1–38n.).

The three versions of the classical story of Orpheus and Eurydice best known to the Middle Ages are in Ovid's *Metamorphoses* 10–11, Virgil's *Georgics* 4, and *The Consolation of Philosophy* 3, metre 12, by the sixth-century writer Boethius, who moralized the story as a warning against the perils of looking back on the pleasures of the world. In all of these versions Orpheus finally loses Eurydice, but there are eleventh-century Latin accounts, discussed by Friedman (1970), 164–75, and P. Dronke, *Classica and Mediaevalia*, 23 (1962), 198–215, where, as in the present poem, he succeeds in bringing her back.

In *Sir Orfeo*, the story has been reinterpreted as a Celtic folk-tale. The abductor of Heurodis (Eurydice) is the Fairy King who takes her to his kingdom, the Other World rather than Hades. Other stories derived from Celtic folk-beliefs tell how mortals, sometimes at the point of death, were snatched by the fairies and taken to their world of light and splendour. Occasionally they could be brought back, as in the late twelfth-century story by Walter Map in which a Breton knight recovered his 'dead' wife from the fairies and later had children by her (*De nugis curialium* iv.8). There is an illuminating account of the whole subject by Allen (1964).

Such folk-tales were passed down by the Celtic-speaking inhabitants of Brittany in the form of musical compositions evidently accompanied by oral narratives. They were taken up by French writers, notably Marie de France who composed a series of verse *lais* in the later twelfth century. A fragmentary English translation of one of Marie's *lais*, the *Lay le Freine*, also survives in the Auchinleck manuscript. *Sir Orfeo* is probably an adaptation of a

French Breton lay. No French version survives, but there are references in French romances to a musical 'Lai d'Orphey'. A late sixteenth-century Scottish poem about Orpheus may be another translation of the same lost French *lai*; see M. Stewart, *Scottish Studies*, 17 (1973), 1–16.

The Breton lay seems to have enjoyed something of a vogue in English. *Sir Launfal* is another example, based ultimately on Marie de France's *Lanval*. Chaucer's Franklin claims to be telling a Breton lay, and he gives an interesting account of the genre in the Prologue to his tale. The author of *Sir Orfeo* is more successful than any other medieval English writer in capturing the world of Celtic folk-beliefs, the mysterious powers of the fairies and their eerie kingdom at once beautiful and terrifying.

In the text, the feminine nominative pronoun is generally *sche*, but occasionally *hye* (81, 337) or *he* (408, 446). Forms of the third person plural pronoun are *þai* (except for *hye*, 91, and *he*, 185), *hem* and *her*. In the present tense of verbs, the ending of both the third person singular and the plural is *-eþ*. There are contracted forms such as *he fint*, 'he finds' (239), *last*, 'lasts' (335) and *sitt*, 'sits' (443).

Editions

Fourteenth Century Verse and Prose, ed. Kenneth Sisam (Oxford, 1921), pp. 13–31

Sir Orfeo, ed. A. J. Bliss, 2nd edn (Oxford, 1966)

Facsimile

The Auchinleck Manuscript, introduced by Derek Pearsall and I. C. Cunningham (London, 1979)

Other Texts

Walter Map, *De nugis curialium*, ed. and trans. M. R. James, revised edn (Oxford, 1983)

The Lais of Marie de France, trans. Glyn S. Burgess and Keith Busby (Harmondsworth, 1986)

Studies

Dorena Allen, 'Orpheus and Orfeo: The Dead and the *Taken*', *Medium Ævum*, 33 (1964), 102–11

John Block Friedman, *Orpheus in the Middle Ages* (Cambridge, Mass., 1970)

D. M. Hill, 'The Structure of "Sir Orfeo"', *Medieval Studies*, 23 (1961), 136–53

E. Hoepffner, 'The Breton Lais', in *Arthurian Literature in the Middle Ages*, ed. R. S. Loomis (Oxford, 1959), pp. 112–21

Howard Rollin Patch, *The Other World* (Cambridge, Mass., 1950)

A. C. Spearing, *Readings in Medieval Poetry* (Cambridge, 1987), pp. 56–82

We redeþ oft and findeþ ywrite,
And þis clerkes wele it wite,
Layes þat ben in harping
Ben yfounde of ferli þing.
Sum beþe of wer and sum of wo,
And sum of joie and mirþe also,
And sum of trecherie and of gile,
Of old aventours þat fel while,
And sum of bourdes and ribaudy,
And mani þer beþ of fairy.
Of al þinges þat men seþ,
Mest o love, for soþe, þai beþ.
In Breteyne þis layes were wrouȝt,
First yfounde and forþ ybrouȝt,
Of aventours þat fel bi dayes,
Wherof Bretouns made her layes.
When kinges miȝt our yhere
Of ani mervailes þat þer were,
þai token an harp in gle and game
And maked a lay and ȝaf it name.
Now of þis aventours þat weren yfalle
Y can tel sum, ac nouȝt alle.
Ac herkneþ, lordinges þat beþ trewe,
Ichil ȝou telle of Sir Orfewe.
   Orfeo mest of ani þing
Loved þe gle of harping.
Siker was everi gode harpour

1–38 The opening lines have been lost from the Auchinleck manuscript. Bliss reconstructs them, taking lines 1–13 and 17–22 from another Breton lay in the manuscript, *Lay le Freine*, which evidently had the same prologue, and basing lines 14–16 and 23–38 on the text in the Harley manuscript. See Bliss's edition, pp. xlvi–xlviii, for a full account of the procedure.

11 **men seþ** 'one sees'; i.e. 'are to be found'. See 5.4.3.

13 **Breteyne** 'Brittany'.

14–16 These lines, omitted in the Auchinleck manuscript, are based on the Harley manuscript, with *ybrouȝt* from the Ashmole manuscript for the rhyme.

17 **our** 'anywhere' (a reduced form of *owhere*).

20 The title of the *lai* had great significance. See, for example, the ending of Marie de France's *Chaitivel*, where, after mooting various titles, she concludes that 'each name is appropriate and supported by the subject matter'.

25–38 These lines come after ll. 39–46 in the Harley text, but Bliss argues convincingly that they were part of the lost prologue in the Auchinleck manuscript.

Of him to have miche honour.
Himself he lerned for to harp
And leyd þeron his wittes scharp;
He lerned so þer noþing was
A better harpour in no plas.
In al þe warld was no man bore
Þat ones Orfeo sat bifore,
And he miȝt of his harping here,
Bot he schuld þenche þat he were
In on of þe joies of Paradis,
Swiche melody in his harping is.
  Orfeo was a king
In Inglond, an heiȝe lording,
A stalworþ man and hardi bo,
Large and curteys he was also;
His fader was comen of King Pluto
And his moder of King Juno,
Þat sumtime were as godes yhold
For aventours þat þai dede and told.
Þis king sojournd in Traciens,
Þat was a cité of noble defens,
For Winchester was cleped þo
Traciens, wiþouten no.
Þe king hadde a quen of priis
Þat was ycleped Dame Herodis,
Þe fairest levedi, for þe nones,
Þat miȝt gon on bodi and bones,
Ful of love and of godenisse;
Ac no man may telle hir fairnise.

29 'He taught himself to play the harp.'

34 'Who ever sat before Orfeo.'

35 **And** 'if'.

36 **Bot he** refers back to *no man* in l. 33, so 'every man . . . would think'.

37 **on of þe joies** there were reputedly fourteen joys of Paradise, seven each for the body and the soul.

42 **Large** 'generous'.

43–4 Pluto is king of the underworld, and in Chaucer's Merchant's Tale, *Canterbury Tales* IV 2227, he is *kyng of Fayerye.* Juno is goddess of marriage. For *of King Juno*, probably a scribal error, the Harley manuscript has more sensibly *cam of Yno.* There does not seem to be particular significance in the identity of Orfeo's ancestors except that they are the nobility of a pre-Christian past (l. 45).

49–50 The identification of Thrace (*Traciens*) with Winchester, the ancient royal city of Alfred and the kings of Wessex, is not in the other manuscripts. The poet, or more probably a reviser, made a consistent effort to set the story in England. Compare ll. 39–40, also only in the Auchinleck manuscript, and l. 478, *Winchester* again, where the other manuscripts refer to Thrace.

52 **Herodis** Eurydice.

54 'Who could ever live.'

Bifel so in þe comessing of May
When miri and hot is þe day,
And oway beþ winter schours,
And everi feld is ful of flours,
And blosme breme on everi bouȝ
Over al wexeþ miri anouȝ,
þis ich quen, Dame Heurodis,
Tok to maidens of priis,
And went in an undrentide
To play bi an orchard side,
To se þe floures sprede and spring
And to here þe foules sing.
þai sett hem doun al þre
Under a fair ympe-tre,
And wel sone þis fair quene
Fel on slepe opon þe grene.
þe maidens durst hir nouȝt awake,
Bot lete hir ligge and rest take;
So sche slepe til after none,
þat undertide was al ydone.
Ac as sone as sche gan awake,
Sche crid and loþli bere gan make,
Sche froted hir honden and hir fet
And crached hir visage, it bled wete,
Hir riche robe hye al torett,
And was reveyd out of hir witt.
þe tuo maidens hir biside
No durst wiþ hir no leng abide,
Bot ourn to þe palays ful riȝt
And told boþe squier and kniȝt
þat her quen awede wold,
And bad hem go and hir at-hold.
Kniȝtes urn, and levedis also,
Damisels sexti and mo,

57 The May setting with the blossom and the lovely lady is characteristic of romance. This is the *comessing*, 'beginning', of May; in folklore May Day is particularly dangerous.

64 **to** 'two', as in ll. 111 and 135.

65 **in an undrentide** 'in mid-morning'. The time meant by *undren* or *under* varies from 'prime' (9 a.m.) to midday. The significant point is that Heurodis is asleep at noon (l. 75) when meetings with the supernatural are most likely. So Orfeo sees the fairies *in hot undertides* (282).

70 **ympe-tre** 'grafted tree'. Apple trees, which are cultivated by grafting onto a root-stock, were common in the Celtic Other World (see Patch (1950), pp. 52–3), and in romances and ballads fairies may visit those who lie under trees, as in the lay of *Sir Launfal*, 226–31.

In þe orchard to þe quen hye come,
And her up in her armes nome
And brouȝt hir to bed atte last,
And held hir þere fine fast,
Ac ever sche held in o cri,
And wold up and owy.
When Orfeo herd þat tiding,
Never him nas wers for noþing;
He come wiþ kniȝtes tene
To chaumber riȝt bifor þe quene,
And biheld and seyd wiþ grete pité:
'O lef liif, what is te,
þat ever ȝete hast ben so stille
And now gredest wonder schille?
þi bodi þat was so white ycore
Wiþ þine nailes is al totore;
Allas, þi rode þat was so red
Is al wan as þou were ded,
And also þine fingres smale
Beþ al blodi and al pale.
Allas, þi lovesom eyȝen to
Lokeþ so man doþ on his fo.
A, dame, ich biseche merci!
Lete ben al þis reweful cri,
And tel me what þe is and hou,
And what þing may þe help now.'
þo lay sche stille atte last
And gan to wepe swiþe fast,
And seyd þus þe king to:
'Allas mi lord, Sir Orfeo,
Seþþen we first togider were,
Ones wroþ never we nere,
Bot ever ich have yloved þe
As mi liif, and so þou me,
Ac now we mot delen ato;
Do þi best, for y mot go.'
'Allas,' quaþ he, 'forlorn ich am!
Whider wiltow go, and to wham?

95 'But she always kept up the same cry.'

96 **wold up** 'wanted to get up': 5.6.9.

98 'He was never more distressed about anything.'

102 **what is te** 'what's wrong?' (*te* is a form of *þe*, dative, 'with thee'). So also *what þe is*, 115.

122 'We were never once angry.'

126 **Do þi best** 'make the best of it'.

Whider þou gost ichil wiþ þe,
And whider y go þou schalt wiþ me.'
'Nay, nay, sir, þat nouȝt nis;
Ichil þe telle al hou it is.
As ich lay þis undertide
And slepe under our orchard side,
þer come to me to fair kniȝtes
Wele y-armed al to riȝtes,
And bad me comen an heiȝing
And speke wiþ her lord þe king,
And ich answerd at wordes bold,
Y no durst nouȝt, no y nold.
þai priked oȝain as þai miȝt drive;
þo com her king also blive
Wiþ an hundred kniȝtes and mo
And damisels an hundred also,
Al on snowe-white stedes,
As white as milke were her wedes.
Y no seiȝe never ȝete bifore
So fair creatours ycore;
þe king hadde a croun on hed,
It nas of silver no of gold red,
Ac it was of a precious ston,
As briȝt as þe sonne it schon.
And as son as he to me cam,
Wold ich, nold ich, he me nam,
And made me wiþ him ride
Opon a palfray bi his side,
And brouȝt me to his palays
Wele atird in ich ways,
And schewed me castels and tours,
Rivers, forestes, friþ wiþ flours,
And his riche stedes ichon,
And seþþen me brouȝt oȝain hom
Into our owhen orchard,

131 **þat nouȝt nis** 'that can't be'.

137 **an heiȝing** 'in haste'. This use of the verbal noun with *an/on* is found again in l. 308, *on haukin*, 'hawking', and survives in modern *a-ringing* etc.

139 **at wordes bold** 'boldly'.

140 'I didn't dare to and I wouldn't.'

141 'They rode back as fast as they could go.'

142–61 The elegance of the fairies and the richness of their land are characteristic features of descriptions of the Other World. See Patch (1950), pp. 55–9, and compare the account in ll. 349–76.

154 **Wold ich, nold ich** 'whether I was willing or not'. Cf. 7b/153 below.

161 **riche stedes** 'fine estates'.

And said to me þus afterward:
"Loke, dame, tomorwe þatow be
Riȝt here under þis ympe-tre,
And þan þou schalt wiþ ous go
And live wiþ ous evermo;
And ȝif þou makest ous ylet,
Whar þou be, þou worst yfet,
And totore þine limes al,
Þat noþing help þe no schal,
And þei þou best so totorn,
Ȝete þou worst wiþ ous yborn."'
When King Orfeo herd þis cas,
'O we!' quaþ he, 'allas, allas!
Lever me were to lete mi liif
Þan þus to lese þe quen mi wiif.'
He asked conseyl at ich man,
Ac no man him help no can.
Amorwe þe undertide is come
And Orfeo haþ his armes ynome
And wele ten hundred kniȝtes wiþ him,
Ich y-armed stout and grim,
And wiþ þe quen wenten he
Riȝt unto þat ympe-tre.
Þai made scheltrom in ich a side,
And sayd þai wold þere abide
And dye þer everichon
Er þe quen schuld fram hem gon;
Ac ȝete amiddes hem ful riȝt
Þe quen was oway ytuiȝt,
Wiþ fairi forþ ynome;
Men wist never wher sche was bicome.
Þo was þer criing, wepe and wo;
Þe king into his chaumber is go
And oft swoned opon þe ston,

169 **makest ous ylet** 'offer us resistance'.

170 'Wherever you may be, you will be fetched'; *worst* is second person singular of *worþen*. See 5.6.10 for its future sense.

171 'And all your limbs (will be) torn apart.'

173–4 **best** 'will be'. 'Though you'll be torn apart in this way, even so you'll be carried off with us.'

177 'I'd rather give up my life.'

185 The plural ending of *wenten* confirms that *he* is 'they'.

187 **made scheltrom** 'drew up the soldiers'. The OE compound *sceld-truma*, 'shield-troop', denotes the tight formation of warriors with interlocking shields. This massive physical presence is powerless to protect Heurodis.

196 **is go** 'went'; see 5.6.3.

And made swiche diol and swiche mon
þat neiȝe his liif was yspent;
þer was non amendement.
He cleped togider his barouns,
Erls, lordes of renouns,
And when þai al ycomen were,
'Lordinges,' he said, 'bifor ȝou here
Ich ordainy min heiȝe steward
To wite mi kingdom afterward.
In mi stede ben he schal,
To kepe mi londes over al;
For now ichave mi quen ylore,
þe fairest levedi þat ever was bore,
Never eft y nil no woman se.
Into wildernes ichil te
And live þer evermore
Wiþ wilde bestes in holtes hore,
And when ȝe understond þat y be spent,
Make ȝou þan a parlement
And chese ȝou a newe king.
Now doþ ȝour best wiþ al mi þing.'
   þo was þer wepeing in þe halle,
And grete cri among hem alle;
Unneþe miȝt old or ȝong
For wepeing speke a word wiþ tong.
þai kneled adoun al yfere
And praid him, ȝif his wille were,
þat he no schuld nouȝt fram hem go.
'Do way!' quaþ he, 'It schal be so.'
Al his kingdom he forsoke,
Bot a sclavin on him he toke;
He no hadde kirtel no hode,
Schert no no noþer gode;
Bot his harp he tok algate
And dede him barfot out atte ȝate;
No man most wiþ him go.
   O way! what þer was wepe and wo
When he þat hadde ben king wiþ croun

211 In Ovid's *Metamorphoses* 10.79–81, Orpheus renounces all women after his final loss of Eurydice.

215–17 The poet envisages a very English arrangement, as in 1327 when Parliament deposed Edward II and adopted his son as king. *Ȝou* (ll. 216, 217) is dative, 'for yourselves'.

228 **Bot a sclavin** 'only a pilgrim's cloak'.

Went so poverlich out of toun.
Þurth wode and over heþ
Into þe wildernes he geþ;
Noþing he fint þat him is ays,
Bot ever he liveþ in gret malais.
He þat hadde ywerd þe fowe and griis,
And on bed þe purper biis,
Now on hard heþe he liþ,
Wiþ leves and gresse he him wriþ.
He þat hadde had castels and tours,
River, forest, friþ wiþ flours,
Now þei it comenci to snewe and frese,
Þis king mot make his bed in mese.
He þat had yhad kniȝtes of priis
Bifor him kneland, and levedis,
Now seþ he noþing þat him likeþ,
Bot wilde wormes bi him strikeþ.
He þat had yhad plenté
Of mete and drink, of ich deynté,
Now may he al day digge and wrote
Er he finde his fille of rote.
In somer he liveþ bi wild frut
And berien bot gode lite;
In winter may he noþing finde
Bot rote, grases and þe rinde;
Al his bodi was oway duine
For missays, and al tochine.
Lord, who may telle þe sore
Þis king sufferd ten ȝere and more?
His here of his berd, blac and rowe,
To his girdel-stede was growe.
His harp whereon was al his gle
He hidde in an holwe tre,
And when þe weder was clere and briȝt,
He toke his harp to him wel riȝt
And harped at his owhen wille;

239 **ays** 'ease'; 'He finds nothing of comfort to him'.

241–56 This effective set of contrasts between wealth and poverty is reminiscent of homiletic tradition; see e.g. Carleton Brown, *English Lyrics of the XIIIth Century* (Oxford, 1932), No. 48, and the discussion by Felicity Riddy, *Yearbook of English Studies*, 6 (1976), 5–15.

241 **fowe and griis** 'fine furs'; *fowe* is parti-coloured fur, *griis* is grey fur.

252 'Except fierce serpents that slither past him.'

258 'And berries of only little value.'

261 **oway duine** 'wasted away'.

Into alle þe wode þe soun gan schille,
þat alle þe wilde bestes þat þer beþ
For joie abouten him þai teþ,
And alle þe foules þat þer were
Come and sete on ich a brere
To here his harping afine,
So miche melody was þerin;
And when he his harping lete wold,
No best bi him abide nold.
He miȝt se him bisides,
Oft in hot undertides,
þe king o fairy wiþ his rout
Com to hunt him al about
Wiþ dim cri and bloweing,
And houndes also wiþ him berking;
Ac no best þai no nome,
No never he nist whider þai bicome.
And oþerwhile he miȝt him se
As a gret ost bi him te,
Wele atourned, ten hundred kniȝtes,
Ich y-armed to his riȝtes,
Of cuntenaunce stout and fers,
Wiþ mani desplaid baners,
And ich his swerd ydrawe hold;
Ac never he nist whider þai wold.
And oþerwhile he seiȝe oþer þing:
Kniȝtes and levedis com daunceing
In queynt atire gisely,
Queynt pas and softly;
Tabours and trunpes ȝede hem bi,
And al maner menstraci.
And on a day he seiȝe him biside
Sexti levedis on hors ride,

277 **afine** 'to the end'.
282 See 65n.
283–96 The fairy hunt and the fairy army are often mentioned in Celtic folklore, as in the story by the twelfth-century writer Walter Map about King Herla who, after visiting fairyland, was condemned to ride unceasingly with his company (*De nugis curialium* i.11).
287–8 'But they caught no animal, and he never knew where they went to.'
290 **As** 'as it were', i.e. 'what seemed to be'.
294 The displaying of banners would signify that the army is marching to war; compare Chaucer's Knight's Tale, *Canterbury Tales* I 966.
296 'But he never knew where they were off to.'
297–302 Walter Map describes a fairy dance in *De nugis curialium* ii.12.
299–300 'Gracefully in elegant dress, quietly and with elegant steps.'

Gentil and jolif as brid on ris;
Nouȝt o man amonges hem þer nis;
And ich a faucon on hond bere,
And riden on haukin bi o rivere.
Of game þai founde wel gode haunt,
Maulardes, hayroun and cormeraunt.
þe foules of þe water ariseþ,
þe faucouns hem wele deviseþ;
Ich faucoun his pray slouȝ.
þat seiȝe Orfeo and louȝ.
'Parfay,' quaþ he, 'þer is fair game.
þider ichil, bi Godes name!
Ich was ywon swiche werk to se.'
He aros and þider gan te;
To a levedi he was ycome,
Biheld and haþ wele undernome
And seþ bi al þing þat it is
His owhen quen, Dam Heurodis.
Ȝern he biheld hir, and sche him eke,
Ac noiþer to oþer a word no speke;
For messais þat sche on him seiȝe,
þat had ben so riche and so heiȝe,
þe teres fel out of her eiȝe.
þe oþer levedis þis yseiȝe
And maked hir oway to ride;
Sche most wiþ him no lenger abide.
'Allas,' quaþ he, 'now me is wo.
Whi nil deþ now me slo?
Allas, wroche, þat y no miȝt
Dye now after þis siȝt.
Allas, to long last mi liif,
When y no dar nouȝt wiþ mi wiif,
No hye to me, o word speke.
Allas, whi nil min hert breke?

305 'Lovely and happy as bird on branch' – a traditional comparison. A hunting party consisting only of ladies is remarkable.

308 **on haukin** 'hawking'; see 137n.

313 The pointed contrast is with l. 287; these ladies are not fairies. The courtly sport reminds Orfeo of his former life, and for the first time he laughs with pleasure and moves towards the group.

316 **ichil** 'I will (go)'; see 5.6.9.

324 They are prevented from communicating by the enchantment of the fairies. See Lewis J. Owen, *Medium Ævum*, 40 (1971), 249–53.

325 'Because of the wretched condition she saw he was in.'

337 'Speak a single word, nor she to me.'

Parfay,' quaþ he, 'tide wat bitide,
Whider so þis levedis ride,
þe selve way ichil streche.
Of liif no deþ me no reche.'
His sclavain he dede on also spac
And henge his harp opon his bac,
And had wel gode wil to gon;
He no spard noiþer stub no ston.
In at a roche þe levedis rideþ
And he after and nouȝt abideþ.
When he was in þe roche ygo
Wele þre mile oþer mo,
He com into a fair cuntray
As briȝt so sonne on somers day,
Smoþe and plain and al grene,
Hille no dale nas þer non ysene.
Amidde þe lond a castel he siȝe,
Riche and real and wonder heiȝe.
Al þe utmast wal
Was clere and schine as cristal;
An hundred tours þer were about,
Degiselich and bataild stout;
þe butras com out of þe diche
Of rede gold y-arched riche;
þe vousour was anowrned al
Of ich maner divers aumal.
Wiþin þer wer wide wones
Al of precious stones;
þe werst piler on to biholde
Was al of burnist gold.
Al þat lond was ever liȝt,
For when it schuld be þerk and niȝt,

339 **tide wat bitide** 'come what may'.
342 'I don't care about whether I live or die.'
345 'And went with great eagerness.'
346 **spard** 'avoided'. He went by the most direct route.
347 Fairyland is always cut off from the world of mortals, over a river or, as here, through a rock. See Patch (1950), 29–48.
351–76 Bliss, p. xxxix, cites Celtic parallels for this description of fairyland, with its brightness, its crystal and its precious metal.
356 **real** 'royal, glorious'.
358 **schine** 'brilliant' (an adjective).
360 'Wonderful and with strong battlements.'
363–4 'The arching (of the buttresses) was all decorated with every kind of different enamel.' The emendation *anowrned* was suggested by Sisam, though it is possible that the reading *avowed* is an otherwise unrecorded word meaning 'coloured', as Bliss suggests.

þe riche stones li3t gonne
As bri3t as doþ at none þe sonne.
No man may telle no þenche in þou3t
þe riche werk þat þer was wrou3t;
Bi al þing him þink þat it is
þe proude court of Paradis.
In þis castel þe levedis ali3t;
He wold in after 3if he mi3t.
   Orfeo knokkeþ atte gate;
þe porter was redi þerate
And asked what he wold have ydo.
'Parfay,' quaþ he, 'ich am a minstrel, lo!
To solas þi lord wiþ mi gle,
3if his swete wille be.'
þe porter undede þe 3ate anon
And lete him in to þe castel gon.
   þan he gan bihold about al,
And sei3e liggeand wiþin þe wal
Of folk þat were þider ybrou3t
And þou3t dede and nare nou3t.
Sum stode wiþouten hade,
And sum non armes nade,
And sum þurth þe bodi hadde wounde,
And sum lay wode ybounde,
And sum armed on hors sete,
And sum astrangled as þai ete,
And sum were in water adreynt,
And sum wiþ fire al forschreynt;
Wives þer lay on child-bedde,
Sum ded and sum awedde,

371 **li3t gonne** 'shone'. Trevisa, *Properties*, p. 839, says of the carbuncle that it 'schyneþ as fuyre whos schynynge is not overcome by night'.

376 This recalls medieval descriptions of heaven, which were based on the Apocalypse (Revelation) 21, e.g. verse 11, 'And the light thereof was like to a precious stone'. Cf. *Pearl* 985–1080.

378 **wold** 'wished to go' (5.6.9).

381 **wold have ydo** 'wanted done'.

384 'If he wishes' (*be* is subjunctive).

388–90 'And caught sight of people lying within the wall who were brought there and thought dead but were not.' In Celtic folk-belief many of those who apparently die suddenly are not actually dead but are 'taken' by the fairies. See Allen (1964), 102–11.

394 Madness was a sign that the sufferer's spirit had already been taken; see Allen (1964), 105. Mad people were restrained: 'þe medicines of hem (manias) is þat he be ibounde . . .' (Trevisa, *Properties*, p. 350).

396 **astrangled** 'choked'.

400 'Some dead, and some mad.' They are 'dead' by conventional wisdom; cf. l. 390.

And wonder fele þer lay bisides
Riȝt as þai slepe her undertides;
Eche was þus in þis warld ynome,
Wiþ fairi þider ycome.
þer he seiȝe his owhen wiif,
Dame Heurodis, his lef liif,
Slepe under an ympe-tre;
Bi her cloþes he knewe þat it was he.
And when he hadde bihold þis mervails alle
He went in to þe kinges halle;
þan seiȝe he þer a semly siȝt,
A tabernacle blisseful and briȝt,
þerin her maister king sete
And her quen fair and swete;
Her crounes, her cloþes schine so briȝt
þat unneþe bihold he hem miȝt.
When he hadde biholden al þat þing,
He kneled adoun bifor þe king.
'O lord,' he seyd, 'ȝif it þi wille were,
Mi menstraci þou schust yhere.'
þe king answerd: 'What man artow
þat art hider ycomen now?
Ich, no non þat is wiþ me,
No sent never after þe.
Seþþen þat ich here regni gan,
Y no fond never so folehardi man
þat hider to ous durst wende
Bot þat ichim wald ofsende.'
'Lord,' quaþ he, 'trowe ful wel,
Y nam bot a pover menstrel,
And, sir, it is þe maner of ous
To seche mani a lordes hous;
þei we nouȝt welcom no be,
Ȝete we mot proferi forþ our gle.'
 Bifor þe king he sat adoun
And tok his harp so miri of soun,
And tempreþ his harp as he wele can,

402 'Just as they were when they took their daytime sleep.' On the dangers of this, see 65n.
408 **it was he** 'it was she'.
413 **her** 'their' (and in ll. 414–15).
415 **schine** 'shone' (past tense plural).
428 'Unless I had chosen to send for him.'
430 **Y nam bot** 'I am only'.
433 'Even though we may not be welcome.'

And blisseful notes he þer gan,
þat al þat in þe palays were
Com to him for to here,
And liggeþ adoun to his fete,
Hem þenkeþ his melody so swete.
þe king herkneþ and sitt ful stille,
To here his gle he haþ gode wille;
Gode bourde he hadde of his gle,
þe riche quen also hadde he.
When he hadde stint his harping
þan seyd to him þe king:
'Menstrel, me likeþ wele þi gle.
Now aske of me what it be;
Largelich ichil þe pay.
Now speke and tow miȝt asay.'
'Sir,' he seyd, 'ich biseche þe
þatow woldest ȝive me
þat ich levedi briȝt on ble
þat slepeþ under þe ympe-tre.'
'Nay,' quaþ þe king, 'þat nouȝt nere!
A sori couple of ȝou it were,
For þou art lene, rowe and blac,
And sche is lovesum wiþouten lac.
A loþlich þing it were forþi
To sen hir in þi compayni.'
'O sir,' he seyd, 'gentil king,
Ȝete were it a wele fouler þing
To here a lesing of þi mouþe.
So, sir, as ȝe seyd nouþe,
What ich wold aski, have y schold,
And nedes þou most þi word hold.'
þe king seyd, 'Seþþen it is so,
Take hir bi þe hond and go.
Of hir ichil þatow be bliþe.'

446 **he** 'she'.

450 **what it be** 'whatever you want'. The 'rash promise' is a common folk-tale motif. King Mark is similarly obliged to hand over to Sir Bleoberys 'the fayreste lady in your courte that me lyste to chose' (*The Works of Sir Thomas Malory*, ed. E. Vinaver, 2nd edn (Oxford, 1967), p. 396). Compare also Chaucer's Franklin's Tale, *Canterbury Tales* V 988–98, where Dorigen playfully promises Aurelius her love if he will remove the rocks from the coast.

452 **and tow miȝt asay** 'and you can find out'.

457 See 131n.

458 'You would make a sorry couple.'

465 **lesing** 'false word'. Orfeo reminds the king of his promise.

471 'I wish you joy of her!'

He kneled adoun and þonked him swiþe,
His wiif he tok bi þe hond
And dede him swiþe out of þat lond,
And went him out of þat þede;
Ri3t as he come, þe way he 3ede.
So long he haþ þe way ynome,
To Winchester he is ycome,
þat was his owhen cité,
Ac no man knewe þat it was he.
No forþer þan þe tounes ende
For knoweleche no durst he wende,
Bot wiþ a begger ybilt ful narwe,
þer he tok his herbarwe
To him and to his owhen wiif
As a minstrel of pover liif,
And asked tidinges of þat lond
And who þe kingdom held in hond.
þe pover begger in his cote
Told him everich a grot,
Hou her quen was stole owy
Ten 3er gon wiþ fairy,
And hou her king en exile 3ede,
Bot no man nist in wiche þede,
And hou þe steward þe lond gan hold,
And oþer mani þinges him told.
Amorwe o3ain none-tide
He maked his wiif þer abide;
þe beggers cloþes he borwed anon
And heng his harp his rigge opon,
And went him into þat cité
þat men mi3t him bihold and se.
Erls and barouns bold,
Burjays and levedis him gun bihold.
'Lo!' þai seyd, 'swiche a man!
Hou long þe here hongeþ him opan.
Lo, hou his berd hongeþ to his kne!
He is yclongen also a tre.'
And as he 3ede in þe strete,
Wiþ his steward he gan mete

482 **For knoweleche** 'for fear of being recognized'.
483 **ybilt ful narwe** 'housed very meanly'.
485 **To him** 'for himself'.
492 'By the fairies ten years ago.'
507 In l. 266 his beard had reached his waist.
508 'He's as wizened as a tree-trunk.'

And loude he sett on him a crie:
'Sir steward,' he seyd, 'merci!
Ich am an harpour of heþenisse;
Help me now in þis destresse.'
Þe steward seyd, 'Com wiþ me, come!
Of þat ichave þou schalt have some.
Everich gode harpour is welcom me to
For mi lordes love Sir Orfeo.'
In þe castel þe steward sat atte mete,
And mani lording was bi him sete;
Þer were trompours and tabourers,
Harpours fele and crouders;
Miche melody þai maked alle,
And Orfeo sat stille in þe halle
And herkneþ when þai ben al stille.
He toke his harp and tempred schille;
Þe blifulest notes he harped þere
Þat ever ani man yherd wiþ ere;
Ich man liked wele his gle.
Þe steward biheld and gan yse,
And knewe þe harp als blive.
'Menstrel,' he seyd, 'so mot þou þrive,
Where hadestow þis harp and hou?
Y pray þat þou me telle now.'
'Lord,' quaþ he, 'in uncouþe þede
Þurth a wildernes as y ȝede,
Þer y founde in a dale
Wiþ lyouns a man totorn smale,
And wolves him frete wiþ teþ so scharp;
Bi him y fond þis ich harp,
Wele ten ȝere it is ygo.'
'O,' quaþ þe steward, 'now me is wo!
Þat was mi lord Sir Orfeo.
Allas, wreche, what schal y do
Þat have swiche a lord ylore?
A, way, þat ich was ybore!
Þat him was so hard grace yȝarked

512 **merci** 'take pity'.
518 'For my lord Sir Orfeo's love.' See 5.3.2.
522 **crouders** players on the 'crowd', a Celtic stringed instrument.
525 **when** 'for the time when'.
527 **blifulest** 'most delightful' (superlative of *blitheful*).
531 'And recognized the harp at once.'
532 **so mot þou þrive** 'as you may prosper'; i.e. 'on your life, tell me . . .'.
547 'That such a hard fate was ordained for him.'

And so vile deþ ymarked!'
Adoun he fel aswon to grounde;
His barouns him tok up in þat stounde
And telleþ him hou it geþ:
It nis no bot of mannes deþ.
  King Orfeo knewe wele bi þan
His steward was a trewe man
And loved him as he auȝt to do,
And stont up and seyt þus, lo:
'Steward, herkne now þis þing.
Ȝif ich were Orfeo þe king,
And hadde ysuffred ful ȝore
In wildernisse miche sore,
And hadde ywon mi quen owy
Out of þe lond of fairy,
And hadde ybrouȝt þe levedi hende
Riȝt here to þe tounes ende,
And wiþ a begger her in ynome,
And were miself hider ycome
Poverlich to þe þus stille
For to asay þi gode wille,
And ich founde þe þus trewe,
Þou no schust it never rewe.
Sikerlich, for love or ay,
Þou schust be king after mi day.
And ȝif þou of mi deþ hadest ben bliþe,
Þou schust have voided also swiþe.'
  Þo al þo þat þerin sete
Þat it was King Orfeo underȝete,
And þe steward him wele knewe,
Over and over þe bord he þrewe
And fel adoun to his fet,
So dede everich lord þat þer sete,
And al þai seyd at o criing:
'Ȝe beþ our lord, sir, and our king!'

551 **hou it geþ** 'the way things are' (*geþ*, 'goes').
552 'There is no remedy for a man's death'; a proverb (Whiting, D78).
553 **King** Orfeo resumes the title last used in l. 175.
bi þan 'by that'; *þan* is dative of *þat*, as again in l. 597. See 4.3.6.
565 'And had put her up with a beggar.'
568 **asay** The steward is tested as the fairy king was (l. 452).
571 **for love or ay** 'without question' (*ay*, 'fear').
574 'You would have quitted at once.'
575 **þo al þo** 'when all those'.
578 The steward knocks a table over in his eagerness.
581 **at o criing** 'with one cry' – the general recognition of Orfeo as king.

Glad þai were of his live.
To chaumber þai ladde him als bilive,
And baþed him and schaved his berd
And tired him as a king apert,
And seþþen wiþ gret processioun
þai brouȝt þe quen in to þe toun
Wiþ al maner menstraci.
Lord, þer was grete melody!
For joie þai wepe wiþ her eiȝe
þat hem so sounde ycomen seiȝe.
  Now King Orfeo newe coround is,
And his quen Dame Heurodis,
And lived long afterward,
And seþþen was king þe steward.
Harpours in Bretaine after þan
Herd hou þis mervaile bigan
And made herof a lay of gode likeing
And nempned it after þe king;
þat lay 'Orfeo' is yhote;
Gode is þe lay, swete is þe note.
þus com Sir Orfeo out of his care;
God graunt ous alle wele to fare. Amen.

592 'Because they saw them so safely returned.'

601–2 Compare the ending of Marie de France's *Guigemar*: 'From this tale which you have heard was the lai *Guigemar* composed, which is played on harp and rote. The melody is sweet to the ear.'

6

The Cloud of Unknowing

The Cloud of Unknowing is a mystical treatise, probably composed in the later fourteenth century. Its unidentified author also wrote other works of a similar kind, including a translation of the *Mystical Theology* of Pseudo-Dionysius (ed. Hodgson 1955 and 1982). That Greek treatise was composed about AD 500 and later translated into Latin (see text 11, 114n.); it became the chief authority for the so-called *via negativa* or 'way of negation' in mystical contemplation. This way required that the mind should be cleared, as far as possible, of all images and categories derived from human experience. In *The Cloud* the author counsels a beginner (see 104n.) on the difficulties and rewards of following the way. He uses imagery of clouds (21n.) to convey the mental darkness in which the journey must be undertaken. His subject is the most advanced kind of mystical activity, excluding even pious meditations on such matters as the incarnate Christ; yet the author expresses his most taxing thoughts in natural idiomatic English, and shows a sympathetic awareness of the many pitfalls. The whole treatise consists of seventy-four chapters, of which four are edited here.

The Cloud survives in some ten copies from the fifteenth century, and it continued to be copied in Catholic circles until the seventeenth. The present text is based, following Hodgson, on British Library MS Harley 674 (Har^1). The language of this manuscript belongs to the North-East Midlands and is probably close to the author's own. In verbs, the present plural normally ends in *-en* or *-e*; the verb 'to be' has either *ben* or *aren*. Third person plural pronouns are *þei* (always), *þeire* (*here* only once) and *hem* (*þeim* three times).

Editions

Phyllis Hodgson, *The Cloud of Unknowing and The Book of Privy Counselling*, EETS 218 (1944, revised edn 1958)

Phyllis Hodgson, *The Cloud of Unknowing and Related Treatises* (Analecta Cartusiana, Salzburg, 1982)

Phyllis Hodgson, *Deonise Hid Divinite*, EETS 231 (1955, revised edn 1958)

Studies

Phyllis Hodgson, Introductions to her editions

Alastair Minnis, '*The Cloud of Unknowing* and Walter Hilton's *Scale of Perfection*', in A. S. G. Edwards, ed., *Middle English Prose: A Critical Guide to Major Authors and Genres* (New Brunswick, 1984), pp. 61–81 [with bibliography]

Wolfgang Riehle, *The Middle English Mystics* (London, 1981)

Þe þrid chapitre. How þe werk of þis book schal be wrouȝt, and of þe worþines of it bifore alle oþer werkes.

Lift up þin herte unto God wiþ a meek steryng of love, and mene himself and none of his goodes. And þerto loke þee loþe to þenk on ouȝt bot hymself, so þat nouȝt worche in þi witte ne in þi wille bot only himself. And do þat in þee is to forȝete alle þe creatures þat ever God maad and þe werkes of hem, so þat þi þouȝt ne þi desire be not directe ne streche to any of hem, neiþer in general ne in special. Bot lat hem be and take no kepe to hem.

Þis is þe werk of þe soule þat moste plesiþ God. Alle seintes and aungelles han joie of þis werk and hasten hem to helpe it in al here miȝt. Alle feendes ben wood whan þou þus doste, and proven for to felle it in alle þat þei kun. Alle men levyng in erþe ben wonderfuli holpen of þis werk, þou wost not how. Ȝe, þe soules in Purgatori ben esed of þeire peine by vertewe of þis werk. Þiself arte clensid and maad vertewos by no werk so mochel. And ȝit it is þe liȝtest werk of alle when a soule is holpen wiþ grace in sensible liste, and sonnest done. Bot elles it is hard and wonderful to þee for to do.

1–2 The heading for this and succeeding chapters is carried over here from the 'table of þe chapitres', which, in Har[1] and some other manuscripts, follows the Prologue and precedes Chapter 1. At the head of each chapter, Har[1] has only 'Here biginneþ þe þrid chapitre' etc.

4 **loke þee loþe** 'make sure that you find it hateful'. 'That' is omitted after *loke*: *MED loken* v. (2) 9 (b). *Loþe* is an impersonal use of 'loathe' (third person singular present subjunctive), with *þee* as its indirect object: literally, 'it may be hateful to you'.

5 The terms *witte* ('intellect') and *wille* denote two of the three main faculties or *miȝtes* (cf. 45, 62–5 below) which the author distinguishes in angels and human beings (the third is memory). Compare the following distinctions between *þouȝt* and *desire* (7), *reson* and *affeccion* (24–5), *knowyng* and *lovyng* (60–1).

6 **do þat in þee is** 'do whatever in you lies'. 'Facere quod in se est' ('to do whatever in one lies') was a common theologians' phrase expressing the limit of human effort, beyond which only God's grace could help towards salvation. See 129–30 below.

8 **be not directe ne streche** 'may not be turned away nor reach out'. *Directe* is a past participle, *streche* a third person singular present subjunctive.

12–13 **proven for to felle it** 'endeavour to frustrate it'.

17 **sensible liste** 'felt longing'. That pleasurable feeling, when it comes as a special gift of grace, makes the work of the contemplative easy.

Lette not þerfore, bot travayle þerin tyl þou fele lyst. For at þe first tyme when þou dost it, þou fyndest bot a derknes and as it were a cloude of unknowyng, þou wost never what, savyng þat þou felist in þi wille a nakid entent unto God. þis derknes and þis cloude is, howsoever þou dost, bitwix þee and þi God, and letteþ þee þat þou maist neiþer see him cleerly by liȝt of understonding in þi reson ne fele him in swetnes of love in þin affeccion. And þerfore schap þee to bide in þis derknes as longe as þou maist, evermore criing after him þat þou lovest; for ȝif ever schalt þou fele him or see him, as it may be here, it behoveþ alweis be in þis cloude and in þis derknes. And ȝif þou wilte besily travayle as I bid þee, I triste in his mercy þat þou schalt come þerto.

þe feerþe chapitre. Of þe schortnes of þis werk, and how it may not be comen to by þe corioustee of witte ne by ymaginacion.

But forþi þat þou schuldest not erre in þis worching, and wene þat it be oþerwise þen it is, I schal telle þee a lityl more þerof, as me þinkeþ. þis werk askeþ no longe tyme er it be ones treulich done, as sum men wenen, for it is þe schortest werke of alle þat man may ymagyn. It is neiþer lenger ne schorter þen is an athomus; þe whiche athomus, by þe diffinicion of trewe philisophres in þe sciens of astronomye, is þe leest partie of tyme, and it is so litil þat for þe littilnes of it it is undepartable and neiȝhonde incompre- hensible. þis is þat tyme of þe whiche it is wretyn: Alle tyme þat is ȝoven to þee, it schal be askid of þee how þou haste dispendid it.

21 **a cloude of unknowyng** The author imagines two clouds: a cloud of unknowing above the contemplative, in which God is hidden from him, and a cloud of forgetting beneath, which should cut him off from all thoughts of created things (cf. 182–3). Pseudo-Dionysius speaks of a 'caligo ignorantiae' ('darkness of unknowing'); but the image of a cloud derives from Exodus, where Moses (interpreted as a type of the contemplative) communes with God at the top of Mount Sinai in a 'very thick cloud': Exodus 19.16 and 24.15–18.

22 **a nakid entent** 'a pure act of will'. This initial act of will involves no knowledge of God, nor even at this first stage any felt longing for him.

23 **letteþ þee** 'stands in your way'.

27–8 **as it may be here** 'so far as that is possible here (on earth)'.

32 **corioustee of witte** 'speculative mental activity'.

ymaginacion Later, in Chapter 65, the author defines 'imagination' as a mental faculty 'þorow þe whiche we portray alle ymages of absent and present þinges'.

37 **athomus** the smallest measurable unit of time, as the author explains. It is *undepartable* or 'indivisible' (40) – the meaning of the word 'atom' in Greek. Medieval astronomers calculated it at 15/94 of a second: see *OED atom* 7.

41–2 **Alle tyme . . . dispendid it** The author recalls one of the Meditations of St Anselm: 'What reply will you make on that day (of Judgement) when an account is required of you for all the time you have been granted, even to the twinkling of an eye (*usque ad ictum oculi*)? How have you spent it?' (*PL* 158.723). *Ictus oculi*, the time taken to blink, is the Latin equivalent of the Greek *atomos*.

And skilful þing it is þat þou ȝeve acompte of it; for it is neiþer lenger ne schorter bot even acording to one only steryng þat is wiþinne þe principal worching miȝt of þi soule þe whiche is þi wille. For even so many willinges or desiringes, and no mo ne no fewer, may be and aren in one oure in þi wille as aren athomus in one oure. And ȝif þou were reformid bi grace to þe first state of mans soule as it was bifore sinne, þan þou schuldest evermore bi help of þat grace be lorde of þat stering or of þoo sterynges, so þat none ȝede forby, bot alle þei schulde streche into þe soverein desirable and into þe heiȝest wilnable þing, þe whiche is God.

For he is even mete to oure soule by mesuring of his godheed, and oure soule even mete unto him bi worþines of oure creacion to his ymage and to his licnes. And he by him one wiþouten moo, and none bot he, is sufficient at þe fulle and mochel more to fulfille þe wille and þe desire of oure soule; and oure soule bi vertewe of þis reformyng grace is mad sufficient at þe fulle to comprehende al him by love, þe whiche is incomprehensible to alle create knowable miȝt, as is aungel and mans soule – I mene by þeire knowyng and not by þeire lovyng, and þerfore I clepe hem in þis caas 'knowable' miȝtes. Bot siþ alle resonable creatures, aungel and man, haþ in hem, ilchone by hymself, o principal worching miȝt þe whiche is clepid a knowable miȝt and anoþer principal worching miȝt þe whiche is clepid a lovyng miȝt; of þe whiche two miȝtes, to þe first, þe whiche is a knowyng miȝt, God þat is maker of hem is evermore incomprehensible, and to þe secound, þe whiche is þe lovyng myȝt, in ilchone seerly he is al comprehensible at þe fulle – in so mochel þat o lovyng soule only in itself by vertewe of love schuld com-

43 **skilful** 'reasonable'. Since the impulses or 'stirrings' of the will, which are the proper objects of God's judgements, occupy no more than a single 'atom' of time, it is reasonable that we should be held to account for every such moment.

44 **even acording to** 'exactly commensurate with', that is, 'exactly the length of time taken by'.

45 **principal worching miȝt** Chapter 63 explains that the two 'principal active faculties' are reason and the will. Cf. 62–5 below.

51 **none ȝede forby** 'no (impulses) passed by', that is, none undirected towards God.

53 **even mete to** 'exactly commensurate with'. God adapts or 'measures' himself to our limited capacities – perhaps a reference to the Incarnation.

55 **by him one wiþouten moo** 'in himself alone without any other'.

62 **siþ** 'since, because'. The series of subordinate clauses which this conjunction introduces has not given place to a main clause by the time the sentence (as punctuated here) ends, at l. 72. Hodgson (1982) adopts *seþ* from other manuscripts, taking it as the imperative plural of the verb 'see'. This solves the syntactic problem, at the cost of some awkwardness ('Only see [that] all reasonable creatures . . .'); but the same manuscripts have the form *seþ* at l. 102 below, where only the conjunction can be meant.

prehende in it hym þat is sufficient at þe fulle, and mochel more wiþoute comparison, to fille alle þe soules and aungelles þat ever may be. And þis is þe eendles merveilous miracle of love, þe whiche schal never take eende; for ever schal he do it, and never schal he seese for to do it. See who bi grace see may, for þe felyng of þis is eendles blisse and þe contrary is eendles pyne.

And þerfore whoso were refourmyd by grace þus to continow in keping of þe sterynges of hys wille schuld never be in þis liif – as he may not be wiþouten þees sterynges in kynde – wiþouten som taast of þe eendles swetnes, and in þe blisse of heven withouten þe fulle food. And þerfore have no wonder þof I stere þee to þis werk. For þis is þe werk, as þou schalt here after, in þe whiche man schuld have contynowed ȝif he never had synned, and to þe whiche worching man was maad, and alle þing for man to help him and forþer him þerto, and by þe whiche worching a man schal be reparailed aȝein. And for þe defaylyng in þis worching a man falleþ depper and depper in synne, and ferþer and ferþer fro God; and by kepyng and contynowel worching in þis werk only, wiþouten mo, a man evermore riseþ hier and hier fro synne, and nerer and nerer unto God.

And þerfore take good keep into tyme, how þat þou dispendist it; for noþing is more precious þan tyme. In oo litel tyme, as litel as it is, may heven be wonne and lost. A token it is þat time is precious: for God, þat is ȝever of tyme, ȝeveþ never two tymes togeder, bot ich one after oþer; and þis he doþ for he wil not reverse þe ordre or þe ordinel cours in þe cause of his creacion. For tyme is maad for man, and not man for tyme. And þerfore God, þat is þe rewler of kynde, wil not in þe ȝevyng of tyme go before þe steryng of kynde in a mans soule, þe whiche is even acordyng to o tyme only; so þat man schal have none excusacion aȝens God in þe dome and at þe

70–1 **mochel more wiþoute comparison** 'incomparably more over and above that'.

73 **ever schal he do it** God, that is, will always make himself comprehensible by the power of love in men's wills.

74 **See who bi grace see may** 'let him see who has grace to see'.

77 **keping of** 'watching over', 'controlling'.

77–8 **as he may not . . . in kynde** 'seeing that he cannot, in the nature of things, be without such impulses'.

79–80 **fulle food** 'complete satisfaction' – as against 'tastes' on earth.

85 **reparailed** 'restored to his original condition', that is, as created by God before the Fall.

95 **þe cause of his creacion** The prime 'purpose of God's creation' was to create man. So its 'order' requires that all created things, including time, should serve man and not vice versa.

97 **go before þe steryng of kynde** 'outrun (fail to keep pace with) natural impulse'.

ȝevyng of acompte of dispendyng of tyme, seiing: 'þou ȝevest two tymes at ones, and I have bot o steryng at ones.'

Bot sooroufuly þou seist now: 'How schal I do? And siþ þis is soþ þat þou seist, how schal I ȝeve acompte of iche tyme seerly – I þat into þis day, now of foure and twenty ȝere age, never toke hede of tyme? Ȝif I wolde now amende it, þou wost wel, bi verrey reson of þi wordes wretyn before, it may not be after þe cours of kynde ne of comoun grace þat I schuld mowe kepe or elles make aseeþ to any mo tymes þan to þoo þat ben for to come. Ȝe, and moreover wel I wote bi verrey proef þat of þoo þat ben to come I schal on no wise, for habundaunce of freelté and slownes of sperite, mowe kepe one of an hondred; so þat I am verrely conclude in þeese resons. Help me now, for þe love of Ihesu!'

Riȝt wel hast þou seide 'for þe love of Ihesu'; for in þe love of Ihesu þere schal be þin help. Love is soche a miȝt þat it makiþ alle þing comoun: love þerfore Ihesu, and alle þing þat he haþ it is þin. He by his godheed is maker and ȝever of tyme; he bi his manheed is þe verrey keper of tyme; and he bi his godheed and his manheed togeders is þe trewist domesman and þe asker of acompte of dispending of tyme. Knyt þee þerfore bi him by love and by beleve, and þan by vertewe of þat knot þou schalt be comoun parcener wiþ him and wiþ alle þat by love so ben knittyd unto him: þat is to sey, wiþ oure lady Seinte Mary þat ful was of alle grace in kepyng of tyme, wiþ alle þe aungelles of heven þat never may lese tyme, and with alle þe seintes in heven and in erþe þat by þe grace of Ihesu kepen tyme ful justly in vertewe of love. Loo! here liþ counforte; construe þou cleerly and pike þee sum profite. Bot of oo þing I warne þee amonges alle oþer. I cannot see who may trewliche chalenge comunité þus wiþ Ihesu and his just moder, his hiȝe aungelles, and also wiþ his seyntes, bot ȝif it be soche one þat doþ þat in hym is, wiþ helping of grace, in kepyng of tyme; so þat he be

104 **foure and twenty ȝere age** *The Cloud* is addressed in the first place to a single 'spiritual friend in God', who is setting out at the age of twenty-four to live the life of contemplation.

107–8 **þat I schuld . . . mo tymes** 'that I should be able to control or else make amends for any more moments of time'.

109 **verrey proef** 'experience itself', contrasted with *verrey reson* (105). The author's reasoning has proved that, since moments come one after another, the past is irrevocably past; but the disciple's own experience is enough to make him pessimistic about the future.

111 **I am verrely conclude in þeese resons** 'I am utterly confounded by these considerations'.

119 **Knyt þee þerfore bi him** 'so bind yourself to his side'.

128 **chalenge comunité** 'lay claim to common possession'.

129–30 **doþ þat in hym is** See 6n. above.

seen to be a profiter on his partye, so litil as is, unto þe comunité, as ich one of hem doþ on his.

And þerfore take kepe to þis werk and to þe merveylous maner of it wiþinne in þi soule. For ȝif it be trewlich conceyved, it is bot a sodeyn steryng, and as it were unavisid, speedly springing unto God as sparcle fro þe cole. And it is merveylous to noumbre þe sterynges þat may be in one oure wrouȝt in a soule þat is disposid to þis werk; and ȝit in o steryng of alle þeese he may have sodenly and parfitely forȝeten alle create þing. Bot fast after iche steryng, for corupcion of þe flesche, it falleþ doune aȝein to som þouȝt or to some done or undone dede. Bot what þerof? For fast after it riseþ aȝen as sodenly as it did bifore.

And here mowe men schortly conceyve þe maner of þis worching, and cleerly knowe þat it is fer fro any fantasie or any fals ymaginacion or queynte opinion, þe whiche ben brouȝt in, not by soche a devoute and a meek blynde stering of love, bot by a proude, coryous and an ymaginatiif witte. Soche a proude, corious witte behoveþ algates be born doun and stifly troden under fote, ȝif þis werke schal trewly be conceyvid in pureté of spirite. For whoso heriþ þis werke ouþer be red or spoken, and weneþ þat it may or schuld be comen to by travayle in þeire wittes – and þerfore þei sitte and sechin in þeire wittes how þat it may be, and in þis coriousté þei travayle þeire ymaginacion paraventure aȝens cours of kynde, and þei feyne a maner of worching þe whiche is neiþer bodily ne goostly – trewly þis man, whatsoever he be, is perilously disseyvid; in so mochel þat, bot ȝif God of his grete goodnes schewe his mercyful myracle and make hym sone to leve werk and meek hym to counsel of provid worchers, he schal falle ouþer into frenesies or elles into oþer grete mischeves of goostly sinnes and devels disseites, þorow þe whiche he may liȝtly be lorne, boþe liif and soule wiþouten any eende. And þerfore for Goddes love beware in þis werk, and travayle not in þi wittes ne in þin ymaginacion on no wise. For I telle þee trewly, it may not be comen to by travaile in þeim; and þerfore leve þeim and worche not wiþ þeim.

And wene not, for I clepe it a derknes or a cloude, þat it be any

131 **a profiter . . . as is** 'making his own contribution, however little it may be'.

141 **Bot what þerof?** 'but what does that matter?'

146–7 **a proude, coryous and an ymaginatiif witte** 'an arrogant, ingenious and speculative mind'.

149–50 **For whoso . . . spoken** 'for whoever hears readings or conversation concerning this activity'.

154–5 **neiþer bodily ne goostly** The author insists on the distinct integrity of both the spiritual and the physical realms. Laborious speculation may lead into a never-never land of fancy, where the two realms are confused together 'against the natural order of things'.

cloude congelid of þe humours þat fleen in þe ayre, ne ȝit any derknes soche as is in þin house on niȝtes when þi candel is oute. For soche a derknes and soche a cloude maist þou ymagin wiþ coriousté of witte, for to bere before þin iȝen in þe liȝtest day of somer; and also aȝenswarde in þe derkist niȝt of wynter þou mayst ymagin a clere schinyng liȝt. Lat be soche falsheed; I mene not þus. For when I sey derknes, I mene a lackyng of knowyng; as alle þat þing þat þou knowest not or elles þat þou hast forȝetyn, it is derk to þee, for þou seest it not wiþ þi goostly iȝe. And for þis skile it is not clepid a cloude of þe eire, bot a cloude of unknowyng þat is bitwix þee and þi God.

Þe fifþe chapitre. Þat in þe tyme of þis werk alle þe cretures þat ever have ben, ben now, or ever schal be, and alle þe werkes of þoo same creatures, scholen be hid under þe clowde of forȝetyng.

And ȝif ever þou schalt come to þis cloude and wone and worche þerin as I bid þee, þee byhoveþ, as þis cloude of unknowyng is aboven þee bitwix þee and þi God, riȝt so put a cloude of forȝetyng bineþ þee bitwix þee and alle þe cretures þat ever ben maad. Þee þinkeþ paraventure þat þou arte ful fer fro God forþi þat þis cloude of unknowing is bitwix þee and þi God; bot sekirly, and it be wel conseyved, þou arte wel ferþer fro hym when þou hast no cloude of forȝetyng bitwix þee and alle þe creatures þat ever ben maad. As ofte as I sey 'alle þe creatures þat ever ben maad', as ofte I mene not only þe self creatures bot also alle þe werkes and þe condicions of þe same creatures. I outetake not o creature, wheþer þei ben bodily creatures or goostly, ne ȝit any condicion or werk of any creature, wheþer þei be good or ivel; bot schortly to sey, alle schuld be hid under þe cloude of forȝetyng in þis caas.

For þof al it be ful profitable sumtyme to þink of certeyne condicions and dedes of sum certein special creatures, neverþeles ȝit in þis werke it profiteþ lityl or nouȝt. Forwhy mynde or þinkyng of any creature þat ever God maad, or of any of þeire dedes ouþer, it is a maner of goostly liȝt, for þe iȝe of þi soule is openid on it and even ficchid þerapon, as þe iȝe of a schoter is apon þe prik þat he

166 **humours** 'vapours'. In the encyclopaedia of Bartholomaeus Anglicus, clouds are described as being made 'of many vapoures gadred into one body in þe myddel regioun of þe eyr, iþickened togedres by cooldnesse of place' (trans. Trevisa, *Properties*, p. 577, ll. 29–31).

181 **þee byhoveþ** 'it will be necessary for you', governing *put* (182). The present tense form has a future sense: see 5.6.1.

183–4 **þee þinkeþ** 'it will seem to you'.

196 **mynde** 'recollection'.

198 **goostly liȝt** The spiritual 'cloud of forgetting' is threatened by such a 'spiritual light'.

199 **prik** 'bull's eye', the spot at the centre of the target.

schoteþ to. And o þing I telle þee, þat alle þing þat þou þinkest apon it is aboven þee for þe tyme and bitwix þee and þi God; and in so muchel þou arte þe ferþer fro God þat ouȝt is in þi mynde bot only God. Ȝe, and ȝif it be cortesye and semely to sey, in þis werk it profiteþ litil or nouȝt to þink of þe kyndenes or þe worþines of God, ne on oure Lady, ne on þe seintes or aungelles in heven, ne ȝit on þe joies in heven – þat is to say, wiþ a special beholding to hem, as þou woldest bi þat beholding fede and encrees þi purpos. I trowe þat on no wise it schuld be so in þis caas and in þis werk. For þof al it be good to þink apon þe kindenes of God and to love hym and preise him for hem, ȝit it is fer betyr to þink apon þe nakid beyng of him and to love him and preise him for himself.

Þe six chapitre. A schort conceyte of þe werk of þis book, tretid by questyon.

But now þou askest me and seiest: 'How schal I þink on himself, and what is hee?' And to þis I cannot answere þee bot þus: 'I wote never.' For þou hast brouȝt me wiþ þi question into þat same derknes and into þat same cloude of unknowyng þat I wolde þou were in þiself. For of alle oþer creatures and þeire werkes – ȝe, and of þe werkes of God self – may a man þorou grace have fulheed of knowing and wel to kon þinke on hem; bot of God himself can no man þinke. And þerfore I wole leve al þat þing þat I can þink, and chese to my love þat þing þat I cannot þink. Forwhi he may wel be loved, bot not þouȝt. By love may he be getyn and holden, bot bi þouȝt neiþer. And þerfore, þof al it be good sumtyme to þink of þe kyndnes and þe worþines of God in special, and þof al it be a liȝt and a party of contemplacion, neverþeles ȝit in þis werk it schal be casten down and keverid wiþ a cloude of forȝetyng. And þou schalt step aboven it stalworþly bot listely, wiþ a devoute and a plesing stering of love, and fonde for to peerse þat derknes aboven þee, and smyte apon þat þicke cloude of unknowyng wiþ a scharp darte of longing love, and go not þens for þing þat befalleþ.

202 **þat** follows from *in so muchel*: 'just so much . . . to the extent that'.

207 **as** 'as if'. The author does not deny the value of pious meditations on God's goodness, the Virgin, saints etc.; but these can only hinder that higher work of contemplation with which he is here concerned.

219 **wel to kon þinke on hem** 'be able to think clearly about them'.

223 **neiþer** that is, neither be got nor held.

225 **party** 'part'. A later chapter, Chapter 8, assigns such 'goodly goostly meditacions' to the 'lower party of contemplative liif'.

227 **stalworþly bot listely** 'vigorously but also craftily'. *Listely* (*MED listeli* adv.) has its root in OE *list*, 'craft, cunning'. Elsewhere, in Chapters 46 and following, the author recommends a variety of mental tricks and devices that will further the work of contemplation. He cites the ME proverb, 'Better is list than lither (crude) strength': Whiting L381. Cf. 2/172–3.

7

William Langland: *Piers Plowman*

Piers Plowman is the only known writing by William Langland, an elder contemporary (born probably in the 1330s) of Geoffrey Chaucer. It was by far the most widely read of Middle English alliterative poems, to judge by the survival of fifty-two manuscripts. These copies represent the poem in at least three distinct forms: the 'A Text' probably composed about 1370, the 'B Text' at the end of the 1370s, and the 'C Text' by the middle 1380s. Langland evidently worked on the poem, revising and adding to it, over a long period. The A Text is unfinished, breaking off after a Prologue and eleven 'passus' (the sections into which *Piers* is divided). The B Text revises and continues the poem, completing it in a Prologue and twenty passus. The C Text, from which both our extracts come, is a revision of B left uncompleted, probably at the poet's death about 1385.

Like the *Gawain*-poet's *Pearl* and Chaucer's *Parliament of Fowls*, *Piers Plowman* is a dream poem; but unlike them it consists of a series of dreams. These range over many topics, but their chief concerns are, successively: the moral reform of contemporary society (C Passus I–IX); the quest by the dreamer, Long Will, for understanding of 'Do-Well', the good life upon which salvation may depend (C X–XVII); and the history of mankind's salvation, in which the triumph of Christ is followed by the decline of the Church into its present state of weakness (C XVIII–XXII). The first of these phases, from which the following extracts are taken, consists of two dreams: that of Holy Church and her adversary Lady Meed (C I–IV), and that of the Pilgrimage to Truth (C V–IX). The first extract (7a, C V 1–104) is a waking interlude between these dreams. Long Will is questioned by Reason and Conscience about his own way of life: what contribution does he himself make to the life of the Christian community? This episode (which evidently refers to Langland's own circumstances) looks forward to the ensuing dream, from which the second extract (7b, C VIII) comes. Here, the people's pilgrimage to Truth (that is, God) takes the form of work on a half acre of land presided over by Piers the Plowman, the hero after whom Langland named his poem. What Piers demands of the people is what Reason demanded of Will: a contribution to the life of society, as a necessary condition of salvation. In Langland's poem, secular and religious issues are inseparable, because for him Society is, ideally, one and the same as the Church.

Although William Langland lived part of his life in London (see 7a/1–5 here), his origins lay in the West of England. He makes three, otherwise unmotivated, references to the Malvern Hills (C Prologue 6, V 110, IX 297), and he was probably brought up thereabouts, though an early note in one manuscript says that he was the son of an Oxfordshire gentleman, Stacy de Rokayle. He may have received his education as a 'clerk' at the Great Malvern Priory. The language of the particular C manuscript upon which the present texts are based, Huntington Library MS HM 143, has been identified as belonging to the Malvern area, in South-West Worcestershire (Samuels, in Alford's *Companion*). It may therefore be supposed to represent Langland's own English quite closely.

The following linguistic features are especially distinctive: the spelling *oe* for /o:/ and /ɔ:/, as in *boek* (7a/38) and *hoem* (7b/108); the forms *ȝut* for 'yet' (7a/94 etc.) and *ar* for 'ere, before' (7b/94, 108 etc.); and the form *a* for unstressed 'he' (7a/96, 7b/19 etc.). In verbs, the present plural ending varies between *-en* and *-eth* (e.g. 7b/27, 29). The Old English infinitive ending of weak verbs, *-ian*, is represented by *-y*, *-ye*(*n*), or *-ie*(*n*), as in *wedy* (7b/66), *lovye* (7b/218), *gladyen* (7b/126). The present plural of the verb 'to be' takes three forms: *aren* (7b/45), *ben* or *beeþ* (7a/59, 7b/52), and occasionally *is* (7b/87). The forms of the third person plural pronouns are regularly *þey*, *her*(*e*) and *hem* (e.g. 7b/225–6).

Editions

W. W. Skeat, *The Vision of William concerning Piers the Plowman, in Three Parallel Texts*, 2 vols (London, 1886)

George Kane, *Piers Plowman: The A Version* (London, 1960)

George Kane and E. Talbot Donaldson, *Piers Plowman: The B Version* (London, 1975)

J. A. W. Bennett, *Piers Plowman: The Prologue and Passus I—VII of the B Text* (Oxford, 1972)

A. V. C. Schmidt, *The Vision of Piers Plowman: A Critical Edition of the B-Text*, new edn (London, 1995)

Derek Pearsall, *Piers Plowman: An Edition of the C-Text*, new edn (Exeter, 1994)

Studies

John A. Alford, ed., *A Companion to Piers Plowman* (Berkeley, 1988)

John A. Alford and M. Teresa Tavormina, eds, *The Yearbook of Langland Studies*, Vol. 1 (1987) – [continuing]

Robert J. Blanch, ed., *Style and Symbolism in Piers Plowman* (Knoxville, 1969)

J. A. Burrow, *Langland's Fictions* (Oxford, 1993)

E. Talbot Donaldson, *Piers Plowman: The C-Text and its Poet* (New Haven, 1949; rpt. Hamden, 1966)

Robert W. Frank, *Piers Plowman and the Scheme of Salvation* (New Haven, 1957; rpt. Hamden, 1969)

Malcolm Godden, *The Making of Piers Plowman* (London, 1990)

George Kane, *Piers Plowman: The Evidence for Authorship* (London, 1965)

Elizabeth D. Kirk, *The Dream Thought of Piers Plowman* (New Haven, 1972)

Derek Pearsall, *An Annotated Critical Bibliography of Langland* (Ann Arbor, 1990)

James Simpson, *Piers Plowman: An Introduction to the B-Text* (London, 1990)

(*7a*)

Thus y awakede, woet God, whan y wonede in Cornehull,
Kytte and y in a cote, yclothed as a lollare
And lytel ylet by, leveth me for sothe,
Amonges lollares of Londone and lewede ermytes,
For y made of tho men as resoun me tauhte.
For as y cam by Consience with Resoun y mette,
In an hot hervest whenne y hadde myn hele
And lymes to labory with, and lovede wel fare
And no dede to do but to drynke and to slepe.
In hele and in inwitt oen me apposede;
Romynge in remembraunce, thus Resoun me aratede:
'Can thow serven,' he sayde, 'or syngen in a churche,

1 Will, the dreamer, awakes from his first dream to find himself at home in Cornhill, a busy London thoroughfare.

2 **Kytte** Kit (Katherine) is mentioned again as Will's wife at C XX 472.

yclothed as a lollare A *lollare*, understood as 'loller about, idler', is in *Piers* especially one who uses religion as an excuse for not working. He is associated with ignorant hermits (line 4 here) and with begging in churches (ll. 30–2). Compare 7b/74 and 287. The clothes in question here are presumably the 'long clothes' to which Will later refers (l. 41) as evidence that he is exempt from manual labour.

5 **made of** 'composed verses about'. *Piers Plowman* launches several attacks on 'religious' layabouts; but in what follows, its maker questions his own right to do so.

6 Conscience and Reason figured in Will's previous dream, where they prevail over Lady Meed.

10 **In hele and in inwitt** 'sound in body and in mind'.

11 'As I mused on the past, Reason reproached me thus.'

12 **thow** Reason consistently addresses Will with the familiar singular form. Will uses the respectful plural in reply at l. 82.

Or koke for my cokeres or to þe cart piche,
Mowen or mywen or make bond to sheves,
Repe or been a rype-reve and aryse erly,
Or have an horn and be hayward and lygge þeroute nyhtes
And kepe my corn in my croft fro pykares and theves,
Or shap shon or cloth, or shep and kyne kepe,
Heggen or harwen, or swyn or gees dryve,
Or eny other kynes craft þat to þe comune nedeth,
That þou betere therby þat byleve the fynden?'
'Sertes,' y sayde, 'and so me God helpe,
Y am to wayke to worche with sykel or with sythe,
And to long, lef me, lowe to stoupe,
To wurche as a werkeman eny while to duyren.'
'Thenne hastow londes to lyve by,' quod Resoun, 'or lynage rryche
That fynde the thy fode? For an ydel man þow semest,
A spendour þat spene mot or a spille-tyme,
Or beggest thy bylyve aboute at men hacches,
Or faytest uppon Frydayes or feste-dayes in churches,
The whiche is lollarne lyf, þat lytel is preysed
There ryhtfulnesse rewardeth ryht as men deserveth –
Reddet unicuique iuxta opera sua –
Or thow art broke, so may be, in body or in membre
Or ymaymed thorw som myshap, whereby thow myhte be excused?'
'When y ȝong was, many ȝer hennes,
My fader and my frendes foende me to scole,

15–17 Both the reeve and the hayward were officials of the lord of the manor. The *rype-reve* was a foreman with responsibility for work at reaping (*rype*) time. The *hayward* supervised enclosed land, here protecting the crop from thieves and animals.

16 **nyhtes** 'of a night', adverbial genitive. See 5.3.2.

21 'So that you may thereby benefit those who provide you with food.' *Betere* is a verb, *byleve* a noun. *þat* means 'those who': see 5.4.6.

22 **and so me God helpe** 'and as God may help me'.

24 **to long** 'too tall'. The dreamer elsewhere refers to himself as 'Long Will'.

25 **eny while to duyren** 'to last for any length of time'.

28 'A compulsive spender or a time-waster.'

29 **men hacches** 'men's half-doors', here of the kitchen or buttery.

30 **faytest** *Faytours* are those who beg on false pretences, out of idleness not true need. Compare 7b/73, 128, 179.

Frydayes special days in the Church calendar, as weekly commemorations of the Crucifixion.

31 **lollarne** 'of lollers'. Cf. 2n. above. The *-ne* genitive plural ending goes back to OE *-ena* in weak nouns.

32a 'He will render to every man according to his works' (Psalm 61.13 (AV 62.12), adapted).

36 'My father and my relatives provided for my schooling.' Cf. 11/56 and *Canterbury Tales* I 299–302.

Tyl y wyste witterly what holy writ menede
And what is beste for the body, as the boek telleth,
And sykerost for þe soule, by so y wol contenue;
And foend y nere, in fayth, seth my frendes deyede,
Lyf þat me lykede but in this longe clothes.
And yf y be labour sholde lyven and lyflode deserven,
That laboure þat y lerned beste þerwith lyven y sholde:
In eadem vocacione qua vocati estis sitis.
And so y leve in London and opelond bothe;
The lomes þat y labore with and lyflode deserve
Is *pater-noster* and my prymer, *placebo* and *dirige*,
And my sauter som tyme, and my sevene phalmes.
This y segge for here soules of suche as me helpeth,
And tho þat fynden me my fode fouchen saf, y trowe,
To be welcome when y come, oþerwhile in a monthe;
Now with hym, now with here, on this wyse y begge
Withoute bagge or botel but my wombe one.
And also moreover me thynketh, syre Resoun,
Me sholde constrayne no clerc to no knaves werkes;
For by þe lawe of *Levytici* þat oure lord ordeynede
Clerkes ycrouned, of kynde understondynge,
Sholde nother swynke ne swete ne swerien at enquestes
Ne fyhte in no faumewarde ne his foe greve:
Non reddas malum pro malo.

39 **by so y wol contenue** 'provided that I am willing to persevere'. Cf. l. 104.

41 **longe clothes** as worn by clerics, in this case a cleric in minor orders.

43 **þerwith** referring back to *laboure*.

43a 'Be in the same calling to which you are called' (I Corinthians 7.20, adapted).

45–7 The 'tools' (*lomes*) with which Will earns his living are the Lord's Prayer, his Primer or book of devotions, the Office for the Dead, the Psalter, and the Seven Penitential Psalms. *Placebo* and *dirige* are the opening words of two services for the dead, Vespers and Matins respectively.

48 **This** 'these' (as at l. 41). Will recites prayers, psalms and offices for his benefactors, living and dead. See Donaldson, *C-Text*, Ch. VII.

50 **To be welcome** 'that I will be welcome'.

52 Langland elsewhere argues that a beggar should be content with what he can eat and drink to satisfy his immediate needs.

53–81 Will's tirade on the privileges of clerics, the deplorable elevation of churls and illegitimates to clerical office, and the general breakdown of social distinctions expresses legitimate complaints, but in a blustering tone that casts doubt on the purity of his motives.

54 **Me** 'one', indefinite pronoun. See 5.4.3.

55 God tells Aaron that priests of the tribe of Levi ('*Levytici*') are to possess nothing and live off tithes: Numbers 18.20–4. Psalm 15, quoted below at 60a, echoes Numbers 18.20.

56 **of kynde understondynge** 'by common understanding'.

57 **swerien at enquestes** 'testify on oath in lay courts of law'. Clerics had their own ecclesiastical courts.

58a 'Do not repay evil with evil' (I Pet 3.9).

For hit ben eyres of hevene, alle þat ben ycrouned,
And in quoer and in kyrkes Cristes mynistres:
Dominus pars hereditatis mee, etc. Et alibi: Clemencia non constringit.
Hit bycometh for clerkes Crist for to serve,
And knaves uncrounede to carte and to worche.
For sholde no clerke be crouned but yf he come were
Of frankeleynes and fre men and of folke ywedded.
Bondemen and bastardus and beggares children,
Thyse bylongeth to labory, and lordes kyn to serve
God and good men, as here degré asketh,
Somme to synge masses, or sitten and wryten,
Redon and resceyven þat resoun ouhte to spene.
Ac sythe bondemen barnes haen be mad bisshopes,
And barnes bastardus haen be erchedekenes,
And soutares and here sones for sulver han be knyhtes,
And lordes sones here laboreres and leyde here rentes to wedde,
For the ryhte of this reume ryden aȝeyn oure enemyes
In confort of the comune and the kynges worschipe,
And monkes and moniales, þat mendenantes sholde fynde,
Imade here kyn knyhtes and knyhtes fees ypurchased,
Popes and patrones pore gentel blood refused
And taken Symondes sones seyntwarie to kepe,
Lyf-holynesse and love hath be longe hennes,

59 **hit ben** 'they are'. See 5.2.

60a 'The Lord is the portion of my inheritance, etc. And elsewhere: Mercy does not constrain.' The first quotation, Psalm 15.5 (AV 16.5), continues: '. . . and of my cup: it is thou that wilt restore my inheritance to me'. Quoted at the ceremony of tonsuring clerics, it was taken to support their right not to 'swink or sweat' for their livelihood. The second quotation (source unknown) is perhaps intended to justify their exemption from imposing legal or military sanctions on others.

64 **frankeleynes** gentlemen holding freehold lands. Cf. Chaucer's Franklin in the *Canterbury Tales.*

65 **Bondemen** 'villeins'. These were unfree tenants, subject, unlike free men, to the will of the lord of their manor in such matters as the services they owed him for the use of his land.

66 'It is for these to labour, and for the nobly born to serve.'

69 **resceyven** This perhaps refers to the duties of clerks in the secular world, serving 'good men' by keeping account of their receipts and expenses. On *þat* = 'that which', see 5.4.6.

70–81 This sentence reaches its main clause only at l. 80, after a long series of 'since . . .' clauses.

73–5 Lords' sons, in order to fulfil their military obligations, have been forced to raise money by pledging their landed incomes (*rentes*) to rich upstarts such as knighted shoemakers, whose 'labourers' they therefore become.

76 **þat mendenantes sholde fynde** 'who should be providing for beggars'.

77 **Imade** 'have made'. *Have* is to be understood from ll. 70–2, as with the ensuing past participles, *ypurchased*, *refused* and *taken.*

79 **Symondes sones** Simon Magus (Acts 8) offered money in an attempt to buy the apostles' gift of the laying on of hands. Hence those who buy clerical office are 'Simon's sons', or simoniacs.

And wol, til hit be wered out or oþerwyse ychaunged.
Forthy rebuke me ryhte nauhte, Resoun, y yow praye,
For in my consience y knowe what Crist wolde y wrouhte:
Preyeres of a parfit man and penaunce discret
Is the levest labour þat oure lord pleseth.
Non de solo', y sayde, 'for sothe *vivit homo*,
Nec in pane et in pabulo; the *pater-noster* wittenesseth,
Fiat voluntas dei þat fynt us alle thynges.'
  Quod Consience, 'By Crist, y can nat se this lyeth;
Ac it semeth no sad parfitnesse in citees to bygge,
But he be obediencer to prior or to mynistre.'
  'That is soth,' y saide, 'and so y beknowe
That y have ytynt tyme and tyme myspened;
Ac ȝut I hope, as he þat ofte hath ychaffared
And ay loste an loste, and at þe laste hym happed
A boute suche a bargayn he was þe bet evere
And sette al his los at a leef at the laste ende,
Suche a wynnyng hym warth thorw wordes of grace –
  Simile est regnum celorum thesauro abscondito in agro;
    Mulier que invenit dragmam –
So hope y to have of hym þat is almyghty
A gobet of his grace, and bigynne a tyme
That alle tymes of my tyme to profit shal turne.'

81 **hit** that is, the present state of affairs, which will either pass away in the nature of things or else be changed by some positive action.

83 **what Crist wolde y wrouhte** 'what kind of work Christ would wish me to do'.

86–8 Two sayings support the claim that God will provide. The first (Matthew 4.4) reads in the Latin of the Vulgate Bible: 'Non in solo pane vivit homo', that is, 'Not in bread alone (*solo*) doth man live (but in every word that proceedeth from the mouth of God)'. Langland quotes the words correctly in a similar context at C XV 245a; but in the version here Will adds *in pabulo* and punningly takes *solo* as a noun, ablative of Latin *solum*, 'soil': 'Not from the soil doth man live, nor in bread and in food'. Cf. 7b/17. The second saying is adapted from the Lord's Prayer (Matthew 6.10): 'Let the will of God, who provides us with everything, be done'.

90 'But it seems no kind of regular perfection to beg in cities.' Conscience cannot see that Will's claim to perfection (l. 84) applies to his particular way of life.

91 **obediencer** an officer under obedience to a prior or superior of a religious order (*mynistre*) – in this case, charged with collecting money on their behalf.

95 **an** unstressed form of *and.*

96 **A boute** 'he bought'. *A* is an unstressed form of *he.*

97 **leef** a thing of no value, like the pea of 7b/166.

98 **wordes of grace** 'fortunate chances'. *Word* is the OE *wyrd*, 'fate'.

98a 'The kingdom of heaven is like unto a treasure hidden in a field (Matthew 13.44); The woman who found the groat (referring to Luke 15.8–9)'. The two parables concern, first, a man's joy at winning heaven and, second, joy in heaven over a sinner's repentance.

99 **So hope y** resuming the sentence begun at l. 94 with *Ac ȝut I hope.*

'Y rede the,' quod Resoun tho, 'rape the to bigynne
The lyif þat is louable and leele to thy soule.'
'Ye, and contynue,' quod Consience; and to þe kyrke y wente.

(*7b*)

Quod Perkyn þe plouhman, 'Be seynt Petur of Rome,
Ich have an half aker to erye by þe heye waye.
Haved ich y-ered þis half aker and ysowed hit aftur,
Y wolde wende with ȝow and þe way teche.'
'That were a long lettyng,' quod a lady in a slayre;
'What sholde we wommen worche þe whiles?'
'Y preye ȝow, for ȝoure profit,' quod Peres to þe ladyes,
'That somme sowe þe sak for shedynge of the whete;
And ȝe worthily wymmen with ȝoure longe fyngres,
That ȝe on selk and on sendel to sowe whan tyme is
Chesibles for chapeleynes churches to honoure.
Wyves and wyddewes, wolle an flex spynneth.
Consience conseyleth ȝow cloth for to make
For profit of the pore and plesaunce of ȝowsulven;
For y shal lene hem lyflode, but þe lond faylle,
As longe as y leve, for the Lordes love of hevene;
And alle manere men þat by þe molde is susteyned
Helpeth hym worche wyȝtly þat wynneth ȝoure fode.'
'By Crist,' quod a knyhte tho, 'a kenneth us þe beste,
Ac on þe teme treuely ytauhte was y nevere.
Y wolde y couthe,' quod the knyhte, 'by Crist and his moder;
Y wolde assaie som tyme, for solace as hit were.'
'Sikerliche, sire knyhte,' sayde Peris thenne,
'Y shal swynke and swete and sowe for us bothe
And labory for tho thow lovest al my lyf-tyme,
In covenant þat thow kepe holy kerke and mysulve
Fro wastores and fro wikked men þat þis world struyen,
And go hunte hardelyche to hares and to foxes,

1 **Perkyn** 'Peterkin', a familiar form of 'Peter', like 'Piers'. Piers Plowman has just described the road that the people have to follow on their pilgrimage to Truth, and here offers himself as their guide.

8 **for** 'to prevent'.

10 The line combines two constructions: 'I pray you that you sew . . .' and 'I pray you to sew . . .'.

16 **Lordes love of hevene** On the word-order, see 5.3.2.

19 **a kenneth** 'he teaches'.

25 **thow lovest** Piers uses the comradely singular *thou* to the knight, but not consistently (cf. 35ff.).

28–31 Hunting and hawking had practical functions in the Middle Ages, when men were on the defensive against wild nature (the reverse of the present situation).

To bores and to bokkes þat breketh adoun myn hegges,
And afayte thy faucones to culle þe wylde foules,
For þey cometh to my croft my corn to diffoule.'
Courteisliche the knyhte thenne comesed thise wordes:
'By my power, Peres, y plyhte the my treuthe
To defende þe in fayth, fyhte thow y sholde.'
'And ȝut a poynt,' quod Peres, 'y preye ȝow of more.
Loke ȝe tene no tenaunt but treuthe wol assente,
And when ȝe mersyen eny man late Mercy be taxour
And Mekenesse thy mayster, maugré Mede chekes.
And thogh pore men profre ȝow presentes and ȝyftes,
Nym hit nat an auntur thow mowe hit nauht deserve,
For thow shalt ȝelden hit, so may be, or sumdel abuggen hit.
Misbede nat thy bondeman, the bette may the spede;
Thogh he be here thyn underlynge, in hevene paraunter
He worth rather reseyved and reverentloker sitte:
Amice, ascende superius.
At churche in the charnel cherles aren evele to knowe,
Or a knyhte or a knave, or a quene fram a queene.
Hit bicometh to the, knyhte, to be corteys and hende,
Treuwe of thy tonge, and tales loth to here
Bute they be of bounté, of batayles or of treuthe.
Hoold nat with non harlotes ne here nat here tales,
Ac nameliche at þe mete suche men eschewe,
For hit beeþ þe develes dysors to drawe men to synne;
Ne countreplede nat Consience ne holy kyrke ryhtes.'
'Y assente, by seynt Gyle,' sayde the knyht thenne,
'For to worche by thy wit, and my wyf bothe.'
'And y shal parayle me,' quod Perkyn, 'in pilgrimes wyse
And wende with alle tho þat wolden lyve in treuthe.'

34 **thow** 'though'.

38 **maugré Mede chekes** 'in spite of all Meed can do'. Idiomatic, like Chaucer's 'maugree his heed' (*Canterbury Tales* I 1169). Lady Meed, the villainess of the previous dream, represents the corrupt principle of bribery and other undeserved payment (cf. l. 40 here).

41 Any excess beyond what has been duly earned must be paid back or otherwise compensated for.

44–44a 'He shall be sooner received and more honourably seated: "Friend, go up higher"' (Luke 14.10, from the Parable of the Marriage Feast).

45 **charnel** The charnel-house was a vault where bones of those dug up to make room for new graves were dumped.

evele to knowe 'hard to tell apart'.

46 **quene** 'common woman'. The word's similarity to the distinct but related *queene* supports the argument here.

52 **hit beeþ** 'these are'.

54 **seynt Gyle** St Giles, patron saint of beggars.

55 'To act as you think right, and my wife will too.'

And caste on hym his clothes of alle kyn craftes,
His cokeres and his coffes, as Kynde Wit hym tauhte,
And heng his hopur on his hales in stede of a scryppe.
A buschel of breedcorn brouht was þerynne,
'For y wol sowen hit mysulf, and sethe wol y wende
To pilgrimages, as palmeres doen, pardon to wynne.
My plouh-pote shal be my pykstaff and pyche ato þe rotes
And helpe my coltur to kerve and clanse þe forwes.
And alle þat helpen me erye or elles to wedy
Shal have leve by oure Lord to go and glene aftur me
And maken hym merye þermyde, maugrey ho bigruchen hit.
And alle kyne crafty men þat conne lyve in treuthe
Y shal fynde hem fode þat fayfulleche libbeth,
Save Jacke þe jogelour and Jonet of þe stuyves
And Danyel þe dees-playere and Denote þe baude
And Frere Faytour and folk of þat ordre,
That lollares and loseles lele men holdeth,
And Robyn þe rybauder for his rousty wordes.
Treuthe telde me ones, and bad me telle hit forthere:
Deleantur de libro vivencium, y sholde nat dele with hem,
For holy chirche is hote of hem no tythe to aske,
  Quia cum justis non scribantur.
They ben ascaped good auntur; now God hem amende.'
  Dame 'Worch when tyme is' Peres wyf hehte;
His douhter hihte 'Do rihte so or thy dame shal þe bete';
His sone hihte 'Soffre thy sovereynes have her wille;

60 Piers takes a sower's seed-basket (*hopur*) in place of a pilgrim's bag (*scryppe*): cf. the similar substitution in l. 64. In the event, work on the half acre turns out to *be* the 'pilgrimage' to Truth (despite ll. 62–3 here). Piers is Truth's 'pilgrim at the plough' (l. 111).

63 **pardon to wynne** So in the next passus the 'pilgrimage' to Truth on the half acre wins Truth's 'pardon'.

64 **plouh-pote** a long spade for clearing earth and weeds from the blade of the plough.

67–8 Piers anticipates the harvest. The right to glean was controlled by manorial customs.

68 **maugrey ho bigruchen hit** 'in spite of whoever may begrudge it'.

72 **Denote** a pet form of 'Denise'.

74 'Whom honest men consider idlers and wastrels.'

77, 78a 'Let them be blotted out of the book of the living . . . for with the just let them not be written': Psalm 68.29 (AV 69.28), adapted.

78 Since the Church does not accept tithes from the ill-gotten gains of Jack and the rest, they have no right to share in the food Piers provides.

79 'They have been lucky to escape', i.e. to have been spared God's judgement so long.

81 **thy dame** 'your mother'. The names take the form of exhortations addressed by Piers to his wife, daughter and son. Hence the son's name can shade off into a speech of fatherly advice: ll. 82–91.

Deme hem nat, yf thow doest thow shalt hit dere abygge.
Consayle nat so þe comune þe kyng to desplese,
Ne hem þat han lawes to loke lacke hem nat, y hote þe.
Lat God yworthe with al, as holy writ techeth.
Super cathedram Moysi sedent, etc. . . .
Maystres as þe mayres is, and grete menne, senatours,
What þei comaunde as by þe kyng countreplede hit nevere;
Al þat they hoten, y hote, heiliche thow soffre hem,
And aftur here warnynge and wordynge worche þou þeraftur:
. . . Omnia que dicunt facite et servate.
Ac aftur here doynge ne do thow nat, my dere sone,' quod Peres.
'For now y am olde and hoer and have of myn owene,
To penaunces and pilgrimages y wol passe with this oþere.
Forthy y wol, ar y wende, do wryte my biqueste.
In Dei nomine, amen. Y make hit mysulve.
He shal have my soule þat alle soules made,
And defenden hit as fro þe fende, and so is my beleve,
Til y come til his acountes as my crede telleth;
To have a remissioun and a relees on þat rental y leve.
The kyrke shal have my caroyne and kepe my bones,
For of my corn and my catel he craved my tythe.
Y payede hit prestly for perel of my soule;
He is holdyng, y hope, to have me on his masse
And menege me in his memorie amonges alle cristene.
My wyf shal have of þat y wan with treuthe and no more

86 **Lat God yworthe with al** 'let God do his will in all things'.

86a '(The scribes and the Pharisees) sit on the chair of Moses . . .' (Matthew 23.2). The quotation, continued at l. 90a, concerns the proper attitude to authority: even evil-living authorities are to be obeyed.

88 **as by þe kyng** 'since it is by the king's authority'.

90a '. . . All things they say unto you, do and observe (but according to their works do ye not. For they say, and do not)' (Matthew 23.3, adapted).

92 **have of myn owene** 'have possessions of my own', referring either to the expenses of the proposed pilgrimage or (more likely) to his need to make a will.

93 **this oþere** 'these other people'.

94 **do wryte my biqueste** 'have my will written'. It was customary to make one's Last Will and Testament before setting out on what might be a dangerous pilgrimage. Piers's will follows common form, bequeathing first soul, then body, then possessions.

95 'In the name of God, amen': the customary opening formula.

99 **a remissioun and a relees** a legal phrase, used when some obligation was remitted or set aside. Piers trusts that, at the Day of Judgement, his unexpiated sins will be forgiven, just as unpaid rent may be remitted.

103–4 Piers's parish priest is to remember him at Mass in the Commemoration for the Dead, since he has paid his tithes promptly.

105–8 Piers claims that all his possessions were come by honestly (*with treuthe*) and that no debts remain outstanding; so there is no need to make restitution, as testators often did in wills, for unpaid debts or ill-gotten gains.

And delen hit amonges my douhteres and my dere childres;
For thouh y dey today my dette is yquited –
I bar hoem þat y borwed ar y to bedde ȝede.
And with þe resudue and þe remenant, by the rode of Lukes,
Y wol worschipe þerwith Treuthe al my lyve,
And ben a pilgrym at þe plouh for profit to pore and ryche.'
  Now is Perkyn and þis pilgrimes to þe plouh faren.
To erien this half aker holpen hym monye,
Dikares and delvares digged up þe balkes.
Therwith was Perkyn apayed, and payede wel hem here huyre.
Oþer werkemen þer were þat wrouhten fol ȝerne,
Uch man in his manere made hymsulve to done,
And somme to plese Perkyn afeelde pykede wedes.
At hey prime Peres leet þe plouh stande
And oversey hem hymsulve; ho-so beste wrouhte
He sholde be huyred þeraftur when hervost tyme come.
  And thenne seet somme and songen at the ale
And holpe erye this half aker with 'hey trollilolly!'
Quod Peres þe plouhman, al in puyre tene:
'But ȝe aryse þe rather and rape ȝow to worche
Shal no grayn þat here groweth gladyen ȝow at nede,
And thow ȝe deye for deul, þe devel have þat reche!'
Tho were faytours aferd and fayned hem blynde
And leyde here legges alery, as suche lorelles conneth,
And maden here mone to Peres how þei may nat worche:
'And we praye for ȝow, Peres, and for ȝoure plouh bothe,
That God for his grace ȝoure grayn multiplye
And ȝelde ȝow of ȝoure almesse þat ȝe ȝeven us here.
We may nother swynke ne swete, suche sekenes us ayleth,
Ne have none lymes to labory with, lord God we thonketh.'
  'Ȝoure preyeres,' quod Peres, 'and ȝe parfyt weren,
Myhte helpe, as y hope; ac hey Treuthe wolde

108 **bar hoem** 'returned'. Cf. Deuteronomy 24.10–15 on the prompt payment of debts.

109 Customarily a testator left two-thirds of his goods to be divided between his wife and children, reserving a third (the *resudue* and *remenant* here) to be bequeathed for any purpose – a peculiar purpose in this case, since Piers does not expect to die on his 'pilgrimage'.

Lukes Lucca, Italy, where there is an image of the crucified Christ.

110 **Treuthe** God, the personification of justice and fidelity.

117 **made hymsulve to done** 'put himself to work'.

127 'And the devil take anyone who bothers with you, even though you die in misery.'

129 **alery** 'awry', perhaps with the leg strapped back on itself to simulate amputation.

135 Cf. 7a/8 above.

That no faytrye were founde in folk þat goth a-beggeth.
Ʒe been wastours, y woet wel, and waste and devouren
That lele land-tilynge men leely byswynken.
Ac Treuthe shal teche ȝow his teme to dryve
Or ȝe shal ete barly breed and of þe broke drynke,
But yf he be blynde or broke-legged or bolted with yren –
Suche poore,' quod Peres, 'shal parte with my godes,
Bothe of my corn and of my cloth to kepe hem fram defaute.
And ankerus and eremytes þat eten but at nones
And freres þat flateren nat and pore folke syke,
What! y and myn wolle fynde hem what hem nedeth.'
  Thenne gan Wastor to wrath hym and wolde have yfouhte,
And to Peres þe plouhman profrede to fyhte
And bad hym go pisse with his plogh, pyvische shrewe!
A Bretener cam braggyng, a bostede Peres also:
'Wolle thow, nulle thow,' quod he, 'we wol have oure wille,
And thy flour and thy flesch feche whenne us liketh,
And maken us murye þermyde, maugreye ho begrucheth.'
Peres the plouhman tho pleynede hym to þe knyhte
To kepe hym and his catel as covenant was bitwene hem:
'Awreke me of this wastors þat maketh this world dere;
They acounteth nat of corsynges, ne holy kyrke nat dredeth.
For ther worth no plenté,' quod Perus, 'and þe plouh lygge.'
Courteisliche the knyhte thenne, as his kynde wolde,
Warnede Wastour and wissede hym betere,
'Or y shal bete the by the lawe and brynge þe in stokkes.'
'I was nat woned to worche,' quod Wastour, 'and now wol y nat bygynne.'
And leet lyhte of þe lawe and lasse of the knyhte,
And sette Peres at a pes, to playne hym whare he wolde.
  'Now by Crist,' quod Peres the plouhman, 'y shal apayre ȝow alle,'
And houped aftur Hunger, þat herde hym at the furste.

142 **barly breed** inferior to wheat bread.

143 **bolted with yren** probably referring to leg-braces, rather than to prison fetters.

151 **pyvische** a general term of abuse in colloquial ME (Modern 'peevish').

152 **Bretener** Bretons were notorious boasters.

153 **Wolle thow, nulle thow** 'whether you wish it or not' (*nulle* represents *ne wulle*).

155 **maugreye ho begrucheth** see 68n. here.

158 **maketh this world dere** 'cause high prices', by consuming where they do not produce.

161 **as his kynde wolde** 'as his nature was'. Courtesy is natural in knights. Cf. l. 47.

165 **leet lyhte of** 'set little store by'.

'Y preye the,' quod Perus tho, 'pur charité, sire Hunger,
Awreke me of this wastors, for þe knyhte wil nat.'
Hunger in haste tho hente Wastour by þe mawe
And wronge hym so by þe wombe þat al watrede his yes;
A boffatede þe Bretoner aboute the chekes
þat a lokede lyke a lenterne al his lyf aftur;
And beet hem so bothe he barste ner her gottes
Ne hadde Peres with a pese-loof preyede hym byleve.
'Have mercy on hem, Hunger,' quod Peres, 'and lat me ȝeve hem benes,
And þat was bake for Bayard hit may be here bote.'
Tho were faytours afered and flowen into Peres bernes
And flapton on with flales fro morwen til even,
That Hunger was nat hardy on hem for to loke.
For a potte ful of potage þat Peres wyf made
An heep of eremytes henten hem spades,
Sputeden and spradden donge in dispit of Hunger.
They corven here copes and courtepies hem made
And wenten as werkemen to wedynge and to mowynge
Al for drede of here deth, such duntes ȝaf Hunger.
Blynde and broke-legged he botened a thousend
And lame men he lechede with longes of bestes.
Prestes and oþer peple towarde Peres they drowe
And freres of alle þe fyve ordres, alle for fere of Hunger;
For þat was bake for Bayard was bote for many hungry,
Drosenes and dregges drynke for many beggares.
There was no ladde þat lyvede þat ne lowede hym to Peres
To be his holde hewe, thow he hadde no more
But lyflode for his labour and his love at nones.
Tho was Peres proude and potte hem alle a-werke
In daubynge and in delvynge, in donge afeld berynge,
In threschynge, in thekynge, in thwytinge of pynnes,
In alle kyne trewe craft þat man couthe devyse.
Was no beggare so bold, but yf a blynd were,
þat durste withsitte þat Peres sayde for fere of syre Hunger;

174 Sunken and translucent cheeks are compared to the sides of a horn lantern.

176 **Ne hadde** 'had not', following on from *barste* (175), 'would have burst'. **pese-loof** a loaf made of peas, eaten by the poor.

178 **Bayard** a horse name. Horses were fed a 'bread' made of beans. So: 'And what was baked for horses may save their lives'.

185 The 'long clothes' of clerics (cf. 7a/41) hampered physical work.

191 **fyve ordres** the four main orders, Dominicans, Franciscans, Augustinians and Carmelites, together with the Crutched Friars.

192 Cf. l. 178 and n.

196 **love** 'loaf', provided, with cheese etc., for a fieldworker's lunch.

201 **a** the unstressed form of *he*: 'unless he were blind'.

And Peres was proud þerof and potte hem alle to swynke
And ȝaf hem mete and money as þei myhte deserve.
  Tho hadde Peres pitee uppon alle pore peple
And bade Hunger in haste hye hym out of contraye
Hoem to his owene ȝerd and halde hym þere evere.
'Y am wel awroke of wastours thorw thy myhte.
Ac y preye the,' quod Peres, 'Hunger, ar thow wende,
Of beggares and biddares what beste be to done?
For y woet wel, be Hunger went, worche þei wol ful ille.
Meschef hit maketh they ben so meke nouthe,
And for defaute this folk folweth myn hestes;
Hit is nat for love, leve hit, thei labore thus faste
But for fere of famyen, in fayth,' sayde Peres.
'Ther is no filial love with this folk, for al here fayre speche;
And hit are my blody bretherne, for God bouhte us alle.
Treuthe tauhte me ones to lovye hem uchone
And to helpe hem of alle thynges ay as hem nedeth.
Now wolde y wyte ar thow wendest what were þe beste,
How y myhte amayster hem to lovye and to labory
For here lyflode; lere me now, sire Hunger.'
  'Now herkene,' quod Hunger, 'and holde hit for a wysdom.
Bolde beggares and bygge þat mowe here breed byswynke,
With houndes bred and hors breed hele hem when þei hun-
    gren,
And abave hem with benes for bollyng of here wombe;
And yf þe gromes gruche, bide hem go and swynke,
And he shal soupe swettere when he hit hath deserved.
Ac yf thow fynde eny folke þat fals men han apayred,
Conforte hem with thy catel, for so comaundeth Treuthe,
Love hem and lene hem, and so lawe of kynde wolde:
  Alter alterius onera portate.

211 **be Hunger went** 'once Hunger has gone'.

212 'It is hardship that makes them be so submissive at present.'

216 **filial love** i.e. love such as should exist between sons? Cf. l. 217. But the word is not otherwise recorded in English until the sixteenth century; and other manuscripts read *final*, 'thoroughgoing'.

217 **blody bretherne** 'blood-brothers', referring to the blood with which God 'bought' or redeemed us all.

226 'And give them an unpleasant diet of beans, for fear of their bellies swelling.' The identity and meaning of the verb is uncertain: we adopt *abave*, 'dismay, confound'. All B-Text manuscripts read *abate*, 'appease'. The second half-line is probably ironical (no fear of *them* getting fat), but may refer to the swollen bellies of famine victims.

231a 'Bear ye one another's burdens (and so you shall fulfil the law of Christ)' (Galatians 6.2). Christ's law coincides with the promptings of nature itself – the *lawe of kynde* (231).

And alle manere men þat thow myhte aspye
In meschief or in malese, and thow mowe hem helpe,
Loke by thy lyve lat hem nat forfare.
Yf thow hast wonne auht wikkedliche, wiseliche despene hit:
Facite vobis amicos de mammona iniquitatis.'
'Y wolde nat greve God,' quod Peres, 'for al þe good on erthe.
Myhte y synneles do as thow sayst?' sayde Peres þe plouhman.
'Ȝe, y bihote the,' quod Hunger, 'or elles þe Bible lyeth.
Go to oure bygynnynge tho God the world made,
As wyse men haen wryten and as witnesseth Genesis,
þat sayth with swynke and with swoet and swetynge face
Bytulie and bytravayle trewely oure lyflode:
In sudore and *labore vultus tui vesceris pane tuo.*
And Salomon þe sage with þe same acordeth:
The slowe caytif for colde a wolde no corn tylye;
In somer for his sleuthe he shal have defaute
And go a-bribeth and a-beggeth and no man beten his hunger:
Piger propter frigus noluit arare; mendicabitur in yeme et non dabitur ei.
Mathew maketh mencioun of a man þat lente
His sulver to thre maner men and menyng they sholden
Chaffare and cheve þerwith in chele and in hete,
And þat best labored best was alloued
And ledares for here laboryng over al þe lordes godes.
Ac he þat was a wreche and wolde nat travaile
The lord for his lachesse and his luther sleuthe
Bynom hym al þat he hadde and ȝaf hit to his felawe
þat leely hadde ylabored; and thenne the lord sayde:
"He þat hath shal have and helpe þer hym liketh,

233 **and** 'if'.

234 'Take care, upon your life, that you do not let them die.'

235a 'Make unto you friends of the mammon of iniquity' (Luke 16.9), i.e. use even wicked winnings (235) for good ends.

236–7 Piers is worried by the first, harsher, part of Hunger's advice (ll. 224–8).

242–242a 'We should till and labour faithfully for our livelihood: "In sweat and labour of thy face shalt thou eat thy bread"' (adapted from Genesis 3.19 and 3.17).

243 **Salomon** King Solomon, the traditional author of the Book of Proverbs.

246a 'Because of the cold, the sluggard would not plough; there will be begging in the winter, and it shall not be given him.' The text, Proverbs 20.4, is adapted to English conditions by substituting *yeme*, 'winter', for the Vulgate's *aestate*, 'summer'. The original reading has been represented, however, in Hunger's own version, l. 245.

247–58 The Parable of the Talents, Matthew 25.14–30.

248 **thre maner men** i.e. three men of different dispositions.

and menyng 'intending that'.

251 'And were given responsibility, because of their good work, for all the lord's possessions.'

256 **helpe þer hym liketh** 'give help where he pleases'. Cf. Matthew 25.29: 'For to every one that hath shall be given, and he shall abound'.

And he þat nauht hath shal nauht have and no man ȝut helpen hym,
And þat he weneth wel to have y wol hit hym bireve."
And lo what þe sauter sayth to swynkares with handes:
"Yblessed be al tho that here bylyve biswynketh
Thorw eny lele labour as thorw lymes and handes":
Labores manuum tuarum quia manducabis, etc.
This aren evidences,' quod Hunger, 'for hem þat wolle nat swynke
That here lyflode be lene and lyte worth here clothes.'
'By Crist,' quod Peres þe plouhman tho, 'this proverbis y wol shewe
To beggares and to boys þat loth ben to worche.
Ac ȝut y praye ȝow,' quod Peres, 'pur charité, syre Hunger,
Yf ȝe can or knowe eny kyne thynges of fisyk,
For somme of my servauntes and mysulf bothe
Of al a woke worche nat, so oure wombe greveth us.'
'Y wot wel,' quod Hunger, 'what sekenesse ȝow ayleth:
Ȝe han manged over-moche, þat maketh ȝow to be syke.
Ac ete nat, y hote, ar hunger the take
And sende the of his sauce to savery with thy lyppes;
And kepe som til soper tyme, and site nat to longe
At noon ne at no tyme and nameliche at þe sopere.
Lat nat sire Sorfeet sittien at thy borde,
And loke þou drynke no day ar thow dyne sumwhat.
And thenk þat Dives for his delicat lyf to þe devel wente
And Lazar þe lene beggare þat longede after croumes –
And ȝut hadde he hem nat, for y, Hunger, culde hym –
And sethen y say hym sitte as he a syre were
In al manere ese and in Abrahames lappe.

257 **ȝut** 'yet, furthermore'. Whereas the good servant can help others out of his abundance, the bad can expect no help in his destitution.

258 'And I will deprive him of what he is confident of having.'

261a 'For thou shalt eat the labours of thy hands (blessed art thou)': Psalm 127.2 (AV 128.2).

265 **boys** a contemptuous word in ME: 'fellows'.

269 **Of al a woke** 'for a whole week'.

271 **manged** 'eaten': an unusual French loan-word, used here in contempt of Frenchified luxury: cf. 334 below.

273 'And send you some of his sauce with which to add relish to your palate.'

278–82 The parable of the rich man (*dives*, 'rich') and Lazarus, in Luke 16.19–31, is adapted to the mouth of Hunger.

281 The main sentence resumes after the parenthesis as if there had been no *þat* in l. 279.

282 Abraham's bosom (Luke 16.22) is the limbo where the faithful who died before the redemption, like Abraham, await the reward of heaven.

And ȝif thow þe pore, Peres y þe rede:
Alle þat grat in thy gate for Godes love aftur fode
Part with hem of thy payne, of potage or of sowl;
Lene hem som of thy loef thouh thow þe lasse chewe.
And thouh lyares and lach-draweres and lollares knocke,
Lat hem abyde til the bord be drawe ac bere hem none croumes
Til alle thyne nedy neyhbores have noen ymaked.
And yf thow dyete the thus, y dar legge myn eres
That Fysik shal his forred hodes for his fode sulle
And his cloke of Callabre for his comune legge,
And be fayn, be my fayth, his fysik to leete
And lerne to labory with lond lest lyflode hem fayle.
Ther ar many luther leches, ac lele leches fewe;
They don men deye thorw here drynkes ar destyné hit wolde.'
'By seynte Poul,' quod Peres, 'thow poyntest neyh þe treuthe
And leelyche sayst, as y leve, Lord hit þe forȝeld!
Wende nouthe when thow wold, and wel thow be evere
For thow hast wel awroke me and also wel ytauhte me.'
'Y behote the,' quod Hunger, 'þat hennes ne wol y wende
Ar y have ydyned be þis day and ydronke bothe.'
'Y have no peny,' quod Peres, 'polettes for to begge,
Ne noþer goos ne gries, but two grene cheses
And a fewe croddes and craym and a cake of otes
And bred for my barnes of benes and of peses.
And ȝut y say, be my soule, y have no salt bacoun
Ne no cokeney, be Crist, colloppes to make.
Ac y have poret-ployntes, parsilie and skalones,
Chibolles and chirvulles and cheries sam-rede,
And a cow with a calf and a cart-mare

283 The text of the first half of this line is very uncertain. See Textual Notes, p. 318.

287 **lach-draweres** These are evidently people who cause householders to let them in (draw their latches) and then take advantage of the privilege.

288 **drawe** 'put away'. The *bord* or table stood on trestles in the hall.

289 **noen** 'their noonday meal'.

292 **cloke of Callabre** a cloak trimmed with squirrel fur from Calabria. Physicians were commonly paid with articles of clothing.

299 **wel thow be evere** 'may you always prosper'.

302 **be þis day** 'before this day is out'.

303 **begge** 'buy'.

306 These poor kinds of bread (cf. 176–8) form part of the subsistence diet of peasants in the lean time before harvest.

308 'Nor any little eggs, by Christ, with which to make bacon and eggs.' A *cokeney* was a small 'cock's egg' (hence a spoiled child or milksop, hence a townsman, a Cockney).

309–10 'But I have leeks, parsley and shallots, spring onions and chervil and half-ripe cherries.'

To drawe afeld my donge þe while þe drouthe lasteth.
And by this lyflode we mote lyve til Lamasse tyme,
And by that y hope to have hervost in my croftes;
Thenne may y dyhte þi dyner as me dere lyketh.'
Alle þe pore peple tho pese-coddes fette,
Benes and bake aples they brouhten in here lappe,
And profrede Pers this present to plese with Honger.
Hunger eet al in haste and askede aftur more.
Pore folk for fere tho fedde Honger ȝerne
With craym and with croddes, with cresses and oþere erbes.
By that hit nyhed neyh hervost and newe corn cam to chepyng,
And thenne were folk fayn and fedde Hunger dentiesliche,
And thenne Gloton with gode ale garte Hunger slepe.
And tho wolde Wastor nat worche bote wandren aboute,
Ne no beggare eten bred þat benes ynne were,
Bote of cler-matyn and coket and of clene whete,
Ne noon halpenny ale in none wyse drynke
Bote of the beste and of þe brouneste þat brewestares sullen.
Laborers þat han no lond to lyve on but here handes
Deynede noȝt to dyne a-day of nyhte-olde wortes.
May no peny-ale hem pay ne no pece of bacoun
But hit be fresh flesch or fisch yfried or ybake,
And þat *chaut* and *pluchaut* for chillyng of his mawe.
And but yf he be heyliche yhuyred, elles wol he chydde
And þat he was werkeman ywrouhte warien þe tyme.
Aȝenes Catones consayle comseth he to gruche:
Paupertatis onus pacienter ferre memento.

312 Dung was spread before what Chaucer calls the 'drought of March' broke.

313 **Lamasse** the 'loaf mass', celebrating on 1 August the beginning of the harvest.

315 **as me dere lyketh** 'as it pleases me best'.

322 The work on the half acre has now extended from seed-time to harvest. So it is no longer possible to regard it as a mere short interruption to the pilgrimage to Truth. See 60n. above.

324 **Gloton** one of the Seven Deadly Sins, whose confessions were recorded in the previous passus.

327 **cler-matyn and coket** kinds of fine white bread.

328 **halpenny ale** cheap beer, at a halfpenny a gallon. 'Penny ale' (l. 332) was also a cheap sort.

331 'Would not condescend to eat one day any vegetables picked the day before.'

334 'And that *chaud* and *plus chaud* (warm and warmer) for fear of a chill on the stomach.' Cf. 271n.

335 **heyliche yhuyred** 'employed for a high wage'. Shortage of labour after the Black Death of 1349 led to a general rise in wage demands.

336 'And curse the time that he was ever made a labourer.'

338 'Be sure to bear the burden of poverty with patience.' From the Distichs of

And thenne a corseth þe kyng and alle þe kynges justices,
Suche lawes to lerne laboreres to greve.
Ac whiles Hunger was here maister ther wolde non chyde
Ne stryve aȝeynes his statuyt, a lokede so sturne.
   Ac y warne ȝow, werkmen, wynneth whiles ȝe mowe,
For Hunger hiderwardes hasteth hym faste.
He shal awake thorw water wastors to chaste,
And ar fewe ȝeres be fulfeld famyne shal aryse,
And so sayth Saturne, and sente us to warne.
Thorw flodes and thorw foule wederes fruyttes shollen fayle;
Pruyde and pestilences shal moche peple feche.
Thre shypes and a schaef with an viii folwynge
Shal brynge bane and batayle on bothe half þe mone;
And thenne shal deth withdrawe and derthe be justice
And Dawe þe delvare dey for defaute,
But yf God of his goodnesse graunte us a trewe.

Cato (I 21), a collection of maxims set as an elementary Latin text in medieval schools.

342 **his statuyt** Hunger's 'statute' is implicitly contrasted with the contemporary Statutes of Labourers, which attempted ineffectively to curb workers' demands.

343–54 A prophecy of impending disasters, expressed, in part, in the customary riddling style.

347 **Saturne** the most maleficent of the god-planets: cf. Chaucer's Knight's Tale, *Canterbury Tales* I 2453–69.

349 **moche peple feche** 'carry off many people'.

350 This line presumably conceals a prophetic date – the date at which the natural disasters of flood, tempest, famine and pestilence will be augmented by universal warfare among men. A *schaef* or sheaf contained 24 arrows, but the numerical value of a ship is obscure. So: $x + 24 + 8 = ?$

351 **on bothe half þe mone** 'in all parts of the world'?

352 **deth** commonly referring to the plague at this time.

353 **Dawe** pet form of 'David' (cf. Modern 'Dawson').

8

Patience

The poems *Pearl*, *Cleanness* (or *Purity*), *Patience* and *Sir Gawain and the Green Knight* are preserved in only one manuscript: British Library MS Cotton Nero A X. The four are generally ascribed to the same unnamed author, partly on the grounds of shared dialect and similarities of style, technique and theme, but finally on the argument that it is more likely that there was one writer of such exceptional literary powers in a small part of the country than that there were several. The date of composition can be judged only on such imprecise criteria as details of dress and architecture and on literary-historical grounds, from which a date in the last quarter of the fourteenth century seems probable.

The rather humble manuscript, of about the same dimensions as this book, is written in a small, ungainly script, dated about 1400, and includes twelve clumsy illustrations. The dialect of the poems is North-West Midlands; the *Linguistic Atlas* places it in Cheshire, on the border with Staffordshire.

The poet shares with other alliterative writers of this region a distinctive vocabulary that includes ranges of synonyms for certain key concepts. The synonyms for 'man, knight, being' (referring also to God) are used so frequently that they are worth memorizing: *burne*, *freke*, *gome*, *haþel*, *lede*, *renk*, *schalk*, *segge*, *tulk* and *wyȝe*. Another characteristic feature to observe is the use of adjectives as nouns, such as *busy* (8/157), 'busy activity', and *schene* (8/440), 'brightness, bright sun'.

In this dialect the spelling *-tz* is used for the third person singular of the verbs *gotz*, 'goes', *hatz* 'has', and *watz*, 'was'. Otherwise verbs in the present tense end in *-ez* or *-es* in both the second and third persons singular: *þou sparez* (8/484), *he nevenes* (9/10). The present plural has a variety of endings, illustrated by *pynez* and *put* (8/79), *begynes* (8/76) and *sytten* (9/351). In the past tense, the second person singular of weak verbs (4.5.4) sometimes ends in *-dez*, as in *þou travayledez* (8/498). The plural of the imperative has the endings *-ez* or *-es*, e.g. *berez* (8/211), and the present participle ends in *-and*, e.g. *fannand* (9/181).

Personal pronouns are *ho*, 'she', *þay*, 'they', *hem* and sometimes confusingly *hym*, 'them', *her* and *hor* 'their', and *hores*, 'theirs'.

Patience is a retelling of the Old Testament Book of Jonah, at times (e.g. ll. 305–36) following the biblical account very closely, at other times (e.g. ll. 73–96, 253–304) expanding quite considerably. The story of Jonah is used as an exemplum to illustrate the necessity of patience, so that the poem has a structure similar to the sermon delivered by Chaucer's Pardoner. In a Prologue (ll. 1–60) the poet explains the nature and importance of patience: it is the *suffraunce*, 'endurance', that overcomes suffering, it is the reverse of anger, and it is the last of the Beatitudes, the blessing for those 'that can control their heart'. If we try to escape what is demanded of us we will, like Jonah, only make difficulties for ourselves.

The interest of the poem centres on Jonah, whose character is strikingly developed from the biblical narrative. Although his preaching to the Ninevites has a powerful effect, the emphasis is not on his qualities as a preacher but on his failing as a man – petulant, quarrelsome, fearful and selfish. Traditionally Jonah was viewed as a type or foreshadowing of Christ; in this poem he becomes the antitype, steadily refusing to respond to God. The world about him – the winds, the sailors, the whale, the Ninevites and the ivy – shows obedience; only Jonah disobeys. His lack of patience shows up in contrast to God's patience with man's rebelliousness: 'Couþe I not þole bot as þou, þer þryved ful fewe' (521). Jonah is a richly comic figure, defeated not by God's wrath but by his mercy.

The poem is composed for the most part in syntactic groups or 'sentences' of four lines which are marked off by slashes in the manuscript.

Editions

J. J. Anderson, *Patience* (Manchester, 1969)

Malcolm Andrew and Ronald Waldron, *The Poems of the Pearl Manuscript* (London, 1978)

A. C. Cawley and J. J. Anderson, *Pearl, Cleanness, Patience, Sir Gawain and the Green Knight* (London and New York, 1976)

Facsimile

Pearl, Cleanness, Patience, and Sir Gawain and the Green Knight, introduced by Sir Israel Gollancz, EETS 162 (1923)

Studies

J. J. Anderson, 'The Prologue of *Patience*', *Modern Philology*, 63 (1965–6), 283–7

Malcolm Andrew, 'Jonah and Christ in *Patience*', *Modern Philology*, 70 (1972–3), 230–3

A. C. Spearing, *The Gawain-Poet* (Cambridge, 1970)
David Williams, 'The Point of *Patience*', *Modern Philology*, 68 (1970–1), 127–36

Pacience is a poynt, þaȝ hit displese ofte;
When hevy herttes ben hurt wyth heþyng oþer elles,
Suffraunce may aswagen hem and þe swelme leþe,
For ho quelles uche a qued and quenches malyce.
For quoso suffer cowþe syt, sele wolde folȝe,
And quo for þro may noȝt þole, þe þikker he sufferes.
þen is better to abyde þe bur umbestoundes
þen ay þrow forth my þro, þaȝ me þynk ylle.
  I herde on a halyday at a hyȝe masse
How Mathew melede þat his mayster his meyny con teche;
Aȝt happes he hem hyȝt and ucheon a mede
Sunderlupes for hit dissert upon a ser wyse:
Thay arn happen þat han in hert poverté,
For hores is þe hevenryche to holde for ever;
þay ar happen also þat haunte mekenesse,
For þay schal welde þis worlde and alle her wylle have;
Thay ar happen also þat for her harme wepes,
For þay schal comfort encroche in kythes ful mony;
þay ar happen also þat hungeres after ryȝt,
For þay schal frely be refete ful of alle gode;
Thay ar happen also þat han in hert rauþe,
For mercy in alle maneres her mede schal worþe;
þay ar happen also þat arn of hert clene,
For þay her savyour in sete schal se with her yȝen;
Thay ar happen also þat halden her pese,

1 **poynt** 'good quality, virtue'.

3 **Suffraunce** 'endurance', defining patience. The concept is further explored through the play on the two meanings of *suffer* in ll. 5–6. In l. 4, *ho*, 'she', refers back to *suffraunce*; compare the personification of the Beatitudes in ll. 30–3.

5–8 'For if anyone could endure misfortune, happiness would follow, and if anyone as a result of impatience is unable to endure, he suffers the more severely. Then it is better to put up with the buffet sometimes, though I may dislike it, than always express my impatience.'

10–12 'How Matthew said his master taught his disciples; he promised them eight blessings and for each one individually a reward for its merit in a different way.' There follows in ll. 13–28 a fairly close translation of the Beatitudes in the Sermon on the Mount in Matthew 5.3–10.

13 The Gospel has 'blessed are the poor in spirit'.

17 The Gospel has 'blessed are they that mourn', which was generally interpreted as a reference to the penitent sorrowing for sin.

25 **halden her pese** 'remain at peace'. The Vulgate *pacifici* was understood both as 'peacemakers' and 'those who are peaceful at heart'. The poet emphasizes the latter interpretation.

For þay þe gracious Godes sunes schal godly be called;
þay ar happen also þat con her hert stere,
For hores is þe hevenryche, as I er sayde.
These arn þe happes alle aȝt þat us bihyȝt weren
If we þyse ladyes wolde lof in lyknyng of þewes:
Dame Povert, dame Pitee, dame Penaunce þe þrydde,
Dame Mekenesse, dame Mercy, and miry Clannesse,
And þenne dame Pes and Pacyence put in þerafter.
He were happen þat hade one; alle were þe better.
Bot syn I am put to a poynt þat poverté hatte,
I schal me porvay pacyence and play me with boþe;
For in þe tyxte þere þyse two arn in teme layde,
Hit arn fettled in on forme, þe forme and þe laste,
And by quest of her quoyntyse enquylen on mede;
And als, in myn upynyoun, hit arn of on kynde,
For þeras povert hir proferes, ho nyl be put utter,
Bot lenge wheresoever hir lyst, lyke oþer greme,
And þereas povert enpresses, þaȝ mon pyne þynk,
Much, maugré his mun, he mot nede suffer;
Thus poverté and pacyence arn nedes playferes.
Syþen I am sette with hem samen, suffer me byhoves;
þenne is me lyȝtloker hit lyke and her lotes prayse
þenne wyþer wyth and be wroth and þe wers have.
Ȝif me be dyȝt a destyné due to have,

27 This differs from the Vulgate, which has 'Blessed are they that suffer persecution for justice' sake'. The poet's interpretation of this as 'those who can control their heart' acts as a definition of patience directed towards the case of Jonah to follow.

28 The eighth Beatitude is granted the same reward as the first, as the poet says in ll. 37–40.

31 **Pitee** applying to the fourth Beatitude (l. 19), evidently has the sense of the Latin *pietas*, 'piety, sense of right'. For some examples of the common personification of the virtues as ladies, see *MED merci* n. (1), 6.

35 Matthew refers to 'the poor in spirit' rather than the materially poor, but in Luke 6.20 they are simply 'ye poor'. Those faced with poverty are, like the poet himself, obliged to learn patience.

36 **play me** 'enjoy myself, have fun' (with the *ladyes*).

37–9 'In the text where these two are linked, they are placed within one framework as the first and the last, and as a legacy of their excellence receive the same reward.' (See 28n.) *In teme layde*, 'coupled together' (*teme*, 'team'), perhaps with a play on the sense 'spoken of' (*teme*, 'theme').

42 **lyke oþer greme** 'whether you like it or not'. Both verbs are impersonal and subjunctive.

43 **þaȝ mon pyne þynk** 'even though it may seem hard' (5.6.8).

44 **maugré his mun** 'despite anything he may say'; *mun*, 'mouth'.

46–7 'Since I am stuck with them both together I have to endure it; then it is easier for me to like it and praise their behaviour.'

49–50 'If I am ordained to have an inevitable fate, what good does it do me to be indignant or resentful?'

What dowes me þe dedayn oþer dispit make?
Oþer ȝif my lege lorde lyst on lyve me to bidde
Oþer to ryde oþer to renne to Rome in his ernde,
What grayþed me þe grychchyng bot grame more seche?
Much ȝif he me ne made, maugref my chekes,
And þenne þrat moste I þole and unþonk to mede,
þe had bowed to his bode, bongré my hyure.
Did not Jonas in Judé suche jape sumwhyle?
To sette hym to sewrté, unsounde he hym feches.
Wyl ȝe tary a lyttel tyne and tent me a whyle,
I schal wysse yow þerwyth as holy wryt telles.

Hit bitydde sumtyme in þe termes of Judé,
Jonas joyned watz þerinne Jentyle prophete;
Goddes glam to hym glod, þat hym unglad made,
With a roghlych rurd rowned in his ere:
'Rys radly', he says, 'and rayke forth even.
Nym þe way to Nynyvé wythouten oþer speche,
And in þat ceté my saȝes soghe alle aboute
þat in þat place at þe poynt I put in þi hert.
For iwysse hit arn so wykke þat in þat won dowellez
And her malys is so much, I may not abide,
Bot venge me on her vilanye and venym bilyve.
Now sweȝe me þider swyftly and say me þis arende.'
When þat steven watz stynt þat stowned his mynde,
Al he wrathed in his wyt and wyþerly he þoȝt:

53 As an example the poet supposes his lord were to order him to travel to Rome. 'What would protesting do for me except invite more trouble?' This leads into the story of Jonah who showed just such reluctance towards his Lord.

54 A difficult line. Perhaps 'it would be too much (to expect) that he would not compel me, despite anything I could do'. Compare *Cleanness* 21–2.

55–6 'And then I should have to endure compulsion and displeasure as a reward, (I) who might have yielded to his bidding, with his good will as my reward.' The French noun *bongré*, 'good will, thanks', is the opposite of *unþonk* in the two parallel phrases.

57 **Judé** Judaea, including Samaria (l. 116). Neither is named in the Book of Jonah.

58 'To bring himself to safety he lands himself trouble.'

62 **Jentyle prophete** 'prophet of the Gentiles', and perhaps also 'gentle (noble) prophet'.

68 **poynt** 'point in time': 'which I shall put into your heart in that place when the time comes.'

71 **venge me** 'I shall avenge myself'. For this use of the present tense see 5.6.1, and compare the verbs in ll. 78–80.

72 **me . . . me** 'for me, on my behalf', in both cases.

73–96 In the biblical account Jonah 'rose up to flee into Tharsis from the face of the Lord: and he went down to Joppe and found a ship going to Tharsis' (Jonah 1.3). The poet expands greatly to describe Jonah's reaction.

'If I bowe to his bode and bryng hem þis tale
And I be nummen in Nunivé, my nyes begynes.
He telles me þose traytoures arn typped schrewes;
I com wyth þose tyþynges, þay ta me bylyve,
Pynez me in a prysoun, put me in stokkes,
Wryþe me in a warlok, wrast out myn yȝen.
þis is a mervayl message a man for to preche
Amonge enmyes so mony and mansed fendes,
Bot if my gaynlych God such gref to me wolde,
For desert of sum sake þat I slayn were.
At alle peryles,' quoþ þe prophete, 'I aproche hit no nerre.
I wyl me sum oþer waye þat he ne wayte after.
I schal tee into Tarce and tary þere a whyle,
And lyȝtly when I am lest he letes me alone.'
   þenne he ryses radly and raykes bilyve,
Jonas toward port Japh, ay janglande for tene
þat he nolde þole for noþyng non of þose pynes,
þaȝ þe fader þat hym formed were fale of his hele.
'Oure syre syttes', he says, 'on sege so hyȝe
In his glowande glorye, and gloumbes ful lyttel
þaȝ I be nummen in Nunnivé and naked dispoyled,
On rode rwly torent with rybaudes mony.'
þus he passes to þat port his passage to seche,
Fyndes he a fayr schyp to þe fare redy,
Maches hym with þe maryneres, makes her paye
For to towe hym into Tarce as tyd as þay myȝt.
Then he tron on þo tres and þay her tramme ruchen,
Cachen up þe crossayl, cables þay fasten,

75 The line recalls l. 56.

76 'And if I am captured in Nineveh, my troubles will begin.'

83 **Bot if** 'unless'.

84 'That I should be killed by reason of some offence.'

85 **At alle peryles** 'whatever the consequences'.

86 **I wyl me** The verb of motion is omitted after the auxiliary verb (5.6.9): 'I will (betake) myself'.

87 **Tarce** Tarshish.

89 An ironic echo of l. 65.

90 **Japh** Joppa.

92 'Even though the Father who made him was indifferent to (?) his well-being.' The meaning of *fale* is uncertain.

96 'Cruelly torn apart on a cross by many ruffians.' The New Testament describes Jonah as a type or foreshadowing of Christ (Luke 11.30; Matthew 12.40). See Spearing (1970), 86–7; Andrew (1972–3), 230–3.

99 'Agrees a price with the sailors and pays them.'

101 'Then he stepped on to those boards (i.e. that ship), and they prepare their tackle.' The Book of Jonah has nothing corresponding to this lively and detailed description of the ship setting sail.

Wiȝt at þe wyndas weȝen her ankres,
Spynde spak to þe sprete þe spare bawelyne,
Gederen to þe gyde-ropes, þe grete cloþ falles.
Þay layden in on ladde-borde and þe lofe wynnes;
Þe blyþe breþe at her bak þe bosum he fyndes,
He swenges me þys swete schip swefte fro þe haven.
Watz never so joyful a Jue as Jonas watz þenne,
Þat þe daunger of dryȝten so derfly ascaped;
He wende wel þat þat wyȝ þat al þe world planted
Hade no maȝt in þat mere no man for to greve.
Lo, þe wytles wrechche! For he wolde noȝt suffer,
Now hatz he put hym in plyt of peril wel more.
Hit watz a wenyng unwar þat welt in his mynde,
Þaȝ he were soȝt fro Samarye, þat God seȝ no fyrre.
Ȝise, he blusched ful brode – þat burde hym by sure;
Þat ofte kyd hym þe carpe þat kyng sayde,
Dyngne David on des þat demed þis speche
In a psalme þat he set þe sauter withinne:
'O folez in folk, felez oþerwhyle,
And understondes umbestounde, þaȝ ȝe be stape fole.
Hope ȝe þat he heres not þat eres alle made?
Hit may not be þat he is blynde þat bigged uche yȝe.'

Bot he dredes no dynt þat dotes for elde,
For he watz fer in þe flod foundande to Tarce;
Bot I trow ful tyd overtan þat he were,
So þat schomely to schort he schote of his ame.
For þe welder of wyt þat wot alle þynges,
Þat ay wakes and waytes, at wylle hatz he slyȝtes;
He calde on þat ilk crafte he carf with his hondes;

103–4 'They swiftly weigh their anchors at the windlass, quickly fastened to the bowsprit the bowline kept in reserve.' The *bawelyne* is *spare* because it is used only in difficult sailing conditions to hold the sail steady.

105 **grete cloþ** 'mainsail'.

106–8 'They set a course to port and gain the luff (turn into the wind). The favourable wind at their back finds the belly of the sail; it turns this fine ship swiftly from the harbour.' On *me* in l. 108, see 5.3.3.

110 **daunger** 'power'.

111 **þat wyȝ** there is a similar periphrasis for God in 9/256.

116 **were soȝt from Samarye** 'had gone from Samaria'.

117–18 'Indeed he (God) looked with wide-open eyes, of that he (Jonah) should have been sure; the words which that king (David) said often taught him that.'

121–4 'O fools among the people, consider once in a while, and understand sometimes, even though you are quite mad. Do you think that he who made all ears does not hear? It is not possible that he who formed each eye is blind.' A paraphrase of Psalm 93.8–9 (AV 94.8–9).

130 **waytes** 'watches'.

131 **crafte** 'creation', i.e. the winds.

þay wakened wel þe wroþeloker for wroþely he cleped:
'Ewrus and Aquiloun þat on est sittes,
Blowes boþe at my bode upon blo watteres.'
þenne watz no tom þer bytwene his tale and her dede,
So bayn wer þay boþe two his bone for to wyrk.
Anon out of þe norþ-est þe noys bigynes,
When boþe breþes con blowe upon blo watteres,
Roȝ rakkes þer ros with rudnyng anunder,
þe see souȝed ful sore, gret selly to here;
þe wyndes on þe wonne water so wrastel togeder
þat þe wawes ful wode waltered so hiȝe
And efte busched to þe abyme, þat breed fysches
Durst nowhere for roȝ arest at þe bothem.
When þe breth and þe brok and þe bote metten,
Hit watz a joyles gyn þat Jonas watz inne,
For hit reled on roun upon þe roȝe yþes;
þe bur ber to hit baft, þat braste alle her gere.
þen hurled on a hepe þe helme and þe sterne,
Furst tomurte mony rop and þe mast after,
þe sayl sweyed on þe see, þenne suppe bihoved
þe coge of þe colde water, and þenne þe cry ryses.
ȝet corven þay þe cordes and kest al þeroute,
Mony ladde þer forth lep to lave and to kest,
Scopen out þe scaþel water þat fayn scape wolde;
For be monnes lode never so luþer, þe lyf is ay swete.
  þer watz busy overborde bale to kest,
Her bagges and her feþer-beddes and her bryȝt wedes,
Her kysttes and her coferes, her caraldes alle,
And al to lyȝten þat lome, ȝif leþe wolde schape;
Bot ever watz ilyche loud þe lot of þe wyndes,
And ever wroþer þe water and wodder þe stremes.

133 Classical writers give Eurus as an east wind and Aquilo as a north-northeast wind. Hence they sit in the easterly quarter (l. 133), and their combined force is a northeasterly (l. 137). St Paul is shipwrecked after a 'tempestuous wind called Euroaquilo' (Acts 27.14).

137–62 This magnificent storm-scene is not biblical, but is a topos found in several alliterative poems; see Nicolas Jacobs, *Speculum*, 47 (1972), 695–719.

138 **con blowe** 'blew'. For this construction with *con*, see 5.6.3.

151–2 **þenne suppe . . . water** 'then the ship had to drink the cold water'.

155–6 'Those who were keen to escape scooped out the dangerous water; for however unpleasant one's journey, life is always sweet.' See 5.4.6.

157–68 Compare: 'And the mariners were afraid and the men cried to their god: and they cast forth the wares that were in the ship into the sea, to lighten it of them' (Jonah 1.5).

160 **ȝif leþe wolde schape** 'to see if relief would come about'.

þen þo wery forwroȝt wyst no bote,
Bot uchon glewed on his god þat gayned hym beste:
Summe to Vernagu þer vouched avowes solemne,
Summe to Diana devout and derf Neptune,
To Mahoun and to Mergot, þe mone and þe sunne,
And uche lede as he loved and layde had his hert.
  þenne bispeke þe spakest, dispayred wel nere:
'I leve here be sum losynger, sum lawles wrech,
þat hatz greved his god and gotz here amonge us.
Lo, al synkes in his synne and for his sake marres.
I louve þat we lay lotes on ledes uchone,
And whoso lympes þe losse, lay hym þeroute,
And quen þe gulty is gon, what may gome trawe
Bot he þat rules þe rak may rwe on þose oþer?'
þis watz sette in asent, and sembled þay were,
Herȝed out of uche hyrne to hent þat falles.
A lodesmon lyȝtly lep under hachches
For to layte mo ledes and hem to lote bryng;
Bot hym fayled no freke þat he fynde myȝt,
Saf Jonas þe Jwe þat jowked in derne;
He watz flowen for ferde of þe flode lotes
Into þe boþem of þe bot and on a brede lyggede,
Onhelde by þe hurrok for þe heven wrache,
Slypped upon a sloumbe-selepe, and sloberande he routes.
þe freke hym frunt with his fot and bede hym ferk up;
þer Ragnel in his rakentes hym rere of his dremes!
Bi þe haspede hater he hentes hym þenne,
And broȝt hym up by þe brest and upon borde sette,
Arayned hym ful runyschly what raysoun he hade
In such slaȝtes of sorȝe to slepe so faste.

163 'Then those worn out with labouring knew no remedy.' *Wery* followed by a past participle with prefix *for-* is an idiom.

164–8 The gods are supplied by the poet: Vernagu is a giant Saracen in the Charlemagne romances; Mahoun is Mahomet, portrayed as a false god in the Middle Ages (see 10/20); Mergot is mentioned in the Charlemagne romances as a heathen god.

173 'I recommend we cast lots for each person.'

174 **lympes þe losse** 'incurs the loss', i.e. 'loses'.

181–8 'Jonas went down into the inner part of the ship and fell into a deep sleep' (Jonah 1.5).

181 'But no man escaped his search.'

185 'Huddled up near the rudder (?) to avoid (*for*) the vengeance of heaven.' The *hurrok* is perhaps a band to keep the rudder in position.

186 **sloumbe-selepe** 'deep sleep'. Sleeping commonly symbolizes lack of moral vigilance, as in Luke 12.36–40.

188 'May Ragnel in his fetters wake him from his dreams.' *þer* introduces a wish (5.6.6). Ragnel is the name of a devil in the *Chester Plays* and elsewhere.

Sone haf þay her sortes sette and serelych deled,
And ay þe lote upon laste lymped on Jonas.
Þenne ascryed þay hym sckete and asked ful loude:
'What þe devel hatz þou don, doted wrech?
What seches þou on see, synful schrewe,
With þy lastes so luþer to lose us uchone?
Hatz þou, gome, no governour ne god on to calle,
Þat þou þus slydes on slepe when þou slayn worþes?
Of what londe art þou lent, what laytes þou here,
Whyder in worlde þat þou wylt and what is þyn arnde?
Lo, þy dom is þe dyȝt for þy dedes ille!
Do gyf glory to þy godde er þou glyde hens.'
'I am an Ebru', quoþ he, 'of Israyl borne.
Þat wyȝe I worchyp, iwysse, þat wroȝt alle þynges,
Alle þe worlde with þe welkyn, þe wynde and þe sternes,
And alle þat wonez þer withinne, at a worde one.
Alle þis meschef for me is made at þys tyme
For I haf greved my God and gulty am founden.
Forþy berez me to þe borde and baþes me þeroute;
Er gete ȝe no happe, I hope for soþe.'
He ossed hym by unnynges þat þay undernomen
Þat he watz flawen fro þe face of frelych dryȝtyn;
Þenne such a ferde on hem fel and flayed hem withinne
Þat þay ruyt hym to rowwe and letten þe rynk one.
Haþeles hyȝed in haste with ores ful longe,
Syn her sayl watz hem aslypped, on sydez to rowe,
Hef and hale upon hyȝt to helpen hymselven,
Bot al watz nedles note, þat nolde not bityde;
In bluber of þe blo flod bursten her ores:
Þenne hade þay noȝt in her honde þat hem help myȝt.
Þenne nas no coumfort to kever ne counsel non oþer

197 **What seches þou** 'why are you trying'.

200 **when þou slayn worþes** 'when you are about to be killed'. On the tense, see 5.6.10.

202 'Where in the world do you want to go to . . .?'

204 **Do gyf** imperative (5.6.7).

208 **at a worde one** 'with a single word'.

212 **Er** 'before that'. The sense of *hope*, 'believe', is usual in Northern texts; e.g. 9/140, 14/67.

213 **hym** plural, as in l. 216.

216 **ruyt hym** reflexive, 'hasten'.

218 'Since their sail had got away from them . . .'

219 'Heave and pull energetically to help themselves.'

220 **nedles note** 'pointless effort'. The Vulgate has 'And the men rowed hard to return to land: but they were not able, because the sea tossed and swelled upon them' (Jonah 1.13).

Bot Jonas into his juis jugge bylyve.
Fyrst þay prayen to þe prynce þat prophetes serven
þat he gef hem þe grace to greven hym never
þat þay in balelez blod þer blenden her handez,
þaȝ þat haþel wer his þat þay here quelled.
Tyd by top and bi to þay token hym synne;
Into þat lodlych loȝe þay luche hym sone.
He watz no tytter outtulde þat tempest ne sessed,
þe se saȝtled þerwith as sone as ho moȝt.
þenne þaȝ her takel were torne þat totered on yþes,
Styffe stremes and streȝt hem strayned a whyle,
þat drof hem dryȝlych adoun þe depe to serve,
Tyl a swetter ful swyþe hem sweȝed to bonk.
þer watz lovyng on lofte when þay þe londe wonnen
To oure mercyable God on Moyses wyse,
With sacrafyse up set and solempne vowes,
And graunted hym on to be God and graythly non oþer.
    þaȝ þay be jolef for joye, Jonas ȝet dredes;
þaȝ he nolde suffer no sore, his seele is on anter,
For whatso worþed of þat wyȝe fro he in water dipped,
Hit were a wonder to wene ȝif holy wryt nere.

Now is Jonas þe Jwe jugged to drowne;
Of þat schended schyp men schowved hym sone.
A wylde walterande whal, as wyrde þen schaped,
þat watz beten fro þe abyme, bi þat bot flotte
And watz war of þat wyȝe þat þe water soȝte,
And swyftely swenged hym to swepe and his swolȝ
        opened.
þe folk ȝet haldande his fete, þe fysch hym tyd hentes;
Withouten towche of any tothe he tult in his þrote.

224 'Except to condemn Jonah to his punishment at once.'

225 'The prince that prophets serve' is Jonah's God.

227 'By immersing their hands in innocent blood.'

231 'No sooner was he thrown out than that storm ceased.' The construction with *ne*, which is based on French usage, is discussed by Anderson (1969), 61.

235 'That drove them relentlessly down to serve (i.e. at the command of) the deep sea.'

236 **a swetter** 'a pleasanter (current)'.

238 **on Moyses wyse** 'according to the manner of Moses'; as described in the next lines.

240 **on** 'alone'.

244 'It would be a strange thing to believe if it were not for Holy Writ.' Actually the details of the next 58 lines are not biblical.

249 **soȝte** 'was falling into', past tense of *seke*.

251 In illustrations of this episode, as indeed in the picture in this manuscript, Jonah is shown going into the whale's mouth as the sailors hold on to his feet.

Thenne he swengez and swayves to þe se-boþem
Bi mony rokkez ful roȝe and rydelande strondes,
Wyth þe mon in his mawe malskred in drede,
As lyttel wonder hit watz ȝif he wo dreȝed;
For nade þe hyȝe heven-kyng þurȝ his honde-myȝt
Warded þis wrech man in warlowes guttez,
What lede moȝt lyve bi lawe of any kynde
Þat any lyf myȝt be lent so longe hym withinne?
Bot he watz sokored by þat syre þat syttes so hiȝe,
Þaȝ were wanlez of wele in wombe of þat fissche,
And also dryven þurȝ þe depe and in derk walterez.
Lorde, colde watz his cumfort, and his care huge,
For he knew uche a cace and kark þat hym lymped,
How fro þe bot into þe blober watz with a best lachched
And þrwe in at hit þrote withouten þret more
As mote in at a munster dor, so mukel wern his chawlez.
  He glydes in by þe giles þurȝ glaym ande glette,
Relande in by a rop, a rode þat hym þoȝt,
Ay hele over hed hourlande aboute,
Til he blunt in a blok as brod as a halle,
And þer he festnes þe fete and fathmez aboute,
And stod up in his stomak þat stank as þe devel.
Þer in saym and in sorȝe þat savoured as helle,
Þer watz bylded his bour þat wyl no bale suffer.
And þenne he lurkkes and laytes where watz le best
In uche a nok of his navel, bot nowhere he fyndez
No rest ne recoverer, bot ramel ande myre
In wych gut so ever he gotz; bot ever is God swete;
And þer he lenged at þe last and to þe lede called:
'Now prynce, of þy prophete pité þou have!

254 **rydelande strondes** perhaps 'flowing currents', but the gloss 'winnowing sands' by Andrew and Waldron (1978) is also possible.

258 **warlowes** 'the devil's'; often applied specifically to the Devil, as well as more generally to a monster. On the association of the whale with the Devil, see 274–5n.

259–60 'What man might believe that by any law of nature any creature could have remained alive so long inside him?'

262 **þaȝ were** 'though he was'; *were* is subjunctive after *þaȝ* (5.6.6), with the subject *he* unexpressed (5.4.2), as again in l. 266.

266–7 'How he was taken by a creature out of the boat into the seething water, and tumbled into its throat without any more struggle.'

268 This remarkable simile of the mote in the minster door has been much commented on; see Burrow (1971), 134–5.

270 **rop** 'intestine' (OE *ropp*).

274–5 The hellish associations of the whale go back to Matthew 12.40: 'For as Jonas was in the whale's belly three days and three nights; so shall the Son of man be in the heart of the earth three days and three nights.'

þaȝ I be fol and fykel and falce of my hert,
Dewoyde now þy vengaunce þurȝ vertu of rauthe;
Thaȝ I be gulty of gyle as gaule of prophetes,
þou art God, and alle gowdez ar grayþely þyn owen;
Haf now mercy of þy man and his mysdedes,
And preve þe lyȝtly a lorde in londe and in water.'
With þat he hitte to a hyrne and helde hym þerinne
þer no defoule of no fylþe watz fest hym abute;
þer he sete also sounde, saf for merk one,
As in þe bulk of þe bote þer he byfore sleped.
  So in a bouel of þat best he bidez on lyve
þre dayes and þre nyȝt, ay þenkande on dryȝtyn,
His myȝt and his merci, his mesure þenne;
Now he knawez hym in care þat couþe not in sele.
Ande ever walteres þis whal bi wyldren depe,
þurȝ mony a regioun ful roȝe, þurȝ ronk of his wylle,
For þat mote in his mawe mad hym, I trowe,
þaȝ hit lyttel were hym wyth, to wamel at his hert;
Ande as sayled þe segge, ay sykerly he herde
þe bygge borne on his bak and bete on his sydes.
þen a prayer ful prest þe prophete þer maked
On þis wyse, as I wene; his wordez were mony:

'Lorde, to þe haf I cleped in carez ful stronge;
Out of þe hole þou me herde of hellen wombe.
I calde, and þou knew myn uncler steven.
þou diptez me of þe depe se into þe dymme hert;
þe grete flem of þy flod folded me umbe.
Alle þe gotez of þy guferes and groundelez powlez
And þy stryvande stremez of stryndez so mony
In on daschande dam dryvez me over.
And ȝet I sayde as I seet in þe se-boþem:
"Careful am I, kest out fro þy cler yȝen
And desevered fro þy syȝt, ȝet surely I hope
Efte to trede on þy temple and teme to þyselven."

291 **saf for merk one** 'except only for the darkness'.

300 **hym wyth** 'in comparison with him (the whale)'.

301–2 'And as the man travelled along, certainly he always heard the mighty water on its (the whale's) back and beating on its sides.'

305–36 The prayer is closely translated from Jonah 2.3–10, which in turn is based on Psalm 68 (AV 69).

308 'You plunged me into the murky heart of the deep sea.' Compare 'And thou hast cast me forth into the deep in the heart of the sea, and a flood hath compassed me: all thy billows and thy waves have passed over me' (Jonah 2.4).

312 **on daschande dam** 'one rushing flood'.

316 'To walk again in your temple and belong to you.'

I am wrapped in water to my wo stoundez,
þe abyme byndes þe body þat I byde inne,
þe pure poplande hourle playes on my heved;
To laste mere of uche a mount, man, am I fallen.
þe barrez of uche a bonk ful bigly me haldes
þat I may lachche no lont, and þou my lyf weldes;
þou schal releve me, renk, whil þy ryȝt slepez,
þurȝ myȝt of þy mercy þat mukel is to tryste.
For when þ'acces of anguych watz hid in my sawle,
þenne I remembred me ryȝt of my rych lorde,
Prayande him for peté his prophete to here,
þat into his holy hous myn orisoun moȝt entre.
I haf meled with þy maystrés mony longe day,
Bot now I wot wyterly þat þose unwyse ledes
þat affyen hym in vanyté and in vayne þynges,
For þink þat mountes to noȝt her mercy forsaken.
Bot I dewoutly awowe, þat verray betz halden,
Soberly to do þe sacrafyse when I schal save worþe,
And offer þe for my hele a ful hol gyfte
And halde goud þat þou me hetes; haf here my trauthe!'
  Thenne oure Fader to þe fysch ferslych biddez
þat he hym sput spakly upon spare drye.
þe whal wendez at his wylle and a warþe fyndez,
And þer he brakez up þe buyrne as bede hym oure Lorde.
þenne he swepe to þe sonde in sluchched cloþes;
Hit may wel be þat mester were his mantyle to wasche.
þe bonk þat he blosched to and bode hym bisyde
Wern of þe regiounes ryȝt þat he renayed hade.
  þenne a wynde of Goddez worde efte þe wyȝe bruxlez:

317 **to my wo stoundez** 'to my agonies of distress'. The Vulgate has 'even to the soul' (Jonah 2.6).

319 **þe pure poplande hourle** 'the billowing surge itself'; *pure* is used as an intensive.

320 'To the farthest limit of each mountain, Lord, have I fallen.' It translates 'I went down to the lowest parts of the mountains' (Jonah 2.7).

321 The Vulgate has 'The bars of the earth have shut me up for ever'.

329 'I have meddled with (or struggled against) your mysterious ways for many a long day.' So Jonah resolves to question God's plan no longer.

332 'Give up their (share of) mercy for something (*þink*) that amounts to nothing.' The Vulgate has 'forsake their own mercy' (Jonah 2.9).

333 **þat . . . halden** 'what will faithfully be kept'.

336 'And keep to what you command me – have here my word on it!'

338 **spare drye** 'bare dry land'.

342 'It may well be that it was necessary to wash his mantle.' Dirty clothes traditionally symbolize the filth of sin.

343 'The shore that he was looking at and the habitation right by him.'

'Nylt þou never to Nynivé bi no kynnez wayez?'
'Ȝisse, Lorde,' quoþ þe lede, 'lene me þy grace
For to go at þi gre; me gaynez non oþer.'
'Ris, aproche þen to prech! Lo, þe place here.
Lo, my lore is in þe loke. Lauce hit þerinne!'
þenne þe renk radly ros as he myȝt,
And to Ninivé þat naȝt he neȝed ful even.
Hit watz a cété ful syde and selly of brede,
On to þrenge þerþurȝe watz þre dayes dede;
þat on journay ful joynt Jonas hym ȝede
Er ever he warpped any worde to wyȝe þat he mette,
And þenne he cryed so cler þat kenne myȝt alle;
þe trwe tenor of his teme he tolde on þis wyse:
'Ȝet schal forty dayez fully fare to an ende,
And þenne schal Ninivé be nomen and to noȝt worþe.
Truly þis ilk toun schal tylte to grounde;
Up-so-doun schal ȝe dumpe depe to þe abyme
To be swolȝed swyftly wyth þe swart erþe,
And alle þat lyvyes hereinne lose þe swete.'
þis speche sprang in þat space and spradde alle aboute
To borges and to bacheleres þat in þat burȝ lenged;
Such a hidor hem hent and a hatel drede
þat al chaunged her chere and chylled at þe hert.
þe segge sesed not ȝet, bot sayde ever ilyche:
'þe verray vengaunce of God schal voyde þis place!'
þenne þe peple pitosly pleyned ful stylle
And for þe drede of dryȝtyn doured in hert.
Heter hayrez þay hent þat asperly bited,
And þose þay bounden to her bak and to her bare sydez,
Dropped dust on her hede and dymly bisoȝten
þat þat penaunce plesed him þat playnez on her wronge.
And ay he cryes in þat kyth tyl þe kyng herde,

346 'Will you never go to Nineve on any account?', and, with a play on another sense of *waye*, 'by no route of any kind'. The expression *no kynnez* has its origin in an OE genitive phrase meaning 'of no kind'.

348 **me gaynez non oþer** 'nothing else profits me'.

350 **loke** past participle, 'locked, enclosed'. Following this, *lauce* has both its primary sense 'set free' and its secondary sense 'utter'.

353–5 'It was a city very extensive and astonishing in its breadth, one that it was three days' effort to travel through. Jonah walked one whole day's journey altogether.' The sense of *journay* here is 'distance travelled in one day'. These lines translate Jonah 3.3–4: 'Now Ninive was a great city of three days' journey. And Jonas began to enter into the city one day's journey.'

364 **swete** 'sweat, life-blood'.

368 'That their mood quite changed and they grew cold in their heart.'

371–6 The Vulgate says only that they 'put on sackcloth' (Jonah 3.5).

376 **plesed** is past tense subjunctive, 'might please'.

And he radly upros and ran fro his chayer,
His ryche robe he torof of his rigge naked,
And of a hep of askes he hitte in þe myddez;
He askez heterly a hayre and hasped hym umbe,
Sewed a sekke þerabof and syked ful colde;
þer he dased in þat duste with droppande teres,
Wepande ful wonderly alle his wrange dedes.
þenne sayde he to his serjauntes: 'Samnes yow bilyve!
Do dryve out a decré, demed of myselven,
þat alle þe bodyes þat ben withinne þis borȝ quyk,
Boþe burnes and bestes, burdez and childer,
Uch prynce, uche prest and prelates alle,
Alle faste frely for her falce werkes.
Sesez childer of her sok, soghe hem so never,
Ne best bite on no brom ne no bent nauþer,
Passe to no pasture, ne pike non erbes,
Ne non oxe to no hay, ne no horse to water.
Al schal crye, forclemmed, with alle oure clere strenþe;
þe rurd schal ryse to hym þat rawþe schal have.
What wote oþer wyte may ȝif þe wyȝe lykes
þat is hende in þe hyȝt of his gentryse?
I wot his myȝt is so much, þaȝ he be myssepayed,
þat in his mylde amesyng he mercy may fynde;
And if we leven þe layk of oure layth synnes
And stylle steppen in þe styȝe he styȝtlez hymselven,
He wyl wende of his wodschip and his wrath leve
And forgif us þis gult ȝif we hym God leven.'
þenne al leved on his lawe and laften her synnes,
Parformed alle þe penaunce þat þe prynce radde,
And God þurȝ his godnesse forgef as he sayde,
þaȝ he oþer bihyȝt, withhelde his vengaunce.

380 'He jumped into the middle of a heap of ashes.'

387 'That all the people that are alive in this city.'

388–94 The Vulgate has 'let neither men nor beasts, oxen nor sheep, taste any thing: let them not feed nor drink water' (Jonah 3.7).

391 **soghe hem so never** 'however much it may trouble them'; the verb is impersonal (5.6.8) and subjunctive. With *so never*, 'however', cf. *never so*, ll. 156, 420.

397–8 'Who knows or can know whether the Lord, who is generous in the great extent of his kindness, will be pleased?'

401–5 There is play on *leven*, 'give up', past tense *laften* (401, 403, 405), and *leven*, 'believe' (404, 405).

402 'And walk quietly in the path that God himself ordains.'

407 **as he sayde** i.e. as *þe prynce* said he would.

408 'Withheld his vengeance even though he (God) had vowed otherwise.'

Muche sorȝe þenne satteled upon segge Jonas;
He wex as wroth as þe wynde towarde oure Lorde.
So hatz anger onhit his hert, he callez
A prayer to þe hyȝe prynce for pyne on þys wyse:
'I biseche þe, syre, now þouself jugge.
Watz not þis ilk my worde þat worþen is nouþe
þat I kest in my cuntré when þou þy carp sendez
þat I schulde tee to þys toun þi talent to preche?
Wel knew I þi cortaysye, þy quoynt soffraunce,
þy bounté of debonerté and þy bene grace,
þy longe abydyng wyth lur, þy late vengaunce;
And ay þy mercy is mete, be mysse never so huge.
I wyst wel when I hade worded quatsoever I cowþe
To manace alle þise mody men þat in þis mote dowellez,
Wyth a prayer and a pyne þay myȝt her pese gete,
And þerfore I wolde haf flowen fer into Tarce.
Now, Lorde, lach out my lyf, hit lastes to longe!
Bed me bilyve my bale-stour and bryng me on ende;
For me were swetter to swelt as swyþe, as me þynk,
þen lede lenger þi lore þat þus me les makez.'
þe soun of oure soverayn þen swey in his ere,
þat upbraydes þis burne upon a breme wyse:
'Herk, renk, is þis ryȝt so ronkly to wrath
For any dede þat I haf don oþer demed þe ȝet?'
  Jonas al joyles and janglande upryses
And haldez out on est half of þe hyȝe place,
And farandely on a felde he fettelez hym to bide,
For to wayte on þat won what schulde worþe after.
þer he busked hym a bour, þe best þat he myȝt,
Of hay and of ever-ferne and erbez a fewe,
For hit watz playn in þat place for plyande grevez
For to schylde fro þe schene oþer any schade keste.
He bowed under his lyttel boþe, his bak to þe sunne,

410 A common alliterative simile, but yet a reminder of the obedient winds as an instrument of God's wrath.

413 **þouself** 'you yourself' (5.4.4).

414–15 'Wasn't this very thing that has now happened the word that I spoke (i.e. what I said) in my country, when you sent your message?' This translates 'Is not this what I said, when I was yet in my own country?' (Jonah 4.2).

426–8 'Give me my death blow quickly and put an end to me, for it would be pleasanter for me to die at once, it seems to me, than to go on spreading your teaching that makes me untruthful in this way.'

434 'And goes out on the east side of the great city.'

436 **wayte** 'look': 'in order to see what would happen afterwards in that town'.

439 **playn . . . for** 'bare of'.

And þer he swowed and slept sadly al nyȝt,
þe whyle God of his grace ded growe of þat soyle
þe fayrest bynde hym abof þat ever burne wyste.
  When þe dawande day dryȝtyn con sende,
þenne wakened þe wyȝ under wodbynde,
Loked alofte on þe lef þat lylled grene.
Such a lefsel of lof never lede hade,
For hit watz brod at þe boþem, boȝted on lofte,
Happed upon ayþer half, a hous as hit were,
A nos on þe norþ syde and nowhere non ellez,
Bot al schet in a schaȝe þat schaded ful cole.
þe gome glyȝt on þe grene graciouse leves,
þat ever wayved a wynde so wyþe and so cole;
þe schyre sunne hit umbeschon, þaȝ no schafte myȝt
þe mountaunce of a lyttel mote upon þat man schyne.
þenne watz þe gome so glad of his gay logge,
Lys loltrande þerinne, lokande to toune,
So blyþe of his wodbynde he balteres þerunder,
þat of no diete þat day – þe devel haf! – he roȝt.
And ever he laȝed as he loked þe loge alle aboute,
And wysched hit were in his kyth þer he wony schulde,
On heȝe upon Effraym oþer Ermonnes hillez:
'Iwysse, a worþloker won to welde I never keped.'
And quen hit neȝed to naȝt, nappe hym bihoved;
He slydez on a sloumbe-slep sloghe under leves,
Whil God wayned a worme þat wrot upe þe rote,
And wyddered watz þe wodbynde bi þat þe wyȝe wakned.
And syþen he warnez þe west to waken ful softe,
And sayez unte Zeferus þat he syfle warme,
þat þer quikken no cloude bifore þe cler sunne,
And ho schal busch up ful brode and brenne as a candel.

442 **sadly** 'heavily'.

446 **wodbynde** a general term for a clinging plant. The Vulgate has *hedera*, 'ivy'.

450 'Covered on every side like a house.' The poet has invented the description of the bower.

451 The *nos* refers to some kind of projection such as a porch.

454–6 'Which a wind so mild and so cool stirred all the time. The bright sun shone around it, though no shaft of light, even to the extent of a little speck (i.e. in the smallest degree), could shine on that man.'

457–64 These lines are an expansion of 'Jonas was exceeding glad of the ivy' (Jonah 4.6).

460 'So that he didn't bother about any food that day – the Devil have it!'

463 Mount Ephraim and Mount Hermon are both mentioned frequently in the Old Testament.

464 **keped** 'wanted'.

469 **þe west** 'the west wind' (Zephyr).

Þen wakened þe wyȝe of his wyl dremes
And blusched to his wodbynde þat broþely watz marred,
Al welwed and wasted þo worþelych leves;
Þe schyre sunne hade hem schent er ever þe schalk wyst.
And þen hef up þe hete and heterly brenned,
Þe warm wynde of þe weste wertes he swyþez.
Þe man marred on þe molde þat moȝt hym not hyde;
His wodbynde watz away, he weped for sorȝe.
With hatel anger and hot heterly he callez:
'A, þou maker of man, what maystery þe þynkez
Þus þy freke to forfare forbi alle oþer?
With alle meschef þat þou may, never þou me sparez.
I kevered me a cumfort þat now is caȝt fro me,
My wodbynde so wlonk þat wered my heved,
Bot now I se þou art sette my solace to reve.
Why ne dyȝttez þou me to diȝe? I dure to longe.'
Ȝet oure Lorde to þe lede laused a speche:
'Is þis ryȝtwys, þou renk, alle þy ronk noyse,
So wroth for a wodbynde to wax so sone?
Why art þou so waymot, wyȝe, for so lyttel?'
'Hit is not lyttel,' quoþ þe lede, 'bot lykker to ryȝt.
I wolde I were of þis worlde wrapped in moldez.'
'Þenne byþenk þe, mon, if þe forþynk sore,
If I wolde help my hondewerk, haf þou no wonder.
Þou art waxen so wroth for þy wodbynde,
And travayledez never to tent hit þe tyme of an howre,
Bot at a wap hit here wax and away at anoþer,
And ȝet lykez þe so luþer, þi lyf woldez þou tyne.
Þenne wyte not me for þe werk, þat I hit wolde help,
And rwe on þo redles þat remen for synne.
Fyrst I made hem myself of materes myn one,
And syþen I loked hem ful longe and hem on lode hade.
And if I my travayl schulde tyne of termes so longe,
And type doun ȝonder toun when hit turned were,
Þe sor of such a swete place burde synk to my hert,

479 'The man who could not shelter himself suffered on the bare earth.'
482 **what . . . þynkez** 'what accomplishment does it seem to you'.
493 **lykker to ryȝt** 'more like what is right', that is, 'rather a matter of justice'.
494 **of** 'out of'.
495–6 'Then reflect, sir, if this greatly upsets *you*, don't be surprised if I wanted to help the work of my hands.'
501 'Then do not blame me for wanting to help my handiwork.'
503 **materes** presumably the four elements of earth, air, fire and water. **myn one** 'by myself alone'.
505 **of termes so longe** 'of such long duration', that is, 'that took so long'.
506 **turned** 'converted'. So also *wyl torne*, 'will be converted', l. 518.

So mony malicious mon as mournez þerinne.
And of þat soumme ȝet arn summe, such sottez formadde
As lyttel barnez on barme þat never bale wroȝt,
And wymmen unwytté þat wale ne couþe
Þat on hande fro þat oþer, for alle þis hyȝe worlde,
Bitwene þe stele and þe stayre disserne noȝt cunen,
What rule renes in roun bitwene þe ryȝt hande
And his lyfte, þaȝ his lyf schulde lost be þerfor;
And als þer ben doumbe bestez in þe burȝ mony
Þat may not synne in no syt hemselven to greve;
Why schulde I wrath wyth hem, syþen wyȝez wyl torne
And cum and cnawe me for kyng and my carpe leve?
Wer I as hastif as þou, heere, were harme lumpen;
Couþe I not þole bot as þou, þer þryved ful fewe.
I may not be so malicious and mylde be halden,
For malyse is noȝt to mayntyne boute mercy withinne.'
Be noȝt so gryndel, godman, bot go forth þy wayes,
Be preue and be pacient in payne and in joye,
For he þat is to rakel to renden his cloþez
Mot efte sitte with more unsounde to sewe hem togeder.
Forþy when poverté me enprecez and paynez innoȝe
Ful softly with suffraunce saȝttel me bihovez;
Forþy penaunce and payne topreve hit in syȝt
Þat pacience is a nobel poynt, þaȝ hit displese ofte. Amen.

509–15 'And of that number there are furthermore some, such people without reason as small children in the lap, who never did wrong, and madwomen that for all this great world could not tell one hand from the other, (people who) cannot recognize the difference between the rung and the upright of a ladder (or recognize) what mysterious rule exists between (i.e. how to distinguish between) the right hand and one's left, even though one's life should be lost for it.' The Vulgate ends: 'persons that know not how to distinguish between their right hand and their left, and many beasts'. Lines 513–15 do not conform to the usual four-line grouping (see Headnote), and it may be that one line has been lost before l. 513.

517 **synne in no syt** 'do any evil'.

520 'If I were as hasty as you, sir, wrong would be done.'

522–3 'I could not be so severe and yet be regarded as merciful, for severity is not to be exercised unless there is mercy in it.'

523–4 Modern punctuation is forced to make a sharp distinction between God's speech and the poet's final comments. The manuscript has no punctuation and makes no such distinction: see ch. 7. However, *godman* is the preacher's form of address; compare the Pardoner's '"Goode men", I seye', *Canterbury Tales* VI 352 and 377.

529 'I am obliged quietly to reconcile myself to patience.'

530 **topreve hit in syȝt** 'make it obvious'.

531 As in *Pearl* and *Gawain*, the end of the poem echoes the beginning.

9

Sir Gawain and the Green Knight

Sir Gawain and the Green Knight follows *Patience* as the last item in British Library MS Cotton Nero A X. Unlike the other three poems in the manuscript, all of which are on religious themes, *Gawain* is a romance set in the court of King Arthur. The first episode from the poem, given here, recounts the New Year visit of the Green Knight to the court and the strange beheading-game that he offers them.

Several other versions of the beheading-game are known, the earliest in the Irish story *Bricriu's Feast*, and others in French. The closest parallel is *Le Livre de Carados* of the thirteenth century, in which a knight arriving at Arthur's court challenges the king's nephew Carados to a beheading-game, returning to the court a year after his beheading to give the return blow. Translations of these and other analogues are given by E. Brewer, *From Cuchulainn to Gawain* (Cambridge, 1973).

Gawain falls into four sections marked by large flourished capitals in the manuscript. In the second section, Sir Gawain sets off northwards to find the Green Knight as he had promised, arriving on Christmas Eve at a castle where he is lavishly entertained over the Christmas season, and is persuaded into an agreement with his host whereby each will exchange whatever he wins. In the third section, while the host goes hunting, his wife on three occasions visits Sir Gawain in his bedroom. On two evenings Gawain and the lord of the castle exchange kisses for hunting spoils, but Gawain fails to hand over the lady's gift of the third day, a magic, life-saving girdle. In the last section, Gawain rides to meet the Green Knight to receive his return blow at the Green Chapel nearby. After two feigned strokes, the Green Knight cuts Sir Gawain slightly, revealing that he was his host at the castle, and reproving him for his failure to keep his agreement. Sir Gawain returns home to Arthur's court, bitterly ashamed at his failure in *trawþe*.

The emphasis on the knightly virtue of *trawþe*, loyalty to a pledged word, runs throughout the poem (see note to ll. 394–403). It is Gawain's failure, as he sees it, in *trawþe* that leads to his humiliation, though both the Green Knight and Arthur take a more generous view of Gawain's conduct.

The unrhymed alliterative lines of *Patience* and *Erkenwald* are in *Gawain* divided into verse-paragraphs of irregular length by the addition of a rhyming section of five lines, rhyming: *a* (the one-stress 'bob') *baba* (the 'wheel' of three stresses). The 'bob and wheel' is sometimes used to remarkable effect, as in ll. 146–50 and 296–300.

For comments on style and vocabulary, the date, authorship and the manuscript, see the Headnote to *Patience* above.

Editions

Malcolm Andrew and Ronald Waldron, *The Poems of the Pearl Manuscript* (London, 1978)

J. A. Burrow, *Sir Gawain and the Green Knight* (Harmondsworth, 1972; New Haven, 1982)

A. C. Cawley and J. J. Anderson, *Pearl, Cleanness, Patience, Sir Gawain and the Green Knight* (London and New York, 1976)

J. R. R. Tolkien and E. V. Gordon, revised N. Davis, *Sir Gawain and the Green Knight* (Oxford, 1967)

Studies

David Aers, *Community, Gender, and Individual Identity* (London, 1988), pp. 153–78

Marie Borroff, *Sir Gawain and the Green Knight: A Stylistic and Metrical Study* (New Haven, 1962)

J. A. Burrow, *A Reading of Sir Gawain and the Green Knight* (London, 1965)

A. C. Spearing, *The Gawain-Poet* (Cambridge, 1970)

Siþen þe sege and þe assaut watz sesed at Troye,
þe borȝ brittened and brent to brondez and askez,
þe tulk þat þe trammes of tresoun þer wroȝt
Watz tried for his tricherie, þe trewest on erthe,
Hit watz Ennias þe athel and his highe kynde
þat siþen depreced provinces and patrounes bicome

1–19 This account of the foundation of Britain by Brutus, great-grandson of Aeneas who had fled from the ruins of Troy, goes back to Geoffrey of Monmouth, *The History of the Kings of Britain* 1.3 and 16.

3 **þe tulk** either Aeneas (*Ennias*, l. 5) or Antenor. For discussion of the interpretation and punctuation of ll. 1–7, see ch. 7.

5 **highe kynde** 'noble kindred'. Geoffrey describes the victorious colonization of Europe by the Trojans.

Welneȝe of al þe wele in þe west iles.
Fro riche Romulus to Rome ricchis hym swyþe,
With gret bobbaunce þat burȝe he biges upon fyrst
And nevenes hit his aune nome as hit now hat;
Ticius to Tuskan and teldes bigynnes,
Langaberde in Lumbardie lyftes up homes,
And fer over þe French flod Felix Brutus
On mony bonkkes ful brode Bretayn he settez
Wyth wynne;
Where werre and wrake and wonder
Bi syþez hatz wont þerinne,
And oft boþe blysse and blunder
Ful skete hatz skyfted synne.

Ande quen þis Bretayn watz bigged bi þis burn rych,
Bolde bredden þerinne baret þat lofden,
In mony turned tyme tene þat wroȝten.
Mo ferlyes on þis folde han fallen here oft
Þen in any oþer þat I wot syn þat ilk tyme.
Bot of alle þat here bult of Bretaygne kynges,
Ay watz Arthur þe hendest as I haf herde telle;
Forþi an aunter in erde I attle to schawe,
Þat a selly in siȝt summe men hit holden
And an outtrage awenture of Arthurez wonderez.
If ȝe wyl lysten þis laye bot on littel quile,

7 **west iles** 'western lands', i.e. Europe.
8 **Fro** 'when', as also in l. 62.
ricchis hym 'goes'. On the use of the historic present, see 5.6.1.
11 'Ticius goes to Tuscany and establishes settlements.' The legendary founder of Tuscany is elsewhere named Tuscus. On the omission of the verb of motion, see 5.6.9.
12 **Langaberde** the legendary ancestor of the Langobardi or Lombards.
lyftes up 'sets up, builds'.
13 **þe French flod** the English Channel.
Felix Brutus The Latin epithet *felix*, 'fortunate, faithful', was used as a title for founders of cities.
17 **Bi syþez** 'from time to time'.
19 'Have very rapidly alternated since.'
21 **Bolde** 'bold men'. This use of an adjective as a noun is especially characteristic of alliterative verse; so also *riche*, 'noble people, courtiers', l. 66 etc. See 5.5.3.
22 'Who caused trouble in many a turbulent time.'
25 **of Bretaygne** qualifies *kynges*: 'But of all the kings of Britain who lived here.'
26 Arthur was a descendant of Brutus, according to Geoffrey of Monmouth.
27 **in erde** here means no more than 'truly'.
30–4 The narrator announces that he will recite his story to his audience as he himself heard it related *in toun*, 'among a group of people'. It is not, however, a tale orally handed down, but a text of considerable antiquity, *stad and stoken*, 'set down and fixed (in writing)'.

I schal telle hit as tit, as I in toun herde
With tonge;
As hit is stad and stoken
In stori stif and stronge,
With lel letteres loken
In londe so hatz ben longe.

Þis kyng lay at Camylot upon Krystmasse
With mony luflych lorde, ledez of þe best,
Rekenly of þe Rounde Table alle þo rich breþer,
With rych revel oryȝt and rechles merþes.
Þer tournayed tulkes by tymez ful mony,
Justed ful jolilé þise gentyle kniȝtes,
Syþen kayred to þe court caroles to make,
For þer þe fest watz ilyche ful fiften dayes,
With alle þe mete and þe mirþe þat men couþe avyse;
Such glaum ande gle glorious to here,
Dere dyn upon day, daunsyng on nyȝtes,
Al watz hap upon heȝe in hallez and chambrez
With lordez and ladies as levest him þoȝt.
With all þe wele of þe worlde þay woned þer samen,
Þe most kyd knyȝtez under Krystes selven
And þe lovelokkest ladies þat ever lif haden,
And he þe comlokest kyng þat þe court haldes;
For al watz þis fayre folk in her first age
On sille;
Þe hapnest under heven,
Kyng hyȝest mon of wylle;
Hit were now gret nye to neven
So hardy a here on hille.

35–6 'Embodied in an authentic text as it has long been here.' The sense of *letteres* is probably 'written account, narrative', as in *The Destruction of Troy* 26, 'By lokyng of letturs þat lefte were of olde'; see *MED lettre* 3 (a). Some editors would interpret the lines as a reference to the antiquity of the alliterative tradition, taking *lel* to mean 'correct' rather than 'truthful', and *letteres* to mean '(alliterating) letters'.

39 **Rekenly** qualifies *lay at Camylot*: 'All those noble brothers of the Round Table (lodged at Camelot) in splendour.'

43 **caroles** are dances accompanied by song. The term is fully discussed in R. L. Greene, *The Early English Carols* (2nd edn, Oxford, 1977), esp. pp. xxviii–xxix.

44 **ilyche ful** 'equally lavish'.

49 **as levest him þoȝt** 'as seemed best to them'; see 5.6.8.

51 **under Krystes selven** that is, 'on earth'.

54 **first age** 'the early part of youth, after childhood and before full maturity' (Mary Dove, *The Perfect Age of Man's Life* (Cambridge, 1986), 136). Cf. ll. 86–9, where the suggestion of youthfulness becomes more prominent.

55 **On sille** literally 'on the floor', hence 'in the hall'.

56–9 'The most fortunate people on earth, their king a man pre-eminent in courage; it would today be very difficult to name so bold a company on a castle-mound.'

Wyle Nw 3er watz so 3ep þat hit watz nwe cummen,
þat day doubble on þe dece watz þe douth served.
Fro þe kyng watz cummen with kny3tes into þe halle,
þe chauntré of þe chapel cheved to an ende,
Loude crye watz þer kest of clerkez and oþer,
'Nowel!' nayted onewe, nevened ful ofte;
And syþen riche forth runnen to reche hondeselle,
3e3ed 3eres 3iftes on hi3, 3elde hem bi hond,
Debated busyly aboute þo giftes.
Ladies la3ed ful loude, þo3 þay lost haden,
And he þat wan watz not wrothe – þat may 3e wel trawe.
Alle þis mirþe þay maden to þe mete tyme;
When þay had waschen worþyly þay wenten to sete,
þe best burne ay abof, as hit best semed,
Whene Guenore ful gay grayþed in þe myddes,
Dressed on þe dere des, dubbed al aboute,
Smal sendal bisides, a selure hir over
Of tryed tolouse, of tars tapites innoghe,
þat were enbrawded and beten wyth þe best gemmes
þat my3t be preved of prys wyth penyes to bye
In daye.
þe comlokest to discrye
þer glent with y3en gray,
A semloker þat ever he sy3e
Soth mo3t no mon say.

Bot Arthure wolde not ete til al were served,
He watz so joly of his joyfnes and sumquat childgered;

60 'While New Year was so fresh it had only just arrived'; that is, on New Year's Day.

65 '"Noel!" was proclaimed anew, often called out.'

67–8 'Announced New Year's presents loudly, handed them over, eagerly argued about those gifts.' It is no longer clear what custom is here referred to; evidently some game in which the losers do not feel too distressed (l. 69).

71 '. . . until dinner time.'

73 'In each case (*ay*) the best man in the more honoured position (*abof*) . . .' What is described is a medieval banquet with a high table at which the guests are ranked according to precedence, rather than a Round Table where all are equal.

74 **Whene Guenore** 'Queen Guenevere'.

75–7 'Arrayed on the high dais, adorned all around, with fine fabric at her side, a canopy of excellent cloth of Toulouse over her, and many wall-hangings of Tharsian fabric.'

79–80 'That could be proved of value to buy with money', i.e. 'that money might buy'. The 'bob' line (80) is a tag meaning 'ever'.

81 **comlokest** 'most lovely person' (4.4.3), referring to Guenevere.

83–4 'Truly no one could say that he had ever seen a more attractive lady.' *Semloker* is a comparative adjective used as a noun.

86 'He was so vigorous in his youthfulness and somewhat boyish' (*ch* alliterates with *j*). *Childgered* is literally 'with the behaviour of a child'. Taken together with the

His lif liked hym ly3t, he lovied þe lasse
Auþer to longe lye or to longe sitte,
So bisied him his 3onge blod and his brayn wylde.
And also anoþer maner meved him eke,
Þat he þur3 nobelay had nomen: he wolde never ete
Upon such a dere day er hym devised were
Of sum aventurus þyng an uncouþe tale,
Of sum mayn mervayle þat he my3t trawe,
Of alderes, of armes, of oþer aventurus;
Oþer sum segg hym biso3t of sum siker kny3t
To joyne wyth hym in justyng, in jopardé to lay,
Lede, lif for lyf, leve uchon oþer,
As fortune wolde fulsun hom, þe fayrer to have.
Þis watz kynges countenaunce where he in court were
At uch farand fest among his fre meny
In halle.
Þerfore of face so fere
He sti3tlez stif in stalle;
Ful 3ep in þat Nw 3ere
Much mirthe he mas with alle.

Thus þer stondes in stale þe stif kyng hisselven,
Talkkande bifore þe hy3e table of trifles ful hende;
There gode Gawan watz grayþed Gwenore bisyde,
And Agravayn a la Dure Mayn on þat oþer syde sittes –
Boþe þe kynges sister-sunes and ful siker kni3tes.

---

lines that follow, this is a remarkable description of a boyish king, developing the description of the court *in her first age* (l. 54). The Green Knight is to refer insultingly to the court's youthfulness, l. 280.

87 'An energetic life pleased him . . .'

91ff. Arthur's refusal to eat until he has seen a marvel is a standard feature in romance, and appears in the closest analogue, the Carados story.

92–3 **er . . . tale** 'until there was related to him an unknown tale of some daring action'. Arthur will not eat until he has heard a story previously unknown but credible (ll. 92–5), or received a challenge (ll. 96–9).

96–9 'Or someone requested him for a trusty knight to fight with him in a joust, a knight (*lede*) to put at risk (his) life for (the other's) life, each one allow the other to have the advantage, as fortune might reward them.'

104 **sti3tlez . . . in stalle** 'stands'.

109–13 The seating is in this arrangement:

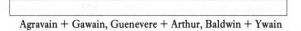

Agravain + Gawain, Guenevere + Arthur, Baldwin + Ywain

Guenevere is in the middle of the high table (l. 74), on the left of the place where Arthur will sit. To the left of the Queen is Gawain, and on his other side is his brother Agravain *a la Dure Mayn*, 'of the Hard Hand'. They are sons of Arthur's sister and King Lot of Orkney.

Bischop Bawdewyn abof biginez þe table,
And Ywan, Uryn son, ette with hymselven.
þise were diȝt on þe des and derworþly served,
And siþen mony siker segge at þe sidbordez.
þen þe first cors come with crakkyng of trumpes,
Wyth mony baner ful bryȝt þat þerbi henged,
Nwe nakryn noyse with þe noble pipes,
Wylde werbles and wyȝt wakned lote,
þat mony hert ful hiȝe hef at her towches,
Dayntés dryven þerwyth of ful dere metes,
Foysoun of þe fresche, and on so fele disches
þat pine to fynde þe place þe peple biforne
For to sette þe sylveren þat sere sewes halden
    On clothe.
  Iche lede as he loved hymselve
  þer laght withouten loþe;
  Ay two had disches twelve,
  Good ber and bryȝt wyn boþe.

Now wyl I of hor servise say yow no more,
For uch wyȝe may wel wit no wont þat þer were;
Anoþer noyse ful newe neȝed bilive,
þat þe lude myȝt haf leve liflode to cach,
For uneþe watz þe noyce not a whyle sesed,
And þe fyrst cource in þe court kyndely served,
þer hales in at þe halle dor an aghlich mayster,
On þe most on þe molde on mesure hyghe;
Fro þe swyre to þe swange so sware and so þik,
And his lyndes and his lymes so longe and so grete,
Half etayn in erde I hope þat he were,
Bot mon most I algate mynn hym to bene,

112 **biginez þe table** 'sits at the place of honour', on Arthur's right hand.

113 **with hymselven** 'with him' (Bishop Baldwin). The diners, as was customary, are seated in pairs. Ywain, son of King Urien, is the hero of a famous romance by Chrétien de Troyes (*c.* 1177).

114–15 Those at the high table (*des*) are served first, and then (*siþen*) those at the side tables.

123 'That (it was) difficult . . .'

126 **loved hymselve** 'liked for himself'.

128 'In each case two people had twelve dishes.'

131 **no wont þat þer were** 'that there was no shortage'.

132 **Anoþer noyse** in addition to the noise of drums and pipes.

133 'So that the man (Arthur) might have leave to take food'; cf. 91ff.

134 On the double negative *uneþe . . . not*, see 5.7.

137 'The largest on earth in height.' For *On þe most*, 'the very greatest', see 5.5.2.

140–1 'I suppose he was really half a giant, but at any rate I declare him to be the largest man.' For *in erde*, see 27n., and for this sense of *hope*, see 8/212n.

And þat þe myriest in his muckel þat my3t ride;
For of bak and of brest al were his bodi sturne,
Both his wombe and his wast were worthily smale,
And alle his fetures fol3ande in forme þat he hade
Ful clene.
For wonder of his hwe men hade,
Set in his semblaunt sene;
He ferde as freke were fade,
And overal enker grene.

Ande al grayþed in grene þis gome and his wedes,
A strayt cote ful stre3t þat stek on his sides,
A meré mantile abof, mensked withinne
With pelure pured apert, þe pane ful clene
With blyþe blaunner ful bry3t, and his hod boþe
þat watz la3t fro his lokkez and layde on his schulderes;
Heme wel-haled hose of þat same grene,
þat spenet on his sparlyr, and clene spures under
Of bry3t golde upon silk bordes barred ful ryche;
And scholes under schankes þere þe schalk rides.
And alle his vesture verayly watz clene verdure,
Boþe þe barres of his belt and oþer blyþe stones
þat were richely rayled in his aray clene
Aboutte hymself and his sadel upon silk werkez,
þat were to tor for to telle of tryfles þe halve
þat were enbrauded abof wyth bryddes and fly3es,
With gay gaudi of grene, þe golde ay inmyddes.

143 **al** 'although': 'for although his body was forbidding in back and chest'.

145 **fol3ande in forme** 'in proportion to (literally 'following') the shape'. The visitor, though huge, has the flat stomach and slender waist and the proportionate features of an elegant knight.

146 **clene** 'elegant' (or adverb, 'elegantly').

148 'Set plain to see in his appearance.'

149 'He behaved as a knight who was hostile (?).' According to *MED*, the meanings of *fade* range from 'acting as an intruder' to 'bold'.

151–9 The knight wears clothes of green: a tight-fitting tunic (*cote*), over that an elegant furred mantle or gown and a hood thrown back over his shoulders. His tight hose is also green, and his gold spurs are fastened with silk bands.

154 Fur that is *pured* has been trimmed so as to show only one colour.

155 **boþe** 'as well'; that is, his hood was also green.

158 'That fastened on his calf.' Hose was made separately for each leg and tied at the top; the Wife of Bath's 'hosen weren of fyn scarlet reed / Ful streite yteyd' (*Canterbury Tales* I 456–7).

160 **scholes** 'shoeless'. Soled hose was worn without shoes, here an indication that the knight has not come equipped for combat (see ll. 267–71).

165–6 'It would be too difficult to tell of half the little things that were embroidered on it . . .'

þe pendauntes of his payttrure, þe proude cropure,
His molaynes and alle þe metail anamayld was þenne,
þe steropes þat he stod on stayned of þe same,
And his arsounz al after and his aþel scurtes,
þat ever glemered and glent al of grene stones.
þe fole þat he ferkkes on fyn of þat ilke,
Sertayn;
A grene hors gret and þikke,
A sted ful stif to strayne,
In brawden brydel quik;
To þe gome he watz ful gayn.

Wel gay watz þis gome gered in grene,
And þe here of his hed of his hors swete.
Fayre fannand fax umbefoldes his schulderes,
A much berd as a busk over his brest henges,
þat wyth his hiȝlich here þat of his hed reches
Watz evesed al umbetorne abof his elbowes,
þat half his armes þerunder were halched in þe wyse
Of a kyngez capados þat closes his swyre;
þe mane of þat mayn hors much to hit lyke,
Wel cresped and cemmed wyth knottes ful mony,
Folden in wyth fildore aboute þe fayre grene,
Ay a herle of þe here, anoþer of golde.
þe tayl and his toppyng twynnen of a sute,
And bounden boþe wyth a bande of a bryȝt grene,
Dubbed wyth ful dere stonez as þe dok lasted,
Syþen þrawen wyth a þwong, a þwarle knot alofte,
þer mony bellez ful bryȝt of brende golde rungen.
Such a fole upon folde ne freke þat hym rydes

168–72 The equipment of the horse is similarly green and gold. The *payttrure* or peytrel is a breast-strap; the *cropure* or crupper goes round the hindquarters; *molaynes* are perhaps studs on the bridle; *arsounz* are the bows at the front and back of the saddle.

171 **after** 'in the same fashion'.

173 'The horse that he rides on bright with the same (colour).' As in the previous stanza, the poet keeps to the last the information about the green skin, in this case of the horse.

180 **of his hors swete** 'a match for his horse'.

183–6 The great beard and the fine hair from his head are clipped level above his elbows, thus covering his arms in the fashion of a short cape. A *capados* is apparently a hood with a cape attached.

187–90 The horse's green mane is curled and combed, and interwoven with a strand of gold thread for every strand of hair.

191 'The tail and his forelock match up' (*OED twin v.*[2]). *Sute* is the same noun as *swete*, l. 180.

193 **as þe dok lasted** 'as far as the dock (fleshy part of the tail) lasted'.

Watz never sene in þat sale wyth syȝt er þat tyme
With yȝe.
He loked as layt so lyȝt,
So sayd al þat hym syȝe;
Hit semed as no mon myȝt
Under his dynttez dryȝe.

Wheþer hade he no helme ne hawbergh nauþer,
Ne no pysan ne no plate þat pented to armes,
Ne no schafte ne no schelde to schwve ne to smyte,
Bot in his on honde he hade a holyn bobbe
þat is grattest in grene when grevez ar bare,
And an ax in his oþer, a hoge and unmete,
A spetos sparþe to expoun in spelle quoso myȝt.
þe lenkþe of an elnȝerde þe large hede hade,
þe grayn al of grene stele and of golde hewen,
þe bit burnyst bryȝt with a brod egge,
As wel schapen to schere as scharp rasores.
þe stele of a stif staf þe sturne hit bi grypte,
þat watz wounden wyth yrn to þe wandez ende
And al bigraven with grene in gracios werkes,
A lace lapped aboute þat louked at þe hede
And so after þe halme halched ful ofte,
Wyth tryed tasselez þerto tacched innoghe
On botounz of þe bryȝt grene brayden ful ryche.
þis haþel heldez hym in and þe halle entres,
Drivande to þe heȝe dece, dut he no woþe,
Haylsed he never one, bot heȝe he overloked.
þe fyrst word þat he warp, 'Wher is', he sayd,

199 'He looked at them as swiftly (*lyȝt*) as lightning (*layt*)'.

201–2 'It appeared that no-one could survive under his blows.'

203 **Wheþer** 'yet, even so'. Despite his threatening appearance, the knight has not come armed for combat.

206–7 The branch of holly is a symbol of peace (see ll. 265–6), and like the knight it is green.

209 'A cruel blade to describe in words, if anyone might.'

211 This massive axe-head has a spike (*grayn*) at the back, made of green steel and gold.

214 'The grim fellow gripped it by the handle of a strong shaft.' *Stele* is OE *stela*, 'stalk' (not OE *stēle*, 'steel' as in l. 211). The axe-shaft is bound with iron, with elegant green engraving; around it is looped a lace with tassles attached by bright green studs.

221–7 The Green Knight, acting according to the custom of hostile challengers in romances, rides straight up to the high table, greeting none of the courtiers, and unceremoniously demands to know where the king is. Arthur is not seated in his place (ll. 107–8).

'þe governour of þis gyng? Gladly I wolde
Se þat segg in syȝt and with hymself speke
Raysoun.'
To knyȝtez he kest his yȝe,
And reled hym up and doun,
He stemmed and con studie
Quo walt þer most renoun.

Ther watz lokyng on lenþe þe lude to beholde,
For uch mon had mervayle quat hit mene myȝt
þat a haþel and a horse myȝt such a hwe lach
As growe grene as þe gres and grener hit semed
þen grene aumayl on golde glowande bryȝter.
Al studied þat þer stod and stalked hym nerre
Wyth al þe wonder of þe worlde what he worch schulde,
For fele sellyez had þay sen, bot such never are;
Forþi for fantoum and fayryȝe þe folk þere hit demed.
þerfore to answare watz arȝe mony aþel freke,
And al stouned at his steven and ston-stil seten
In a swoghe sylence þurȝ þe sale riche,
As al were slypped upon slepe so slaked hor lotez
In hyȝe.
I deme hit not al for doute,
Bot sum for cortaysye;
Bot let hym þat al schulde loute
Cast unto þat wyȝe.

þenn Arþour bifore þe hiȝ dece þat aventure byholdez
And rekenly hym reverenced, for rad was he never,
And sayde 'Wyȝe, welcum iwys to þis place!
þe hede of þis ostel, Arthour I hat.
Liȝt luflych adoun and lenge, I þe praye,
And quatso þy wylle is we schal wyt after.'
'Nay, as help me', quoþ þe haþel, 'he þat on hyȝe syttes,

225 **þe governour of þis gyng** 'the master of this company'. The words are abrupt and perhaps a little disrespectful.

229 **reled hym** 'rolled them' (his eyes).

230 'He paused and looked to see.' *Con* forms a past tense; see 5.6.3.

237 'All those who were standing there looked intently and approached closer to him.' The reference is to the servants, rather than the knights who remained seated *ston-stil* (l. 242).

239 **such never are** 'never anything like it before'.

246–9 'I suppose it was not entirely because of fear, but partly out of courtesy; at any rate they let him to whom all had to defer (i.e. Arthur) deal with that man.' The subject pronoun 'they' is not expressed; see 5.4.2.

253 A direct answer to the Green Knight's question of 224–5.

256 An emphatic form of 'So help me God!'

To wone any quyle in þis won hit watz not myn ernde;
Bot for þe los of þe, lede, is lyft up so hy3e,
And þy bur3 and þy burnes best ar holden,
Stifest under stel-gere on stedes to ryde,
Þe wy3test and þe worþyest of þe worldes kynde,
Preue for to play wyth in oþer pure laykez,
And here is kydde cortaysye as I haf herd carp –
And þat hatz wayned me hider iwyis at þis tyme.
3e may be seker bi þis braunch þat I bere here
Þat I passe as in pes and no ply3t seche;
For had I founded in fere in fe3tyng wyse,
I have a hauberghe at home and a helme boþe,
A schelde and a scharp spere schinande bry3t,
Ande oþer weppenes to welde, I wene wel als;
Bot for I wolde no were, my wedez ar softer.
Bot if þou be so bold as alle burnez tellen,
Þou wyl grant me godly þe gomen þat I ask
    Bi ry3t.'
  Arthour con onsware
  And sayd, 'Sir cortays kny3t,
  If þou crave batayl bare,
  Here faylez þou not to fy3t.'

'Nay, frayst I no fy3t, in fayth I þe telle!
Hit arn aboute on þis bench bot berdlez chylder.
If I were hasped in armes on a he3e stede,
Here is no mon me to mach for my3tez so wayke.
Forþy I crave in þis court a Crystemas gomen,
For hit is 3ol and Nwe 3er and here ar 3ep mony.
If any so hardy in þis hous holdez hymselven,
Be so bolde in his blod, brayn in hys hede,

258 **for** '(I have come here) because'. The knight gives three reasons: (a) Arthur's personal fame, (b) the repute of the knights as warriors, (c) the court's reputation for courtesy. Towards the end of the poem (2457ff.) he explains more specifically that the purpose was to test 'þe grete renoun of þe Rounde Table'.

262 **oþer pure laykez** noble sports other than the jousting of l. 260.

267 **in fere** probably 'in a group', that is, 'with a band of knights'; *MED fere* n. (2).

in fe3tyng wyse 'equipped for combat'.

271 **for I wolde no were** 'because I didn't want a battle'.

273 **gomen** 'game'; a word used eighteen times in the poem, with varying degrees of irony.

275 **con onsware** 'answered'.

277 **bare** that is, 'without armour', as again in l. 290. Arthur, anxious to retrieve the honour of the court, misunderstands the request and asserts that the knight will find a combatant if he wants one.

285 'If anyone in this castle thinks himself so brave.'

þat dar stifly strike a strok for anoþer,
I schal gif hym of my gyft þys giserne ryche,
þis ax þat is hevé innogh to hondele as hym lykes;
And I schal bide þe fyrst bur as bare as I sitte.
If any freke be so felle to fonde þat I telle,
Lepe ly3tly me to and lach þis weppen;
I quit-clayme hit for ever, kepe hit as his auen;
And I schal stonde hym a strok stif on þis flet,
Ellez þou wyl di3t me þe dom to dele hym anoþer,
    Barlay;
  And 3et gif hym respite
  A twelmonyth and a day.
  Now hy3e and let se tite
  Dar any herinne o3t say.'

If he hem stowned upon fyrst, stiller were þanne
Alle þe heredmen in halle, þe hy3 and þe lo3e.
þe renk on his rouncé hym ruched in his sadel
And runischly his rede y3en he reled aboute,
Bende his bresed bro3ez blycande grene,
Wayved his berde for to wayte quoso wolde ryse.
When non wolde kepe hym with carp, he co3ed ful hy3e
Ande rimed hym ful richly and ry3t hym to speke.
'What, is þis Arþures hous', quoþ þe haþel þenne,
'þat al þe rous rennes of þur3 ryalmes so mony?
Where is now your sourquydrye and your conquestes,
Your gryndellayk and your greme and your grete wordes?
Now is þe revel and þe renoun of þe Rounde Table
Overwalt wyth a worde of on wy3es speche,

287 **for** 'in exchange for'. A very general reference to the beheading game.

291 **to fonde þat I telle** 'to attempt what I suggest'.

294 **stonde hym** 'take from him'.

295–6 **Ellez** as a conjunction means 'provided that': 'on condition that you will grant me the right to strike him another (blow) in return'. The meaning of *barlay* is uncertain, though it has been identified with the cry 'barley' used as a truce-term by children in the North-West Midlands; see I. and P. Opie, *The Lore and Language of Schoolchildren* (Oxford, 1959), 135, 146–9.

298 'A year and a day'; 'a period constituting a term for certain purposes, in order to ensure the completion of a full year' (*OED year*, 7b). This phrase, together with *quit-clayme*, *dom* and *respite*, reinforces the legal formality of the contract, in contrast to the knight's description of it as a *Crystemas gomen.*

299 **hy3e** imperative, 'hurry up'.

306 **wayte** 'observe': 'turned his beard from side to side to see who would get up'.

307 **kepe hym with carp** 'engage him in conversation', that is, 'reply to him'.

308 'And drew himself up very proudly and prepared to speak.'

310 **þat . . . of** 'about which'.

For al dares for drede withoute dynt schewed!'
Wyth þis he laȝes so loude þat þe lorde greved,
þe blod schot for scham into his schyre face
    And lere;
  He wex as wroth as wynde,
  So did alle þat þer were;
  þe kynge, as kene bi kynde,
  þen stod þat stif mon nere,

Ande sayde, 'Haþel, by heven þyn askyng is nys,
And as þou foly hatz frayst, fynde þe behoves.
I know no gome þat is gast of þy grete wordes.
Gif me now þy geserne, upon Godez halve,
And I schal bayþen þy bone þat þou boden habbes.'
Lyȝtly lepez he hym to and laȝt at his honde.
þen feersly þat oþer freke upon fote lyȝtis.
Now hatz Arthure his axe and þe halme grypez
And sturnely sturez hit aboute, þat stryke wyth hit þoȝt.
þe stif mon hym bifore stod upon hyȝt,
Herre þen ani in þe hous by þe hede and more;
Wyth sturne schere þer he stod he stroked his berde,
And wyth a countenaunce dryȝe he droȝ doun his cote,
No more mate ne dismayd for hys mayn dintez
þen any burne upon bench hade broȝt hym to drynk
    Of wyne.
  Gawan þat sate bi þe quene,
  To þe kyng he can enclyne:
  'I beseche now with saȝez sene
  þis melly mot be myne.

'Wolde ȝe, worþilych lorde,' quoþ Wawan to þe kyng,

315 **dares** 'are cowering' (plural).

319 **as wroth as wynde** a rather common alliterative simile, as in 8/410.

321 'The King, as a bold man by nature.'

324 **fynde þe behoves** 'it is right that you find it'.

328–9 Arthur goes up to the knight and takes the axe from him. The knight then dismounts.

331 **þat stryke wyth hit þoȝt** 'intending to strike with it'.

336 **hys mayn dintez** 'Arthur's powerful practice blows'.

337 **þen** 'than if'.

341 **saȝez sene** 'plain words'. For adjectival *sene*, see also l. 148.

343–61 Gawain addresses Arthur with the polite *ȝe*, in contrast to the Green Knight's more abrupt *þou* (see 5.4.1). His whole speech is characterized by elaborate courtesy: he asks Arthur to command him to leave the table and he hopes Guenevere at his side will not be offended; he argues that the king himself should not have to deal with such an arrogant proposal, but that he, the least of the knights, whose only virtue is kinship with Arthur, has a right to it, having asked first to take on this foolish business.

343 **Wolde ȝe** a conditional clause, 'if you would'; see 5.9.1 (iii).

Wawan this is a regular form of Gawain's name necessary for the alliteration.

'Bid me boȝe fro þis benche and stonde by yow þere,
þat I wythoute vylanye myȝt voyde þis table,
And þat my legge lady lyked not ille,
I wolde com to your counseyl bifore your cort ryche;
For me þink hit not semly, as hit is soþ knawen,
þer such an askyng is hevened so hyȝe in your sale,
þaȝ ȝe ȝourself be talenttyf, to take hit to yourselven,
Whil mony so bolde yow aboute upon bench sytten,
þat under heven I hope non haȝerer of wylle
Ne better bodyes on bent þer baret is rered.
I am þe wakkest, I wot, and of wyt feblest,
And lest lur of my lyf, quo laytes þe soþe.
Bot for as much as ȝe ar myn em I am only to prayse,
No bounté bot your blod I in my bodé knowe;
And syþen þis note is so nys þat noȝt hit yow falles,
And I have frayned hit at yow fyrst, foldez hit to me;
And if I carp not comlyly, let alle þis cort rych
Bout blame.'
Ryche togeder con roun,
And syþen þay redden alle same
To ryd þe kyng wyth croun,
And gif Gawan þe game.

þen comaunded þe kyng þe knyȝt for to ryse,
And he ful radly upros and ruchched hym fayre,
Kneled doun bifore þe kyng and cachez þat weppen;
And he luflyly hit hym laft and lyfte up his honde
And gef hym Goddez blessyng and gladly hym biddes
þat his hert and his honde schulde hardi be boþe.

345 **vylanye** 'discourtesy'. It is what characterizes a villein, a person of low birth.

346 'And provided that my liege lady were not displeased.' Guenevere will be left with an empty place on either side.

347 **com to your counseyl** 'come to consult with you'.

348–50 The construction is 'It would seem to me improper ... (for you) to take it on yourself'. The clause is interrupted by the subordinate clauses: *þer* ... 'in a situation where', and *þaȝ* ... 'even though'.

352 '(So bold) that I believe there are none on earth firmer in courage.'

355 'And my life would be the least loss, if anyone wants to know the truth.'

356 **Bot for as much as** 'only in as much as'.

359 **foldez hit** 'it belongs to'.

360 **rych** is probably a verb, 'make arrangements'. Gawain hopes that if his offer is not acceptable the court will come to some other arrangement *bout blame*, that is, without rebuking him for his intervention.

362 **Ryche** an adjective used as a noun; see 21n.

363 **same** 'together, with one accord'.

369 **he** Arthur. 'He courteously gave it up to him.'

‘Kepe þe, cosyn,’ quoþ þe kyng, ‘þat þou on kyrf sette,
And if þou redez hym ryȝt, redly I trowe
þat þou schal byden þe bur þat he schal bede after.’
Gawan gotz to þe gome with giserne in honde,
And he baldly hym bydez, he bayst never þe helder.
þen carppez to Sir Gawan þe knyȝt in þe grene:
‘Refourme we oure forwardes er we fyrre passe.
Fyrst I eþe þe, haþel, how þat þou hattes
þat þou me telle truly, as I tryst may.’
‘In god fayth,’ quoþ þe goode knyȝt, ‘Gawan I hatte
þat bede þe þis buffet, quatso bifallez after,
And at þis tyme twelmonyth take at þe anoþer
Wyth what weppen so þou wylt, and wyth no wyȝ ellez
On lyve.’
þat oþer onswarez agayn:
‘Sir Gawan, so mot I þryve
As I am ferly fayn
þis dint þat þou schal dryve.

‘Bigog,’ quoþ þe grene knyȝt, ‘Sir Gawan, me lykes
þat I schal fange at þy fust þat I haf frayst here;
And þou hatz redily rehersed bi resoun ful trwe
Clanly al þe covenaunt þat I þe kynge asked,
Saf þat þou schal siker me, segge, bi þi trawþe,
þat þou schal seche me þiself whereso þou hopes
I may be funde upon folde, and foch þe such wages
As þou deles me today bifore þis douþe ryche.’
‘Where schulde I wale þe?’ quoþ Gauan, ‘Where is þy [place?
I wot never where þou wonyes, bi hym þat me wroȝt,

372–4 ‘“Make sure, nephew,” said the King, “that you place one blow, and if you manage him properly I fully believe that you’ll survive the blow that he’ll offer you afterwards.”’ Arthur seems to imply, rather too optimistically, that Gawain can dispatch the knight with one blow.

376 **he bayst never þe helder** ‘he was not at all disconcerted’.

381–5 Gawain formally states his name and the terms of the agreement he is accepting.

383 **take at þe anoþer** ‘I’ll take a return blow from you’.

384–5 **and . . . lyve** ‘and from no other man alive’; i.e. not from the Green Knight’s deputy after his death.

387–8 ‘Upon my life (literally, ‘so may I prosper as’) I am very glad.’

394–403 The knight asks Gawain to confirm *bi þi trawþe* that he himself will make the journey to receive the return blow. Gawain points out that he needs directions on where to find the knight, and assures him he will do all he can to get to the appointed place, *by my seker traweþ*. The word *trawþe* may here be translated ‘pledge of honour’. After the return blow Gawain admits his failure in *trawþe* (l. 2383).

399 **bi . . . wroȝt** i.e. ‘by God’.

Ne I know not þe, knyʒt, þy cort ne þi name.
Bot teche me truly þerto and telle me howe þou hattes,
And I schal ware alle my wyt to wynne me þeder;
And þat I swere þe for soþe and by my seker traweþ.'
'Þat is innogh in Nwe Ʒer; hit nedes no more',
Quoþ þe gome in þe grene to Gawan þe hende.
'Ʒif I þe telle trwly quen I þe tape have
And þou me smoþely hatz smyten, smartly I þe teche
Of my hous and my home and myn owen nome,
Þen may þou frayst my fare and forwardez holde.
And if I spende no speche, þenne spedez þou þe better,
For þou may leng in þy londe and layt no fyrre.
Bot slokes!
Ta now þy grymme tole to þe
And let se how þou cnokez.'
'Gladly, sir, for soþe',
Quoþ Gawan; his ax he strokes.

The grene knyʒt upon grounde grayþely hym dresses,
A littel lut with þe hede, þe lere he discoverez,
His longe lovelych lokkez he layd over his croun,
Let þe naked nec to þe note schewe.
Gauan gripped to his ax and gederes hit on hyʒt,
Þe kay fot on þe folde he before sette,
Let hit doun lyʒtly lyʒt on þe naked,
Þat þe scharp of þe schalk schyndered þe bones
And schrank þurʒ þe schyire grece and schade hit in [twynne,
Þat þe bit of þe broun stel bot on þe grounde.
Þe fayre hede fro þe halce hit to þe erþe,
Þat fele hit foyned wyth her fete þere hit forth roled;
Þe blod brayd fro þe body, þat blykked on þe grene,

402 **ware alle my wyt** 'use all my intelligence', that is, 'do everything in my power'.

407 **teche** is parallel to *telle*: 'if I tell you . . . and inform you promptly . . . then you may . . .'

409 **frayst my fare** an idiom, meaning perhaps 'find out what I shall do', or 'come and see how I am'. *Frayst* may mean 'test' or 'seek'; *fare* may mean 'behaviour' or 'condition'.

412 **slokes** imperative plural, 'let's stop!' or 'that's enough!'

424–5 'So that the sharp weapon severed the bones of the man, and slipped through the white fat and split it in two.' The two lines alliterate on the fricative *sch*, strongly contrasting with the plosive *b* and *t* of l. 426.

426 **broun** as in OE the meaning is 'shining' when the reference is to metal.

429 The *þat*-clause qualifies *blod*: 'The blood that shone on the green (skin) poured from the body'. See 5.9.4.

And nawþer faltered ne fel þe freke never þe helder,
Bot styþly he start forth upon styf schonkes
And runyschly he raȝt out þereas renkkez stoden,
Laȝt to his lufly hed and lyft hit up sone,
And syþen boȝez to his blonk, þe brydel he cachchez,
Steppez into stel-bawe and strydez alofte,
And his hede by þe here in his honde haldez;
And as sadly þe segge hym in his sadel sette
As non unhap had hym ayled, þaȝ hedlez he were
    In stedde.
  He brayde his bluk aboute,
  þat ugly bodi þat bledde;
  Moni on of hym had doute
  Bi þat his resounz were redde.

For þe hede in his honde he haldez up even,
Toward þe derrest on þe dece he dressez þe face,
And hit lyfte up þe yȝe-lyddez and loked ful brode
And meled þus much with his muthe as ȝe may now here:
'Loke, Gawan, þou be grayþe to go as þou hettez,
And layte as lelly til þou me, lude, fynde,
As þou hatz hette in þis halle, herande þise knyȝtes.
To þe Grene Chapel þou chose, I charge þe, to fotte
Such a dunt as þou hatz dalt; disserved þou habbez
To be ȝederly ȝolden on Nw Ȝeres morn.
þe Knyȝt of þe Grene Chapel men knowen me mony;
Forþi me for to fynde, if þou fraystez, faylez þou never.
þerfore com, oþer recreaunt be calde þe behoves.'
With a runisch rout þe raynez he tornez,
Halled out at þe hal dor, his hed in his hande,
þat þe fyr of þe flynt flaȝe fro fole hoves.

437–9 'The knight seated himself in his saddle as firmly as if no misadventure had troubled him, even though he was without his head there.'

441 **ugly** 'gruesome'.

442–3 'Many a person was afraid of him by the time that his words were uttered.'

445 **þe derrest** either plural, 'the noblest knights', or singular, referring to Guenevere, whose horrified reaction is implied by l. 470. At the end of the poem (ll. 2460–2) the Green Knight says that one purpose of his visit was to frighten Guenevere to death.

447 **his** 'its' (4.3.3).

450 **herande** 'in the hearing of'.

451 **þou chose** imperative, 'go'.

454 The knight fulfils the promise of l. 408, but with a troubling imprecision.

455 'Therefore if you ask you won't fail to find me.'

456 **recreaunt** 'one who admits defeat'.

459 **fole hoves** 'the hooves of the horse' (4.2.4).

To quat kyth he becom knwe non þere,
Never more þen þay wyste from queþen he watz wonnen.
What þenne?
Þe kyng and Gawen þare
At þat grene þay laȝe and grenne;
Ȝet breved watz hit ful bare
A mervayl among þo menne.

Þaȝ Arþer þe hende kyng at hert hade wonder,
He let no semblaunt be sene, bot sayde ful hyȝe
To þe comlych quene wyth cortays speche:
'Dere dame, today demay yow never.
Wel bycommes such craft upon Cristmasse,
Laykyng of enterludez, to laȝe and to syng,
Among þise kynde caroles of knyȝtes and ladyez.
Neverþelece to my mete I may me wel dres,
For I haf sen a selly, I may not forsake.'
He glent upon Sir Gawen and gaynly he sayde:
'Now, sir, heng up þyn ax; þat hatz innogh hewen.'
And hit watz don abof þe dece on doser to henge,
Þer alle men for mervayl myȝt on hit loke
And bi trwe tytel þerof to telle þe wonder.
Þenne þay boȝed to a borde, þise burnes togeder,
Þe kyng and þe gode knyȝt, and kene men hem served
Of alle dayntyez double as derrest myȝt falle.
Wyth alle maner of mete and mynstralcie boþe,
Wyth wele walt þay þat day til worþed an ende

460–1 None of the courtiers have any more idea of where he went than they have of where he came from. Cf. the fairy hunt in 5/288, 'never he nist whider þai bicome'.

464 **grene** 'green man'.

465–6 'Yet it was very openly accounted among those men as a marvel.' So Arthur may begin eating.

471–3 Arthur speciously places the adventure in the category of standard Christmas entertainment: performing of interludes, singing and *caroles*. The 'interlude' at this date was an entertainment, not necessarily dramatic, during a feast. On the meaning of *caroles*, see 43n.

474–5 'Nevertheless I may indeed begin my meal, for I can't deny I've seen an extraordinary sight.' Arthur concedes that this is not *entirely* the expected Christmas fare.

476 **gaynly** perhaps here 'aptly', though the adverb is often used rather imprecisely. The expression 'hang up your axe', here used literally, had the proverbial sense, also appropriate here, of 'rest after your work'. See Whiting A251, and compare *The Owl and the Nightingale* 658, 'Hong up þin ax!', where it means 'Give up!'.

480 'And by the authentic evidence of it (the axe) they might describe the wonderful event.' The axe hanging above the table was proof of the story. (*To telle* is, like *loke*, dependent on *myȝt*; 5.6.5).

483 **as derrest myȝt falle** 'as might suit the noblest knights'.

In londe.
Now þenk wel, Sir Gawan,
For woþe þat þou ne wonde
Þis aventure for to frayn
Þat þou hatz tan on honde.

487–90 The poet addresses Gawain with a note of warning: 'Now think carefully, Sir Gawain, that you do not hesitate because of the danger to attempt this adventure that you have undertaken.'

10

St Erkenwald

The alliterative poem *St Erkenwald* survives in just one manuscript, British Library MS Harley 2250. This copy was made in 1477, but the poem was most likely composed in the 1390s or early 1400s. The dialect of the copy is assigned by the *Linguistic Atlas* to Cheshire; and the opening reference to *London in Englond* points to the same county (see 1n.). Nothing is known of the author's identity. So far as linguistic evidence goes, the poem might have been written by the author of *Sir Gawain and the Green Knight* (text 9 here) – to whom, indeed, it has sometimes been ascribed. Yet its style tells against this identification: it is less exuberant, sparer and more concise. See also Benson (1965).

Like Chaucer's Prioress's Tale (text 16b here), the poem would have been described in the Middle Ages as a *miraculum* or 'miracle'. Its subject is a miracle brought about through the agency of Erkenwald, an Anglo-Saxon saint of the seventh century. Erkenwald was Bishop of London, and his cult was celebrated there at St Paul's Cathedral – an episcopal church with which the poet may well have had connections. The miracle in question does not figure elsewhere in the saint's dossier. It appears to have been a pious invention of the poet himself, suggested by similar stories concerning St Gregory's part in the posthumous salvation of a pagan Roman emperor, Trajan. Like these, the *Erkenwald* story addresses a large theological question which medieval Christians found troublesome: could those who lived virtuously according to their lights, but without knowledge of the Christian faith, be saved? And if so, how? In the B Text of *Piers Plowman* (XI 141–69, XII 281–92) Langland gives a liberal version of the Trajan story: the emperor was so outstandingly just and merciful that it required only the longings and tears of Gregory to bring him out of hell. But a different version, found in an early commentary on Dante's *Commedia*, makes Trajan's salvation depend on his being resuscitated and baptized by Gregory; and this is closer, in its theological conservatism, to the *Erkenwald* story. See Whatley (1986). In the Middle English poem it is indeed the pagan judge's outstanding virtues which induce God to preserve his body and clothes undecayed (ll. 267–70); but his soul is not admitted to heaven until the saint has administered the sacrament of baptism – the climax of the poem (316n.). So here, as not in Langland, the Church and its sacraments have an essential part to play.

The vivid and sharply focused narrative matches the clarity of the theology it serves. The poem is divided exactly into two equal halves (177n.). The first half is devoted to the discovery of the corpse and the bishop's solemn preparations for his encounter with it; the second half describes that encounter in dialogue which, with deceptive naturalness, answers precisely all the questions raised by the strange contents of the tomb (questions put by the bishop, ll. 185–8). The baptismal climax is a *tour de force* of the theological imagination. A single tear, falling on the exposed flesh of the judge's face, has completed the conditions of baptism, *and þe freke syked* – 'the man sighed' (l. 323). The consequences, both spiritual and physical, then follow with the speed and inevitability of a chemical reaction; and the poem ends in a clamour of bells.

The following points may be noted in the language of this North-West Midland text. The spelling *qu-* corresponds to modern *wh-* (which is never used) in words like *quen*, 'when', *quile*, 'while' and *quo*, 'who', as well as to modern *qu-*, as in l. 133. In verbs, the second person singular of the present tense has the ending -(*e*)*s* (*þou says*, 159). The plural also often has *-es*, though *-en* and *-e* are also used. The present participle always ends in *-and*(*e*), and is to be distinguished from the verbal noun in *-ing* (*blysnande* 87, as against *moulyng* 86). Among the third person pronouns, note *ho*, 'she', and the plural set *þai*, 'they', *hor*, 'their' and *hom*, 'them'.

Editions

H. L. Savage, *St Erkenwald* (New Haven and London, 1926)
C. Peterson, *St Erkenwald* (Philadelphia, 1977)

Studies

L. D. Benson, 'The Authorship of *St Erkenwald*', *Journal of English and Germanic Philology*, 64 (1965), 393–405

G. Whatley, 'Heathens and Saints: *St Erkenwald* and its Legendary Context', *Speculum*, 61 (1986), 330–63

At London in Englond noȝt full long sythen
Sythen Crist suffrid on crosse and Cristendome stablyd,
Ther was a byschop in þat burgh, blessyd and sacryd;
Saynt Erkenwolde as I hope þat holy mon hatte.
In his tyme in þat toun þe temple alder-grattyst
Was drawen doun, þat one dole, to dedifie new,
For hit hethen had bene in Hengyst dawes
þat þe Saxones unsaȝt haden sende hyder.
þai bete oute þe Bretons and broȝt hom into Wales
And pervertyd all þe pepul þat in þat place dwellid.
þen wos this reame renaide mony ronke ȝeres,
Til Saynt Austyn into Sandewich was send fro þe pope.
þen prechyd he here þe pure faythe and plantyd þe trouthe,
And convertyd all þe communnatés to Cristendame newe.
He turnyd temples þat tyme þat temyd to þe devell,
And clansyd hom in Cristes nome and kyrkes hom callid;
He hurlyd owt hor ydols and hade hym in sayntes,
And chaungit chevely hor nomes and chargit hom better;
þat ere was of Appolyn is now of Saynt Petre,
Mahoun to Saynt Margrete oþir to Maudelayne,
þe Synagoge of þe Sonne was sett to oure Lady,
Jubiter and Jono to Jesu oþir to James.
So he hom dedifiet and dyght all to dere halowes
þat ere wos sett of Sathanas in Saxones tyme.
    Now þat London is nevenyd hatte þe New Troie,

1 **in Englond** Cheshire, the poet's native country, regarded itself as somewhat separate from the rest of England. Its earls enjoyed special, semi-royal privileges.

1–2 **sythen/Sythen** 'after the time that' ('afterwards after'). The poet's chronology is foreshortened. Erkenwald became bishop of London in AD 675.

6 **þat one dole** 'one part of it'.

7 **Hengyst** Hengest, with Horsa, led the pagan Saxons, who in the fifth century conquered Christian Britain (*Bretons* 9) and caused its relapse into paganism. Cf. 3/168 above.

12 **Austyn** St Augustine of Canterbury began the reconversion of England in 597. He was sent by Pope Gregory.

Sandewich A major Channel port in the Middle Ages, one of the Cinque Ports.

15–24 Gregory instructed Augustine that pagan shrines 'should be changed from the worship of devils to the service of the true God' (Bede's *History* 1.30). Erkenwald, a century later, was continuing this cleansing process.

17 **hade hym in** 'brought in'.

19 'That which previously had belonged to Apollo . . .' See 5.4.6.

20 **Mahoun** Mahomet, often cited as a pagan god.

Maudelayne St Mary Magdalene.

21 **Synagoge of þe Sonne** The poet lumps together all kinds of non-Christians with their 'synagogues' (pagan temples): nature-worshippers (the sun), Muslims (Mahomet), and worshippers of Classical gods (Apollo, Jupiter, Juno). All were followers of Satan (24). Cf. 8/165–7 above.

25 'What is now known as London was called "the New Troy".' The Trojan Brutus, legendary founder of Britain (cf. 9/13 above), named his principal city 'Troia Nova'. The poet later refers to pagan London simply as 'Troy' (251, 255).

þe metropol and þe mayster-toun hit evermore has bene.
þe mecul mynster þerinne a maghty devel aght,
And þe title of þe temple bitan was his name,
For he was dryghtyn derrest of ydols praysid
And þe solempnest of his sacrifices in Saxon londes.
þe thrid temple hit wos tolde of Triapolitanes:
By all Bretaynes bonkes were bot othire twayne.
Now of þis Augustynes art is Erkenwolde bischop
At love London toun and the lagh teches,
Syttes semely in þe sege of Saynt Paule mynster
þat was þe temple Triapolitan as I tolde are.
þen was hit abatyd and beten doun and buggyd efte new,
A noble note for þe nones and New Werke hit hatte.
Mony a mery mason was made þer to wyrke,
Harde stones for to hewe with eggit toles,
Mony grubber in grete þe grounde for to seche
þat þe fundement on fyrst shuld þe fote halde;
And as þai makkyd and mynyd a mervayle þai founden
As ȝet in crafty cronecles is kydde þe memorie,
For as þai dyȝt and dalfe so depe into þe erthe
þai founden fourmyt on a flore a ferly faire toumbe;
Hit was a throgh of thykke ston thryvandly hewen,
With gargeles garnysht aboute alle of gray marbre.
The sperl of þe spelunke þat spradde hit olofte
Was metely made of þe marbre and menskefully planed
And þe bordure enbelicit with bryȝt golde lettres;
Bot roynyshe were þe resones þat þer on row stoden.
Full verray were þe vigures, þer avisyd hom mony,
Bot all muset hit to mouth and quat hit mene shuld;
Mony clerke in þat clos with crownes ful brode

28 The legal rights (*title*) in the temple – its endowments etc. – were 'assigned to his name', that is, to the devil in whose name it was dedicated and who therefore 'owned' it (l. 27).

31 'It was reckoned the third temple of the Triapolitans', i.e. of the three metropolitan cities. According to Geoffrey of Monmouth, *History of the Kings of Britain* 4.19, pagan Britain had three chief religious centres, of which London was one.

32 'In all parts of Britain there were only two others', at York and Caerusk.

33 **art** 'province'. Archbishops of Canterbury, as successors of St Augustine, ruled the southern province, including London.

38 **New Werke** Part of the fabric of St Paul's Cathedral constructed in the thirteenth century was in fact later known as the New Work. Perhaps the poet thought it much older.

41 **grounde** 'solid ground', upon which the new foundations (*fundement* 42) could rest securely.

49 'The lid of the tomb which shut it on top.'

53–4 'The shapes (of the letters) were perfectly distinct, as many could see; but everyone was at a loss to pronounce it (the text) or understand what it might mean.'

Þer besiet hom aboute noȝt to bryng hom in wordes.
Quen tithynges token to þe toun of þe toumbe-wonder
Mony hundrid hende men highid þider sone;
Burgeys boghit þerto, bedels and othire,
And mony a mesters mon of maners dyverse;
Laddes laften hor werke and lepen þiderwardes,
Ronnen radly in route with ryngand noyce;
Þer comen þider of all kynnes so kenely mony
Þat as all þe worlde were þider walon within a honde-quile.
Quen þe maire with his meynye þat mervaile aspied,
By assent of þe sextene þe sayntuaré þai kepten,
Bede unlouke þe lidde and lay hit byside;
Þai wold loke on þat lome quat lengyd withinne.
Wyȝt werkemen with þat wenten þertill,
Putten prises þerto, pinchid one-under,
Kaghten by þe corners with crowes of yrne,
And were þe lydde never so large þai laide hit by sone.
Bot þen wos wonder to wale on wehes þat stoden
That myȝt not come to to knowe a quontyse strange,
So was þe glode within gay, al with golde payntyd,
And a blisfull body opon þe bothum lyggid,
Araide on a riche wise in riall wedes.
Al with glisnande golde his gowne wos hemmyd,
With mony a precious perle picchit þeron,
And a gurdill of golde bigripid his mydell;
A meche mantel on lofte with menyver furrit,
Þe clothe of camelyn ful clene with cumly bordures;
And on his coyfe wos kest a coron ful riche
And a semely septure sett in his honde.
Als wemles were his wedes withouten any tecche
Oþir of moulyng oþir of motes oþir moght-freten,
And als bryȝt of hor blee in blysnande hewes
As þai hade ȝepely in þat ȝorde bene ȝisturday shapen;

56 'Laboured there in vain to make words out of them (the letters).'

64 **þat as** 'that it was as if . . .'

66 The mayor seeks permission of the sacristan (the ecclesiastical officer responsible for care of the building) before taking charge of a holy place.

68 **quat** 'to see what'.

72 'And however large the lid was . . .', i.e. although it was very large.

74 **come to to knowe** 'manage to understand'. For *come to*, 'succeed', see *MED comen* v. 4a (d).

81 It was a peculiar privilege of judges to wear a mantle furred with miniver.

83–4 The coif or cap, like the miniver mantle, identifies the body as a lawyer's; but the crown and sceptre present puzzles, which the judge solves later (221–4, 253–6).

And als freshe hym þe face and the flesh nakyd
Bi his eres and bi his hondes þat openly shewid
With ronke rode as þe rose and two rede lippes,
As he in sounde sodanly were slippid opon slepe.
þer was spedeles space to spyr uschon oþir
Quat body hit myȝt be þat buried wos ther,
How long had he þer layne, his lere so unchaungit,
And al his wede unwemmyd? þus ylka weghe askyd.
'Hit myȝt not be bot such a mon in mynde stode long.
He has ben kyng of þis kith, as couthely hit semes,
He lyes dolven þus depe; hit is a derfe wonder
Bot summe segge couthe say þat he hym sene hade.'
Bot þat ilke note wos noght, for nourne none couthe,
Noþir by title ne token ne by tale noþir,
þat ever wos brevyt in burgh ne in boke notyd
þat ever mynnyd such a mon, more ne lasse.
 þe bodeword to þe byschop was broght on a quile
Of þat buried body al þe bolde wonder.
þe primate with his prelacie was partyd fro home,
In Esex was Sir Erkenwolde an abbay to visite.
Tulkes tolden hym þe tale with troubull in þe pepul
And suche a cry aboute a cors crakit evermore;
The bischop sende hit to blynne by bedels and lettres
And buskyd þiderwarde bytyme on his blonke after.
By þat he come to þe kyrke kydde of Saynt Paule,
Mony hym metten on þat meere þe mervayle to tell;
He passyd into his palais and pes he comaundit
And devoydit fro þe dede and ditte þe durre after.
þe derke nyȝt overdrofe and day-belle ronge,
And Sir Erkenwolde was up in þe ughten ere þen,
þat welnegh al þe nyȝt hade naityd his houres
To biseche his soverayn of his swete grace
To vouchesafe to revele hym hit by a visoun or elles.

89 **hym þe face** 'his face'. See 5.3.3.

93 'There was time spent in vain as people asked each other.'

97 'A man such as that must have been long remembered.' The onlookers are surprised not to be able to identify a man of such evident importance, apparently so recently buried.

99–100 '. . . it would be very strange if someone were not able to claim to have seen him.'

108 Bede, *History* 4.6, records that Erkenwald founded an abbey at Barking in Essex, some ten miles east of St Paul's.

Sir a title for priests as well as knights.

109–10 'Men told him what had happened, including the disturbance among the people and such a continual uproar raised around a dead body.'

113 **kydde of Saynt Paule** 'well known as St Paul's'.

'þagh I be unworthi,' al wepand he sayde,
'Thurgh his deere debonerté digne hit my Lorde:
In confirmyng þi Cristen faith, fulsen me to kenne
þe mysterie of þis mervaile þat men opon wondres.'
And so long he grette after grace þat he graunte hade,
An ansuare of þe Holy Goste, and afterwarde hit dawid.
Mynster-dores were makyd opon quen matens were songen;
þe byschop hym shope solemply to synge þe hegh masse.
þe prelate in pontificals was prestly atyrid,
Manerly with his ministres þe masse he begynnes
Of *Spiritus Domini* for his spede on sutile wise,
With queme questis of þe quere with ful quaynt notes.
Mony a gay grete lorde was gedrid to herken hit,
As þe rekenest of þe reame repairen þider ofte,
Till cessyd was þe service and sayde þe later ende;
þen heldyt fro þe autere all þe hegh gynge.
þe prelate passid on þe playn, þer plied to hym lordes,
As riche revestid as he was he rayked to þe toumbe;
Men unclosid hym þe cloyster with clustred keies,
Bot pyne wos with þe grete prece þat passyd hym after.
The byschop come to þe burynes, him barones besyde,
þe maire with mony maȝti men and macers before hym.
þe dene of þe dere place devysit al on fyrst,
þe fyndynge of þat ferly with fynger he mynte.
'Lo, lordes,' quod þat lede, 'suche a lyche here is
Has layn loken here on logh, how long is unknawen;
And ȝet his colour and his clothe has caȝt no defaute,
Ne his lire ne þe lome þat he is layde inne.
þer is no lede opon lyfe of so long age
þat may mene in his mynde þat suche a mon regnyd,
Ne noþir his nome ne his note nourne of one speche;
Queþer mony porer in þis place is putte into grave

123–4 'May my Lord in his precious mercy grant it: in confirmation of thy Christian faith, help me to explain.' The shift from *his* to *thy* marks the beginning of Erkenwald's prayer to God.

132 **Spiritus Domini** the Mass of the Holy Spirit (cf. 127), which begins 'The spirit of the Lord fills the whole earth'.

138 'The prelate crossed the floor, with lords bowing to him.' After celebrating Mass at the high altar, the bishop processes down the church to the tomb.

140 **cloyster** 'enclosed area', in the crypt?

141 'But there was a crush among the big crowd which followed him.'

144 **þe dene** In a cathedral's hierarchy, the dean ranked next to the bishop.

148 See 263n.

152 'Or reveal a single thing about his name or his occupation.'

153–4 'Yet there is many a poorer man buried here whose memory is set down in our burial-register for ever.'

þat merkid is in oure martilage his mynde for ever;
And we have oure librarie laitid þes long seven dayes,
Bot one cronicle of þis kyng con we never fynde.
He has non layne here so long, to loke hit by kynde,
To malte so out of memorie bot mervayle hit were.'
'þou says soþe,' quod þe segge þat sacrid was byschop,
'Hit is mervaile to men, þat mountes to litell
Toward þe providens of þe prince þat paradis weldes,
Quen hym luste to unlouke þe leste of his myȝtes.
Bot quen matyd is monnes myȝt and his mynde passyd,
And al his resons are torent and redeles he stondes,
þen lettes hit hym ful litell to louse wyt a fynger
þat all þe hondes under heven halde myȝt never.
þereas creatures crafte of counsell oute swarves,
þe comforth of þe creatore byhoves þe cure take.
And so do we now oure dede, devyne we no fyrre;
To seche þe soth at oureselfe ȝee se þer no bote;
Bot glow we all opon Godde and his grace aske,
þat careles is of counsell and comforthe to sende,
And þat in fastynge of ȝour faith and of fyne bileve.
I shal avay ȝow so verrayly of vertues his
þat ȝe may leve upon long þat he is lord myȝty
And fayne ȝour talent to fulfille if ȝe hym frende leves.'

Then he turnes to þe toumbe and talkes to þe corce,
Lyftand up his egh-lyddes he loused such wordes:
'Now, lykhame þat þou lies, layne þou no leng!
Sythen Jesus has juggit today his joy to be schewyd,
Be þou bone to his bode, I bydde in his behalve;
As he was bende on a beme quen he his blode schadde,
As þou hit wost wyterly and we hit wele leven,

154 **þat . . . his** 'whose': see 5.4.6.
157 **to loke hit by kynde** 'to judge by the natural signs'.
158 **bot mervayle hit were** 'unless something extraordinary has occurred'.
161 **Toward** 'in face of, in comparison with'.
165 'Then it causes him (God) very little trouble to set free with a finger.'
167–8 'Where the power of created beings fails to reach a solution, the benevolence of the Creator must undertake the remedy.'
172 **careles** 'free, generous'.
173 **þat** '(does) that'.
177 The extra-large capital letter with which this line begins in the manuscript (used elsewhere only for the poem's first line) marks the precise half-way point in the 352-line poem. The bishop's exchanges with the body, which begin here, occupy its second half.
179 **lykhame þat þou lies** 'corpse that you are, lying there'. Editors emend *þou* to *þus* or *þer*, perhaps rightly.
183 The dead know (*wost*) what the living can only believe (*leven*).

Ansuare here to my sawe, councele no trouthe!
Sithen we wot not qwo þou art, witere us þiselwen
In worlde quat weghe þou was and quy þow þus ligges,
How long þou has layne here and quat lagh þou usyt,
Queþer art þou joyned to joy oþir juggid to pyne.'
Quen þe segge hade þus sayde and syked þerafter,
þe bryȝt body in þe burynes brayed a litell,
And with a drery dreme he dryves owte wordes
þurgh sum lant goste-lyfe of hym þat al redes.
'Bisshop,' quod þis ilke body, 'þi boode is me dere;
I may not bot bogh to þi bone for bothe myn eghen.
To þe name þat þou nevenyd has and nournet me after
Al heven and helle heldes to and erthe bitwene.
Fyrst to say the þe sothe quo myselfe were:
One þe unhapnest hathel þat ever on erth ȝode,
Never kyng ne cayser ne ȝet no knyȝt nothyre,
Bot a lede of þe lagh þat þen þis londe usit.
I was committid and made a mayster-mon here
To sytte upon sayd causes; þis cité I ȝemyd
Under a prince of parage of paynymes lagh,
And uche segge þat him sewid þe same fayth trowid.
þe lengthe of my lying here þat is a lewid date,
Hit is to meche to any mon to make of a nombre.
After þat Brutus þis burgh had buggid on fyrste,
Noȝt bot fife hundred ȝere þer aghtene wontyd
Before þat kynned ȝour Criste by Cristen acounte:
A þousand ȝere and þritty mo and ȝet threnen aght.

192 'By virtue of some spirit-life granted by Him who rules all.' We take *goste-lyfe* to be a compound improvised in order to denote the peculiar kind of life here enjoyed by the dead man. But the word-order is awkward (*lant*... *of* 'granted by'), and the line has been much emended. Emending *al* to *lyfe* would restore alliteration to the second half-line.

194 **for bothe myn eghen** an emphasizing phrase (cf. 2/381), originally, 'even if I were to lose both eyes as a result'. So: 'I cannot for the life of me do other than submit to your command.'

198 'Quite the most unfortunate man...' See 5.5.2.

202 **sayd causes** 'cases which come to court': Latin *causam dicere.*

205 **lewid date** 'uncalculable period'? *Lewid*, usually 'ignorant, unlettered', here perhaps indicates that the period in question is beyond the calculations of the learned. Our difficulties with ll. 207–10 bear this out.

207–10 The reference to the founding of London by Brutus (25n.) evidently does no more than cast the ensuing calculations back into the remote past. The next two lines then seem to state that the judge died 482 years before Christ's birth ('five hundred years with eighteen lacking'). This is the important point: that he lived as a pagan, before Christ. Line 210 may then be taken as an answer to the third of the bishop's five questions: 'How long þou has layne here?' (187): 1054 years ('a thousand and thirty and thrice eight'). This puts Erkenwald in the wrong century, since 1054 − 482 = AD 572; but the error matters little.

I was an heire of anoye in þe New Troie
In þe regne of þe riche kyng þat rewlit us þen,
The bolde Breton Sir Belyn – Sir Berynge was his brothire;
Mony one was þe busmare boden hom bitwene
For hor wrakeful werre quil hor wrath lastyd.
þen was I juge here enjoynyd in gentil lawe.'
  Quil he in spelunke þus spake, þer sprange in þe pepull
In al þis worlde no worde ne wakenyd no noice,
Bot al as stille as þe ston stoden and listonde
With meche wonder forwrast, and wepid ful mony.
The bisshop biddes þat body: 'Biknowe þe cause,
Sithen þou was kidde for no kynge, quy þou þe croun weres.
Quy haldes þou so hegh in honde þe septre
And hades no londe of lege men ne life ne lym aghtes?'
'Dere sir,' quod þe dede body, 'devyse þe I thenke,
Al was hit never my wille þat wroght þus hit were.
I wos deputate and domesmon under a duke noble,
And in my power þis place was putte altogeder.
I justifiet þis joly toun on gentil wise
And ever in fourme of gode faithe, more þen fourty
    wynter.
þe folke was felonse and fals and frowarde to reule –
I hent harmes ful ofte to holde hom to riȝt;
Bot for wothe ne wele, ne wrathe ne drede,
Ne for maystrie ne for mede, ne for no monnes aghe,
I remewit never fro þe riȝt by reson myn awen
For to dresse a wrang dome, no day of my lyve,
Declynet never my consciens for covetise on erthe
In no gynful jugement no japes to make,
Were a renke never so riche, for reverens sake;
Ne for no monnes manas, ne meschefe ne routhe,

211 'I was an inheritor of affliction . . .', i.e. by Adam's fall. St Paul calls unbelievers 'by nature children of wrath' (Ephesians 2.1–3, cf. Colossians 3.6 and Romans 4.13–16). Contrast 7a/59 above.

213–15 Belinus, king of Britain, quarrelled with his brother Brennius, but the two were eventually reconciled. Geoffrey of Monmouth, who tells the story (*History of the Kings of Britain* 3.1–10), emphasizes Belinus' concern for justice in the kingdom.

224 'And possessed no land held by vassals, nor had (royal) power over life and limb.'

229 **gentil** 'gentile', i.e. pagan, as in l. 216; but *gentil* can also mean 'noble': the judge is a noble pagan. See 8/62n.

234 **no monnes aghe** 'fear of no man'.

235 **by reson myn awen** 'according to my own judgement'.

237 **Declynet** *I* is probably to be understood, from l. 235: 'I never diverted my conscience (from the straight path) for any kind of avarice.'

239 **for reverens sake** 'out of deference to him'.

Non gete me fro þe hegh gate to glent out of ryȝt
Als ferforthe as my faith confourmyd my hert.
Þagh had bene my fader bone, I bede hym no wranges,
Ne fals favour to my fader, þagh fell hym be hongyt.
And for I was ryȝtwis and reken and redy of þe laghe,
Quen I deghed for dul denyed all Troye;
Alle menyd my dethe, þe more and the lasse,
And þus to bounty my body þai buriet in golde,
Cladden me for þe curtest þat courte couthe þen holde,
In mantel for þe mekest and monlokest on benche,
Gurden me for þe governour and graythist of Troie,
Furrid me for þe fynest of faith me withinne.
For þe honour of myn honesté of heghest enprise
Þai coronyd me þe kidde kynge of kene justises
Þer ever wos tronyd in Troye oþir trowid ever shulde,
And for I rewardid ever riȝt þai raght me the septre.'
Þe bisshop baythes hym ȝet with bale at his hert,
Þagh men menskid him so, how hit myȝt worthe
Þat his clothes were so clene. 'In cloutes, me thynkes,
Hom burde have rotid and bene rent in rattes long sythen.
Þi body may be enbawmyd, hit bashis me noght
Þat hit thar ryne no rote ne no ronke wormes;
Bot þi coloure ne þi clothe – I know in no wise
How hit myȝt lye by monnes lore and last so longe.'
'Nay, bisshop,' quod þat body, 'enbawmyd wos I never,
Ne no monnes counsell my cloth has kepyd unwemmyd,
Bot þe riche kyng of reson, þat riȝt ever alowes
And loves al þe lawes lely þat longen to trouthe;
And moste he menskes men for mynnyng of riȝtes
Þen for al þe meritorie medes þat men on molde usen;
And if renkes for riȝt þus me arayed has,
He has lant me to last þat loves ryȝt best.'
'Ȝea, bot sayes þou of þi saule,' þen sayd þe bisshop;

242 'In so far as my faith regulated my conscience.'

243–4 'Though it had been my father's murderer, I gave him no wrong decisions, nor false favour for my father, even though it fell to him to be hanged.' See 5.4.2 on omission of subject pronouns.

248 **to bounty** 'in my honour'.

251 He wears a 'gurdill of golde' (80).

255 **oþir trowid ever shulde** 'or was believed ever likely to be'.

262 'That no rot need touch it, nor any foul worms.' See ch. 7.

263 **coloure** The reference must be to cloth, not complexion (cf. 148). The corpse mentions only cloth in reply.

267 **þat riȝt ever alowes** 'who always gives credit for justice'.

273 'Yes, but speak about your soul . . .'

'Quere is ho stablid and stadde, if þou so streȝt wroghtes?
He þat rewardes uche a renke as he has riȝt servyd
Myȝt evel forgo the to gyfe of his grace summe brawnche.
For as he says in his sothe psalmyde writtes:
"þe skilfulle and þe unskathely skelton ay to me."
Forþi say me of þi soule, in sele quere ho wonnes,
And of þe riche restorment þat raȝt hyr oure Lorde.'
þen hummyd he þat þer lay and his hedde waggyd,
And gefe a gronyng ful grete and to Godde sayde:
'Maȝty maker of men, thi myghtes are grete;
How myȝt þi mercy to me amounte any tyme?
Nas I a paynym unpreste þat never thi plite knewe,
Ne þe mesure of þi mercy ne þi mecul vertue,
Bot ay a freke faitheles þat faylid þi laghes
þat ever þou, Lord, wos lovyd in? Allas þe harde stoundes!
I was non of þe nombre þat þou with noy boghtes
With þe blode of thi body upon þe blo rode.
Quen þou herghdes helle-hole and hentes hom þeroute,
þi loffynge oute of limbo, þou laftes me þer,
And þer sittes my soule þat se may no fyrre,
Dwynande in þe derke deth þat dyȝt us oure fader,
Adam oure alder, þat ete of þat appull
þat mony a plyȝtles pepul has poysned for ever.
Ȝe were entouchid with his tethe and take in þe glotte,
Bot mendyd with a medecyn ȝe are made for to lyvye –
þat is fulloght in fonte with faitheful bileve,
And þat han we myste alle merciles, myselfe and my soule.

275 Cf. Psalm 7.9: 'Judge me, O Lord, according to my justice.'

276 'Could hardly fail to give you some share of his grace.'

278 Rendering Psalm 14 (AV 15) 1–2: 'Lord . . . who shall rest in thy holy hill? He that walketh without blemish, and worketh justice.' The *skilfulle* 'worketh justice', the *unskathely* is 'without blemish'.

287–8 '. . . but always was a man without faith who did not know those laws in which you, Lord, have always been glorified?'

291–2 The Harrowing of Hell is narrated in the apocryphal Gospel of Nicodemus. Between the Crucifixion and the Resurrection, Christ descended into a region of Hell known as the 'limbo of the fathers' and rescued the souls of such as Abraham.

292 **þi loffynge** 'thy remnant' (so *MED*; perhaps to be emended to *leffynge*, 'leaving'?). The biblical 'remnant', Latin *reliquiae*, are those 'saved according to the election of grace' (Romans 11.5, cf. Romans 9.27).

297 'You were poisoned by his teeth and involved in the corruption.' The reference is to Adam's teeth, which became poisonous after biting into the forbidden apple. But other editors emend *tethe* to *teche*, 'fault, sin'.

299 Baptism (*fulloght*) and true belief are the medicine required to counteract the poison of original sin.

Quat wan we with oure wele-dede þat wroghtyn ay riȝt,
Quen we are dampnyd dulfully into þe depe lake,
And exilid fro þat soper so, þat solempne fest,
þer richely hit arne refetyd þat after right hungride?
My soule may sitte þer in sorow and sike ful colde,
Dymly in þat derke dethe þer dawes never morowen,
Hungrie inwith helle-hole, and herken after meeles
Longe er ho þat soper se oþir segge hyr to lathe.'
  þus dulfully þis dede body devisyt hit sorowe
þat alle wepyd for woo þe wordes þat herden,
And þe bysshop balefully bere doun his eghen,
þat hade no space to speke, so spakly he ȝoskyd,
Til he toke hym a tome and to þe toumbe lokyd,
To þe liche þer hit lay, with lavande teres.
'Oure Lord lene', quod þat lede, 'þat þou lyfe hades,
By Goddes leve, as longe as I myȝt lacche water,
And cast upon þi faire cors and carpe þes wordes,
"I folwe þe in þe Fader nome and his fre Childes
And of þe gracious Holy Goste", and not one grue lenger.
þen þof þou droppyd doun dede, hit daungerde me lasse.'
With þat worde þat he warpyd, þe wete of his eghen
And teres trillyd adoun and on þe toumbe lighten,
And one felle on his face, and þe freke syked.
þen sayd he with a sadde soun: 'Oure Savyoure be lovyd!
Now herid be þou, hegh God, and þi hende Moder,
And blissid be þat blisful houre þat ho the bere in!
And also be þou, bysshop, þe bote of my sorowe
And þe relefe of þe lodely lures þat my soule has levyd in!
For þe wordes þat þou werpe and þe water þat þou sheddes,
þe bryȝt bourne of þin eghen, my bapteme is worthyn.

302 **lake** 'pit (of Hell)'. So Latin *lacus* in the Vulgate Bible.

304 Alluding to the Beatitude: 'Blessed are they that hunger and thirst after justice: for they shall have their fill' (Matthew 5.6). But they are excluded from the heavenly banquet if, like the judge, they lack faith and baptism.

308 'For a long time before she (the soul) see that supper or find anyone to invite her to it.'

316 'With God's leave, just long enough for me to fetch some water.' In what follows, the conditions for a valid baptism are met, as it were, by accident. The Trinity is invoked hypothetically (ll. 318–19 represent what Erkenwald hopes to be able to say), and the necessary water falls by chance from the bishop's eye on to the judge's flesh.

319 **not one grue lenger** 'not a moment longer'.

320 'Then, even though you dropped down dead, it would distress me little.'

324 **Oure Savyoure** The judge now counts himself among the saved. Contrast 'ȝour Criste' (209).

þe fyrst slent þat on me slode slekkyd al my tene;
Ryȝt now to soper my soule is sette at þe table.
For with þe wordes and þe water þat wesche us of payne,
Liȝtly lasshit þer a leme loghe in þe abyme
þat spakly sprent my spyrit with unsparid murthe
Into þe cenacle solemply þer soupen all trewe;
And þer a marciall hyr mette with menske alder-grattest,
And with reverence a rowme he raȝt hyr for ever.
I heere þerof my hegh God and also þe, bysshop,
Fro bale has broȝt us to blis, blessid þou worth!'
Wyt this cessyd his sowne, sayd he no more,
Bot sodenly his swete chere swyndid and faylid
And all the blee of his body wos blakke as þe moldes,
As roten as þe rottok þat rises in powdere.
For as sone as þe soule was sesyd in blisse,
Corrupt was þat oþir crafte þat covert þe bones,
For þe ay-lastande life þat lethe shall never
Devoydes uche a vayneglorie þat vayles so litelle.
þen wos lovyng oure Lord with loves uphalden,
Meche mournyng and myrthe was mellyd togeder.
þai passyd forthe in procession and alle þe pepull folowid,
And all þe belles in þe burgh beryd at ones.

333 **us** cf. l. 300.

335 'Which made my spirit quickly spring . . .' *Sprent* is from OE *sprengan*, 'to cause to spring'.

336 **cenacle** 'dining-room': Latin *cenaculum*, used in the Vulgate for the room of the Last Supper and hence, here, of the heavenly banquet.

337–8 The marshal assigned each guest his place (*rowme*) at a feast.

340 Omission of relative pronoun *who* before *has*: see 5.4.6.

345 **sesyd in** 'possessed of', a legal term implying rightful possession.

346 The *crafte*, or device, covering the bones is the flesh.

352 In saints' lives, a miraculous ringing of bells 'withouten hond' (*Troilus* 3.188) commonly marks solemn or joyful moments. Cf. Boccaccio's *Decameron* 2.1: 'When [Arrigo] died, all the bells of the cathedral in Treviso began to ring of their own accord. This was taken as a miracle, and everyone said that Arrigo must be a saint.' The present line is probably to be understood accordingly.

11

John Trevisa: *Dialogue between a Lord and a Clerk*

John Trevisa was born about 1342, studied at Oxford University, became a Fellow there, and was ordained priest in 1370. He enjoyed the patronage of Thomas IV, Lord Berkeley, of Berkeley Castle, Gloucestershire, and became his chaplain and also vicar of the town of Berkeley. He died in 1402. His chief writings are translations of three major Latin works of the period: the *Polychronicon* of Ranulph Higden, a world history; the *De Proprietatibus Rerum* of Bartholomaeus Anglicus, an encyclopaedia; and a book of advice for rulers, the *De Regimine Principum* of Aegidius Romanus.

Trevisa's *Dialogue between a Lord and a Clerk* accompanies his English *Polychronicon*, along with a letter (not printed here) dedicating the translation to 'my worþy and worschypfol lord Sire Thomas, lord of Berkeleye'. The Latin *Polychronicon* is a vast history of the world, written by Ranulph Higden, a monk in the Benedictine abbey of Chester, in the 1320s and subsequently worked on by him up to his death in the 1360s. The book soon became a bestseller, and survives in more than 100 manuscripts. See Taylor (1966). Trevisa's English version was under way in 1385, and he completed it in April 1387. Although the prefatory *Dialogue* is set at Berkeley (see 126n.), it is to be read as an expository fiction modelled on other such dialogues in Latin. Its subject is translation. Trevisa compliments his patron by attributing to 'Dominus' all the good arguments for his own translating activity, reserving for himself, in the person of 'Clericus', only the reactionary objections against it. It was a common form of apology for medieval writers to claim that they undertook some great task only because they were urged or commanded to do so.

The *Dialogue* survives in five of the fourteen manuscripts of the English *Polychronicon*. See Waldron (1988). The present text is based, closely following Waldron, on British Library MS Cotton Tiberius D VII. Its Western dialect, according to the *Linguistic Atlas*, is exactly that of the Berkeley area of Gloucestershire. Voicing of /f/ to /v/ at the beginning of native words appears in *vor*, 'for', *vaste*, 'fast', etc. In verbs, the present plural indicative ending is always *-eþ* (the form for the verb 'to be' is *buþ*). Past participles commonly have the prefix *y-*. Among the personal pronouns, note that 'Dominus' uses *þou* to 'Clericus' (48), while 'Clericus' uses the respectful *ȝe*, *ȝow* (44, 145): see 5.4.1. The unstressed and reduced form *a* is used for both *he* (11) and *hy*, 'they' (37). Other forms of the third person plural pronoun are *here*, 'their' and *ham* or *hem*, 'them'. The form for 'these' is *þeus*(*e*). Monosyllabic adjectives in the definite declension (see 4.4.1) have *-e*, e.g. *þe vurste makyng* (27).

Edition

Ronald Waldron, 'Trevisa's Original Prefaces on Translation: A Critical Edition', in E. D. Kennedy, R. Waldron and J. S. Wittig, eds, *Medieval English Studies Presented to George Kane* (Woodbridge, 1988), pp. 285–99 [with full MS variants]

Studies

A. S. G. Edwards, 'John Trevisa', in A. S. G. Edwards, ed., *Middle English Prose: A Critical Guide to Major Authors and Genres* (New Brunswick, 1984), pp. 133–46 [with bibliography]

John Taylor, *The Universal Chronicle of Ranulf Higden* (Oxford, 1966)

Ronald Waldron, 'John Trevisa and the Use of English', *Proceedings of the British Academy*, 74 (1988), 171–202

Dominus Seþthe þet Babyl was ybuld men spekeþ dyvers tonges, so þat dyvers men buþ straunge to oþer and knoweþ noȝt of here speche. Speche ys noȝt yknowe bote ȝif hyt be lurned. Commyn lurnyng of speche ys by huyryng; and so alwey deef ys alwey dombe, vor he may noȝt hure speche vor to lurne. So men of ser contrayes and londes þat habbeþ dyvers speches, ȝef noþer of ham haþ lurned oþeres speche, neyþer of ham wot what oþer meneþ, þey hy meete and have greet neode of informacion and of loore, of talkyng and of speche. Be þeo neode never so gret, neyþer of ham understondeþ oþeres speche no moore þan ganglyng of gees. For jangle

1 **Babyl** Until the building of the Tower of Babel 'the earth was of one tongue, and of the same speech'; but God's revenge upon the builders was to 'confound their tongue, that they may not understand one another's speech' (Genesis 11.1–9). Hence the diversity of human language, for which various remedies were sought – including translation, the subject of the present dialogue.

4 **alwey deef** 'someone deaf from birth'.

10 **ganglyng** 'cackling', a variant of the following *jangle*.

10–12 'For however vigorously one of them cackles, the other is none the wiser, even though he may be cursing him rather than wishing him good day.' The *a* (11) is unstressed 'he'.

þe on nevere so vaste þet oþer ys nevere þe wyser, þey a schrewe hym in stude of good morowe. þis ys a gret meschef þat volweþ now mankuynde; bote God of hys mercy and grace haþ ordeynd doubel remedy. On ys þat som man lurneþ and knoweþ meny dyvers speches; and so bytwene strange men of þe whoche noþer understondeþ oþeres speche such a man may be mene and telle eyþer what þoþer wol mene. þe oþer remedy ys þat on langage ys ylurned, yused and yknowe in meny nacyons and londes; and so Latyn ys ylurned, yknowe and yused specialych a þys half Grees in al þe nacions and londes of Europa. þarfore clerkes of here godnes and cortesy makeþ and wryteþ here bokes in Latyn vor here wrytyng and bokes scholde be understonde in dyvers nacyons and londes. And so Ranulph monk of Chester wrot yn Latyn hys bookes of cronykes þat discreveþ þe world aboute yn lengthe and yn brede, and makeþ mencyon and muynde of doyngs and of dedes, of mervayls and of wondres, and rekneþ þe ȝeres to hys laste dayes fram þe vurste makyng of hevene and of erþe. And so þarynne ys noble and gret informacion and lore to hem þat can þarynne rede and understonde. þarvore ich wolde have þeus bokes of cronyks translated out of Latyn ynto Englysch, for þe mo men scholde hem understonde and have þereof konnyng, informacion and lore.

Clericus þeus bokes of cronyks buþ ywryte yn Latyn, and Latyn ys yused and understonde a þys half Grees yn al þe nacions and londes of Europa; and comynlych Englysch ys noȝt so wyde understonde, yused and yknowe, and þe Englysch translacion scholde no man understonde bote Englyschmen alone. þanne how scholde þe mo men understonde þe cronyks þey a were translated out of Latyn, þat ys so wyde yused and yknowe, into Englysch, þat ys noȝt yused and yknowe bote of Englyschmen alone?

Dominus þes question and doute ys esy to assoyle; vor ȝef þeus cronyks were translated out of Latyn into Englysch, þanne by so meny þe mo men scholde understonde ham as understondeþ Englysch and no Latyn.

Clericus ȝe cunneþ speke and rede and understonde Latyn. þanne hyt nedeþ noȝt to have such an Englysch translacion.

Dominus Y denye þys argument; for þey I cunne speke and rede and understonde Latyn, þer ys moche Latyn in þeus bokes of cronyks þat y can noȝt understonde, noþer þou wiþoute studyinge

16 **mene** 'an intermediary', with wordplay on *mene*, 'mean' (17).

19 **a þys half Grees** 'on this side of Greece', i.e. not Byzantium.

23 **Ranulph** Ranulph Higden. See Headnote. His *Polychronicon* is divided into seven *bookes*, the first of which describes the geography of the world. The remaining six are devoted to the history of the world from the beginning to the present.

26 **hys** 'its', the world's. See 4.3.3.

37 **þey a** 'even though they': *þey* is 'though'; *a* is unstressed 'they'.

and avysement and lokyng of oþer bokes. Also, þey hyt were noȝt neodful vor me, hyt is neodfol vor oþere men þat understondeþ no Latyn.

Clericus Men þat understondeþ no Latyn may lerne and understonde.

Dominus Noȝt alle: for som may noȝt vor oþer maner bysynes, som vor elde, som vor defaute of wyt, som vor defaute of katel oþer of frendes to vynde ham to scole, and som vor oþere dyvers defautes and lettes.

Clericus Hyt neodeþ noȝt þat al soche knowe þe cronykes.

Dominus Spek noȝt to streytlych of þyng þat neodeþ; for streytlych to speke of þyng þat neodeþ, onlych þyng þat ys and may noȝt fayle nedeþ to be, and so hyt neodeþ þat God be, for God ys and may noȝt faile. And so vor to speke, no man nedeþ to knowe þe cronykes, vor hyt myȝte and may be þat no man ham knoweþ. Oþerwyse to speke of þyng þat neodeþ, somwhat neodeþ vor to susteyne oþer to have oþer þinges þarby, and so mete and dryngke nedeþ vor kepyng and sustenaunce of lyf. And so vor to speke, no man neodeþ to knowe þe cronyks. Bote in þe þridde manere to speke of þing þat neodeþ, al þat ys profytable nedeþ; and so vor to speke, al men neodeþ to knawe þe cronykes.

Clericus þanne hy þat understondeþ no Latyn mowe axe and be informed and ytauȝt of ham þat understondeþ Latyn.

Dominus þou spekst wonderlych, vor þe lewed man wot noȝt what a scholde axe, and namelych of lore of dedes þat come nevere in hys muynde, noþer wot comynlych of whom a scholde axe. Also noȝt al men þat understondeþ Latyn habbeþ such bokes to informe lewed men. Also som konneþ noȝt, and som wol noȝt, and som mowe noȝt a whyle; and so hyt neodeþ to han an Englysch translacion.

Clericus þe Latyn ys boþe good and fayr. þarvore hyt neodeþ noȝt to han an Englysch translacion.

Dominus þis reson ys worþy to be plonged yn a plod and leyd in

56 **to vynde ham to scole** 'to provide for their schooling'. Cf. 7a/36. In both passages, *frendes* probably has its Old Norse sense, 'relatives'.

59–60 **streytlych** 'strictly, narrowly'. In what follows (59–69), the lord distinguishes three kinds of necessity: some things must in strict necessity exist (God); others are necessary for the support of other things (food and drink); and others are necessary in that they are beneficial (chronicles). The distinction is a scholastic one, going back to Aristotle's *Metaphysics* 5.5.

64 **somwhat** 'some thing'.

77 **mowe noȝt a whyle** 'cannot for the time being', ironically echoing a Latinist's excuse.

81–2 The idea here and at 96–7 appears to be that the argument is so contemptibly stupid that it is good for nothing but to be pulverized and dissolved away in water (*plod*, 'pool, puddle').

pouþer of lewednes and of schame. Hyt myȝte wel be þat þou makest þys reson onlych in murthe and in game.

Clericus þe reson mot stonde bot hyt be assoyled.

Dominus A blere-yȝed man, bote he were al blynd of wyt, myȝte yseo þe solucion of þis reson; and þey a were blynd a myȝte grope þe solucion, bote ȝef hys velyng hym faylede. Vor ȝef þis reson were oȝt worþ, by such manere argement me myȝt preove þat þe þre score and ten, and Aquila, Symachus, Theodocion, and he þat made þe vyfte translacion, and Origenes were lewedlych ocupyed whanne hy translated holy wryt out of Hebrew into Grw; and also þat Seint Jerom was lewedlych ocupyed whanne he translatede holy writ out of Hebreu ynto Latyn; vor þe Hebreu ys boþe good and feyre and ywryte by inspiracion of þe Holy Gost. And al þeuse vor here translacions buþ hyȝlych ypreysed of al holy cherche. þanne þe vorseyde lewed reson ys worþy to be pouþred, yleyd a water and ysouced. Also holy wryt in Latyn ys boþe good and fayr, and ȝet for to make a sermon of holy wryt al yn Latyn to men þat konneþ Englysch and no Latyn hyt were a lewed dede; vor hy buþ nevere þe wyser vor þe Latyn bote hyt be told hem an Englysch what hyt ys to mene, and hyt may noȝt be told an Englysch what þe Latyn ys to mene withoute translacion out of Latyn in Englysch. þanne hyt nedeþ to have an Englysch translacion. And for to kepe hyt in muynde þat hyt be noȝt vorȝut, hyt ys betre þat such a translacion be ymad and ywryte þan yseyd and noȝt ywryte. And so þis vorseyde lewed reson scholde meeve no man þat haþ eny wyt to leve þe makyng of Englysch translacion.

Clericus A gret del of þeuse bokes stondeþ moche by holy wryt, by holy doctors and by philosofy. þanne þeuse bokes scholde noȝt be translated ynto Englysch.

84 'The objection must stand unless it can be countered.'

85–7 'A short-sighted man, provided he was not entirely without intelligence, could see the answer to this objection; and even if he were completely blind, he could still feel the answer, provided his sense of touch did not fail.'

88 **me** 'one': the unstressed form of *man*, not a form of the pronoun *I*.

88–91 Early translations of the Hebrew Old Testament into Greek were gathered together in parallel columns by Origen (AD *c.*185–*c.*254) in his *Hexapla*. The 'three score and ten' are the translators said to have produced the Greek Old Testament known as the Septuagint (Latin *septuaginta*, 'seventy'); Aquila, Symmachus and Theodotion all produced further versions in the second century. Origen included these four in his *Hexapla*, along with an anonymous 'fifth translation' (the 'Quinta').

92 **Seint Jerom** St Jerome (*c.*342–420) translated the Old Testament from Hebrew into Latin as part of his standard, or 'Vulgate', version of the whole Bible.

95 **vor here translacions** 'on account of their translations'.

96–7 **a water** 'in water'. See 81–2n.

108 **stondeþ moche by** 'draw largely upon'.

Dominus Hyt ys wonder þat þou makest so feble argementys and hast ygo so long to scole. Aristoteles bokes and oþere bokes also of logyk and of philosofy were translated out of Gru into Latyn. Also, atte prayng of Kyng Charles, John Scot translatede Seint Denys hys bokes out of Gru ynto Latyn. Also holy wryt was translated out of Hebrew ynto Gru and out of Gru into Latyn, and þanne out of Latyn ynto Frensch. Þanne what haþ Englysch trespased þat hyt myȝt noȝt be translated into Englysch? Also Kyng Alvred, þat foundede þe unyversité of Oxenford, translatede þe beste lawes into Englysch tonge and a gret del of þe Sauter out of Latyn into Englysch, and made Wyrefryth byschop of Wyrcetre translate Seint Gregore hys bokes Dialoges out of Latyn ynto Saxon. Also Cedmon of Whyteby was inspired of þe Holy Gost and made wonder poesyes an Englysch nyȝ of al þe storyes of holy wryt. Also þe holy man Beda translatede Seint John hys gospel out of Latyn ynto Englysch. Also þou wost where þe Apocalips ys ywryte in þe walles and roof of a chapel boþe in Latyn and yn Freynsch. Also þe gospel and prophecy and þe ryȝt fey of holy churche mot be tauȝt and ypreched to Englyschmen þat conneþ no Latyn. Þanne þe gospel

112 **Aristoteles bokes** Aristotle's works in Latin translations were prime authorities for medieval scholars in the West.

114 **John Scot** John Scotus Erigena (*c.*810–*c.*877), under the patronage of the Carolingian Charles the Bald, translated from Greek into Latin certain theological writings ascribed to Dionysius the Areopagite (Acts 17.34). This Dionysius was also wrongly identified with St Denys, the patron saint of France.

117 **Frensch** Translations of the Bible into French were already current in the thirteenth century, giving rise in the fourteenth to a great two-volume vernacular Bible.

Englysch The 'Wycliffite' translation of the Bible, with which Trevisa's name has been associated, was begun before Wycliffe's death in 1384; but Trevisa shows no awareness of it here. See David C. Fowler, 'John Trevisa and the English Bible', *Modern Philology*, 58 (1960), 81–98.

118 **Kyng Alvred** Alfred the Great of Wessex (849–99), fancifully supposed founder of Oxford University, produced a set of vernacular laws, in which passages are translated from the Latin Bible. He is also said to have left an Anglo-Saxon translation of the Psalms unfinished at the time of his death. In Alfred's Preface to his translation of Gregory's *Pastoral Care* (No. 5 in *A Guide to Old English*), he advocates translation and, like Dominus here, cites renderings of the Hebrew Old Testament as precedents.

121 **Wyrefryth** Werferth, Bishop of Worcester (*Wyrcetre*), made his translation of Gregory's *Dialogues* at the request of King Alfred. Trevisa's parish of Berkeley belonged to the Worcester diocese.

122 **Cedmon** According to Bede, *History* 4.24, Cædmon was the first to retell biblical stories in Anglo-Saxon verse. He was a farmhand attached to the monastery of Whitby in the later seventh century. See No. 9 in *A Guide to Old English.*

125 **Beda** Bede (*c.*673–735) is said to have been engaged on a translation of St John's Gospel at the time of his death.

126 **þe Apocalips** Passages from an Anglo-Norman translation of the Book of Revelation are still to be seen inscribed on the roof beams in the morning room, formerly the chapel, of Berkeley Castle. Clericus would be expected to know this (*þou wost*), since Trevisa was Berkeley's chaplain.

and prophecy and þe ryȝt fey of holy cherche mot be told ham an Englysch, and þat ys noȝt ydo bote by Englysch translacion. Vor such Englysch prechyng ys verrey Englysch translacion, and such Englysch prechyng ys good and neodful; þanne Englysch translacion ys good and neodfol.

Clericus Ȝef a translacion were ymad þat myȝte be amended yn eny poynt, som men hyt wolde blame.

Dominus Ȝef men blameþ þat ys noȝt worþy to be blamed, þanne hy buþ to blame. Clerkes knoweþ wel ynow þat no synfol man doþ so wel þat he ne myȝte do betre, noþer makeþ so good a translacyon þat he ne myȝte make a betre. Þarvore Orygenes made twey translacions and Jerom translatede þryes þe Sauter. Y desire no translacion of þeus bokes þe beste þat myȝte be, for þat were an ydel desyre vor eny man þat ys now here alyve; bote ich wolde have a skylfol translacion þat myȝt be knowe and understonde.

Clericus Wheþer ys ȝow levere have a translacion of þeuse cronyks in ryme oþer yn prose?

Dominus Yn prose, vor comynlych prose ys more cleer þan ryme, more esy and more pleyn to knowe and understonde.

Clericus Þanne God graunte grace greiþlyche to gynne, wyt and wysdom wysly to wyrche, myȝt and muynde of ryȝt menyng, to make translacion trysty and truwe, plesyng to þe Trynyté, þre persones and o god in majesté, þat ever was and evere schal be, and made hevene and erþe and lyȝt vor to schyne, and departede lyȝt and derknes, and clepede lyȝt Day and derknesse Nyȝt, and so was maad evetyde and morowe tyde on day þat had no morow tyde. Þe secunde day he made þe firmament betwene watres, and departede þe watres þat were under þe firmament vram watres þat were above þe firmament and clepede þe firmament Hevone. Þe þridde day he gadrede þe watres þat buþ under hevene ynto on place and made þe erþe unheled and clepede þe gadryngs of watres Sees and drye

131–4 The argument is summed up in the form of a scholastic syllogism: *major premiss* English preaching is English translation; *minor premiss* English preaching is good and necessary; *conclusion* English translation is good and necessary.

137 **þat** 'that which'.

140 **Orygenes** The reference is evidently to Origen's own contributions to his *Hexapla* (88–91n.), revising the text of the Greek Septuagint.

141 **Jerom** Before making his Latin version of the Psalms from the Hebrew original (92n.), St Jerome had made two earlier versions from the Greek.

145 'Would you rather have . . .?' An impersonal construction: 5.6.8.

149–78 The argument being now over, Clericus breaks into a heavily alliterated prayer for God's help in his translation, following it with a summary of biblical events from Creation to Last Judgement – an abbreviated example of the very 'holy writ in English' for which Dominus has argued.

155 **on day þat had no morow tyde** Genesis 1.5: 'And there was evening and morning one day'; but this one day, the first, itself had no morning.

erþe Lond, and made tren and gras. Þe verþe day he made sonne and moone and sterres and sette hem yn þe fermament of hevene, þar vor to schyne and to be toknes and sygnes to departe tymes and ȝeres and nyȝt and day. Þe vyfte day he made voules and bryddes yn aer and fysches yn þe water. Þe sixte day he made bestes of þe lond and man of erþe and put hym yn paradys for he scholde worche and wone þarynne. Bote man brak God hys heste. He vyl ynto synne and was pot out of paradys ynto wo and sorowe, worþy to be dampned to þe peyne of helle wiþoute eny ende. Bot þe Holy Trynyté hadde mersy of man, and þe Vader sende þe Sone, and þe Holy Gost alyȝte on a mayde, and þe Sone tok vlesch and blod of þat blysfol mayde, and deyde on þe rode to save mankynde, and aros þe þridde day gloryous and blysfol, and tauȝte hys disciples, and styȝ into hevene whanne hit was tyme, and schal come atte day of dome and deme quyk and ded. Þanne al men þat buþ ywryte yn þe bok of lyf schal wende wiþ hym ynto þe blysse of hevene, and be þere in body and in soul, and se and knowe hys godhede and manhede in joye wiþout eny ende. *Explicit Dialogus.*

169–75 Following the Apostles' Creed.

12

John Gower: *Confessio Amantis*

John Gower was an old man when he died in 1408. His formative years were apparently spent in Kent and Suffolk; and in later life he took up residence in St Mary's Priory, Southwark, on the south side of London Bridge. He was a gentleman landowner, who also played a part in the legal and official business of London. Chaucer, when setting out for Italy in 1378, gave power of attorney to Gower; and he submitted *Troilus and Criseyde* to him for correction (*Troilus* 5.1856). Gower in his turn refers to Chaucer in his *Confessio Amantis* (8.2941*–57*). Gower's three principal works show his facility in all the three literary languages of late fourteenth-century England. They are: *Mirour de l'Omme*, a long didactic poem in French, completed in the late 1370s; *Vox Clamantis*, a Latin poem concerned with the social evils of the reign of Richard II, among them the Peasants' Revolt of 1381; and the English *Confessio Amantis*. *Confessio Amantis* survives in more than fifty manuscripts (with excerpts in several more), representing the poem in three successive forms, the latest of which was completed in 1392–3. The poem was printed in 1483 (by Caxton) and 1532, and continued throughout the Tudor period to be recognized as a vernacular classic. Puttenham, in 1589, cites Gower and Chaucer as the first true masters of the 'art of English poesy'.

Confessio Amantis ('A Lover's Confession') represents Genius, a priest of Venus, hearing the confession of Amans. He interrogates him about each of the Seven Deadly Sins in turn (see *Ancrene Wisse*, text 4 here), illustrating them and their various sub-species with stories drawn mainly from ancient history and legend. As a dependant of the goddess Venus, Genius represents the power and interests of human love, and he advises Amans accordingly, guiding him in the conduct of his love-affair. Yet Genius is also a priest, and as such he represents another, higher, power, and is concerned with sin as the Church understood it. These two interests conflict on occasion, but less often than might be expected. The civilized, and ineffectual, love of Amans is hardly such as to incur the wrath of the Church – indeed, it even serves to foster certain Christian virtues such as humility. Furthermore, when Amans at last gives it up, in the beautiful closing pages of the poem, he does so not merely because the priest there reminds him of higher truths – the law of reason and the love of God – but also because, as we then learn, he is an old man and no longer fit to serve Venus. Thus, in his case, the law of nature points to the same conclusion as does the law of God.

The following extract consists of Book 1, lines 2399–2661 of *Confessio Amantis*. The manuscript upon which the text is based, Bodleian Fairfax 3, so exactly represents what Gower wrote that it is thought to have been copied under his personal supervision. It faithfully preserves the delicate art of his octosyllabic couplets. As in the best texts of Chaucer's verse, final *-e* is to be pronounced as a syllable, except where it is lost by elision before words beginning with a vowel or (in certain cases) an *h*. Thus: 'I rede͡ how þat þis proudė vicė' (11), where the *-e* elides before *how*, while *proude* has two syllables (on inflexional *-e* in the definite form of adjectives, see 4.4.1). Or again: 'Above͡ allé͡ oþré͡ aȝein þis vicė' (54). The Fairfax scribe carefully observes the distinction between *hire*, 'her' and *here*, 'their', as in 94–5 here. Gower's English reflects in some details his early connections with Kent and Suffolk: e.g. the present participle inflexion *-ende* (*thenkende*, 'thinking', 167), the form *oghne*, 'own' (adj.), and the shortened forms of the third person singular of verbs (*þenkþ* 256). One idiosyncrasy is his habit of shifting words which belong after conjunctions to a position before them (cf. 56, 135, 190–1 here). However, his usage is in general much like that of his London contemporary Chaucer.

Editions

G. C. Macaulay, *The Complete Works of John Gower*, 4 vols (Oxford, 1899–1902)

G. C. Macaulay, *The English Works of John Gower*, EETS e.s. 81–2 (1900–1901)

J. A. W. Bennett, *Selections from John Gower*, Clarendon Medieval and Tudor Series (Oxford, 1968)

Studies

John H. Fisher, *John Gower: Moral Philosopher and Friend of Chaucer* (New York, 1964)

W. P. Ker, 'Gower', in *Essays on Medieval Literature* (London, 1905), pp. 101–34

C. S. Lewis, *The Allegory of Love* (Oxford, 1936), Chapter V

A. J. Minnis, ed., *Gower's Confessio Amantis: Responses and Reassessments* (Cambridge, 1983)

Derek A. Pearsall, 'Gower's Narrative Art', *Publications of the Modern Languages Association*, 81 (1966), 475–84

Derek A. Pearsall, 'Gower's Latin in the *Confessio Amantis*', in A. J. Minnis, ed., *Latin and Vernacular: Studies in Late-Medieval Texts and Manuscripts* (Cambridge, 1989), pp. 13–25

M. L. Samuels and J. J. Smith, *The English of Chaucer and his Contemporaries* (Aberdeen, 1988), Chapters 3 and 9

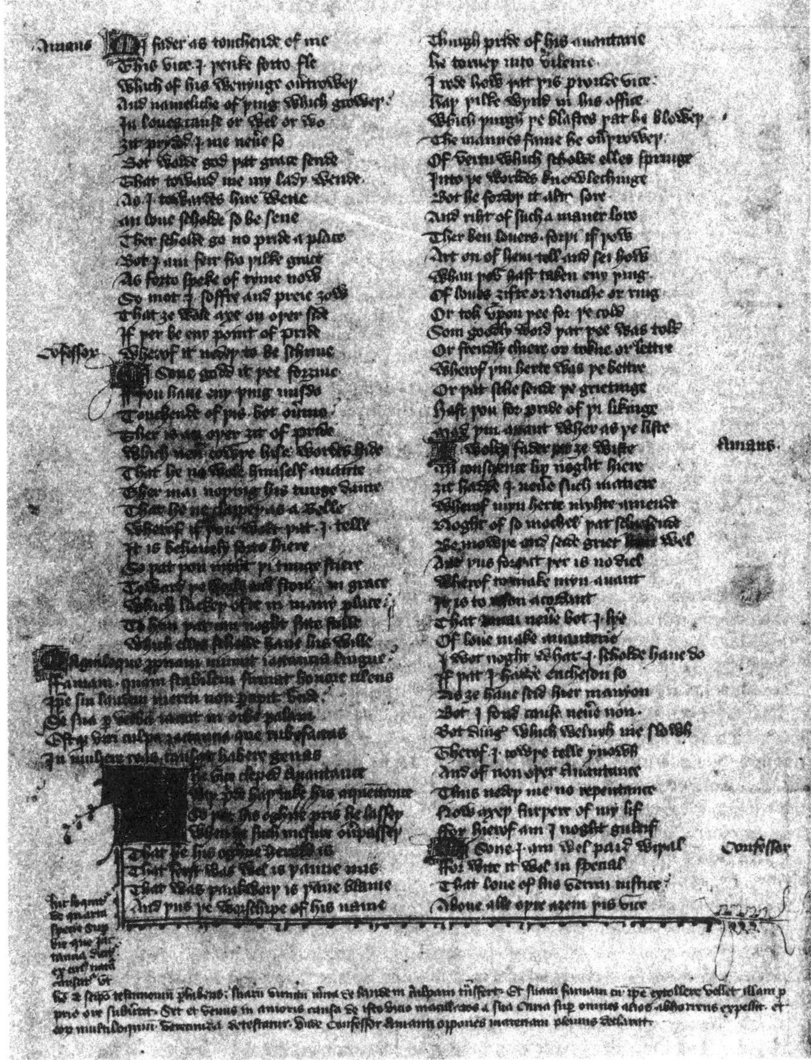

A page from *Confessio Amantis* (MS Fairfax 3). Reproduced by permission of the Bodleian Library.

Magniloque propriam minuit iactancia lingue
Famam, quam stabilem firmat honore cilens.
Ipse sui laudem meriti non percipit, unde
Se sua per verba iactat in orbe palam.
Estque viri culpa iactancia, que rubefactas
In muliere reas causat habere genas.

Confessor

The vice cleped Avantance
Wiþ Pride haþ take his aqueintance,
So þat his oghne pris he lasseþ
When he such mesure overpasseþ
That he his oghne herald is.
That ferst was wel is þanne mis,
That was þankworþ is þanne blame,
And þus þe worschipe of his name
Thurgh pride of his avantarie
He torneþ into vilenie.
I rede how þat þis proude vice
Haþ þilke wynd in his office
Which þurgh þe blastes þat he bloweþ
The mannes fame he overþroweþ
Of vertu, which scholde elles springe
Into þe worldes knowlechinge;
Bot he fordoþ it alto sore.
And riht of such a maner lore

Latin Verses The Prologue and the eight books of *Confessio Amantis* are divided into sections introduced by headnotes in Latin elegiac couplets. Like the Latin prose side-notes (not printed here, but see plate on p. 225), these have no precedent in English poetry. The new format marks the new ambitiousness of Gower's project. The subject of Book 1 is the sin of pride; and the present verses introduce the fourth of its five 'species', boastfulness (*iactancia*): 'The boastfulness of a bragging tongue lessens a man's own proper reputation, whereas by silence he confirms his true distinction. Not hearing from others the praise that he deserves, he glorifies himself in his own words before the world. In the male, moreover, boasting is a fault, since in the woman it causes guilty cheeks to blush.'

4 **mesure** 'proper moderation', i.e. in speaking of one's own merits.

5 **herald** One function of the herald was the public proclamation of a knight's victory and renown: cf. 127–8 here.

6 'What was originally good then becomes bad.'

11–17 The Confessor's source is not known. For the association of vainglory with wind and trumpets, compare *Ancrene Wisse* on pride, No. 4 here, ll. 1–11. In Chaucer's *House of Fame*, the god of winds, Aeolus, acts as trumpeter to the goddess Fame, bringing honour to some and shame to others.

14–15 **fame . . . Of vertu** 'reputation for virtue'.

18–19 'And there are lovers who belong to just such a school of thought.' The Confessor here turns from boasting in general to boasting in love. Male lovers were supposed to be secretive. Boasting of favours received put the lady's honour at risk: cf. the last couplet of the Latin headnote above, and Chaucer's *Troilus* 3.281–322.

Ther ben lovers; forþi if þow
Art on of hem, tell and sei how.
Whan þou hast taken eny þing
Of loves ȝifte, or nouche or ring,
Or tok upon þee for þe cold
Som goodly word þat þee was told,
Or frendly chiere or tokne or lettre,
Wherof þin herte was þe bettre,
Or þat sche sende þe grietinge,
Hast þou for pride of þi likinge
Mad þin avant wher as þe liste?

Amans I wolde, fader, þat ȝe wiste
Mi conscience liþ noght hiere.
Ȝit hadde I nevere such matiere
Wherof myn herte myhte amende –
Noght of so mochel þat sche sende
Be mowþe and seide 'Griet him wel'.
And þus, for þat þer is no diel
Wherof to make myn avant,
It is to reson acordant
That I mai nevere, bot I lye,
Of love make avanterie.
I wot noght what I scholde have do
If þat I hadde encheson so
As ȝe have seid hier manyon,
Bot I fond cause nevere non.
Bot Daunger, which welnyh me slowh,
Therof I cowþe telle ynowh,
And of non oþer avantance.
Thus nedeþ me no repentance:
Now axeþ furþere of my lif,
For hierof am I noght gultif.

Confessor Mi sone, I am wel paid wiþal;
For wite it wel in special
That love of his verrai justice

19 **þow** The Confessor uses the familiar singular pronoun, the Lover the more formal plural *ȝe* (30). See 5.4.1.

23–4 A lover might comfort himself, as if with clothing on a cold day, with the report of some friendly remark about him made by his lady.

27 **þat** 'when', continuing the series of subordinate clauses begun at l. 21.

31 'I have no guilty conscience on that point.'

34 'Not even as much as her sending a message.'

43 'As you have just said many men have.'

45 **Daunger** the disdain or standoffishness of the lady towards her lover, personified here as in the *Romance of the Rose*: cf. the Chaucerian *Romaunt of the Rose* 3130ff., and *Troilus* 2.1376.

Above alle oþre aȝein þis vice
At alle times most debateþ,
Wiþ al his herte and most it hateþ.
And ek in alle maner wise
Avantarie is to despise,
As be ensample þou myhte wite
Which I finde in þe bokes write.
  Of hem þat we Lombars now calle
Albinus was þe ferst of alle
Which bar corone of Lombardie,
And was of gret chivalerie
In werre aȝein diverse kinges.
So fell amonges oþre þinges
That he þat time a werre hadde
Wiþ Gurmond, which þe Geptes ladde
And was a myhti kyng also;
Bot natheles it fell him so
Albinus slowh him in þe feld.
Ther halp him nowþer swerd ne scheld
That he ne smot his hed of þanne,
Wherof he tok awey þe panne,
Of which he seide he wolde make
A cuppe for Gurmoundes sake,
To kepe and drawe into memoire
Of his bataille þe victoire.
And þus whan he þe feld haþ wonne
The lond anon was overronne
And sesed in his oghne hond,
Wher he Gurmondes dowhter fond,
Which Maide Rosemounde hihte,
And was in every mannes sihte

56 Sometimes, strangely, Gower puts words that belong after an *and* before it. So here, *wiþ al his herte* belongs with *hateþ*. See 5.9.5 and cf. l. 135.

59 **ensample** The ensuing illustrative story, or *exemplum*, exemplifies boasting in general (*in alle maner wise*, 57). As the Latin side-note (omitted here) observes, it is directed 'against those who boast either of their prowess in arms or of their success in love': cf. ll. 160–3 and 253–7. Gower's source was a well-known twelfth-century historical work, the *Pantheon* of Godfrey of Viterbo: ed. G. Waitz, in G. H. Pertz, ed., *Monumenta Germaniae Historica*, Scriptores Vol. 22 (Hanover, 1872), pp. 214–16; also *PL* 198.936–8.

61 **Lombars** 'Lombards'. The story is first related in the eighth century by Paul the Deacon in his *History of the Lombards* (*PL* 95.475–6, 498–500).

68 **Geptes** the Gepidi, a barbarian people who fought with the Lombards in the mid-sixth century.

72–3 'Neither sword nor shield could help him in preventing him [Albinus] from then cutting his head off.'

81 **sesed** 'seised', a legal term: 'taken into possession'.

A fair, a freissh, a lusti on.
His herte fell to hire anon,
And such a love on hire he caste
That he hire weddeþ ate laste;
And after þat long time in reste
Wiþ hire he duelte, and to þe beste
Thei love ech oþer wonder wel.
Bot sche which kepþ þe blinde whel,
Venus, whan þei be most above
In al þe hoteste of here love,
Hire whiel sche torneþ, and þei felle
In þe manere as I schal telle.
 This king, which stod in al his welþe
Of pes, of worschipe and of helþe,
And felte him on no side grieved
As he þat haþ his world achieved,
Tho þoghte he wolde a feste make;
And þat was for his wyves sake,
That sche þe lordes ate feste
That were obeissant to his heste
Mai knowe. And so forþ þerupon
He let ordeine and sende anon
Be lettres and be messagiers,
And warnede alle hise officiers
That every þing be wel arraied.
The grete stiedes were assaied
For joustinge and for tornement,
And many a perled garnement
Embroudred was aȝein þe dai.
The lordes in here beste arrai
Be comen ate time set.
On jousteþ wel, anoþer bet,
And oþerwhile þei torneie;
And þus þei casten care aweie
And token lustes upon honde;

85 **a lusti on** 'a vivacious creature' (*on*, 'one').

92–6 The wheel of the blind goddess Fortune (cf. 226–7) is here attributed to the goddess of love: cf. the Chaucerian *Romaunt of the Rose* 4353–66.

93 **most above** 'at the highest point' (in their fortunes as lovers).

103–5 'So that at the feast she may get to know the lords who were subject to him.'

106 'He caused orders to be given and messages to be sent at once.' See 5.6.5.

111 Jousts were for single combat, tournaments for mass encounters. Cf. 116–17 below.

113 **aȝein** 'in preparation for'.

119 'And engaged in pleasures.'

And after, þou schalt understonde,
To mete into þe kinges halle
Thei come, as þei be beden alle.
And whan þei were set and served,
Thanne after, as it was deserved,
To hem þat worþi knyhtes were,
So as þei seten hiere and þere,
The pris was ȝove and spoken oute
Among þe heraldz al aboute;
And þus beneþe and ek above
Al was of armes and of love,
Wherof abouten ate bordes
Men hadde manye sondri wordes,
That of þe merþe which þei made
The king himself began to glade,
Wiþinne his herte and tok a pride,
And sih þe cuppe stonde aside
Which mad was of Gurmoundes hed,
As ȝe have herd, whan he was ded,
And was wiþ gold and riche stones
Beset and bounde for þe nones,
And stod upon a fot on heihte
Of burned gold, and wiþ gret sleihte
Of werkmanschipe it was begrave
Of such werk as it scholde have,
And was policed ek so clene
That no signe of þe skulle is sene,
Bot as it were a gripes ey.
The king bad bere his cuppe awey

121 **mete** a noun, 'food'.

127–8 Compare l. 5 above, and note there. These knights are not 'their own heralds'.

129 i.e. among those sitting on both the low and the high tables.

135 See 56n.

136 **aside** 'on a side table'.

140 **for þe nones** 'for the purpose'.

144 'With the most suitable kind of decoration.'

147 **gripes ey** 'griffin's egg', the name of a kind of drinking-vessel, referred to in late medieval wills. It was made from a large eggshell, perhaps an ostrich's, set in a surround and on a base of precious metals: *OED Gripe's egg* and *MED grip(e* n. (3) (d). Such bejewelled eggshells were attributed to griffins, perhaps because those fabulous creatures 'kepen þe mounteyns in þe whiche ben gemmes and precious stones' (Trevisa, *Properties*, p. 1207; cf. *Paradise Lost* 2.943). In the source, Godfrey's *Pantheon*, the skull is simply 'bound in gold'; but Gower vividly imagines an ornate contemporary cup, in which the skull, like the eggshell in a 'griffin's egg', would be heavily overlaid. Hence Gower's Rosemounde, more plausibly than Godfrey's, can drink from it in ignorance of its origin and significance.

Which stod tofore him on þe bord
And fette þilke. Upon his word
This skulle is fet and wyn þerinne,
Wherof he bad his wif beginne:
'Drink wiþ þi fader, dame', he seide.
And sche to his biddinge obeide,
And tok þe skulle, and what hire liste
Sche drank, as sche which noþing wiste
What cuppe it was; and þanne al oute
The kyng in audience aboute
Haþ told it was hire fader skulle,
So þat þe lordes knowe schulle
Of his bataille a soþ witnesse,
And made avant þurgh what prouesse
He haþ his wyves love wonne,
Which of þe skulle haþ so begonne.
Tho was þer mochel pride alofte.
Thei speken alle, and sche was softe,
Thenkende on þilke unkynde pride
Of þat hire lord so nyh hire side
Avanteþ him þat he haþ slain
And piked out hire fader brain
And of þe skulle had mad a cuppe.
  Sche soffreþ al til þei were uppe,
And þo sche haþ seknesse feigned
And goþ to chambre and haþ compleigned
Unto a maide which sche triste,
So þat non oþer wyht it wiste.
This mayde Glodeside is hote,
To whom þis lady haþ behote

150 **fette** an infinitive depending, like *bere* (148), on *bad* (148): 'The king ordered his cup to be carried away . . . and that same (the skull-cup) to be fetched.' See 5.6.5.

151 **wyn þerinne** 'wine (is put) in it'.

153 The emphatic reversal of stress in the first foot (*Drink wiþ þi fader*), rare in Gower's verse, marks the saying which forms the core of the story: 'Bibe cum patre tuo' in Godfrey's *Pantheon*.

162 **avant** 'boast'. This word, with *avanteþ* (169) and *avant* (187), marks the point at which the story touches its announced theme.

164 His wife had begun the feast at his command (l. 152) by drinking from the skull.

168 'In that her husband, sitting so near at her side.'

171 **had** a past participle, depending on *haþ* (169). Albinus boasts that he 'has had' the cup made. The past tense would be *hadde*, with two syllables.

172 **uppe** 'risen from the table'.

176 'On the understanding that no one else should know it.' The queen takes her waiting-woman into her confidence.

Of ladischipe al þat sche can,
To vengen hire upon þis man
Which dede hire drinke in such a plit
Among hem alle for despit
Of hire and of hire fader boþe;
Wherof hire þoghtes ben so wroþe,
Sche seiþ þat sche schal noght be glad
Til þat sche se him so bestad
That he nomore make avant.
And þus þei felle in covenant
That þei acorden ate laste
Wiþ suche wiles as þei caste
That þei wol gete of here acord
Som orped knyht to sle þis lord;
And wiþ þis sleihte þei beginne
How þei Helmege myhten winne,
Which was þe kinges boteler,
A proud, a lusti bacheler,
And Glodeside he loveþ hote.
And sche, to make him more assote,
Hire love granteþ, and be nyhte
Thei schape how þei togedre myhte
Abedde meete; and don it was
This same nyht. And in þis cas
The qwene hirself þe nyht secounde
Wente in hire stede, and þere haþ founde
A chambre derk wiþoute liht,
And goþ to bedde to þis knyht.
And he, to kepe his observance,
To love doþ his obeissance,
And weneþ it be Glodeside;
And sche þanne after lay aside
And axeþ him what he haþ do,
And who sche was sche tolde him þo,
And seide: 'Helmege, I am þi qwene.

179 **ladischipe** 'favour, patronage'. The queen promises to use all her influence to advance the damsel's career at court.

181 **dede hire drinke** 'caused her to drink'.

191 **of here acord** 'to join in their agreement'.

193–4 **beginne / How** 'begin to consider how'.

195 **boteler** 'butler'. The butler was a court officer charged with responsibility for the royal wine.

196 **bacheler** 'young knight'. The butlership was a knightly office; cf. Sir Lucan the Butler in Malory.

207–8 The sexual act is here described in courtly euphemisms: Love is a god whose rituals demand observance, and a lord whose commands require obedience.

Now schal þi love wel be sene
Of þat þou hast þi wille wroght:
Or it schal sore ben aboght,
Or þou schalt worche as I þee seie.
And if þou wolt be such a weie
Do my plesance and holde it stille,
For evere I schal ben at þi wille,
Boþe I and al myn heritage.'
Anon þe wylde loves rage
In which no man him can governe
Haþ mad him þat he can noght werne,
Bot fell al hol to hire assent.
And þus þe whiel is al miswent
The which Fortune haþ upon honde;
For how þat evere it after stonde,
Thei schope among hem such a wyle
The king was ded wiþinne a whyle.
So slihly cam it noght aboute
That þei ne ben descoevered oute,
So þat it þoghte hem for þe beste
To fle, for þere was no reste;
And þus þe tresor of þe king
Thei trusse and mochel oþer þing,
And wiþ a certein felaschipe
Thei fledde and wente awey be schipe,
And hielde here rihte cours fro þenne
Til þat þei come to Ravenne,
Wher þei þe dukes helpe soghte.
And he, so as þei him besoghte,
A place granteþ forto duelle;
Bot after, whan he herde telle
Of þe manere how þei have do,
This duk let schape for hem so
That of a puison which þei drunke

215 'For the one upon whom you have worked your will.'

216 **Or** 'either'.

219 **holde it stille** 'keep it secret'.

225 'But consented to her wishes completely.' In Godfrey's *Pantheon* it is the queen's threats, not Helmege's sudden infatuation with her, that wins his consent.

226–7 See 92–6n.

228 **stonde** subjunctive: 'should turn out'.

231–2 'It was not so secretly done that they escaped discovery.'

240 Gower treats the events at Ravenna, described by Godfrey, in summary fashion. The deaths of Rosemounde and Helmege are not relevant to the Confessor's theme.

246 **let schape** 'caused it to be brought about'.

Thei hadden þat þei have beswunke.
  And al þis made avant of pride.
Good is þerfore a man to hide
His oghne pris, for if he speke
He mai lihtliche his þonk tobreke.
In armes liþ non avantance
To him which þenkþ his name avance
And be renomed of his dede;
And also who þat þenkþ to spede
Of love he mai him noght avaunte;
For what man þilke vice haunte
His pourpos schal ful ofte faile.
In armes he þat wol travaile,
Or elles loves grace atteigne,
His lose tunge he mot restreigne,
Which berþ of his honour þe keie.

249 'And proud boasting caused all this.'
252 'He may easily shatter the goodwill of others.'

13
Lyrics

a–f RAWLINSON LYRICS

A single strip of parchment bound into a Bodleian Library manuscript, MS Rawlinson D 913, preserves a number of short poems in English and French. They were written down in the early fourteenth century in the south of England. The English poems are of a more popular character than the Harley and Grimestone lyrics which follow here (13g–k, l–r). The large amount of repetition and redundancy, especially noticeable in 13a, c and f, suggests song – in some cases most probably also accompanied by dance. In particular, 13b has the form of a dance-song or 'carol': the burden or refrain ('Icham of Irlaunde' etc.) to be sung by dancers dancing in a ring, and the stanza ('Gode sire' etc.) to be sung by a soloist. Similarly, 13c ('Maiden in the mor lay'), which happens to be referred to in a fourteenth-century sermon, is there described as 'a certain song, namely a *karole*'. The least song-like of the poems is 13d, an extremely enigmatic piece of love-narrative.

Editions and Studies

J. A. Burrow, *Essays on Medieval Literature* (Oxford, 1984), pp. 1–26

R. T. Davies, *Medieval English Lyrics: A Critical Anthology* (London, 1963)

Richard Leighton Greene, *The Early English Carols*, 2nd edn (Oxford, 1977)

Rossell Hope Robbins, *Secular Lyrics of the XIVth and XVth Centuries* (Oxford, 1952)

Siegfried Wenzel, 'The Moor Maiden – A Contemporary View', *Speculum*, 49 (1974), 69–74

(*a*)

Of everykune tre,
Of everykune tre,
þe haweþorn blowet swotes,
Of everykune tre.

My lemmon sse ssal boe,
My lemmon sse ssal boe,
þe fairest of every kinne
My lemmon sse ssal boe.

(*b*)

Icham of Irlaunde
Ant of the holy londe
Of Irlande.

Gode sire, pray ich þe
For of saynte charité
Come ant daunce wyt me
In Irlaunde.

(*c*)

Maiden in the mor lay,
In the mor lay,
Sevenyst fulle ant a –
Sevenist fulle ant a –
Maiden in the mor lay,
In the mor lay,
Sevenistes fulle ant a day.

Welle was hire mete,
Wat was hire mete?

a/3 **blowet swotes** 'blossoms most sweetly'. See 4.4.4.

a/5 'My mistress she must be.'

b/1 'I am from Ireland.' W. B. Yeats adapted this carol burden (see Headnote) for his own poem, 'I am of Ireland'.

b/4–7 This stanza may have been meant for repetition by a female soloist, inviting individual male dancers to join her in the centre of the dance-ring.

b/5 An entreaty: 'For the sake of holy charity'.

c/1 The mysterious 'maiden' sleeps out on the moor for seven nights in a shelter of roses and lilies, eating primroses and violets and drinking spring water. Scholars have identified her, variously, with the Virgin Mary, Mary Magdalene, a dead child, a water-sprite etc.; but it is doubtful whether the singers would have known or cared who she was.

c/3 **Sevenyst** 'seven nights', an uninflected plural (contrast l. 7). Here *s* represents the 'yogh' sound (2.3). Compare *alnist* (e/1, 2) and *noust* (e/3) here, and 2/78 (*mist*) above.

þe primerole ant the –
þe primerole ant the –
Welle was hire mete,
Wat was hire mete?
þe primerole ant the violet.

Welle was hire dryng,
Wat was hire dryng?
þe chelde water of the –
þe chelde water of the –
Welle was hire dryng,
Wat was hire dryng?
þe chelde water of the welle-spring.

Welle was hire bour,
Wat was hire bour?
þe rede rose an te –
þe rede rose an te –
Welle was hire bour,
Wat was hire bour?
þe rede rose an te lilie flour.

(*d*)

Wer þer ouþer in þis toun
Ale or wyn,
Isch hit wolde bugge
To lemmon myn.

Welle wo was so hardy
Forte make my lef al blody.

þaut he were þe kynges sone
Of Normaundy,
ȝet icholde awreke boe
For lemman myn.

Welle wo was me tho,
Wo was me tho;
þe man that leset þat he lovet
Hym is al so.

c/15–28 These stanzas are much abbreviated in the manuscript (see Textual Notes). They have been expanded on the model of the second stanza.

d/5–6 'It was a very unhappy thing that anyone should be so bold as to make my beloved all bloody.' The circumstances of this assault are quite obscure. It apparently involved the loss, but not the death, of the mistress.

d/9 **icholde** 'I would' (*ich wolde*).

d/11 'It was a very unhappy thing for me then.'

d/13–14 'That is how it is for the man who loses what he loves.'

So sse me lerde –
Ne no more I ne can,
But Crist ich hire biteche
þat was my lemman.

(*e*)

Alnist by þe rose rose,
Alnist bi the rose I lay.
Darst ich noust þe rose stele,
Ant ȝet I bar þe flour awey.

(*f*)

Al gold Jonet is þin her,
Al gold Jonet is þin her.
Save þin Jankyn, lemman dere,
Save Jankyn, lemman dere,
Save þin onlie dere.

g–k HARLEY LYRICS

In about 1340 a scribe accustomed to copying documents in Ludlow (on the border of Shropshire and Herefordshire) compiled a wide-ranging anthology of texts in Latin, French and English, now in the British Library, MS Harley 2253. It includes a remarkable series of English lyrics, both religious and secular, many of them highly sophisticated in their use of language and their stanza-structures. Four poems of secular love are chosen here. They show the influence of French and troubadour traditions: 13g is in carol form with a burden (see Headnote to 13a–f above), 13h is a fine example of a *reverdie* or spring-song, while 13j is a variety of the *pastourelle* in which the lover pleads with his lady at her window. Characteristic is the juxtaposition of rhetorical figures with down-to-earth colloquialisms, seen at its most striking in 13j.

Many of the lyrics were composed in other parts of the country, and show traces of dialects other than that of the Harley scribe. 'She' is often *he*, 'they' is *þey* in 13j/38, 'them' is *hem* and 'their' is *huere*. The present third person singular verb ending is *-eþ*; the

e/1 **Alnist** 'all night'. Cf. c/3n. above.

e/4 **flour** If the rose-bush represents the beloved, then the 'flower' is her maidenhood.

f/3 **Jankyn** a familiar form of 'John': like 'Janet', a common name (cf. Wife of Bath's Prologue, *Canterbury Tales* III 303, 548).

plural ending is usually the expected *-eþ* of the South-West Midlands, but sometimes the Midland *-e(n)* (*lete* 13j/38, *waxen* 13h/15), or the Northern *-es* (*wowes* 13h/19).

Edition

G. L. Brook, *The Harley Lyrics*, 4th edn (Manchester, 1968)

Facsimile

Facsimile of British Museum MS. Harley 2253, introduction by N. R. Ker, EETS 255 (1965)

Studies

Derek Pearsall, *Old English and Middle English Poetry* (London, 1977), pp. 120–32

Carter Revard, 'Richard Hurd and MS. Harley 2253', *Notes and Queries*, 224 (1979), 199–202

Rosemary Woolf, in *The Middle Ages* (Sphere History of Literature, Vol. I), ed. W. F. Bolton, 2nd edn (London, 1986), pp. 287–92

(*g*)

Bytwene Mersh ant Averil
  When spray biginneþ to springe,
þe lutel foul haþ hire wyl
  On hyre lud to synge.
  Ich libbe in love-longinge
  For semlokest of alle þynge,
  He may me blisse bringe:
    Icham in hire baundoun.

  An hendy hap ichabbe yhent,
  Ichot from hevene it is me sent,
  From alle wymmen mi love is lent,
    Ant lyht on Alysoun.

On heu hire her is fayr ynoh,
  Hire browe broune, hire eȝe blake,

g/1–8 Here, as even more strikingly in 13k below, there is an abrupt transition from the traditional spring-opening to the love-lament. Contrast the next poem, 13h, where the connection between the two is more explicitly made.

g/3 **haþ hire wyl** 'delights'.

g/7 **He** 'she'.

g/8 **baundoun** 'power'. The image of the lover in thrall to or imprisoned by his mistress is a common one in courtly poetry.

g/9–12 The burden of the carol, repeated after each stanza.

g/9 'I have had wonderful good fortune.'

g/13 **her** 'hair'.

Wiþ lossum chere he on me loh,
Wiþ middel smal ant wel ymake.
Bote he me wolle to hire take
Forte buen hire owen make,
Longe to lyven ichulle forsake
Ant feye fallen adoun.

An hendy hap etc.

Nihtes when y wende ant wake
(Forþi myn wonges waxeþ won),
Levedi, al for þine sake
Longinge is ylent me on.
In world nis non so wyter mon
Þat al hire bounté telle con,
Hire swyre is whittore þen þe swon,
Ant feyrest may in toune.

An hendy hap etc.

Icham for wowyng al forwake,
Wery so water in wore,
Lest eny reve me my make
Ychabbe yȝyrned ȝore.
Betere is þolien whyle sore
Þen mournen evermore.
Geynest under gore,
Herkne to my roun.

An hendi etc.

(*h*)

Lenten ys come wiþ love to toune,
Wiþ blosmen ant wiþ briddes roune,
Þat al þis blisse bryngeþ.
Dayeseȝes in þis dales,
Notes swete of nyhtegales,
Uch foul song singeþ.

g/17 **Bote he** 'unless she'.
g/22 **Nihtes** 'at night' (genitive singular); see 5.3.2.
g/29 **in toune** 'anywhere'. Cf. 13h/1.
g/32 Perhaps 'weary as agitated water'. The meaning of *wore* may be 'disturbance, motion', related to OE *wōrian*, 'to move round'.
g/37 'Most gracious of women.' *Under gore*, 'in a gown', is a conventional phrase in this sort of epithet.
h/1 **to toune** 'into the world'. The opening six lines are very similar to those of a debate poem, *The Thrush and the Nightingale*, in Carleton Brown, *English Lyrics of the XIIIth Century*, No. 52.

þe þrestelcoc him þreteþ oo,
Away is huere wynter wo
  When woderove springeþ.
þis foules singeþ ferly fele
Ant wlyteþ on huere wynne wele,
  þat al þe wode ryngeþ.

þe rose rayleþ hire rode,
þe leves on þe lyhte wode
  Waxen al wiþ wille.
þe mone mandeþ hire bleo,
þe lilie is lossom to seo,
  þe fenyl ant þe fille.
Wowes þis wilde drakes,
Miles murgeþ huere makes,
  Ase strem þat strikeþ stille.
Mody meneþ, so doþ mo;
Ichot ycham on of þo
  For love þat likes ille.

þe mone mandeþ hire lyht,
So doþ þe semly sonne bryht,
  When briddes singeþ breme.
Deawes donkeþ þe dounes,
Deores wiþ huere derne rounes
  Domes forte deme.
Wormes woweþ under cloude,
Wymmen waxeþ wounder proude,
  So wel hit wol hem seme.
Ȝef me shal wonte wille of on,
þis wunne weole y wole forgon
  Ant wyht in wode be fleme.

(*j*)

My deþ y love, my lyf ich hate
  For a levedy shene;

h/11 **wynne wele** 'blissful joy', as in l. 35.
h/20 **Miles** probably 'animals'; a rare Welsh loan.
h/23–4 'I know I am one of those unhappy for love.'
h/29–30 Perhaps 'Animals whisper to their secret loves in order to speak their minds'. In this reading *derne*, 'secret (ones)', is an adjective used as a noun; see 5.5.3.
h/31 **cloude** 'earth'.
h/32–3 'Women become very splendid, so well does it (i.e. spring, love, etc.) suit them.' *Proude* may connote haughtiness and also elegance in dress.
h/34 'If I shall fail to have my joy of one.'

Heo is brith so daies liht,
  þat is on me wel sene;
Al y falewe so doþ þe lef
  In somer when hit is grene;
ȝef mi þoht helpeþ me noht,
  To wham shal y me mene?

Sorewe ant syke ant drery mod
  Byndeþ me so faste
þat y wene to walke wod
  ȝef hit me lengore laste;
My serewe, my care, al wiþ a word
  He myhte awey caste.
'Whet helpeþ þe, my swete lemmon,
  My lyf þus forte gaste?'

'Do wey, þou clerc, þou art a fol!
  Wiþ þe bydde y noht chyde.
Shalt þou never lyve þat day
  Mi love þat þou shalt byde.
ȝef þou in my boure art take,
  Shame þe may bityde;
þe is bettere on fote gon
  þen wycked hors to ryde.'

'Weylawei! Whi seist þou so?
  þou rewe on me, þy man!
þou art ever in my þoht
  In londe wher ich am.
ȝef y deȝe for þi love
  Hit is þe mykel sham.
þou lete me lyve ant be þi luef,
  Ant þou my swete lemman.'

j/11 'That I think I shall go mad.'

j/14 **He** 'she'.

j/15 **Whet helpeþ þe** 'in what way does it help you'.

j/17 **clerc** is deliberately vague. It commonly means a student, often, but not necessarily, one preparing for the priesthood. Compare, for example, the *clerks* in Chaucer's Reeve's Tale. This lover, however, reveals (l. 57) that he is no longer a student, and so is perhaps now in minor orders, like Will in No. 7a above.

j/18 'I don't want to get into an argument with you.'

j/21 **take** 'captured, seized'.

j/23–4 Apparently proverbial: 'it is better for you to travel on foot than on a horse that will throw you'.

j/28 'Wherever I go.'

j/30 **þe** 'to you'.

'Be stille, þou fol! Y calle þe riþt.
  Cost þou never blynne?
þou art wayted day ant nyht
  Wiþ fader ant al my kynne.
Be þou in mi bour ytake,
  Lete þey for no synne
Me to holde ant þe to slon;
  þe deþ so þou maht wynne.'

'Swete ledy, þou wend þi mod;
  Sorewe þou wolt me kyþe.
Ich am al so sory mon
  So ich was whylen blyþe.
In a wyndou þer we stod
  We custe us fyfty syþe.
Feir biheste makeþ mony mon
  Al is serewes mythe.'

'Weylawey! Whi seist þou so?
  Mi serewe þou makest newe.
Y lovede a clerke al par amours;
  Of love he wes ful trewe.
He nes nout blyþe never a day
  Bote he me sone seȝe.
Ich lovede him betere þen my lyf;
  Whet bote is hit to leȝe?'

'Whil y wes a clerc in scole;
  Wel muchel y couþe of lore.
Ych have þoled for þy love
  Woundes fele sore,
Fer from þe ant eke from men
  Under þe wode-gore.
Swete ledy, þou rewe of me.
  Nou may y no more!'

'þou semest wel to ben a clerc,
  For þou spekest so shille.
Shalt þou never for mi love
  Woundes þole grylle.

j/34 **Cost** a form of 'canst' (4.5.7).
j/35–6 **wayted . . . Wiþ** 'spied on by'.
j/37 **Be þou** 'if you are'.
j/38–9 'However wicked it may be, they will not hesitate (*Lete*) to imprison me and slay you.'
j/48 **is** 'his'.
j/51 **par amours** 'passionately'.

Fader, moder ant al my kun
  Ne shal me holde so stille
Þat y nam þyn ant þou art myn
  To don al þi wille.'

(*k*)

When þe nyhtegale singes
  Þe wodes waxen grene,
Lef ant gras ant blosme springes
  In Averyl, y wene,
Ant love is to myn herte gon
  Wiþ one spere so kene,
Nyht ant day my blod hit drynkes;
  Myn herte deþ me tene.

Ich have loved al þis ȝer
  Þat y may love namore,
Ich have siked moni syk,
  Lemmon, for þin ore;
Me nis love never þe ner
  Ant þat me reweþ sore.
Swete lemmon, þench on me;
  Ich have loved þe ȝore.

Swete lemmon, y preye þe
  Of love one speche.
Whil y lyve in world so wyde
  Oþer nulle y seche.
Wiþ þy love, my swete leof,
  Mi blis þou mihtes eche.
A swete cos of þy mouþ
  Mihte be my leche.

Swete lemmon, y preȝe þe
  Of a love-bene:
Ȝef þou me lovest ase men says,
  Lemmon, as y wene,
Ant ȝef hit þi wille be,
  Þou loke þat hit be sene.

k/5–7 The traditional image of the wounding dart of love is here presented with unusual vigour.

k/8 **deþ** 'causes'.

k/18 'For one expression of love.'

k/23–4 These lines continue the image of love's wound that only one surgeon can heal.

So muchel y þenke upon þe
  þat al y waxe grene.

Bitwene Lyncolne ant Lyndeseye,
  Norhamptoun ant Lounde,
Ne wot y non so fayr a may
  As y go fore ybounde.
Swete lemmon, y preȝe þe
  þou lovie me a stounde.
    Y wole mone my song
    On wham þat hit ys on ylong.

l–r GRIMESTONE LYRICS

In 1372 a Franciscan friar, John of Grimestone, compiled an anthology of pieces (National Library of Scotland MS Advocates 18.7.21) suitable to be quoted in sermons. The quotations are arranged alphabetically under topics (*Abstinencia*, etc.) for ease of reference. Many are Latin; but there are also 239 English poems, generally short enough to be readily used by a preacher. The seven poems selected here all occur in the section headed *Passio Christi* and were primarily intended for use in Good Friday sermons. Six of them take the form of imagined addresses: by the crucified Christ to man (m, n, q); by man to the crucified Christ (p); by man to the infant Christ, anticipating the Crucifixion (l); and by both Christ and man (r).

Grimestone was a Norfolk man, and certain features of his Norfolk English deserve notice. *Sh-* and *wh-* words have *s-* and *w-* respectively (*salt*, 'shalt', l/10; *seld*, 'shield', n/2; *wan*, 'when', l/8; *wy*, 'why', r/2). Final *-th* appears as *-t* (*det*, 'death', n/3; *endet*, 'endeth', l/30). Words with final *-ght* in Modern English have *-th* (*fith*, 'fight', n/1; *þouth*, 'thought', n/7). A more general feature of South-Eastern English is the *e* from Old English *y*, where Modern English commonly has *i*: *senne*, 'sin', r/8 (OE *synn*); *mende*, 'mind', r/20 (OE *mynd*).

Editions and Studies

Carleton Brown, *Religious Lyrics of the XIVth Century*, 2nd edn (Oxford, 1952)

k/32 i.e. green with sickness. Cf. l. 2 above.

k/33–4 Lincoln, Lindsey, Northampton and Lound are all in the East Midlands, at no very great distance apart.

k/36 'As (the one) I am in chains for.'

k/40 'About the one whom it concerns.'

Douglas Gray, *Themes and Images in the Medieval English Religious Lyric* (London, 1972)

Siegfried Wenzel, *Preachers, Poets, and the Early English Lyric* (Princeton, 1986)

Edward Wilson, *A Descriptive Index of the English Lyrics in John of Grimestone's Preaching Book*, Medium Ævum Monographs, n.s. 2 (Oxford, 1973)

Rosemary Woolf, *The English Religious Lyric in the Middle Ages* (Oxford, 1968)

(*l*)

Lullay, lullay litel child, child, reste þe a þrowe.
Fro hey3e hider art þu sent with us to wone lowe;
Pore an litel art þu mad, unkut an unknowe,
Pine an wo to suffren her for þing þat was þin owe.
  Lullay, lullay litel child, sorwe mauth þu make,
  þu art sent into þis werd as tu were forsake.

Lullay, lullay litel grom, king of alle þingge.
Wan I þenke of þi methchef, me listet wol litel singge;
But caren I may for sorwe, 3ef love wer in myn herte,
For swiche peines as þu salt dri3en were nevere non so smerte.
  Lullay, lullay litel child, wel mauth þu cri3e,
  For þan þi bodi is bleyk an blak, sone after sal ben dri3e.

Child, it is a weping dale þat þu art comen inne.
þi pore clutes it proven wel, þi bed mad in þe binne;
Cold an hunger þu must þolen as þu were geten in senne,
An after dey3en on þe tre for love of al mankenne.
  Lullay, lullay litel child, no wonder þou þu care,
  þu art comen amonges hem þat þi det3 sulen 3are.

l/1 This lullaby addressed to the Christ child is adapted from an earlier secular lullaby (Carleton Brown (1952), No. 28). Where the earlier poem laments the general miseries of human life, as in l. 15 here, Grimestone's version concentrates on sorrows specific to Christ: the contrast between his present earthly and his past heavenly existence (2–6), and especially his future passion and death on the cross.

l/4 The 'thing that was your own' is humanity, which God himself created.

l/6 'You are sent into this world as if you have been abandoned.' Cf. Matthew 27.46. *Werd* is a Norfolk form, as in o/1 below.

l/8 **me listet wol litel singge** 'I have very little desire to sing'.

l/12 **bleyk an blak** 'pale and wan' (not 'black').

dri3e 'dry, withered', in death.

l/13 **weping dale** 'vale of tears'.

l/14 **binne** that is, the manger.

l/15 **as** 'as if'.

l/17 **þou** 'though'.

l/18 'You have come among those who will prepare your death.'

Lullay, lullay litel child, for sorwe mauth þu grete.
Þe anguis þat þu suffren salth sal don þe blod to swete;
Naked, bunden saltu ben an seiþen sore bete,
No þing fre upon þi bodi of pine sal be lete.
  Lullai, lullay litel child, it is al for þi fo,
  Þe harde bond of love-longging þat þe hat bunden so.

Lullay, lullay litel child, litel child, þin ore!
It is al for oure owen gilt þat þu art peined sore;
But wolde we ȝet kinde be an liven after þi lore
An leten senne for þi love, ne keptest þu no more.
  Lullay, lullay litel child, softe slep an faste;
  In sorwe endet everi love but þin at þe laste. Amen.

(*m*)

Ȝe þat pasen be þe weyȝe,
  Abidet a litel stounde.
Beholdet, al mi felawes,
  Ȝef ani me lik is founde.
To þe tre with nailes þre
  Wol fast I hange bounde.
With a spere al þoru mi side
  To min herte is mad a wounde.

(*n*)

I am Jesu þat cum to fith
  Withouten seld an spere;
Elles were þi det idith
  Ȝif mi fithting ne were.

l/20 Referring to Christ's agony in the garden: 'His sweat became as drops of blood' (Luke 22.44).

l/22 'No part of your body will be left free of pain.'

l/25 **þin ore** '(I beg for) your mercy'.

l/27–8 'But yet, if we would only be loving and live by your teaching and abandon sin for love of you, you would no more be troubled.'

m/1–4 The biblical source (reproduced in part by Grimestone along with his poem) is Lamentations 1.12: 'O all ye that pass by the way, attend, and see if there be any sorrow like to my sorrow.' These words, originally a lament by the city of Jerusalem, were customarily transferred to Christ on the cross, e.g. in Good Friday services (and in Handel's *Messiah*). Cf. No. 14 below, ll. 253–8.

m/4 **me lik** 'like me', in sorrow.

m/5 **nailes þre** one for each hand and one through both feet. Cf. No. 14 below, ll. 102, 120, 141.

n/1 Here the crucified Christ appeals to man, speaking as a warrior who has fought the powers of evil on his behalf – a common conception, as in *Piers Plowman* B XVIII.

n/3–4 'Otherwise your death would be ordained, if it were not for my fighting.'

Siþen I am comen an have þe broth
  A blisful bote of bale,
Undo þin herte, tel me þi þouth,
  þi sennes grete an smale.

(*o*)

Gold an al þis werdis wyn
  Is nouth but Cristis rode.
I wolde ben clad in Cristis skyn
  þat ran so longe on blode,
An gon t'is herte an taken myn in:
  þer is a fulsum fode.
þan ȝef I litel of kith or kyn,
  For þer is alle gode. Amen.

(*p*)

  Luveli ter of loveli eyȝe,
  Qui dostu me so wo?
  Sorful ter of sorful eyȝe,
  þu brekst myn herte ato.

þu sikest sore;
þi sorwe is more
  þan mannis muth may telle.
þu singest of sorwe,
Manken to borwe
  Out of þe pit of helle. Luveli etc.

I prud an kene,
þu meke an clene
  Withouten wo or wile.
þu art ded for me
An I live þoru þe,
  So blissed be þat wile. Luveli etc.

o/2 'Is as nothing without Christ's cross.'

o/5 'And go to his heart and find my dwelling place.'

o/6 **fulsum fode** 'plentiful supply of food'. So Christ can provide all the essentials of life: clothing, lodging and food.

o/7 'Then I would care little about kith or kin.'

p/1–4 This is the burden of the 'carol' (see 13b above and its Headnote), to be repeated after each stanza. It is addressed to the suffering Christ, who is imagined as weeping.

p/2 'Why do you cause me such sorrow?'

p/13 **wo** 'evil' (OE *wōh*), to be distinguished from *wo*, 'woe' (OE *wā*) in ll. 2 and 18.

þi moder seet
Hou wo þe beet,
   An þerfore ȝerne sche ȝerte.
To hire þu speke
Hire sorwe to sleke:
   Swet suet wan þin herte.   Luveli etc.

þin herte is rent,
þi bodi is bent
   Upon þe rode tre.
þe weder is went,
þe devel is schent,
   Crist, þoru þe mith of þe.   Luveli etc.

(*q*)

Love me brouthte
An love me wrouthte,
   Man, to be þi fere.
Love me fedde
An love me ledde
   An love me lettet here

Love me slou
An love me drou
   An love me leyde on bere.
Love is my pes;
For love I ches
   Man to byȝen dere.

Ne dred þe nouth,
I have þe south
   Boþen day an nith.
To haven þe

p/18 'How great is your grief' (*beet*, 'is').

p/20 Christ addresses Mary from the cross in John 19.25–7.

p/22 'Her loving appeal won your heart.' In devotional amplifications of the crucifixion scene, Mary is represented as appealing to Christ to spare her the suffering his pain causes her.

p/26 'The storm has passed.' Another fourteenth-century poem incorporates this same stanza (Carleton Brown (1952), No. 90, ll. 15–18) and reads *wrong* for *þe weder* here.

q/1–3 The speaker is the crucified Christ. His love for mankind brought him to earth and caused him to become man's companion and equal.

q/6 **me lettet** 'causes me to remain, detains me'.

q/16–17 'I am happy to possess you.' Taken with the following line, this suggests the idea, common at the time, of Christ winning mankind like a knight winning his lady by force of arms.

Wel is me:
  I have þe wonnen in fith.

(*r*)

Undo þi dore, my spuse dere;
Allas! wy stond I loken out here?
  Fre am I, þi make.
Loke mi lokkes an ek myn heved
An al my bodi with blod beweved
  For þi sake.

Responsio peccatoris:
Allas! allas! hevel have I sped;
For senne Jesu is fro me fled,
  My trewe fere.
Withouten my gate he stant alone,
Sorfuliche he maket his mone
  On his manere.

Ideo, þerfore:
Lord, for senne I sike sore;
Forȝef, an I ne wil no more.
With al my mith senne I forsake
An opne myn herte þe inne to take,
For þin herte is cloven oure love to kecchen,
þi love is chosen us alle to fecchen.
Min herte it þerlede, ȝef I wer kende,
þi swete love to haven in mende.
Perce myn herte with þi lovengge,
þat in þe I have my dwellingge. Amen.

r/1–6 The language of Christ's appeal to sinful man derives from the Song of Songs (5.2), where the woman's beloved was customarily identified as Christ and the woman as humanity: 'The voice of my beloved knocking: Open to me, my sister, my love, my dove, my undefiled: for my head is full of dew, and my locks of the drops of the nights.' Cf. also the Apocalypse (Revelation) 3.20: 'Behold, I stand at the gate and knock.' Grimestone gives the Latin of both passages at the head of his poem.

r/7–12 The 'sinner's response'. Lines 1–12 appear in a thirteenth-century manuscript as a separate poem, but with the order of the two stanzas reversed (Woolf (1968), 51). Grimestone evidently adapted and reordered this earlier piece, and added the couplet conclusion (13–22).

r/7 **hevel have I sped** 'things have gone badly with me'.

r/13–22 The penitent conclusion (*ideo*, 'therefore'), added by Grimestone.

r/18 'Your love has been chosen to rescue us all.'

r/19 'It would pierce my heart, if I had natural feelings.'

r/22 Compare o/5 above.

14

The York Play of the Crucifixion

There are references to the performance of a cycle of mystery plays at York from the late fourteenth century. A list of plays with the craft guilds responsible for producing them was drawn up in 1415, and subsequently revised in line with developments in the cycle. Considerably later, at some time between 1463 and 1477, the texts of forty-five plays were written down as the official register of the cycle for the city corporation. This is now MS Additional 35290 in the British Library. The plays continued to be performed in York until at least 1569, and the register was used as a check on the arrangements for these performances. The York cycle of plays encompasses the whole of the history of salvation, from the Fall of the Angels to the Last Judgement, with particular emphasis given to the life of Christ.

The organizations responsible for staging and financing the individual plays were the city's craft guilds. The plays were staged on pageant wagons which followed a prescribed route through the city, each stopping in turn at some twelve stations to perform its play. The performance took place annually on the feast of Corpus Christi in late May or June, beginning at daybreak and ending after midnight.

The play of the Crucifixion was staged, appropriately enough, by the Pinners, whose craft was to make pins, nails and hooks. Its principal source is, of course, the account of the Crucifixion in the Gospels, and it draws also on Latin and vernacular meditations that envisage Christ nailed to the cross as it lies on the ground, a cross with the holes for the nails too far apart for the body that has shrunk in pain. Like all the York Plays it is written in rhyming stanzas, in this case a twelve-line stanza of eight four-stress lines followed by four three-stress lines, rhyming *abababab cdcd*, and with much alliteration.

The following features are characteristic of the Northern dialect of the text: the third person plural pronouns are *þai* and *þei*, *þame*, *þare* and *þer*; the present plural of verbs ends in *-s* when not preceded by a pronoun subject: *has* (5), *walkis* (253), but *þei wirke* (261); the imperative plural often ends in *-s*: *commes* (32), *gose* (78), but *take* (1); the present participle ends in *-and*: *doand* (267); the past participle of strong verbs ends in *-en*: *geven* (5), *comen* (7).

Editions

Richard Beadle, *The York Plays* (London, 1982)
Lucy Toulmin Smith, *York Plays* (Oxford, 1885)

Facsimile

The York Play, introduced by Richard Beadle and Peter Meredith (Leeds, 1983)

Studies

Richard Beadle, ed., *The Cambridge Companion to Medieval English Theatre* (Cambridge, 1994)
Alexandra F. Johnston and Margaret Rogerson, *Records of Early English Drama: York* (Toronto, 1979)
V. A. Kolve, *The Play Called Corpus Christi* (Stanford, 1966)
Rosemary Woolf, *The English Mystery Plays* (London, 1972)

1 Soldier Sir knyghtis, take heede hydir in hye,
This dede on dergh we may noght drawe.
Ȝee wootte youreselffe als wele as I
Howe lordis and leders of owre lawe
Has geven dome þat þis doote schall dye.
2 Sold. Sir, alle þare counsaile wele we knawe.
Sen we are comen to Calvarie
Latte ilke man helpe nowe as hym awe.
3 Sold. We are alle redy, loo,
þat forward to fullfille.
4 Sold. Late here howe we schall doo
And go we tyte þertille.

1 Sold. It may noȝt helpe her for to hone
If we schall any worshippe wynne.
2 Sold. He muste be dede nedelyngis by none.
3 Sold. þanne is goode tyme þat we begynne.
4 Sold. Late dynge hym doune, þan is he done.
He schall nought dere us with his dynne.
1 Sold. He schall be sette and lerned sone
With care to hym and all his kynne.

2 **on dergh . . . drawe** 'draw out in length', so 'delay'. The first soldier is evidently the leader of the group.

11 **Late here** 'make heard', that is 'tell us'. On the construction of *let* followed by an infinitive with passive sense, see 5.6.5, and cf. below *Late dynge hym doune*, 'strike him down' (17), and *Late bere* (178).

19 **sette and lerned** contemptuous: 'put to school and taught a lesson'.

2 Sold. þe foulest dede of all
Shalle he dye for his dedis.
3 Sold. That menes crosse hym we schall.
4 Sold. Behalde, so right he redis!

1 Sold. Thanne to þis werke us muste take heede
So þat oure wirkyng be noght wrange.
2 Sold. None othir noote to neven is nede,
But latte us haste hym for to hange.
3 Sold. And I have gone for gere goode speede,
Bothe hammeres and nayles large and lange.
4 Sold. þanne may we boldely do þis dede;
Commes on, late kille þis traitoure strange!
1 Sold. Faire myght ȝe falle in feere
þat has wrought on þis wise.
2 Sold. Us nedis nought for to lere
Suche faitoures to chastise.

3 Sold. Sen ilke a thyng es right arrayed,
The wiselier nowe wirke may we.
4 Sold. þe crosse on grounde is goodely graied
And boorede even as it awith to be.
1 Sold. Lokis þat þe ladde on lenghe be layde
And made me þane unto þis tree.
2 Sold. For alle his fare he schalle be flaied;
That one assaie sone schalle ye see.
3 Sold. Come forthe, þou cursed knave;
Thy comforte sone schall kele.
4 Sold. Thyne hyre here schall þou have.
1 Sold. Walkes oon! Now wirke we wele.

Jesus Almyghty God, my fadir free,
Late þis materes be made in mynde.
þou badde þat I schulde buxsome be
For Adam plyght for to be pyned.
Here to dede I obblisshe me

21–2 There is a play on *dede*, 'death', and *dedis*, 'deeds'.
27 'There is no need to talk about any other business.'
32 **strange** the Northern form of 'strong'.
33–4 'May things turn out well for all of you who have acted in this way.'
40 The holes have already been bored to take the nails.
42 **made me** 'fastened'; see 5.3.3. The *tree* is the wood of the cross.
43 'Despite all his boasting, he'll be terrified.'
44 **one assaie** 'in the event'.
48 **Walkes oon** 'carry on'; the imperative plural, addressed to the soldiers.
52 **Adam plyght** 'Adam's sin'. *Adam* is genitive; see 4.2.4.
53 'Here I submit myself to death.'

Fro þat synne for to save mankynde,
And soveraynely beseke I þe
That þai for me may favoure fynde
And fro þe fende þame fende,
So þat þer saules be saffe
In welthe withouten ende;
I kepe nought ellis to crave.

1 Sold. We, herke, sir knyghtis, for Mahoundis bloode!
Of Adam kynde is all his þoght.
2 Sold. þe warlowe waxis werre þan woode,
þis doulfull dede ne dredith he noght.
3 Sold. þou schulde have mynde, with mayne and moode,
Of wikkid werkis þat þou haste wrought.
4 Sold. I hope þat he hadde bene as goode
Have sesed of sawes þat he uppe-sought.
1 Sold. Thoo sawes schall rewe hym sare,
For all his saunteryng sone.
2 Sold. Ille spede þame þat hym spare
Tille he to dede be done.

3 Sold. Have done belyve, boy, and make þe boune
And bende þi bakke unto þis tree.
4 Sold. Byhalde, hymselffe has laide hym doune
In lenghe and breede as he schulde bee.
1 Sold. This traitoure here teynted of treasoune,
Gose faste and fette hym þan ȝe thre,
And sen he claymeth kyngdome with croune,
Even as a kyng here have schall hee.

2 Sold. Now certis I schall noȝt fyne
Or his right hande be feste.
3 Sold. þe lefte hande þanne is myne.
Late see who beres hym beste.

60 **kepe** 'care, wish', a common early sense.

61 **Mahoundis bloode** the Roman soldiers have their version of the oath *by Cristes blod. Mahound* is a form of the name Mahomet; see 8/164–8n.

63 **werre** 'worse'; a Northern form (ON *verre*).

65 **with mayne and moode** 'wholeheartedly'.

67–8 'I reckon he'd have done as well to have left off the stories he made up.' Note here and elsewhere the common Northern sense of *hope*, 'think'.

70 **For** 'despite'.

73 **boy** a contemptuous term in ME.

80 'He will be treated just like a king here.'

82 **Or** 'until'.

84 **beres hym** 'conducts himself', so 'gets on'.

4 Sold. Hys lymmys on lenghe þan schalle I lede
And even unto þe bore þame bringe.
1 Sold. Unto his heede I schall take hede
And with myne hande helpe hym to hyng.
2 Sold. Nowe sen we foure schall do þis dede
And medill with þis unthrifty thyng,
Late no man spare for speciall speede
Tille that we have made endyng.
3 Sold. þis forward may not faile;
Nowe are we right arraiede.
4 Sold. This boy here in oure baile
Shall bide full bittir brayde.

1 Sold. Sir knyghtis, saie, nowe wirke we oght?
2 Sold. ȝis certis, I hope I holde þis hande,
And to þe boore I have it brought
Full boxumly withouten bande.
1 Sold. Strike on þan harde, for hym þe boght.
2 Sold. ȝis, here is a stubbe will stiffely stande,
Thurgh bones and senous it schall be soght.
This werke is wele, I will warande.
1 Sold. Saie sir, howe do we þore?
þis bargayne may not blynne.
3 Sold. It failis a foote and more,
þe senous are so gone ynne.

4 Sold. I hope þat marke amisse be bored.
2 Sold. þan muste he bide in bittir bale.
3 Sold. In faith, it was overe-skantely scored;
þat makes it fouly for to faile.
1 Sold. Why carpe ȝe so? Faste on a corde
And tugge hym to, by toppe and taile.

91 'Let everyone work with exceptional effort.'

93 **may** is used as a future auxiliary, 'shall', as again in l. 106. In l. 208 *myght* is used in the same sense.

97–108 The manuscript confuses the speakers in this stanza. The individual tasks have been apportioned in ll. 81–8. In the arrangement adopted here, the first soldier is in charge at the head, while the second drives the nail into the right hand. Then (l. 105) the first soldier asks how the third soldier is coping with the left hand. He replies that the hand falls far short of the nail-hole.

101 **for hym þe boght** 'for the sake of him who redeemed you'; the oath is a pointed anachronism. On the lack of a relative pronoun see 5.4.6.

108 **gone ynne** 'shrunk'.

111 **overe-skantely scored** 'negligently marked', since the holes to take the nails were made too far apart.

113 **Faste** imperative verb, 'fasten'.

114 **by toppe and taile** that is, 'lengthwise'.

3 Sold. Ȝa, þou comaundis lightly as a lorde;
Come helpe to haale, with ille haile!
1 Sold. Nowe certis þat schall I doo
Full snelly as a snayle.
3 Sold. And I schall tacche hym too,
Full nemely with a nayle.

þis werke will holde, þat dar I heete,
For nowe are feste faste both his hende.
4 Sold. Go we all foure þanne to his feete,
So schall oure space be spedely spende.
2 Sold. Latte see what bourde his bale myght beete;
Tharto my bakke nowe wolde I bende.
4 Sold. Owe! þis werke is all unmeete;
This boring muste all be amende.
1 Sold. A, pees man, for Mahounde!
Latte no man wotte þat wondir.
A roope schall rugge hym doune,
Yf all his synnous go asoundre.

2 Sold. þat corde full kyndely can I knytte
þe comforte of þis karle to kele.
1 Sold. Feste on þanne faste þat all be fytte;
It is no force howe felle he feele.
2 Sold. Lugge on ȝe both a litill ȝitt.
3 Sold. I schalle nought sese, as I have seele!
4 Sold. And I schall fonde hym for to hitte.
2 Sold. Owe, haylle!
4 Sold. Hoo nowe, I halde it wele.
1 Sold. Have done. Dryve in þat nayle
So þat no faute be foune.
4 Sold. þis wirkyng wolde noȝt faile
Yf foure bullis here were boune.

1 Sold. Ther cordis have evill encressed his paynes
Or he wer tille þe booryngis brought.

116 **with ille haile** 'bad luck to you', so 'damn you'.
122 **hende** the Northern plural of 'hand' is required for the rhyme.
125 'Let's see what bit of fun can relieve his pain.'
132 **Yf** 'even though'.
136 'It doesn't matter how painfully he may feel it.'
138 **as I have seele** 'my word on it'; literally 'so may I have bliss'.
139 **hitte** i.e. the nail through the hand.
140 **I halde it wele** 'I think that's fine.'
144 That is, even if a team of oxen were attached (*boune*, 'bound') to the cross.
145 **Ther** 'these'.
146 **Or** 'before', followed by the subjunctive; see 5.6.6.

2 Sold. Ȝaa, assoundir are bothe synnous and veynis
On ilke a side, so have we soughte.
3 Sold. Nowe all his gaudis nothyng hym gaynes;
His sauntering schall with bale be bought.
4 Sold. I wille goo saie to oure soveraynes
Of all þis werkis howe we have wrought.
1 Sold. Nay sirs, anothir thyng
Fallis firste to youe and me;
þei badde we schulde hym hyng
On heghte þat men myght see.

2 Sold. We woote wele so ther wordes wore,
But sir, þat dede will do us dere.
1 Sold. It may not mende for to moote more;
þis harlotte muste be hanged here.
2 Sold. The mortaise is made fitte þerfore.
3 Sold. Feste on youre fyngeres þan in feere.
4 Sold. I wene it wolle nevere come þore;
We foure rayse it noȝt right to-yere.
1 Sold. Say, man, whi carpis þou soo?
Thy liftyng was but light.
2 Sold. He menes þer muste be moo
To heve hym uppe on hight.

3 Sold. Now certis I hope it schall noght nede
To calle to us more companye.
Me thynke we foure schulde do þis dede
And bere hym to ȝone hille on high.
1 Sold. It muste be done, withouten drede.
No more, but loke ȝe be redy,
And þis parte schalle I lifte and leede;
On lenghe he schalle no lenger lie.
Therfore nowe makis you boune,
Late bere hym to ȝone hill.
4 Sold. Thanne will I bere here doune
And tente his tase untill.

2 Sold. We twoo schall see tille aythir side,
For ellis þis werke wille wrie all wrang.

150 'His babbling will be paid for in suffering.'

158 **do us dere** 'cause us trouble', as well as more generally 'do us harm'. The soldiers vigorously complain of their great sufferings; e.g. ll. 189–94.

161 **mortaise** the slot or pit that has been prepared in advance for the cross.

164 **rayse** present tense for the future. See 5.6.1.

180 'And take care of his toes.' The fourth soldier takes responsibility for the foot of the cross (see l. 85).

3 Sold. We are redy.
4 Sold. Gode sirs, abide,
And late me first his fete up fang.
2 Sold. Why tente ȝe so to tales þis tyde?
1 Sold. Lifte uppe!
4 Sold. Latte see!
2 Sold. Owe, lifte alang!
3 Sold. Fro all þis harme he schulde hym hyde
And he war God.
4 Sold. þe devill hym hang.
1 Sold. For grete harme have I hente!
My schuldir is in soundre.
2 Sold. And sertis I am nere schente,
So lange have I borne undir.

3 Sold. This crosse and I in twoo muste twynne,
Ellis brekis my bakke in sondre sone.
4 Sold. Laye downe agayne and leve youre dynne;
þis dede for us will nevere be done.
1 Sold. Assaie, sirs, latte se yf any gynne
May helpe hym uppe withouten hone,
For here schulde wight men worschippe wynne
And noght with gaudis al day to gone.
2 Sold. More wighter men þan we
Full fewe I hope ȝe fynde.
3 Sold. þis bargayne will noght bee,
For certis me wantis wynde.

4 Sold. So wille of werke nevere we wore.
I hope þis carle some cautellis caste.
2 Sold. My bourdeyne satte me wondir soore;
Unto þe hill I myght noght laste.
1 Sold. Lifte uppe and sone he schall be þore.
Therfore feste on youre fyngeres faste.
3 Sold. Owe lifte!
1 Sold. We loo!
4 Sold. A litill more.
2 Sold. Holde þanne!

185 'Why do you spend so much time talking?'

188 **And he war God** cf. Luke 23.35: 'Let him save himself if he be Christ.'

196 **for** 'by'.

200 'And not go around all day amusing themselves.' *Schulde* (199) is followed by two infinitives, *wynne* and *to gone*, on which see 5.6.5.

206 The source for this accusation of witchcraft is the apocryphal Gospel of Nicodemus (in M. R. James, *The Apocryphal New Testament* (Oxford, 1924), 96).

211 **We loo!** an exclamation, 'Phew!'.

1 Sold. Howe nowe?
2 Sold. þe werste is paste.
3 Sold. He weyes a wikkid weght.
2 Sold. So may we all foure saie
Or he was heved on heght
And raysed in þis array.

4 Sold. He made us stande as any stones,
So boustous was he for to bere.
1 Sold. Nowe raise hym nemely for þe nonys
And sette hym be þis mortas heere,
And latte hym falle in alle at ones,
For certis þat payne schall have no pere.
3 Sold. Heve uppe!
4 Sold. Latte doune, so all his bones
Are asoundre nowe on sides seere.
1 Sold. þis fallyng was more felle
þan all the harmes he hadde.
Nowe may a man wele telle
þe leste lith of þis ladde.

3 Sold. Me thynkith þis crosse will noght abide
Ne stande stille in þis morteyse ȝitt.
4 Sold.. Att þe firste tyme was it made overe-wyde;
þat makis it wave, þou may wele witte.
1 Sold. Itt schall be sette on ilke a side
So þat it schall no forther flitte.
Goode wegges schall we take þis tyde
And feste þe foote, þanne is all fitte.
2 Sold. Here are wegges arraied
For þat, both grete and smale.
3 Sold. Where are oure hameres laide
þat we schulde wirke withall?

4 Sold. We have þem here even atte oure hande.
2 Sold. Gyffe me þis wegge, I schall it in dryve.
4 Sold. Here is anodir ȝitt ordande.
3 Sold. Do take it me hidir belyve.
1 Sold. Laye on þanne faste.
3 Sold. Ȝis, I warrande.
I thryng þame same, so motte I thryve.

223–8 Compare Psalm 21.15 and 18 (AV 22.14 and 17).
246 'I'm packing them in tight together, I promise you.'

Nowe will þis crosse full stabely stande;
All yf he rave, þei will noght ryve.
1 Sold. Say, sir, howe likis you nowe
þis werke þat we have wrought?
4 Sold. We praye youe, sais us howe
ȝe fele, or faynte ȝe ought?

Jesus Al men þat walkis by waye or strete,
Takes tente ȝe schalle no travayle tyne.
Byholdes myn heede, myn handis and my feete,
And fully feele nowe or ȝe fyne
Yf any mournyng may be meete
Or myscheve mesured unto myne.
My fadir, þat alle bales may bete,
Forgiffis þes men þat dois me pyne:
What þei wirke wotte þai noght;
Therfore, my fadir, I crave
Latte never þer synnys be sought,
But see þer saules to save.

1 Sold. We, harke! He jangelis like a jay.
2 Sold. Me thynke he patris like a py.
3 Sold. He has ben doand all þis day
And made grete menyng of mercy.
4 Sold. Es þis þe same þat gune us say
That he was Goddis sone almyghty?
1 Sold. Therfore he felis full felle affraye,
And demyd þis day for to dye.
2 Sold. *Vath qui destruit templum!*
3 Sold. His sawes wer so, certayne.
4 Sold. And sirs, he saide to some
He myght rayse it agayne.

248 **All yf** 'even though'.

253–64 Christ's dignified speech is based on two biblical texts: from the Old Testament, 'O all ye that pass by the way, attend, and see if there be any sorrow like to my sorrow' (Lamentations 1.12), and from the Gospels the words from the cross, 'Father, forgive them, for they know not what they do' (Luke 23.34). Both were used in the liturgy for Holy Week, and the former is the basis of several lyrics on the Passion; see No. 13m above, and Rosemary Woolf, *The English Religious Lyric in the Middle Ages* (Oxford, 1968), 42–4.

260 **Forgiffis** imperative, the formal plural, addressed to *my fadir*.

267 **ben doand** 'been at it', that is, chattering.

268 **menyng of** 'lamentation for'. Or the reading may be *mevyng*, 'agitation'.

269 **gune us say** 'said to us'; see 5.6.3.

271–2 'For that reason he is suffering very dreadful pain and is condemned to die today.'

273 'O he who destroys the temple.' The scornful words from Matthew 27.40 and Mark 15.29, alluding to Christ's prophecy of his Resurrection (John 2.19).

1 Sold. To mustir þat he hadde no myght,
For all the kautelles þat he couthe keste.
All yf he wer in worde so wight,
For all his force nowe is he feste.
Als Pilate demed is done and dight,
Therfore I rede þat we go reste.
2 Sold. þis race mon be rehersed right
Thurgh þe worlde both este and weste.
3 Sold. ȝaa, late hym hynge here stille
And make mowes on þe mone!
4 Sold. þanne may we wende at wille.
1 Sold. Nay, goode sirs, noght so sone.

For certis us nedis anodir note:
þis kirtill wolde I of you crave.
2 Sold. Nay, nay sir, we will loke be lotte
Whilke of us foure fallis it to have.
3 Sold. I rede we drawe cutte for þis coote –
Loo, se howe sone! – alle sidis to save.
4 Sold. The schorte cutte schall wynne, þat wele ȝe woote,
Whedir itt falle to knyght or knave.
1 Sold. Felowes, ȝe thar noght flyte,
For þis mantell is myne.
2 Sold. Goo we þanne hense tyte;
þis travayle here we tyne.

283 'This course of events must be accurately reported.'
286 **mowes** 'grimaces, faces'. The expression *make mowes on þe mone* is elsewhere used as a euphemism for 'be left on the gallows'.
289 'Because in fact another matter demands our attention.'
291 **loke be lotte** 'draw lots to see'.
294 **alle sidis to save** 'to protect everyone's interests'.
300 'We're wasting our efforts here.'

15

Geoffrey Chaucer: *The Parliament of Fowls*

Geoffrey Chaucer was born in the early 1340s and died in 1400. His first datable work was the dream-vision poem, *The Book of the Duchess*, written to commemorate Blanche, Duchess of Lancaster, who died in 1368. In the 1380s he was writing *Troilus and Criseyde*, and he left *The Canterbury Tales* unfinished at his death.

For much of his life he was associated with the court circle. The earliest record of him is as a page in the service of the Countess of Ulster who was married to one of Edward III's sons; later records show regular payments of royal annuities, as well as payments for travelling abroad on the king's business and for services in royal administration. He spent most of his life in London, living for a time at Aldgate (1374–86) when he was controller of customs in the port of London. In the 1390s he retired to Kent. During his lifetime he was recognized as a poet not only in England, honoured by his friend Gower at the end of the *Confessio Amantis*, but also in France, where the poet Deschamps wrote a poem in his praise.

Chaucer's language is well represented by the Fairfax manuscript of *The Parliament of Fowls* and the Hengwrt manuscript of *The Canterbury Tales*, both copied by London scribes. The following points may be noted. The plural forms of the third-person pronoun are *they*, *hem*, 'them', and *hir*, 'their'. The third-person singular verb-ending in the present tense is *-eth*, which is sometimes assimilated into a stem ending in *d* or *t* (e.g. *slyd* for *slydeth*, 15/3; *stant*, 'stands', 16b/62). The plural of the present tense ends in *-e* or *-en*. In the Reeve's Tale, however, Chaucer uses the dialect forms in *-s*, for both singular and plural, to represent the speech of his Northern students (see note to 16a/169).

In his early poems Chaucer wrote in the four-stress line used in the *Owl and the Nightingale*, *Sir Orfeo* and by Gower in the *Confessio Amantis*. In the works here, though, he writes a five-stress line (ten or eleven syllables), which is rarely found before his time. The Reeve's Tale is written in rhyming couplets, whereas both *The Parliament of Fowls* and the Prioress's Tale are in 'rhyme-royal' stanzas of seven lines. The principles to be observed in the pronunciation of final *-e* are explained in the Headnote to Text 12. The feature is well preserved in the Hengwrt text of the *Canterbury Tales*, but less so in the Fairfax manuscript of *The Parliament of Fowls*.

Editions

Walter W. Skeat, *The Complete Works of Geoffrey Chaucer*, 6 vols (Oxford, 1894)

Larry D. Benson, *The Riverside Chaucer* (Boston, 1987; Oxford, 1988)

General Studies

Derek Brewer, ed., *Writers and Their Background. Geoffrey Chaucer* (London, 1974)

E. Talbot Donaldson, *Speaking of Chaucer* (New York, 1970)

Charles Muscatine, *Chaucer and the French Tradition* (Berkeley, 1957)

Derek Pearsall, *The Life of Geoffrey Chaucer* (Oxford, 1992)

Paul Strohm, *Social Chaucer* (Cambridge, Mass., 1989)

The Parliament of Fowls is a dream-vision poem in which the narrator, having read a classic work on the place of man in the universe, dreams of a garden of love in which the birds are assembled under the watchful eye of Nature to choose their mates on St Valentine's Day. The poem was probably written in the early 1380s, and the discussion of the birds may allude to the negotiations for the hand of Anne of Bohemia, who became Richard II's wife in 1382.

Chaucer used the dream-vision form for several poems. In the *Parliament* it allows him to bring together a wide variety of discordant attitudes towards love and sexuality, as represented by Venus, Nature, and a group of noisy birds anxious to select partners and fly away. In his preface to the dream the narrator explains his dependence on books for his understanding of the nature of the good life, and he ends the poem, still unsatisfied, avowing his determination to read further books for enlightenment.

Chaucer names three Latin sources: Cicero's *Somnium Scipionis* (line 31); Macrobius, who provided a commentary to that work (line 111); and *de Planctu Naturae* by Alanus de Insulis (line 316). The description of the temple of Venus closely follows an Italian work of *c.*1340, Giovanni Boccaccio's *Teseida* (the major source for the Knight's Tale); and Chaucer is also indebted to the *Roman de la Rose* (see notes to lines 176–82 and 216) and to Dante's *Divine Comedy* (see note to lines 127–40).

The poem is preserved in fourteen manuscripts and a print by Caxton, which present a wide range of variant readings. The text here is based on Bodleian Library MS Fairfax 16, a mid-fifteenth-century collection of 'courtly' poems, including many by Chaucer, and also by Lydgate, Hoccleve and others. The first poem in the manuscript, Chaucer's *Complaint of Mars*, is illustrated by a magnificent frontispiece with the arms of John Stanley, an official in the royal household.

Editions

D. S. Brewer, *The Parlement of Foulys*, 2nd edn (Manchester, 1972)
The Riverside Chaucer (see above).

Facsimile

Bodleian Library MS Fairfax 16, introduced by John Norton-Smith (London, 1979)

Studies

J. A. W. Bennett, *The Parlement of Foules: An Interpretation* (Oxford, 1957)
P. M. Kean, *Chaucer and the Making of English Poetry*, vol. i: *Love Vision and Debate* (London, 1972), pp. 67–85
A. J. Minnis, *The Shorter Poems*, Oxford Guides to Chaucer (Oxford, 1995), pp. 252–321.
A. C. Spearing, *Medieval Dream-Poetry* (Cambridge, 1976)

The lyf so short, the crafte so longe to lerne,
Th'assay so harde, so sharpe the conquerynge,
The dredeful joy, that alwey slyd so yerne,
Al this meene I be love, that my felynge
Astonyeth with his wonderful worchyng
So soore ywys, that whan I on hym thynke,
Nat wote I wel wher that I wake or wynke.

For al be that I knowe not love in dede,
Ne wote how he quyteth folke her hire,
Yet hapeth me in bookes ofte to rede
Of hys miracles and of hys cruelle yre.
There rede I wel he wol be lorde and sire;
Dar I not seyn – hys strokes ben so sore –
But God save suche a lorde! I kan no more.

1 The opening account of love includes a number of rhetorical devices, beginning with a well-known maxim 'ars longa, vita brevis'.
4–5 'I say all this about love, that bewilders my understanding.'
7 **wher that** 'whether'.
8 **al be that** 'although'.
13–14 **Dar I not seyn . . . / But** 'I dare not say anything . . . except'.

Of usage, what for luste, what for lore,
On bookes rede I ofte, as I yow tolde.
But why that I speke al this: not yore
Agon hit happed me for to beholde
Upon a booke, was write wyth lettres olde;
And therupon, a certeyn thing to lerne,
The longe day ful fast I rad and yerne.

For out of olde feldys, as men seyth,
Cometh al this new corne fro yere to yere;
And oute of olde bokes, in good feythe,
Cometh al thys new science that men lere.
But now to purpose of my firste matere:
To rede forth hit gan me so delyte,
That al the day thought me but a lyte.

This booke of which I make mension
Entitled was al there, I shal yow telle,
'Tullius of the Dreme of Scipion';
Chapitres hyt had seven, of hevene and helle
And erthe, and soules that theryn duelle;
Of which, as shortly as I kan hyt trete,
Of his sentence I wol you tel the grete.

First telleth hyt, whan Scipion was come
Into Aufryke, how he mette Massynysse,
That hym for joy in armes hath ynome.
Than telleth he hir speche and al the blysse
That was betwixt hem, til the day gan mysse,
And how his auncestre, Aufrikan so dere,
Gan on his slepe that nyght to hym appere.

Than tolde he hym that fro a sterry place,
How Aufrikan hath hym Cartage yshewed,

15 **what for** 'partly for'.

22 **men seyth** 'is said' (5.4.3).

27 **gan** See 5.6.3.

28 'That the whole day seemed as nothing to me.'

30 'Was given the full title . . .'.

31 *The Dream of Scipio* was written in 51 BC as the final part of the *Republic* by Marcus Tullius Cicero. Chaucer would have known it as a separate work with a commentary by Macrobius (about AD 400), both translated by W. H. Stahl, *Macrobius: Commentary on the Dream of Scipio* (New York, 1952).

35 **his** 'its'.

36–42 The Roman general Scipio relates how he visited Massinissa, the king of Numidia, who talked of Scipio's ancestor Africanus. That night Africanus appeared to Scipio in a dream, telling him that he would destroy Carthage and Numantia.

39 **he** Scipio, who narrates his dream to his friend Laelius (hence *hym* in line 43).

And warned hym before of al hys grace,
And seyde hym what man, lered other lewede,
That loveth comune profyt, wel ythewede,
He shal unto a blysful place wende,
There joy is that lasteth without ende.

Than asked he yf the folke that here be dede
Have lyfe and dwellynge in another place;
And Aufrikan seyde, ye, withoute drede,
And oure present worldes lyves space
Meneth but a maner dethe, what wey we trace,
And ryghtfull folke shul goo, whan they dye,
To hevene; and shewed hym the Galoxye.

Than shewede he hym the lytel erthe that here is
At regarde of hevenes quantyté;
And aftir shewed he hym the nyne speris,
And aftir that the melodye herd he
That cometh of thilke speres thries thre,
That welle ys of musyke and melodye
In this worlde here, and cause of armonye.

Than bad he hym, syn the erthe was so lite,
And was somedel fulle of harde grace,
That he ne shuld hym in the worlde delyte.
Than tolde he hym, in certeyne yeres space,
That every sterre shulde come into his place
There hit was first; and al shal oute of mynde
That in this worlde was doon of al mankynde.

45 **hys grace** his destiny to defeat Carthage.

46 **what** 'whatever'.

47 **comune profyt** 'the public good'. In the *Dream* Africanus says that there is a place in the afterlife for all of those who work for the common good. The phrase is fully discussed by Bennett, pp. 33–5.

wel ythewede 'endowed with good qualities' (referring to *what man*).

54 **what wey we trace** 'whichever way we turn'.

56 In *The House of Fame* Chaucer writes of 'the Galaxie, / Which men clepeth the Milky Wey' (936–7). Africanus describes it as the home of the virtuous dead.

58 'By comparison with the size of the heavens.'

59–63 Africanus explains that there are nine circles or spheres; the outermost is the celestial sphere containing the stars, then come the seven spheres of the planets (including sun and moon), and finally the innermost sphere of earth. The movement of the spheres produces harmonious music, which, though inaudible on earth, is imitated by gifted musicians.

62 **welle** 'spring', i.e. 'source'; as again in l. 129.

67–9 In the *Dream* Scipio is told that all the heavenly bodies will return to their original positions at the end of the 'Great Year', reckoned by Macrobius to be 15,000 of our years.

69 For non-expression of the verb of motion after *shal*, see 5.6.9.

Than prayed hym Scipion to tel hym alle
The wey to come to that hevene blysse,
And he seyde, 'Know thyselfe first immortalle,
And loke ay besely thou werke and wysse
To comune profyte, and thou shalt never mysse
To come swiftely unto that place dere
That ful of blysse ys and soules clere.

'But brekers of the lawe, soth to seyne,
And lecherous folke, after that they be dede,
Shul alwey whirle aboute th'erthe in peyne
Til many a worlde be passed, out of drede,
And than, foryeven al hir wikked dede,
Than shul they come unto that blysful place,
To which to come God sende ech lover grace!'

The day gan faile and the derke nyght,
That reveth bestes from her besynesse,
Berefte me my boke for lake of lyght,
And to my bed I gan me for to dresse,
Fulfilled of thought and besy hevenesse;
For bothe I had thinge which that I nolde,
And eke I ne had thynge that I wolde.

But fynally my spiryte, at the laste,
Forwery of my labour al the day,
Tooke reste, that made me to slepe faste,
And in my slepe I mette, as I lay,
How Aufrikan, ryght in that selfe aray
That Scipion hym sawe before that tyde,
Was comen, and stoode ryght at my beddys side.

The wery hunter slepynge in hys bed
To woode ayeine hys mynde gooth anoon,

71–7 Africanus tells Scipio in the *Dream* that the body alone is mortal, and continues: 'The noblest efforts are in behalf of your native country; a soul thus stimulated and engaged will speed hither to its destination and abode without delay.'

74 **wysse** 'guide (others)'.

78–84 Souls of those enslaved by passion, says Africanus, 'hover close to the earth, and return to this region only after long ages of torment'.

82–3 'And, with all their wretched deeds forgiven, then ...' (*dede* is a plural form).

85–6 These lines are based on Dante's *Inferno*, ii. 1–3.

90–1 If Chaucer were looking for light on human love in the *Dream*, he would not have found it.

99–105 Discussing the classification of dreams, Macrobius comments: 'Nightmares may be caused by mental or physical distress, or anxiety about the future: the patient experiences in dreams vexations similar to those that disturb him during the

The juge dremeth how hys plees ben sped,
The cartar dremeth how his cartes goone,
The ryche of golde, the knyght fyght with his fone,
The seke meteth he drynketh of the tonne,
The lover meteth he hath hys lady wonne.

Can not I seyne yf that the cause were
For I redde had of Aufrikan beforne
That made me to mete that he stood there;
But thus seyde he, 'Thou hast the so wel borne
In lokynge of myn olde booke al totorne,
Of which Macrobye roght noght a lyte,
That somedel of thy labour wolde I the quyte.'

Cytherea, thou blysful lady swete,
That with thy firebronde dauntest whom the lest,
And madest me thys sweivene for to mete,
Be thou my helpe in this, for thou maist best;
As wisly as I sawe the northe-northe-west
When I beganne my swevene for to write,
So yeve me myght to ryme and to endyte!

This forseyde Aufrikan me hent anoon,
And forth with hym unto a gate broght
Ryght of a parke, walled with grene stoon;
And over the gate, with letres large ywroght,
There were vers writen, as me thoght,
On eyther halfe, of ful gret difference,
Of which I shal yow sey the pleyn sentence:

'Thorgh me men goon into that blysful place
Of hertes hele and dedely woundes cure;

---

day.' Chaucer's examples here are taken from *De Sexto Consulatu Honorii*, 3–10, by the poet Claudian, a contemporary of Macrobius.

101 **plees ben sped** 'cases are progressing'.

111 Macrobius' opinion of the *Dream* was that 'there is nothing more complete than this work, which embraces the entire body of philosophy'.

113 The proem, beginning with an account of the god of love, ends with an invocation to *Cytherea*, a name for Venus (Aphrodite) born from the sea-foam off the island of Cythera. With her firebrand she enflames lovers with the fire of love. Her planetary position in the unpropitious north-north-west (l. 117) may suggest the narrator's lack of success in love; cf. l. 8. It may also be a reference to the date of composition; the planet was in its most northerly position in May 1382.

114 **the lest** 'pleases you', i.e. 'you want' (5.6.8).

125 **of ful gret difference** 'very sharply contrasting'.

127–40 The inscriptions over the gate recall that over the gate of Dante's Hell, *Per me si va* . . .: 'Through me one goes into the city of mourning; through me one goes to eternal sorrow; through me one goes among the lost people . . . Abandon all hope, you who enter' (*Inferno* iii. 1–9).

Thorgh me men goon unto the welle of grace,
There grene and lusty May shal ever endure.
This is the wey to al good aventure;
Be glad, thou reder, and thy sorwe of caste!
Al open am I; passe in, and hye the faste.'

'Thorgh me men goon,' than spake that other side,
'Unto the mortale strokes of the spere,
Of which Disdayne and Daunger is the gyde,
There tree shal never frute ne leves bere.
This streme yow ledeth unto the sorwful were
Thereas the fyssh in prison is al drye;
Th'eschewynge ys only the remedye.'

These vers of golde and blak ywriten were,
Of which I gan a stounde to beholde,
For with that oon encresed ay my fere,
And with that other gan myn hert to bolde.
That oon me hette, that other did me colde;
No wytte had I, for errour, for to chese
To entre or flee, or me to save or lese.

Ryght as betwix adamauntes twoo
Of evene myght a pece of iren ysette
That hath no myght to meve to nor froo –
For what that on may hale, that other lette –
Ferde I, that nyste wher that me was bette
To entre or leve, til Affrikan my gyde
Me hente, and shoofe in at the gates wyde,

And seyde, 'Hyt stondeth writen in thy face,
Thyn errour, though thou tel hyt not to me;
But drede the not to come in to this place,
For this writynge ys nothing ment be the,
Ne be noon but he loves servant be;

135 Compare 13k/6 for the fatal spear of love, in this case directed by the lady's disdain.

136 **Disdayne and Daunger** Personifications from the world of courtly love; see note to 12/45.

138 **were** a fish-trap made in the river (see *OED weir* 2). Here the trapped fish gasps for lack of water.

140 'Avoidance is the only remedy.'

141 The verses of gold are lines 127–33; those of black are 134–40.

146 **errour** here and in l. 156 means 'perplexity' (OF *irrour*), not 'error' (OF *errour*).

151 **on** 'one'.

152 'So it was with me, knowing not whether it was better for me . . .'

For thou of love hast lost thy taste, y gesse,
As seke man hath of swete and bitternesse.

'But natheles, although thou be dulle,
That thou canst not do, yet thou maist hyt se;
For many a man that may not stonde a pulle,
Yet lyketh hym at the wrastelynge to be,
And demeth yit whethir he do bet or he;
And yf thou haddest kunnynge for to endite,
I shal the shewen mater of to wryte.'

With that my honde in hys he toke anoon,
Of which I comfort kaught and went in faste;
But Lorde, so I was glad and wel begoon!
For over al, where I myn eyen caste,
Weren trees claad with levys that ay shal laste,
Eche in his kynde, with coloure fressh and grene
As emerawde, that joy was to sene:

The bylder oke, and eke the hardy asshe,
The peler elme, the cofre unto careyne,
The boxtre piper, holme to whippes lasshe,
The saylynge firre, the cipresse deth to pleyn,
The sheter ewe, the aspe for shaftes pleyne,
The olyve of pes, and eke the drunken vyne,
The victor palme, the laurere to devyne.

163 **That** 'that which, what'.

164 **stonde a pulle** 'withstand a wrestling-hold'. Compare 9/294.

166 'And still judges whether that one does better than the other.'

168 'I shall show you subjects to write about.'

169–70 Similarly Dante's guide, Virgil, comforts him by taking his hand and leading him through the gate of Hell (*Inferno* iii. 19–20). See Bennett, pp. 68–9.

171 **wel begoon** 'well content'.

176–82 The catalogue of noble trees and their uses draws on classical tradition and in particular on the examples of the *Roman de la Rose* and Boccaccio's *Teseida*, xi. 22–4. See the Middle English *Romaunt of the Rose*, 1349–90, in *The Riverside Chaucer*, and Bennett, pp. 72–3.

177 **peler** 'pillar', here 'vine-prop'. Elm was used to support vines and to make coffins.

178 Boxwood can be used for whistles. Perhaps the holm-oak was used for whip-handles.

179 Ships' masts are made of fir; the cypress is traditionally used at funerals to symbolize mourning.

180 **sheter** 'shooter, for shooting'. The yew was for bows, the aspen tree for spear-shafts and arrows.

182 Palms symbolize victory; eating laurel leaves was supposed to give powers of divination.

A gardyn sawh I, ful of blossomed bowis
Upon a ryver in a grene mede,
Theras swetnes evermor ynowh is,
With floures white, blew, yelow and rede,
And colde well-stremes nothinge dede,
And swymmynge ful of smale fisshes lyght
With fynnes rede and scales sylver-bryght.

On every bowgh the briddes herde I synge
With voys of aungel in her armony,
That besyed hem her briddes forthe to bryngе.
The lytel conyes to her pley gunnen hye;
And further al aboute y gan espye
The dredful roo, the buk, the hert and hynde,
Squerel, and bestis smale of gentil kynde.

On instrumentes of strynges in acorde
Herde I pley, and ravysshinge swetnesse,
That God, that maker ys of al and lorde,
Ne herde never bettir, as I gesse;
Therewith a wynde, unnethe hyt myght be lesse,
Made in the leves grene a noyse softe
Accordant to the foulys songe on lofte.

The aire of that place so attempre was
That never was grevance ther of hoot ne colde;
Ther growen eke every holsome spice and gras;
No man may there wexe seke ne olde.
Yet was there more joy a thousande folde
Than man kan telle: never wolde hyt nyght,
But ay clere day to any mannys syght.

Under a tree, besyde a welle, I say
Cupide our lorde hys arwes forge and fyle,
And at hys fete hys bowe al redy lay;

183–98 The description of the paradisaical garden draws in part on Boccaccio's account of the blossom, bird-song, little animals and music in the garden of Venus in *Teseida*, vii. 51–3. A translation of the passage is given by Brewer, p. 138, and Chaucer's handling of the *topos* is discussed by Bennett, pp. 70–7.

187 **nothinge dede** i.e. 'full of life'.

192 **forthe to brynge** 'to rear, bring up'.

201 'In addition a breeze that could scarcely be less strong . . .' Cf. l. 264.

211–17 In the *Teseida*, vii. 54, Cupid is forging his arrows, while his daughter tempers them in the water of the spring. The daughter is named *Voluttà*, 'Sensual Desire', though a variant reading has *Voluntade*, which perhaps accounts for Chaucer's 'Wille'. Assisting her are Ease and Memory who tip the arrows with the metal heads (Brewer, p. 138). For Chaucer's modifications see Bennett, pp. 78–87.

211 **say** 'saw'.

And Wille hys doghtre tempred al the while
The hedes in the welle, and with hir file
She touched hem after as they shul serve,
Somme to slee, and somme to wounde and kerve.

Thoo was I war of Plesaunce anon-ryght,
And of Array and Lust and Curtesye,
And of the Crafte that kan and hath the myght
To do by force a wyght to do folye.
Dysfigured was she, I shal not lye;
And by hymselfe, under an oke, I gesse,
Sawgh I Delyte, that stoode with Gentilesse.

I sawgh Beauté, withoute any atire,
And Yowthe ful of game, and Jolyté,
Foolhardynesse, Flatery, and Desire,
Messagery, Mede, and other thre –
Her names shul noght be tolde for me –
And upon pelers grete of jasper longe
I sawgh a temple of bras founded stronge.

Aboute the temple daunceden alway
Wommen ynow, of which somme were
Faire of hemself, and somme of hem gay;
In kirtels al disshevelé went they there,
That was hir office alwey, fro yere to yere;
And on the temple, of dowves white and faire
Saugh I sittynge many a hundred paire.

Before the temple-dore ful soberly
Dame Pes sate, a curtyne in hir honde;
And hir beside, wonder discretly,
Dame Pacience sittynge ther I fonde

216 'She sharpened them to suit the use to which they would be put.' In the *Romaunt of the Rose*, 937–70, Love's knight, 'Swete-Lokyng', has ten arrows, five of which are of gold, that cause injuries of varying degrees.

218–24 Closely modelled on Boccaccio, who names *Leggiadria*, 'Gracefulness', *Adornezza*, 'Adornment', *Affabilitate*, *Cortesia* and *l'Arti*, and *Van Diletto*, 'Vain Delight' standing together with *Gentilezza* (*Teseida*, vii. 55). See Bennett, pp. 87–9.

220–1 Boccaccio refers to 'the arts that can force others to commit folly'.

226 **Jolyté** 'Cheerfulness, Pleasantness'; for which Boccaccio has *Piacevolezza*.

227–9 Boccaccio names Foolhardiness, Flattery and Pimping (*Ruffiania*). The last of these presumably prompted Chaucer's *Messagery*, 'sending messages between lovers', and *Mede*, 'reward, payment', as well as his coy reference to the *other thre*.

230–1 In the Italian the temple is on columns of copper, which, like brass, is a metal of Venus.

234 That is, some were naturally beautiful and others attractively dressed.

240 Peace is 'the tranquillity that love requires for its enjoyment' (Bennett, p. 91). Her curtain is presumably to ensure the lovers' privacy.

With face pale, upon an hille of sonde;
And alder-next, within and ek withoute,
Behest and Arte, and of her folke a rowte.

Withyn the temple, of syghes hoote as fire
I herde a swogh that gan aboute renne,
Which syghes were engendred with desire,
That maden every auter for to brenne
Of newe flawme; and aspyed I thenne
That al the cause of sorwes that they drye
Come of the bitter goddys Jalousye.

The god Priapus sawgh I as I wente
Withyn the temple in soverayne place stonde,
In suche array as whan the asse hym shente
With crie be nyght, and with his ceptre in honde;
Ful besely men gunne assay and fonde
Upon his hede to sette, of sondry hewe,
Garlondes ful of fressh floures newe.

And in a prevy corner in disporte
Fond I Venus and hir porter Rychesse,
That was ful noble and hawteyn of hir porte;
Derke was that place, but afterward lyghtnesse
I saugh a lyte, unnethe hyt myght be lesse,
And on a bed of golde she lay to reste
Til that the hoote sonne gan to weste.

Hir gilte heeres with a golde threde
Ybounden were untressed, as she lay,
And naked fro the brest unto the hede
Men myght hir see, and, sothely for to say,
The remenant kevered wel to my pay
Ryght with a subtil keverchefe of Valence;
There was no thikker clothe of no defence.

243 **upon an hille of sonde** Chaucer's addition, perhaps implying that the patience of a lover is not firmly based.

245 'Promise and Artfulness, and a crowd of their (*her*) people.'

253–9 Chaucer and Boccaccio draw on the story in Ovid, *Fasti*, i. 415–40. The god Priapus was about to ravish the nymph Lotis, when the ass brayed and woke her. Priapus, 'his private parts only too well prepared', was mocked by all. Hence *in suche array*, 'in such condition'.

261 **hir porter Rychesse** 'her doorkeeper Wealth', guarding access to Venus.

264 See 201n.

272 **keverchefe of Valence** a scarf of cloth woven in Valence (France).

273 **of no defence** i.e. to protect her from sight.

The place yafe a thousande savours swoote,
And Bacus, god of wyne, sate hir beside,
And Ceres next, that dooth of hunger boote;
And, as I seide, amyddes lay Cipride,
To whom on knes two yonge folkes criede
To ben hir helpe; but thus I lete hir lye,
And ferther in the temple I gan espye

That, in dyspite of Diane the chaste,
Ful many a bowe ybroke henge on the walle
Of maydens suche as gonne hyr tymes waste
In hir servise; and peynted over alle
Of many a storye, of which I touche shalle
A fewe, as of Calixte and Athalante,
And many a mayde of which the name I wante.

Semyramus, Candace and Ercules,
Biblys, Dido, Tesbe and Piramus,
Tristram, Isoude, Paris and Achilles,
Eleyne, Cleopatre and Troylus,
Silla, and eke the moder of Romulus:
Alle these were peynted on that other syde,
And al her love, and in what plite they dide.

Whan I was comen ayen into the place
That I of spake, that was so swoote and grene,
Forth welke I thoo, myselven to solace.
Tho was I war where ther sate a quene,
That as of lyght the somer sonne shene
Passeth the sterre, ryght so over mesure
She fairer was than any creature.

And in a launde, upon an hille of floures,
Was sette this noble goddesse of Nature;

276 Ceres, goddess of food, 'brings relief from hunger'.

277 **Cipride** Another name for Venus, from her cult in Cyprus.

281–7 Diana is the virgin huntress. Both Callisto and Atalanta were virgins who resisted love in vain. Their stories are told in Ovid's *Metamorphoses*, ii. 409–507 and x. 560–707.

288–94 On the opposite wall are painted tragic lovers, most of them well known. Boccaccio lists Semiramis (who committed incest), Hercules, Biblis (who went mad for love of her brother), and Pyramus and Thisbe. Candace seduced Alexander the Great. *Isoude* is Isolde, *Eleyne* is Helen of Troy. Scylla betrayed her city out of love for Minos; Rhea Silvia died as a punishment for giving birth to Romulus and Remus, founders of Rome.

294 **dide** 'died'.

303 Nature represents the glory and perfection of God's creation, the beauty of the ordered world, and human love working within the framework of the divine plan. See Bennett, pp. 194–212.

But natheles, my ryghtful ordenaunce
May I not let for al this worlde to wynne,
That he that most ys worthy shal begynne.

'The tercel egel, as that ye knowen wele
The foule royal aboven yow in degree,
The wyse and worthy, secré, trewe as stele,
The whiche I have formed, as ye may see,
In every parte as hit best lyketh mee –
Hyt nedeth noght hys shappe yow to devyse –
He shal first chese and speken in his gyse.

'And aftir hym, by order shul ye chese,
Aftir youre kynde, everyche as yow lyketh,
And as youre happe ys, shul ye wynne or lese;
But which of yow that love moste entriketh,
God sende hym hyr that sorest for hym syketh.'
And therwythalle the tercel gan she calle
And seyde, 'My sone, the choys is to the falle.

'But natheles, in thys condicioun
Mote be the choys of everych that ys here,
That she agree to hys eleccioun,
Whoso he be that shulde ben hir fere.
This is oure usage alwey, fro yere to yere,
And whoso may at this tyme have hys grace,
In blisful tyme he come into this place.'

With hed enclyned and with ful humble chere
This real tercel spake and taried noght:
'Unto my sovereyne lady, and noght my fere,
I chese, and chesse with wille and hert and thought,
The formel on youre honde so wel ywrought,
Whos I am alle and ever wol hir serve,
Doo what hir lyste, to doo me lyve or sterve;

'Besechynge hir of mercy and of grace,
As she that ys my lady sovereyne;
Or let me dye present in thys place.
For, certes, longe may I not lyve in peyne,
For in myn herte ys korven every veyne.

391 'I cannot diverge from (my decree), even to gain the whole world.'
395 **secré** Discretion is a necessary virtue in a lover, without which he is an *avauntour* (430) and a *jangler* (457).
401 **Aftir youre kynde** meaning both 'according to your species' and 'in line with your natural inclination'.
407–8 'But nevertheless the choice of everyone here must meet this condition.'

Of braunches were hir halles and hir boures,
Ywrought aftir hir crafte and hir mesure;
Ne ther nas foule that cometh of engendrure
That there ne were prest in hir presence
To take hir dome and yeve hir audience.

For this was on seynt Valentynes day,
Whan every foule cometh there to chese his make
Of every kynde that men thynke may;
And that so huge a noyse gan they make,
That erthe and aire and tree and every lake
So ful was, that unnethe was ther space
For me to stonde, so ful was al the place.

And ryght as Alayne, in the Pleynt of Kynde,
Devyseth Nature of suche array and face,
In suche array men myght hir there fynde.
This noble emperesse, ful of grace,
Bad everey foule to take her oune place,
As they were wont alwey fro yere to yere,
Seynt Valentynes day, to stonden there.

That ys to sey, the fowles of ravyne
Were hyest sette, and than the foules smale
That eten as that nature wolde enclyne,
As worme, or thynge of whiche I tel no tale;
But watir-foule sate lowest in the dale,
And foule that lyveth by seede sate on the grene,
And that so fele that wonder was to sene.

There myght men the royal egle fynde,
That with his sharpe looke perceth the sonne,
And other egles of a lower kynde,
Of which that clerkes wel devysen konne.
There was the tiraunte with his fethres donne
And grey, I mene the goshauke, that doth pyne
To briddes for his outrageouse ravyne.

308 'To take judgement from Nature and give her a hearing.'
309 This is one of the earliest references to the tradition that birds choose their mates on St Valentine's Day, 14 February.
316 'The Complaint of Nature', *de Planctu Naturae*, by Alanus de Insulis (*c.* 1128–1202), gave a celebrated description of the goddess lamenting the sinfulness of mankind. It describes the birds as decorations on Nature's robe.
320 **her** is plural, 'their'.
325 'That eat according to their natural appetites.'
331 The eagle was supposed to have such good sight that it could look at the sun without being blinded.

The gentil faucoune, that with his fete distreyneth
The kynges honde; the hardy sperhauke eke,
The quayles foo; the merlyon that peyneth
Hymself ful ofte the larke for to seke;
There was the dowve with hir eyen meke;
The jalouse swanne, ayens hys deth that syngeth;
The owle eke that of dethe the bode bryngeth;
The crane the geaunte, with his trompes soune;
The thefe, the choghe, and eke the janglynge pye;
The scornynge jay; the eles foo, heroune;
The fals lapwynge, ful of trecherye;
The stare, that the counseylle kan bewrye;
The tame ruddok and the cowarde kyte;
The cok, that orlogge ys of thropes lyte;

The sparow, Venus sone; the nyghtyngale
That clepeth forth the fressh leves newe;
The swalow, mordrer of the foules smale
That maken hony of floures fressh of hewe;
The wedded turtel with hys hert trewe;
The pecok with his aungels fethers bryght;
The fesaunt, scorner of the cok be nyght;

The waker goos; the cukkow ever unkynde;
The papenjay ful of delycacye;
The drake, stroyer of hys oune kynde;

337 **gentil** is the standard epithet for the nobler birds of prey.
342 'The fierce swan that sings at the approach of his death'; hence the expression 'swan-song'.
343 Alanus calls the owl 'the prophet of misery'.
345 Choughs (jackdaws etc.) pick up bright objects, and so have a reputation for stealing gold and silver.
346 The heron is 'the enemy of eels'.
347 The lapwing pretends its wing is broken to draw predators away from its nest.
348 The allusion is to the chattering of starlings.
351 **Venus sone** The sparrow has a reputation for lechery; e.g. 'lecherous as a sparwe' (*Canterbury Tales* I 626).
352 The nightingale is the harbinger of summer.
353–4 Some authorities classified the bee as a kind of bird; e.g. Trevisa, *Properties*, 609.
355 For the turtle-dove's faithfulness see ll. 582–8.
357 From Alanus, who says that the wild cock (rather than the pheasant) mocks the domestic fowl for its laziness.
358 **waker** 'watchful', because the cackling of geese roused the Romans when the Capitol was attacked at night.
unkynde 'unnatural', because cuckoos lay eggs in other birds' nests.
359 **delycacye** 'lasciviousness'. Parrots are traditionally lecherous.
360–2 The drake was reputed sometimes to kill the duck in the heat of passion. A stork, discovering that his mate has been unfaithful, 'betiþ hire and stikeþ hire

The storke, wreker of avowtrie;
The hoote cormeraunte of glotonye;
The raven wys, the crow with voys of care;
The throstel olde; the frosty feldefare.

What shulde I seyn? Of foules every kynde
That in this worlde han fetheres and stature
Men myghte in that place assembled fynde
Before that noble goddesse of nature.
And eche of hem did hys besy cure
Benygnely to chese or for to take,
By hir accorde, hys formel or hys make.

But to the poynte: Nature helde on hir honde
A formel egle, of shappe the gentileste
That ever she amonge hir werkes fonde,
The moste benigne and the goodlyeste;
In hir was every vertu at his rest,
So ferforthe, that Nature hirselfe had blysse
To looke on hir, and ofte hir beke to kysse.

Nature, the vyker of th'almyghty lorde,
That hoot, colde, hevy, lyght, moiste and drye
Hath knyt be evene noumbre of accorde,
In esy vois began to speke and seye:
'Foules, take hede of my sentence, I prey,
And, for youre ease, in furtherynge of youre nede,
As faste as I may speke, I wol me spede.

'Ye knowe wel how seynt Valentynes day,
Be my statute and thorgh my governaunce,
Ye come for to chese – and flee youre way –
Youre makes, as I prik yow with plesaunce.

wiþ his bille and sleþ hire' (Trevisa, *Properties*, 619). The cormorant's practice of swallowing large fish whole gives it a reputation for gluttony.
363 'Now þe crowe clepiþ rayne wiþ unworþy voys' (Trevisa, *Properties*, 620, citing Virgil's *Georgics*).
379 **vyker** 'deputy, representative', as she is called in Alanus. Chaucer elsewhere applies the word to the Virgin.
380–1 Nature, as God's viceregent, binds together the basic elements of creation in due proportion. Boethius describes how God 'byndest the elementis by nombres proporcionables, that the coolde thinges mowen accorde with the hote thinges, and the drye thinges with the moyste' (Chaucer's *Boece*, 3, metre 9. 18–21). See Bennett, p. 133; Kean, i. 75–7.
384 **furtherynge of youre nede** 'advancing your necessary business'. The formal expression introduces a speech containing such legal terms as *statute*, *governaunce* and *ordenaunce*.

Havynge rewarde oonly to my trouthe,
My dere herte, have on my woo somme routhe.

'And yf I be founde to hir untrewe,
Dysobeysaunt, or wilful negligent,
Avauntour, or in processe love a newe,
I pray to yow thys be my jugement,
That with these foules y be al torent,
That ylke day that ever she me fynde
To hir untrewe or in my gylte unkynde.

'And syn that noon loveth hir so wel as I,
Althogh she never of love me behette,
Than oght she be myn thourgh hir mercy,
For other bonde kan I noon on hir knette.
For never for no woo ne shal I lette
To serven hir, how ferre so that she wende;
Sey what yow lyste, my tale ys at an ende.'

Ryght as the fressh rede rose newe
Ayene the somer sonne coloured ys,
Ryght so for shame al wexen gan the hewe
Of thys formel whan she herde al thys.
Neyther she answerde wel, ne seyde amys,
So sore abasshed was she, til that Nature
Seyde, 'Doghter, drede yow noght, I yow assure.'

Another tercel egle spake anoon
Of lower kynde, and seyde, 'That shulde not be!
I love hir bet than ye do, by seynt John,
Or atte lest I love hyr as wel as ye,
And lenger have served hir, in my degre;
And yf she shulde have loved for long lovyng,
To me allone had ben the guerdonynge.

'I dar eke seye, yf she me fynde fals,
Unkynde, jangler, or rebel any wyse,
Or jalouse, do me hongen by the hals!
And but I bere me in hir servise
As wel as my wytte kan me suffise,
Fro poynt to poynt, hir honour for to save,
Take she my lyfe, and al the good I have.'

426 **rewarde** 'regard'; hence 'considering only my fidelity'.
454 **for** 'in return for'. The second eagle denies the prior claim advanced by the first in l. 437.
458 For *do* + infinitive see 5.6.5.

The thirdde tercel egle answerde thoo,
'Now, sirs, ye seen the lytel leyser here,
For every foule cryeth out to ben agoo
Forth with hys make or with hys lady dere;
And eke Nature hirselfe ne wol nought here,
For taryinge here, noght half that I wolde sey;
And but I speke, I mote for sorwe dey.

'Of longe servise avaunte I me nothinge,
But as possible ys me to dye today
For woo, as he that hath ben langwysshynge
Thise twenty wynter, and wel happen may
A man may serven bette, and more to pay,
In halfe a yere, although hyt were no more,
Than somme man dooth that hath served ful yore.

'I ne say not thys by me, for I ne kan
Do no servise that may my lady plese;
But I dar sey I am hir trewest man
As to my dome, and faynest wolde hir ese;
At short wordes, til that deth me sese,
I wol ben hirs, whethir I wake or wynke,
And trew in al that herte may bethynke.'

Of al my lyfe, syn that day I was borne,
So gentil plee in love or other thinge
Ne herde never no man me beforne,
Who that had leyser and kunnynge
For to rehersen hir chere and her spekynge;
And from the morwe gan this speche last
Til dounwarde went the sonne wonder fast.

The noyse of foules for to ben delyvered
So lowde ronge, 'Have doon and let us wende!'
That wel wende I the woode had al toshyvered.
'Come of!' they cride, 'Allas! ye wol us shende!
Whan shal youre cursed pledynge have an ende?
How shulde a juge eyther party leve,
For yee or nay, withouten any preve?'

467 **here** verb, 'hear'.
468 **For taryinge here** 'to avoid delay here'.
474 **more to pay** 'more satisfactorily'.
477 **by me** 'about myself'.
480 **As to my dome** 'in my own estimation'.
481 **At short wordes** 'in short'.
495 **pledynge** See note to 2/5.

The goos, the cokkowe, and the duk also
So criden 'Kek, kek!' 'Kukkowe!' 'Quek, quek!' hye,
That thorgh myn eres the noyse went tho.
The goos seyde tho, 'Al thys nys worthe a flye!
But I kan shape hereof a remedye,
And wol sey my veyrdit faire and swythe
For watir-foule, whoso be wrothe or blythe.'

'And I for worme-foule,' seyde the foole cukkowe,
'For I wol, of myn oune auctorité,
For comune spede take on me the charge nowe,
Fore for to delyveren us ys grete charité.'
'Ye may abyde a while yet, pardé,'
Quod the turtel, 'yf hyt be youre wille;
A wyght may speke, hym were as good be stille.

'I am a sede-foule, oon the unworthieste,
That wot I wel, and lytel of kunnynge,
But better ys that a wightys tonge reste
Than entremete hym of suche doynge
Of which he neyther rede kan nor synge.
And whoso hyt dothe, ful foule hymself acloyeth,
For office uncommytted ofte anoyeth.'

Nature, which that alway had an ere
To murmour of the lewdenesse behynde,
With facound voys seyde, 'Holde your tonges there!
And I shal soone, I hope, a counseylle fynde
Yow to delyveren, and from this noyse unbynde;
I jugge of every folke men shal one calle
To seyne the veirdit for yow foules alle.'

Assented were to thys conclusyon
The briddes alle; and the foules of ravyne
Han chosen first, by pleyn eleccion,
The tercelet of the faucon, to dyffyne

507 **For comune spede** 'for the general good'. Ironically it is the selfish cuckoo who echoes the phrase from the *Dream of Scipio*; see 47n.

511 'A person may speak, (though) it would have been as well for him to have remained silent.'

512 **oon the unworthieste** 'the least worthy'; see 5.5.2.

516 i.e. which he knows nothing about.

518 **uncommytted** 'not commissioned'; so 'Because taking on a job you haven't been asked to do often causes annoyance'.

524 **folke** in this case a group of birds. The parallel is with the election of local representatives to the national parliament.

Al her sentence, and as hym lyst, to termyne;
And to Nature hym gonnen to presente,
And she accepteth hym wyth glad entente.

The tercelet seyde thanne in this manere:
'Ful harde were hyt to preven hyt by reson
Who loveth best this gentil formel here,
For everych hath suche replicacion
That by skylles may non be broght adon.
I kan not seen that argumentys avaylle;
Than semeth hit ther moste be bataylle.'

'Al redy!' quod these egles tercels thoo.
'Nay, sirs,' quod he, 'yf that I dorst hyt sey,
Ye doon me wrong, my tale ys not ydoo.
For sirs, taketh noght agrefe, I pray,
Hyt may nought as ye wolde, in thys wey.
Oures ys the voys that han the charge in honde,
And to the juges doome ye moten stonde.

'And therfore pes! I seye, as to my witte,
Me wolde think how that the worthieste
Of knyghthode, and lengest had used hitte,
Moste of estaate, of blode the gentyleste,
Were syttynge for hir, yf that hir leste;
And of these three she woote hirselfe, I trowe,
Which that he be, for hyt is lyght to knowe.'

The watir-foules han her hedes leyde
Togedir, and of shorte avysement,
Whan everych had hys large golé seyde,
They seyden sothely, al by on assent,
How that the goos, 'with hir faucond gent,
That soo desireth to pronounce oure nede,
Shal telle oure tale,' and preyde to God hir spede.

And for these watir-foules tho began
The goos to speke, and in hir cakelynge
She seyde, 'Pes! Now take kepe every man,
And herkeneth which a reson I shal forth brynge;

530 **termyne** 'adjudicate', a legal word, only here in Chaucer, reinforcing the parliamentary terminology of this passage.

544 **Hyt may nought** 'It may not proceed'. The verb is not expressed; see 5.6.9.

547 **as to my witte** 'as I understand it'.

549 '. . . and he who had longest practised it' (with 'zero' relative pronoun; see 5.4.6).

555 **of shorte avysement** 'following a brief consultation'.

My wytte ys sharpe, I love no taryinge.
I sey, y rede hym, though he were my brother,
But she wol love hym, lat hym love another!'

'Loo here, a parfyte reson of a goos!'
Quod the sperhauke; 'never mote she thee!
Loo, suche hyt ys to have a tonge loos!
Now pardé, foole, yet were hit bet for the
Have holde thy pes, than shewede thy nycetė!
Hyt lyth not in hys wytte nor in hys wille,
But sooth ys seyde: "A foole kan noght be stille".'

The laughtre aroose of gentil foules alle,
And ryght anoone the sede-foules chosen hadde
The turtel trewe, and gan hir to hem calle,
And prayden hir to sey the sothe sadde
Of thys matere and asked what she radde;
And she ansuerde that pleynly hyr entente
She wolde shewe, and sothely what she mente.

'Nay, God forbede a lover shulde chaunge!'
The turtel seyde, and wexe for shame al rede;
'Thoogh that hys lady evermore be straunge,
Yet let hym serve hir ever tyl he be dede.
Forsoth, I preyse noght the gooses rede;
For thoygh she deyed, I wolde noon other make;
I wol ben hirs, til that the deth me take.'

'Wel bourded,' quod the duk, 'by my hatte!
That men shulden alwey loven causeles,
Who kan a reson fynde or wytte in that?
Daunceth he murye that ys murtheles?
Who shulde rechche of that ys rechcheles?
Ye, quek!' quod the duk ful wel and faire,
'There ben moo sterres, God woot, than a paire!'

'Now fye, cherle!' quod the gentil tercelet,
'Out of the dunghille come that word ful ryght.
Thou kanst noght see which thing is wel beset;
Thou farest be love as owles doon by lyght:

573 'It isn't within his intelligence or willpower', viz. to keep quiet.
574 A common proverb in various forms.
587 'For even if she died I'd not wish for another mate.'
593 **that** 'anyone who' (5.4.6). 'Why care about one who doesn't care about himself?'
595 i.e. there are many more fish in the sea.
599 'You react towards love as owls do towards light.' For owls, see 2/240–3 and 363–70.

The day hem blent, ful wel they see by nyght.
Thy kynd ys of so lowe a wrechednesse,
That what love is, thou kanst neyther see ne gesse.'

Thoo gan the cukkow put hym forth in pres
For foule that eteth worme, and seyde blyve,
'So I,' quod he, 'may have my make in pes,
I reche not how longe that ye stryve;
Lat eche of hem be soleyne al her lyve!
This ys my rede, syn they may not acorde;
This shorte lesson nedeth noght recorde.'

'Yee, have the gloton filde ynogh hys paunche,
Than ar we wel!' seyde the emerlyon;
'Thou mordrere of the haysogge on the braunche
That broght the forth, thou rewful gloton!
Lyve thou soleyn, wormes corrupcion!
For no fors ys of lakke of thy nature.
Goo, lewde be thou, while the worlde may dure!'

'Now pes,' quod Nature, 'I commaunde here;
For I have herde al youre opynyon,
And in effecte yet be we never the nere;
But fynally, this ys my conclusyon,
That she hirselfe shal have hir eleccion
Of whom hir lyste, whoso be wrooth or blythe;
Hym that she cheest, he shal han hir as swithe.

'For syth hyt may not here discussed be
Who loveth hir best, as seyde the tercelet,
Than wol I doon thys favour to hir, that she
Shal have ryght hym on whom hir hert is sette,
And he hir that hys hert hath on hir knette.
This juge I, Nature, for I may not lye;
To noon estaat I have noon other eye.

'But as for counseylle for to chese a make,
Yf I were Reson, than wolde y
Counseylle yow the royal tercel take,

603 **put hym forth in pres** 'thrust himself forward'.
609 **recorde** has passive sense, 'to be repeated'. See 5.6.5.
612 **haysogge** the tiny hedge-sparrow which is overwhelmed by the huge fledgling in its nest.
613 **broght the forth** cf. 192n.
615 'For the loss of your species is of no consequence.'
630 'I have no special regard for any worldly status.'
632 For Reason personified see text 7a.

As seyde the tercelet ful skilfully,
As for the gentilest and moste worthy
Whiche I have wroght so wel to my plesaunce,
That to yow ought to ben a suffisaunce.'

With dredeful vois the formel hir answerde:
'My ryghtful lady, goddesse of nature,
Sooth ys that I am ever under youre yerde,
As ys everych other creature,
And moste be youres while my lyf may dure;
And therfore graunte me my firste boone,
And myn entent yow wol I sey ryght soone.'

'I graunte hyt yow,' quod she; and ryght anoon
This formel egle spake in thys degré:
'Almyghty quene, unto this yere be doon
I aske respite for to avysen me,
And after that to have my choyse al fre.
Thys al and somme that I wolde speke and seye;
Ye gete no more although ye do me deye.

'I wolle noght serven Venus ne Cupide
Forsoth as yet, by no maner wey.'
'Now syn hyt may noon other weyes betide,'
Quod Nature, 'here ys no more to sey.
Than wolde I that these foules were awey,
Eche with hys make, for taryinge lenger here.'
And seyde hem thus, as ye shal after here:

'To yow speke I, yee terceletys,' quod Nature.
'Beth of good hert and serveth, al thre.
A yere ys not so longe to endure,
And eche of yow peyne hym, in hys degre,
For to do wel, for, God wote, quyte ys she
Fro yow thys yere. What after so befalle,
This entremesse ys dressed for yow alle.'

And whan thys werke al wroght was to an ende,
To every foule Nature yafe hys make
By evene acorde, and on her wey they wende.
A, Lorde! the blysse and joy that they make!
For eche of hem gan other in wynges take,

647 **unto** 'until'.
653 **by no maner wey** 'in any way at all'.
657 **for** see 468n.
665 'This intermission applies to all of you.'
668 **evene acorde** 'mutual agreement', echoing l. 381.

And with her nekkes eche gan other wynde,
Thonkyng alwey the noble goddesse of kynde.

But firste were chosen foules for to synge,
As yere by yere was alwey hir usaunce
To synge a roundel at her departynge,
To do Nature honour and plesaunce.
The note, I trowe, maked was in Fraunce;
The wordes were suche as ye may here fynde,
The next vers, as I now have in mynde.

Que bien ayme a tarde oublie.

'Nowe welcome somor, with thy sonne softe,
That hast thes wintres wedres ovireshake,
And drevyne away the longe nyghtes blake!'

Saynt Valentyne, that ert ful hye olofte,
Thus syngen smal foules for thy sake:
'Nowe welcome somor, with thy sonne softe,
That hast thes wintres wedres ovireshake.'

Wele han they cause for to gladen ofte,
Sethe ech of hem recoverede hathe hys make;
Ful blisseful mowe they synge when they wake:
'Nowe welcome somor, with thy sonne softe,
That hast thes wintres wedres ovireshake,
And drevyne away the longe nyghtes blake!'

And with the showtynge, whan hir song was do
That foules made at her flyght away,
I wooke, and other bookes toke me to
To rede upon, and yet I rede alway;
I hope, ywyse, to rede so sommday
That I shal mete somme thyng for to fare
The bet; and thus to rede I wol not spare.

675 **roundel** a French lyric form used by writers such as Machaut. It usually consists of three stanzas on two rhymes, with the opening lines used as a refrain. The text of the roundel is here printed in italics, since its authenticity is dubious and it is not preserved complete in any manuscript. See Textual Notes.

679a A saying found quite widely in French: 'He who loves well forgets slowly.' The line perhaps indicates the setting (the *note*) to which the roundel might be sung.

680 **somor** 'spring', as often when contrasted with winter.

16

Chaucer: *The Canterbury Tales*

Chaucer is thought to have begun *The Canterbury Tales* in about 1387, after completing *Troilus and Criseyde* and leaving *The Legend of Good Women* unfinished. He evidently worked on it until his death in 1400, at which time the project was still very far from complete. In the General Prologue, the Host of the Tabard Inn – who presides over the company of 'nyne and twenty' pilgrims – proposes a plan: each pilgrim is to tell two tales on the road to Canterbury and two more on the way back (I 788–809). In the event, Chaucer left just twenty-four tales, two of them fragments; and the work as we have it ends, not with the projected dinner back at the Tabard, but with the Parson's Tale, a sombre exposition of the sacrament of penance. Yet, thanks to those who put the pieces together for publication shortly after Chaucer's death, the *Tales* enjoyed immediate success. No fewer than fifty-five manuscripts, complete or nearly so, survive from the fifteenth century. Chaucer had done enough to realize his prime intention: to match a variety of occupations among his 'sundry folk' with a matching variety of literary types among the stories they tell: romance, fabliau, moral 'example', saint's life, miracle story, 'tragedy', beast fable . . .

The two short tales presented here, a comic fabliau and a grave Miracle of the Virgin, illustrate the range of literary types. They also show something of the various principles governing Chaucer's assignment of tales to tellers. The Miracle of the Virgin is assigned to a prioress because such stories were supposed to appeal particularly to religious women – a matter of the sociology of literary taste; but the fabliau is assigned to a reeve (an estate foreman), not because such men particularly liked tales of that comic kind, but because, being 'cherles', they might themselves figure in such tales as characters – a matter of the literary decorum of low comedy. The Reeve's Tale also has another, dramatic, motivation, as an anti-miller story rooted in an occupational hostility between reeves and millers (see 16a/7–8n). For yet another interest in the rich Canterbury project was to represent the friendly or hostile relations existing between members of different occupations – lawyers and country gentlemen, friars and summoners, cooks and manciples – in Chaucer's England.

The present texts are based on the Hengwrt Manuscript, National Library of Wales MS Hengwrt 154 (Peniarth 392D), the earliest and in many ways the best of the surviving copies, made very few years after the poet's death.

Editions

N. F. Blake, *The Canterbury Tales by Geoffrey Chaucer, Edited from the Hengwrt Manuscript* (London, 1980)

Benson and Skeat editions: see Headnote to text 15 above.

Studies

W. F. Bryan and Germaine Dempster, *Sources and Analogues of Chaucer's Canterbury Tales* (Chicago, 1941)

Helen Cooper, *The Canterbury Tales*, Oxford Guides to Chaucer (Oxford, 1989)

Donald R. Howard, *The Idea of the Canterbury Tales* (Berkeley, 1976)

V. A. Kolve, *Chaucer and the Imagery of Narrative: The First Five Canterbury Tales* (Stanford, 1984)

Derek Pearsall, *The Canterbury Tales* (London, 1985)

16a Chaucer: The Reeve's Tale

The Reeve's is the third tale told on the journey to Canterbury, following those of the Knight and the Miller. Like the latter, it belongs to a literary genre which had flourished in thirteenth-century France, the 'fabliau'. Fabliaux are short comic tales in verse, dealing mainly with sexual or other advantages won by tricks and stratagems: see Per Nykrog, *Les Fabliaux* (Copenhagen, 1957) and C. Muscatine, *The Old French Fabliaux* (New Haven, 1986). The story told by the Reeve has analogues among French fabliaux (especially *Le Meunier et les ii Clers*, 'The Miller and the Two Clerks'), and also in Boccaccio's *Decameron* (Ninth Day, Tale 6): see Bryan and Dempster and especially Benson and Andersson (the latter with translations). Since the Reeve is angry with the Miller (see 7–8n), his tale of an outwitted and humiliated miller acquires extra point in its Canterbury context. Here, as elsewhere, Chaucer seizes the opportunities, offered by fabliau, of representing contemporary realities: see Bennett on the world of Cambridge and its environs, and Tolkien on the Northern speech of the two Cambridge students.

Editions

Benson and Skeat editions: see Headnote to text 15 above

Studies

J. A. W. Bennett, *Chaucer at Oxford and at Cambridge* (Oxford, 1974)

L. D. Benson and T. M. Andersson, *The Literary Context of Chaucer's Fabliaux* (Indianapolis and New York, 1971), pp. 79–201

Bryan and Dempster (*Canterbury Tales* Headnote), pp. 124–47

T. W. Craik, *The Comic Tales of Chaucer* (London, 1964), pp. 30–47

J. Hines, *The Fabliau in English* (Harlow, 1993)

Kolve (*Canterbury Tales* Headnote), pp. 217–56

Pearsall (*Canterbury Tales* Headnote), pp. 183–92

J. R. R. Tolkien, 'Chaucer as a Philologist: *The Reeve's Tale*', *Transactions of the Philological Society* (1934), 1–70

The Prologe of the Reves Tale.

Whan folk hadde laughen at this nyce cas
Of Absolon and hende Nicholas,
Diverse folk diversely they seyde,
But for the moore part they lowe and pleyde;
Ne at his tale I seigh no man hym greve
But it were oonly Osewold the reve:
By cause he was of carpenters craft
A litel ire is in his herte ylaft.
He gan to grucche and blamed it a lite.
'So the ik,' quod he, 'ful wel koude I thee quyte
With bleryng of a proud millerys iye
If þat me liste speke of rybaudye;
But ik am oold, me list no pley for age;
Gras tyme is doon, my fodder is now forage.

1 **nyce cas** 'silly business', referring to the comic tale just told by the Miller.

7–8 Oswald, a 'sclendre colerik man' (General Prologue I 587), is angry because the Miller represented a carpenter as a cuckolded husband. He himself was trained as a carpenter (General Prologue I 613–14). As a reeve, or foreman on a manorial estate, he would in any case be ill-disposed towards millers, whose cheating habits he goes on to illustrate in his tale.

10 **So the ik** 'as I may prosper'. The form *ik* 'I', unique in Chaucer's works, is an East Midland and Northern form appropriate to the Reeve, who comes from north Norfolk (General Prologue I 619–20). Since it was evidently obsolescent there by Chaucer's time, it is appropriate also to an older speaker. See also 32n, 69n, and 84n.

11 'With the outwitting of a proud miller' (literally 'blearing his eye'), as in the ensuing story.

13 **me list no pley for age** 'because I am old no silly game (*pley*) gives me pleasure'. Cf. 2/213.

This white top writeth myne olde yerys,
Myn herte is also mowled as myne herys;
But if ik fare as dooth an open-ers –
That ilke fruyt is ever lenger the wers
Til it be roten in mollok or in stree –
We olde men, I drede, so fare we:
Til we be roten kan we noght be rype.
We hoppe alwey whil þat the world wol pipe,
For in oure wil ther stiketh evere a nayl
To have an hoor heed and a grene tayl
As hath a leek; for thogh oure myght be goon
Oure wil desireth folie evere in oon,
For whan we may noght doon than wol we speke.
Yet in oure asshen olde is fyr yreke.
Foure gleedes have we, whiche I shal devyse –
Avauntyng, lyyng, anger, coveitise;
Thise foure sparkles longen unto eelde.
Oure olde lemes mowe wel been unweelde,
But wil ne shal noght faillen, that is sooth.
And yet ik have alwey a coltes tooth,
As many a yeer as it is passed henne
Syn þat my tappe of lyf bigan to renne.
For sikerlik, whan ik was bore, anon
Deeth drogh the tappe of lyf and leet it goon,
And evere sith hath so the tappe yronne
Til þat almoost al empty is the tonne.
The streem of lyf now droppeth on the chymbe.
The sely tonge may wel rynge and chymbe
Of wrecchednesse þat passed is ful yoore;
With olde folk save dotage is namoore.'
  Whan þat oure Hoost hadde herd this sermonyng,
He gan to speke as lordly as a kyng.
He seyde, 'What amounteth al this wit?

15 **writeth** 'indicates'.

17 **open-ers** 'open-arse, medlar', so called because, when ripe, its contents dribble out of its open end.

18 'That same fruit becomes worse and worse the older it gets.'

32 **lemes** 'limbs', a Norfolk form (see 10n).

34 **a coltes tooth** i.e. the appetites of a young horse.

35 'Despite the many years that have passed by now' (*henne* 'hence', i.e. counting back from now).

41 Instead of jetting out as they once did, the contents of the almost empty barrel now drop weakly down onto its projecting rim (*chymbe*).

42–4 The point seems to be that old people enjoy recalling hard times in the past, having no other pleasure in their senility.

45–6 The Host, landlord of the Tabard Inn in Southwark, acts as a temporary festive *kyng*, ruling over the pilgrims on their Canterbury journey.

What shal we speke al day of holy writ?
The devel made a reve for to preche,
Or of a souter a shipman or a leche.
Sey forth thy tale and tarie noght the tyme:
Lo, Depeford, and it is half-wey pryme;
Lo, Grenewych, ther many a sherewe is inne;
It were al tyme thy tale to bigynne.'
'Now, sires,' quod this Osewold the reve,
'I pray yow alle þat ye noght yow greve
Thogh I answere and somdel sette his howve,
For leveful is with force force of showve.
This dronken miller hath ytoold us heer
How þat bigiled was a carpenter,
Paraventure in scorn for I am oon;
And by youre leve I shal hym quyte anon;
Right in his cherles termes wol I speke.
I pray to God his nekke mote tobreke.
He kan wel in myn eye seen a stalke,
But in his owene he kan noght seen a balke.'

At Trompyngtoun, nat fer fro Cantebrygge,
Ther gooth a brook and over that a brygge,
Upon the which brook ther stant a melle;
And this is verray sooth þat I yow telle.
A miller was ther dwellyng many a day,
As any pecok he was proud and gay.
Pipen he koude and fisshe, and nettes beete,
And torne coppes, and wel wrastle and sheete;

48 **What** 'why'.

49–50 'It is the devil's doing for a reeve to become a preacher, or a shoemaker to be a sailor or physician.'

52–3 By 7.30 a.m. (*half-wey pryme*) on the first day, the pilgrims have reached Deptford, some four miles from Southwark and within sight of Greenwich, where Chaucer was probably living at the time of writing, in the late 1380s.

57 **somdel sette his howve** 'get the better of him somewhat', literally, 'adjust his headgear'.

58 'For it is permissible to repel force with force.' A legal maxim. Whiting F491.

65–6 Matthew 7.3: 'And why seest thou the mote that is in thy brother's eye; and seest not the beam that is in thy own eye?' *Stalke* corresponds to the Vulgate Bible's *festuca* 'piece of straw', where the English version has *mote*.

67 The village of Trumpington, about three miles from Cambridge. See Bennett for the local details.

69 **melle** 'mill', a Norfolk form (see 10n).

73 **Pipen** 'play the bagpipes', like the pilgrim Miller (General Prologue I 565–6).

74 **torne coppes** 'up-end drinking cups' (cf. 295–6 below)? or 'make wooden cups'?

wel wrastle Compare the pilgrim Miller, at whom the Reeve is aiming: 'At wrastlynge he wolde have alwey the ram' (General Prologue I 548).

And by his belt he baar a long panade,
And of a swerd ful trenchaunt was the blade;
A joly popper baar he in his pouche –
Ther was no man for peril dorste hym touche;
A Sheffeld thwitel baar he in his hose.
Round was his face and camuse was his nose;
As piled as an ape was his skulle.
He was a market-beter atte fulle:
Ther dorste no wight hand upon hym legge
That he ne swoor he sholde anon abegge.
A theef he was for sothe of corn and mele,
And þat a sleigh and usant for to stele.
His name was hoten deynous Symkyn.
A wif he hadde, comen of noble kyn,
The person of the toun hir fader was.
With hir he yaf ful many a panne of bras
For þat Symkyn sholde in his blood allye.
She was yfostred in a nonnerye,
For Symkyn wolde no wyf, as he sayde,
But she were wel ynorissed and a mayde,
To saven his estaat of yemanrye;
And she was proud and peert as is a pye.
A ful fair sighte was it upon hem two:
On halidayes biforn hir wolde he go
With his tipet wounden aboute his heed,
And she cam after in a gyte of reed,
And Symkyn hadde hosen of the same.
Ther dorste no wight clepen hire but dame.
Was noon so hardy þat wente by the weye
That with hire dorste rage or ones pleye,
But if he wolde be slayn of Symkyn
With panade or with knyf or boydekyn;
For jalous folk been perilouse everemo –
Algate they wolde hir wyves wenden so.

79 His *thwitel*, or knife, was made of fine Sheffield steel.

82 **market-beter** apparently, someone who made trouble at markets.

84 **abegge** 'pay for it', a Norfolk form (see 10n).

87 **Symkyn** a diminutive of Simon(d). The students never use this familiar form in addressing him.

90 The village parson provides for his illegitimate daughter a dowry of brass pans (items sometimes specified in medieval wills).

91 **in his blood allye** 'marry into his family'.

95 'To preserve his standing as prosperous freeholder.'

97 'It was a very fine sight to see the two of them.'

108 'Or at any rate they like their wives to think so.'

And eek, for she was somdel smoterlich,
She was as digne as water in a dich
And ful of hoker and of bismare.
Hir thoghte þat a lady sholde hir spare,
What for hir kynrede and hir nortelrye
That she hadde lerned in the nonnerye.
  A doghter hadde they bitwix hem two
Of twenty yeer, withouten any mo,
Savyng a child þat was of half-yeer age;
In cradel it lay and was a propre page.
This wenche thikke and wel ygrowen was,
With camuse nose and eyen greye as glas,
With buttokes brode and brestes rounde and hye;
But right fair was hir heer, I wol nat lye.
The person of the toun, for she was so feir,
In purpos was to maken hir his heir
Bothe of his catel and his mesuage,
And straunge he made it of hir mariage.
His purpos was for to bistowe hir hye
Into som worthy blood of auncetrye;
For holi cherches good moot been despended
On holi cherches blood þat is descended;
Therfore he wolde his holy blood honoure,
Thogh þat he holy chirche sholde devoure.
  Greet sokne hath this miller out of doute
With whete and malt of al the land aboute,
And nameliche ther was a greet collegge
Men clepeth the Soler Halle at Cantebregge:
Ther was hir whete and eek hir malt ygrounde.
And on a day it happed in a stounde

109–10 'And also, because she was of somewhat dubious origin (*smoterlich* 'besmirched'), she was as stand-offish as ditchwater.' The proverbial comparison (Whiting D268) here implies that the wife was 'stinking with pride' (*OED*) and hence unpleasant to deal with.

112 **hir spare** 'keep herself aloof'.

118 **propre page** 'fine little boy'.

126 **straunge** 'difficult'; i.e. the parson was reserving her for some suitably well-born husband. The Reeve stresses the social pretensions of the family in gleeful anticipation of their subsequent dishonouring.

133 **sokne** 'the exclusive right claimed by a mill-owner to grind and take toll of all the grain of a manor or town' (Bennett, p. 91).

134 Wheat for bread, malt for beer.

136 **Men clepeth** 'one calls', literally. The singular verb shows that *men* is the unstressed indefinite pronoun: see 5.4.3.

Soler Halle King's Hall (later merged with Trinity College, Cambridge), so called because of its *solers* or sunny rooms: see Bennett, pp. 93–7. The college had an unusually large number of north-country students: see 160–1 below.

Syk was the maunciple on a maladie;
Men wenden wisly þat he sholde dye,
For which this millere stal bothe mele and corn
An hondred tyme moore than biforn;
For therbiforn he stal but curteisly,
But now he was a theef outrageously,
For which the wardeyn chidde and made fare;
But therof sette the millere noght a tare,
He craked boost and swoor it was noght so.
  Thanne were ther yonge poure scolers two
That dwelten in the halle of which I seye.
Testyf they were and lusty for to pleye,
And oonly for hir myrthe and reverye
Upon the wardeyn bisily they crye
To yeve hem leve but a litel stounde
To go to mille and seen hir corn ygrounde;
And hardily they dorste leye hir nekke
The millere sholde noght stelen hem half a pekke
Of corn by sleighte, ne by force hem reve;
And atte laste the wardeyn yaf hem leve.
John highte that oon and Aleyn highte that oother;
Of oon town were they born þat highte Strother,
Fer in the north, I kan noght telle where.
This Aleyn maketh redy al his gere
And on an hors the sak he caste anon.
Forth gooth Aleyn the clerk and also John
With good swerd and with bokeler by hir syde.
John knew the wey, hym neded no gyde,
And at the mille the sak adoun he layth.
Aleyn spak first: 'Al hayl, Symond, yfayth.
How fares thy faire doghter and thy wyf?'

139 **maunciple** the college officer concerned with its food supplies.

140 **wenden wisly** 'thought for certain'. See 308n.

143 **curteisly** 'courteously', that is, with some regard for decency and discretion.

145 **wardeyn** the head of the college.

146 'But the miller cared nothing for that.' Cf. 7a/97. *Tares* are worthless weeds.

147 **craked boost** 'blustered'.

150 **lusty for to pleye** 'eager to have fun'.

159 **Aleyn** a name particularly common in the North. See next note.

160 **Strother** an unidentified village (*town*) 'far in the North'. The word ('a place overgrown with brushwood') occurs in a number of Northumberland and Durham place-names. A well-known Border family, the de Strothers, held lands around Kirknewton in Glendale, north Northumberland. Aleyn de Strother was constable of Roxburgh Castle in 1366. Chaucer may have inferred the place from the name of this family.

169 **fares** The form with -(*e*)*s* ending for the third person plural of the present

'Aleyn welcome,' quod Symkyn, 'by my lyf,
And John also. How now, what do ye here?'
'By God,' quod John, 'Symond, nede has na peere;
Hym boes serve hymself þat has na swayn,
Or ellis he is a fool, as clerkes sayn.
Oure maunciple, I hope he wol be deed,
Swa werkes ay the wanges in his heed;
And therfore is I come and eek Alayn
To grynde oure corn and carie it heem agayn.
I pray yow speed us heythen what ye may.'
'It shal be doon,' quod Symkyn, 'by my fay.
What wol ye doon whil þat it is in hande?'
'By God, right by the hoper wol I stande,'
Quod John, 'and se howgates the corn gas in.
Yet saw I nevere, by my fader kyn,
How þat the hoper wagges til and fra.'
Aleyn answerde, 'John, wiltow swa?
Thanne wol I be byneth, by my crown,
And se howgates the mele falles down
Into the trogh; that sal be my desport,
For, John, yfaith, I may been of youre sort,
I is as ille a millere as ar ye.'
  This millere smyled of hir nycetee
And thoghte, 'Al this nys doon but for a wyle.

---

tense establishes the students as Northern speakers (cf. *werkes* 176). The -*(e)s* ending for the third person singular (e.g. *has* 172, *boes* 173) is also Northern, and abnormal in Chaucer: see 4.5.2. On the students' dialect, see 1.2.1. The main Northernisms are noted here ('Nth'). For a full discussion, see Tolkien's article.

172 **nede has na peere** 'necessity has no equal', i.e., there is no alternative. Proverbial: Whiting N51, N52. Long *a* for long *o*, as in *na* here, is a Northernism prominent in the students' speech: e.g. *gas* 183, *fra* 185, *banes* 219, *atanes* 220, *twa* 275.

173 'One who has no servant must look after himself.' *Boes* is Nth for Chaucerian *bihoveth* 'it is necessary'.

175 **hope** 'expect', comically Nth.

176 'The back teeth are giving him such a pain in his head.' *Werkes* 'ache', word and ending Nth; *wanges* Nth.

177 **is** Nth for first person singular (cf. 191, 232, 348, 385); also for second person singular (274).

178 **heem** 'home'. This form, where we would expect Nth *haam* (172n), is paralleled in the Ellesmere MS by *geen* for *gane* 'gone' (224) and *neen* for *naan* (331, 333). These are hard to account for, unless they reflect a Nth sound change of /a:/ to /ɛ:/.

179 'Please do your best to help us get away quickly.' *Heythen* 'hence', Nth.

183 **howgates** 'how', Nth, like *gas* 'goes'.

185 **til and fra** 'to and fro', Nth.

186 **swa** 'so', Nth.

187 **by my crown** an oath, lit. 'by the top of my head'.

189 **sal** 'shall', Nth (cf. 233, 248, etc.).

191 **ille** 'bad', Nth (Scandinavian, see 3.2).

They wene þat no man may hem bigile,
But by my thrift, yet shal I blere hir iye
For al the sleighte in hir phislophye.
The moore queynte crekys þat they make,
The moore wol I stele whan I take;
In stede of flour yet wol I yeve hem bren.
The grettest clerkes been noght the wisest men,
As whilom to the wolf thus spak the mare.
Of al hir art counte I noght a tare.'
Out of the dore he gooth ful pryvely
Whan þat he saugh his tyme softely.
He looketh up and doun til he hath founde
The clerkes hors theras it stood ybounde
Bihynde the mille under a leefsel,
And to the hors he gooth hym faire and wel;
He strepeth of the bridel right anon.
And whan the hors was laus he gynneth gon
Toward the fen ther wilde mares renne
And forth with 'wehe' thurgh thikke and thenne.
This millere gooth ayein; no word he seyde,
But dooth his note and with the clerkes pleyde
Til þat hir corn was faire and wel ygrounde.
  And whan the mele was sakked and ybounde,
This John gooth out and fynt his hors away,
And gan to crye 'Harrow and weilaway!
Oure hors is lost. Alayn, for Goddes banes,
Step on thy feet. Com of, man, al atanes.
Allas, oure wardeyn has his palfrey lorn.'
This Alayn al forgat bothe mele and corn;
Al was out of his mynde his housbondrye.
'What, whilk wey is he gane?' he gan to crye.
The wyf cam lepyng inward with a ren;

195 'But, as I may thrive, I shall still outwit them.'

196 **phislophye** the miller's version of *philosophye*.

197 'The more clever tricks they play.' *Creke* (the modern 'creek') suggests a winding or devious course here: 'a crooked device', *OED creek* 7.

200–1 In the fable, a wolf wants to buy a foal. The mare tells him that, if he can read and is a scholar, he may find the price written on her hind foot, and then she kicks him. Hence the proverbial conclusion in l. 200 (Whiting C291).

202 'I care nothing for all their learning.' Cf. 146 and n.

207 **leefsel** 'lean-to of poles thatched with reeds' (Bennett, p. 113).

213 **gooth ayein** 'returns'.

219 **banes** 'bones', Nth.

220 **Com of** 'hurry up'.

atanes 'at once', Nth.

224 **whilk** 'which', Nth.

She seyde, 'Allas, youre hors gooth to the fen
With wilde mares as faste as he may go.
Unthank come on his hand þat boond hym so
And he þat bettre sholde have knyt the reyne.'
'Allas,' quod John, 'Aleyn, for Cristes peyne,
Lay doun thy swerd and I wol myn alswa.
I is ful wight, God waat, as is a ra;
By God hert, he sal nat scape us bathe.
Why ne had thow pit the capil in the lathe?
Il-hail! by God, Alayn, thow is a fonne.'
This sely clerkes haan ful faste yronne
Toward the fen, bothe Alayn and eek John;
And whan the millere seigh þat they were gon,
He half a busshel of hir flour hath take
And bad his wyf go knede it in a cake.
He seyde, 'I trowe the clerkes were aferd;
Yet kan a millere maken a clerkes berd
For al his art. Ye, lat hem goon hir weye.
Lo wher he gooth. Ye, lat the children pleye;
They gete hym noght so lightly by my croun.'
Thise sely clerkes rennen up and doun
With 'Keep, keep! Stand, stand! Jossa, warderere!
Ga whistle thow, and I sal kepe hym heere.'
But shortly, til þat it was verray nyght
They koude noght, thogh they dide al hir myght,
Hir capyl cacche, he ran alwey so faste,
Til in a dych they caughte hym at the laste.

226 **fen** the low-lying wetland in which Cambridge stands, then little cultivated, but with some drainage ditches (252).

228 **Unthank come on** 'curses upon'.

231 **alswa** 'also', Nth.

232 'I am very quick, God knows, like a roe-deer.' Nth long *a* for long *o* (*waat, ra*), and Nth *is*, as again at 235 (177n).

233 More Northernisms: *God* uninflected genitive (4.2.4); *sal* 'shall'; *bathe* 'both' as at 258 and 337.

234 **pit** 'put', Nth.

lathe 'barn', Nth.

235 **Il-hail** 'bad luck to you', Nth.

fonne 'fool', Nth.

236 **sely** 'wretched', commonly applied in Chaucer to victims of others, as at 246 and 254 here.

240 **cake** 'flat loaf'.

241 **aferd** 'suspicious'.

242 To *make* (trim?) someone's beard is to outwit him.

244 **he** the horse, still in view across the flat fenland.

245 **by my croun** See 187n.

247 'Watch him! . . . stay where you are! . . . down this way . . . look out behind!'

248 **kepe** 'watch'. *Ga* and *sal* are Northern forms.

Wery and weet as beest is in the reyn
Comth sely John and with hym comth Aleyn.
'Allas,' quod John, 'the day þat I was born,
Now ar we dryven til hethyng and til scorn.
Oure corn is stoln; men wil us foolis calle,
Bathe the wardeyn and oure felawes alle,
And namely the millere, weilawey.'
Thus pleyneth John as he gooth by the wey
Toward the mille, and Bayard in his hond.
The millere sittyng by the fyr he fond,
For it was nyght, and ferther myghte they noght;
But for the love of God they hym bisoght
Of herberwe and of ese as for hir peny.
The millere seide agayn, 'If ther be eny,
Swich as it is yet shal ye have youre part.
Myn hous is streyt, but ye han lerned art;
Ye kan by argumentz make a place
A myle brood of twenty foot of space.
Lat se now if this place may suffise,
Or make it rowm with speche as is your gyse.'
'Now, Symond,' seyde this John, 'by seint Cutberd,
Ay is thou myrie, and that is faire answerd.
I have herd seye men sal taa of twa thynges,
Swilk as he fyndes or taa swilk as he brynges.
But specialy I pray thee, hoost deere,
Get us som mete and drynke and make us cheere,
And we wol payen trewely atte fulle.
With empty hand men may none haukes tulle.
Lo heere oure silver, redy for to spende.'
This millere into town his doghter sende
For ale and breed, and rosted hem a goos,
And boond hir hors, it sholde namoore go loos,

256 **til hethyng** 'to contempt', both Nth.

261 **Bayard** a common horse name.

265 **as for** 'in return for'.

266 **agayn** 'in reply'.

268 'My house is small, but you have taken a university course.' The miller sarcastically suggests that education in such subjects as logic and rhetoric might actually have some practical use.

273 Cuthbert, a Northumberland saint whose remains were venerated in Durham Cathedral, is appropriately invoked by John. See 160n.

275–6 'I have heard it said that a man must take one of two things, either such as he finds or else such as he brings.' The clerks, in the end, take both. 'Take as one finds' is proverbial (Whiting T15). Northernisms: *sal*, *taa*, *twa*, *swilk*, *fyndes*, *brynges*.

278 **make us cheere** 'entertain us'.

280 **tulle** 'lure'. Proverbial: Whiting H89.

And in his owene chambre hem made a bed,
With shetes and with chalons faire yspred,
Noght from his owene bed ten foot or twelve.
His doghter hadde a bed al by hirselve
Right in the same chambre by and by.
It myghte be no bet; and cause why?
Ther was no rowmer herberwe in the place.
They soupen and they speken hem to solace
And drynken evere stroong ale at the beste.
Aboute mydnyght wente they to reste.
Wel hath this millere vernysshed his heed,
Ful pale he was fordronke and noght reed;
He yexeth and he speketh thurgh the nose
As he were on the quakke or on the pose.
To bedde he goth, and with hym goth his wyf;
As any jay she light was and jolyf,
So was hir joly whistle wel ywet.
The cradel at hir beddes feet is set
To rokken and to yeve the child to sowke.
And whan þat dronken al was in the crowke,
To bedde wente the doghter right anon,
To bedde gooth Aleyn and also John;
Ther nas namoore, hem neded no dwale.
This millere hath so wisly bibbed ale
That as an hors he fnorteth in his sleep,
Ne of his tayl bihynde he took no keep;
His wyf bar hym a burdon, a ful strong,
Men myghten hir routyng heren a furlong;
The wenche routeth eek *par compaignye*.
  Aleyn the clerc, that herde this melodye,
He poked John and seyde, 'Slepestow?
Herd thow evere slyk a sang er now?

289 **by and by** 'nearby'.
292 **hem to solace** 'to pass the time pleasantly'. *Hem* is reflexive (5.4.5).
295 To 'varnish one's head' is to get very drunk ('well oiled').
296 **fordronke** 'very drunk', as his pallor indicates – recalling the pilgrim Miller 'that fordronken was al pale' (I 3120).
298 'As if he was hoarse or had a cold.'
301 i.e. she had had a good drink (as in Modern 'wet one's whistle').
307 'That was the end of it, no sleeping potion was necessary for them.'
308 **wisly** 'surely, thoroughly' (not 'wisely'; the vowel is short).
310 'Nor did he bother to restrain his backside.'
312 **a furlong** i.e. a long way off.
313 **par compaignye** 'to keep them company'.
316 **slyk a sang** 'such a song', Nth.

Lo, swilk a complyng is ymel hem alle;
A wilde fyr on thair bodyes falle.
Wha herkned evere swilk a ferly thyng?
Ye, they sal have the flour of il endyng.
This lang nyght ther tydes me na reste,
But yet na force, al sal be for the beste;
For, John,' seyde he, 'als evere moot I thryve,
If þat I may, yon wenche wol I swyve.
Som esement has lawe shapen us,
For, John, ther is a lawe þat says thus,
That gif a man in a point be agreved,
That in another he sal be releved.
Oure corn is stoln, soothly it is na nay,
And we han had an ille fit today;
And syn I sal have naan amendement
Agayn my los, I wil have esement.
By Goddes saule, it sal naan other be.'
This John answerde, 'Aleyn, avyse thee.
The millere is a perilous man,' he sayde,
'And gif þat he out of his sleep abrayde
He myghte doon us bathe a vileynye.'
Aleyn answerde, 'I counte hym noght a flye,'

317 'See what an evening service they are having among themselves.' *Swilk* 'such' and *ymel* 'among' are both Northernisms; and so, we suppose, is *complyng*. The majority of manuscripts, including Hengwrt and Ellesmere, read *couplyng*; but a minority has some form of 'compline' (the last church service of the day, sung before retiring), which gives much better sense. Words with *-yng* for *-yn* are recorded in the North, including *complyng* for 'compline' in Gavin Douglas; and three *Canterbury Tales* manuscripts read *complyng* here. If that is what Chaucer wrote, the unusual form would explain an early 'correction' to *couplyng*.

318 **wilde fyr** 'erysipelas', an acute inflammation of the skin.

thair Nth. See 3.2. The form occurs only here in Chaucer's works.

319 **Wha** 'who', Nth (also *swilk*).

320 **the flour of il endyng** 'the best kind of bad end' (*il* Nth). *Flour* is the normal Chaucerian spelling of *flower*: but Aleyn also punningly alludes to the miller's occupation.

321–2 Northernisms: *lang*, *tydes* (*-s* ending), *na* 'no', *sal* 'shall'.

324 **yon** 'yonder' ('that girl over there'), Nth.

327 **gif** 'if', Nth.

a point 'one point' (long *a*, 'one', Nth). Some manuscripts note the legal maxim 'Qui in uno gravatur, in alio debet relevari'. Aleyn is evidently studying law. Cf. 331–2n.

329 **it is na nay** 'there's no denying it'.

330 **ille fit** 'bad time' (*ille* Nth).

331–2 *Amendement* here represents full compensation for the stolen corn, as against partial redress or *esement*.

333 **saule** 'soul', Nth.

334 **avyse thee** 'be careful'.

336 **gif þat** 'if'.

And up he rist and by the wenche he crepte.
This wenche lay uprighte and faste slepte
Til he so neigh was er she myghte espie
That it hadde been to late for to crie,
And shortly for to seyn, they were at oon.
Now pley Aleyn, for I wol speke of John.
This John lith stille a furlang wey or two
And to hymself he maketh routhe and wo.
'Allas', quod he, 'this is a wikked jape;
Now may I seyn þat I is but an ape.
Yet has my felawe somwhat for his harm,
He has the milleris doghter in his arm.
He auntred hym and has his nedes sped
And I lye as a draf-sak in my bed;
And whan this jape is tald another day
I sal ben halden a daf, a cokenay.
I wil arise and auntre it by my fayth;
Unhardy is unsely, thus men sayth.'
And up he roos, and softely he wente
Unto the cradel and in his hand it hente
And baar it softe unto his beddes feet.
Soone after this the wyf hir rowtyng leet
And gan awake and wente hir out to pisse,
And cam agayn and gan hir cradel mysse
And groped heer and ther, but she foond noon.
'Allas,' quod she, 'I hadde almoost mysgoon;
I hadde almoost goon to the clerkes bed.
Ey, *benedicite*, thanne had I foule ysped.'
And forth she gooth til she the cradel fond;
She gropeth alwey forther with hir hond
And foond the bed and thoghte noght but good

339 **rist** 'rises', present tense, as at 395.

340 **uprighte** 'on her back'.

345 **furlang wey** strictly two-and-a-half minutes, one eighth of the time customarily taken to walk a mile (20 minutes). A Northern form, *-lang*, spills over into the narrative here.

346 **maketh routhe and wo** 'expresses his self-pity and misery'.

349 **has** Nth (also 350, 351).

351 'He took a risk and has got what he wanted.'

353 **tald** Nth (like *halden* 354).

354 **cokenay** 'milksop, weakling'. The word, originally 'cock's egg', came to be applied to pampered children (and later to pampered Londoners, whence 'cockney').

356 **Unhardy is unsely** literally 'unbold is unsuccessful', i.e. Fortune favours the brave. On *men*, see 136n above.

366 'Hey, bless us, then I would have ended up badly.' *Benedicite* has only three syllables (*bendisté*), as usual.

By cause þat the cradel by it stood,
And nyste wher she was for it was derk,
But faire and wel she creep in to the clerk
And lyth ful stille and wolde have caught a sleep.
Withinne a while this John the clerk up leep
And on this goodewyf he leyth on soore.
So murie a fyt ne hadde she nat ful yoore;
He priketh harde and depe as he were mad.
This joly lyf han thise two clerkes lad
Til þat the thridde cok bigan to synge.
  Aleyn wax wery in the dawenynge
For he hadde swonken al the longe nyght,
And seyde, 'Farewel, Malyn, swete wight.
The day is come, I may no lenger byde,
But everemo wherso I go or ryde
I is thyn awen clerk, swa have I sel.'
'Now, deere lemman,' quod she, 'go, farewel.
But er thow go, o thyng I wol thee telle:
Whan that thow wendest homward by the melle,
Right at the entree of the dore bihynde
Thow shalt a cake of half a busshel fynde
That was ymaked of thyn owene mele
Which þat I heelp my sire for to stele.
And, good lemman, God thee save and kepe.'
And with that word almoost she gan to wepe.
Aleyn up rist and thoghte, 'Er þat it dawe
I wol go crepen in by my felawe,'
And fond the cradel with his hond anon.
'By God,' thoghte he, 'al wrang I have mysgon.
Myn heed is toty of my swynk tonyght;
That maketh me þat I go noght aright.
I woot wel by the cradel I have mysgo –
Here lyth the millere and his wyf also.'

372 **creep** 'crept', past tense (an OE strong verb, weak in Modern English; cf. *leep* 'leapt' 374, *heelp* 'helped' 392, and see 4.5.1).

375 **goodewyf** 'mistress of the house'.

379 Cocks were thought to crow three times a night, the third at one hour before dawn.

382 **Malyn** a pet form of 'Maud', associated by Chaucer elsewhere with a country girl (*Canterbury Tales* VII 3384).

385 Northernisms: *I is*, *awen* 'own', *swa* 'so', *sel* 'happiness'. The dawn parting of lovers is an episode that calls romance to mind: cf. *Troilus* 3.1415–1533.

386 **lemman** 'sweetheart' (also 393), a word not used by Chaucer in elevated contexts.

398 **wrang** 'wrong', Nth.

399 **toty of my swynk** 'befuddled with my labours'.

And forth he gooth on twenty devele way
Unto the bed theras the millere lay.
He wende have cropen by his felawe John
And by the millere in he creep anoon,
And caughte hym by the nekke and softe he spak.
He seyde, 'Thou, John, thow swynes-hed, awak,
For Cristes saule, and here a noble game;
For by that lord þat called is seint Jame,
As I have thries in this shorte nyght
Swyved the milleris doghter bolt upright,
Whil thow hast as a coward been agast.'
'Ye, false harlot,' quod the millere, 'hast?
A, false traytour, false clerk,' quod he,
'Thou shalt be deed, by Goddes dignytee.
Who dorste be so bold to disparage
My doghter, that is come of swich lynage?'
And by the throte-bolle he caughte Alayn,
And he hente hym despitously agayn
And on the nose he smoot hym with his fest;
Doun ran the blody streem upon his brest.
And in the floor with nose and mouth tobroke
They walwen as doon two pigges in a poke;
And up they goon and doun agayn anoon
Til þat the millere sporned on a stoon,
And doun he fil bakward upon his wyf,
That wiste nothyng of this nyce stryf,
For she was falle aslepe a litel wight
With John the clerk that waked hadde al nyght,
And with the fal out of hir sleep she brayde.
'Help, holy cros of Bromholm,' she sayde.

403 **on twenty devele way** an often jocular curse ('Tel on, a devel wey!' says the Host to the drunk Miller), here addressed to the consequences of Aleyn's mistake: 'to his utter ruin'.

405 'He intended to have crept in beside his mate John.'

409 **saule** 'soul', the last of the Northernisms.

410 St James was known especially from his pilgrimage centre at Compostela, Spain.

414 **hast?** 'have you?'

417 **disparage** The relevant sense is *OED* 1: 'to degrade or dishonour by marrying to one of inferior rank'.

420 'And he (i.e. Aleyn) grappled with him violently in return.'

426 **sporned on a stoon** 'tripped over a stone'.

429 **wight** 'bit, while'.

432 **Bromholm** in the Reeve's own county of Norfolk. Its priory possessed a relic of Christ's cross, an object of reverence and pilgrimage.

'*In manus tuas*, Lord, to thee I calle.
Awake, Symond, the feend is on us falle.
Myn herte is broken. Help, I nam but ded.
Ther lyth oon upon my wombe and up myn hed.
Help, Symkyn, for the false clerkes fighte.'
  This John sterte up as faste as evere he myghte,
And graspeth by the walles to and fro
To fynde a staf; and she sterte up also,
And knew the estres bet than dide this John,
And by the wal a staf she foond anon,
And saugh a litel shymeryng of a light
For at an hole in shoon the moone bright,
And by that light she saugh hem bothe two,
But sikerly she nyste who was who
But as she saugh a whit thyng in hir iye;
And whan she gan this white thyng espye
She wende the clerk hadde wered a voluper,
And with the staf she drow ay ner and ner
And wende han hit this Aleyn atte fulle,
And smoot the millere on the piled skulle
That doun he gooth and cryde, 'Harrow, I dye.'
Thise clerkes bette hym wel and lete hym lye,
And greithen hem and tooke hir hors anon
And eek hir mele and on hir wey they gon,
And at the mille yet they toke hir cake
Of half a busshel flour ful wel ybake.
  Thus is the proude millere wel ybete,
And hath ylost the gryndyng of the whete,
And payed for the souper every del
Of Aleyn and of John, that bette hym wel.
His wyf is swyved, and his doghter als.
Lo, swich it is a millere to be fals!
And therfore this proverbe is seyd ful sooth:

433 **In manus tuas** 'Into thy hands [I commend my spirit]', Luke 23.46, words used at the point of death.

435 **I nam but ded** 'I am as good as dead'. She refers, not to heartbreak, but to some injury to her chest.

441 **estres** i.e. the ins and outs of the house.

447 'Except that with her eye she saw something white.'

450 **drow ay ner and ner** 'drew ever nearer and nearer'. Cf. 16b/68.

452 **piled** 'bald', cf. 81 above.

457 **yet** 'furthermore'.

458 **half a busshel flour** After words expressing measure, like 'bushel', the thing measured is often put in apposition (see 5.3.2).

Hym thar nat wene wel þat yvele dooth;
A gilour shal hymself bigiled be.
And God, that sitteth heighe in magestee,
Save al this compaignie grete and smale.
Thus have I quyt the Millere in my tale.

Here endeth the Reves Tale.

466 'He who does evil need expect no good.' Proverbial: Whiting E185. *Hym thar* 'he need', an impersonal expression (5.6.8).

467 Another proverb: Whiting G491. Medieval literary theory advises ending with proverbs – in this case, with a personal edge to them.

16b Chaucer: The Prioress's Tale

Like *St Erkenwald* (text 10), the Prioress's Tale is a *miraculum*, in this case a Miracle of the Virgin. Such stories were popular in England, especially among devout women readers. Other Middle English examples are collected in Beverly Boyd, *The Middle English Miracles of the Virgin* (San Marino, 1964). The story told by the Prioress has many analogues (Bryan and Dempster, below), though Chaucer's exact source is not known. Since it concerns the death of a small boy, this particular *miraculum* suits its teller, who is described in the General Prologue as so 'pitous' that she wept to see a mouse in a trap (I 143–5). In the preface to his modernization of the Tale, William Wordsworth remarked that the Prioress's 'fierce bigotry . . . forms a fine background for her tender-hearted sympathies with the Mother and Child'; but the *torment* and *shameful deth* meted out to the murderer and also to the Jews *that of this mordre wiste* (176–82) have understandably provoked many readers since. In judging Chaucer's own attitude to such 'fierce bigotry', it should be recalled that, since Edward I banished them in 1290, there had been no Jews in England. Hence the story is set in a remote and unspecified *Asye*, unlike the similar story of Jewish child-murder told in the *Peterborough Chronicle* (1/74–82 here). There is also a theological consideration. The Bible represents the Jewish people as responsible, in the person of Herod, for the Massacre of the Innocents, and also, corporately, for the death of Christ (Matthew 27.25). Accordingly, in the Prioress's version of the murdered innocent and his grieving mother, there is a strong sense of history repeating itself, as part of a long-running confrontation between God and his adversaries (see notes to 1–7, 122, 128–33, 175, and compare 1/76–8).

Editions

Beverly Boyd, *The Prioress's Tale*, The Variorum Chaucer vol. II (Norman, 1987)

Benson and Skeat editions: see Headnote to text 15 above

Studies

Bryan and Dempster (*Canterbury Tales* Headnote), pp. 447–85

Cooper (*Canterbury Tales* Headnote), pp. 287–98

Pearsall (*Canterbury Tales* Headnote), pp. 246–52

Florence Ridley, *The Prioress and the Critics* (Berkeley, 1965)

The Proheme of the Prioresse Tale.
Domine dominus noster.

O Lord, oure Lord, thy name how merveilous
Is in this large world ysprad – quod she –
For nat oonly thy laude precious
Parfourned is by men of dignytee,
But by the mouth of children thy bountee
Parfourned is, for on the brest soukynge
Somtyme shewen they thyn heryynge.

Wherfore in laude, as I best kan or may,
Of thee and of the white lilye flour
Which þat the bar and is a mayde alway,
To telle a storie I wol do my labour;
Nat that I may encressen hir honour,
For she hirself is honour and the roote
Of bountee next hir sone, and soules boote.

O moder mayde, O mayde moder free,
O bussh unbrent brennyng in Moyses sighte,
That ravysedest doun fro the deitee
Thurgh thyn humblesse the goost þat in th'alighte,
Of whos vertu whan he thyn herte lighte
Conceyved was the fadres sapience,
Help me to telle it in thy reverence.

Lady, thy bountee, thy magnificence,
Thy vertu, and thy grete humylitee,
Ther may no tonge expresse in no science;

1–7 The opening of the Prioress's 'proheme', or prologue, is based on Psalm 8.2–3 (AV 1–2): 'O Lord our Lord [*Domine dominus noster*]: how admirable is thy name in the whole earth! For thy magnificence is elevated above the heavens. Out of the mouth of infants and of sucklings thou hast perfected praise, because of thy enemies: that thou mayst destroy the enemy and the avenger.' The passage was familiar from liturgical uses, in the Little Office of the Virgin and the Mass of the Holy Innocents. The reference to the destruction of God's enemies, not represented in these lines, anticipates the conclusion of the Tale.

9 **lilye flour** a common symbol of the Virgin, from Song of Songs 2.2.

16 Alluding to the burning bush seen by Moses (Exodus 3.2), another common type or symbol of Mary. The bush remained unburnt (*unbrent*), just as Mary remained a virgin.

18 **the goost þat in th'alighte** 'the Holy Spirit who alighted in thee'.

20 **sapience** 'wisdom'. Christ, whose incarnation is here described, is commonly referred to as the Wisdom of God the Father. Compare *Piers Plowman* B XVI 36–7.

22 **magnificence** 'glory' (*magnificentia* in Psalm 8.2, quoted above 1–7n).

24 **in no science** i.e. in the language of any learned discipline.

For somtyme, lady, er men praye to thee,
Thow goost biforn of thy benygnytee
And getest us the light of thy prayere
To gyden us unto thy sone so deere.

My konnyng is so wayk, O blisful queene,
For to declare thy grete worthynesse
That I ne may the weighte nat sustene,
But as a child of twelve month old or lesse
That kan unnethe any word expresse
Right so fare I; and therfore I yow preye,
Gideth my song that I shal of yow seye.
Explicit prohemium.

Here bigynneth the Prioresse tale of Alma redemptoris mater.

Ther was in Asye in a greet citee
Amonges Cristen folk a Jewerye,
Sustened by a lord of that contree
For foul usure and lucre of vileynye,
Hateful to Crist and to his compaignye,
And thurgh this strete men myghte ryde and wende
For it was free and open at eyther ende.

A litel scole of Cristen folk ther stood
Doun at the ferther ende, in which ther weere
Children an heep ycomen of Cristen blood
That lerned in that scole yeer by yere
Swich manere doctrine as men used there –
This is to seyn, to syngen and to rede
As smale children doon in hir childhede.

Among thise children was a wydwes sone,
A litel clergeon seven yeer of age,

26–8 'In your graciousness, you go in advance and procure for us by your intercession the light to guide us on our way to your beloved son.' Close to Dante, *Paradiso* 33.16–18 (St Bernard's praise of Mary): 'Thy graciousness [*benignità*] not only succours whoever asks, but often freely runs ahead of [*precorre*] the asking.'

37 **Jewerye** 'Jewish quarter', here a street occupied by Jews (*this strete* 41). There is still a Jewry Street in London.

39 The Jews are here associated with usury, lending money at interest (forbidden to Christians), and with 'filthy lucre', excessive profits from sales. Some manuscripts, including Hengwrt, give the biblical original of the latter phrase as a gloss: 'turpe lucrum' (I Timothy 3.8).

51 The age of seven marked the end of infancy, the age of innocence (see ll. 86, 114, 156, 183), and the customary beginning of school-days. The boy is in his first term (cf. 88n).

That day by day to scole was his wone,
And eek also, wher as he say th'ymage
Of Cristes moder, hadde he in usage,
As hym was taught, to knele adoun and seye
His *Ave Marie* as he goth by the weye.

Thus hath this wydwe hir litel sone ytaught
Oure blisful lady, Cristes moder deere,
To worshipe ay, and he forgat it naught,
For sely child wol alwey soone lere.
But ay whan I remembre on this matere,
Seint Nicholas stant evere in my presence
For he so yong to Crist dide reverence.

This litel child his litel book lernynge
As he sat in the scole at his prymer,
He *Alma redemptoris* herde synge
As children lerned hir antiphoner,
And as he dorste, he drow hym ner and ner
And herkned ay the wordes and the note
Til he the firste vers koude al by rote.

Nat wiste he what this Latyn was to seye
For he so yong and tendre was of age;
But on a day his felawe gan he preye
T'expounden hym this song in his langage
Or telle hym why this song was in usage:
This prayde he hym to construe and declare
Ful often tyme upon hise knowes bare.

His felawe, which þat elder was than he,
Answerde hym thus: 'This song, I have herd seye,
Was maked of oure blisful lady free

52 'Who was accustomed to go every day to school': see 5.6.9.

53 **wher as he say** 'wherever he saw'.

54 **hadde he in usage** 'it was his custom'.

56 **Ave Marie** 'Hail Mary'.

60 'For a good child will always be quick to learn.' Proverbial: Whiting C219.

62 St Nicholas, patron saint of schoolboys, is said to have observed fast-days even as a baby at the breast (cf. ll. 6–7 above), and as a boy he was an exceptionally quick learner.

65 **prymer** a Latin book of devotions, here used as a Latin reader.

66 **Alma redemptoris** 'Gracious [mother] of the Redeemer', an anthem in praise of Mary as Virgin Mother and help of sinners.

67 **antiphoner** 'anthem book', from which older children (l. 78) are learning to chant in another part of the schoolroom.

68 'And, as far as he dared, he drew nearer and nearer.'

71 'He did not know what this Latin meant.'

Hir to salue and eek hir for to preye
To been oure help and socour whan we deye.
I kan namoore expounde in this matere;
I lerne song, I kan but smal gramere.'

'And is this song maked in reverence
Of Cristes moder?' seyde this innocent.
'Now certes I wol do my diligence
To konne it al er Cristemasse is went.
Thogh þat I for my prymer shal be shent
And shal be beten thries in an houre,
I wol it konne oure lady for to honoure.'

His felawe taughte hym homward prively
Fro day to day til he koude it by rote,
And thanne he soong it wel and boldely
Fro word to word acordyng with the note.
Twyes a day it passed thurgh his throte,
To scoleward and homward whan he wente;
On Cristes moder set was his entente.

As I have seyd, thurghout the Juerye
This litel child as he cam to and fro
Ful murily wolde he synge and crye
O Alma redemptoris everemo.
The swetnesse his herte perced so
Of Cristes moder, that to hir to preye
He kan nat stynte of syngyng by the weye.

Oure firste foo, the serpent Sathanas,
That hath in Jewes herte his waspes nest,
Up swal and seyde, 'O Hebrayk peple, allas,
Is this to yow a thyng that is honest,
That swich a boy shal walken as hym lest
In youre despit and synge of swich sentence
Which is agayns oure lawes reverence?'

84 'I am learning singing, I know only a little Latin.'

88 'To learn it all before the Christmas holiday is over.' The boy is in his first, Michaelmas, term.

89 'Even though I will be punished for (neglecting) my primer.'

92 **homward** 'on the way home'.

93 **Fro day to day** i.e. a little each day.

95 'With every word correctly fitted to the tune.'

106 **Sathanas** a Vulgate Latin form of 'Satan'.

110 **boy** usually a contemptuous term in Middle English, as here.

as hym lest 'just as he pleases'. See 5.6.8 on such impersonal verbs.

111 **In youre despit** 'in defiance of you'.

112 **oure lawes** Satan identifies himself with the Jewish people, against God and his Christians. Many manuscripts, however, read *youre* not *oure*.

Fro thennes forth the Jewes han conspired
This innocent out of this world to chace.
An homycide therto han they hired
That in an aleye hadde a privee place;
And as the child gan forby for to pace,
This cursed Jew hym hente and heeld hym faste
And kitte his throte and in a pit hym caste.

I seye that in a wordrobe they hym threwe
Wheras thise Jewes purgen hir entraille.
O cursed folk of Herodes al newe,
What may youre yvel entente yow availle?
Mordre wol out, certeyn it wol nat faille,
And namely theras th'onour of God shal sprede;
The blood out cryeth on youre cursed dede.

O martir souded to virginitee,
Now maystow syngen, folwyng everė in oon
The white lamb celestial – quod she –
Of which the grete evangelist, seint John,
In Pathmos wroot, which seith þat they þat gon
Biforn this lamb and synge a song al newe
That nevere flesshly womman they ne knewe.

This poure wydwe awaiteth al that nyght
After hir litel child, but he cam noght;
For which, as soone as it was dayes lyght,
With face pale of drede and bisy thoght
She hath at scole and elliswhere hym soght,

117 'And as the child was going past.' On *gan*, see 5.6.3.

120 **wordrobe** 'privy', the pit in which the Jews *purgen hir entraille*, 'empty their bowels'.

122 The reference to Herod the Great, King of the Jews, recalls his Massacre of the Innocents ('all the men children that were in Bethlehem and in all the borders thereof, from two years old and under', Matthew 2.16). The modern Jews re-enact (*al newe*) what 'Herod's folk' did at the time of Christ's birth.

124 A proverb: Whiting M806.

126 God says to Cain, after he has murdered Abel, 'The voice of thy brother's blood crieth to me from the earth' (Genesis 4.10).

128–33 In his vision on the island of Patmos, St John saw the Lamb of God 'and with him an hundred forty-four thousand . . . And they sung as it were a new canticle . . . These are they who were not defiled with women: for they are virgins. These follow the Lamb whithersoever he goeth': Apocalypse (Revelation) 14.1–4. The passage was read at the Mass of the Holy Innocents, associating the 144,000 with the children massacred by Herod. See 122n above.

128 **evere in oon** 'continually'.

133 **flesshly** The gloss *carnaliter* in the Hengwrt MS identifies this as an adverb: 'in a carnal way'.

Til fynally she gan so fer espie
That he last seyn was in the Jewerie.

With modres pitee in hir brest enclosed
She goth as she were half out of hir mynde
To every place wheras she hath supposed
By liklyhede hir litel child to fynde,
And evere on Cristes moder meke and kynde
She cryde, and at the laste thus she wroghte:
Among the cursed Jues she hym soghte.

She frayneth and she prayeth pitously
To every Jew that dwelte in thilke place
To telle hir if hir child wente oght forby.
They seyde nay; but Jesu of his grace
Yaf in hir thought inwith a litel space
That in that place after hir sone she cryde
Wher he was casten in a pit bisyde.

O grete God, that parfournest thy laude
By mouth of innocèntz, lo here thy myght!
This gemme of chastitee, this emeraude,
And eek of martirdom the ruby bright,
Ther he with throte ycorven lay upright
He *Alma redemptoris* gan to synge
So loude that al the place gan to rynge.

The Cristen folk that thurgh the strete wente
In coomen for to wondre upon this thyng,
And hastily they for the provost sente.
He cam anon withouten tariyng
And herieth Crist that is of hevene kyng
And eek his moder, honour of mankynde;
And after that the Jewes leet he bynde.

This child with pitous lamentacioun
Up taken was, syngynge his song alway;

139 'Till at last she got so far as to discover.'

150 **wente oght forby** 'had by any chance passed by'.

152 'Within a short time put it into her mind.'

155–6 Recalling Psalm 8, here as at ll. 5–6, but now using the term 'innocents'.

157–8 The emerald is a 'clean stone' which 'voideth lechery': *English Mediaeval Lapidaries*, EETS o.s. 190 (1933), 20–1, 40, 121. The red ruby symbolizes the blood of martyrdom.

159 **upright** 'flat on his back'.

164 **provost** a term for chief magistrate used only of foreign towns, in this case, Asiatic.

168 **leet he bynde** 'he caused to be bound' (5.6.5).

170 **Up taken was** 'was lifted up' (out of the *pit*).

And with honour of greet processioun
They carien hym unto the nexte abbay.
His moder swownyng by his beere lay;
Unnethe myghte the peple that was there
This newe Rachel bryngen fro his beere.

With torment and with shameful deth echon
This provost dooth thise Jewes for to sterve
That of this mordre wiste, and that anon.
He nolde no swich cursednesse observe.
Yvel shal have that yvel wol disserve;
Therfore with wilde hors he dide hem drawe,
And after that he heng hem by the lawe.

Upon his beere ay lyth this innocent
Biforn the chief auter whil the masse laste;
And after that the abbot with his covent
Han sped hem for to buryen hym ful faste;
And whan they holy water on hym caste,
Yet spak this child whan spreynd was holy water
And song *O alma redemptoris mater*.

This abbot, which þat was an holy man,
As monkes ben, or ellis oghten be,
This yonge child to conjure he bigan,
And seyde, 'O deere child, I halsen thee
In vertu of the Holy Trinitee,
Tel me what is thy cause for to synge,
Sith þat thy throte is kit to my semynge.'

'My throte is kit unto my nekke-boon,'
Seyde this child, 'and as by wey of kynde

175 **newe Rachel** In his account of the Massacre of the Innocents, Matthew cites from an Old Testament prophecy of Jeremiah: 'A voice in Rama was heard, lamentation and great mourning; Rachel bewailing her children and would not be comforted, because they are not' (Matthew 2.18, from Jeremiah 31.15). So the boy's mother is another 'new Rachel', like the grieving mothers of the Innocents. This use of *newe*, as at l. 122, expresses the typological idea that modern events are foreshadowed in the Bible, just as Old Testament events there foreshadow those in the New.

177 'This magistrate causes these Jews to be put to death.'

179 'He had no wish to countenance such wickedness.'

180 Proverbial: Whiting E178.

181 **he dide hem drawe** 'he caused them to be drawn', that is, dragged through the streets to their hanging.

186 **Han sped hem** 'hastened' (5.4.5).

187 Following the Requiem Mass, the corpse is sprinkled with holy water, according to custom.

196 **to my semynge** 'as it seems to me'.

198 **as by wey of kynde** 'in the natural way of things'.

I sholde have dyed, ye, longe tyme agoon;
But Jesu Crist, as ye in bokes fynde,
Wol þat his glorie laste and be in mynde;
And for the worship of his moder deere
Yet may I synge *O alma* loude and clere.

'This welle of mercy, Cristes moder swete,
I loved alwey as after my konnynge;
And whan þat I my lyf sholde forlete
To me she cam and bad me for to synge
This antheme verraily in my deiynge,
As ye han herd; and whan þat I had songe
Me thoughte she leyde a greyn upon my tonge.

'Wherfore I synge and synge moot, certeyn,
In honour of that blisful mayden free
Til fro my tonge of taken is the greyn;
And after that thus seyde she to me:
"My litel child, now wol I fecche thee
Whan þat the greyn is fro thy tonge ytake.
Be nat agast, I wol thee nat forsake."'

This holy monk, this abbot hym mene I,
His tonge out caughte and took awey the greyn,
And he yaf up the goost ful softely.
And whan this abbot hadde this wonder seyn
His salte teerys trikled doun as reyn,
And gruf he fil al plat upon the grounde
And stille he lay as he hadde leyn ybounde.

The covent eek lay on the pavement
Wepynge, and heryen Cristes moder deere;
And after that they ryse and forth been went
And toke awey this martir from his beere,
And in a toumbe of marbilstones cleere
Enclosen they this litel body swete.
Ther he is now, God leve us for to meete!

205 'I always praised so far as I knew how.' *Love* is 'praise' (OE *lofian*), not 'love' (OE *lufian*). See *MED loven* v.(2).

208 **in my deiynge** 'as I lay dying'.

210 **greyn** This 'grain' (which takes the part played in other versions of the story by a lily, a gem, or a pebble) has prompted much scholarly speculation: see the notes in the Riverside and Variorum editions. The word may simply denote a small bit of something which Chaucer chooses not to specify; but *MED grain* n. cites this occurrence under sense 3(b): 'precious stone; small bits of gold or gems'.

227 **ryse** probably past tense plural, 'rose'.

forth been went 'went out' (from the abbey church?).

231 'May God grant us to meet again where he now is' (i.e. in Paradise).

O yonge Hugh of Lyncoln, slayn also
With cursed Jewes, as it is notable,
For it is but a litel while ygo,
Preye eek for us, we synful folk unstable,
That of his mercy God so merciable
On us his grete mercy multiplie,
For reverence of his moder Marie. Amen.

Here endeth the Prioresse Tale.

232 'Little St Hugh' of Lincoln was a boy supposedly martyred by Jews in 1255. His relics were venerated in Lincoln Cathedral. Compare the *Peterborough Chronicle* story of St William of Norwich, 1/74–82 here.

Textual Notes

These notes record all significant departures from the manuscripts used in this volume as the basis of a text. The reading of the text is followed, after the square bracket, by the rejected manuscript reading and also (e.g. in No. 7) by the readings of other manuscripts consulted.

1. *The Peterborough Chronicle* Sole manuscript: Bodleian Library MS Laud Misc. 636.

55 þoleden] þolenden. 81 þurh] þur.

2. *The Owl and the Nightingale* Base manuscript: British Library MS Cotton Caligula A IX (C). Also cited: Jesus College, Oxford, MS 29 (J). Not noted: *d/ð* variants.

7 aiþer] asþer C; eyþer J. 11 oþeres] oþere C; oþres J. 17 vaste] J; waste C. 21 Bet] J; Het C. 47 Wenst] West C; Wenest J. 51 vote] J; note C. 59 ȝif] ȝis C; If J. 62 þe] J; se C. 86 *Line from* J; C *omits.* 89 fliȝst] fliȝt C; flyhst J. 104 fule] J; fole C. 115 loþe custe] J; loþ wiste C. 116 Segget] Seggeþ J; Segge C. 118 oȝe] oȝer C; owe J. 120 he] J; hi C. 144 noþerward] noþerwad C; neþerward J. 149 ȝaf] yaf J; ȝas C. 151 hwaþer] hweþer J; ware C. 164 among] J; amon C. 174 ek] J; eck C. 178 unwreste] J; unwerste C. 184 foȝe] soȝe C; soþe J. 185 ur] J; hure C. 187 Wo] Hwo J; þu C. 211 nu] J; him C. 223 schrichest] schirchest C; scrichest J. 225 þincheþ] J; þinchest C. 242 sihst] sichst C; syst J. bow ne rind] *altered from* bos ne strind C; bouh of lynd J. 249 þustre] J; þurste C. 255 hattest] J; attest C. 267 þarevore] warevore C; hwer vore J. 272 wunne] wune C; ynne J. 273 kende] cunde C, J. 274 me] J; C *omits.* 284 þeȝ] þeyh J; Yif C. 303 werse] worse C; wrse J. 317 bold] J; blod C. 325 a] J; ad C. 347 ure] ouer C, J. 359 of þan] J; oþþan C. 370 lesse] J; lasse C. 376 gencheþ] J; gengþ wel C. aweyward] J; awaiwart C.

3. Laȝamon, *Brut* Base manuscript: British Library MS Cotton Caligula A IX (C). Also cited: British Library MS Cotton Otho C XIII (O). Not noted: *d/ð* variants.

1 tydinge] O; tidende C. 12 Heo] He C, O. 26 heo] he C; hii O. 43 biginnen] bigunnen C; bigynne O. 49 riche] richen C; rich O. 75 fordo] O; fordon C. 77 swyn] O; C *omits.* 83 þat] O; þa C. 84 water] O; wate C. 104 cleopede] cheopede C. 123 swiðe] O; swi C (*also at 142*). 125 Wihtere] Whitere C. 128 Grim] grum C (*crossed out and corrected in margin in later hand to* Colgrim); Colgrim O. 131 him] him him C. 135 Go we mid isunde and] O; Gumen mine gode C. 144 fæiesið] fæiesih C. 159 aðele] alðele C. 161 to] O; C *omits.* 163 eower] eorwer C. 169 Octa and Ossa] O; and Ossa Octa C.

4. *Ancrene Wisse* Base manuscript: Corpus Christi College, Cambridge, MS 402 (A). Also cited: British Library MS Cotton Cleopatra C VI (C).

50 esken] C; ahte esken A. 65 feondes fode] C; feode A.

5. *Sir Orfeo* Base manuscript: National Library of Scotland MS Advocates 19.2.1 (A). Also cited: British Library MS Harley 3810 (H); British Library MS Ashmole 61 (Ash).

13 In Breteyne þis layes were wrouȝt] In Breteyne bi hold time / þis layes were wrouȝt so seiþ þis rime A; In Brytayn þis layes arne ywrytt H; That in þe leys ben iwrouȝht Ash. 14–16 *text based on* H, A *omits.* 14 ybrouȝt] brouȝht Ash; ygete H. 23–38 þat beþ trewe . . . harping is] *lost in* A; *text based on* H *with alterations to language of* A. (*Lines 25–38 follow 39–46 in* H). 29 lerned] lernyd Ash; loved H. 33 al] Ash; H *omits.* 36 Bot] Ash; H *omits.* 38 melody] Ash; joy and melody H. 39 A *resumes.* 41 A stal-worþ] T; stalworþ A. 57 Bifel] Uifel A; Hit byfel H, Ash. 140 Y no] Y n A. 219 þo] Lo A. 230 no (1)] ne Ash; A *omits.* 345 wel] *last two letters smudged in* A. 363 anowrned] avowed *or* anowed A. 388 seiȝe] seiȝe ful A. 406 lef] liif A. 450 aske] alke A. 482 he] A *omits.* 521 trompours] trompour A.

6. *The Cloud of Unknowing* Base manuscript: British Library MS Harley 674 (Har[1]). Also cited: Cambridge University Library MS Kk vi 26 (Kk).

24 neiþer] Kk; not Har[1]. 33 schuldest] Kk; schalt Har[1]. 55 him one] Kk; himself Har[1]. 63 hymself] Kk; hemself Har[1]. 68 seerly] Kk; diversly Har[1]. 77 hys] Kk; þe Har[1]. 84 worching] Kk; Har[1] *omits.* 103 tyme seerly] Kk; þing diversly Har[1]. 148 troden] Kk; troden doun Har[1]. 209 apon] onpon Har[1]. 220 þing þat] þing þat þat Har[1]. 225 ȝit] Kk; Har *omits.*

7a and 7b. Langland, *Piers Plowman* Base manuscript: Huntington Library MS HM 143 (X). Also cited, the other manuscripts of the 'i'-group: Bodleian Library MS Douce 104 (D); Bodleian Library MS Digby 102 (Y); British Library MS Addit. 34779 (P^2); British Library MS Addit. 35157 (U); London University Library MS S.L.V. 88 (I).

(7a)
21 therby] the by X, D, Y, P^2, U, I. 30 feste-dayes] Y, D, P^2, U, I; feste day X. 35 ȝong] ȝong ȝong X. 43a *qua*] D, Y, U, I; *quia* X; P^2 *omits.* 62 knaves] P^2, D, U, I; knave X, Y. 76 mendenantes] P^2, D, U, I; mendenant X, Y. 81 or] X *omits.* 84 discret] U, D, Y, P^2, I; desirede X. 98a *que*] Y, U; *qui* X, D, P^2, I.

(7b)
2 waye] X *omits.* 4 wolde] U, D, P^2; wol X, Y, I. 5 a lady] D, Y, P^2, U, I; þat lady X. 18 wyȝtly] *Skeat*; wittiliche X, Y, U, I; witterly D, P^2. 20 on þe teme] *A and B Texts*; on teme U; on tyme (?) P^2; in tyme X, Y; on þat tyme D; one tyme I. 22 assaie] X *omits.* 77 *Deleantur*] *Deliantur* X. 90 wordynge] worchynge X, D, Y, P^2, I; U *omits.* 93 pilgrimages] I, D, Y, U; pilgrimage P^2; pilgrimes X. 135 have] D; X, Y, P^2, U, I *omit.* 166 pes] U, D, P^2; mase X; ase Y, I. 176 byleve] Y, D, P^2, U, I; blyne X. 180 flales] fuales X. 196 labour] lalour X. 226 abave] Y, U (*or* abane); abane I; bane (*or* bave) X, D; abaite P^2. 228 he hit] hit X. 242 Bytulie] U Y; Bytuyle X; By tyling D; Bi toille P^2; *torn* I. 242a *sudore*] *sudure* X. 246a *arare*] Y U, I; *arrare* X, D P^2. 278 Dives] .on. X. 283 And ȝif thow þe pore] And if þou þe pore I; And ȝif þe pore D; And ȝeve þou pore P^2 (be of *added in different ink after* þou); And ȝif thow pouer X; And yf þow have power U; And ȝit thou pouer Y. 287 lach-draweres] lechdraweres X. 307 say] D; saide X Y, U, I; P^2 *omits.* 313 Lamasse] I, D; lowe masse X, Y, P^2, U. 315 þi] D, U; my X, Y, P^2, I. 333 fresh] U, D; X, Y, P^2 I *omit.*

8. *Patience* Sole manuscript: British Library MS Cotton Nero A X.

3 aswagen] aswagēd. 35 syn] fyn. 73 stowned] stownod. 84 For] Fof. 94 glowande] g..wande (*letters lost*). 122 ȝe] he. 152 colde] clolde. 166 Neptune] Nepturne. 189 hater] MS *omits.* 194 þe] þe þe. 211 baþes] baþeþes. 240 on] un. 245 to] to to. 294 þre nyȝt] þe nyȝt. 313 sayde] say. 348 non] mon. 411 he] ye. 459 þerunder] þer unde. 512 for] fol. 520 as þou] a þou. 522 malicious] malcio*us.* 523 noȝt] noȝ.

9. *Sir Gawain and the Green Knight* Sole manuscript: British Library MS Cotton Nero A X.

46 glaum ande] glaumande. 58 were] werere. 88 longe lye] lenge lye. 95 Of alderes] Of of alderes. 113 with] wit. 124 sylveren] sylvener. 144 Both] bot. 168 þe proude] pe proude. 182 as] as as. 203 hawbergh] hawbrgh. 210 lenkþe] hede. hede] lenkþe. 236 glowande] lowande. 282 so] fo. 312 gryndellayk] n *lost.* 343 Wawan] Gawan. 384 so] fo. 425 schade] scade. 432 runyschly] ruyschly. 438 he were] ho we.

10. *St Erkenwald* Sole manuscript: British Library MS Harley 2250.

49 The] Thre. 97 mynde] myde. 103 boke] boko. 104 mon] more. 119 naityd] nattyd. 206 is] MS *omits.* 262 no (1)] ne. 286 þe] þi. 292 me] ne. 306 Dymly] Dynly. 321 of his] of *followed by space.*

11. Trevisa, *Dialogue between a Lord and a Clerk* Base manuscript: British Library MS Cotton Tiberius D VII (C). Also cited: British Library MS Harley 1900 (H); British Library MS Stowe 65 (S).

1 *Dominus*] S; C, H *omit.* 23 bookes] S, H; book C. 63 ham] S, H; C *omits.* 76 som (2)] S; C *omits.* 155 on day . . . tyde] H; C *omits.* 178 in joye . . . ende] H; C *omits.*

12. Gower, *Confessio Amantis* Base manuscript: Bodleian Library MS Fairfax 3.

No variants.

13a–13f. Lyrics From Bodleian Library MS Rawlinson D 913.

(13a) 7 every kinne] y *and* k *illegible.*
(13b) 4 þe] ȝe.
(13c) 3, 4 ant a] MS *omits.* 8 was] wat. 15–21 *Expanded from* Welle wat was hire dryng þe chelde water of þe welle spring. 24–8 *Expanded from* þe rede rose ante lilie flour.
(13d) 13 lovet] levet. 16 I ne] in.

13g–13k. Lyrics From British Library MS Harley 2253.

(13g) 30 hendy hap] hend.
(13h) 11 wynne] wynter. 22 doþ] doh.

(13j) 61 þe] MS *omits.* 66 shille] stille.
(13k) 23 mouþ] imou*er*þ.

13l–13r. Lyrics From National Library of Scotland MS Advocates 18.7.21.

(13l) 5 *etc* Lullay lullay] Lullay l. 10 smerte] snerte.
(13p) 19 ȝerte] ȝepte.

14. The York Play Sole manuscript: British Library MS Addit. 35290.

1 1 Soldier] Primus Miles *and so throughout.* 26 wrange] wronge. 69 sare] sore. 81 fyne] feyne. 97 nowe] howe. oght] nowe. 99–100 *marked for* iii Miles. 101 *marked for* ii Miles. 118 snelly] snerly. 122 hende] handis. 154 and] MS *omits.* 155 þei] I. 183 4 Sold.] *marked for* iii Miles. 230 morteyse] moteyse. 278 keste] kaste.

15. Chaucer, *The Parliament of Fowls* Base manuscript: Bodleian Library MS Fairfax 16 (F). Also cited from the same 'b'-group: Bodleian Library MS Bodley 638 (B). Readings from the 'a'-group generally cited from Cambridge University Library MS Gg 4.27 (Gg). Other 'a'-group manuscripts cited: St John's College, Oxford, MS LVII (J), Trinity College, Cambridge, MS R.3.19 (R), Bodleian Library MS Digby 181 (D).

3 dredeful] Gg; slyder F. 5 with his wonderful] Gg; soo with a dredeful F. 31 Scipion] R; the Cipion F. 34 hyt] Gg; F *omits.* 46 other] Gg; or F. 64 syn] Gg; see F. was] Gg; that is F. 71 hym] Gg; he F. to] Gg; F *omits.* 72 that] Gg; F *omits.* 73 immortalle] Gg; mortalle F. 78 to] Gg; for to F. 82 foryeven] Gg; foryeven hem F. 108 made] Gg; F *omits.* 114 firebronde] Gg; firy bronde F. 135 strokes] Gg; stroke F. 140 Th'eschewynge] B; Th'escwynge F. 152 nyste] Gg; I ne wiste F. 156 to] Gg; F *omits.* 169 With] Gg; And with F. 172 eyen] Gg; eyn F. 178 boxtre piper] Gg; box pipe tre F. 194 al] Gg; F *omits.* 197 strynges] Gg; strynge F. 201 be] B, Gg; F *omits.* 209 Than] Gg; No F. 215 hir] Gg; harde F. 216 touched] B, R; couched F, Gg. 221 do by force] R; goo before F. 231 bras] B, Gg; glas F. 232 daunceden] Gg; daunced F. 237 of dowves] Gg; saugh I F. 238 Saugh I sittynge] Gg; of dowves white F. 240 honde] Gg; hande F. 244 ek] Gg; F *omits.* 273 of no] Gg; of F. 278 two] Gg; the F. 284 peynted] B, Gg; peyted F. 311 Of] B, Gg; On F. 313 aire] Gg; see F. 319 grace] B, Gg; gace F. 338 hardy] Gg; F *omits.* 346 eles] Gg; egles F. 358 the cukkow] B, Gg; cukkow F. 359 papenjay] B, Gg; papjay F. 363 raven . . . with] Gg; ravenes and the crowes with her F.

370 Benygnely] Gg; Benyngly F. 375 and the] Gg; and F. 381 Hath] B, Gg; Halfe F. 383 hede] Gg; F *omits*. 386 how] Gg; how that F. 389 Youre] Gg; With youre F. 390 ordenaunce] Gg; governaunce F. 402 lese] B, Gg; lesse F. 420 or] B, Gg; of F. 436 Althogh] B; As thogh F. 467 Nature] Gg; F *omits*. 476 ful] B, Gg; F *omits*. 480 ese] Gg; plese F. 482 hirs] B; hirse F. 498 cokkowe] Gg; duk F. duk] Gg; cokkowe F. 523 to] Gg; for to F. 556 gole] Gg; goler F. 612 of the] Gg; of F. 637 ought] Gg; hyt ought F. 652 Cupide] B, Gg; Cipride F. 665 for] Gg; fro F. *680–4 and 687–9 are copied in a much later hand in* Gg. *Otherwise the roundel is in* D *(680–3, 687–9) and* J *(683–4, 687–9) only. 685–6 and 690–2 are conjectural reconstructions.* 680 thy] D; Gg *omits*. 682 longe] D, J; large Gg. 683 Valentyne] Volantyne Gg. 689 synge] D, J; ben Gg.

16a and 16b. Chaucer, *Canterbury Tales* Base manuscript: National Library of Wales MS Hengwrt 154 (Peniarth 392D) (Hg). Also cited: Huntington Library MS Ellesmere 26 C 9 (El).

16a The Reeve's Tale

13 pley] El; pleye Hg. 24 heed] El; heer Hg. 32 olde lemes] El; lymes Hg. 34 ik] El; I Hg. 90 of] El; a Hg. 117 half] El; hal Hg. 139 the] El; this Hg. 165 hir] El; his Hg. 168 Symond yfayth] El; Symkyn in fayth Hg. 173 boes] El; bihoves Hg. 183 howgates] *other MSS*; how Hg; how that El. 188 howgates] *other MSS*; how Hg. 190 yfaith] El; in faith Hg. 257 stoln] El; stole Hg. 258 Bathe] El; Bothe Hg. 275 taa] El; tak Hg. 276 taa] El; tak Hg. 287 ten] El; but ten Hg. 317 complyng] *other MSS*; couplyng Hg, El (*see footnote*). 336 gif] El; if Hg. 353 tald] El; told Hg. 360 rowtyng] El; routynt Hg. 385 swa] El; so Hg. 394 she] El; he Hg. 423 in] El; on Hg. 434 us] El; me Hg. 464 swich] El; which Hg.

16b The Prioress's Tale

41 myghte] El; Hg *damaged*. wende] El; Hg *damaged*. 42 open at eyther ende] El; Hg *damaged*. 76 to construe] El; Hg *damaged*. 77 Ful often tyme upon hise knowes bare] El; Hg *damaged*. 111 of swich] El; Hg *damaged*. 112 lawes reverence] El; Hg *damaged*. 116 hadde] El; at Hg. 146 laste thus she] El; Hg *damaged*. 147 Among the cursed Jues she hym soghte] El; Hg *damaged*. 181 hors he dide] El; Hg *damaged*. 182 heng hem by the lawe] El; Hg *damaged*. 216 fro thy tonge] El; Hg *damaged*. 217 Be nat agast I wol thee nat forsake] El; Hg *damaged*. 223 plat] El; flat Hg.

Glossary

This glossary aims to include all words that might cause difficulty to the reader, but explanations given in the notes are not repeated here. The following abbreviations are used:

acc.	accusative	neut.	neuter
adj.	adjective	nom.	nominative
adv.	adverb	num.	numeral
art.	article	pa.	past tense
comp.	comparative	pl.	plural
conj.	conjunction	poss.	possessive
dat.	dative	pp.	past participle
def.	definite	ppl. adj.	participial adjective
demons.	demonstrative	pr.	present tense
fem.	feminine	prep.	preposition
fut.	future	pron.	pronoun
gen.	genitive	pr. p.	present participle
imp.	imperative	refl.	reflexive
impers.	impersonal	rel.	relative
indef.	indefinite	sg.	singular
interj.	interjection	subj.	subjunctive
interrog.	interrogative	superl.	superlative
masc.	masculine	v.	verb
n.	noun	vbl. n.	verbal noun

Variation between *ȝ* and *gh*, *þ*, *ð* and *th*, *i* and *y* is not noted, nor are other variant spellings in straightforward cases, e.g. with or without final *-e*, with variation in the inflexion *-es*, *-is*, *-ez*, etc. Regular -(*e*)*s* plurals of nouns are not generally listed, nor are the inflexional cases of nouns and adjectives ending in *-e* generally defined, since the grammatical significance of this ending is often uncertain; see 4.4.1-2 and the individual Headnotes. Inflexional forms are, however, recorded where they might cause difficulty, especially for strong verbs. Verbs are listed under the infinitive form where it occurs, and in the more complex entries the inflexional forms are given first within parentheses, followed by the meanings. A definition is not repeated if it is the same as that of the immediately preceding form of the word.

So that the user is spared a certain amount of hunting around the glossary, different spellings of the same word are sometimes glossed separately.

In the alphabetical arrangement, *ȝ* follows *g*, *æ* is treated as *ae* (so between *ad* and *af*), *þ* and *ð* are treated as *th* (so between *te* and *ti*), *y* as a vowel is treated as *i*, but as a consonant it follows *w*.

Occurrences of words are cited by text number and line: 3/25 refers to text 3 (Laȝamon's *Brut*), line 25, though not all occurrences are cited, and line references are not given for words frequently occurring in common senses.

In the etymologies the following abbreviations are used for languages:

AN	Anglo-Norman	Norw	Norwegian
Dan	Danish	ODan	Old Danish
Du	Dutch	OE	Old English
Icel	Icelandic	OF	Old French
Lat	Latin	OI	Old Icelandic
MDu	Middle Dutch	ON	Old Norse
ME	Middle English	Sw	Swedish
MLG	Middle Low German		

A star indicates a form unrecorded and reconstructed. Note also 'cf.' ('compare'), 'prec.' ('preceding entry'), and 'prob.' ('probably').

a, on(e) *indef. art.* a(n); **on** *masc. nom.* 3/11; **ænne, enne** *acc.* 3/54, 138 [OE *ān*]

a *pron.* he 7b/152 (2), 173, 174 (1), 11/73, 86 [OE *hē*]

a *see* **a(n)**

abatyd *pp.* demolished 10/37 [OF *abatre*]

abbotrice *n.* abbacy 1/56, 64 [OE *abbodrice*]

a-beggeth *prep.* + *vbl. n.* a-begging 7b/138, 246 [OE *on* + ? *bedecian* or OF *begart*]

abide *v.* delay 8/70, stay fixed 14/229; **abideþ** *pr. 3 sg.* tarries 5/348; **abidet** *imp. pl.* stay 13m/2; **abod** *pa. 3 sg.* waited 2/41 [OE *ābīdan*]

abydyng *n.* bearing 8/419 [from prec.]

abygge *see* **abuggen**

abyme *n.* depths, deep sea 8/143, 248, 318, abyss 10/334 [OF *abi(s)me*]

abiten *v.* bite 2/77; **abiteð** *pr. 3 sg.* savages 3/101 [OE *ābītan*]

ablendeð *pr. pl.* blind 4/50 [OE *āblendan*]

abod *see* **abide**

aboght *see* **abuggen**

abolȝen *pp.* enraged 3/61, 76 [ME *abelgen*, OE *ābelgan*]

aboute, abute(n) *adv.* round about 2/16, around 4/33, all round 11/24; **abuton** *prep.* around 1/23 [OE *onbūtan*]

abreiden *v.* awaken 4/41; **abrayde** *pr. 3 sg. subj.* 16a/336 [OE *ābregdan*]

a-bribeth *prep.* + *vbl. n.* cadging 7b/246 [OE *on* + OF *briber*]

abuggen, abygge *v.* compensate for 7b/41, pay for 7b/83; **aboght** *pp.* 12/216 [OE *ābycgan*]

abute(n), abuton *see* **aboute**

ac, ah, oc *conj.* but; and 4/57, furthermore 2/83 [OE *ac*]

acces *n.* attack 8/325 [OF *acces*]

ac(c)ordant *adj.* in ~ *to* in accordance with 12/38, in harmony with 15/203 [OF *accordant*]

ac(c)orde *n.* harmony 15/197, agreement 15/371, 381, 668 [OF *accord*]

acloyeth *pr. 3 sg.* overburdens 15/517 [AN *acloyer*]

acompte *n.* account 6/43, 100, 103; **acountes** *pl.* reckoning 7b/98 [OF *acompte*]

acorden *pr. pl.* agree 12/189 [OF *acorder*]

acountes *see* **acompte**

acounteth *pr. pl.* in ~ *nat of* care nothing for 7b/159 [OF *aconter*]

adai *adv.* in the daytime 2/89, 219, 227 [OE *on* + *dæg*]

adamauntes *n. pl.* magnets 15/148 [OF *adamaunt*]

adel *adj.* addled 2/133 [OE *adela* 'filth']

adiȝte *pr. 1 sg.* order, arrange 2/326 [OE *ādihtan*]

adreynt *pp.* drowned 5/397 [ME *adrenchen*, OE *ādrencan*]

adun, ado(u)n *adv.* below 2/208, down 4/19, 13g/20, downwards 3/154; *broght* ~ defeated 15/537 [OE *of dūne* 'from the hill']

adunest *pr. 2 sg.* assault with din 2/337 [cf. OE *dynian*]

æc *see* **ek(e)**

æfne *see* **efne**

ælc *adj.* every 1/70 [OE *ǣlc*]

ælmes *see* **almesse**

ænne *see* **a** *indef. art.*, **on** *pron.*

ær *adv.* previously 1/72 [OE *ǣr*]

æuwer *see* **ȝe**

æv(e)re *see* **ever**

ævric *see* **everich**

afayte *imp.* train 7b/30 [OF *afaitier*]

afe(e)lde *adv.* in the field 7b/118, 198, 312 [OE *on* + *feld*]

afere *v.* frighten 2/221; **aferd** *pp.* 7b/128 [OE *āfǣran*]

affeccion *n.* emotions 6/25 [OF *affection*]

affyen *pr. pl. refl.* in ~ *hym* trust 8/331 [OF *afier*]

affraye *n.* attack 14/271 [AN *affrai*]

after, aftur *prep.* according to 6/106, 7b/90, 91, along 9/218 [OE *æfter*]

agayn *adv.* in reply 9/386, back 16a/362; *prep.* in return for 16a/332 [OE *ongēan*]

agayns, agænes *prep.* against 1/13, 16b/112 [cf. OE *ongēan*]

ageasten *v.* terrify 4/23; **agast** *ppl. adj.* frightened 16a/413, 16b/217 [cf. OE **gǣstan**]

aghlich *adj.* terrifying 9/136 [ON *agi* + OE *-lic*]

aght *see* **awith**

aghtene *num.* eighteen 10/208 [OE *eahtatēne*]

agon *v.* pass away 2/355; **agoo** *pp.* gone 15/465; **agon** *adv.* ago 15/18 [OE *āgān*]

agon *pa. 3 sg.* began to 3/47, 132, 160 [OE *āginnan*]

agrefe *adv.* amiss 15/543 [OF *a grief*]

agreved *pp.* injured 16a/327 [OF *agrever*]

aȝaf *pa. 3 sg.* uttered 2/139 [OE *āgifan*]

aȝe(i)n *adv.* again 6/140, 142, **ayeine** back 15/100 [OE *ongēan*]

aȝe(i)n, aȝens, aȝe(y)nes *prep.* against; in return for 4/69 (1), in preparation for 12/113, **ayene** facing 15/443 [as prec.]

aȝenswarde *adv.* conversely 6/170 [OE *ongēan* + *-weard*]

aȝt *num.* eight 8/29 [OE *eahta*]

aȝte *adj.* valiant 2/385, 389 [OE *āwiht*, *āht* 'aught']

ah *see* **ac**

ahȝere, ahne *see* **oghne**

ahof *pa. 3 sg.* raised 3/154 [OE *āhebban*]

ahte *n.* possession 4/50 [OE *ǣht*]

ay *adv.* always [ON *ei*]

ay-lastande *pr. p.* everlasting 10/347 [prec. + OE *lǣstan*]

aiþer, aythir *see* **eiþer**

aiware *adv.* everywhere 2/216 [OE *ǣg-hwǣr*]

akende *pa.* gave birth to 3/65 [OE *ācennan*]

al *n.* everything 1/46, 58; ~ *and somme* the whole thing 15/650 [OE *eall*]

al, all *adj.* all; **alre** *gen. pl.* of all 3/33, 72, 95 [OE *eall*]

al, alle *adv.* entirely 1/51, 53, 15/419 [as prec.]

al, all *conj.* although 10/226; ~ *yf* even though 14/248, 279 [OE *eall*]

alang *adv.* along 14/186 [OE *andlang*]

alder *n.* ancestor 10/295; **alderen** *pl.* forefathers 3/32, **alderes** lords 9/95 [OE *ealdor*]

alder-grattyst *superl. adj.* greatest of all 10/5, 337 [OE *ealra* + *grēat* + *-ost*]

alder-next *adv.* closest of all 15/244 [OE *ealra* + *nēhsta*]

algate(s) *adv.* at any rate 5/231, by all means 6/148 [ON *alla götu* + *-s*]

alihte, aliȝt(e) *pa.* dismounted 3/6, 5/377, alighted 11/171 [OE *ālīhtan*]

all *see* **al**

alloued *pp.* commended 7b/250 [OF *alouer*]

almesse, ælmes *n. sg.* alms 7b/133, *on* ~ begging 1/42 [OE *ælmesse*]

alofte *adv.* at the top 9/194, on horseback 9/435, in the air 12/165 [ON *á lopti*]

als(e), also *demons. adv.* too, also 8/40, 9/270, the same 1/66, just as 8/291, accordingly 2/298, just so, likewise 2/129, 237 [OE *ealswā*]

als(e), also, as *rel. adv. & conj.* as 1/2, 20, as if 2/146, 7b/281, 9/244, 10/88, 92[OE *ealswā*]

alswa *rel. adv.* as 3/41, 123 OE [*ealswā*]

alswic *adj.* just such 1/2 [OE *eall* + *swilc*]

alto *adv.* all too 12/17[OE *eall* + *tō*]

alwey *adv.* always [OE *ealne weg*]

amayster *v.* compel 7b/221 [OF *amaistrer*]

amende *v.* recover 12/33 [OF *amender*]

amendement *n.* remedy 5/200, full compensation 16a/331 [OF *amendement*]

amesyng *n.* gentleness 8/400 [OF *amesir*]

amidde *adv.* from amongst them 2/124, in the middle 3/155; *prep.* in the middle of 5/355 [OE *on middan*]

amyddes *adv.* in the middle 15/277; *prep.* from amongst 5/191 [OE *on middan*]

amys *adv.* wrongly, anything wrong 15/446 [? ON *á mis*]

among *adv.* at times 2/6 [OE *on* + *gemang*]

amonges *prep.* among 12/66 [from prec.]

amorwe *adv.* on the next day 5/181, 497 [OE *on* + *morgen*]

amounte *v.* be sufficient 10/284 [OF *amounter*]

an *conj.* and 2/7, 192, 278, 7a/95, 7b/12, 13c/24, 13l/3 [OE *and*]

a(n) *prep.* in 2/54, 134, 323 (1), 3/24, 58, 11/100, 124, 130, into 3/8, on 3/20, 68, at 2/323 (2), 325 [OE *on*]

an *see* **on, one**

anamayld *pp.* enamelled 9/169 [AN *enamailler*]

anan *adv.* then 3/63, **ano(o)n** straight away, immediately 15/100, 120, 16a/406, 16b/178; *ryght* ~ straight away 15/576 [OE *on āne*]

and *conj.* if 6/185 (2), 7b/136, 160, 233 [OE *and*]

ane *see* **one**

angoise, anguych *n.* anguish 4/25, 8/325 [OF *anguisse*]

aniȝt *adv.* in the night-time 2/89, 219, 227 [OE *on niht*]

ankerus *n. pl.* anchorites 7b/146 [OE *ancer*]

anon-ryght *adv.* at once 15/218 [OE *on āne* + *riht*]

anoon *see* **anan**

anouȝ *adv.* very 5/62 [OE *genōg*]

ant *conj.* and [OE *and*]

anter *see* **a(u)nter**

anunder *adv.* underneath 8/139 [OE *on* + *under*]

apayed *pp.* pleased 7b/115 [OF *apayer*]

apayre *v.* punish 7b/167; **apayred** *pp.* ruined 7b/229 [OF *empeirier*]

apert *adv.* for all to see 5/586, 9/154 [OF *apert*]

apposede *pa.* questioned 7a/10 [OF *aposer*]

aray *see* **ar(r)ay**

arayned *pa.* questioned 8/191 [AN *arainer*]

ar(e) *see* **er(e)**

are(n), arn *see* **be(n)**

ar(e)nde *n.* message 8/72, business 8/202 [OE *ǣrende*]

arest *v.* lie still 8/144 [OF *arester*]

arȝe *adj.* afraid 9/241 [OE *earh*]

armes *n. pl.* deeds of arms [OF *armes*]

armonye *n.* harmony 15/63, 191 [OF *harmonie*]

arnde *see* **ar(e)nde, irnen**

ar(r)ay *n.* fashion 14/216, adornment 15/219, dress 15/96, 317 [AN *arai*]

arrayed *pp.* prepared 12/109, organized 14/37, 94, provided 14/237 [AN *araier*]

art *n.* learning 16a/202, 243 [OF *art*]

arte, artow *see* **be(n)**
as *see* **als(e)**
asay *see* **assaie**
ascaped *pa.* escaped 8/110 [AN *ascaper*]
ascryed *pa.* shouted at 8/195 [AN **ascrier*]
askeþ *see* **axe**
askez *n. pl.* ashes 9/2 [ON *aska*]
askyng *n.* request 9/323, 349 [OE *acsung*]
asneasen *v.* pierce 4/34 [OE *āsnǣsan*]
asperly *adv.* sharply 8/373 [from OF *aspre*]
aspille *v.* spoil 2/348 [OE *āspillan*]
assay *n.* attempt 15/2 [OF *assai*]
assaie, asay *v.* try, test; **assaied** *pp.* tried out 12/110 [OF *assaier*]
assaut *n.* assault 9/1 [OF *assaut*]
asshen *n. pl.* ashes 16a/28 [OE *æsce*]
assoyle *v.* resolve 11/40 [OF *assoiler*]
assote *v.* dote 12/198 [OF *assoter*]
aswagen *v.* comfort 8/3 [OF *assuager*]
aswon *adj.* swooning 5/549 [cf. OE pp. *ge-swōgen*]
at *prep.* of, from 5/179; **at(t)e** *prep.* + *def. art.* at the [OE *æt*]
atfliþ *pr. 3 sg.* fails 2/37 [OE *ætflēon*]
athel *adj.* noble [OE *æþele*]
athes *n. pl.* oaths of allegiance 1/11 [OE *āþ*]
at-hold *v.* restrain 5/88 [OE *æthēaldan*]
atird *pp.* equipped 5/158 [OF *atirer*]
atywede *pa.* showed 1/79 [OE *ātēowian*]
ato, atwa *adv.* in two 3/140, 7b/64, 13p/4 [OE *on twā*]
atourned *pp.* equipped 5/291 [OF *atourner*]
atprenche *v.* get the better of 2/248 [cf. ME *atwrenchen?*]
atschet *pa. 3 sg.* failed 2/44 [cf. ME *sheten*]
atstonden *v.* make a stand 3/89; **atstod** *pa. 3 sg.* stopped 3/137, 156 [OE *ætstondan*]
at(t)e *see* **at**
atteigne *v.* attain 12/261 [OF *ateigner*]
attempre *adj.* temperate 15/204 [OF *atem-pré*]
attle *pr. 1 sg.* intend 9/27 [ON *ætla*]
atwa *see* **ato**
auctorité *n.* authority 15/506 [OF *autorité*]
audience *n.* a hearing 15/308 [OF *audience*]
auen *see* **oghne**
auȝt *see* **awith**
auht *see* **o(u)ȝt**
aumayl *n.* enamel 9/236 [AN **aumail*]
auncetrye *n.* ancestry, lineage 16a/128 [cf. OF *ancesserie*]
aune *see* **oghne**
a(u)nter, auntur, awenture, aventure *n.* adventure 9/27, 29, fortune 15/131; **aven-turus** *pl.* 9/95; *an* ~ for fear that 7b/40, *on* ~ in the balance 8/242, *good* ~ by good luck 7b/79 [OF *aventure*]
auntre *v.* risk 16a/355 [OF *aventurer*]
auter *n.* altar 15/249, 16b/184 [OE *alter*, OF *auter*]
auþer *see* **other**
avay *v.* inform 10/174 [OF *aveier*]
avance *v.* advance 12/254 [OF *avancer*]
avant *n.* boast 12/29, 37, 162 [cf. OF *avanter*]
avantance *n.* boasting 12/1, 47, 253 [from prec.]
avantarie *n.* boasting 12/9, 58; **avanterie** 12/40 [as prec.]
avaunte *v. refl.* in ~ *him* boast 12/257; **avanteþ** *pr. 3 sg.* 12/169 [OF *avanter*, *avaunter*]
avauntyng *n.* boasting 16a/30 [as prec.]
avauntour *n.* boaster 15/430 [as prec.]
aventure, aventurus *see* **a(u)nter**
Averil *n.* April 13g/1, 13k/4 [OF *avril*]
avyse *v.* devise 9/45; ~ *me* consider 15/648 [OF *aviser*]
avysement *n.* consultation 11/49 [OF *avise-ment*]
avowtrie *n.* adultery 15/361 [OF *avoutrie*]
awæmmen *v.* destroy 3/90 [cf. OE *gewem-man*]
awede *v.* go mad 5/87 [OE *āwēdan*]
awenture *see* **a(u)nter**
a-werke *prep.* + *n.* to work 7b/197 [OE *on* + OE *weorc*]
awith *pr. 3 sg.* ought 14/40; **awe** *pr. impers. subj.* in *him* ~ he ought 14/8; **auȝt, ouhte, aght** *pa.* was bound 5/555, ought 7a/69, possessed 10/27 [OE *āgan*]
awowe *pr. 1 sg.* swear 8/333 [OF *avouer*]
awreke *imp.* avenge 7b/158, 170; **awreke, awroke** *pp.* 2/262, 7b/208, 300, 13d/9 [OE *āwrecan*]
axe *v.* ask; **askeþ** *pr. 3 sg.* demands 6/35, requires 7a/67 [OE *ācsian*, *āscian*]
aye(i)ne *see* **aȝe(i)n**

baar *see* **bere** *v.*
bacheleres *n. pl.* young men 8/366 [OF *bacheler*]
bad(de) *see* **bid(e)**
baft *adv.* from the stern 8/148 [OE *be-æftan*]
baile *n.* custody 14/95 [OF *bail*]
bayn *adj.* willing 8/136 [ON *beinn* 'direct']
bayþen *v.* grant 9/327; **baythes** *pr. 3 sg.* asks 10/257 [ON *beiða*]
balde *adj.* bold 3/94, 118, 133; **baldest** *superl.* 3/105 [OE *bald*]
baldly *adv.* boldly 9/376 [OE *baldlīce*]
bale *n.*[1] harm 8/276, evil 13n/6, anguish 10/257, torment 14/110; *pl.* sorrows 14/259 [OE *balu*]
bale *n.*[2] packages 8/157 [? OF *bale*]
balefully *adv.* in distress 10/311 [OE *balu* + *full* + *-līce*]

balke *n.* beam 16a/66; **balkes** *n. pl.* unploughed places 7b/114 [OE *balca*]
balteres *pr. 3 sg.* rolls about 8/459 [ON, cf. Dan *baltre*]
ban *n. pl.* bones 3/173 [OE *bān*]
bande *n.* rope 14/100 [ON *band*]
bane *n.* slaughter 7b/351 [OE *bana* 'killer']
banne *n.* troop 2/390 [OE *gebann*, OF *ban*]
bar *n.* boar 3/76 [OE *bār*]
bar *see* **bere**
bare *adj.* without armour 9/290; *as n.* open 2/56, 150 [OE *bær*]
baret *n.* fighting 9/21, 353 [OF *barat*]
bargayne *n.* business, job 14/106, 203 [OF *bargaine*]
barnes *see* **bearnes**
barred *pp.* striped 9/159 [cf. OF *barre*]
barste *see* **bersteð**
bashis *pr. 3 sg.* surprises 10/261 [OF *baissier*]
baþes *imp. pl.* plunge 8/211 [OE *baþian*]
baude *n.* procuress 7b/72 [? cf. OF *baudetrot*]
be *prep.* by 1/17, 7b/1, 302, 12/35 [OE *be*]
be *see* **be(n)**
bearm *n.* bosom 4/36 [OE *bearm*]
bearnes *n. gen.* child's 4/40; **barnes** *pl.* children 7a/70, 7b/306; *gen.* 7a/71 [OE *bearn*]
bebyried *see* **biburien**
becom *see* **bicometh**
bede *pr. 1 sg.* offer 9/382; **bede** *pa.* ordered 8/187, 340, 10/67; **boden** *pp.* asked 9/327, exchanged 10/214 [OE *bēodan*, cf. OE *biddan*]
bedels *n. pl.* town officials 10/59, 111 [OF *bedel*]
beden *see* **bid(e)**
beere *see* **bere** *n.*[1]
beet *see* **be(n)**
beete *see* **bete(n)**
before *adv.* in front 9/422 [OE *beforan*]
beforen *prep.* before 1/76 [as prec.]
begæt *pa.* obtained 1/64; ~ *in* recovered 1/66 [ME *bigeten*, OE *begetan*]
begrave *see* **bigraven**
beh *see* **buȝen**
behalve *n.* in *in his* ~ in his name 10/181 [OE *bī* + *half*]
behote, bihote *pr. 1 sg.* promise 7b/238, 301; **behette** *pa.* 15/436; **behote** *pp.* 12/178, **bihyȝt** promised to 8/29 [OE *behātan*]
behoveþ, -es *pr. 3 sg.* is necessary, must 6/28, 148; *impers.* it is necessary for 9/456; **behoved, bihoved** *pa.* 1/58, 8/465 [OE *behōfian*]
beknowe *pr. 1 sg.* acknowledge 7a/92; **biknowe** *imp.* explain 10/221 [OE *becnāwan*]
belamp *pa.* happened 1/74 [OE *belimpan*]
beleve *n.* belief, faith 6/119, 7b/97 [cf. OE *gelēafa*]
belyve *adv.* quickly [OE *bī* + *līf*]
beme *n.* tree 10/182 [OE *bēam*]
bemen *n. pl.* trumpets 4/4 [OE *bēme*]
bemere *n.* trumpeter 4/7; *pl.* 4/1 [from prec.]
bemin *v.* trumpet 4/8 [as prec.]
be(n) *v.* be; illustration of forms: **ben** *infinitive* 1/2, **beon** 4/6, **bon** 2/262, **by** 8/117, **boe** 13d/9, **buen** 13g/18; **icham** *pr. 1 sg.* + *pron.* I am 13g/8, 31; **arte** *2 sg.* 6/15, **ert** 15/683, **artow** *2 sg.* + *pron.* are you 5/421; **beoð** *3 sg.* 3/111, **betz** will be 8/333; **beet** 13p/18; **boþ** *pl.* 2/75, 178, **beoð** 3/33, will be 3/39, **buþ** 11/2, **ben** 5/4, 6/13, 8/2, **beþe** 5/5, **be** 12/115, **aren** 6/47, **arn** 9/280, **is** 7b/87; **bo** *2 sg. subj.* 2/171, 295; **bo** *3 sg. subj.* 2/137, 166, 233, **beo** 4/87, **beon** 3/99; **bo** *pl. subj.* 2/97, 181; **beth** *imp. pl.* 15/660; **wæs** *pa. sg.* 3/76, **watz** 9/1, **wes** 1/3, 13j/52; **wæron** *pa. pl.* 1/12, **waren** 1/15, **wern** 8/268, 344, **wore** 14/157, 205, **weoren** 3/72; **weoren** *pa. sg. subj.* 3/80; **be** *pp.* 7a/70, **bene** 10/7 [OE *bēon*]
bende *pa.* bent 9/305; *pp.* stretched 10/182 [OE *bendan*]
bene *adj.* lovely 8/418 [? OF *bien*]
benigne *adj.* gracious 15/375; **benygnely** *adv.* with good will 15/370 [OF *benigne*]
bent *n.* field 8/392, battlefield 9/353 [OE *beonet*]
beom *n.* beam 1/30 [OE *bēam*]
beo(n), beoð *see* **be(n)**
beorkeð *pr. pl.* bark 3/115 [OE *beorcan*]
beornes *n. pl.* men 3/133 [OE *beorn*]
berdlez *adj.* without beards 9/280 [OE *beardleas*]
bere *n.*[1] bier 13q/9, **beere** 16b/173, 175, 228 [OE *bēr*]
bere *n.*[2] noise 5/78 [OE *gebēru*]
bere *v.* (**bar, baar** *pa.*, **ber(e)** 8/148, 10/326; **bore, ybore, born** *pp.*) bear, carry; take 7b/288, push 6/148; ~ *doun* lower 10/311, ~ *to* hit 8/148, *the/me* ~ conduct yourself/myself, behave 15/109, 459 [OE *beran*]
berefte *pa.* deprived (of) 15/87 [OE *berēafian*]
beryd *pa.* rang out 10/352 [OE *gebǣran* 'behave']
bernes *n. pl.* barns 7b/179 [OE *bern*]
bersteð *pr. 3 sg.* bursts 4/48; **barste, braste** *pa. sg.* 7b/175, smashed 8/148; **bursten** *pl.* shattered 8/221 [OE *berstan*]
beset *pp.* set 12/140; *wel* ~ proper 15/598 [OE *besettan*]
besy, bisy *adj.* anxious 15/89, 16b/137 [OE *bisig*]
besyed *see* **bisied**

besily *adv.* energetically 6/29, **besely** diligently 15/74, eagerly 15/257 [OE *bisig* + *-līce*]
besynesse *n.* activity 15/86 [from OE *bisig*]
best *n.* beast [OF *beste*]
bestad *pp.* in *so* ~ in such circumstances 12/186 [ME *be-* + ON *staddr*]
beswunke *see* **byswynke**
bet *comp. adj.* in *þe* ~ the better off 7a/96; **bet(te)** *comp. adv.* rather 2/21, 23, better 2/172, 182, 12/116; *the* ~ the better 7b/42 [OE *bet*]
bete *v.* beat; **bette** *pa.* 16a/454, 462; **ybete, beten** *pp.* set 9/78, beaten 16a/459 [OE *bēatan*]
bete(n) *v.* relieve 7b/246, cure 14/259, **beete** repair 16a/73 [OE *bētan*]
beth *see* **be(n)**
bethynke *v.* think of 15/483 [OE *beþencan*]
beweved *pp.* covered 13r/5 [OE *bewǣfan*]
bewrye *v.* betray 15/348 [OE *be-* + *wrēgan*]
by *adv.* to one side 10/72 [OE *bī*]
bi *prep.* concerning 2/46; ~ *þat* by the time that 8/468, when 10/113 [OE *bī*]
by *see* **be(n)**
bibbed *pp.* drunk 16a/308 [? Lat *bibere*]
biburien *v.* bury 4/80; **bebyried** *pa.* 1/80 [OE *bebyrgan*]
bichermet *pr. pl.* scream at 2/279 [OE *be-* + *cierman*]
bicometh, bicumeþ, bycommes *pr. 3 sg.* is fitting 7a/61, 9/471; ~ *to* is fitting for 2/271, 7b/47; **bicome, becom** *pa.* became 9/6, went 9/460; **bicome** *pl.* went to 5/288; **bicume, bicome** *pp.* gone away, separated 2/137, *was* ~ had got to 5/194 [OE *becuman*]
biddares *n. pl.* beggars 7b/210 [OE *biddere*]
bid(e) *v.* (**bad(de)** *pa.*; **beden** *pp.*) bid, command 3/170, 5/88, 7b/76, 227, invite 12/122 [OE *biddan*]
bide *v.* await 9/290, wait for 9/376, dwell 8/318, remain 8/293, 16a/383, endure 14/96, get 13j/20; ~ *in* endure 14/110 [OE *bīdan*]
bidon *v.* befoul 4/81; **bidoð** *pr. pl.* 4/81 [OE *be-* + *dōn*]
bifore *prep.* in preference to 6/2 [OE *beforan*]
bifuleð *pr. 3 sg.* befouls 4/74 [OE *befȳlan*]
bigeorede *pp. pl.* equipped 3/108 [OE *be-* + *gerwan*]
biges *pr. 3 sg.* builds 9/9; **buggyd, bigged** *pp.* 10/37, 207, established 9/20 [ON *byggva*]
bygge *adj.* strong 7b/224 [unknown]
bygge *v.* beg 7a/90 [OE *bedecian* or OF *begart*]
bigly *adv.* strongly 8/321 [unknown]
bigog *interj.* by God 9/390 [OE *bī* + *gog* for *God*]
bigraven, begrave *pp.* engraved 9/216, 12/143 [OE *begrafan*]
bigredet *pr. pl.* cry out at 2/67, **bigredeþ** 2/279; **bigrede** *subj. pl.* 2/304 [OE *be-* + *grǣdan*]
bigripid *pa.* enclosed tightly 10/80 [OE *begrīpan*]
bigrowe *pp.* overgrown 2/27 [OE *be-* + *grōwan*]
biȝæten *pp. as n.* possessions 3/119 [cf. OE v. *begitan*]
byȝen, bugge *v.* purchase 13q/12, ~ *to* buy for 13d/3; **boute** *pa.* bought 7a/96; **bohton** *pa. pl.* 1/75 [OE *bycgan*]
bihalt, bihaldeð *see* **biholde**
bihalves *prep.* near 3/5, 116; *adv.* nearby 3/26 [OE *bī* + *half*]
bihedde *pa. 3 sg.* guarded 2/102 [OE *behēdan*]
biheste *n.* promise 13j/47 [OE *behǣs*]
bihyȝt *see* **behote**
biholde *v.* in ~ *on* look at 5/367; **bihalt** *pr. 3 sg.* looks at 4/48; **bihaldeð** *pl.* look 4/17; **bihold** *pa. sg.* gazed at 2/30, 108; **bihold(en)** *pp.* beheld 5/409, 417 [OE *behaldan*]
bihote *see* **behote**
bihoved *see* **behoveþ**
biis *n.* fine cloth 5/242 [OF *bysse*]
biknowe *see* **beknowe**
bylded *pp.* built 8/276, **ybuld** 11/1 [OE **byldan*]
bylder *n. as adj.* used for building 15/176 [from prec.]
bile *n.* bill 2/79, 269 [OE *bile*]
biledet *pr. pl.* in *narewe* ~ pursue closely 2/68 [OE *belǣdan*]
bileve *v.* keep silent 2/42, desist 7b/176; **bilæfde** *pa.* left 3/3; **bilæfved** *pp.* abandoned 3/116 [OE *belǣfan*]
byleve, bylyve *n.* livelihood 7a/21, 29, 7b/260 [OE *bilēofa*]
b(i)lyve *adv.* quickly, at once; *als, also* ~ at once, quickly [OE *bī* + *līf*]
bynde *n.* clinging plant 8/444 [OE *binde*]
bineþ *prep.* beneath 6/183 [OE *beneoþan*]
bynom *pa.* deprived of 7b/254 [OE *beniman*]
biqueste *n.* will 7b/94 [cf. OE *-cwiss*]
bireved *pp.* deprived 2/120 [OE *berēafian*]
byrieden *pa. pl.* buried 1/78 [OE *byrgan*]
bischricheþ *pr. pl.* screech at 2/67 [imitative]
bisy *see* **besy**
byside *adv.* aside 10/67, nearby 16b/154 [OE *be sīdan*]
bisied *pa.* stirred 9/89; **besyed** *pa. refl.* in ~ *hem* busied themselves 15/192 [OE *bysigian*]

bisiliche *adv.* busily 4/44 [OE *bisig* + *-līce*]
bismare *n.* superciliousness 16a/111 [OE *bismer*]
bismuddet *pp.* beslobbered 4/60 [? imitative]
bismulret *pp.* besmeared 4/60 [? imitative]
bisne *adj.* poor-sighted 2/97, 243 [OE *bīsene*]
biso3ten *pa.* implored 8/375 [OE *be-* + *sēcan*]
bispeke *pa.* spoke 8/169 [OE *besprecan*]
bispel *n.* parable 2/127 [OE *bīspell*]
biswike *v.* deceive 2/158 [OE *beswīcan*]
byswynke *v.* work for, deserve 7b/224; **byswynken** *pr. pl.* 7b/140, **biswynketh** 7b/260; **beswunke** *pp.* 12/248 [OE *beswincan*]
bit *n.* sharp edge 9/212, 426; **biten** *pl.* blows 3/127 [ON *bit*]
bitan *pp.* assigned to 10/28 [OE *be-* + ON *taka*]
biteche *pr. 1 sg.* commit (to) 13d/17 [OE *betǣcan*]
bitelle *v.* in *me* ~ justify myself 2/263 [OE *betellan*]
bityde *v.* happen 8/220, come to 13j/22; *pr. 3 sg. subj.* in *so hit* ~ may it so happen 2/52; **bitydde** *pa.* 8/61 [OE *be-* + *tīdan*]
bytyme *adv.* in good time 10/112 [OE *bī* + *tīma*]
bivore(n) *prep.* at the head of 3/57, before 3/134, 4/5, in the presence of 4/28, 59 [OE *beforan*]
bivoren *adv.* in advance 4/22; **bivorenhond** 4/26 [OE *beforan*]
blac *adj.* dirty 5/265, 459 [OE *blæc*]
blaunner *n.* ermine 9/155 [AN **blaunc-ner*]
blawen *v.* blow 4/5 [OE *blāwan*]
ble(e), bl(e)o *n.* colour 10/87, 343, bright colour 13h/16, appearance 2/152, complexion 5/455 [OE *blēo*]
blenche *v.* dodge, escape 2/170 [OE *blencan*]
blent *pr. 3 sg.* blinds 4/46, 15/600 [OE *blendan*]
blessyd *pp.* ordained 10/3 [OE *blētsian*]
blete *n.* (the) open 2/57 [OE *blēat*]
blycande *pr. p.* shining 9/305; **blykked** *pa.* shone 9/429 [OE *blīcan*]
blynne *v.* stop 10/111, 13j/34, be delayed 14/106 [OE *blinnan*]
blysnande *pr. p.* shining 10/87 [? OE *blysian*]
blisse *n.* joy 4/48 [OE *bliss*]
blis(se)ful, blysfol *adj.* beautiful 5/412, 438, 10/76, blessed 11/172, 173 [from prec.]
blyþe *adj.* happy, lovely [OE *blīþe*]
blive *see* **b(i)lyve**
blo *adj.* dark [ON *blár*]
blo *see* **ble(e)**
blok, bluk *n.* torso 9/440, compartment of the body 8/272 [? OF *bloc*]
blonke *n.* horse 9/434, 10/112 [OE *blanca*]
blosme *n.* blossom 5/61, 13k/3; **blosme(n)** *pl.* 2/16, 13h/2 [OE *blosma*]
blossomed *pp.* covered with blossom 15/183 [from prec.]
bluber *n.* seething 8/221 [? imitative]
bluk *see* **blok**
blunder *n.* trouble 9/18 [? ON *blunda* 'doze']
blunt *pa.* stopped 8/272 [uncertain]
blusched *pa.* in ~ *to* looked at 8/474 [OE *blyscan*]
bo *adv.* as well 5/41 [OE *bā*]
bobbaunce *n.* display 9/9 [OF *bobaunce*]
bobbe *n.* branch 9/206 [unknown]
bode, boode *n.* bidding, command, message [OE *bod*]
boden *see* **bede**
bodeð *pr. 3 sg.* portends 4/32; **bodieð** *pr. pl.* 4/22 [OE *bodian*]
bodeword *n.* message 10/105 [OE *bod* + *word*]
boe *see* **be(n)**
boek *n.* book, Bible 7a/38 [OE *bōc*]
boghit, bo3e *see* **bu3en**
bo3e, bowe *n.* bough 2/15, 125 [OE *bōg*]
bo3ted *pp.* vaulted 8/449 [cf. OE *byht*]
bohton *see* **by3en**
boy *n.* wretch 14/73, 95 [cf. AN **abuié*]
boydekyn *n.* dagger 16a/106 [? Celtic]
bokeler *n.* buckler, small shield 16a/165 [OF *boucler*]
bokkes *n. pl.* bucks, male deer 7b/29 [OE *buc*]
bolde *adj.* great 10/106 [OE *bald*]
bolde *v.* become bold 15/144 [OE **baldian*]
bon *see* **be(n)**
bond *n.* binding 7a/14 [ON *band*]
bondeman *n.* villein 7b/42; **bondemen** *gen. pl.* 7a/70 [ON *bóndi* + OE *man*]
bone *n.* request 9/327, **boone** 15/643 [ON *bón*]
bone *adj.* obedient 10/181 [ON *búinn*]
bonk *n.* shore 8/236; *pl.* hills 9/14 [ON **banki*]
boode *see* **bode**
boond *pa.* tied 16a/228, 284 [OE *bindan*]
bo(o)re *n.* nail-hole 14/86, 99 [cf. OE *borian*]
booryngis *n. pl.* nail-holes 14/146 [from OE *borian*]
boote *see* **bote**
borde *n.* table 5/578, 9/481, ship's side 8/211; *upon* ~ on deck 8/190; *pl.* tables 12/131 [OE *bord*]
bordes *n. pl.* bands 9/159 [OE *borda*]
bore *see* **bere**
bores *n. pl.* boars 7b/29 [OE *bār*]
borges *n. pl.* citizens 8/366 [OF *burgeis*]
bor3 *n.* town, city [OE *burg*]

born *see* **bere**
borwe *v.* redeem 13p/9; **borwed** *pa.* borrowed 5/499 [OE *borgian*]
bostede *pa.* threatened 7b/152 [? AN **boster*]
bot *pa.* in ~ *on* cut into 9/426 [ME *biten*, OE *bītan*]
bot, but(e) *conj.* but; but that 8/176, nothing but 4/52, except 4/12, 7a/41, 8/521, unless 7a/91, 7b/15, 49, 12/39, 13j/54; ~ *ȝif* unless; *adv.* only 6/20, 101, 7b/146 [OE *būte*]
bote, boote *n.* help, use 10/170, 13j/56, remedy 10/327, 13n/6, cure, salvation 7b/178, 192 [OE *bōt*]
botened *pa.* cured 7b/188 [OE *bōtian*]
boþ *see* **be(n)**
boþe *n.* booth, shelter 8/441 [ODan **bóð*]
bothe *adv.* too 7b/131, 9/268, 484 [ON *báðir*]
bothem, bothum *n.* bottom [OE *botm*]
botounz *n. pl.* buttons 9/220 [OF *botoun*]
bouel *n.* bowel 8/293 [OF *bouel*]
bounde, bunden *pp.* plated 12/140, bound 13l/21, 24 [OE *bindan*]
boune *adj.* ready [ON *búinn*]
bounté, bountee *n.* moral virtue 7b/49, generosity 8/418, goodness 9/357, excellence 13g/27 [OF *bounté*]
bour *n.* bower 8/276, 437, chamber, shelter y13c/22, 23, 26, bedroom 13j/21, 37 [OE *būr*]
bourde *n.* entertainment 5/445; *pl.* frivolity 5/9 [OF *bourde*]
bourded *pp.* joked 15/589 [OF *bourder*]
bourne *n.* stream 10/330 [OE *burna*]
boustous *adj.* massive 14/218 [uncertain]
bout *prep.* without 9/361 [OE *būtan*]
boute *see* **byȝen**
bowe *see* **boȝe**
bowe(d) *see* **buȝen**
boxumly *adv.* without resistance 14/100 [from OE **būhsum*]
bradne *see* **brod(e)** *adj.*
brayd, brayed, bræid *pa.* lifted 3/61, 121, spurted 9/429, twisted 9/440, stirred 10/190, started 16a/431; **brawden, brayden, ibroide** *pp.* embroidered 9/177, 220, woven 3/10 [OE *bregdan*]
brayde *n.* affliction 14/96 [cf. OE *brægd*]
brayn *adj.* mad 9/286 [shortening of ME *braynwod*?]
brak *pa. sg.* broke 11/167 [OE *brecan*]
brakez *pr. 3 sg.* vomits 8/340 [? OE **bracian*]
braste *see* **bersteð**
brawden *see* **brayd**
breað *n.* smell 4/76, 88 [OE *brǣþ*]
breche *n.* clearing 2/14 [OE *brǣc*]
bredde(n) *pa.* had offspring 2/101, multiplied 9/21 [OE *brēdan*]
brede *n.* plank 8/184 [OE *bred*]
breed *ppl. adj.* terrified 8/143 [OE *brēgan*]
breedcorn *n.* grain for making bread 7b/61 [OE *brēad* + *corn*]
bre(e)de *n.* breadth 2/174, 11/24, 14/76 [OE *brǣdu*]
breme *adj.* glorious 5/61, wild 2/202, stern 8/430; *adv.* loudly 13h/27 [OE *brēme*]
bren *n.* bran 16a/199 [? OF *bran*]
brenne *v.* burn 8/472; **brenned** *pa.* 8/477; **brendon, brenden** *pa. pl.* 1/38, 46; **brent** *pp.* 9/2; **brende** *ppl. adj.* refined 9/195 [ON *brenna*]
breosten *n. acc. sg.* breast 3/62; *dat.* 3/61 [OE *brēost*]
brere *n.* briar, thorn-branch 5/276 [OE *brǣr*]
bres *n.* brass 4/68 [OE *bræs*]
bresed *adj.* bristling 9/305 [unknown]
breth *n.* wind 8/145; *pl.* 8/138 [OE *brǣþ*]
brevyt *pp.* reported 10/103 [OE *gebrēfan*]
brewestares *n. pl.* female brewers, alewives 7b/329 [OE *brēowan* + *-estre*]
brid *n.* small bird, young bird 2/124; **bridde** *pl.* 2/111, 123, **briddes** 2/107, 11/164; *gen.* of birds 13h/2 [OE *brid*]
bryniges *n. pl.* coats of mail 1/22 [ON *brynja*]
brith *adj.* bright 13j/3 [OE *beorht*]
brittened *pp.* destroyed 9/2 [OE *brytnian*]
brode *n.* brood 2/93, 130 [OE *brōd*]
brod(e) *adj.* large 8/472, **brood** broad 16a/270; **bradne** *masc. acc. sg.* 3/115 [OE *brād*]
brode *adv.* open-eyed 9/446 [OE *brāde*]
broȝez *see* **browe**
brohte, brouthte, broȝt *pa.* brought 1/60, 13q/1, drove 10/9; **broth, ybrouȝt, brouht** *pp.* brought 13n/5, 5/389, put 7b/61 [ME *bringen*, OE *bringan*]
brok(e) *n.* brook 7b/142, sea 8/145 [OE *brōc*]
broke *pp.* injured 7a/33 [OE *brecan*]
brom *n.* broom 8/392 [OE *brōm*]
brondez *n. pl.* bits of charred wood 9/2 [OE *brond*]
brood *see* **brod(e)**
broth *see* **brohte**
broþely *adv.* suddenly 8/474 [ON *bráðliga*]
brouht, brouthte *see* **brohte**
browe *n.* eyebrow 13g/14; **broȝez** *pl.* 9/305 [OE *brū*]
bruxlez *pr. 3 sg.* reproves 8/345 [ON *brigzla*]
buen *see* **be(n)**
bugge *see* **byȝen**
buggyd *see* **biges**
buȝen, boȝe, bowe *v.* go; *pr. 1 sg.* submit 8/75; **buhȝeð** *imp. pl.* advance 3/94; **beh, bowed, boghit** *pa.* came 3/5, went 3/48, 8/441, 10/59; *refl.* ~ *him* made his way 3/79, 88 [OE *būgan*]
bulk *n.* hold 8/292 [ON *búlki*]

bunden *see* **bounde**
bur *n.* blow 9/290, gale 8/148 [ON *byrr*]
burde *pa.* ought to 8/507; *impers.* in *hom* ~ they ought to 10/260 [OE *byrian*]
burdez *n. pl.* women 8/388 [OE **byrde*]
burdon *n.* musical accompaniment 16a/311 [OF *burdon*]
burgeys, burjays *n. pl.* citizens 5/504, 10/59 [OF *burgeis*]
burȝe, burgh *n.* town, city [OE *burg*]
burȝen *v.* save 3/79 [OE *beorgan*]
burynes *n.* burial-place 10/142, 190 [OE *byrignes*]
burne *n.* corselet, coat of mail 3/10, 156; **burnen** *pl.* 3/7 [OE *byrne*]
burn(e) *n.* man, knight; **buyrne** 8/340 [OE *beorn*]
burned *pp.* burnished, polished 12/142 [OF *burnir*]
burnist *pp.* polished 5/368, 9/212 [OF *burnir, burniss-*]
bursten *see* **bersteð**
busch *v.* in ~ *up* rise 8/472; **busched** *pa.* plunged 8/143 [ON *búask*]
busy *adj. as n.* bustle 8/157 [OE *bisig*]
busk *n.* bush 9/182 [ON *buski*]
busked, -yd *pa.* made 8/437, hurried 10/112 [ON *búask*]
busmare *n.* insult 10/214 [OE *bīsmer*]
but(e) *see* **bot**
bute(n) *prep.* without; except 2/357; *world* ~ *ende* eternally 4/65 [OE *būtan*]
buþ *see* **be(n)**
buve *adv.* above 2/208 [OE *bufan*]
buxsome *adj.* obedient 14/51 [OE **būhsum*]

cace *see* **cas**
cach(ch)e, kecchen *v.* obtain 13r/17; **cach(ch)ez** *pr. 3 sg.* takes 9/368, seizes 9/434; **cachen** *pr. pl.* in ~ *up* hoist 8/102; **kaught** *pa.* took 15/170; **kaghten** *pa. pl.* took hold 10/71; **caȝt** *pp.* taken 8/485, received 10/148 [AN *cacher*]
cæse *n.* cheese 1/40 [OE *cēse*]
cayser *n.* emperor 10/199 [Lat *Caesar*, OE *cāsere*]
caytif *n.* wretch 7b/244 [OF *caitif*]
camelyn *n.* fine material 10/82 [AN *camelin*]
camuse *adj.* (of a nose) pug 16a/80, 120 (OF *camus*]
can, con *auxiliary v. forming past tense* did
can *see* **con**
canceler *n.* chancellor 1/8 [AN *canceler*]
canges *n. gen.* fool's 4/47 [? ON]
capil *n.* horse 16a/234, 251 [ON *kapall*]
caraldes *n. pl.* casks 8/159 [ON *kerald*]
care *n.* unhappiness, sorrow [OE *caru*]
careful *adj.* sorrowful 8/314 [OE *carful*]
careyne *see* **caroyne**
caren *v.* grieve 13l/9; *pr. 2 sg. subj.* 13l/17 [OE *carian*]
carf *see* **kerve**
carited *n.* feasting on saints' days 1/58 [AN *caritet*]
carle *n.* fellow 14/206 [ON *karl*]
carlmen *n. pl.* men 1/18 [prec. + OE *man*]
caroyne *n.* body 7b/100, **careyne** 15/177 [AN *caroine*]
carpe *n.* teaching 8/519 [ON *karp*]
carpe *v.* talk, speak, say [ON *karpa*]
cartar *n.* charioteer 15/102 [from next]
cartes *n. pl.* chariots 15/102 [? ON *kartr*]
cas, cace *n.* misfortune, sad event 5/175, 8/265 [OF *cas*]
castel-weorces *n. pl.* building of castles 1/15 [AN *castel* + OE *weorc*]
casten *see* **kest(e)**
catel *n.* property 7b/101, 157, 230 [AN *catel*]
cautellis, kautelles *n. pl.* spells 14/206, 278 [OF *cautele*]
cemmed *pp.* combed 9/188 [OE *cemban*]
ceptre *n.* sceptre 15/256 [OF *ceptre*]
certis, certes *adv.* indeed14/81, 15/424, 16b/87 [OF *certes*]
cessyd *pp.* ended 10/136 [OF *cesser*]
ceste *n.* chest 1/26 [OE *cest*]
chace *v.* drive 16b/114 [OF *chacier*]
chaffare *v.* trade 7b/249; **ychaffared** *pp.* 7a/94 [OE *cēap* 'bargain' + *faru* 'journey']
chalons *n. pl.* blankets 16a/286 [OF *Chalons-(sur-Marne)*]
charge *n.* responsibility 15/507, 545 [OF *charge*]
chargit *pa.* dedicated 10/18 [OF *charger*]
charren *v. refl.* in *him* ~ turn back 3/78 [OE **cearran*]
chaste *v.* punish 7b/345 [OF *chastier*]
chauling *n.* scolding 2/284 [cf. OE *ceafl*]
chaumber *n.* private room 5/584 [OF *chambre*]
chauntré *n.* singing 9/63 [OF *chaunterie*]
chawlez *n. pl.* jaws 8/268 [OE *ceafl*]
chearre *n.* time, occasion 4/90 [OE *cerr*]
chelde *adj.* cold 13c/17, 18, 21 [OE *cēald*]
chele *n.* cold 7b/249 [OE *ciele*]
chepyng *n.* market 7b/322 [OE *cīeping*]
chere, chiere *n.* face, expression, look 4/27, 10/342, 12/25, 13g/15, behaviour 15/414, 488; *pl.* 4/13 [OF *ch(i)ere*]
cherle *n.* wretch, peasant, churl 15/596, 16a/63; *pl.* 7b/45 [OE *ceorl*]
chese *v.* choose 6/221, 15/146, 388; **chesse** *pr. 1 sg.* 15/417; **cheest** *3 sg.* 15/623; **chese** *imp.* 5/217; **ches** *pa.* 13q/11 [OE *cēosan*]
chesibles *n. pl.* chasubles, church vestments 7b/11 [OF *chesible*]

cheste *n.* strife 2/177, 183 [OE *cēast*]
cheve *v.* prosper 7b/249; **cheved** *pp.* come 9/63 [OF *chevir*]
chevely *adv.* promptly 10/18 [from OF *chef*]
chyd(d)e *v.* quarrel 2/287, complain angrily 7b/335, 341; *pa.* 2/112, 16a/145 [OE *cīdan*]
chiere *see* **chere**
chymbe *v.* chime, ring out (like a bell) 16a/42 [? OF *chimbe*]
chirme *n.* clamour 2/305 [OE *cierm*]
cild *n.* child 1/75; **childer** *pl.* children [OE *cild*, pl. *cildru*]
circe *n.* church 1/45, 59 [OE *cirice*]
cyrceiærd *n.* churchyard 1/45 [OE *cirice* + *geard*]
clackes *pr. 2 sg.* make clacking sounds 2/81 [ON *klaka*]
clæf *pa. 3 sg.* cut 3/140; **cloven** *pp.* split 13r/17 [ME *cleven*, OE *clēofan*]
clanly *adv.* entirely 9/393 [OE *clǣnlīce*]
clannesse *n.* purity 8/32 [OE *clǣnnes*]
clanse *v.* clear 7b/65; *pa.* purified 10/16 [OE *clǣnsian*]
cle(e)re *adj.* pure 15/77, bright 16b/229 [OF *cler*]
clene *adj.* elegant [OE *clǣne*]
cleopien, clepe *v.* (**cleopede, clupede, cleped** *pa.*; **clepid, ycleped** *pp.*) call, call out [OE *cleopian*]
clerc, clerke *n.* priest, cleric 7a/54, 10/55, student 16a/164; **cler(e)kes** *pl.* clergymen 1/48, learned men 5/2, chaplains 9/64, scholars 15/333 [late OE *clerc*, OF *clerc*]
clergeon *n.* schoolboy 16b/51 [OF *clerjon*]
clivre *n.* claw 2/78; *pl.* 2/84, 155, 270 [OE *clifer*]
clos *n.* cathedral precinct 10/55 [OF *clos*]
closes *pr. 3 sg.* encloses 9/186 [cf. OF *clos*]
cloude *n.* ground 13h/31 [OE *clūd*]
cl(o)utes *n. pl.* rags 10/259, swaddling clothes 13l/14 [OE *clūt*]
cloven *see* **clæf**
clumbe *pa. 2 sg.* climbed 3/165; **iclumben** *pp.* 3/161, 4/91 [OE *climban*]
clupede *see* **cleopien**
cnawe *v.* recognize 8/519; **knwe** *pa.* knew 9/460; **knawen, knowe** *pp.* acknowledged (to be) 9/348, known 11/144 [OE *cnāwan*]
cnif-warpere *n.* knife-thrower 4/28-9 [OE *cnīf* + *weorpan*]
cnihten *n. gen. pl.* of knights 3/84, 105, 168 [OE *cniht*]
cnokez *pr. 2 sg.* strike 9/414 [OE *cnocian*]
coffes *n. pl.* mittens 7b/59 [unknown]
cofre *n.* coffin 15/177 [OF *coffre*]
cogge *n.* cog-wheel 2/86 [? from ON]
coȝed *pa.* cleared throat 9/307 [OE *cohhetan*]
coyfe *n.* lawyer's cap 10/83 [OF *coife*]
cokeres *n. pl.*[1] haymakers 7a/13 [? from ON]
cokeres *n. pl.*[2] leggings 7b/59 [OE *cocer*]
colblake *adj.* coal-black 2/75 [OE *col* + *blæc*]
colde *v.* grow cold 15/145 [OE **caldian*]
colde *adv.* sadly 8/382 [OE *calde*]
cole *adv.* coolly 8/452 [from OE *cōl*]
coltur *n.* coulter, front cutting-blade of plough 7b/65 [OE *culter*]
comen *v.* (**kimeð** *pr. 3 sg.* 4/59; **com, come** *pa.*; **coman, coomen, come** *pa. pl.*; **icume, ycome, cummen, comen, come** *pp.*) come, arrive; ~ *to* achieve 6/31-2, 163 [OE *cuman*]
comenci *pr. 3 sg. subj.* begins 5/247 [OF *comencier*]
comynlych *adv.* in general, usually 11/34, 74, 147 [from OF *comun*]
comlych *adj.* lovely 9/469; **comlokest** *superl.* most handsome 9/53 [OE *cymlic*]
comlyly *adv.* graciously 9/360 [from prec.]
committid *pp.* appointed 10/201 [Lat *committere*]
comseth *pr. 3 sg.* begins 7b/337; **comesed** *pa.* uttered 7b/32 [from OF *comencier*]
comune *n.* community 7a/20, 75, common people 7b/84, allowance of food 7b/292 [OF *comune*]
comunité *n.* common good 6/131; **communnatés** *pl.* communities 10/14 [OF *comunité*]
con, can *v.* (**kan** *pr. 1 sg.* 15/14; **can** *pr. 3 sg.* 2/249; **cunnen** *pl.* 1/55, 4/12, **kun** 6/13, **con** 8/27, **conne** 7b/69, **konne** 15/333, **can** 7b/267, **cunneþ** 11/44, **conneth** 7b/129, **konneþ** 11/76; **cunne** *1 sg. subj.* 2/47; **kunne** *3 sg. subj.* 2/188; **couþe, cowþe, koude** *pa.*) can; know 2/249, 13j/58, know how 7b/129, understand 7b/267, learn 16b/91; ~ *of* know about 2/48 [OE *cunnan*]
con *see* **can** *auxiliary*
conceyte *n.* summary 6/212 [from OF *concevoir*]
conclusyon *n.* decision 15/526, 620 [OF *conclusion*]
conyes *n. pl.* rabbits 15/193 [AN *conil*, pl. *conys*]
conjure *v.* appeal solemnly to 16b/192 [OF *conjurer*]
consayle *imp.* advise 7b/84 [OF *conseiller*]
consayle *see* **counsaile** n.
construen *v.* translate 16b/76; **construe** *imp.* understand 6/126 [Lat *construere*]
coote *n.* coat 14/293 [OF *cote*]
copes *n. pl.* cloaks 7b/185 [OE *cāp*]
corce *n.* corpse 10/177 [OF *cors*]
coryous *adj.* ingenious 6/147 [OF *curios*]
coriousté *n.* ingenious speculation 6/152, 169 [OF *curioseté*]

coron *see* **croun**
coround *see* **crouned**
corsynges *n. pl.* cursings, anathemas 7b/159 [from OE *cursian*]
corteys *adj.* courteous 7b/47 [OF *corteis*]
corven *see* **kerve**
cos *n.* kiss 13k/23 [OE *coss*]
cote *n.* cottage 5/489, 7a/2 [OE *cote*]
councele *imp.* conceal 10/184 [OF *conceler*]
counsaile, counseylle, counsell, consayle *n.* wisdom, skill 10/266, decision 14/6, advice 7b/337, 15/631, plan 15/522, secret 15/348 [OF *counseil*]
countenaunce *n.* custom 9/100 [OF *countenaunce*]
countreplede *imp.* argue against 7b/53, 88 [AN *contrepleder*]
cours *n.* process 6/106, 153 [OF *cours*]
courtepies *n. pl.* short coats 7b/185 [? MDu *korte pîe*]
couþe *see* **con**
couthely *adv.* plainly 10/98 [OE *cūþlīce*]
cove *adv.* swiftly 2/379 [OE *cāfe*]
coveitise *n.* covetousness 16a/30 [OF *coveitise*]
covena(u)nt *n.* agreement 9/393, 12/188; *in ~ þat* on condition that 7b/26 [OF *covenant*]
covent *n.* company of monks 16b/185, 225 [AN *covent*]
covert *pa.* enveloped 10/346 [OF *covrir*]
cowþe *see* **con**
crached *pa.* scratched 5/80 [uncertain]
craft *n.* doings 9/471, skill 15/1, art 15/220, 305 [OE *cræft*]
crafty *adj.* learned 10/44; *~ men* skilled labourers 7b/69 [OE *cræftig*]
craym *n.* cream 7b/305, 321 [OF *craime*]
crakkyng *n.* sounding 9/116 [OE *cracian*]
crave *pr. 1 sg.* request 9/283; *2 sg. subj.* 9/277; **craved** *pa.* demanded as of right 7b/101 OE *crafian*]
create *pp.* created 6/59 [Lat *creatus*]
creep *pa.* crept 16a/372, 406 [OE *crēopan*]
cresped *pp.* curled 9/188 [OE *cirpsian*]
croddes *n. pl.* curds 7b/305, 321 [unknown]
croft *n.* field 7a/17, 7b/31; *pl.* 7b/314 [OE *croft*]
crohhe *n.* jug 4/59 [OE *crōh*]
cronykes *n. pl.* chronicles 11/24, 29, 32 [OF *cronique*]
crossayl *n.* mainsail 8/102 [OE *cros* + *segl*]
crosse *v.* crucify 14/23 [from ON *kross*, OE *cros*]
croumes *n. pl.* crumbs 7b/279, 288 [OE *cruma*]
croun, coron *n.* top of head 9/419, crown 10/83, 12/63; **crownes** *pl.* tonsures 10/55 [OF *coro(u)ne*]
crouned, ycrouned, coround *pp.* tonsured 7a/56, 59, 63, crowned 5/593 [OF *coroner*]
crowes *n. pl.* crowbars 10/71 [OE *crāwe*]
crowke *n.* jug 16a/304 [OE *crūce*]
cuchene *n.* kitchen 4/58 [OE *cycene*]
culle *v.* kill 7b/30; **culde** *pa.* 7b/280 [unknown; cf. OE *cwellan*]
cumly *adj.* lovely 10/82 [cf. OE *cȳmlic*]
cummen *see* **comen**
cunde *n.* nature 2/276 [OE *cynd*]
cun(ne) *n.* family 2/271, race, kin 3/35, 167, 169; **cunnes** *gen.* 3/29 [OE *cynn*]
cunne(n) *see* **con**
cure *n.* in *did hys besy ~* was busily occupied 15/369 [OF *cure*]
curt *n.* court 4/14, 71; **curz** *pl.* 4/72 [AN *curt*]
curtest *superl. adj.* most excellent 10/249 [OF *curteis* + *-est*]
custe *n.* character 2/9 [OE *cyst*]
custe *pa. pl.* in *~ us* kissed one another 13j/46 [OE *cyssan*]
cuþ(est) *see* **kyþe**
cutte *n.* cut stick, lot 14/293, 295 [from ME *cutten*, OE **cyttan*]
cuvertur *n.* bedspread 4/54 [OF *coverture*]

dæ- *see* **de-**
daf *n.* fool 16a/354 [cf. OE *gedæfte*, 'meek']
dayes, dawes *n. pl.* days 10/7; *bi ~* once upon a time 5/15 [OE *dæg*]
dayeseȝes *n. pl.* daisies 13h/4 [OE *dæges ēage*]
dairim *n.* daybreak 2/328 [OE *dæg-rima*]
daisterre *n.* day-star 2/328 [OE *dæg-steorra*]
dale *n.* part 4/83 [OE *dāl*]
dales *n. pl.* valleys 3/164, 13h/4 [OE *dæl*]
dalfe *pa.* dug 10/45; **dolven** *pp.* buried 10/99 [ME *delven*, OE *delfan*]
dalt *see* **delen**
dar *pr. 1 sg.* dare 7b/290; **durst(e)** *pa.* 5/73, 427, 7b/202, **darst** 13e/3, **dorst** 15/541, **dorste** 16a/78, 83 [OE *durran*]
dare *pr. 1 sg.* stay hidden 2/384 [OE *darian*]
dased *pa.* lay distraught 8/383 [ON *dasask*]
daubynge *n.* plastering 7b/198 [from OF *dauber*]
dauntest *pr. 2 sg.* subjugate 15/114 [AN *daunter*]
dawes *pr. 3 sg.* dawns 10/306; **dawe** *pr. 3 sg. subj.* 16a/395; **dawande** *pr. p.* 8/445; **dawid** *pa.* 10/127 [OE *dagian*]
dawes *see* **dayes**
debateþ *pr. 3 sg.* fights 12/55 [OF *debattre*]
debonerté *n.* kindness 8/418 [OF *deboneretė*]
dece, des *n.* dais, high table [OF *deis*]
declare *v.* explain 16b/76 [OF *declarer*]

dede *n.*[1] deed 14/2; *in* ~ from experience 15/8; **dædes** *pl.* 1/53, **dede** 15/82 [OE *dǣd*]
dede *n.*[2] death 14/64, 72 [cf. OE *dēaþ*]
ded(e) *see* **do(n)**
dedifie *v.* dedicate 10/6, 23 [OF *dediier* and *edifiier*]
de(e)d *adj.* dead 15/50, 16a/175, 416; **dede** *as n.* dead body 10/116 [OE *dēad*]
dees-playere *n.* dicer 7b/72 [OF *dé*, pl. *dés* + OE *plegian*]
defaylyng *n.* failing 6/85 [OF *defaillir*]
defaute *n.* damage 10/148, want 7b/145, 213, 245, lack 11/55; *pl.* 11/56 [OF *defaute*]
defens *n.* fortification 5/48 [OF *defens*]
defoule *n.* defilement 8/290 [from ME *defoulen*, OF *defoler*]
degre(e) *n.* status 7a/67, rank 15/394, manner 15/646; *in my/hys* ~ as well as I/he can 15/453, 662 [OF *degré*]
dey(e), deyȝen, diȝe *v.* die 7b/296, 353, 8/488, 13l/16; **deȝe** *pr. 1 sg.* 13j/29; **deyede, deghed** *pa.* 7a/40, 10/246 [prob. ON *deyja*]
deynous *adj.* haughty, 'stuck up' 16a/87 [from OF *desdeignous*]
del *n.* part 11/108, 120, bit 16a/461; **dæle** *pl.* 3/8 [OE *dǣl*]
delen *v.* (**dælde** *pa.*; **dalt** *pp.*) share 7b/106, divide 3/8, deliver 9/397, 452; ~ *ato* part from one another 5/125 [OE *dǣlan*]
delicat *adj.* luxurious 7b/278 [OF *delicat*]
delyvere(n) *v.* release 15/508, 523; *pp.* 15/491 [OF *delivrer*]
delvare *n.* digger 7b/353; *pl.* 7b/114 [from OE *delfan*]
delvynge *n.* digging 7b/198 [as prec.]
demay *imp. refl.* be dismayed 9/470 [OF *demaier*]
deme *v.* judge; **demed** *pa.* spoke 8/119, decreed 14/281; **demed, idemet** *pp.* judged 4/6, decreed 8/432; ~ *of* ordained by 8/386 [OE *dēman*]
denyed *see* **dunede**
dentiesliche *adv.* on dainties 7b/323 [from OF *deintie*]
deor(e) *n.pl.* animals 3/112, 117 [OE *dēor*]
deore *see* **dere** *adj.*
deorling *n.* darling 4/36 [OE *dēorling*]
deovel *n.* devil 4/37; **deofles** *gen.* 4/8; **deovles, deoflen** *pl.* 1/16, 4/23, 32 [OE *dēofol*]
departe *v.* separate 11/163; **departede** *pa.* 11/153, 156 [OF *departir*]
depreced *pa.* subjugated 9/6 [OF *depresser*]
deputate *n.* deputy 10/227 [Lat *deputatus*]
dere *v.* frighten 14/18 [OE *derian*]
dere, deore, dære *adj.* dear, precious, splendid, expensive; **derrest** *superl.* most honoured 10/29 [OE *dēore*]
dere *adv.* at a high price 7b/83, 13q/12 [from prec.]
derf(e) *adj.* mighty 8/166, great 10/99 [ON *djarfr*]
derfly *adv.* boldly 8/110 [from prec.]
derne *n.* hiding place 8/182 [OE *derne*]
derthe *n.* famine 7b/352 [OE *dēore* + *-th*]
derworþly *adv.* honourably 9/114 [OE *dēorwurþlīce*]
des *see* **dece**
deserve(n) *v.* earn 7a/42; *pr. 1 sg.* 7a/45 [OF *deservir*]
desevered *pp.* separated 8/315 [OF *desevrer*]
despende *v.* spend 16a/129; **despene** *imp.* make use of 7b/235 [OF *despendre*]
despit *see* **dispit**
desport *n.* amusement 16a/189 [AN *desport*]
dest, deð *see* **do(n)**
devyne *pr. pl. subj.* speculate 10/169, prophesy 15/182 [OF *deviner*]
devyse *v.* inform 10/225, describe 15/333, 398, specify 16a/29; **devyseth** *pr. 3 sg.* describes 15/317; **deviseþ** *pr. pl.* see 5/312; **devysit** *pa.* described 10/144 [OF *deviser*]
devoydes *pr. 3 sg.* eliminates 10/348; **dewoyde** *imp.* remove 8/284; **devoydit** *pa.* stayed away 10/116 [OF *devoidier*]
devout *adj.* holy 8/166 [OF *devot*]
dewoutly *adv.* devoutly 8/333 [from prec.]
diche *n.* moat 5/361 [OE *dīc*]
dide *see* **do(n)**
diel *n.* in *no* ~ nothing 12/36 [OE *dǣl*]
dyffyne *v.* pronounce 15/529 [OF *definer*]
diffoule *v.* trample down 7b/31 [OF *defoler*]
diȝe *see* **dey(e)**
diȝele *adj.* secluded 2/2 [OE *dīegel*]
dyhte *v.* prepare 7b/315; **dyȝttez** *pr. 2 sg.* appoint 8/488; **dyght, dyȝt** *pa.* 10/23, worked 10/45, prepared 10/294; *pp.* appointed 8/203, set 9/114, arranged 14/281 [OE *dihtan*]
dikares *n.pl.* ditchers 7b/114 [ON *dík* + *-er*]
dim *adj.* gloomy 2/369, faint 5/285 [OE *dim*]
dymly *adv.* abjectly 8/375; **dimluker** *comp.* more quietly 4/8 [from prec.]
dyn *n.* sound 9/47 [OE *dyne*]
dynge *v.* strike 14/17 [? OE **dingan*]
dyngne *adj.* noble 8/119 [OF *digne*]
dynt, dunt *n.* stroke, blow [OE *dynt*]
diol *n.* lamentation 5/198 [OF *diol*]
dipped *pa.* plunged 8/243 [OE *dippan*]
discoverez *pr. 3 sg.* uncovers 9/418 [OF *descovrir*]
discret *adj.* judicious 7a/84 [OF *discret*]
discretly *adv.* modestly 15/241 [from prec.]
discreveþ *pr. pl.* describe 11/24 [OF *descrivre*]

dysobeysaunt *adj.* disobedient 15/429 [OF *desobeissant*]
dysors *n. pl.* minstrels 7b/52 [OF *disor*]
dispendist *pr. 2 sg.* spend 6/90; **dispendid** *pp.* 6/42 [OF *despendre*]
dispit, despit *n.* defiance 7b/184, 15/281; *for ~ of* in contempt of 12/182 [OF *despit*]
dispoyled *pp.* stripped 8/95 [OF *despoiller*]
disshevelé *adj.* with hair loose 15/235 [OF *deschevelé*]
distreyneth *pr. 3 sg.* grasps 15/337 [from OF *destreindre*]
ditte *pa.* shut 10/116 [OE *dyttan*]
dyvers *adj.* various 11/1, 2, 6 [OF *divers*]
doctrine *n.* teachings 16b/47 [OF *doctrine*]
dolven *see* **dalfe**
dom(e), doome *n.* judgement; doom 8/203, Last Judgement 4/5, 6/99 [OE *dōm*]
domesman, -mon *n.* judge 6/118, 10/227 [from prec.]
do(n) *v.* (**dest** *pr. 2 sg.* 2/49, **dostu** *2 sg. + pron.* 2/218; **deð** *3 sg.* 4/15, **dooth** 16b/177; **doð** *pl.* 4/2, **don** 7b/296, **doen** 7b/63, **dois** 14/260; **doþ** *imp. pl.* 5/218; **dide** *pa.* 1/8, **dude** 3/10, **dede** 5/580; **ydo(o)** *pp.* 5/381, 15/542, **ydone** 5/76, **do(o)n** 9/478, 15/70) do; cause 2/49, 13l/20, 14/260, cause to 7b/296, 8/443, 15/458, put 1/8, 18, 22, carry out 1/10, finish 15/542; *~ on* put on 3/10, 5/343, *refl.* in *~ him* go 5/232, 474; *imp. ~ way/wey* enough! 5/226, 13j/17; *pp.* finished 5/76, achieved 11/131, placed 9/478 [OE *dōn*]
donkeþ *pr. pl.* moisten 13h/28 [ON, cf. Icel *dökk* 'pool']
donne *adj.* dun coloured 15/334 [OE *dun*]
doon *see* **do(n)**
doote *n.* fool 14/5 [cf. MDu *doten*]
dorst(e) *see* **dar**
doser *n.* wall-hanging 9/478 [OF *dosser*]
dostu *see* **do(n)**
doted *ppl. adj.* foolish 8/196 [from ME *doten*, ? OE **dotian*]
dotes *pr. 3 sg.* is foolish 8/125 [as prec.]
doulfull *adj.* miserable 14/64 [OF *dol* + *-full*]
dounes *see* **dunes**
doured *pa.* grieved 8/372 [? from OF *dur*]
doute *n.* uncertainty 11/40 [OF *doute*]
douth *n.* company [OE *duguþ*]
dowellez *pr. pl.* dwell 8/69, 422; **duelte** *pa.* 12/90 [OE *dwellan*]
draf-sak *n.* sack of chaff, rubbish-sack 16a/352 [OE **dræf* + *sacc*]
draheð *pr. pl.* draw 4/1; **drogh, droȝ, drou, drowe** *pa.* drew, came 7b/190, 9/335, drew on 13q/8, opened 16a/38; **ydrawe, drawen** *pp.* drawn 5/295, pulled 10/6 [OE *dragan*]
drapen *pa. pl.* killed 1/25, 33 [OE *drepan*]
drede *n.* in *withouten ~* undoubtedly 14/173, 15/52, *out of ~* undoubtedly 15/81 [from next]
drede *imp.* in *~ the/yow not* do not fear 15/157, 448 [OE *ondrǣdan*]
dredfule, dredeful *adj.* terrifying 4/41, full of fear 15/3, timid 15/195, 638 [from prec.]
dreȝed *see* **driȝen**
dreme, dream *n.* sound 2/314, 4/3, voice 10/191 [OE *drēam*]
drery *adj.* sad 10/191, 13j/9 [OE *drēorig*]
dresse *v.* deliver 10/236, get ready 15/88; **dressez** *pr. 3 sg.* turns 9/445; *hym ~* prepares himself 9/417 [OF *drecier*]
drevyne *see* **dryve**
dryȝe *adj.* impassive 9/335 [ON *drjúgr*]
driȝen *v.* suffer 13l/10; **drye** *pr. pl.* 15/251; **dreȝed** *pa.* 8/256 [OE *drēogan*]
dryȝtyn, dryghtyn, drihte(n) *n.* lord, God [OE *dryhten*]
drihtliche *adj.* noble 3/164 [OE *dryhtlic*]
dryng *n.* drink 13c/15, 16, 19 [OE *drinc*]
dryve *v.* strike 9/389; *~ out* issue 8/386; **drivande** *pr. p.* coming 9/222; **dryven, drevyne** *pp.* brought 9/121, driven 15/682 [OE *drīfan*]
droȝ, drogh, drou, drowe *see* **draheð**
drosenes *n. pl.* dregs 7b/193 [from OE *drōs*]
drouthe *n.* drought 7b/312 [OE *drūgað*]
druncwile *n.* the drunkard 4/70 [OE *druncen-wille*]
dubbed *pp.* adorned 9/193 [OF *aduber*]
dude *see* **do(n)**
duelte *see* **dowellez**
dul *n.* grief 10/246 [OF *dul*, *dol*]
dulfully *adv.* miserably 10/302, 309 [from prec.]
dulle *adj.* lacking in feeling 15/162 [MDu *dul*]
dumpe *v.* plunge 8/362 [ON, cf. Dan *dumpe*]
dun *adv.* down 4/37 [from OE *of dūne* 'from the hill']
dunede, denyed *pa.* resounded 3/60, 10/246 [OE *dynian*]
dunes, dounes *n. pl.* uplands 3/164, 13h/28 [OE *dūn*]
dunt *see* **dynt**
dure *pr. 1 sg.* last 8/488 [OF *durer*]
durre *n.* door 10/116 [OE *duru*]
durst *see* **dar**
dusten *v.* fling 4/33 [? OE **dystan*]
dut *pa.* feared 9/222 [OF *duter*]
dwynande *pr. p.* languishing 10/294 [OE *dwīnan*]

eani *adj.* any 4/77 [OE *ǣnig*]
eardingstowe *n.* dwelling-place 2/28 [OE *eardung-stow*]

earen *n. pl.* ears 4/19 [OE *ēar*]
earmite *n.* hermit 4/79; **eremytes** *pl.* 7b/146 [OF *ermite*]
eateliche *adj.* horrible 4/23, 35 [OE *atelic*]
eaver *see* **ever**
eawles *n. pl.* flesh-hooks 4/33 [OE *āwol*]
eawt *n.* anything 4/17 [OE *āwiht*]
eche *v.* increase 13k/22 [OE *ēcan*]
echeliche *adv.* eternally 4/42 [OE *ēcelīce*]
echon *pron.* every one 16b/176 [OE *ǣlc ān*]
edwiten *v.* criticize 4/17 [OE *edwītan*]
eek *see* **ek(e)**
eelde *see* **elde**
eet *see* **eten**
efne *adv.* indeed 2/313 [OE *efne*]
efne *prep.* immediately upon 3/120, **æfne** 3/153 [OE *efne*]
efte *adv.* then 4/2, 8/143, again 5/211, 8/345, 10/37 [OE *eft*]
efter *prep.* to obtain 1/19 [OE *æfter*]
egge *n.* edge 9/212 [OE *ecg*]
eggit *pp.* sharp-edged 10/40 [from prec.]
ehe, e(i)ȝe, iȝe *n.* eye 4/16, 5/327, 6/174, 13g/14; **eȝene, (e)yȝen** *pl.* 2/75, 5/111, 6/169, 9/82, **ehnen** 4/13, **eȝe** 2/144, **yes** 7b/172 [OE *ēage*]
ey *n.* egg 2/104; **eye** *dat.* 2/133 [OE *ǣg*]
ei *adj.* any 4/52; *pron.* anyone 4/15 [OE *ǣnig*]
eyres *n. pl.* heirs 7a/59 [OF *eir*]
eiþer, eyther, aiþer, aythir *adj.* each 14/181, 15/125; *pron.* each one 2/7, 9, 11/17, both 4/18 [OE *ǣgþer*]
ek(e), æc, eek *adv.* also, too [OE *ēac*]
elde *n.* old age 8/125, 11/55, **eelde** 16a/31 [OE *eldo*]
eleccio(u)n *n.* choice 15/409, 621 [AN *eleccioun*]
elles, ellis *adv.* else, otherwise; in another way 10/121 [OE *elles*]
elnȝerde *n.* ell-rod (45 inches) 9/210 [OE *eln* + *gerd*]
em *see* **eom**
emerawde *n.* emerald 15/175 [OF *emeraude*]
emerlyon *n.* merlin 15/611 [OF *esmerillon*]
en *prep.* in 5/493 [OF *en*]
enbawmyd *pp.* embalmed 10/261, 265 [OF *embaumer*]
enbelicit *pp.* decorated 10/51 [OF *embellir*]
enbrawded *pp.* embroidered 9/78 [AN *enbrouder*]
encheson *n.* occasion 12/42 [OF *enchaison*]
enclyne *v.* bow 9/340 [OF *encliner*]
encrees, encressen *v.* increase 6/207, 16b/12; **encressed** *pp.* 14/145 [OF *encreistre*]
encroche *v.* obtain 8/18 [OF *encrocher*]
ende *n.* outskirts 5/481, 564 [OE *ende*]
endyte *v.* relate, compose 15/119, 167 [AN *enditer*]
engendrure *n.* procreation 15/306 [OF *engendreure*]
englene *n. gen. pl.* of angels 4/4, 41 [OE *engel*]
enjoynyd *pp.* appointed 10/216 [OF *enjoindre*]
enker grene *adj.* bright green 9/150 [ON *einkar* + OE *grēne*]
enne *see* **a** *indef. art.*
enpresses, enprecez *pr. 3 sg.* oppresses 8/43, 528 [OF *enpresser*]
enprise *n.* renown 10/253 [OF *enprise*]
entente *n.* opinion 15/580, wish 15/644, mind 16b/98, 123; *wyth glad* ~ gladly 15/532 [OF *entente*]
entremete *v.* in ~ *hym of* involve himself in 15/515 [OF *entremetre*]
entriketh *pr. 3 sg.* ensnares 15/403 [OF *entriquer*]
eom, em *n.* uncle 1/3, 9/356 [OE *ēam*]
eorðlich *adj.* earthly 4/49 [OE *eorþlic*]
eower *see* **ȝe**
erbes *n. pl.* plants, vegetables 7b/321, grasses 8/393, 438 [OF *erbe*]
erchedekenes *n. pl.* archdeacons 7a/71 [OE *ercediacon*, Lat *archidiaconus*]
er(e), ar(e) *conj.* before, previously [OE *ǣr*]
eremytes *see* **earmite**
erye, erien *v.* plough 7b/2, 66, 113; **y-ered** *pp.* 7b/3 [OE *erian*]
ernde *n.* business 8/52, mission 9/257 [OE *ǣrende*]
ert *see* **be(n)**
ese *n.* rest 16a/256 [AN *ese*]
ese *v.* please 15/480 [from prec.]
esement *n.* redress 16a/325, 332 [OF *aisement*]
esy *adj.* pleasant 15/382 [AN *aisé*]
esken *n. pl.* ashes 4/44, 50 [OE *æsce*]
espye *v.* see 15/280 [OF *espier*]
estaate *n.* rank 15/550, 630 [OF *estat*]
este *n.* pleasure 2/353 [OE *ēst*]
Estren *n.* Easter 1/76 [OE *ēastre*]
eten *v.* eat 7b/326; **ete, eet** *pa.* 5/396, 7b/319 [OE *etan*]
ethalt *pr. 3 sg.* retains 4/52 [OE *oþhealdan*]
eþe *pr. 1 sg.* beg 9/379 [OE *ge-ǣþan*]
euch *adj.* each 4/49; *pron.* 4/33 [OE *ǣghwilc*]
even *adv.* exactly; directly 8/65, 352, straight 9/444 [OE *efen*]
evene *adj.* equal 15/149, proportionate 15/381 [OE *efen*]
ever, æv(e)re, eaver *adv.* always; continually 1/51, repeatedly 3/146; ~ *in oon* all the time 16a/26 [OE *ǣfre*]
everemo *adv.* always 16a/107, 384, 16b/102 [OE *ǣfre mā*]
ever-ferne *n.* species of fern 8/438 [OE *eforfearn*]

everich, ævric *adj.* every; ~ *a* every 5/490 [OE *ǣfre ǣlc*]
everichon *pron.* every one 5/189 [prec. + OE *ān*]
everykune *adj.* every kind of 13a/1, 2, 4 [OE *ǣfre ǣlc* + *cynn*]
evesed *pp.* clipped 9/184 [OE *efsian*]
evetyde *n.* evening time 11/155 [OE *efen* + *tīd*]
evidences *n. pl.* authoritative proofs 7b/262 [OF *evidence*]
evill *adv.* terribly 14/145 [OE *yfel*]
excusacion *n.* defence 6/99 [OF *excusation*]

facound *adj.* eloquent 15/521 [OF *facond*]
fader *n. gen.* father's 12/159, 170, 16a/184 [OE *fæder*]
fæht *see* **fith** *v.*
fæie, feye *adj.* doomed to death, dead 3/64, 81, 103, 13g/20 [OE *fǣge*]
fæiescipe *n.* slaughter 3/74 [from prec.]
fæstliche *adv.* resolutely 3/46 [OE *fæstlīce*]
faȝerest *see* **feir**
fay *see* **fey**
fayfulleche *adv.* faithfully 7b/70 [from AN *fei*]
faile *v.* not exist 11/61, 62; **faylid** *pa.* disappeared 10/342 [OF *faillir*]
fayn(e) *adj.* happy 7b/293, 323, eager 10/176; **faynest** *adv. superl.* most gladly 15/480 [OE *fægen*]
fayned *pa.* feigned 7b/128 [OF *feindre*]
fayre *adv.* well 9/367 [OE *fægre*]
fairy, fayryȝe *n.* enchantment 5/10, 9/240 [OF *faierie*]
faith *n.* in *in* ~ truly 14/111 [OF *feid*]
faytour *n.* false beggar 7b/73; *pl.* 7b/128, 179, impostors 14/36 [OF *faitour*]
faytrye *n.* malingering 7b/138 [from prec.]
falewe *pr. 1 sg.* lose colour 13j/5 [OE *fealwian*]
falles *pr. 3 sg.* befalls 8/178, is fitting 9/358, gets 14/292; **vyl, fel(l), fil** *pa. sg.* fell 11/167, 16a/427, (it) befell 12/66, 70; **fel, feollen, vullen** *pa. pl.* fell 3/70, 144, 146, occurred 5/8, 15; **yfalle, fallen** *pp.* 5/21, 9/23 [OE *feallan*]
falt *pr. 3 sg.* folds, grows weak 2/37; **folden** *pp.* plaited 9/189 [OE *faldan*]
famyen *n.* famine 7b/215 [OF *famine*]
fand *see* **fynde**
fange *v.* receive 9/391, take 14/184 [ON *fanga*]
fannand *pr. p.* spreading out (like a fan) 9/181 [from OE *fann*]
fantoum *n.* illusion 9/240 [OF *fantome*]
farand *adj.* splendid 9/101 [ON *farandi*]
farandely *adv.* pleasantly 8/435 [from prec.]
fare *n.* journey 1/39, 8/98; *made* ~ made a fuss 16a/145 [OE *faru*]
fare(n) *v.* (**farþ** *pr. 3 sg.*; **fareþ** *pl.*; **faren** *subj. pl.* 3/46; **ferde** *pa.*, **for** 1/63; **faren** *pp.*) travel 1/39, 2/386, go 1/63, 3/56, 7b/112, come 8/359; *wele* ~ prosper 5/604, 7a/8, ~ *bi* be in the case of 2/245 [OE *faran*]
faste *adv.* firmly 13j/10, 14/210, vigorously 7b/214, immediately 6/139, much, copiously 5/118, soundly 15/94 [OE *fæste*]
fastynge *n.* confirmation 10/173 [from OE *fæstan*]
fastrede *adj.* secure in judgement 2/211 [OE *fæst-rǣd*]
fathmez *pr. 3 sg.* gropes 8/273 [OE *fæþmian*]
faucond *n.* eloquence 15/558 [OF *faconde*]
faukun, faucun, faucoune *n.* falcon 2/101, 111, 123, 15/337 [OF *faucon*]
faumewarde *n.* vanguard 7a/58 [from OF *avangarde*]
faute *n.* fault 14/142 [OF *faute*]
fax *n.* hair 9/181 [OE *feax*]
feareð *pr. 3 sg.* in ~ *abuten* busies himself with 4/44 [OE *faran*]
feche *v.* take 7b/154 [OE *feccean*]
feere *n.* in *in* ~ together 14/33, 162 [OE *gefēre*]
feersly *see* **ferslych**
feerþe *adj.* fourth 6/31 [OE *fēorþa*]
fees *n. pl.* in *knyhtes* ~ landed estates held by a knight 7a/77 [AN *fee*]
fehteð *see* **fith** *v.*
fey *n.* faith 11/128, 130, **fay** 16a/180 [AN *fei*]
feye *see* **fæie**
feyne *pr. pl.* invent 6/154 [OF *feindre*]
feir *adj.* attractive 13j/47; **faȝerest** *superl.* fairest 3/168 [OE *fæger*]
fel *see* **falles**
felaschipe *n.* company of people 12/237 [OE *fēolaga* from ON *félagi* + OE *-scipe*]
feldefare *n.* fieldfare (winter thrush) 15/364 [OE *feldefare*]
fele *adj.* & *adj. as n.* many [OE *fela*]
fell *see* **falles**
felle *adj.* fierce 9/291, painful 14/225, 271 [OF *fel*]
felonse *adj.* wicked 10/231 [OF *felons*]
fende, feond *n.* devil 4/28, 39, 7b/97; *pl.* fiends 8/82 [OE *fēond*]
fende *v.* in *þame* ~ save themselves 14/57 [from OF *defendre*]
fenyl *n.* fennel (herb) 13h/18 [OE *fenol*, OF *fenoil*]
feolahes *n. pl.* companions 4/75 [OE *fēolaga* from ON *félagi*]
feolde *pa.* felled 3/128 [OE *gefællan*]
feollen *see* **falles**
fer, feor *adj.* far; far away 13j/61; *adv.* far,

ferre 15/440; **fyrre** *comp.* farther 8/116, 9/378, 411, 10/169 [OE *feorr*]
ferde *n.*[1] army 3/8, 50, 57 [OE *ferd*, *fyrd*]
ferde *n.*[2] fear 8/183, 215 [from ME pp. *forferd*, OE **forferan*]
ferde *see* **fare(n)**
fere *n.* companion 2/223, 13q/3, 13r/9 [OE *gefēra*]
fere *adj.* proud 9/103 [OF *fier*]
ferforthe *adv.* in *so* ~ so much so 15/377 [OE *feorr* + *forþ*]
ferk *v.* jump 8/187 [OE *fercian*]
ferly *n.* marvel 10/145; *pl.* strange events 9/23 [from next]
ferli *adj.* wonderful 5/4, 16a/319; *adv.* wonderfully 10/46, amazingly 13h/10 [ON *ferligr*]
ferre *see* **fer**
fers *adj.* fierce 5/293 [AN *fers*]
ferslych, feersly *adv.* sternly 8/337, proudly 9/329 [from prec.]
fest *n.* fist 16a/421 [OE *fȳst*]
feste *imper.* fasten 14/135, 162; *pp.* placed 8/290, fixed 14/82, 122, made fast 14/280 [OE *fæstan*]
festnes *pr. 3 sg.* in ~ *þe fete* gains a foothold 8/273 [OE *fæstnian*]
fette *imper.* lay hold of 14/78; *pa.* fetched 7b/316; **fet** *pp.* 12/151 [OE *fetian*]
fettelez *pr. 3 sg. refl.* prepares 8/435 [?cf. OE *fetel* 'belt']
fetures *n. pl.* parts of the body 9/145 [OF *feture*]
ficchid *pp.* fixed 6/199 [OF *ficher*]
fil *see* **falles**
fylden *pa. pl.* filled 1/14 [OE *fyllan*]
fildore *n.* gold thread 9/189 [OF *fil d'or*]
fille *n.* chervil (aromatic herb) 13h/18 [OE *fille*]
fynde *v.* (**fynt** *pr. 3 sg.*, **fynden** *pl.*; **fand, fond, foend, foond** *pa.*; **yfounde, foune, funde** *pp.*) find 5/426, 7a/40, 12/44, 14/142, compose 5/4, 14, provide for 7a/76, provide with 1/57, 7a/27, 7b/70 [OE *findan*]
fyne *v.* stop 14/81; *pr. pl.* 14/256 [OF *finer*]
fyne *adj.* pure 10/173 [OF *fin*]
fine *adv.* very 5/94 [from prec.]
fyrre *see* **fer**
fyrst, furste *n.* in *on* ~ from the start, at first 10/42, 144, 207, *at the* ~, *upon* ~ right away 7b/168, 9/9 [OE *fyrst*]
fisyk *n.* medicine 7b/267, 291, 293 [OF *fisique*]
fyt *n.* time 16a/330, 376 [OE *fitt*]
fith *n.* fight 13q/18 [OE *feoht*]
fith, viȝte *v.* fight 13n/1; **fehteð** *pr. 3 sg.* 3/97; **fæht** *pa. 3 sg.* 3/149 [OE *fihtan*, *feohtan*]
fytte *adj.* right 14/135 [uncertain]
flæh, flaȝe *see* **flon**
flayed *pa.* terrified 8/215 [OE **flēgan*, cf. ON *fleyja*]
flales *n. pl.* flails 7b/180 [? OF *flaiel*]
flapton *pa. pl.* lashed 7b/180 [cf. Du *flappen*]
flawen *see* **flon**
flawme *n.* flame 15/250 [AN *flaume*]
flec, flesch *n.* meat 1/40, 7b/154 [OE *flǣsc*]
flee(n) *see* **flon**
flem *n.* flow 8/309 [OE *flēam*]
fleme *n.* fugitive 13h/36 [OE *flēma*]
fleoteð *pr. pl.* float 3/110 [OE *flēotan*]
flet *n.* hall-floor 9/294 [OE *flett*]
flex *n.* flax 7b/12 [OE *flæx*]
flicð *see* **flon**
flyȝes *n. pl.* butterflies 9/166 [OE *flēge*]
flyte *v.* quarrel 14/297 [OE *flītan*]
flitte *v.* move 14/234 [ON *flytja*]
flod *n.* sea [OE *flōd*]
flon *v.* (**flo** *pr. 1 sg.*; **fliȝst** *2 sg.*; **fliȝt, flicð, flihð, fliȝeð** *3 sg.*; **floþ, flee(n)** *pl.*; **flo** *imp.*; **flæh, flaȝe** *pa.*; **flowen, flugen, flugæn** *pa. pl.*; **flowen, flawen** *pp.*) flee 1/43, 3/84, 115, 7b/179, 8/183, fly 2/33, 89, 150, 3/123, 6/166 [OE *flēon*]
flotte *pa.* floated 8/248 [OE *flotian*]
fnast *n.* breath 2/44 [OE *fnǣst*]
fnorteth *pr. 3 sg.* snores 16a/309 [cf. OE *fnora*, 'sneezing']
fo *see* **fo(o)**
fo *pr. pl. subj.* ~ *on* proceed 2/179 [OE *fōn*]
foch *v.* receive 9/396 [OE *feccean*]
foend *see* **fynde**
foȝe *n.* decency 2/184 [OE *gefōg*]
foȝle *see* **fuȝel**
foyned *pa.* kicked 9/428 [from OF *foine*]
foysoun *n.* abundance 9/122 [OF *foisoun*]
fol *adj.* foolish 8/283 [OF *fol*]
fol *adv.* very 7b/116 [OE *ful*]
folde *n.* earth, land, country [OE *folde*]
folden *see* **falt**
fole *n.* horse 9/196 [OE *fola*]
folȝi *pr. 1 sg.* follow 2/389; **folȝeþ** *3 sg.* 2/307, **volweþ** afflicts 11/12; **fulieð** *pr. pl.* follow 3/114; **fuleden** *pa. pl.* 3/124 [OE *folgian*]
folwe *pr. 1 sg.* baptize 10/318 [OE *fulwian*]
fond *see* **fynde**
fonde *v.* try 6/228, 14/139, 15/257 [OE *fondian*]
fo(o) *n.* enemy 5/112, 15/339, 16b/106; **fone** *pl.* 15/103 [OE *gefā*]
foole *adj.* lecherous 15/505 [OF *fol*]
for, vor *conj.* for 2/43, 202, 11/5(1), 40, because 8/113, in order that 11/21, 30, 166 [OE *for*]
for, vor *prep.* because of 1/49, 2/19, despite 14/280; ~ *þat* because 2/365, ~ *to* (with infinitive) to, in order to [as prec.]

for *see* **fare(n)**
forage *n.* winter feed 16a/14 [OF *fourrage*]
forbaren *pa. pl.* spared 1/45, 47 [OE *forberan*]
forbi *prep.* more than 8/483 [OE *fora(n)* + *bī*]
force *n.* in *na* ~ no matter 16a/322 [OF *force*]
forclemmed *ppl. adj.* starving 8/395 [OE *for-* + *clemman*]
forcursæd *pp.* excommunicated 1/52 [OE *for-* + *cursian*]
fordemen *v.* destroy 3/102; **fordemed** *pp.* 3/39 [OE *fordēman*]
fordoþ *pr. 3 sg.* destroys 12/17; **fordo(n)** *pp.* 1/53, 3/75 [OE *fordōn*]
fordrunke *pp.* very drunk 4/61 [OE *fordruncen*]
forfare *v.* destroy 8/483 [OE *forfaran*]
forgef *pa.* forgave 8/407 [cf. ON *fyrirgefa*]
forgon *v.* give up 13h/35 [OE *forgān*]
forȝef *imp.* forgive 13r/14 [OE *forgiefan*]
forȝeld *pr. 3 sg. subj.* repay 7b/298 [OE *forgieldan*]
forȝete *v.* forget 6/6; **forȝeten** *pp.* 6/139, **vorȝut** 11/104 [OE *forgietan*]
forholen *pp.* concealed 1/79 [OE *forhelan*]
forlete *v.* lose 16b/206; *pr. 1 sg.* abandon 2/36 [OE *forlētan*]
forlore(ne) *pp.* broken 1/13, damned 1/52, 3/38, lost 4/72 [OE *forlēosan*]
formel n. female (bird) 15/371, 373 [from OF *formel*]
formeste, vormeste *superl. adj.* first 3/129, *as n.* leader 3/64 [OE *fyrmest*]
forn *adv.* in ~ *to* in front of 3/121 [OE *foran*]
forre *adv.* far 2/386 [OE *feorr*]
forred *see* **furrid**
forsake *v.* refuse 13g/19 [OE *forsacan*]
forschreynt *pp.* scorched to death 5/398 [OE *forscrencan*]
forseyde *adj.* previously mentioned 15/120 [OE *foresægd*]
forsworen(e) *pp.* perjured 1/12, 52, 3/38 [OE *forswerian*]
fort *conj.* until 2/41, 332 [OE *for* + *to*]
forte *prep.* (with infin.) to, in order to 4/6, 13g/18, 13j/16 [OE *for* + *to*]
forþ, vorþ *adv.* in ~ *go* go on your way 2/297, ~ *mid* together with 3/158, ~ *þerupon* immediately after 12/105 [OE *forþ*]
forþer *v.* assist 6/84 [OE *fyrþrian*]
forther(e) *adv.* further 16a/368, more widely 7b/76 [OE *furþor*]
forthy, forþe, vorþi *adv.* therefore; for that reason 2/65, 277, 13g/23 [OE *forþī*]
forþi *conj.* in ~ *þat* in order that 6/33, because 1/2, 6/184 [as prec.]
forðward *adv.* onward 3/40 [OE *forþweard*]
forwake *pp.* deprived of sleep 13g/31 [OE *for-* + *wacan*]
forward *n.* contract, agreed business 14/10, 93; *pl.* agreements 9/378, 409 [OE *foreweard*]
forwery *adj.* *in* ~ *of* exhausted by 15/93 [OE *for-* + *wērig*]
forwes *n. pl.* furrows 7b/65 [OE *furh*]
forwhy *conj.* for 6/196, 221 [OE *forhwī*]
forwrast *pp.* seized 10/220 [OE *for* + *wrǣstan*]
fot(e) *n.* footing 10/42, base 12/141 [OE *fōt*]
fotte *v.* receive 9/451 [cf. OE *fettan*]
fouchen *pr. pl.* in ~ *saf* vouchsafe, grant 7a/49 [OF *voucher*]
foules *see* **fuȝel**
fouly *adv.* terribly 14/112 [OE *fūlīce*]
foundande *pr. p.* travelling 8/126; **founded** *pp.* set out 9/267 [OE *fundian*]
founded *pp.* built 15/231 [OF *fonder*]
foune *see* **fynde**
fourme *n.* in *in* ~ *of* in accord with 10/230 [OF *fourme*]
frayneth *pr. 3 sg.* asks 16b/148; *pp.* 9/359 [OE *frægnian*]
frayst *pr. 1 sg.* ask for 9/279; *pp.* 9/324, 391 [ON *freista*]
fram, fron, vram, vrom *prep.* from [OE *fram*]
fre(e) *adj.* noble 9/101, 13r/3, 14/49, gracious 10/318, free 7a/64 [OE *frēo*]
freelté *n,* frailty 6/110 [OF *fraileté*]
freke *n.* man, knight [OE *freca*]
frelych *adj.* gracious 8/214; **frely** *adv.* abundantly 8/20, willingly 8/390 [OE *frēolic*, *frēolīce*]
frendes *n. pl.* relatives 7a/36, 40, 11/56 [ON *frændi*]
frenesies *n. pl.* frenzies, fits 6/158 [OF *frenesie*]
frere *n.* friar 7b/73 [OF *frere*]
fresche *adj. as n.* fresh food 9/122 [OF *fresche*]
frete *pa.* devoured 5/539 [OE *fretan*]
friþ *n.* woodland 5/160, 246 [OE *fyrþ*]
fro *adj.* well-born 2/134 [OE *frēo*]
fro *prep.* from; *conj.* after 8/243, when 9/62 [ON *frá*]
fron *see* **fram**
froted *pa.* rubbed together 5/79 [OF *froter*]
frowarde *adj.* recalcitrant 10/231 [ON *frá* + OE *-weard*]
frunt *pa.* kicked 8/187 [OF *fronter*]
fuelkunne *n. dat. pl.* kinds of birds 2/65 [OE *fugol* + *cynn*]
fuȝel *n.* bird 3/123; **foules** *pl.* 5/68; **foȝle** *dat. pl.* 2/277 [OE *fugol*]
ful *adv.* very [OE *full*]
ful(e), vul(e) *adj.* foul 1/21, 2/32, 35, 4/88, foul (with excrement) 2/236; **fuleste** *superl.* 4/80 [OE *fūl*]

hærdliche *adv.* violently 3/154 [from OE *heard*]
hærnes *n. pl.* brains 1/24 [ON *hjarni*]
hafde *see* **habbe, hefed**
haggen *n. pl.* hags 4/86 [? cf. OE *hægtesse*]
haȝe *see* **high(e)**
haylle *see* **ha(a)le**
haylsed *pa.* greeted 9/223 [ON *heilsa*]
hayre *n.* hair-shirt 8/381; *pl.* 8/373 [OE *hǣr*]
hayroun *n.* heron 5/310 [OF *hairon*]
halce *see* **hals**
halched *pp.* enclosed 9/185, fastened 9/218 [OE *halsian*]
halde(n) *see* **hold**
hale *n.* nook 2/2 [OE *halh*]
halechen *adj. as n. pl.* saints 1/54 [OE *hālga*]
hales *see* **ha(a)le, hals**
halfe *see* **halve**
hali *adj.* holy 1/79, 4/79 [OE *hālig*]
halyday *n.* feast day 8/9; *pl.* 16a/98 [OE *hāligdæg*]
halled *see* **ha(a)le**
halm *n.* helm 3/16 [OE *helm* or ON *hjálmr*]
halme *n.* shaft 9/218, 330 [OE *halm*]
halowes *n. pl.* saints 10/23 [OE *hālga*]
halp *see* **healp**
hals, hales, halce *n.* neck 1/31, 7b/60, 9/427 [OE *hals*]
halsen *pr. 1 sg.* implore 16b/193 [OE *halsian*]
halve, halfe *n.* side 2/109, 15/125; *upon Godez* ~ in God's name 9/326 [OE *half*]
ham, hamseolf, hamseolven *see* **hi**
han *see* **habbe**
hapeth *pr. impers.* in ~ *me* it happens to me 15/10; **happed** *pa.* 7a/95, 15/18 [from next]
hap(pe) *n.* good fortune 8/212, happiness 9/48, fortune 15/402 [ON *happ*]
happen *adj.* blessed 8/13 [ON *heppinn*]
hardelyche *adv.* boldly 7b/28, **hardily** *adv.* confidently 16a/155 [from OE *heard*]
hardi *adj.* bold, courageous 5/41, 7b/181, 9/371, 16a/103, tough 15/176 [OF *hardi*]
hare *see* **hi**
harke *see* **herke**
harlot(te) *n.* scoundrel 14/160, 16a/414; *pl.* 7b/50 [OF *harlot*]
harme *n.* wrongdoing 8/17; *pl.* injuries 10/232 [OE *hearm*]
harping *n.* in *in* ~ composed to the harp 5/3 [from OE *hearpian*]
harrow *interj.* alas, help 16a/218, 453 [OF *haro*]
harwen *v.* harrow 7a/19 [from ON *hervi*]
hasped *pa.* wrapped 8/381; *pp.* buckled 9/281; **haspede** *ppl. adj.* with a buckle 8/189 [OE *hæpsian*]
hastow *see* **habbe**
hatel *adj.* cruel 8/367, bitter 8/481 [OE *hatol*]
hater *n.* clothing 8/189 [OE *hæteru* pl.]
haþel *n.* man, knight, (in address) sir [OE *hæleþ*]
hat(te) *see* **hoten**
hatz *see* **habbe**
haunt *n.* in *gode* ~ great plenty 5/309 [OF *hant*]
haunte *pr. pl.* practise 8/15; *pr. 3 sg. subj.* 12/258 [OF *hanter*]
havec(k) *n.* hawk 2/303, 307; **havekes** *gen.* 2/271 [OE *hafoc*]
havet *see* **habbe**
hawbergh, hauberghe *n.* coat of mail 9/203, 268 [OF *hauberc*]
hawteyn *adj.* proud 15/262 [OF *hautain*]
healp, halp, heelp *pa.* helped 4/79, 12/72; **holpe(n)** *pa. pl.* 7b/113, 123; *pp.* 6/14 [OE *helpan*]
heatien *v.* hate 4/86 [OE *hatian*]
Hebrayk *adj.* Hebrew 16b/108 [Lat *Hebraicus*]
heep *see* **hepe**
heere *pr. 1 sg.* praise 10/339; **herieth** *3 sg.* 16b/166; **heryen** *pl.* 16b/226; **herid** *pp.* 10/325 [OE *herian*]
heete *see* **hoten**
hef *pa.* rose 9/120; ~ *up* increased 8/477 [OE *hebban*]
hefden *see* **habbe**
hefed, heved *n.* head 1/22, **hæved** 1/23, **hafde** 3/16, **hæfd** 3/139, **hæfved** 3/158, **hade** 5/391 [OE *hēafod*]
hegge *n.* hedge 2/59 [OE *hegg*]
heggen *v.* hedge 7a/19 [from prec.]
hegh, heȝe, hehe, hey(ȝe) *see* **high(e)**
heglice, heiliche *see* **hiȝlich**
hehte *see* **hoten**
heihte *see* **hyȝt**
helde *see* **hold**
helder *adv.* in *never þe* ~ not at all 9/430 [ON *heldr*]
heldez *see* **hælden**
hele *n.* health 7a/7, 10, 15/128, safety 8/335 [OE *hǣlu*]
hele *imp.* restore 7b/225 [OE *hǣlan*]
helede *pa.* covered 3/13 [OE *helan*]
helle *n. gen.* of Hell 4/42 [OE *hell*]
hellen *adj.* of Hell 8/306 [from prec.]
hem *see* **hi**
heme *adj.* attractive 9/157 [OE *gehǣme*]
hende *n. pl.* hands 14/122 [ON pl. *hendr*]
hende *adj.* gracious, worthy, noble, courteous [OE *gehende*]
henge, hyng, hongen *v.* hang; **hongeþ** *pr. 3 sg.* 5/506; **heng(e)** *pa.* 3/20, 5/344, 7b/60; **hengen** *pl.* 1/77 (see 1/20 note) [ON *hengja*, OE *hangian*, OE *hōn*]

fuleden *see* **folȝi**
fuleþ *pr. 3 sg.* befouls 2/100; *pr. pl.* 2/96; **ifuled** *pp.* 2/110 [cf. OE *fūlian*]
fulfeld *pp.* completed 7b/346, **fulfilled** full 15/89 [OE *fullfyllan*]
fulheed *n.* fullness 6/218 [OE *full* + **-hǣdu*]
fulieð *see* **folȝi**
fulle *adj. as n.* in *at þe* ~ completely 6/56, 58, 68, thoroughly 16a/82, 451 [OE *full*]
fulliche *adv.* filthily 4/75 [OE *fūlice*]
fulste *n.* help 3/39 [OE *fylst*]
fulsten *pr. 3 sg. subj.* help 3/46, 64 [OE *fylstan*]
fulðe *n.* filth 4/75 [OE *fylþ*]
funde *see* **fynde**
furrid *pa.* put fur on 10/252; **forred** *pp.* 7b/291 [OF *furrer*]
furste *see* **fyrst**
fuse(n) *pr. pl. subj.* let (us) hasten 3/34, 40 [OE *fȳsan*]
fust *n.* fist, hand 9/391 [OE *fȳst*]

gadering *n.* council 1/6; **gadryngs** *pl.* gatherings 11/160 [from OE *gadrian*]
gadrede *see* **gedereð**
gæde *see* **ȝede**
gæildes *n. pl.* taxes 1/36 [OE *gield*]
gær(e) *n.* year 1/1, 57, 70 [OE *gēar*]
gæt *adv.* previously 1/43 [OE *gēt*]
gay *adj.* lovely, finely dressed 15/234, 16a/72 [OF *gai*]
gayn *adj.* obedient 9/178 [ON *gegn*]
gayned *pa.* suited 8/164 [ON *gegna*]
gaynlych *adj.* gracious 8/83 [from ON *gegn*]
game *n.* entertainment 5/19 [OE *gamen*]
gan *see* **gynne**
gargeles *n. pl.* gargoyles, grotesque heads 10/48 [OF *gargouille*]
garnement *n.* garment 12/112 [OF *garnement*]
garnysht *pp.* decorated 10/48 [OF *garnir, garniss-*]
garte *pa.* made 7b/324 [ON *gøra*]
gast *ppl. adj.* afraid 9/325 [OE *gæstan*]
gaste *v.* ruin 13j/16 [? OF *gaster*]
gat *n.* goat 3/96; **gaten** *pl.* 3/100 [OE *gāt*]
gate *n.* in *hegh* ~ high road (of justice) 10/241 [ON *gata*]
gaudi *n.* ornaments 9/167 [OF *gaudie*]
gaudis *n. pl.* tricks 14/149, 200 [cf. AN *gaudir*]
gaule *n.* scum 8/285 [OE *galla*]
geaunte *n.* giant 15/344 [OF *jaiant*]
gedereð, -es *pr. 3 sg.* gathers 4/52, lifts up 9/421; **gederen** *pr. pl.* in ~ *to* pull at 8/105; **gadrede** *pa.* gathered 11/159; **gadered, gedrid** *pp.* accumulated 1/4, assembled 10/134 [OE *gadrian*]
gef(e) *see* **gif** *v.*
genge *see* **gynge**
gent *adj.* fine 15/558 [OF *gent*]
gentil(e), gentel *adj.* noble, well-born 7a/78, 15/196, 337, gentile, pagan 10/216, 229; **gentileste** *superl.* noblest, most exquisite 15/373, 550 [OF *gentil*]
gentilesse *n.* nobility, good breeding 15/224 [OF *gentillesse*]
gere *n.* tools 14/29 [ON *gervi*]
gered *pp.* dressed 9/179 [from prec.]
geserne *see* **giserne**
gestes *n. pl.* guests 1/58 [ON *gestr*]
gete *pa.* got, diverted 10/241; **getyn, geten** *pp.* got 6/222, begotten 13l/15 [ON *geta*]
geþ *see* **go(n)**
gyde-ropes *n. pl.* guy-ropes 8/105 [OF *guide* + OE *rāp*]
gif *v.* give 9/288; **gef** *pr. 3 sg. subj.* 8/226; **gyf** *imp.* 8/204; **gef(e)** *pa.* 9/370, 10/282 [OE *giefan* or ON *gefa*]
gif *conj.* if 1/48 [OE *gif*]
gile *n.* trickery 5/7, deceit 8/285 [OF *guile*]
giles *n. pl.* gills 8/269 [? ON, cf. Sw *gäl*]
gilour *n.* trickster, deceiver 16a/467 [OF *guileor*]
gylte *n.* in *in my* ~ by my fault 15/434 [OE *gylt*]
gilte *adj.* golden 15/267 [from OE *gegyld*]
gynful *adj.* dishonest 10/238 [from *gyn*, OF *engin*]
gynge *n.* company 10/137, **genge** 3/56 [ON *gengi*]
gyn(ne) *n.* vessel 8/146, contraption 14/197 [from OF *engin*]
gynne *v.* begin 11/149; **gon, gan** *pa.* 3/78, 5/425, 7b/149, (forming past tense with infinitive) 3/4, 5/78; **gun(ne), gonne(n)** *pa. pl.* 5/504, 14/269, 15/193, 15/331, did 15/283 [from OE *onginnan*]
girdel-stede *n.* waist 5/266 [OE *gyrdel* + *stede*]
gyse *n.* style 15/399, custom, way 16a/272 [OF *guise*]
giserne, geserne *n.* axe 9/288, 326, 375 [OF *guiserne*]
gyte *n.* dress 16a/100 [OF *guite*]
gladyen, glade *v.* make glad 7b/126, rejoice 12/134, 15/687 [OE *gladian*]
gladur *comp. adj.* more glad 2/19 [OE *glæd*]
glaym *n.* slime 8/269 [uncertain]
gla(u)m *n.* voice 8/63, noise 9/46 [ON *glaumr*]
gle, gleo *n.* music; entertainment 4/12, pleasure 5/267, rejoicing 9/46 [OE *glēo*]
gleedes *n. pl.* burning coals 16a/29 [OE *glēd*]
glemered *pa.* gleamed 9/172 [? ON, cf. Du *glimmeren*]

glent *v.* deviate 10/241; *pa.* glanced 9/82, 476, shone 9/172 [ON **glenta*]

glette *n.* filth 8/269 [OF *glette*]

glew *adj.* prudent 2/193 [OE *glēaw*]

glewed *see* **glow**

gliden *v.* travel silently 3/44; **glyde** *pr. 2 sg. subj.* pass 8/204; **glod** *pa.* came 8/63 [OE *glīdan*]

glyʒt *pa.* looked 8/453 [uncertain]

glisnande *pr. p.* glistening 10/78 [OE *glisnian*]

glode *n.* open space 10/75 [uncertain]

gloumbes *pr. 3 sg.* worries 8/94 [unknown]

glow *pr. pl. subj.* call 10/171; **glewed** *pa.* called 8/164 [OE *gleowian*]

glowande *adj.* shining 8/94 [OE *glōwan*]

gobet *n.* portion 7a/100 [OF *gobet*]

god(e), good *n.* good 2/329, wealth 1/17, 45, possession(s) 5/230, 7b/236; **goodes, gowdez** *pl.* creations 6/4, good things 8/286 [OE *gōd*]

goded *pa.* endowed 1/60 [OE *gōdian*]

godhede *n.* goodness 2/351 [OE *gōd* + **-hǣdu*]

godly *adv.* properly 8/26, honourably 9/273 [from OE *gōd*]

goldfaʒe *adj. pl.* adorned with gold 3/109 [OE *gold-fāh*]

golé *n.* mouthful 15/556 [OF *golee*]

gome *n.* man, knight; anyone 8/175 [OE *guma*]

gomen *n.* game 4/48, 9/283 [OE *gomen*]

go(n) *v.* go; **geþ** *pr. 3 sg.* 5/238, **gotz** 8/171, 280, 9/375; **goon** *pr. pl.* 15/127, 129, 134; **gose** *imp. pl.* 14/78; **ygo, goon** *pp.* gone 5/349, 11/112, ago 5/541 [OE *gān*]

gon, gonnen *see* **gynne**

good *see* **god(e)**

goodely *adv.* well 14/39 [from OE *gōd*]

goostly *adj.* spiritual 6/155 [OE *gastlic*]

gose *see* **go(n)**

gotez *n. pl.* currents 8/310 [OE *gota*]

gottes *n. pl.* guts 7b/175 [OE pl. *guttas*]

governaunce *n.* rule 15/387 [OF *governance*]

governe *v.* in *him* ~ control himself 12/223 [OF *governer*]

gowdez *see* **god(e)**

grace *n.* fortune 15/45, 65, good fortune 15/412, favour 15/421 [OF *grace*]

graciouse, gracios *adj.* lovely 8/453, elegant 9/216 [OF *gracious*]

grayþe *adj.* ready 9/448; **graythist** *superl.* most powerful 10/251 [ON *greiðr*]

grayþed, graied *see* **greithen**

graythly, greiþlyche *adv.* truly 8/240, 286, promptly 9/417, 11/149 [ON *greiðliga*]

grame *n.* harm 2/49 [OE *grama*]

granti *pr. 1 sg.* grant 2/201 [AN *granter*]

grat *pr. pl.* cry out 7b/284 [ME *greden*, OE *grēdan*]

grattest *superl. adj.* in ~ *in grene* greenest 9/207 [OE *grēat*]

graunte *n.* in ~ *hade* received assent 10/126 [OF *grant*]

gre *n.* in *at þi* ~ as you wish 8/348 [OF *gré*]

grede *v.* shout 2/308; **gredest** *pr. 2 sg.* cry out 5/104 [OE *grēdan*]

gref *n.* harm 8/83 [OF *gref*]

greithen *pr. pl. refl.* in ~ *hem* get ready 16a/455; **grayþed, graied** *pp.* set 9/74, 109, arrayed 9/151, prepared 14/39 [ON *greiða*]

greiþlyche *see* **graythly**

greme *n.* martial spirit 9/312 [ON *gremi*]

grene *n.* grass 5/72 [OE *grēne*]

grene *adj.* green, unripe 7b/304 [OE *grēne*]

grennin *v.* gnash the teeth 4/24; **grenne** *pr. pl.* grin 9/464 [OE *grennian*]

grennunge *n.* gnashing 4/23 [from prec.]

gres(se) *n.* grass 5/244, 9/235 [OE *græs*]

gret *adj.* full 2/43, **grete** *as n.* important part, essence 15/35 [OE *grēat*]

grete *n.* earth 10/41 [OE *grēot*]

grete *v.* weep 13l/19; **grette** *pa.* in ~ *after* wept for 10/126 [OE *grētan*]

grevance *n.* discomfort 15/205 [OF *grevance*]

greve *v.* injure 7a/58, harm, bring harm to 8/112, 517, offend 8/226; *refl.* become angry 16a/5, 56; **greveth** *pr. 3 sg.* hurts 7b/269; **greved** *pa.* became angry 9/316 [OF *grever*]

grevez *n. pl.* groves 8/439, 9/207 [OE *grǣfa*]

gries *n.* pig 7b/304 [ON *griss*]

grylle *adj.* painful 13j/68 [cf. OE *gryllan*]

grim *adj.* hideous 4/27 [OE *grim*]

grimliche *adv.* cruelly 4/41 [from prec.]

gryndel *adj.* angry 8/524 [? from next]

gryndellayk *n.* fierceness 9/312 [ON *grindill* 'storm' + *leikr*]

grislich *adj.* dreadful 2/224, 315; **grisliche** *adv.* horribly 4/5 [OE *grislic*, *grislīce*]

grom *n.* lad 13l/7; *pl.* men 7b/227 [cf. MDu *grom* 'offspring']

grot *n.* small thing, detail 5/490 [OE *grot*]

groundelez *adj.* bottomless 8/310 [OE *grundlēas*]

Gru *see* **Grw**

grubber *n.* digger 10/41 [cf. OE **grybban*]

gruc(c)he *v.* grumble 7b/337, 16a/9; *pr. pl.* 7b/227 [OF *gruchier*]

gruf *adv.* face down 16b/223 [ON *á grúfu*]

grulde *pa. 3 sg. subj.* twanged 2/142 [unknown]

grunde *n.* in *bi* ~ near the ground 2/278 [OE *grund*]

grurefule *adj.* terrible 4/5 [from OE *gryre*]

Grw, Gru *n.* Greek 11/91, 113, 115 [OF *Greu*]

Glossary

guerdonynge *n.* reward 15/455 [from OF *gueredon*]

guferes *n. pl.* depths 8/310 [OF *goufre*]

gultif *adj.* guilty 12/50 [OE *gyltig*]

gume *n.* man 3/103 [OE guma]

gun(ne) *see* **gynne**

gurden *pa. pl.* girdled 10/251 [OE *gyrdan*]

ʒaf *see* **ʒive**

ʒal *see* **ʒollest**

ʒare *adj.* ready 2/215, **ʒaru** 3/50; **ʒærewe** *pl.* 3/55 [OE *gearu*]

ʒate *n.* gate 5/232, 385 [OE *gæt*]

ʒe *pron. pl.* you; **ʒow** *acc. & dat.*; **ou, ow** *dat.* 2/115, 4/92; **ʒowsulven** *emphatic* yourselves 7b/14; **(e)ower, æuwer** *poss. adj.* your 3/163, 173, 4/90 [OE *gē*, *ēow*, etc.]

ʒe *adv.* yes, indeed 6/14, 108 [OE *gē*]

ʒeddien *v.* speak 3/160 [OE *gieddian*]

ʒede *pa.* went, walked; **ʒæde** 1/23; **ʒode** 10/198; **ieden** *pl.* 1/42 [OE *ēode*]

ʒederly *adv.* promptly 9/453 [from OE *ēdre*]

ʒef *conj.* if [OE *gif*]

ʒef *see* **ʒive**

ʒelde(n) *v.* repay 7b/41, 133; **ʒolden** *pp.* 9/453 [OE *geldan*]

ʒelp *n.* boasting 4/2 [OE *gielp*]

ʒemeles *adj.* heedless 4/40 [OE *gīemelēas*]

ʒemyd *pa.* governed 10/202 [OE *gēman*]

ʒeomerest *superl. adj.* most wretched 3/73 [from OE *geōmor*]

ʒeorne *see* **ʒerne**

ʒeot *imp.* pour 4/68 [OE *gēotan*]

ʒeove *see* **ʒive**

ʒep *adj.* vigorous 9/105; *as n. pl.* 9/284 [OE *gēap*]

ʒepely *adv.* freshly 10/88 [from prec.]

ʒerd *n.* place 7b/207 [OE *geard*]

ʒer(e) *n.* year; *þat oþer* ~ a year or two ago 2/101; **ʒer(e)** *pl.* years 5/264, 6/104, 7a/35 [OE *gēr*]

ʒerne, ʒeorne *adv.* eagerly 4/39, 5/323, 7b/116, loudly 13p/19 [OE *georne*]

ʒerstendæi *n.* yesterday 3/95 [OE *gestrandæg*]

ʒerte *pa.* cried out 13p/19 [? OE **gierran*]

ʒet(e), ʒut, ʒit(t) *adv.* yet; further 2/309, 363, 3/104, up to now 5/103, as yet 12/32, still 7a/94, longer 14/137, 230 [OE *gēt*]

ʒeve *see* **ʒive**

ʒever *n.* giver 6/93 [from OE *gefan*]

ʒevyng *n.* giving 6/97, 100 [as prec.]

ʒif *conj.* if [OE *gif*]

ʒif *see* **ʒive**

ʒifte *n.* gift 12/22; *pl.* 7b/39 [from ME *ʒiven*]

ʒimston *n.* precious stone 3/17 [OF *gemme* + OE *stān*]

ʒiscere *n.* miser 4/44 [OE *gītsere*]

ʒis(s)e *interj.* yes (answering ne… tion) 8/117, 347 [OE *gīse*]

ʒit(t) *see* **ʒet(e)**

ʒive, ʒeve, yeve *v.* (**ʒeven** *pr*… **ʒeove** *pr. 3 sg. subj.* 4/92; **ʒef, ʒ**… 4/67, 69, 7b/283; **ʒaf, yaf(e)** … 7b/187, 204; **iafen, ʒefven** *p*… **ʒove(n)** *pp.* 6/42, 12/127) give… *giefan*, *gefan*]

ʒivere *n.* the glutton 4/69 [from…

ʒivere *adj.* greedy 4/57 [OE *gīfr*…

ʒode *see* **ʒede**

ʒoʒelinge *n.* yowling 2/40 [imit…

ʒol *n.* Christmas 9/284 [OE *gēol*…

ʒolden *see* **ʒelde(n)**

ʒollest *pr. 2 sg.* yell 2/223; **ʒ**… screamed 2/112 [imitative]

ʒond *pron.* in *þe* ~ that one ove… [OE *geond*]

ʒone *adj.* yonder 14/178 [OE *ge*…

ʒorde *n.* precinct 10/88 [OE *gea*…

ʒore *adv.* for a long time 13g/34, … for a very long time 5/559 [OE…

ʒoskyd *pa.* sobbed 10/312 [OE …

ʒove(n) *see* **ʒive**

ʒow, ʒowsulven *see* **ʒe**

ʒurstendæi *n.* yesterday 3/1… *gystrandæg*]

ʒut *see* **ʒet(e)**

ha *see* **hi**

ha(a)le *v.* pull 14/116, 15/151; **h**… comes 9/136; **haylle** *imp.* … **halled** *pa.* went 9/458 [OF *ha*…

habbe, han, haan *v.* (**habbe** *p*… **ichave** *pron.* + *pr. 1 sg.* I … **ychabbe** 13g/34; **habbez** *pr.*… **hastow** *pr. 2 sg.* + *pron.* hav… **havet** *3 sg.* 2/113, **haveþ** 2/11… **hatz** 9/17, **hat** 13l/24; **habbe**… **haþ** 6/62, **han** 6/11, 8/13, **h**… **hatz** 9/19; **hafde** *pa.* 3/9; **ha**… 5/573; **hadestow** *pa. 2 sg.* + … **had(d)en** *pa. pl.* 1/11, 9/52, … 1/17, 67) have; acquire 1/67… *habban*]

habundaunce *n.* abundance … *abundance*]

hade, hæfd, hæfved *see* **hefed**

hæʒe, hæh, hæhʒere *see* **high(**…

hæhliche *see* **hiʒlich**

hælden *v.* come 3/54; **heldez** … 9/221; **heldes** *pl.* bow 10/196 … moved away 10/137; **hælden** … *pl.* turned 3/126, fell 3/139, 145…

hælle *n.* hell 3/166 [OE *helle*]

haen *see* **habbe**

hen(ne)s *adv.* ago 7a/35, away from here 7a/80, hence 7b/301, 8/204 [from OE *heonane*]
hent *v.* (**hent(e)** *pa. & pp.*) receive 8/178, 10/232, 14/189, seize 7b/171, 8/189, 251, 367, take 7b/183, 8/373, 10/291, engage 3/128 [OE *hentan*]
heold *see* **hold**
heo(m), heore *see* **hi**
heorte *see* **hert**
hepe, heep *n.* heap, large number 16b/45; *bi* ~ to overflowing 2/360 [OE *hēap*]
her *adv.* here 3/173 [OE *hēr*]
herbarwe *n.* lodging 5/484, **herberwe** 16a/265 [OE *herebeorg*]
herdes *n. pl.* herdsmen 2/286 [OE *hirde*]
her(e) *n.* hair 9/180, 13f/1, 2; **herys** *pl.* 16a/16 [OE *hēr*]
heredmen *n. pl.* courtiers 9/302 [OE *hīredmann*]
hereword *n.* praise 4/2 [OE *herian* + *word*]
herghdes *pa. 2 sg.* harrowed 10/291; **herȝed** *pp.* dragged 8/178 [OE *hergian*]
herid *see* **heere**
heryen, herieth *see* **heere**
heryynge *vbl. n.* praise 16b/7 [from OE *herian*]
heritage *n.* inheritable possessions 12/221 [OF *heritage*]
herke, harke *imp.* listen 8/431, 14/61, 265 [OE **hercian*]
herken *v.* listen; ~ *after* long for 10/307 [OE *hercnian*]
herle *n.* strand 9/190 [cf. MLG *herle*]
herre *see* **high(e)**
hert, h(e)orte *n.* heart; **herttes** *pl.* 8/2 [OE *heorte*]
hervest *n.* autumn 7a/7 [OE *hærfest*]
heste *n.* command 11/167, 12/104; *pl.* 7b/213 [OE *hǣs*]
hete *n.* hatred 2/167 [OE *hete*]
heter *adj.* rough 8/373 [? cf. MLG *hetter*]
heterly *adv.* fiercely 8/381, 477, 481 [from prec.]
heþenisse *n.* heathen lands 5/513 [OE *hǣþennes*]
heþyng *n.* abuse 8/2 [ON *hæðing*]
hette *pa.* warmed up 15/145 [OE *hǣtan*]
hette(z) *see* **hoten**
heu *n.* colour 13g/13, **hewe** 15/258 [OE *hēow*]
heved *n. see* **hefed**
hevened *pp.* raised 9/349 [OE *hafenian*]
hevenesse *n.* sorrow 15/89 [OE *hefignes*]
hevenryche *n.* kingdom of Heaven 8/14, 28 [OE *heofonrīce*]
hewe *n.* labourer 7b/195 [OE pl. *hīwan*]
hewen *pp.* shaped 9/211, cut 9/477 [OE *hēawan*]
hi *pron. pl. nom.* they 1/2, 2/12, 95, 11/7, **hye** 5/91, **ho** 2/66, 76, 97, **ha** 4/3, **a** 11/37, **heo** 3/69; **hi** *acc.* them 2/108, 308; **hom** *dat.* 2/62; **he(o)m** *acc. & dat.* them 1/18, 3/67, 4/73, **hom** 10/16, **ham** 4/23, 87, 11/6; **her(e)** *poss. adj.* their 1/9, 5/87, 7b/260, 11/2, **heore** 3/109, **hare** 4/3, 84, **hor** 9/130, 10/17, **huere** 13h/8, **hir** 15/39, 16a/137; **hores** *disjunctive* theirs 8/14; **hamseolf, hamseolven** *pron. refl. and emphatic* themselves 4/24, 81 [OE *hie*, *hēo* etc.]
hi *see also* **ho**
hyder, hidir *adv.* hither [OE *hider*]
hidor *n.* terror 8/367 [OF *hidor*]
hye *v. refl.* in ~ *hym/the* hurry 7b/206, 15/133; **hyȝed, highid** *pa.* hurried 8/217, 10/58 [OE *hīgian*]
hye *see* **hy(ȝ)e**
hielde *see* **hold**
high(e), hyȝe, hæh, hæhȝe, heiȝe, hey(e), hegh *adj.* high 3/16, 5/356, 7b/2; noble 3/132, 9/5, 10/137, exalted 10/325, 339; **hæhȝere** *fem. dat.* high, mighty 3/126; **herre** *comp.* taller 9/333; **heiȝest** *superl.* highest 6/52; **he(y)ȝe** *as n.* a high place 13l/2, *on* ~ on high 8/463, *upon* ~ to the highest degree 9/48; **highe, hyȝe, hæȝe, haȝe, hehe** *adv.* high 3/121, 161, 4/91, 9/120, loudly 9/307, 468, arrogantly 9/349 [OE *hēh*]
highid, hyȝed *see* **hye**
highte *see* **hoten**
hy(ȝ)e *n.* in *in* ~ suddenly 9/245, quickly 14/1 [from OE v. *hīgian*]
hiȝenliche *adv.* hastily 3/4 [from OE *hīgian*]
hiȝlich *adj.* splendid 9/183; **heglice, hæhliche, heiliche, hyȝlych** *adv.* honourably 1/80, nobly 3/89, scrupulously 7b/89, highly 11/95 [OE *hēalic*, *hēalīce*]
hyȝt, heihte *n.* in *upon* ~ to his full height 9/332, *on* ~ on high 9/421, up high 12/141 [OE *hēhþo*]
hihte *see* **hoten**
himward *adv.* in *to* ~ towards him 2/375 [OE *him* + OE *-weard*]
hine *masc. pron. acc.* him 3/3; **hisselven** *emphatic* himself 9/107 [OE *hine*, *his* + *self*]
hyng *see* **henge**
hir *see* **hi**
hyre *n.* wages 14/47 [OE *hȳr*]
hyrne *n.* corner 8/178, 289 [OE *hyrne*]
hit *gen. pron.* its 8/12, 10/309 [OE *hit*]
hit(te) *pa.* in ~ *to* reached 8/289, fell to 9/427 [ON *hitta*]
ho *fem. pron. nom.* she 2/19, 8/4, **hi** 2/10; **hi** *acc.* her 2/29, 30 [OE *heō*, *hīe*]
ho *see also* **hi**
hoem *adv.* home 7b/108, 207 [OE *hām*]

hoer *see* **hore**
hoge *adj.* huge 9/208 [OF *ahoge*]
hoker *n.* scornfulness 16a/111 [OE *hōcor*]
hol *adj.* perfect 8/335 [OE *hāl*]
hold, halde *v.* (**hold, heold, helde, hielde** *pa.*; **holde(n), heolden, halden** *pa. pl.*; **yhold, holde(n), halden** *pp.*) hold; rule 9/53, contain 9/124, keep 1/12, 5/468, observe 1/58, consider 5/45, 9/28, 259; ~ *hym* stay 7b/207, keep himself 8/289, ~ *with* have dealings with 7b/50; **holdyng** *pr. p.* obliged 7b/103 [OE *haldan*]
holde *adj.* faithful 7b/195 [OE *hold*]
holyn *n.* holly 9/206 [OE *holen*]
holpe(n) *see* **healp**
holtes *n. pl.* woods 5/214 [OE *holt*]
hom *see* **hi**
homycide *n.* murderer 16b/115 [OF *homicide*]
honde *n.* hand; *haþ upon* ~ has control of 12/227; **honde-myȝt** power 8/257, **honde-quile** short time 10/64; **honden** *pl.* 5/79 [OE *hond*, *miht*, *hwīl*]
hondele *v.* use 9/289 [OE *hondlian*]
hondeselle *n.* presents 9/66 [OE *hondselen*]
hone *n.* delay 14/198 [uncertain]
hone *v.* delay 14/13 [uncertain]
honest *adj.* honourable 16b/109 [OF *honeste*]
hongen, hongeþ *see* **henge**
honne *adv.* away 2/66 [OE *heonane*]
hoo *interj.* stóp 14/140 [ON *hō*]
hoot *adj. as n.* hot 15/205 [OE *hāt*]
hope *v.* think, believe [OE *hopian*]
hoper *n.* hopper 16a/182, 185 [from OE *hoppian*, 'hop']
hor, hores *see* **hi**
hore, hoer, hoor *adj.* hoar, ancient 5/214, white-haired 7b/92, 16a/24 [OE *hār*]
horte *see* **hert**
hose *n.* stocking 16a/79; *pl.* 3/13, 16a/101 [OE *hosa*]
ho-so *pron.* whoever 7b/120 [OE *hwā* + *swā*]
hote *adv.* passionately 12/197 [OE *hāte*]
hoten, heete *v.* (**hote, hat(te)** *pr. 1 sg.*; **hattes(t)** *2 sg.*; **hat(te)** *3 sg.*; **hoten** *pl.*; **hehte, hihte, highte, hatte** *pa.*; **hettez** *pa. 2 sg.*; **hote(n), yhote, ihaten, hette** *pp.*) call, be called; command 7b/78, 85, 89, 272, promise 9/448, 14/121 (see 5.6.10) [OE *hātan*]
houped *pa.* whooped 7b/168 [imitative]
houres *n. pl.* canonical hours 10/119 [AN *ure*]
hourlande *pr. p.* tumbling 8/271; **hurled** *pa.* crashed down 8/149 [uncertain]
housbondrye *n.* concern with household matters 16a/223 [from OE *hūsbonda*, ON *húsbóndi*]
howe, hwe *n.* hue 2/152, 9/147, 234 [OE *hēow*]
howsoever *adv.* in whatever way 6/23 [OE *hū* + *swā* + *ǣfre*]
hu *adv.* how 2/46, 263, 4/22, 77 [OE *hū*]
hude *pr. 1 sg.* hide 2/265; **hud** *imp.* 2/164 [OE *hȳdan*]
huere *see* **hi**
huyre *n.* wages 7b/115 [OE *hȳr*]
huyred *pp.* employed 7b/121 [OE *hȳrian*]
huyryng *n.* hearing 11/4 [from OE *hȳran*]
hul *n.* hill 3/96; **hulle** *dat.* 3/87, 89; **hulles** *pl.* 3/94 [OE *hyll*]
hule, ule *n.* owl 2/4, 26; **hule** *gen.* 2/28 [OE *ūle*]
humblesse *n.* humility 16b/18 [OF *humblesse*]
hundes *n.* hounds 2/375 [OE *hund*]
hunte *n.* huntsman 3/114 [OE *hunta*]
hupþ *pr. 3 sg.* leaps 2/379 [OE **hyppan*]
hure *v.* hear 11/5 [OE *hȳran*]
hure *adv.* in ~ *and* ~ especially 2/11 [OE *huru*]
hurled *see* **hourlande**
hurne *n.* corner 2/14 [OE *hyrne*]
hus *n.* house, monastery 1/59 [OE *hūs*]
hw- *see also* **wh-**
hwe *see* **howe**
hwitel *n.* blanket 4/55 [OE *hwītel*]
hwucche *adj.* which 4/84 [OE *hwylc*]

i *prep.* in 3/3, 77, 107, 4/57 [from OE *in*]
iafen *see* **ȝive**
ibalded *pp.* emboldened 3/141 [OE *bealdian*]
ibeot *n.* boast 3/118 [OE *gebēot*]
ibere *n.* outcry 2/222 [OE *gebǣru*]
ybete *see* **bete**
ibolwe *pp.* puffed up 2/145 [OE *belgan*, pp. *gebolgen*]
ybore *see* **bere**
iborhen *pp.* saved 4/7 [OE *beorgan*, pp. *geborgen*]
ybounden *pp.* bound 15/268 [OE *bindan*]
ibroide *see* **brayd**
ybroke *pp.* broken 15/282 [OE *brecan*]
ybrouȝt *see* **brohte**
ibrugged *pp.* bridged 3/83 [OE *brycgian*]
ybuld *see* **bylded**
ich *adj.* same 5/63, 455 [OE *ilca*]
ich *pron.* I; **isch** 13d/3; **min(e)** *poss. adj.* my 4/83, 5/205; *pron.* my people 7b/148 [OE *ic*]
ychabbe *see* **habbe**
ychaffared *see* **chaffare**
icham *see* **be(n)**
ichave *see* **habbe**
ich(e) *adj.* each 5/292, 6/94, 103 [OE *ylc*]
ichil, ichulle *see* **wille**

ichot *see* **wit(e)**
iclumben *see* **clumbe**
ycome *see* **comen**
ycore *adj.* & *adv.* (originally pp. of **chese**) excellent 5/148, beautifully 5/105 [OE *cēosan*, pp. *gecoren*]
ycorven *see* **kerve**
ycrouned *see* **crouned**
icume *see* **comen**
idel *adj.* vain 4/2, futile 11/143 [OE *īdel*]
ydo(ne) *see* **do(n)**
ydrawe *see* **draheð**
ieden *see* **ȝede**
yes *see* **ehe**
yfalle *see* **falles**
ifan *n. pl.* foes 3/134 [OE *gefā*]
yfere *adv.* together 5/223 [from OE *gefēra*, 'comrade']
yfostred *pp.* brought up 16a/92 [OE *fōstrian*]
yfounde *see* **fynde**
ifuled *see* **fuleþ**
ygo *see* **go(n)**
igrap *pa. 3 sg.* gripped 3/122, 136; **igripen** *pl.* grasped 3/52 [OE *grīpan*]
iȝe(n) *see* **ehe**
yȝyrned *pp.* desired 13g/34 [OE *giernan*]
ihaten *see* **hoten**
yhere *v.* hear 5/17, 420; **iherd(e)** *pa.* heard 2/3; *pp.* 4/83 [OE *gehēran*]
yhold *see* **hold**
yhote *see* **hoten**
ylaft *see* **leve** *v.*[1]
ilce *see* **ilk(e)**
ilchone *pron.* each one 6/63, 68 [OE *ylc* + *ān*]
ilefde *pa.* believed 2/123 [OE *gelēfan*]
ylent *see* **lent**
ileste *v.* last 2/341; **ilesteþ** *pr. 3 sg.* 2/347 [OE *gelǣstan*]
ylet *see* **lete**
ilich(e) *adj.* like 2/316, 318, 319; unchanging 2/358, 362; *adv.* equally 8/161; *ever* ~ always the same thing 8/369 [OE *gelīc*, *gelīce*]
ilk(e), ilce *adj.*[1] same; *þat* ~ that (same) 9/24 [OE *ilca*]
ilke, ylka *adj.*[2] each; ~ *a* every [from OE *ylc*]
ille *adj.* evil 8/203; *adv.* badly 7b/211 [ON *illr*]
ilome *adv.* frequently 2/49, 290 [OE *gelōme*]
ylore *see* **lese**
ilorned *see* **lerne**
ymad, ymake *see* **makien**
ymarked *pp.* appointed 5/548 [OE *mearcian*]
imeind *see* **meind**
imeteð *pr. 3 sg.* meets 3/77 [OE *gemētan*]
imunde *n.* thought 2/252 [OE *gemynd*]
inmyddes *adv.* in the middle 9/167 [cf. OE *on middan*]
innen *adv.* in *þer* ~ therin 3/22 [OE *innan*]
innogh, inoȝe, ynow(h), ynoh *adj.* enough, many, in plenty; *adv.* very 9/289, 13g/13 [OE *genōg*]
inohreaðe *adv.* soon enough 4/8 [from prec. + OE *hreþe*]
ynome *see* **nym**
ynorissed *pp.* brought up 16a/94 [OF *noriss-*, from *norir*]
insiȝt *n.* in ~ *in* understanding of 2/195 [OE *in* + *sihð*]
into *prep.* up to 6/104 [OE *in tō*]
inwið *adv.* inside 4/68; *prep.* within 10/307, 16b/152 [OE *in* + *wið*]
inwitt *n.* reasoning power 7a/10 [OE *in* + *witt*]
yquited *pp.* paid 7b/107 [OF *quiter*]
yre *n.* anger 15/11 [OF *ire*]
yreke *pp.* covered up 16a/28 [cf. MDu *reken*]
iren *n.* iron band 1/31 [OE *īren*]
irnen *v.* 3/60 (**urneþ** *pr. pl.* 2/375; **arnde** *pa.* 3/57; **ourn** *pa. pl.* 5/85, **urn** 5/89) run, hasten [OE *iernan*]
yronne *see* **renne**
is *see* **be(n)**
isæh *see* **iso(n)**
iscend *see* **schende**
isch *see* **ich**
yse, iseȝ, yseiȝe *see* **iso(n)**
isechen *v.* seek 3/48 [OE *gesēcan*]
yseyd *see* **segge(n)**
isene *adj.* obvious 2/166, evident 2/275, 367, visible 5/354 [OE *gesēne*]
iset, ysett *see* **settez**
ishote *pp.* shot, sent out 2/23 [OE *scēotan*]
isiȝen *pp.* come 3/111 [OE *sīgan*]
iso(n), yse *v.* (**iseȝ** *pa.* 2/29, 108, 109, **isæh** 3/28, 53, 54, **iseh** 3/147, **yseiȝe** 5/328) see [OE *gesēon*]
ysouced *pp.* soused 11/97 [from OF *sous*]
yspent *see* **spende**
ysprad *see* **spradden**
isprunge *pp.* spread 2/300 [OE *springan*]
iswolȝe *see* **swolȝed**
ytauhte *see* **teche**
yþes *n. pl.* waves 8/147, 233 [OE *ȳþ*]
iþoncket *see* **thonketh**
ytynt *see* **tyne**
ytuiȝt *pp.* snatched 5/192 [cf. OE *twiccian*]
yused *see* **usyt**
yvele *adj.* wicked 1/16, 56 [OE *yfel*]
iwar *adj.* aware 2/147 [OE *gewær*]
iweden *n. pl.* gear 3/25 [OE *gewēde*]
ywerd *see* **wered**
iwys(se), iwyis *adv.* indeed [OE *gewis*]
iwivet *pp.* in ~ *o* married 4/85 [OE *wīfian*]
ywon *adj.* accustomed 5/317 [from OE *gewunian*]

ywon *see* **wynne**
iworht, ywrought, ywro(w)ght *see* **wurche(n)**
ywrite *see* **write**

jangelis *pr. 3 sg.* chatters 14/265; **janglande** *pr. p.* grumbling 8/90, 433 [OF *jangler*]
jangler *n.* boaster 15/457 [OF *jangleor*]
janglynge *ppl. adj.* chattering 15/345 [OF *jangler*]
jape *n.* foolishness 8/57, trick 16a/347; *pl.* tricks, false judgements 10/238 [from OF *japer*]
jogelour *n.* entertainer 7b/71; **juglurs** *pl.* clowns 4/12 [OF *joglere, juglere*]
joyned *pp.* appointed 8/62 [OF *joindre*]
jolef, joly(f) *adj.* happy 8/241, fine 16a/77, merry 16a/300 [OF *jolif*]
jolilé *adv.* lustily 9/42 [from prec.]
jowked *pa.* lay asleep 8/182 [OF *jouquier*]
Judeus *n. pl.* Jews 1/75 [Lat *Iudaeus*]
jug(g)e *pr. 1 sg.* decree 15/524, 629; *imp.* judge 8/413; **jugged, -it** *pp.* condemned 8/245, 10/188, decided 10/180 [OF *juger*]
juglurs *see* **jogelour**
justed *pa.* jousted 9/42 [OF *juster*]
justifiet *pa.* administered justice to 10/229 [OF *justifier*]

kaghten *see* **cach(ch)e**
kay *adj.* left 9/422 [ON, cf. Dan *kej*]
kayred *pa.* went 9/43 [ON *keyra*]
kaisere *n.* emperor 3/113 [Lat *Caesar*, OE *cāsere*]
kan *see* **con**
kark *n.* trouble 8/265 [AN *kark*]
karle *n.* man 14/134 [ON *karl*]
katel *n.* wealth 11/55 [AN *catel*]
kaught *see* **cach(ch)e**
kautelles *see* **cautellis**
kealche-cuppe *n.* boozer, toss-pot 4/67 [OE *celc* + *cuppe*]
kecchen *see* **cach(ch)e**
keie *n.* key 12/263 [OE *cǣg*]
kele *v.* cool, be lessened 14/46, 134 [OE *cēlan*]
kende *see* **kynde** *adj.*
kene *adj.* brave 9/482, fierce 2/276, 13p/11, sharp 4/35, 13k/6, wise 10/254; **kennest** *superl.* boldest, bravest 3/95, 113 [OE *cēne*]
kenliche, kenely *adv.* boldly 3/93, extremely 10/63 [OE *cēnlīce*]
kenne *v.* recognize 3/167, understand 8/357 [ON *kenna*]
keorvinde *ppl. adj.* cutting, sharp 4/30, 35 [OE *ceorfan*]
kepe, keep *n.* in *take* ~ *(in)to* pay attention to 6/9, 90, 133 [from next]
kepe *v.* control 6/107; *pr. 2 sg. subj.* protect 7b/26; **kepten** *pa. pl.* took charge of 10/66 [OE *cēpan*]
keping *n.* controlling 6/77, persevering 6/87 [from prec.]
kerke *see* **kyrke**
kerve *v.* cut 7b/65; **carf** *pa.* made 8/131; **corven** *pa. pl.* cut 7b/185, 8/153; **korven, ycorven** *pp.* 15/425, 16b/159 [OE *ceorfan*]
kest(e) *v.* (**kest, caste(n)** *pa. & pp.*) throw, cast; cast (shadow) 8/440, direct (eyes) 9/228, utter 9/64, set 10/83, plan 12/190 [ON *kasta*]
kever *v.* be obtained 8/223; **kevered** *pa.* in ~ *me* got for myself 8/485 [OF *(re)cuvrir*]
keverid *pp.* covered 6/226, **kevered** 15/271 [OF *cuvrir*]
kyd(de) *see* **kyþe**
kimeð *see* **comen**
kyn *see* **kin(ne)**
kynde *n.* nature 6/78, 7b/161, kindred 9/5, 14/62, species 15/174, 15/311 [OE *(ge)cynd*]
kynde *adj.* natural 7b/59, seemly 9/473, **kende** compassionate 13r/19 [OE *(ge)cynde*]
kyndely *adv.* with elegance 9/135, properly 14/133 [from prec.]
kindenes *n. pl.* kindnesses 6/209 [as prec.]
kyne *n. pl.* cattle 7a/18 [OE *cȳ* pl. + *-n*]
kinelond *n.* kingdom 3/163 [OE *cyne-* + *land*]
kinge *n. gen. pl.* of kings 3/53, 66, **kingen** 3/91, 113, 130 [OE *cyning*]
kin(ne), kun *n.* kind 13a/7, family 13j/36, 69, followers 14/20; *alle* ~ all kinds of 7b/58, 69, 200, *eny* ~ any kind of 7b/267; **kynes** *gen.* in *other* ~ of other kind 7a/20; *pl.* kinds 10/63 [OE *cynn*]
kynned *pa.* was born 10/209 [cf. OE *(ge)cennan*]
kynrede *n.* kindred, family connections 16a/113 [OE *cynn* + *rǣden*]
kyrke, kerke *n.* church [ON *kirkja*]
kirtel, kirtill *n.* short coat, tunic 5/229, 14/290; **kirtels** *pl.* gowns 15/235 [OE *cyrtel*]
kysttes *n. pl.* chests 8/159 [ON *kista*]
kyte *n.* kite (large bird) 15/349 [OE *cȳta*]
kyth *n.* country [OE *cȳþ*]
kyþe *v.* show; bring 13j/42; **cuþest** *pr. 2 sg.* 2/90; **cuþ** *pr. 3 sg.* 2/132, 138; **kydde** *pp.* shown 9/263, made known 10/44, acknowledged 10/254, ~ *for* recognized as 10/222; **kyd** *as adj.* famous 9/51 [OE *cȳþan*]
kitte *pa.* cut 16b/119; **kit** *pp.* 16b/196, 197 [OE **cyttan*]
knave *n.* labourer 7b/46; *gen.* 7a/54; *pl.* 7a/62 [OE *cnafa*]

knawen *see* **cnawe**
kneland *pr. p.* kneeling 5/250 [OE *cnēowlian*]
knytte *v.* tie 14/133, **knette** fasten 15/438; **knyt, knette** *pp.* united 15/381, fastened 15/628 [OE *cnyttan*]
knowable *adj.* capable of knowing 6/59 [from OE *cnāwan*]
kn(o)we *see* **cnawe**
knowes *n. pl.* knees 16b/77 [OE *cnēow*]
knowlechinge *n.* recognition 12/16 [from OE *cnāwan*]
koke *v.* put hay into haycocks 7a/13 [ON, cf. Norw *kok* 'heap']
konne(þ) *see* **con**
konnyng, kunnynge *n.* knowledge 11/31, 15/513, skill 15/167, 487, ability 16b/29, 205 [from OE *cunnan*]
korven *see* **kerve**
koude *see* **con**
kun(ne) *see* **con, kin(ne)**

lac *n.* fault 5/460 [cf. MDu *lac*]
lach(che) *v.* (**laȝt, laght** *pa. & pp.*) take; reach 8/322, take on 9/234, pull back 9/156; ~ *out* take away 8/425, ~ *to* pick up 9/433 [OE *læççan*]
lachesse *n.* slackness 7b/253 [AN *lachesse*]
lacke *imp.* criticize 7b/85 [cf. MDu *laken*]
ladde *n.* fellow 7b/194, 14/41 [uncertain]
lad(de) *see* **lede** *v.*
ladliche *adv.* with ill will 4/17 [OE *lāþlīce*]
læc *pa.* in ~ *to* pursued 3/80 [OE *lācan*]
læiden *see* **legge**
læðest *see* **layth**
laft(en), laftes *see* **leve** *v.*[1]
lagh *n.* law; Christian faith 10/34, religion 10/187, 203 [late OE *lagu*, from ON]
laght, laȝt *see* **lach(che)**
laȝe *v.* laugh; **lah(h)eð** *pr. 3 sg.* laughs 4/48, 62; **loh, louȝ, lowe, laȝed** *pa.* laughed 3/159, 5/314, 8/461, smiled 13g/15 [OE *hlæhhan*]
lay(e) *n.* song 5/20, poem 9/30 [OF *lai*]
lay(e) *see* **legge, lien**
layk *n.* folly 8/401; *pl.* games 9/262 [ON *leikr*]
laykyng *n.* performing 9/472 [from ON *leika*]
layne *imp.* lie hidden 10/179 [ON *leyna*]
layt(e) *v.* look for, search; **laitid** *pp.* 10/155 [ON *leita*]
layth *adj.* hateful 8/401; **læðest** *superl.* 3/33 [OE *lāþ*]
lake *n.* lack 15/87 [cf. MDu *lak*]
lange *adv.* long 14/192 [OE *lange*]
lant *see* **lene** *v.*
lapped *pp.* wrapped 9/217 [uncertain]
lare *n.* teaching 4/39 [OE *lār*]
large *adj.* broad 9/210 [OF *large*]
largelich *adv.* generously 5/451 [from prec.]
lasse *adj. as n.* lesser 10/247; **l(e)asse** *adv.* less 4/26, 7b/165 [OE *lǣssa*]
lasseþ *pr. 3 sg.* lessens 12/3 [from prec.]
lasshit *pa.* flashed 10/334 [? imitative]
laste *n.* in *upon* ~ in the end 8/194 [OE *latost*]
lastes *n. pl.* crimes 8/198 [cf. OI *lǫstr*]
lastunge *n.* detraction 4/21 [from ON *lasta*]
lat *see* **lete** *v.*
later *adj.* in ~ *ende* last part 10/136 [OE *lator*]
laude *n.* praise 16b/3, 8 [OF *laude*]
launde *n.* glade 15/302 [AN *launde*]
laus *see* **lose** *adj.*
laused *pa.* uttered 8/489 [from ON *lauss*]
lave *v.* bail 8/154; **lavande** *pr. p.* flowing 10/314 [OE *lafian*, OF *laver*]
laverd *n.* lord 4/15, 60 [OE *hlāford*]
lawe *n.* decree 8/405 [late OE *lagu*, from ON]
le *n.* shelter 8/277 [OE *hlēo*]
leape *pr. 3 sg. subj.* rise 4/90; **leop, le(e)p** *pa.* leapt 3/25, 8/154, 179, 16a/374; **leopen, lepen** *pl.* hurried 10/61; *refl.* in ~ *heom* leapt 3/51 [OE *hlēapan*]
leasse *see* **lasse**
leche *n.* surgeon 13k/24; *pl.* doctors 7b/295 [OE *lǣce*]
lechede *pa.* healed 7b/189 [from prec.]
ledares *n. pl.* controllers 7b/251 [OE *lǣdere*]
lede, lude *n.* man, knight [OE *lēod*]
lede *v.* draw 14/85; **ledeþ** *pr. pl.* in ~ *to* lead against 2/280; **lad(de)** *pa.* led 5/584, 12/68 [OE *lǣdan*]
leele *see* **lele**
leely(che) *see* **lel(l)y**
leest, leste *superl. adj.* smallest 6/39, 14/228; *as n.* least 10/162; *atte* ~ at the least 15/452 [OE *lǣst*]
leet *see* **lete** *v.*
lef *n.* foliage 8/447 [OE *lēaf*]
lef *see* **le(o)f, leve** *v.*[2]
lefsel *n.* shelter of leaves 8/448 [OE *lēafsele*]
lege *adj.* liege 8/51, 10/224 [OF *lege*]
legge, leye *v.* (**leið** *pr. 3 sg.*; **lay(e)** *imp.*; **leyde** *pa.*; **leiden, læiden** *pa. pl.*) lay; set 8/168, put 8/174, impose 1/36, wager 7b/290, 16a/155, pawn, pledge 7b/292; ~ *on* attack 3/34, 68, 16a/375, strike (with hammer) 14/245, ~ *þeron* apply to it 5/30, ~ *to wedde* mortgage 7a/73 [OE *lecgan*]
leȝe *v.* tell lies 13j/56 [OE *lēogan*]
leyser *n.* time to spare 15/464, 487 [OF *leisir*]
leist *pr. 3 sg.* lasts 2/333 [OE *lǣstan*]
lele, leele *adj.* honest, trustworthy 7b/140, 261, 295, serviceable 7a/103 [AN *leel*]
lel(l)y, leely(che) *adv.* faithfully 7b/140, 9/449, trustworthily 7b/298, sincerely 10/268 [from prec.]
leme *n.* beam of light 10/334 [OE *lēoma*]

lemmon, lemman *n.* mistress, beloved [OE *lēof* + *man*]

lene *v.* give (to) 7b/15, 231, 286, grant 8/347, 10/315; **lant** *pp.* granted 10/272 [OE *lǣnan*]

lene *adj.* poor 7b/263 [OE *hlǣne*]

leng *comp. adv.* longer 2/42, 5/84, 10/179, **lenger** 5/330, 16a/18, 383, **lengore** 13j/12 [OE *leng*]

lenge *v.* remain, dwell; **lengyd** *pa.* 10/68 [OE *lengan*]

lenger *comp. adj.* longer 6/37 [OE *lengra*]

lenghe *n.* length 14/76, *on* ~ prostrate, flat out 14/41, 176 [OE *lengu*]

lent, ylent *pp.* come 8/201, 13g/25, gone 13g/11 [OE *lendan*]

lenten *n.* spring 13h/1 [OE *lencten*]

lenþe *n.* in *on* ~ for a long time 9/232 [OE *lengþu*]

leoden *n. gen. pl.* of peoples 3/73 [from OE *lēod*]

le(o)f, lof, l(e)ove, luef, *adj.* dear (to) 2/203, 4/83, 10/34; *me is* ~ my pleasure is 2/281; ~ *liif* dear beloved one 5/102, 406; *as n.* beloved 13j/31, 13k/21; **levest** *superl.* most precious 7a/85 [OE *lēof*]

leop, lep(en) *see* **leape**

lepe *n.* basket 2/359 [OE *lēap*]

lere *n.*[1] cheek 9/318, complexion 10/95 [ON *hlýr*, OE *hlēor*]

lere *n.*[2] flesh 9/418 [OE *līra*]

lere *v.* teach 7b/222, 14/35; *pr. pl.* learn 15/25; **lerde** *pa.* 13d/15 [OE *lǣran*]

lered *ppl. adj.* learned, clerical 1/50, 15/46 [from prec.]

lerne *v.* teach, prescribe 7b/340; **ilorned** *pp.* gained knowledge 2/216 [OE *lēornian*]

les *adj.* untruthful 8/428 [OE *lēas*]

lese *v.* lose 5/178, 6/123; **les** *pa. 3 sg.* 3/71; **ylore** *pp.* 5/209, 545, **lorn(e)** 6/160, 16a/221, **lest** lost from sight 8/88 [OE *lēosan*]

leste *see* **leest, lyst(e)**

lete *n.* appearance 2/35 [OE *gelǣte*]

lete, leete, lette *v.* (**lat, lette** *pr. 3 sg. & imp.*; **let, leet** *pa.*; **ylet** *pp.*) let 7b/119, stop 5/279, prevent 15/151, desist 6/19, abandon 7b/293, cause (to) 12/106; ~ *awai* leave aside 2/177, neglect 2/250, ~ *be(n)* desist from 5/114, leave alone 6/171, ~ *by* esteem 7a/3, ~ *to serven* desist from serving 15/439 [OE *lǣtan*]

lethe *v.* heal 8/3, cease 10/347 [uncertain]

lettes *n. pl.* hindrances 11/57 [from OE *lettan*]

lettyng *n.* delay 7b/5 [as prec.]

leve *v.*[1] abandon 11/107; **laft** *pa.* gave 9/369; **laftes** *pa. 2 sg.* left 10/292; **laften** *pa. pl.* abandoned 8/405, left 10/61; **levyd** *pp.* remained 10/328, **ylaft** left 16a/8 [OE *lǣfan*]

leve *v.*[2] (**leve** *pr. 1 sg.* 7b/99, 298; **lef** *imp. sg.* 7a/24, **leve** 7b/214; **leveth** *imp. pl.* 7a/3) believe; believe to be 10/176, trust 7b/99 [OE *gelēfan*]

leve *v.*[3] *see* **libbe**

levedi *n.* lady [OE *hlǣfdige*]

levest *see* **le(o)f**

lewed(e) *adj.* ignorant 7a/4, 11/72, 76, foolish 11/96, 99, 106, **lewde** vulgar 15/616 [OE *lǣwede*]

lewedlych *adv.* uselessly 11/90, 92 [from prec.]

lewednes *n.* ignorance 11/82, **lewdenesse** incivility 15/520 [from OE *lǣwede*]

libbe, leve *pr. 1 sg.* live 7a/44, 7b/16, 13g/5; **libbeth** *pl.* 7b/70; **levyng** *pr. p.* 6/13 [OE *libban*, *leofian*]

lich *n.* corpse 4/79, 10/146, 314 [OE *līc*]

licnes *n.* likeness 6/55 [OE *gelīcness*]

lien, lye, ligen, ligge *v.* (**lið** *pr. 3 sg.* 3/162, **lyth** 16b/183, **lyeth** 7a/89, **lys** 8/458; **lien** *pl.* 1/65, **ligeð** 3/107; **lygge** *pr. 3 sg. subj.* 7b/160; **lien** *imp.* 3/161; **ligginde** *pr. p.* 3/3, **liggeand** 5/388; **lay** *pa.* 9/37, **lyggid** 10/76) lie; stay 9/37, stay in bed 9/88, lie idle 7b/160, apply 7a/89, be appropriate 12/253, be allocated 1/65 [OE *licgan*]

lyfe *n.* (**live** *dat.*) in *bi his* ~ upon pain of death 3/45, *opon* ~ alive 10/150, *on* ~ alive 8/293, in this life 8/51 [OE *līf*]

lyflode *n.* food, livelihood [OE *līflād*]

lyftes *pr. 3 sg.* builds 9/12; **lyfte** *pa.* lifted 9/369, 433; **lyft** *pp.* raised 9/258 [ON *lyfta*]

ligen, ligg- *see* **lien**

lyght *adj.* easy 15/553; **liȝtest** *superl.* 6/16 [OE *lēoht*]

lyght *see* **lyhte**

lighte *pa.* illuminated 16b/19 [OE *līhtan*]

lyȝt *v.* descend 9/423; **lyȝtis** *pr. 3 sg.* alights 9/329; **liȝt** *imp.* 9/254; **lighten** *pa. pl.* fell 10/322; **lyht** *pp.* 13g/12 [OE *līhtan*]

liȝtly, lightly *adv.* easily 6/160, casually 14/115, probably 8/88, swiftly, quickly 8/179, 288, 9/292, 328, at once 10/334 [OE *lēohtlīce*]

lyhte *adj.* bright 13h/14, **lyght** 15/188 [OE *lēoht*]

likeing, likinge *n.* love 12/28, *of gode* ~ pleasing 5/599 [from next]

liki *v.* please 2/342; **lykes, likeþ** *pr. 3 sg.* pleases; *impers.* it pleases [OE *līcian*]

liklyhede *n.* likelihood, probability 16b/144 [ON *líkligr* + OE *-*hǣdu*]

lyknyng *n.* in *in* ~ *of* by imitating 8/30 [ME *liken*, from *like* adj.]

lylled *pa.* quivered 8/447 [MDu *lillen*]

lymes *n. pl.* limbs 7a/8 [OE *lim*]
lymped *pa.* fell 8/194, happened to 8/265 [OE *limpan*]
lynage *n.* family, relatives 7a/26 [OF *lignage*]
lyndes *n. pl.* loins 9/139 [OE *lendenu*, ON *lendir*]
lire *n.* flesh 10/149 [OE *līra*]
lys *see* **lien**
lyst *n.* desire, longing 6/19 [from next]
lyst(e), lust *pr. impers.* it pleases 8/42, *hym* ~ it may please him 10/162, *him* ~ he desires 2/212, 213, *ne* ~ *me* I have no wish to 2/287, *me* ~ *bet* I would rather 2/39; **lyst(e), leste** *pa.* wished 8/51; *impers.* in *me/þe/hir* ~ I wished to 16a/12, it pleased you/her 12/29, 15/551, she pleased 12/155 [OE *lystan*]
listely *adv.* craftily 6/227 [OE *listelīce*]
lyte *n.* little 15/111, 264, 16a/9 [OE *lȳt*]
lyte *adj.* small 15/64, 350; in ~ *worth* of little value 7b/263 [ON *lȳt*]
lith *n.* bone, joint 14/228 [OE *liþ*]
lyth *see* **lien**
liđ *see* **lien**
liđe(n) *v.* travel 3/4, sail 3/85 [OE *līþan*]
live *see* **lyfe**
lo *interj.* in ~ *what* see what 7b/259 [? from ME *loke*]
lode *n.* in *on* ~ in my care 8/504 [OE *lād*]
lodesmon *n.* steersman 8/179 [OE *lādman*]
lodlich, lodely, loþli(ch) *adj.* hateful 2/32, 71, 91, horrible 5/78, 461, terrible 8/230, 10/328 [OE *lāþlic*]
loef *see* **love**
lof *n.* praise; *of* ~ excellent 8/448 [OE *lof*]
lof *v.* love 8/30, **lovye** 7b/218, 221; **luveden** *pa. pl.* 1/73, **lofden** 9/21 [OE *lufian*]
lof *adj. see* **le(o)f**
lofte *n.* in *on* ~ aloft, above [ON *loft*]
log(g)e *n.* shelter 8/457, 461 [OF *loge*]
loȝe *n.* sea 8/230 [OE *luh* from Gaelic *loch*]
loȝe *adj.* lowly 9/302; **logh** *as n.* in *on* ~ below 10/147; **loghe** *adv.* low 10/334 [ON *lágr*]
loh *see* **laȝe**
loke, lokin *v.* look 4/16, behold 13r/4, watch over 7b/85, 8/504, take care 2/166, 295, 7b/277, 13k/30 [OE *lōcian*]
loken *see* **louked**
lollares *n. pl.* idlers 7b/74, 287 [from MDu *lollen* and *Lollaert*]
loltrande *pr. p.* lounging 8/458 [uncertain]
lome *n.* vessel 8/160, receptacle, tomb 10/68, 149; *pl.* tools 7a/45 [OE *lōma*]
lome *adj.* defective 2/364 [OE *lama*, *loma*]
londe *n.* land, country; **lont** 8/322 [OE *lond*]
long *adj. as n.* in *upon* ~ in the end 10/175 [OE *long*]
longen *pr. pl.* pertain 10/268, 16a/31 [cf. OE *gelang*]
longes *n. pl.* lungs (eaten as offal) 7b/189 [OE *lungen*]
lont *see* **londe**
lording *n.* lord, sir [from OE *hlāford*]
lore, loore *n.* learning 13j/58, knowledge 11/73, teaching 8/350, instruction 11/8, 28, 31, doctrine, way of thinking 12/18, contrivance 10/264 [OE *lār*]
lorelles *n. pl.* wastrels 7b/129 [from OE *-loren*, pp. of *-lēosan*]
lorn(e) *see* **lese**
los *n.* praise 9/258 [OF *los*]
lose *v.* ruin 8/198 [OE *losian*]
lose *adj.* loose 12/262, **laus** 16a/210 [ON *lauss*]
losynger *n.* evildoer 8/170 [OF *losenger*]
lossom *adj.* lovely [OE *lufsum*]
lot(e) *n.*[1] noise 8/161, 9/119; *pl.* 8/183, voices 9/244 [ON *lát*]
lote *n.*[2] casting of lots 8/180 [OE *hlot*]
loþ *adj.* hateful (to) 2/65, 72, 194, reluctant 7b/48 [OE *lāþ*]
loþe *n.* in *withouten* ~ without stint 9/127 [OE *lāþ*]
loþli(ch) *see* **lodlich**
louable *adj.* praiseworthy 7a/103 [OF *louable*]
louȝ *see* **laȝe**
louked *pa.* was fastened 9/217; **loken** *pp.* 9/35, locked 13r/2, enclosed 10/147 [OE *lūcan*]
loused *pa.* uttered 10/178 [from ON *lauss*]
love *n.* loaf 7b/196, **loef** 7b/286 [OE *hlāf*]
love *see* **le(o)f**
love-bene *n.* love-favour 13k/26 [OE *lufu* + *bēne*]
lovelych, lovelokkest *see* **lufly(ch)**
loves *n. pl.* hands 10/349 [? ON *lófi*]
lovesom, -sum *adj.* lovely 5/111, 460 [OE *lufsum*]
lovyd *pp.* glorified, praised 10/288, 324 [OE *lofian*]
lovye *see* **lof**
lovyng *n.* praising 8/237, 10/349 [from OE *lofian*]
lowe *see* **laȝe**
lowede *pa. refl.* in ~ *hym* submitted 7b/194 [from *low* adj., ON *lágr*]
luche *pr. pl.* tip 8/230 [uncertain]
lud *n.* language (of birds) 13g/4 [OE *lǣden*]
lud *adj.* loud 2/6, 4/3; **ludere** *fem. dat. sg.* 3/30, 150; **lude** *adv.* loudly 2/112, 141, 3/93 [OE *hlūd*, *hlūde*]
lude *see* **lede**
luef *see* **le(o)f**
lufly(ch) *adj.* gracious 9/38, beautiful 9/433, **lovelych** lovely 9/419; **lovelokkest** *superl. adj.* loveliest 9/52; **luveliche, luflych** *adv.*

willingly 4/39, amicably 9/254 [OE *luflic, luflīce*]
lugge *imper.* pull 14/137 [? ON]
lur *n.* injury 8/419; *pl.* deprivations 10/328 [OE *lyre*]
lurkkes *pr. 3 sg.* moves cautiously 8/277 [uncertain]
lust *imp.* listen 2/263, 267; **luste** *pa.* listened 2/143, 253 [OE *hlystan*]
lust *see* **lyst(e)**
lust(e) *n.* enjoyment 15/15, desire 15/219 [OE *lust*]
lusti *adj.* vivacious 12/85, vigorous 12/196, 15/130 [from OE *lust*]
lut *pa.* bent 9/418 [OE *lūtan*]
luteþ *pr. 3 sg.* lies low 2/373 [OE *lūtian*]
luther *adj.* wicked, evil 7b/253, 295, 8/198; **luðere** *dat. pl.* 3/32, 68; **luþer** *adv.* badly 8/500 [OE *lȳþre*]
luveden *see* **lof**
luveliche *see* **lufly(ch)**

ma *n.* more 3/169 [OE *mā*]
macers *n. pl.* mace-bearers 10/143 [OF *maissier*]
mach *v.* equal 9/282 [OE *gemæcca*]
macod, maced, mad(e) *see* **makien**
mæi *n.* kinsman 3/2 [OE *mǣg*]
mæste *n.* mast, acorns 3/77 [OE *mæst*]
maghty, maȝti *adj.* powerful 10/27, 143, 283 [from next]
maȝt *n.* power 8/112 [OE *mæht*]
mahen, maht, may *see* **mowe**
may *n.* girl 13g/29, 13k/35 [? OE *mǣg*]
mayn *adj.* great, strong 9/94, 187 [OE *mægen-*, ON *megn*]
maire *n.* mayor 10/65; *pl.* mayors 7b/87 [OF *maire*]
maist, maystow *see* **mowe**
mayster *n.* knight 9/136; **maystres** *pl.* masters 7b/87 [OE *mægester*, OF *maistre*]
mayster-mon *n.* chief official 10/201 [prec. + *man*]
maystrie *n.* compulsion 10/234 [OF *maistrie*]
make *n.* partner, husband 13g/18, 33, 13r/3; *pl.* mates 13h/20 [OE *gemaca*]
makien *v.* (**mas** *pr. 3 sg.*; **macod, makede, maket, makkyd** *pa.*; **maced, makyd, ymake, ymad, mad(e)** *pp.*) make; build 1/13, 10/43, ordain 1/70, compose 11/105, 134, summon 1/6; ~ *in mynde* record 14/50, ~ *opon* throw open 10/128 [OE *macian*]
malais, malese *n.* hardship 5/240, 7b/233 [OF *malaise*]
malicious *adj.* sinful 8/508 [OF *malicius*]
malskred *pp.* bewildered 8/255 [cf. OE *malscrung*, 'enchantment']
malte *v.* melt 10/158 [OE *gemæltan*]
man, me *pron.* one 1/52, 2/142, 340, 3/68, 5/112, 7a/54, anyone 1/39; **men** *pl.* people, they 5/194 [OE *man*]
manace *v.* threaten 8/422 [OF *manacer*]
manas *n.* threat 10/240 [OF *manase*]
mandeþ *pr. 3 sg.* sends forth 13h/16, 25 [OF *mander*]
maner(e) *n.* kind(s) of 11/54, 88, 12/18, custom 9/90; *al* ~ every kind of 5/589; *pl.* respects 8/22, kinds 10/60 [AN *manere*]
manerly *adv.* ceremoniously 10/131 [from prec.]
manifældlice *adj.* of many kinds 1/81 [OE *manig-fealdlīce*]
manken(ne) *n.* mankind 13l/16, 13p/9 [OE *mancyn*]
manred *n.* in ~ *maked* done homage 1/11 [OE *manrǣden*]
mansed *adj.* accursed 8/82 [cf. OE *amansian*]
marbre *n.* marble 10/48 [OF *marbre*]
mare *comp. adj.* greater 1/43, more 4/21; *as n.* more 1/54 [OE *māra*]
marres *pr. pl.* perish 8/172; **marred** *pp.* spoilt 8/474 [OE *merran*]
mas *see* **makien**
mate *adj.* daunted 9/336 [OF *mat*]
matere *n.* subject 15/26; **materes** *pl.* elements 8/503 [OF *matere*]
matyd *pp.* overcome 10/163 [OF *mater*]
maulardes *n. pl.* ducks 5/310 [OF *malart*]
mauth *see* **mowe**
mawe *n.* belly, throat [OE *maga*]
me *see* **man**
meast *superl. adj.* greatest 4/74 [OE *mǣst*]
meaðeleð *pr. 3 sg.* speaks 4/38, pronounces 4/61 [OE *maþelian*]
meche *see* **miche**
mecul *see* **micel**
mede *n.*[1] reward 8/22, bribery 10/234; *pl.* virtues 10/270 [OE *mēd*]
mede *n.*[2] meadow 15/184 [OE *mǣd*]
medill *v.* deal 14/90 [OF *medler*]
meek *v.* in ~ *hym* submit himself meekly 6/157 [from *meek* adj., ON *mjúkr*]
meere *n.* place 10/114 [OE *gemǣre*]
me(e)te *adj.* sufficient 8/420, equal 14/257 [OE *gemǣte*]
me(e)ve *v.* move 15/150, prompt 11/106; **meved** *pa.* 9/90 [AN *mever*]
meind *pp.* mingled 2/131; **imeind** mixed 2/18 [ME *mengen*, OE *mengan*]
meynye *see* **meny**
mekest *superl. adj.* most compassionate 10/250 [ON *mjúkr*]
meled *pa.* spoke 9/447 [OE *mǣlan*]
melle *n.* mill 16a/388 [OE *mylen*]
melly *n.* contest 9/342 [OF *melee*]
mellyd *pp.* mingled 10/350 [OF *meller*]

memorie *n.* commemorative Mass 7b/104 [OF *memorie*]

men *see* **man, mon**

mende *n.* mind 13r/20 [OE *gemynd*]

mende *v.* help 14/159; **mendyd** *pp.* cured 10/298 [AN *mender*]

mendenantes *n. pl.* beggars 7a/76 [OF *mendinant*]

mene *v.*[1] recall 10/151; *imp.* have in mind 6/3; **mente** *pa.* 15/581; **ment** *pp.* in ~ *be* intended for 15/158 [OE *mǣnan*]

mene *v.*[2] (*refl.*) in *me* ~ complain 13j/8; **meneþ** *pr. pl.* complain 13h/22; **menyd** *pa.* lamented 10/247 [OE *mǣnan*]

menege *v.* remember 7b/104 [OE *mynegian*]

meny, meynye *n.* retinue 9/101, followers 10/65 [OF *menie*]

menyng *n.* interpretation 11/150 [from OE *mǣnan*]

menske *n.* courtesy 10/337 [ON *mennska*]

menskefully *adv.* elegantly 10/50 [from prec.]

menskes *pr. 3 sg.* honours 10/269; **menskid** *pa.* 10/258; **mensked** *pp.* adorned 9/153 [as prec.]

menstraci *n.* minstrelsy [OF *menestralsie*]

ment(e) *see* **mene** *v.*[1]

meoster *n.* craft, skill 4/14, 80, occupation 4/26; **mesters** *n. gen.* in ~ *mon* craftsman 10/60 [OF *mester*]

mercyable *adj.* merciful 8/238, 16b/236 [OF *merciable*]

merciles *adj.* obtaining no mercy 10/300 [from OF *merci*]

mere *n.* sea 8/112 [OE *mere*]

meré *see* **miri**

meritorie *adj.* meritorious 10/270 [OF *meritoire*]

merlyon *n.* merlin (small hawk) 15/339 [AN *merilun*]

Mersh *n.* March 13g/1 [AN *marche*]

mershe *n.* marsh 2/304 [OE *mersc*]

mersyen *v.* impose a fine upon 7b/37 [AN *mercier*]

merþes *see* **mirþe**

mervayl *adj.* wonderful 8/81 [OF *merveil*]

mesch(i)ef, methchef, myscheve *n.* misfortune 7b/233, 13l/8, trouble 8/209, 484, 10/240, evil 11/12, injury 14/258; **mischeves** *pl.* evils 6/159 [OF *meschief*]

mese *n.* moss 5/248 [OE *mēos*]

meshe *v.* crush 2/84 [? OE **mǣscan*]

mest *adv.* most(ly) 5/12, 25 [OE *mǣst*]

mesters *see* **meoster**

mesuage *n.* dwelling house 16a/125 [AN *mesuage*]

mesure *n.* restraint 8/295, design 15/305; *over* ~ immeasurably 15/300 [OF *mesure*]

mete *n.* food; mealtime 7b/51 [OE *mete*]

mete *v.* dream 15/108, 115; **mette** *pa.* 15/95 [OE *mǣtan*]

mete *see* **me(e)te**

metely *adv.* fittingly 10/50 [from OE *gemǣte*]

methchef *see* **mesch(i)ef**

metropol *n.* capital 10/26 [OF *metropole*]

meve(d) *see* **me(e)ve**

micel *adj.* great 1/4, much 1/57, 58, **muchele** 3/36, 4/25, 72, **mochel** 12/165, 236, **mecul** 10/27, 286, **mykel** 13j/30, **mukel** large 8/268; **muchel** *as n.* much 13j/58; **mochel, muchel** *adv.* much 13k/31 [OE *micel, mycel*]

miche, meche, much *adj.* much 5/28, 278, 10/206, 220, large 10/81, great 8/70, 9/182 [from prec.]

mid *prep.* with; *adv.* in *oþer* ~ others as well 2/136 [OE *mid*]

middel *n.* waist 13g/16 [OE *middel*]

myddes *n.* middle 9/74 [cf. OE *on middan*]

miȝt *n.* power, faculty 6/45, command 11/150; *pl.* strengths 9/282 [OE *miht*]

myhtes *see* **mowe**

mykel *see* **micel**

milde *adj.* gentle 1/9 [OE *milde*]

mynde *n.* memory 15/69 [OE *gemynd*]

min(e) *see* **ich**

mynyd *pa.* excavated 10/43 [OF *miner*]

mynnyd *pa.* mentioned 10/104 [ON *minna*]

mynnyng *n.* observing 10/269 [from prec.]

minstre *n.* church 1/61, 80 [OE *mynster*]

mint(e) *pa.* intended 1/66, pointed out 10/145 [OE *myntan*]

miri(e), meré *adj.* lovely 5/58, 62, 436, 8/32, elegant 9/153; **myriest** *superl.* 9/142 [OE *myrige*]

mirþe *n.* entertainment 9/45; **merþes** *pl.* joys 9/40 [OE *myrgþ*]

mis *adv.* awry 4/13, wrongly 4/61 [from OE *miss*, 'loss']

misbede *imp.* maltreat 7b/42 [OE *misbēodan*]

myscheve *see* **mesch(i)ef**

mysgo(on) *pp.* gone wrong 16a/364, 398, 401 [OE *mis-* + *gān*]

mislikeþ *pr. pl.* displease 2/344 [OE *mislīcian*]

myspened *pp.* misspent 7a/93 [from OE *mis-* + *spendan*]

misraddest *pa. 2 sg.* advised wrongly 2/160 [OE *misrǣdan*]

missays *n.* hardship 5/262 [OF *messaise*]

mysse *n.* wrong 8/420 [OE *miss*]

misse *v.* fail 15/40, 75; **myste** *pp.* lacked 10/300 [OE *missan*]

myssepayed *pp.* displeased 8/399 [OF *mespaiier*]

mist *see* **mowe**

miswent *pp.* turned in the wrong direction 12/226 [OE *miswendan*]
mith *n.* might 13p/28, 13r/15 [OE *miht*]
mið *prep.* with 4/18 [OE *mid*]
mythe *v.* hide 13j/48 [OE *mīþan*]
mywen *v.* stack 7a/14 [cf. OE *mūwa*]
mo, moo *n.* others 13h/22, 16a/116; *wiþouten* ~ without any other 6/55, 88 [OE *mā*]
mo *adj.* more; *adv.* in *ever* ~ all the time 2/238 [OE *mā*]
mochel *see* **micel**
mod *n.* heart, mind; feeling 2/8 [OE *mōd*]
moder-sunnen *n. pl.* mother-sins 4/84 [OE *mōdor* + *synn*]
mody *adj.* proud 8/422; *as n. pl.* emotional ones 13h/22 [OE *mōdig*]
moght-freten *adj.* moth-eaten 10/86 [OE *moþþe* + *fretan*]
moȝt *see* **mowe**
molde *n.* earth 7b/17, 10/270; *pl.* clods 8/494, 10/343 [OE *molde*]
mollok *n.* rubbish 16a/19 [unknown]
mon *n.* man; **monnen** *gen. pl.* of men 3/95, 125, **men** 7a/29 [OE *mon*]
mon(e) *n.* sorrowing 5/198, complaint 7b/130, 13r/11 [OE **mān*, cf. OE *mǣnan*, 'complain']
mone *v.* utter 13k/39 [ON *muna*, 'remember']
moni *adj.* many [OE *monig*]
moniales *n. pl.* nuns 7a/76 [Lat *monialis*]
monlokest *superl. adj.* noblest 10/250 [OE *mannlic*]
moot *see* **mot(e)**
moote *v.* speak 14/159 [OE *mōtian*]
mor *n.* moor 13c/1, 2, 5 [OE *mōr*]
mordre *n.* murder 16b/178 [OE *morþor*]
mordrer(e) *n.* murderer 15/353, 612 [from prec.]
more *comp. adj. as n.* greater 10/247; *of* ~ in addition 7b/35 [OE *māra*]
morow(e), morwe, mor(o)wen *n.* morning 7b/180, 10/306, 11/155 [OE *morgen*]
mortas *n.* socket 14/220 [OF *mortaise*]
mose *n.* titmouse (small bird) 2/69 [OE *māse*]
mote *n.*[1] city 8/422 [OF *mote*]
mote *n.*[2] speck 8/268, 299; *pl.* spots 10/86 [OE *mot*]
mot(e), moot, motte *pr. sg. & pl.* (**most, muste** *pa.*) must; may 2/52, 9/342, 14/246; *pa.* might 5/233, 330; *impers.* in *us* ~ we must 14/25 [OE *mōt*]
moulyng *n.* mouldering 10/86 [ON **mugla*]
mountes *pr. 3 sg.* amounts 10/160 [OF *monter*]
mowe *v.* be able to 6/107, 110; **may** *pr. 1 sg.* can do 13j/64; **mist** *pr. 2 sg.* might 2/78, **mowe** may 7b/40, **maht** 13j/40, **mauth** 13l/5, 11, 19, **maist** 15/116, **maystow** *2 sg. + pron.* may you 16b/128; **muȝe** *pr. pl.* might 2/62, 182, **mahen** may 4/15, 73, **mowe** 6/143, 11/70, can 7b/224, 343; **mowe** *2 sg. subj.* 7b/233; **moȝt** *pa.* might, was able; **myhtes** *pa. 2 sg.* could 1/39, 13k/22 [OE *mæg* etc.]
mowled *ppl. adj.* gone mouldy 16a/16 [? from ON **mugla*]
much *see* **miche**
muchel(e) *see* **micel**
muckel *n.* dimensions 9/142 [OE *mycelu*]
muȝe *see* **mowe**
muynde *n.* record 11/25, mind 11/74, recall 11/150 [OE *gemynd*]
mukel *see* **micel**
mulne *n.* mill 2/86 [OE *mylen*]
munec *n.* monk 1/72; **munekes** *pl.* monks 1/48, 57 [OE *munuc*]
munster *n.* cathedral 8/268 [OE *mynster*]
munten *n. pl.* hills 3/86 [OF *mount*, OE *munt*]
mur(e)ȝþe, murthe *n.* pleasure 2/341, 355, joy 10/335 [OE *myrgþ*]
murgeþ *pr. pl.* make happy 13h/20 [OE *myrgan*]
murye *adv.* joyfully 15/592 [OE *myrige*]
murily *adv.* merrily 16b/101 [from prec.]
mus *n. pl.* mice 2/87 [OE *mūs*]
muste *see* **mot(e)**
mustir *v.* manifest 14/277 [OF *mustrer*]
muð *n.* mouth 4/13, 13p/7 [OE *mūþ*]

na *adj.* no 1/5, 3/45, 4/6, **nan** 1/11; **nenne** *masc. acc. sg.* 3/28 [OE *nān*]
nabbeþ *pr. pl.* have not 2/252; **nade** *pa.* 5/392, 8/257 [OE *nabban* from *ne* + *habban*]
nadres, neddren *n. pl.* adders 1/24, 4/54 [OE *nǣddre*]
naȝt *n.* night 8/352, 465 [OE *næht*]
naityd *pp.* recited 10/119 [ON *neyta*, 'use']
naked *adj. as n.* naked flesh 9/423 [OE *nacod*]
nakryn *adj.* of drums 9/118 [OF *nacaire*]
nalde *see* **nil**
nam *pr. 1 sg.* am not 5/430, 13j/71; **nis** *pr. 3 sg.* 2/369, 4/50, 13g/26; **nas** *pa. sg.* 5/150, 354, 10/285, **nes** 13j/53; **nare** *pl.* 5/390; **nere** *pa. 3 sg. subj.* 2/22 [OE *nam* etc. from *ne eam* etc.]
nam *see* **nym**
nameliche, namely *adv.* especially 7b/51, 275, 11/73 [from OE *nama*]
nammore, namoore *n.* nothing more 1/38, 16a/44 [OE *nān* + *māra*]
nan, no(o)n *pron.* none 1/41, no-one 10/241, 15/159 [OE *nān*]
nan *see* **na**

nappe *v.* sleep 8/465 [OE *hnappian*]
nare, nas *see* **nam**
narew *adj.* narrow 1/26 [OE *nearu*]
natheles *adv.* nevertheless 12/70, 15/162 [OE *nā þē lǣs*]
nauht(e), nawt *see* **noȝt** *adv.*
nauþer *see* **nother**
ne *adv.* not; *conj.* nor [OE *ne*]
nease *n.* nose 4/78 [? cf. MDu *nese*]
neddren *see* **nadres**
nede *n.* business 15/384, 559 [OE *nēd*]
nedelyngis *adv.* necessarily, absolutely 14/15 [OE *nēadlunga*]
nede(s) *adv.* necessarily 5/468, 8/44, 45 [from OE *nēd*]
neȝed, nyhed *pa.* approached 7b/322, 8/352, 9/132; ~ *to* approached 8/465 [from next]
neh, neiȝe, nyȝ *adv.* nearly 3/123, 5/199, 11/124 [OE *nēah*]
neiȝhonde *adv.* nearly 6/40 [from prec. + OE *hond*]
neyh, nyh, neigh *prep.* near 7b/297, 322, 12/168 [OE *nēah*]
neltu *see* **nil**
nemely *adv.* nimbly, quickly 14/120, 219 [from OE *nǣmel*]
nempned *pa.* named 5/600 [OE *nemnan*]
nenne *see* **na**
ne(o)deþ, nedis *pr. 3 sg.* is necessary (for); **neded** *pa.* 16a/166, 307 [OE *nēodian*]
neodful(e) *adj.* necessary; *as n.* needy 4/55 [from OE *nēod*]
neppes *n. pl.* cups 4/59 [OE *hnæp*]
ner *adj. comp.* nearer 13k/13; **nexte** *superl.* nearest 16b/172 [OE *nērra*]
ner(e) *adv.*[1] nearly 7b/175, 8/169; **ner(r)e** *comp.* more closely 8/85, *never the* ~ no nearer success 15/619 [OE *nēr*]
nere *adv.*[2] never 7a/40 [OE *nǣfre*]
nere, nes *see* **nam**
nevenes *pr. 3 sg.* names 9/10; **nevenyd** *pp.* 10/195 [ON *nefna*]
neves *n. pl.* nephews 1/8 [OE *nefa*]
new(e) *adv.* newly, anew 5/593, 10/6, 14, 37 [OE *nēowe*]
nexte *see* **ner**
nycetë(e) *n.* foolishness 15/572, 16a/192 [OF *nicetë*]
nyȝ *see* **neh**
nyght *v.* become night 15/209 [from OE *niht*]
niȝtes *n. gen.* by night 2/238 [OE *niht*]
niȝtingale *n. pl.* nightingales 2/203 [OE *nihtegala*]
nyh *see* **neyh**
nyhed *see* **neȝed**
nil *pr. 1 sg.* will not 5/211, **nulle** 13k/20; **neltu** *pr. 2 sg. + pron.* will you not 2/150; **nil** *3 sg.* 5/332; **nold(e)** *pa.* would not 2/159, 5/280, did not want 15/90, **nalde** 4/55 [OE *nyllan, ne + willan*]
nym *imp.* (**nom, nam** *pa.*; **namen, nome** *pa. pl.*; **ynome, nomen, nummen** *pp.*) take; seize, capture 1/7, 16, 8/76, 95, 360, adopt 9/91 [OE *niman*]
nys, nyce *adj.* foolish [OF *nice*]
nis *see* **nam**
nist *pa.* knew not 5/288, 494, **nyste** 15/152, 16a/371, 446 [OE *nyste, ne + wyste*]
nith *n.* night 13q/15 [OE *niht*]
nivelin *v.* snivel 4/24 [uncertain]
no *adv.* not 5/333, 424; *as n.* denial 5/50; *conj.* nor 5/150, 354 [OE *nā*]
nobelay *n.* nobleness 9/91 [OF *nobleie*]
node *n. pl.* in *gode* ~ brave deeds 2/388 [OE *nēod*]
noght *adj.* to no avail 10/101 [OE *nōwiht*]
noȝt *n.* nothing; **nohte** *dat.* 3/118 [as prec.]
noȝt, nouȝt, nauht(e), nawt *adv.* not (at all); *ryhte* ~ not at all 7a/82 [as prec.]
noy *n.* suffering 10/289 [from OF *anoi*]
noiþer *see* **noþer**
nok *n.* corner 8/278 [uncertain]
nold(e) *see* **nil**
nome *n.* name [OE *nama, noma*]
nom(en) *see* **nym**
non *adv.* not at all 10/157 [OE *nān*]
non *see* **nan**
none *n.* noon 14/15; *pl.* noon mealtimes 7b/146 [OE *nōn*, Lat *nona*]
nones *adv.* in *for þe* ~ for the purpose 10/38, indeed 5/53, now 14/219 [ME **for þan anes*]
none-tide *n.* midday 5/497 [OE *nōntīd*]
noon *see* **nan**
nortelrye *n.* good breeding 16a/113 [jocular formation on OF *norture*]
notable *adj.* well-known, notorious 16b/233 [OF *notable*]
note *n.*[1] business 2/330, 9/358, 420, construction 10/38, fuss 10/101 [OE *notu*]
note *n.*[2] tune 5/602, 16b/69 [OF *note*]
noþeles *adv.* nonetheless 2/149, 374 [OE *nā þē lǣs*]
noþer, noiþer *pron.* neither; *adj.* in *no* ~ no other 5/230 [OE *nāhwæþer*]
nother, nouther, nowther, nauþer, nothyre, noþir *adv. & conj.* neither, nor [as prec.]
noþerward *adv.* downwards 2/144 [from OE *neoþor*]
noþing *adv.* not at all 5/31, 12/156, 15/158 [OE *nān þing*]
nouche *n.* brooch 12/22 [OF *nuche*]
nouȝt *see* **noȝt**
nourne *v.* state 10/101; **nournet** *pp.* in ~ *me*

after addressed me in the name of 10/195 [cf. Sw *norna*, 'whisper']
noust *adv.* not 13e/3, **nout** 13j/53, **nouth** 13q/13 [OE *nōwiht*]
nouþe *adv.* just now 5/466, 7b/299 [OE *nū þā*]
nowiderwardes *adv.* in no direction 1/32 [from OE *nōhwider*]
nulle *see* **nil**
nummen *see* **nym**
nw(e) *adj.* new 9/105, 118 [OE *nīwe*]

o *see* **on**, *adj. & num.*, *prep.*
obeissant *adj.* obedient 12/104 [OF *obeissant*]
oc *see* **ac**
oen *see* **on**, *pron.*
of *adv.* off 3/158, 15/132, 16b/213; *prep.* from 1/67 [OE *of*]
ofdred *pp.* afraid 4/90 [OE *ofdrǣdan*]
office *n.* service 12/12, duty 15/236 [OF *office*]
ofte *adv.* often [OE *oft*]
oftoned *pp.* annoyed 2/254 [OE *of* + *tēonian*]
oghne *adj.* own; **owe** 2/100, **oʒe** 2/118, **ahne** 4/71, **owhen** 5/163, **owen** 9/408, **aune** 9/10; **ahʒere** *dat. fem.* 3/163; **auen** *pron.* 9/293 [OE *āgen*]
oʒain *adv.* back 5/162; *prep.* towards 5/497 [OE *ongēan*]
oʒt *see* **o(u)ʒt**
ohte *adj.* brave 3/51 [from OE *ōwiht*]
olofte *adv.* above 15/683 [ON *á lopti*]
on *adj. & num.* one 8/40, 9/30, 206, 314, 11/17, **o** 2/333, 6/63, 69, 11/152, **oo** 6/91, **an** 1/64, 4/60, 69 [OE *ān*]
on*á lopti*]
on *adj. & num.* one 8/40, 9/30, 206, 314, 11/17, **o** 2/333, 6/63, 69, 11/152, **oo** 6/91, **an** 1/64, 4/60, 69 [OE *ān*]
on *pron.* one (person) 2/117, 12/20, 85, 116, **oen** 7a/10, **ænne** 3/71 [as prec.]
on, o *prep.* in 1/41, 56, 3/21, on 3/142, 4/17, 40 [OE *on*]
one *adj. & adv.* alone 6/55, 7a/52, 8/216, **ane** 3/99 [OE *ān*]
on(e) *see* **a**
ones *adv.* once 14/221 [OE *ǣnes*]
one-under *adv.* underneath 10/70 [OE *on* + *under*]
onfon *v.* begin 3/42 [OE *onfōn*]
onhit *pp.* taken hold of 8/411 [from OE *hittan*]
only(ch) *adj.* single 6/44, only 11/60 [OE *ānlīc*]
onlicnes *n.* likeness, image 3/23 [OE *onlīcnes*]
onoh *n.* enough 1/29 [OE *genōg*]
onswarez *pr. 3 sg.* answers 9/386 [OE *andswarian*]
ontfule *adj. as n. pl.* envious people 4/14 [from OE *anda*]
oo *adv.* all the time 13h/7 [OE *ā*]
oo *see* **on** *adj. & num.*
opan *prep.* upon 5/506 [OE *up* + *on*]
ope *adj.* open 2/168 [from OE *open*]
opelond *adv.* in the country 7a/44 [OE *uppe* + *lond*]
openlice *adv.* openly 1/54 [OE *openlīce*]
or *adv.* in ~ . . . ~ either . . . or 12/22, 216 [OE *oþþe*]
or *conj.* before 14/146, 215, 256 [OE *ǣr*]
ord *n.* point 4/29 [OE *ord*]
ordainy *pr. 1 sg.* appoint 5/205; **ordande** *pp.* prepared 14/243 [AN *ordeiner*]
ordenaunce *n.* decree 15/390 [OF *ordenance*]
order *n.* in *by* ~ in turn 15/400 [OF *ordre*]
ordinel *adj.* ordered, regular 6/95 [Lat *ordinalis*, OF *ordenel*]
ore *n.* mercy 13k/12 [OE *ār*]
orhel *n.* pride 4/3 [OE *orgel*]
oryʒt *adv.* fittingly 9/40 [OE *on riht*]
orisoun *n.* prayer 8/328 [OF *orison*]
orl *n.* leader 3/56 [OE *eorl*]
orlogge *n.* clock 15/350 [OF *orloge*]
orped *adj.* doughty, valiant 12/192 [OE *orped*]
ossed *pa.* showed 8/213 [uncertain]
ost *n.* army 5/290 [OF (*h*)*ost*]
ostel *n.* dwelling place 9/253 [OF (*h*)*ostel*]
other, ouþir, ouþer, auþer *adv. & conj.* either 6/197, or 1/22, 5/350, 8/2, 11/55, 65(1); ~ . . . *or* either . . . or 6/150, 9/88; ~ . . . *oþer* 2/328, 8/52, 10/86 [OE *oþþe*]
oðer *pron. & adj.* the other 4/34, 13k/20; **oþre** *pl.* 4/31, 12/54, 66 [OE *ōþer*]
oþerwhile *adv.* at other times 5/289, 297, 12/117, from time to time 7a/50 [OE *ōþerhwīle*]
oþerwyse *adv.* in a different way 11/64 [OE *on ōþre wīsan*]
oþre *see* **oðer**
ou *see* **ʒe**
ought *adv.* at all 14/252 [from next]
o(u)ʒt, auht *n.* anything, anything whatever 6/5, 202, 7b/235, 9/300; ~ *worþ* worth anything 11/88 [OE *āwiht*, *āht*]
ouhte *see* **awith**
oure *n.* hour 6/47 [AN *ure*]
ourn *see* **irnen**
ous *see* **we** *pron.*
oute *adv.* openly 12/157, 232 [OE *ūte*]
outetake *pr. 1 sg.* except 6/190 [OE *ūt* + ON *taka*]
ouþer *see* **other**
outrageouse *adj.* excessive 15/336 [OF *outrageus*]

outtrage *adj.* extraordinary 9/29 [OF *outrage*]
over *prep.* in ~ *al(le)* everywhere 15/172, 284 [OE *ofer*]
overdede *n.* excess 2/352 [OE *ofer-* + *dǣd*]
overdrofe *pa.* passed 10/117 [OE *oferdrīfan*]
overloked *pa.* surveyed from above 9/223 [OE *ofer-* + *lōcian*]
overquatie *v.* in *þe* ~ glut yourself 2/353 [OE *ofer-* + OF *quatir*]
oversez, oversey *pa.* looked over 2/30, oversaw, supervised 7b/120 [OE *oferséon*]
oversithon *adv.* too often 1/44 [OE *ofer* + *sīþum*]
overtan *pp.* overtaken 8/127 [OE *ofer-* + ON *taka*]
overvareþ *pr. pl.* overrun 2/387 [OE *oferfaran*]
overwalt *pp.* overturned 9/314 [OE *ofer-* + *wæltan*]
ovireshake *pp.* shaken off 15/681 [OE *ofer-* + *scacan*]
oway, owy *adv.* away [OE *onweg, aweg*]
owe *interj.* expressing surprise 14/127, 140 [uncertain]
owe, ow(h)en *see* **oghne**

pay *n.* in *to (my)* ~ pleasingly 15/271, 474 [OF *paie*]
pay *v.* please 7b/332; **paid** *pp.* satisfied 12/51 [OF *payer*]
payne *n.* bread 7b/285 [OF *pain*]
paynym *n.* pagan 10/203, 285 [OF *painime*]
palfray *n.* lady's horse 5/156 [OF *palefrei*]
palmeres *n. pl.* full-time pilgrims 7b/63 [AN *palmer*]
panade *n.* cutlass 16a/75, 106 [cf. OF *penarde*]
pane *n.* fur edging 9/154 [OF *pane*]
panne *n.* top of skull, brain-pan 12/74 [OE *panne*]
pape *n.* pope 1/63 [OE *pāpa*, Lat *papa*]
papenjay *n.* parrot 15/359 [OF *papingai*]
parage *n.* high rank 10/203 [OF *parage*]
parayle *v.* dress 7b/56 [from OF *apareil*]
paraunter, paraventure *adv.* perhaps [OF *par aventure*]
parcener *n.* sharer 6/120 [AN *parcener*]
pardé *interj.* certainly 15/509, 571 [OF *par Dieu, par Dé*]
parfay *interj.* truly 5/315, 339 [AN *par fay*]
parfyte *adj.* perfect 15/568 [OF *parfit*]
parfitely *adv.* perfectly 6/139 [from prec.]
parfourned *pp.* manifested 16b/4, 6; **parfournest** *pr. 2 sg.* 16b/155 [OF *parfournir*]
parte *v.* in ~ *with* share in 7b/144; *imp.* share 7b/285 [OF *partir*]
partie *n.* division, unit 6/39, part 6/131, 225 [OF *partie*]
passeth *pr. 3 sg.* surpasses 15/300; **passe** *pl.* proceed 9/378; **passyd** *pp.* surpassed 10/163 [OF *passer*]
patris *pr. 3 sg.* prattles 14/266 [from Lat *pater(noster)*]
patro(u)nes *n. pl.* patrons of ecclesiastical livings 7a/78, lords 9/6 [OF *patron*]
pavement *n.* paved floor 16b/225 [OF *pavement*]
peaðereð *pr. 3 sg.* stirs 4/46 [unknown]
peert *adj.* pushy 16a/96 [OF *apert*]
peyneth *pr. 3 sg. refl.* takes pains 15/339; **peyne** *subj. sg.* in *hym* ~ strive 15/662 [OF *pener*]
pelers *n. pl.* columns 15/230 [OF *piler*]
pelure *n.* fur 9/154 [OF *pelure*]
pented *pa.* belonged 9/204 [from OF *apendre*]
perceth *pr. 3 sg.* pierces 15/331 [OF *percer*]
pere *n.* equal 14/222 [OF *per*]
person *n.* parson 16a/89, 123 [OF *persone*]
pes *n.* pea 7b/166; **peses** *pl.* 7b/306 [OE *pise* sg.]
pese *n.* peace 8/423 [AN *pes*]
pese-coddes *n. pl.* pea-pods 7b/316 [OE *pise* + *cod*]
peté *n.* pity 8/327 [OF *pité*]
phalmes *n. pl.* psalms 7a/47 [OE *psalm*, Lat *psalmus*]
philisophres *n. pl.* scientists 6/38 [AN *philosofre*]
piche *v.* pitch (hay) 7a/13, cut 7b/64; **picchit** *pp.* set 10/79 [uncertain]
pie, py *n.* magpie 2/126, 14/266, 16a/96 [OF *pie*]
pykares *n. pl.* pilferers 7a/17 [from next]
pike *imp.* gather 6/126, crop 8/393; **pykede** *pa.* hoed 7b/118 [uncertain]
pykstaff *n.* pilgrim's staff 7b/64 [ON *píkstafr*]
piled *ppl. adj.* stripped of hair, bald 16a/81, 452 [from OE *pilian*]
pinchid *pa.* squeezed 10/70 [AN **pinchier*]
pyne *n.* torment 4/25, 6/75, 10/188, anguish 8/412, 14/260, penance 8/423, pain 13l/4; **pines, pinen** *pl.* torments 1/34, 4/35, 8/91 [OE **pīn*]
pynez *pr. pl.* confine 8/79 [? from OE *gepyndan*]
pinin *v.* torture 4/82; **pined(en)** *pa. pl.* afflicted with (torture) 1/18, 76; **pined** *pp.* tortured 1/20, 77, 14/52 [OE *pinian*]
pining *n. pl.* tortures 1/19, 76 [from prec.]
pynnes *n. pl.* pegs 7b/199 [OE *pinn*]
pysan *n.* neck-armour 9/204 [OF *pizane*]
pitosly *adv.* piteously 8/371 [from AN *pitous*]
play *see* **pleie(n)**

plaidi *v.* plead the case 2/184 [OF *plaidier*]
plaiding *n.* legal dispute 2/12 [from prec.]
playferes *n. pl.* playfellows 8/45 [OE *plega* + *(ge)fēra*]
plain *adj.* flat 5/353, **pleyn** smooth 15/180, open 15/528 [OF *plain*]
playne, pleyn *v.* lament 15/179; ~ *hym* complain 7b/166; **playnez** *pr. 3 sg.* in ~ *on* complains about 8/376; **pleynede** *pa.* 7b/156, lamented 8/371 [OF *plaindre*]
planed *pp.* levelled off 10/50 [OF *planer*]
planted *pa.* established 8/111 [OE *plantian*, OF *planter*]
plat *adv.* flat 16b/223 [OF *plat*]
plate *n.* plate-armour 9/204 [OF *plate*]
pleie(n), play *v.* fool around 2/213, 16a/104, play 4/32, relax 5/66; **pleieð** *pr. 3 sg.* performs 4/29; **pleyde** *pa.* joked 16a/4 [OE *plegian*, *plægian*]
pleyn *adj.* full 15/126 [OF *plain*]
pleyn *see* **plain, playne**
pleynede *see* **playne**
plesaunce *n.* pleasure, desire 15/218, 389, 636, 676 [OF *plaisance*]
plyande *pr. p.* swaying 8/439 [OF *plier*]
plyȝt, plite *n.* hostility 9/266, covenant 10/285 [OE *pliht*]
plyȝtles *adj.* blameless 10/296 [from prec.]
plyhte *pr. 1 sg.* pledge; ~ *my treuthe* plight my troth 7b/33 [OE *plihtan*]
plyt *n.* state 8/114, manner 12/181, **plite** circumstances 15/294 [OF *plit*]
plite *see* **plyȝt**
plonged *pp.* plunged 11/81 [OF *plongier*]
poynt *n.* respect 11/136, *fro* ~ *to* ~ in every respect 15/461 [OF *point*]
poke *n.* sack 16a/424 [OE *pohha*, OF *poque*]
polettes *n. pl.* pullets, chickens 7b/303 [OF *poulet*]
policed *pp.* polished 12/145 [OF *polir*]
pontificals *n. pl.* bishop's robes 10/130 [Lat *pontificalis*]
popper *n.* dagger 16a/77 [from ME *poppen*, 'strike']
pore *see* **pover**
porte *n.* bearing 15/262 [OF *port*]
porvay *v.* acquire 8/36 [AN *porveier*]
potage *n.* soup or stew 7b/182, 285 [OF *potage*]
potte *pa.* put 7b/197, 203; **pot** *pp.* 11/168 [OE *potian*]
pouþer *n.* powder 11/82 [OF *poudre*]
pouþred *pp.* pulverized 11/96 [from prec.]
pover *adj.* poor 5/486; **pore** *as n.* poor people 7b/283 [OF *povre*]
poverlich *adj.* like a poor man 5/236, 567 [from prec.]
powlez *n. pl.* deeps 8/310 [OE *pōl*]
prayng *n.* request 11/114 [from OF *preier*]
preye *v.* pray, beg 16b/73, 81 [OF *preier*]
prelacie *n.* body of prelates 10/107 [AN *prelacie*]
preostes *n.* request 11/114 [from OF *preier*]
preye *v.* pray, beg 16b/73, 81 [OF *preier*]
prelacie *n.* body of prelates 10/107 [AN *prelacie*]
preostes *see* **prost**
present *adv.* here and now 15/423 [OF *present*]
prest *adj.* prompt 8/303, ready 15/307 [OF *prest*]
prestly *adv.* promptly 7b/102, 10/130 [from prec.]
preue *adj.* steadfast 8/525, valiant 9/262 [OF *preu*]
preve *n.* proof 15/497 [OF *preve*]
preven *v.* prove 15/534; **preve** *imp.* show 8/288 [AN *prever*]
prevy *see* **privee**
prik *pr. 1 sg.* urge on 15/389 [OE *prician*]
prime *n.* in *hey* ~ 9 a.m. 7b/119 [OE *prīm*, Lat *prima* (*hora*)]
primerole *n.* primrose 13c/10, 11, 14 [cf. OF *primerose*]
pris, priis *n.* reputation 12/3, 251, praise as victor 12/127; *of* ~ excellent 5/51, 64, 249 [OF *pris*]
prises *n. pl.* levers 10/70 [OF *prise*]
privee, prevy *adj.* secret 16b/116, private 15/260 [OF *privé*]
prively *adv.* secretly, privately 16a/203, 16b/92 [from prec.]
processe *n.* in *in* ~ in course of time 15/430 [OF *proces*]
proferi *v.* in ~ *forþ* offer 5/434; **proferes** *pr. 3 sg. refl.* presents (herself) 8/41; **profrede** *pa.* offered 7b/150, 318 [OF *proffrir*]
prophecy *n.* prophetic books of Old Testament 11/128, 130 [OF *profecie*, Lat *prophetia*]
prost *n.* priest 2/322; **preostes** *gen.* priest's 1/47 [OE *prēost*]
prouesse *n.* prowess 12/162 [OF *proesce*]
proverbis *n. pl.* sayings 7b/264 [OF *proverbe*]
provid *ppl. adj.* experienced 6/158 [OF *prover*]
providens *n.* governing power 10/161 [OF *providence*]
provinces *n. pl.* nations 9/6 [OF *province*]
prud(e) *adj.* proud 4/7, 78, 13p/11; *as n. pl.* 4/1 [OE *prūd*, from OF *prud*]
pruyde *n.* pride 7b/349 [OE *prȳde*]
psalmyde *adj.* in ~ *writtes* psalm writings, Psalter 10/277 [from OE *psalm*, Lat *psalmus*]
puison *n.* poison 12/247 [OF *puison*]

pur *prep.* in ~ *charité* for charity's sake 7b/169, 266 [AN *pur*]
pure, puyre *adj.* pure 7b/124, refined, courtly 9/262 [OF *pur*]
pured *pp.* trimmed 9/154 [OF *purer*]
purper *adj.* dark coloured 5/242 [Lat *purpura*]
put *n.* pit 4/82 [OE *pytt*]

qu- *see also* **wh-**
quarterne *n.* prison 1/24 [OE *cweartern*]
quaþ *see* **quod**
qued *n.* injury 8/4 [OE *cwēad*, 'filth']
queynte *adj.* fanciful 6/145, **quaynt** intricate 10/133, **quoynt** gracious 8/417 [OF *queinte*]
quelles *pr. 3 sg.* alleviates 8/4; **quelled** *pa.* killed 8/228 [OE *cwellan*]
queme *v.* please 2/209 [OE *cwēman*]
queme *adj.* pleasing 10/133 [OE *(ge)cwēme*]
quere *see* **quoer**
questis *n. pl.* singing 10/133 [OF *queste*]
queþen *adv.* whence 9/461 [ON *hvaðan*]
quik *adj.* lively 9/177; *as n.* the living 11/175 [OE *cwic*]
quikken *pr. 3 sg. subj.* develop 8/471 [from prec.]
quile *n.* time 9/30, 257, while 10/105 [OE *hwīl*]
quit-clayme *pr. 1 sg.* give up claim to 9/293 [OF *quiteclamer*]
quyte *v.* repay 15/112, get even with 16a/10, 62; **quyteth** *pr. 3 sg.* in ~ *her hire* rewards 15/9; **quyt** *pp.* 16a/470 [OF *quiter*]
quyte *adj.* free 15/663 [OF *quite*]
quod, quoþ, quaþ *pa.* said 2/117, 5/226, 7a/26, 89, 102, 8/85 [OE *cweþan*]
quoer, quere *n.* choir 7a/60, 10/133 [OF *quer*]
quoynt *see* **queynte**
quontyse *n.* marvel 10/74 [OF *cointise*]
qw- *see* **wh-**

rachenteges *n. pl.* chains 1/29 [OE *racentēah*]
rad *adj.* afraid 9/251 [ON *hræddr*]
rad, radde(st) *see* **redon**
radly *adv.* quickly, promptly [OE *hrædlīce*]
ræie *adj.* bold 3/58 [OE *hrēoh*]
ræse *n.* assault 3/129 [OE *rǣs*]
ræveden *see* **reve**
ræveres *n. pl.* robbers 1/50 [OE *rēafere*]
rage *n.* passion 12/222 [OF *rage*]
rage *v.* romp, flirt 16a/104 [OF *rager*]
raght, raȝt *see* **reche**
rayke *v.* go [ON *reika*]
rayleþ *pr. 3 sg.* displays 13h/13; **rayled** *pp.* set 9/163 [OF *reillier*]
raysoun *see* **reso(u)n**
rak *n.* cloud 8/176; **rakkes** *pl.* 8/139 [cf. ON *rek(i)*]
rakel *adj.* hasty 8/526 [uncertain]
ramel *n.* muck 8/279 [OF *ramaille*]
rape *pr. pl. refl.* hurry 7b/125; *imp. refl.* 7a/102 [ON *hrapa*]
rather *comp. adv.* sooner 7b/125 [OE *hraþor*]
rattes *n. pl.* tatters 10/260 [uncertain]
rauþe *n.* mercy, pity [from OE *hrēow*]
rave *pr. 3 sg. subj.* act wildly 14/248 [AN *raver*]
ravyne *n.* rapaciousness, greed 15/336; *fowles of* ~ birds of prey 15/323 [OF *ravine*]
ravysedest *pa. 2 sg.* in ~ *doun* drew down (by force) 16b/17 [OF *raviss-*, from *ravir*]
real *adj.* royal 15/415 [OF *real*]
reame *see* **reume**
rebel *adj.* disobedient 15/457 [OF *rebelle*]
reche *v.* hand over 9/66; **reches** *pr. 3 sg.* hangs 9/183; **raȝt, raght** *pa.* reached 9/432, granted 10/256, 280, 338 [OE *rǣcan*]
rec(c)he *pr. 1 sg.* care 2/58, 60; **roghte** *pa.* in ~ *of* cared for 15/111 [OE *reccan*]
rechles *n.* incense 4/77 [OE *rēcels*]
rechles *adj.* carefree 9/40 [OE *recceléas*]
recoverede *pp.* won 15/688 [AN *recoverer*]
recoverer *n.* relief 8/279 [AN *recoverer*]
redde(n), rede *see* **redon**
rede *n.* counsel, course of action 2/307, advice 15/586, 608 [OE *rǣd*]
red(e)les *adj.* baffled 10/164; *as n.* foolish ones 8/502 [from prec.]
redy *adj.* in ~ *of* wise in 10/245 [from OE *rǣde*]
redily *adv.* fully 9/392 [from prec.]
redon *v.* read 7a/69; **rede** *pr. 1 sg.* advise 7a/102, 7b/283, 14/282, 293; **redis** *3 sg.* speaks 14/24; **rad(de)** *pa.* ordered 8/406, read 15/21, advised 15/579; **raddest** *2 sg.* advised 2/159; **redden** *pl.* 9/363; **redde** *pp.* spoken 9/443 [OE *rǣdan*]
reed *adj.* red 16a/296; *as n.* 16a/100 [OE *rēad*]
refete, refetyd *pp.* fed 8/20, 10/304 [AN *refeter*]
refourme *imp.* repeat 9/378; **reformyng** *pr. p.* restoring 6/58; **refo(u)rmid** *pp.* restored 6/48, 76 [OF *refo(u)rmer*]
refused *pp.* excluded 7a/78 [OF *refuser*]
regni *v.* reign 5/425 [OF *reignier*]
rehersen *v.* give an account of 15/488; **rehersed** *pp.* repeated 9/392 [OF *rehercer*]
reken *adj.* upright 10/245; **rekenest** *superl. adj. as n.* noblest 10/135 [OE *recen*]
rekenly *adv.* fittingly 9/251 [from prec.]
rekneþ *pr. 3 sg.* enumerates 11/26 [OE *gerecenian*]
reled *pa.* rolled 9/304 [from OE *hrēol* n.]
relees *n.* discharge 7b/99 [OF *reles*]
remen *pr. pl.* cry 8/502 [OE *hrēman*]

remenant *n.* remainder 15/271 [OF *remenant*]

remewit *pa.* departed 10/235 [OF *remuer*]

ren *n.* run 16a/225 [from ON *renna*]

renaide *adj.* renegade from the faith, apostate 10/11 [as next]

renayed *pp.* refused to go to 8/344 [OF *renaier*]

renden *v.* tear 8/526 [OE *rendan*]

renk(e), rynk *n.* man, knight, sir [OE *rinc*, ON *rekkr*, earlier **renkr*]

renne *v.* run 8/52, 15/247, 16a/36; **rennes** *pr. 3 sg.* is current 9/310; **ronnen** *pa. pl.* ran 10/62; **yronne** *pp.* 16a/39, 236 [ON *renna*, OE *rinnan*]

renomed *pp.* in ~ *of* famed for 12/255 [OF *renomer*]

renouns *n. pl.* great reputations 5/202 [OF *renoun*]

rental *n.* rent-roll 7b/99 [AN *rental*]

rentes *n. pl.* incomes 7a/73 [OF *rente*]

repairen *pr. pl.* go 10/135 [OF *repairer*]

repe *v.* reap 7a/15 [OE *reopan*]

replicacion *n.* argument in reply 15/536 [OF *replicacion*]

rered *pp.* stirred up 9/353 [OE *rǣran*]

reso(u)n, raysoun *n.* reason 8/191, statement 9/392, argument 11/81, 83, 96, 15/534; *speke* ~ speak 9/227; *pl.* words 9/443, 10/52 [OF *resoun*, *raisoun*]

rest *n.* in *at his* ~ firmly in its place 15/376 [OE *ræst*]

restorment *n.* recompense 10/280 [OF *restorement*]

reume, reame *n.* realm; **ryalmes** *pl.* 9/310 [OF *realme*, *reaume*]

reve *v.* take away 8/487; *pr. 3 sg. subj.* take from 13g/33, deprive 16a/157; **reveth** *pr. 3 sg.* 15/86; **ræveden** *pa. pl.* plundered 1/38, 47 [OE *rēafian*]

reveyd *pp.* driven 5/82 [AN *riveier*]

revel *n.* revelling 9/40, 313 [OF *revel*]

reverenced *pa.* bowed to 9/251 [from OF *reverence*]

reverye *n.* wildness 16a/151 [OF *reverie*]

revestid *pp.* robed 10/139 [OF *revestir*]

rewe, rwe *v.* regret 5/570, have pity 8/176, 502, make sorry 14/69; **reweþ** *pr. 3 sg.* grieves 13k/14; **rewe** *imp.* have pity 13j/26, 63 [OE *hrēowan*]

rew(e)ful *adj.* sorrowful 5/114, miserable 15/613 [from OE *hrēow*]

riall *adj.* royal 10/77 [AN *rial*]

ryalmes *see* **reume**

rybauder *n.* teller of ribald stories 7b/75 [from OF *ribauder*]

ribaudy *n.* ribaldry 5/9, 16a/12 [OF *ribauderie*]

riche *n.* kingdom 2/357, 361, 3/35 [OE *rīce*]

ric(h)e *adj.* noble, powerful, splendid; *as n.* noble people 9/66; *adv.* splendidly 5/362, 9/159 [OE *rīce*, OF *riche*]

ryd *v.* free 9/364 [OE *ryddan*]

ridend *pr. p.* riding 1/49; **ryden** *pp.* ridden 7a/74 [OE *rīdan*]

rigge *n.* back 5/500, 8/379 [OE *hrycg*, ON *hryggr*]

ryghtful(l) *adj.* just, upright 15/55, 390, by right 15/639 [OE *rihtful*]

riȝt *n.* what is right 2/229, justice 8/323; *pl.* in *to* (*his*) ~ fittingly 5/136, 292 [OE *riht*]

riȝt, ri(g)ht, riþt *adv.* rightly 4/71, 13j/33, duly 8/326, exactly 8/344, upright 14/164, just 15/272, very 15/644; *ful* ~, *wel* ~ straight away 5/85, 191, 270 [OE *rihte*]

riȝte *adj.* very 2/276 [OE *riht*]

ryȝtwys *adj.* just 8/490, 10/245 [OE *rihtwīs*]

ryhtfulnesse *n.* justice 7a/32 [from OE *rihtful*]

rikeneres *n. pl.* calculators 4/47 [from next]

rikenin *v.* calculate 4/47 [OE *gerecenian*]

rinde *n.* bark 5/260 [OE *rind*]

ryngand *pr. p.* ringing, clamorous 10/62 [OE *hringan*]

rynk *see* **renk(e)**

rise *n.* branch [OE *hrīs*]

rist *pr. 3 sg.* rises 16a/339, 395 [OE *rīsan*]

riþt *see* **riȝt** *adv.*

ryve *v.* break off 14/248 [ON *rífa*]

rivere *n.* river bank 5/308, 15/184 [OF *rivere*]

roche *n.* rock 5/347, 349 [OF *roche*]

rode *n.*[1] rood, cross; ~ *tre* cross 13p/25 [OE *rōd*]

rode *n.*[2] red colour 13h/13, (ruddy) complexion 5/107, 10/91 [OE *rudu*]

rode *n.*[3] road 8/270 [OE *rād*]

roghlych *adj.* stern 8/64 [from OE *rūh*]

roghte *see* **rec(c)he**

roȝ(e), rowe *adj.* rough; *as n.* turbulence 8/144 [OE *rūh*]

roynyshe *adj.* mysterious 10/52 [uncertain]

ronge *pa.* rang 15/492 [OE *hringan*]

ronk(e) *adj.* rebellious 8/490, 10/11, fresh 10/91; *as n.* determination 8/298 [OE *ranc*]

ronkly *adv.* arrogantly 8/431 [from prec.]

ronnen *see* **renne**

roo *n.* roe-deer 15/195 [OE *rā*]

rorde, rurd *n.* voice, utterance 2/311, 8/64, noise 8/396 [OE *reord*]

rote *n.* root 5/256, 260 [OE *rōt*]

rotede *pp.* decayed 4/79 [OE *rotian*]

rottok *n.* decayed matter 10/344 [from prec.?]

roun *n.*[1] in *on* ~ around 8/147 [AN *runt*]

roun *n.*[2] song 13g/38, 13h/2 [OE *rūn*]

roun *v.* murmur 9/362; **rowned** *pa.* 8/64 [OE *rūnian*]

rouncé *n.* horse 9/303 [OF *rounci*]
rous *n.* talk 9/310 [ON *hrós*]
rousty *adj.* foul 7b/75 [OE *rūstig*]
rout *n.*[1] company 5/283, crowd 10/62 [OF *route*]
rout *n.*[2] jerk 9/457 [cf. OE *hrūtan*]
routes *pr. 3 sg.* snores 8/186; **routeth** 16a/313 [OE *hrūtan*]
routhe *n.* pity 10/240, 15/427 [from OE *hrēow*]
routyng, rowtyng *n.* snoring 16a/312, 360 [from OE *hrūtan*]
rowe *see* **roȝ(e)**
rowm *adj.* big, spacious 16a/272; *comp.* 16a/291 [OE *rūm*]
rowned *see* **roun**
ruch(ch)ed *pa. refl.* in *hym* ~ turned 9/303, prepared himself 9/367 [OE **ryccan*]
ruddok *n.* robin 15/349 [OE *rudduc*]
rudnyng *n.* red glare 8/139 [from OE *rudian*]
rugge *v.* pull 14/131 [ON *rugga*]
rukelin *v.* heap 4/45; **rukeleð** *pr. 3 sg.* 4/52 [from next]
ruken *n. pl.* piles 4/45 [? ON *hrúka*]
rungen *pa. pl.* rang 9/195 [OE *hringan*]
runisch *adj.* fierce 9/457 [uncertain]
runyschly *adv.* roughly 8/191, fiercely 9/304, 432 [from prec.]
rurd *see* **rorde**
rwe *see* **rewe**

sacryd *pp.* consecrated 10/3, 159 [OF *sacrer*]
sadde *adj.* grave 10/324, serious, real 15/578 [OE *sæd*]
sæ *n.* sea 1/1 [OE *sǣ*]
sæden, sægen, sæin *see* **segge(n)**
saf *prep.* except 8/182; *conj.* in ~ *þat* except that 9/394 [AN *sa(u)f*]
saȝes *see* **sawe**
saȝtled *pa.* became calm 8/232 [OE *sahtlian*]
say *see* **seo**
saym *n.* grease 8/275 [OF *saim*]
saynte *adj.* holy 13b/5 [OF *saint*]
sayntuaré *n.* shrine 10/66 [OF *saintuarie*]
sake *n.* wickedness 8/172 [OE *sacu*]
sale *n.* hall [OE *sæl*, OF *sale*]
sal(th), saltu *see* **schal**
salue *v.* salute, greet 16b/81 [OF *saluer*]
same(n) *adv.* together 9/50, 363 [OE *ætsamne*]
samnes *imp. pl. refl.* assemble 8/385 [OE *samnian*]
sare *adv.* sorely 14/69 [OE *sāre*]
sari *adj.* sorry, grieved 3/2 [OE *sārig*]
satte *see* **sitt**
satteled *pa.* descended 8/409 [? OE **sætlan*]
saunteryng *n.* babbling 14/70, 150 [obscure]
sauter *n.* Psalter [OF *sauter*]
save *v.* preserve 15/461 [OF *sauver*]
save *adj.* saved 8/334 [OF *sauf*]
savyng *prep. and conj.* except 6/21, 16a/117 [from OF *sauver*]
savoured *pa.* smelt 8/275 [OF *savourer*]
savours *n. pl.* scents 15/274 [OF *savour*]
sawe *n.* speech 10/184; **saȝes, sawes** *pl.* commands 8/67, stories 14/274 [OE *sagu*]
saweð *pr. 3 sg.* disseminates 4/89 [OE *sāwan*]
sawle *n.* soul 4/59 [OE *sāwol*]
scærp *adj.* sharp 1/27, 31 [OE *scearp*]
scaft *see* **schafte**
scal *see* **schal**
scale *n.* bowl 4/60 [ON *skál*]
scalen *n. pl.* fish-scales 3/109 [OF *escale*]
scape *v.* escape 16a/233 [from AN *ascaper*]
schadde *pa.* shed 10/182 [OE *sceādan*]
schaef *n.* sheaf 7b/350 [OE *scēaf*]
schafte, scaft *n.* shaft, spear 3/59, 9/205 [OE *scæft*]
schaȝe *n.* thicket 8/452 [OE *sceaga*]
schal *pr. 1 sg.* (**schalt** *2 sg.*, **salt** 13l/10, **salth** 13l/20; **schaltu** *2 sg.* + *pron.*, **saltu** 13l/21; **sc(h)al** *3 sg.*, **sal** 13l/12; **scullen, schul(en), schulle, scholen** *pl.*; **scolde, sholde, sc(h)ulde** *pa.*; **sc(h)uldest, schust** *pa. 2 sg.*) shall, should, would; must 3/68, 5/226, 6/1; *pa.* might 3/27, had to 7a/42 [OE *sceal, scolde*]
schalk *n.* man, knight [OE *scealc*]
schamie *imp. refl.* in ~ *þe* you should be ashamed 2/161 [OE *scamian*]
schankes, schonkes, sconken *n. pl.* legs 3/13, 9/431, *under* ~ on his feet 9/160 [OE *scanca*]
s(c)hap, shape *v.* (**schaped, s(c)hope** *pa.*; **shapen** *pp.*) make 10/88, fashion 7a/18, plan 12/200, 229, decree 8/247, bring about 15/502; *refl.* prepare oneself 6/25, 10/129 [from OE *scieppan*]
scharpe *adv.* shrilly 2/141 [OE *scearpe*]
schawin, schawe, schewe *v.* display 4/3, tell 9/27, be seen 9/420; **shewen** *pr. pl.* show 16b/7; **schawde** *pa.* displayed 4/78; **schewed** *pp.* offered 9/315 [OE *scēawian, sceāwian*]
schede *v.* distinguish 2/197 [OE *scēadan*]
s(c)hende *v.* reproach 2/274, ruin 15/494; **shente** *pa.* put to shame 15/255; **iscend, schent** *pp.* put to shame 3/36, 13p/27, destroyed 8/476, 14/191; **schended** *ppl. adj.* damaged 8/246 [OE *scendan*]
s(c)hene *adj.* beautiful 13j/2, bright 15/299; *as n.* bright sun 8/440 [OE *scēne*]
scheome *see* **s(c)home**
schere *n.* expression 9/334 [OF *chere*]
schere *v.* cut 9/213 [OE *sceran*]
schet *pp.* enclosed 8/452 [OE *scyttan*]

schewe(d) *see* **schawin**
schild(e) *v.* shelter 2/62, shield 8/440; *pr. 1 sg.* 2/57; *imp.* hide 2/163 [OE *scildan*]
schille *v.* ring out 5/272 [OE *scellan*]
schille *adj.* shrill 2/142; *adv.* loudly 5/104, 526, **shille** clearly 13j/66 [OE *scill*]
schyre *adj.* bright 8/476, fair 9/317 [OE *scīr*]
schitworde *n. pl.* foul language 2/286 [OE **scite* + *word*]
scholen *see* **schal**
s(c)home, scome, scheome *n.* shame 2/167, 3/36, 4/73, shameful thing 2/363 [OE *scomu*]
schomely *adv.* shamefully 8/128 [from prec.]
schonkes *see* **schankes**
schope *see* **s(c)hap**
schoter *n.* archer 6/199 [from OE *scēotan*]
schowved *see* **schwve**
schrewes *see* **shrewe**
schrichest *pr. 2 sg.* screech 2/223 [imitative]
schruden *v.* clothe 4/55 [from OE *scrūd*]
schulde(st), schulen, schulle *see* **schal**
schulen *v.* squint 4/13; **schuleð** *pr. pl.* 4/18 [cf. OE *bescȳlan*]
schunien *v.* avoid 4/87; **schuniet** *pr. 3 sg.* 2/229 [OE *scunian*]
schust *see* **schal**
schwve *v.* thrust 9/205; **schowved** *pa.* pushed 8/246, **shoofe** 15/154 [OE *scūfan*]
sckete *adv.* at once 8/195 [ON *skjótt*]
sclavain *n.* cloak 5/343 [AN *esclavine*]
scolde *see* **schal**
scome *see* **s(c)home**
sconken *see* **schankes**
scornynge *ppl. adj.* mocking 15/346 [from OF *escarnir*]
scort *adj.* short 1/26 [OE *sceort*]
screwen *see* **shrewe**
sculde, scullen *see* **schal**
scurtes *n. pl.* saddle-skirts 9/171 [ON *skyrta*]
se *adv.* so 4/88 [OE *swā*]
seche *v.* seek, look for; find 10/41; **south, so(u)ghte** *pp.* sought 13q/14, driven 14/103, driven in nails 14/148, examined 14/263 [OE *sēcan*]
sede *see* **segge(n)**
see *see* **seo**
seele *see* **sele**
seere, seerly *see* **ser(e), serelych**
seese *see* **sese**
seet *see* **seo, sitt**
sege *n.* throne 8/93, bishop's throne 10/35, siege 9/1 [OF *sege*]
segge *n.*[1] man, knight [OE *secg*]
segge *n.*[2] sedge 2/18 [OE *secg*]
segge(n), sægen, sæin, seyn(e) *v.* (**seie** *pr. 1 sg.*; **seist** *2 sg.*; **seið** *3 sg.*, **seyt** 5/556; **segget** *pl.* 2/98; **segge** *2 sg. subj.* 2/60; **segget** *imp. pl.* 2/113; **seiing** *pr. p.* 6/100; **sede** *pa.* 2/33; **sæden** *pa. pl.* 1/54; **yseyd** *pp.*) say, speak, tell, recite; ~ *of* speak about 2/309 [OE *secgan*]
seȝ(e), seiȝe, seigh, seyn *see* **seo**
seyntwarie *n.* sanctuary 7a/79 [AN *sanctuarie*]
seist *see* **segge(n)**
seiþen *adv.* afterwards 13l/21 [OE *siþþan*]
seke *see* **syke**
seker *adj.* sure 9/265 [OE *sicor*]
sekirly *adv.* in truth 6/185 [from prec.]
sekke *n.* sack-cloth 8/382 [OE *sæcc*]
seld *n.* shield 13n/2 [OE *sceld*]
sele, seele *n.* happiness 8/242, 296, felicity 10/279 [OE *sǣl*]
selere *comp. adj.* better 3/28 [OE *sēlra*]
sely *adj.* wretched, poor 16a/42, 236, 246 [OE *gesǣlig*]
selly *n.* wonder [OE *sellic* adj.]
selve, self *adj.* same 5/341, 15/96, actual 6/189 [OE *self(a)*]
sembla(u)nt *n.* expression, faces 4/25, sign 9/468 [OF *sembla(u)nt*]
sembled *pp.* assembled 8/177 [OF *sembler*]
seme *v.* arbitrate between 2/187 [OE *sēman*]
sem(e)ly *adj.* proper 6/203, lovely 5/411, 13h/26; **semlokest** *superl. as n.* 13g/6; **semely** *adv.* fittingly 10/35 [ON *sœmiligr*]
sen *conj.* since 14/7, 79, 89 [OE *siþþan*]
sen *see* **seo**
senatours *n. pl.* statesmen 7b/87 [OF *senateur*, Lat *senator*]
sende *pa.* sent 12/27, 34, sent a message 10/111; **sendez** *pa. 2 sg.* 8/415; **send(e)** *pp.* 10/8, 12 [OE *sendan*]
sendel *n.* fine silk 7b/10 [OF *cendal*]
sene *n.* eyesight 2/240, 368 [OE *sēon*]
sene *ppl. adj.* visible 13j/4 [from OE *sēon*]
senne *n.* sin 13l/15, 13r/8; *pl.* 13n/8 [OE *synn*]
senous *see* **synnous**
sentence *n.* teaching 15/35, meaning 15/126, decision 15/383, 530, subject matter 16b/111 [OF *sentence*]
seo, sene *v.* (**so** *pr. 1 sg.* 2/34; **suþ** *3 sg.* 2/246, **seþ** 5/251, **seet** 13p/17; **see** *imp.*; **s(e)iȝe** *pa.* 5/147, 355, 9/200, **seȝ** 8/116, **sih** 12/136, **say** 7b/281, 16b/53, **seigh** 16a/5, 238, **saugh** 16a/204; **seȝe** *pa. subj.* 13j/54; **sen** *pp.* 9/239, **seyn** 16b/140, 221) see; take care 14/264 [OE *sēon*]
seoc *see* **syke**
seolcuðe *adj.* rare, wonderful 3/111 [OE *seld-cūþ*]
seove(n) *num.* seven 3/88, 4/84, 86 [OE *seofon*]

ser(e), seere *adj.* individual, various 9/124, 11/5, 14/224 [ON *sér*]
serelych, seerly *adv.* individually 6/68, 103, 8/193 [from prec.]
serewe *n.* sorrow 13j/13 [OE *sorh*]
serjauntes *n. pl.* officers 8/385 [OF *serjant*]
sertayn *adv.* indeed 9/174 [OF *certain*]
sertes *adv.* assuredly 7a/22 [OF *certes*]
servyd *pp.* deserved 10/275 [from OF *deservir*]
servin *v.* in ~ *of* perform 4/12; **servið** *pr. pl.* 4/14, 85 [OF *servir*]
servise *n.* food at table 9/130 [OF *servise*]
sese, seese *v.* cease 6/74, 14/138; **sesez** *imp. pl.* stop 8/391; **sesed** *pa.* ceased 8/369; *pp.* ended 9/1, 134 [OF *cesser*]
sese *pr. 3 sg. subj.* seize 15/481 [OF *seisir*]
sete *n.* throne 8/24, place at table 9/72 [ON *sæti*]
sete(n) *see* **sitt**
seþ *see* **seo**
seþþen, sethe(n) *adv.* afterwards 5/162, 7b/62, 281 [OE *siþþan*]
seþþen, seþthe, seth *conj.* since 5/121, 469, 7a/40, 11/1; ~ *þat* since 5/425 [as prec.]
settez *pr. 3 sg.* establishes 9/14; **sett(e)** *pa.* in ~ *a crie on* entreated 5/511, ~ *at a leef/pes* thought nothing of 7a/97, 7b/166; **sett(e), (i)set, ysette** *pp.* arranged 3/9, determined 8/487, seated 12/123, made firm 14/233, placed 15/149; ~ *in asent* agreed 8/177, ~ *of* established by 10/24 [OE *settan*]
sewes *n. pl.* broths 9/124 [OE *sēaw*]
sewid *pa.* followed 10/204 [AN *suer*]
sextene *n.* sacristan 10/66 [OF *secrestein*]
sexti *num.* sixty 5/90 [OE *siextig*]
sh- *see also* **sch-**
sharpe *adj.* painful 15/2 [OE *scearp*]
sheete *v.* shoot, use a bow 16a/74 [OE *scēotan*]
sherewe *see* **shrewe**
shewen *see* **schawin**
sholde *see* **schal**
shon *n. pl.* shoes 7a/18 [OE *scō*]
shoofe *see* **schwve**
shoon *pa.* shone 16a/444 [OE *scīnan*]
shope *see* **s(c)hap**
shrewe *n.* scoundrel 7b/151, **sherewe** 16a/53; **schrewes, screwen** *pl.* 2/287, 8/77 [? OE *scrēawa*, 'shrew-mouse']
sidbordez *n. pl.* side tables 9/115 [OE *sīd* + *bord*]
syfle *pr. 3 sg. subj.* blow 8/470 [OF *siffler*]
siȝe, sih *see* **seo**
siȝt *n.* in *in* ~ to see 9/28 [OE *-siht*]
sih *see* **seo**
syk *n.* sigh, sighing [cf. next]
sike *v.* sigh [OE *sīcan*]
syke, seoc *adj.* sick, ill 3/2, 7b/147, 271; **seke** *as n.* sick an 15/104 [OE *sēoc*]
siker *v.* assure 9/394 [from next]
siker *adj.* certain 5/27, trusty 9/111, 115; **sykerost** *superl.* most certain 7a/39 [OE *sicor*]
sikerliche, sikerlik, sikerly *adv.* certainly, truly [from prec.]
syn *conj.* since 8/35, 9/24 [OE *siþþan*]
synne *adv.* afterwards 8/229 [as prec.]
synnous, senous *n. pl.* sinews 14/103, 132, 147 [OE *sinewe, seonewe*]
syre *n.* lord 7b/281, father 16a/392 [OF *sire*]
syt *n.* evil 8/517 [ON **sýt*]
siþe *n.* time 2/293, 325; **syþe** *pl.* times 13j/46 [OE *sīþ*]
siðen *v.* go 3/85 [OE *sīþian*]
syth(en) *adv.* afterwards, then, since [OE *siþþan*]
syth(en) *conj.* after, since, because; ~ *þat* since 16b/196 [as prec.]
sitt *pr. 3 sg.* (**sittende** *pr. p.* 1/40; **satte, sete, seet** *pa. sg.*; **sete(n), seet** *pl.*; **sete** *pp.*) sit, be seated; remain 1/40, weigh on 14/207 [OE *sittan*]
syttynge *ppl. adj.* suitable 15/551 [from prec.]
skelton *pr. pl.* hasten 10/278 [? ON]
skile *n.* reason 6/174; **skylles** *pl.* 15/537 [ON *skil*]
skylfol *adj.* intelligible 11/144; **skilfulle** *as n.* righteous 10/278 [from prec.]
skilfully *adv.* sensibly 15/634 [from prec.]
skirmi *v.* in ~ *wið* toss 4/33; **skirmeð** *pr. 3 sg.* tosses 4/31, ~ *mid* tosses 4/28 [AN *eskirmir*]
skleatteð *pr. pl.* flap 4/18 [uncertain]
slaȝtes *n. pl.* buffets 8/192 [OE *slæht*]
slayre *n.* veil 7b/5 [? MLG *sleyer*]
slaked *pa.* grew quiet 9/244 [OE *slacian*]
slawe *see* **slowe**
sleigh *adj.* sly 16a/86 [ON *slǿgr*]
sleihte, sleighte *n.* skill 12/142, cunning scheme 12/193, trickery 16a/157, subtleties 16a/196; **slyȝtes** *pl.* devices 8/130 [ON *slægð*]
sleke *v.* abate 13p/21; **slekkyd** *pa.* relieved 10/331 [cf. ON *sløkkva*]
slent *n.* splash 10/331 [ON *sletta* v.]
slep(e) *pa.* slept 1/54, 5/75, 134 [OE *slǣpan*]
sleuthe *n.* sloth 7b/245, 253 [OE *slǣwþ*]
slydez *pr. 3 sg.* slips 8/200, 466, **slyd** slips away 15/3 [OE *slīdan*]
slyȝtes *see* **sleihte**
slypped *pp.* in ~ *upon slepe* fallen asleep 9/244 [MLG *slippen*]
slo *v.* slay, kill 5/332, **slee** 15/217; **slou(ȝ), slo(w)h** *pa.* 5/313, 12/45, 71, 13q/7, struck

3/154; **sloȝen** *pl.* slew 3/32 [OE *slēan*, ON *slá*]
sloberande *pr. p.* dribbling 8/186 [cf. MDu *slubberen*]
slode *pa.* fell 10/331 [OE *slīdan*]
sloumbe-slep *n.* deep slumber 8/466 [OE *sluma* + *slēp*]
slowe *adj.* slothful 7b/244; **slawe** *as n.* slothful man 4/36; **sloghe** *adv.* drowsily 8/466 [OE *slāw*]
sluchched *ppl. adj.* soiled 8/341 [uncertain]
smærte, smerte *adj.* painful 3/127, 13l/10 [OE *smeart*]
smal(e) *adj.* slender, thin; *adv.* into little pieces 5/538 [OE *smæl*]
smartly *adv.* promptly 9/407 [from OE *smeart*]
smat, smo(o)t *pa. sg.* smote, struck 3/62, 136, 138; ~ *to* struck at 3/75, ~ *of* struck off 12/73; **smiten** *pl.* 3/127; *pp.* 9/407 [OE *smītan*]
smoþely *adv.* deftly 9/407 [from OE *smōþ*]
snelly *adv.* quickly 14/118 [OE *snellīce*]
so *adv. & conj.* so, as; as if 2/77, 97, 142, so well that 5/31; ~ *as* just as 12/126, *al* ~ just as 13j/43, ~ *may be* perhaps 7b/41 [OE *swā*]
so *see* **seo**
soberly *adv.* solemnly 8/334 [from OF *sobre*]
soche *adj.* such 6/167 [OE *swylc*]
socour *n.* aid 16b/82 [OF *socours*]
soffraunce *n.* patience 8/417 [AN *suffraunce*]
soffre *imp.* allow, accept, agree to 7b/82, 89 [OE *soffrir*]
softe *adj.* quiet 12/166 [OE *softe*]
soghe *imp.* spread 8/67 [OE *sāwan*]
soghte *see* **seche**
sojournd *pa.* lived 5/47 [AN *sojurner*]
sok *n.* sucking 8/391 [OE *soc*]
sokored *pp.* aided 8/261 [OF *socorre*]
solace *n.* fun 7b/22, comfort 8/487 [OF *solas*]
solas *v.* delight 5/383, **solace** amuse 15/297 [from prec.]
soleyne *adj.* single 15/607, 614 [AN *solein*]
somedel *see* **sumdel**
somwhat *n.* something 16a/349 [OE *sum* + *hwæt*]
sonde *n.* beach 8/341, sand 15/243 [OE *sand*, *sond*]
sondre *see* **so(u)ndre**
sondri *adj.* various 12/132, 15/258 [OE *syndrig*]
sone *adv.* quickly, at once; **sonnest** *superl.* soonest 6/18 [OE *sōna*]
song(en) *pa.* sang 2/26, 7b/122 [OE *singan*]
sooth *see* **soþ(e)**
sor(e) *n.* misery 5/263, 560, 8/507, pain 13g/35 [as next]
sore *adj.* painful 13j/60, 15/13; *adv.* painfully, terribly 8/140, 13k/14, grievously 12/17,
soore heavily 14/207, intensely 15/6, vigorously 16a/375 [OE *sār*, *sāre*]
sorfeet *n.* surfeit, excess 7b/276 [OF *sorfait*]
sorful *adj.* sorrowful 13p/3 [OE *sorhful*]
sorȝe *n.* sorrow; filth 8/275 [OE *sorh*]
sortes *n. pl.* lots 8/193 [OF *sort*]
soþ *adj.* true [OE *sōþ*]
soþ(e), sooth *n.* truth; *for* ~ in truth, truly [OE *sōþ*]
sothely *adv.* truly 15/581 [OE *sōþlīce*]
soþþe *adv.* afterwards 2/324 [OE *seoþþan*]
sotlice *adv.* foolishly 1/4 [from next]
sottes *n. pl.* fools 2/297 [OE *sott*, OF *sot*]
souded *pp.* in ~ *to* enlisted in the service of 16b/127 [OF *souder*]
soughte *see* **seche**
souȝed, swey *pa.* roared 8/140, sounded 8/429 [OE *swōgan*]
soukynge *see* **sowke**
soun, sowne *n.* sound 5/436, voice 8/429, utterance 10/324, 341 [AN *soun*]
sounde *n.* health 10/92 [OE *-sund*]
so(u)ndre *n.* in *in* ~ in pieces 14/190, 194 [phrase from OE *onsundran*]
soupe(n) *v.* eat 7b/228, 16a/292; *pr. pl.* 10/336 [OF *souper*]
sourquydrye *n.* pride 9/311 [OF *surcuiderie*]
soutares *n. pl.* shoemakers 7a/72 [OE *sūtere*, Lat *sutor*]
south *see* **seche**
soverayne *adj.* highest 15/254 [OF *soverein*]
soveraynely *adv.* most of all 14/55 [from prec.]
sovereynes *n. pl.* superiors 7b/82 [as prec.]
sowe *v.* do needlework 7b/10 [OE *siowan*]
sowke *v.* suck 16a/303; **soukynge** *pr. p.* 16b/6 [OE *sūcan*]
sowl *n.* relish eaten with bread 7b/285 [OE *sufel*]
spac *adv.* in *also* ~ quickly 5/343 [ON *spakr*]
space *n.* place 8/365, time 10/312, 14/124, 15/53 [OF *(e)space*]
spæren *n. pl.* spears 3/110 [OE *spere*]
spak(e) *see* **speke**
spakest *superl. adj. as n.* wisest 8/169 [ON *spakr*]
spakly *adv.* at once 8/338, frequently 10/312 [as prec.]
spale *n.* rest 2/258 [OE *spala*]
sparcle *n.* spark 6/136; **sparkles** *pl.* burning bits 16a/31 [cf. OE *spærca*]
spare *v.* cease 15/699 [OE *sparian*]
speche *n.* language 11/3, 4, 5 [OE *spēc*]
special *n.* in *in* ~ particularly 12/52 [OF *especial*, Lat *specialis*]
spede *v.* prosper 12/256; **spedez** *pr. 2 sg.* 9/410; **speddestu** *pa. 2 sg.* + *pron.* did you succeed 2/169; **spede** *impers.* in *may the* ~ it

may prosper for you 7b/42, *ille ~ þame* may it go badly for them 14/71; *refl.* in *me ~* make haste 15/385 [OE *spēdan*]
spe(e)de *n.* success 10/132; *goode ~* quickly 14/29 [OE *spēd*]
speedly, spedely *adv.* swiftly 6/135, profitably 14/124 [OE *spēdlīce*]
speke *pa.* spoke 5/324, **spak(e)** 15/134, 16b/188 [OE *sprecan*]
spelle *n.* mere talk 2/264, sayings 2/294 [OE *spell*]
spelunke *n.* tomb 10/217 [Lat *spelunca*]
spende *pr. 1 sg.* utter 9/410; **(y)spent, spende** *pp.* finished, dead 5/199, 215, employed 14/124 [OE *spendan*]
spene *v.* spend 7a/28, 69, practise 2/165; **spenþ** *pr. 3 sg.* spends, gives of itself 2/362 [? from prec.]
sperhauke *n.* sparrow-hawk 15/338, 569 [OE *spearhafoc*]
speten *v.* spit 2/39; **sput** *pr. 3 sg. subj.* 8/338 [OE *spǣtan, spittan*]
spice *n.* herb 15/206 [OF *espice*]
spire *n.* reeds 2/18 [OE *spīr*]
spiten *n. pl.* fin-spines 3/110 [OE *spitu*]
spradde(n) *pa.* spread 7b/184, 8/365; **ysprad** *pp.* 16b/2 [OE *sprǣdan*]
spray *n.* twig 13g/2 [uncertain]
spreynd *pp.* sprinkled 16b/188 [OE *sprengan*]
spurie *v.* spur 3/122 [from OE *spura*]
spuse *n.* spouse 13r/1 [OF *spus*]
sput *see* **speten**
sputeden *pa. pl.* dug 7b/184 [OE *spittan*]
squerel *n. collective* squirrels 15/196 [AN *esquirel*]
sse *pron.* she 13a/5, 6, 13d/15 [? from OE *hēo*]
stablyd *pa.* established 10/2; *pp.* 10/274 [OF *(e)stablir*]
stadde *pp.* placed 10/274 [ON pp. *staddr*]
stæfne *see* **steven**
stærcliche *adv.* fiercely 3/34 [from OE *stearc*]
stærcne *see* **starc**
stayned *pp.* coloured 9/170 [ON *steina*]
stal *see* **stele**
stale *n.* position 9/107 [OE *stal*]
stalworþ *adj.* stalwart 5/41 [OE *stǣlwyrþe*]
stant *see* **stonde**
starc *adj.* violent 2/5; **stærcne** *masc. acc. sg.* strong 3/59 [OE *stearc*]
stard *pr. 3 sg.* jumps 2/379; **start, sterte** *pa.* sprang 9/431, *~ up* started up 16a/438, 440 [cf. OE *styrtan*]
stare *n.* starling 15/348 [OE *stær*]
stareblind *adj.* completely blind 2/241 [OE *stærblind*]
stature *n.* form 15/366 [OF *stature*]
statute *n.* law 15/387 [OF *statut*]
staven *n. pl.* outlines 3/22 [OE *stæf*]
sted *n.* horse 9/176, 281; **steden** *dat. sg.* 3/25; **stiedes** *pl.* 12/110 [OE *stēda*]
stede *n.* place 5/207, 12/204 [OE *stede*]
stefne *see* **steven**
stek *pa.* clung 9/152 [OE **stecan*]
stel-bawe *n.* stirrup 9/435 [OE *stēle + boga*]
stele *pa. 2 sg.* stole 2/103; **stal** *3 sg.* 16a/141, 143 [OE *stelan*]
stelene *adj. pl.* steel 3/107 [from OE *stēle*]
stel-gere *n.* armour 9/260 [OE *stēle* + ON *gervi*]
stere *pr. 1 sg.* urge 6/80 [OE *stēran*]
steryng *n.* impulse 6/3 [from prec.]
sterne *n.* rudder 8/149 [ON *stjórn*]
sterne *adv.* sternly 2/112 [OE *styrne*]
sternes *n. pl.* stars 8/207 [ON *stjarna*]
sterre *n.* star 15/300 [OE *steorra*]
sterry *adj.* starry 15/43 [from prec.]
sterte *see* **stard**
sterve *v.* die 15/420, 16b/177; **sturven** *pa. pl.* 1/41 [OE *steorfan*]
steven *n.* voice; **stefne** 2/314, 317, 3/150, **stæfne** 3/30 [OE *stefn*]
stiedes *see* **sted**
stif, styffe *adj.* brave, strong, firm, unflinching; uncompromising 2/5; *~ and stronge* powerful 9/34; *adv.* without flinching 9/294 [OE *stīf*]
stifly, stiffely *adv.* firmly 6/148, 14/102, bravely 9/287 [from prec.]
stiheð *pr. 3 sg.* rises 4/91; **styȝ** *pa. sg.* ascended 11/174 [OE *stīgan*]
stikeð *pr. 3 sg.* stays 4/57 [OE *stician*]
stille *adj.* quiet 5/103, 13j/33, inactive 13j/70; *adv.* secretly 5/567, in a low voice 8/371, gently 13h/21 [OE *stille*]
stynte *v.* in *~ of* cease from 16b/105; **stint** *pp.* finished 5/447, 8/73 [OE *styntan*]
stiðimoden *adj.* valiant 3/59 [OE *stīþmōd*]
styþly *adv.* firmly 9/431 [OE *stīþlīce*]
stoc *n.* stump 2/25 [OE *stoc*]
stonde *v.* submit 15/546; **stant, stont** *pr. 3 sg.* stands 3/106, 5/556, 13r/10 [OE *standan, stondan*]
ston-stil *adj.* stone-still 9/242 [OE *stān + stille*]
stounde *n.* while 13k/38, 13m/2; *in þat ~* then 5/550, *in a ~* once 16a/138; *pl.* times 10/288 [OE *stund*]
stouned, stowned *pa.* stunned 8/73, 9/301, were stunned 9/242 [OF *estouner*]
stout *adj.* bold 5/184, 293 [OF *(e)stout*]
stræhte *see* **streche**
stræme *see* **stram**
strayne *v.* restrain 9/176; **strayned** *pa.* controlled, carried along 8/234 [OF *estreindre*]

strayt *adj.* tight 9/152 [OF (*e*)*streit*]
stram *n.* stream 3/83; **stræme** *dat.* 3/107; **stremes** *pl.* currents 8/162, 234, seas 8/311 [OE *strēam*]
stra(u)nge *adj.* foreign 11/2, 15, disdainful 15/584 [OF *stra*(*u*)*nge*]
streche *v.* reach out 6/51, go 5/341; **stræhte** *pa.* held out 3/59 [OE *streccan*]
stree *n.* straw 16a/19 [OE *strēaw*]
streȝt *adj.* direct 8/234, well pulled-down (stretched) 9/152; *adv.* justly 10/274 [OE *streht*, pp. of *streccan*]
stremes *see* **stram**
strenges *n. pl.* cords 1/23 [OE *streng*]
strengthe *n.* force 1/67 [OE *strengþu*]
strepeth *pr. 3 sg.* strips 16a/209 [OE **strēpan*]
strikeþ *pr. 3 sg.* flows 13h/21 [OE *strīcan*]
stryndez *n. pl.* currents 8/311 [uncertain]
stryvande *pr. p.* contending 8/311 [OF *estriver*]
stroyer *n.* destroyer 15/360 [from OF *destruire*]
stronge *adj.* great 8/305 [OE *strang*]
struyen *pr. pl.* destroy 7b/27 [from OF *destruire*]
stub(be) *n.* tree-stump 5/346, nail 14/102 [OE *stub*(*b*)]
stuyves *n. pl.* stews, brothel 7b/71 [OF *estuve*]
sturez, stureð *pr. 3 sg.* brandishes 9/331; ~ *him* occupies himself 4/44 [OE *styrian*]
sturne *adj.* grim 9/334 [OE *styrne*]
sturnely *adv.* grimly 9/331 [from prec.]
sturven *see* **sterve**
subtil *see* **sutile**
suffisaunce *n.* satisfaction enough 15/637 [AN *suffisaunce*]
suffise *v.* permit 15/460 [OF *suffis*-, from *suffire*]
sulle *v.* sell 7b/291; **sullen** *pr. pl.* 7b/329 [OE *syllan*]
sulve *adj.* very 2/69 [OE *sylf*(*a*)]
sumdel *adv.* something about 1/74, somewhat 4/20, 90, in some degree 7b/41, **somedel** rather 15/65; *pron.* part 15/112 [OE *sum* + *dǣl*]
summe *adj. pl.* some 4/12 [OE *sum*]
sumtime *adv.* once 5/45 [OE *sum* + *tīma*]
sumwile, sumwhyle *adv.* once 1/42, 8/57, at times 2/6 [OE *sum* + *hwīl*]
sur *adj.* rueful 4/24 [OE *sūr*]
sustene *v.* support 16b/31, 38 [OF *sustenir*]
sustren *n. pl.* sisters 4/83 [OE *swuster*]
suþ *see* **seo**
suþe *adv.* very 2/2, 12, 155 [OE *swȳþe*]
sutile, subtil *adj.* delicate 15/272; *on ~ wise* in expert fashion 10/132 [OF *sutil*]
swa *adv.* so much 1/20, 4/72, thus 1/25, 4/38, in this way 1/30 [OE *swā*]
swa, swo *conj.* as 3/76, 123, while 3/71, as if 3/80; *riȝt* ~ just as if 2/76 [as prec.]
swærd *see* **sweord(e)**
swayves *pr. 3 sg.* sweeps 8/253 [ON *sveifla*]
swal *pa. 3 sg.* swelled up 2/7, swelled 16b/108 [OE *swellan*]
swange *n.* waist 9/138 [ON *svangi*]
sware *adj.* squarely built 9/138 [from AN *esquarre*]
swart *adj.* black 8/363 [OE *sweart*]
swarves *pr. 3 sg.* in ~ *of* turns aside from 10/167 [OE *sweorfan*]
sweȝe *imp.* hurry 8/72; **sweyed, sweȝed** *pa.* fell 8/151, brought 8/236 [OE *swēgan*]
swey *see* **souȝed**
sweinde *pa.* hung 3/14, struck 3/157; **swenged** swung round 8/250 [OE *swengan*]
swe(i)vene *n.* dream 15/115, 118 [OE *swefn*]
swelme *n.* pain 8/3 [OE **swelm*]
swelte *pr. 3 sg. subj.* may burn 4/68 [OE *sweltan*]
swencten *pa. pl.* oppressed 1/14 [OE *swencan*]
swenged *see* **sweinde**
sweord(e) *n.* sword 3/14, 74, 4/30, **swærd** 3/154; **sweoreden** *pl.* 3/143 [OE *sweord*]
sweore *see* **swyre**
swepe *v.* gather up 8/250; **swepe** *pa.* waded 8/341 [cf. OE *swāpan*]
swete *n.* sweetness 15/161 [from OE *swēte*]
swete *v.* sweat 7a/57, 7b/24, 134 [OE *swǣtan*]
swettere *comp. adv.* more agreeably 7b/228 [OE *swēte*]
swiche, swilce *adj.* such; **swilc** *pron.* such 1/54 [OE *swilc*]
swikedom *n.* treachery 2/167 [OE *swicdōm*]
swikeldom *n.* treachery 2/163 [from OE *swicol*]
swikelhede *n.* treachery 2/162 [as prec.]
swikes *n. pl.* traitors 1/9 [OE *swica*]
swikeþ *pr. 3 sg.* stops 2/336 [OE *swīcan*]
swinc, swinke *n.* hard work, labour 1/57, 7b/241 [OE *swinc*]
swyndid *pa.* faded away 10/342 [OE *swindan*]
swynes-hed *n.* pighead, i.e. sluggish fellow 16a/408 [OE *swīn* + *hēafod*]
swynkares *n. pl.* workers 7b/259 [from next]
swynke *v.* labour, do bodily work; **swonken** *pp.* 16a/381 [OE *swincan*]
swipen *n. pl.* blows 3/69 [OE *swipu*]
swipte *pa.* struck 3/158 [OE *swippan*]
swyre, sw(e)ore *n.* neck 2/73, 3/20, 9/138, 13g/28 [OE *swīra*, *sweora*]
swiþe *adv.* very, greatly, quickly; *as* ~ at once 15/623 [OE *swīþe*]
swyþez *pr. 3 sg.* scorches 8/478 [ON *svíða*]

swyve *v.* copulate with 16a/324; *pp.* 16a/412, 463 [OE *swīfan*, 'move, sweep']
swo *see* **swa**
swoet *n.* sweat 7b/241 [OE *swāt*]
swogh *n.* soft noise 15/247 [from OE *swōgan*]
swoghe *adj.* deathly 9/243 [OE *geswōgen*]
swolȝ *n.* gullet 8/250 [from next]
swolȝed *pp.* swallowed up 8/363, **iswolȝe** swallowed 2/146 [OE *swelgan*]
swonken *see* **swynke**
swo(o)te *adj.* sweet, lovely 4/77, 15/274, 296 [OE *swōt*]
swore *see* **swyre**
swowed, swoned *pa.* fell asleep 8/442, swooned 5/197; **swownyng** *pr. p.* 16b/173 [from OE **geswōgan*, pp. *geswōgen*]
swulc *conj. & prep.* as if 3/110, 166, like 3/109 [OE *swulce*]
swulche *adj. pl.* such 3/112 [OE *swulc*]

ta *pr. pl.* (*as fut.*) will take 8/78; **ta, take** *imp.* take 9/413, pass 14/244; **token** *pa. pl.* spread 10/57; **tan** *pp.* taken 9/490 [ON *taka*]
tabernacle *n.* canopy over throne 5/412 [AN *tabernacle*]
tabourers *n. pl.* drummers 5/521 [from next]
tabours *n. pl.* drums 5/301 [AN *tabur*]
tacche *v.* fasten 14/119; **tacched** *pp.* attached 9/219 [OF *atacher*]
tadden *n. pl.* toads 4/53 [OE *tādige*]
take *see* **ta**
tale *n.* conversation, debate 2/3, speech 2/140, 8/135, report 10/102; **tale** *pl.* speeches 2/257 [OE *talu*]
talent *n.* purpose 8/416, desire 10/176 [OF *talent*]
talenttyf *adj.* desirous 9/350 [OF *talentif*]
tan *see* **ta**
tape *n.* blow 9/406 [cf. OF *taper*]
taxour *n.* assessor (of a fine) 7b/37 [AN *taxour*]
te *def. art.* the 1/58 [from OE *se* etc.]
teames *n. pl.* brood 4/84 [OE *tēam*]
tecche *n.* blemish 10/85 [OF *teche*]
teche *imp.* direct 9/401; **ytauhte** *pp.* taught 7b/20 [OE *tǣcan*]
te(e) *v.* go, travel 5/212, 318, 8/87, 416; **teþ** *pr. pl.* 5/274 [OE *tēon*]
tegædere *adv.* together 1/46 [OE *tōgædere*]
teynted *ppl. adj.* convicted 14/77 [from OF *ateint*]
telle *v.* describe 5/56, count 14/227; **telde** *pa.* told 7b/76 [OE *tellan*]
teme *n.*[1] plough-team 7b/20, 141 [OE *tēam*]
teme *n.*[2] subject 8/358 [OF *tesme*]
temyd *pa.* belonged 10/15 [OE *tēman*]
tempreþ *pr. 3 sg.* tunes 5/437; **tempred** *pa.* 5/526 [OE *temprian*]
tene *num.* ten 5/99 [OE *tīen*]
tene *n.* anger 7b/124, 8/90, suffering 10/331, grief 13k/8 [OE *tēona*]
tene *pr. 2 pl. subj.* penalize 7b/36 [OE *tēonian*]
tenor *n.* purport 8/358 [AN *tenur*]
tente *n.* heed 14/254 [from OF *atente*]
tent(e) *v.* attend (to) 8/59, 14/180, 185, tend 8/498 [? from prec.]
tercel *n.* male (hawk) 15/393, 405, 463 [OF *tercel*]
tercelet *n.* male hawk 15/529, 533 [OF *tercelet*]
termes *n. pl.* regions 8/61 [OF *terme*]
testyf *adj.* headstrong 16a/150 [AN *testif*]
þa *adv.* then 3/1, 47 [OE *þā*]
þa *conj.* when 3/9, 4/78; ~ ... *þa* when ... then 1/5-6 [OE *þā*]
þa *rel. pron.* which 3/24, 87, 120, who 3/26, 65 [OE *se* etc.]
þaȝ, þagh *conj.* though [OE *þēah*]
þan *adv.* then 6/49, 14/42 [OE *þanne*]
þan *conj.* when 13l/12 [as prec.]
þan *pron. dat.* in *after* ~ after that 2/200, *bi* ~ from that 5/553 [OE *se*, dat. *þǣm*]
þankworþ *adj.* creditable 12/7 [OE *þancweorþ*]
thar *pr. pl.* need 14/297 [OE *þearf*]
þar *adv.* there 2/97 [OE *þār*]
þar *conj.* where 1/24, 2/16, 26, 126 [as prec.]
þarafter, þarbi *see* **þeraftur, þerbi**
þar(e)vore *adv.* for that reason 2/274, therefore 11/29, 79, 140 [OE *þār* + *fore*]
þarynne, þarmid *see* **þerinne, þermyde**
ðat *conj.* so that 1/31; **þatow** *conj.* +*pron.* that you 5/165, 454 [OE *þæt*, *þæt* + *þou*]
þat *pron.* that which, what 2/95, 159, 218, 10/166, whatever 8/178 [OE *þæt*]
þaut *conj.* though 13d/7 [OE *þēah*]
þe *rel. pron.* which 3/11, 4/4 (2), 50 (1), who 3/27, 4/50 (2) [OE *þe*]
the *see* **þu**
þear *see* **þer**
þede *n.* country [OE *þēod*]
þeder *adv.* to there 9/402 [OE *þider*]
thee *v.* prosper 15/569 [OE *þēon*]
þeȝ, þeh, þey *conj.* though; just because 2/48, if, even if 2/284, 359, 384, 11/37, 49 [OE *þēah*]
þeines *n. pl.* followers 3/94 [OE *þegn*]
thekynge *n.* thatching 7b/199 [cf. OE *þeccan*]
þen(e) *conj.* than 3/29, 6/34, 9/24 [OE *þænne*]
þenk, þenche *v.* (**þenkþ** *pr. 3 sg.*; **þenkande, thenkende** *pr. p.*; **þohte** *pa.*; **þoȝtest** *pa. 2 sg.*; **þohten** *pl.*) think; intend

to 2/157, 3/85, 10/225, hope (to) 12/254, 256; ~ *in þouȝt* imagine 5/373 [OE *þencan*]
þenkeþ *see* **þinkeþ**
thenne *adj. as n.* thin 16a/212 [OE *þynne*]
þenne *adv.* thence 12/239 [OE *þanon*]
þenne *conj.* when 3/42, 77, 98 [OE *þænne*]
þens *adv.* thence 6/230, **thennes** 16b/113 [from OE *þanon*]
þeo *def. art.* the 11/9 [OE *se* etc.]
þeo *pron.* those 4/83 [OE *þā*]
þeose *see* **þes**
þer *conj.* where; **þear** 4/6 [OE *þǣr*]
þerabof *adv.* on top of it 8/382 [OE *þǣr* + *on* + *bufan*]
þeraftur, þarafter *adv.* accordingly 7b/90; ~ *longe* after a long time 2/45 [OE *þǣr æfter*]
þerate *adv.* at it 5/380 [OE *þǣr æt*]
þerbi, þarbi *adv.* from them 9/117, concerning that 2/98, 244, thereby 11/65 [OE *þǣrbi*]
therbiforn *adv.* before that 16a/143 [OE *þǣr* + *beforan*]
þer(e)as *conj.* where 8/41, 43, 9/432 [OE *þǣr* + *ealswa*]
þereof *adv.* from them 11/31 [OE *þǣrof*]
þerinne, þarynne *adv.* in it, in there, in that place [OE *þǣrinne*]
þerk *n.* darkness 5/370 [OE **þeorc*]
þermyde, þarmid *adv.* therewith 2/81, 156, with it 7b/68, with them 7b/155 [OE *þǣrmid*]
þeroute *adv.* out of there; out of doors 7a/16, overboard 8/174, 211 [OE *þǣrūte*]
þertill *adv.* to it 10/69, 14/12 [OE *þǣr* + ON *til*]
þerto *adv.* to it; furthermore 6/4 [OE *þǣrtō*]
þerwyth *adv.* with it 8/60, at that, then 8/232, 9/121 [OE *þǣrwiþ*]
therwythalle *adv.* then, with that 15/405 [OE *þǣr* + *wiþ* + *eall*]
þes *demons. adj. & pron.* this 4/40, 11/40; **þes, þeos(e)** *pl.* these 4/8, 21, 46, **þeus(e)** 11/29, 47 [OE *þes* etc.]
þet *conj.* until 4/48, so that 4/68 [OE *þæt*]
þewes *n. pl.* virtues 8/30 [OE *þēaw*]
þider *adv.* thither, in that direction [OE *þider*]
þiderward(es) *adv.* to that 2/143, towards there 4/18, 10/61, 112 [from prec.]
þilke *pron.* that one 12/150; *adj.* that same 12/12, 167, 258, these same 15/61 [*þe* from OE *se* + *ilca*]
þin *see* **þu**
þing *n.* in *bi al* ~ from every feature 5/321, 375; **þing** *pl.* matters 5/4, affairs 5/218 [OE *þing*]
þinkeþ, thynkes, þenkeþ *pr. 3 sg. & impers.* (it) seems, *me* ~ it seems to me; **þink** *subj.* it would seem; **þuȝte, þoghte** *pa.* [OE *þyncan*, impers.]
þire *see* **þu**
þis(e) *demons. adj. pl.* these 5/340, 8/422 (1) [OE *þes* etc.]
tho, þoo *demons. adj. & pron. pl.* those 6/108, 7a/49, 7b/25, 8/475, 14/69 [OE *þā*]
tho, þoo *adv.* then [OE *þā*]
tho *conj.* when 7b/239 [OE *þā*]
þode *n. pl.* peoples 2/387 [OE *þēod*]
þoghte *see* **þinkeþ**
þoȝ, þof *conj.* though, even though 2/304, 6/80; ~ *al* although 6/194 [ON *þó*, earlier **þoh*]
þoȝtest, þohte(n) *see* **þenk**
þole(n), þolien *v.* suffer, endure; **þoleden** *pa. pl.* 1/55 [OE *þolian*]
thonketh *pr. pl.* thank 7b/135; **þonked** *pa.* 5/472; **iþoncket** *pp.* 4/87 [OE *þoncian*]
þonne *adv.* thence 2/132 [OE *þanon*]
þore *adv.* there [OE *þār*]
þor(o)u, þor(o)w, tho(u)rgh *prep.* through [OE *þurh*]
þos *demons. adj. fem. nom.* this 2/41; *pl.* these 2/139 [OE *þes* etc.]
þoþer *def. art.* + *pron.* the other 11/17 [*þe* from OE *se* + *ōþer*]
þoþwethere *adv.* even so 1/59 [OE *þēah-hwæþere*]
þou, thow *conj.* though 7b/34, 195, 13l/17 [OE *þēah*]
þouth *n.* thought 13n/7 [OE *þoht*]
þrawen *pp.* tied 9/194 [OE *þrāwan*]
threnen *adv.* thrice 10/210 [OE *þrinen*, from ON]
þrengde *pa.* crushed 1/27 [OE **þrengan*]
þrestelcoc *n.* male thrush 13h/7 [OE *þrostle* + OE *cocc*]
þretest *pr. 2 sg.* in ~ *to* threaten 2/83; **þreatið, þreteþ** *pr. 3 sg.* threatens 4/63, *refl.* in *him* ~ chides 13h/7 [OE *þrēatian*]
þrid(de) *adj.* third [OE *þridda*]
þryes *adv.* three times 11/141, 15/61, 16a/411, 16b/90 [from OE *þrīwa*]
þrin *adv.* in them 4/45, 46 [OE *þǣrinne*]
þriste *adj.* bold 2/171 [OE *þrīste*]
thryvandly *adv.* beautifully 10/47 [from next]
þryved *pa.* prospered 8/521 [ON *þrífask*]
throgh *n.* coffin 10/47 [OE *þrūh*]
þroȝe, þrowe *n.* time, turn 2/260, while 13l/1 [OE *þrāg*]
thropes *n. pl.* villages 15/350 [OE *þrop*]
throstel *n.* thrush 15/364 [OE *þrostle*]
throte-bolle *n.* Adam's apple 16a/419 [OE *þrotbolla*]

þu *pron.* thou 3/161; **the** *acc.* thee 16b/10; **þin** *poss. adj.* thy 13k/12; **þire** *poss. adj. dat. fem.* 3/162 [OE *þū* etc.]
þuȝte *see* **þinkeþ**
þullich *pron.* such 4/69 [OE *þyllic*]
þurȝ, thurgh *prep.* through; **þurth** 5/237, 393 [OE *þurh*]
þurhut *adv.* through and through 4/34; *prep.* right through 3/62 [OE *þurh* + *ūt*]
þusen *n. pl.* thousands 1/33 [OE *þūsend*]
þuster *n.* darkness 2/198, 230, 232 [OE *þȳstru*]
þusternesse *n.* darkness 2/369 [from prec.]
þustre *adj.* dark 2/249 [OE *þȳstre*]
þuvele *n.* thicket 2/278 [OE *þȳfel*]
þwarle *adj.* intricate 9/194 [? cf. OE *þweorh*]
thwytinge *n.* whittling 7b/199 [OE *þwītan*]
þwong *n.* thong 9/194 [OE *þwong*]
tyd *adv.* quickly [cf. ON *títt*]
tyde *n.* time 11/155; *þis* ~ now 14/185, 235 [OE *tīd*]
tidende *n.* tidings 3/49; *pl.* **tydinge** 3/1, **tyþynges** 8/78 [OE *tīdung*, ON *tíðendi*]
tydes *pr. 3 sg.* comes to 16a/321 [OE *tīdan*]
til *conj.* until 1/8 [ON *til*]
tylye *v.* cultivate 7b/244; **tilede** *pa.* 1/52; **tiled** *pp.* 1/40 [OE *tilian*]
til(le) *prep.* to 7b/98 (2), 14/181 [ON *til*]
tylte *v.* tumble 8/361; **tult** *pa.* 8/252 [OE **tyltan*, cf. *tealt* 'unsteady']
tymes *n. pl.* in *by* ~ on occasions 9/41 [OE *tīma*]
tyne *n.* bit 8/59 [uncertain]
tyne *v.* lose 8/500, 14/300, waste 8/505, miss, fail to see 14/254; **ytynt** *pp.* lost 7a/93 [ON *týna*]
type *v.* throw 8/506 [uncertain]
tipet *n.* dangling tip of hood 16a/99 [uncertain]
typped *adj.* consummate 8/77 [ON *typpa* v.]
tired *pa.* dressed 5/586 [from OF *atirer*]
tit(e) *adv.* quickly, at once 9/299, 14/12, 299; *as* ~ quickly 9/31 [cf. ON *títt*]
tyþynges *see* **tidende**
title *n.* inscription 10/102 [OF *title*]
to *n.* toe 8/229 [OE *tā*]
to *adv.* too 2/171, 257, 344, 7b/274, 11/59 [OE *tō*]
toberste *pr. 3 sg. subj.* break 2/122 [OE *tōberstan*]
toblaweð *pr. 3 sg.* blows around 4/89 [OE *tōblāwan*]
tobreke *v.* break in pieces 16a/64; **tobroke** *plp.* shattered 16a/423 [OE *tōbrecan*]
tochan *pa. 3 sg.* split in two 3/63; **tochine** *pp.* weatherbeaten 5/262 [OE *tōcīnan*]
toclæf *pa. 3 sg.* split 3/155 [OE *tōclēofan*]
todeld *pa.* dispersed 1/3 [OE *tōdǣlan*]
todrowe *pa. pl.* tore to pieces 2/126 [from OE *dragan*]
togederes *adv.* together 4/45, 52, **togider** 5/201 [OE *tōgædere*]
toȝeines *prep.* towards 3/54 [OE *tōgegnes*]
to-yere *adv.* this year 14/164 [OE *to* + *gēar*]
token, tokne *n.* sign, proof 6/92, physical evidence 10/102, love token 12/25 [OE *tācn*]
token *see* **ta**
tom(e) *n.* delay 8/135, pause 10/313 [ON *tóm*]
tomurte *pa.* broke 8/150 [uncertain]
tone *n.* insult 2/50 [OE *tēona*]
tonge *n.* pair of tongs 2/156 [OE *tonge*]
tonne *see* **tunne**
torent *pp.* torn to shreds 10/164, 15/432 [OE *torendan*]
torett *pa.* tore up 5/81 [OE *tō* + **rittan*]
torneie *pr. pl.* tourney 12/117; **tournayed** *pa.* 9/41 [OF *to(u)rneier*]
torof *pa.* ripped 8/379 [from ON *rífa*]
toshyvered *pp.* broken in pieces 15/493 [cf. MDu *scheveren*]
tosomne *adv.* together 3/40 [OE *tosomne*]
toswolle *pp.* swollen up 2/145 [OE *tōswellan*]
totered *pa.* tossed 8/233 [MDu *touteren*]
toþen *n. dat. pl.* teeth 3/137 [OE *tōþ*]
totore, totorn *pp.* torn to shreds 5/106, torn apart 5/171, 538, torn 15/110 [OE *tōteran*]
totose *v.* tear to pieces 2/70 [OE *tō* + **tāsian*]
towches *n. pl.* musical notes 9/120 [OF *touche*]
towe *v.* take 8/100 [OE *togian*]
trammes *n. pl.* schemes 9/3 [OF *traime*]
travayl(e) *n.* work 8/505, 14/300, suffering 14/254 [OF *travail*]
travayle *v.* work, labour; tax 6/153; **travayledez** *pa. 2 sg.* worked 8/498 [OF *travaillier*]
trawe *see* **trowe** *v.*
tren *see* **trowe** *n.*
trenchaunt *adj.* cutting, sharp 16a/76 [OF *trenchant*]
trendli *pr. 3 sg. subj.* roll 2/135 [OE *-trendlian*]
tresor *n.* royal treasury 1/3 [OF *tresor*]
trespased *pp.* offended 11/117 [OF *trespasser*]
trete *v.* deal with 15/34 [OF *tretier*]
treulich, trewliche, treuely, trewely *adv.* truly, indeed 6/35, 7b/20, justly 6/127, faithfully 16a/279 [OE *trēowlīce*]
treuthe, trouthe *n.* pledge 1/12, justice 7b/36, 10/268, integrity, honesty 7b/49, 57, 69; **treothes** *pl.* pledges 1/12 [OE *trēowþ*]
trewe *n.* truce, respite 7b/354 [OE *trēow*]
tricherie *n.* treachery 9/4 [OF *tricherie*]

tryed *ppl. adj.* fine 9/219 [OF *trier*]
trillyd *pa.* flowed 10/322 [? ON]
tryst(e) *v.* (**triste** *pa.*) trust 6/29, 12/175, rely on 8/324, believe 9/380 [ON *treysta*]
trysty *adj.* faithful 11/151 [cf. prec.]
trompes *see* **trunpes**
tronyd *pp.* enthroned 10/255 [from OF *trone* n.]
trouthe *see* **treuthe**
trowe *n.* tree 2/135; **tren** *pl.* 11/161 [OE *trēow*]
trowe, trawe *v.* believe, think [OE *trēowian*]
trunpes, trumpes, trompes *n. pl.* trumpets 5/301, 9/116, 15/344 [OF *trumpe*]
trusse *pr. pl.* pack up 12/236 [OF *trusser*]
trwe *adj.* true [OE *trēowe*]
tulk *n.* man, knight [ON *túlkr*, 'interpreter']
tult *see* **tylte**
tun *n.* village 1/49, monastic estate 1/71 [OE *tūn*]
tunne *n.* barrel 4/59, **tonne** 15/104, cask 16a/40 [OE *tunne*]
tunscipe *n.* people of the village 1/49 [OE *tūnscipe*]
turnyd *pa.* converted (to Christian use) 10/15 [OE *turnian*]
turtel *n.* turtle-dove 15/510, 577 [OE *turtla*]
tuteleð *pr. 3 sg.* whispers to 4/37 [uncertain]
twa *num.* two 1/29, 4/69 [OE *twā*]
tweye *num.* two 11/140 [from OE *twēgen*]
twelmonyth *n. as adv.* in a year 9/383 [OE *twelf* + *mōnaþ*]
twengst *pr. 2 sg.* pinch 2/156 [OE *twengan*]
twyes *adv.* twice 16b/96 [from OE *twige*]
twynne *v.* separate 14/193 [from OE *twinn*]

uch(e) *adj.* each; **uchon(e)** *pron.* every one 7b/218, 8/164, **uschon** 10/93 [OE *ylc*, *ylc* + *ān*]
ughten *n.* morning 10/118 [from OE *ūhta*]
ule *see* **hule**
umbe *adv.* about 8/309, 381 [OE *ymbe*]
umbefoldes *pr. 3 sg.* covers 9/181 [prec. + OE *faldan*]
umbetorne *adv.* around 9/184 [OE *ymbe* + OF *tourn*]
unavisid *pp.* unconsidered 6/135 [from OF *aviser*]
unbynde *v.* free 15/523 [OE *unbindan*]
unbrent *pp.* unburnt 16b/16 [from ON *brenna*]
unclene *adj.* gross 2/233 [OE *unclǣne*]
uncler *adj.* feeble 8/307 [from OF *cler*]
uncouþe *adj.* unknown, strange 5/535 [OE *uncūþ*]
uncrounede *ppl. adj.* untonsured 7a/62 [from AN *coruner*]
undede *pa.* opened 5/385 [OE *undōn*]
undep *adj.* shallow 1/26 [OE *undēop*]
undepartable *adj.* indivisible 6/40 [from OF *departable*]
underfangen *pp.* received 1/2; ~ *fram* received by 1/63 [OE *underfōn*, pp. *underfangen*]
undergæton *pa. pl.* understood 1/9, **underȝete** 5/576; *pp.* recognized 2/168 [OE *undergetan*]
undernomen *pa. pl.* understood 8/213; **undernome** *pp.* realized 5/320 [OE *underniman*]
understont *pr. 3 sg.* understands 4/49; **understonde** *pp.* 11/144 [OE *understondan*]
undertide *n.* morning 5/181; *pl.* 5/282 [OE *underntīd*]
underveð *pr. 3 sg.* receives 4/39 [OE *underfōn*]
uneþe *see* **un(n)eþe**
unglad *adj.* unhappy 8/63 [OE *unglæd*]
ungode *adj. as n. dat.* wicked one 2/129, 245 [OE *ungōd*]
unheled *pp.* uncovered (by water) 11/160 [OE *unhelan*]
unkynde *adj.* unnatural 12/167, cruel 15/434, 457 [OE *uncynde*]
unkut *adj.* unrecognized 13l/3 [OE *uncūþ*]
unlouke *v.* unlock, release 10/67, 162 [OE *unlūcan*]
unme(e)te *adj.* excessively large 9/208, wrong 14/127 [OE *un(ge)mǣte*]
unmeþe *n.* immoderation 2/352 [OE *unmǣþ*]
unmilde *adj.* cruel 2/61 [OE *unmilde*]
un(n)eþe *adv.* scarcely 5/221, 416, 9/134 [OE *unēaþe*]
unnynges *n. pl.* indications 8/213 [? from OE *unnan*]
unorne *adj.* feeble 2/317 [OE *unorne*]
unpreste *adj.* unprepared 10/285 [from OF *prest*]
unrede *n.* bad advice 2/161, evil counsel 2/212 [OE *unrǣd*]
unriȝt *n.* wickedness 2/165 [OE *unriht*]
unsaȝt *adj.* warlike 10/8 [from OE *sæht*]
unseli *adj.* wretched 4/14 [OE *unsǣlig*]
unskathely *adj. as n.* innocent 10/278 [from ON *skaði*]
unsounde *n.* trouble 8/527 [OE *un-* + *sund*]
unsparid *pp.* unrestrained 10/335 [OE *un-* + *sparian*]
unte *prep.* unto 8/470 [cf. ON *und-* + OE *tō*]
untellendlice *adj.* unspeakable 1/19 [from OE *tellan*]
unþe(a)w *n.* vice 2/194, 4/88 [OE *unþēaw*]
unthrifty *adj.* inauspicious, unlucky 14/90 [from ON *þrift*]

untressed *pp.* not braided 15/268 [from OF *trecier*]
unwar *adj.* foolish 8/115 [OE *unwær*]
unweelde *adj.* feeble 16a/32 [from OE *wielde*]
unwemmyd *pp.* unspotted 10/96, 266 [OE *unwemmed*]
unwiȝt *n.* monster 2/33, 90; *pl.* 2/218 [OE *un-* + *wiht*]
unwrenche *n.* dirty trick 2/169 [OE *unwrenc*]
unwreste *adj.* bad 2/178; *adv.* poorly, badly 2/342 [OE *unwræste*]
unwroȝen *pp.* exposed 2/162 [OE *unwrēon*]
unwurþ *adj.* cheap 2/339 [OE *un* + *wurþ*]
up *prep.* upon 2/15, 16a/436 [OE *up* + *on*]
upbraydes *pr. 3 sg.* reproaches 8/430, 16a/436 [OE *upbregdan*]
upbroȝte *pa.* uttered 2/200 [OE *up* + *bringan*]
uphalden *pp.* raised 10/349 [OE *up* + *haldan*]
upynyoun *n.* opinion 8/40 [OF *opinion*]
uppart *adv.* upwards 4/91 [OE *upweard*]
uppen *prep.* upon 3/97, 127 [OE *uppan*]
upright *adj.* in *bolt* ~ flat on her back 16a/412 [OE *upriht*]
upros *pa.* got up 8/378 [OE *up* + *rīsan*]
ure *see* **we** *pron.*
urneþ *see* **irnen**
usage *n.* habit 15/15, practice 15/411, use 16b/75 [OF *usage*]
usant *adj.* accustomed 16a/86 [OF *usant*]
usaunce *n.* practice 15/674 [OF *usance*]
uschon *see* **uch(e)**
usyt *pa.* practised 10/187, 200; **yused** *pp.* used 11/18, 19, 33 [OF *user*]
ut *adv.* out 1/43, 2/8, 53, 121 [OE *ūt*]
uthalve *adv.* towards the outer edge 2/110 [cf. OE *ūthealf* n.]
uðen *n. pl.* waves 3/37 [OE *ȳþ*]
utmast *adj.* outermost 5/357 [OE *ūtemest*]
utter *adv.* outside 8/41 [OE *ūtter*]
uvel *n.* evil 4/20 [from next]
uvel(e), uvole *adj.* wicked, evil 2/247, 4/21, hostile 2/8 [OE *yfel*]

vayles *pr. 3 sg.* avails 10/348 [OF *valoir*]
vaire *adj.* beautiful 2/15; **vairur** *comp.* 2/152; **væireste** *superl.* most handsome 3/27 [OE *fæger*]
vaste *adv.* close 3/40 [OE *fæste*]
veyrdit *n.* verdict 15/503, 525 [AN *verdit*]
vengen *v.* avenge 12/180 [OF *vengier*]
venym *n.* venom 8/71 [AN *venim*]
verde *n.* army 3/27 [OE *ferd*, *fyrd*]
verdure *n.* green 9/161 [OF *verdure*]
ver(r)ayly *adv.* truly 9/161, 10/174 [from next]
verrey, verrai *adj.* true 6/117, 11/132, 12/53, itself (intensive) 8/370; ~ *reson* reason itself 6/105, ~ *sooth* the absolute truth 16a/70 [AN *verrey*, *verrai*]
vers *n. pl.* verses 15/124, 141 [OE *fers*, OF *vers*]
vertewos *adj.* virtuous 6/16 [OF *vertuous*]
verþe *adj.* fourth 11/161 [OE *feorþa*]
vertu(e) *n.* power 8/284, 10/286; *pl.* 10/174 [OF *vertu*]
vesture *n.* clothing 9/161 [OF *vesture*]
vyfte *adj.* fifth 11/90, 164 [OE *fīfta*]
viȝte *see* **fith** *v.*
vyl *see* **falles**
vilainie, vilenie *n.* wickedness 4/74, disgrace 12/10, **vileynye** injury 16a/337 [AN *vilainye*, *vilenie*]
visage *n.* face 5/80 [OF *visage*]
vlesch *n.* flesh 11/171 [OE *flǣsc*]
voyde *v.* empty 8/370, leave 9/345 [OF *voider*]
volc *n.* people 3/164 [OE *folc*]
voluper *n.* nightcap 16a/449 [AN *volupier*]
volweþ *see* **folȝi**
vor *see* **for**
vorbisne *n.* proverb 2/98, 244 [OE *fōrebȳsen*]
vorȝut *see* **forȝete**
vormeste *see* **formeste**
vorseyde *ppl. adj.* aforesaid 11/96, 106 [from OE *on foran* + *secgan*]
vorþ *see* **forþ**
vorþi *see* **forthy**
vote *n.* claw 2/51 [OE *fōt*]
vouched *pa.* offered 8/165 [OF *voucher*]
voules *n. pl.* birds 11/164 [OE *fugol*]
vram, vrom *see* **fram**
vul(e) *see* **ful(e)**
vullen *see* **falles**
vurste *adj.* first 11/27 [OE *fyrst*]

wæl *see* **wel(e)**
wæld(e) *n.* plain 3/48, 115 [OE *wald*]
wælle *n.* stream 3/112 [OE *wælla*]
wær *see* **where**
wæron *see* **be(n)**
wages *n. pl.* payment 9/396 [AN *wage*]
wai *interj.* alas 2/120, 5/234; **wailawai, weylawei, weilaway** 2/220, 13j/25, 49, 16a/218 [ON *vei*, OE *weg lā weg*]
wayke *adj.* weak 7a/23, 9/282, 16b/29 [ON *veikr*]
waymot *adj.* angry 8/492 [OE *wēamōd*]
wayned *pa.* sent 8/467; *pp.* brought 9/264 [OE *-wægnan*]
ways *n. pl.* in *in ich* ~ in every way 5/158 [OE *weg*]
wayte *pr. 3 sg. subj.* in ~ *after* keeps a watch on 8/86 [AN *waitier*]

wakien *v.* stay awake 4/42; **wake** *pr. 1 sg.* 13g/22, am awake 15/7, 482; **wakes** *pr. 3 sg.* 8/130 [OE *wacian*]
wakkest *adj. superl.* weakest 9/354 [from OE *wāc*]
wakned *pa.* created 9/119 [OE *wæcnian*]
walden *see* **wille**
wale *n.* in *to* ~ in abundance 10/73 [ON *val*]
wale *v.* find 9/398; **walon** *pp.* made their way 10/64 [from ON *val* n.]
wallinde *ppl. adj.* boiling 4/68 [OE *wallan*]
walt *see* **welde**
walterez *pr. 3 sg.* rolls 8/263, 297; **walterande** *pr. p.* 8/247; **waltered** *pa.* 8/142 [cf. MLG *walteren*]
walwen *pr. pl.* roll about 16a/424 [OE *walwian*]
wamel *v.* feel sick 8/300 [uncertain]
wan *see* **when, wynne**
wandez *n. gen.* haft's 9/215 [ON *vǫndr*]
wanlez *adj.* without hope 8/262 [ON *ván* + OE *-lēas*]
wante *pr. 1 sg.* lack 15/287; **wantis** *3 sg.* is lacking 14/204 [ON *vanta*]
wap *n.* stroke 8/499 [imitative]
war *adj.* cautious 2/170, 192, aware 8/249, 15/218 [OE *wær*]
war *see* **where**
warande *v.* warrant 14/104 [OF *warand*]
warded *pp.* protected 8/258 [OE *weardian*]
waren *see* **be(n)**
warevore *adv.* wherefore 2/268 [OE *hwǣr* + *for*]
warlok *n.* shackle 8/80 [? OE *waru* + *loc*]
warlowe *n.* scoundrel 14/63 [OE *wǣrloga*]
warni *pr. 1 sg.* summon 2/330; **warnez** *pr. 3 sg.* commands 8/469; **warnede** *pa.* 12/108, ~ *before* informed in advance 15/45 [OE *warnian*]
warnynge *n.* commands 7b/90 [from prec.]
warpeð *pr. 3 sg.* (**worp** *imp.*; **warp(yd), warpped, werpe** *pa.*) throw 2/121, 125, 4/31, utter 2/45, 8/356, 9/224, 10/321, 329 [OE *weorpan*]
warsæ, wher(e)so *conj.* wherever 1/52, 9/395, 16a/384 [OE *swā hwǣr* + *swā*]
warth *see* **worthe**
warþe *n.* shore 8/339 [OE *waroþ*]
wast *n.* waist 9/144 [? OE **wæst*]
wasted *pp.* destroyed 8/475 [AN *waster*]
wasto(u)r(e)s *n. pl.* idlers, parasites 7b/27, 139, 158 [AN *wastour*]
wat *see* **what, wite**
watz *see* **be(n)**
wawes *n. pl.* waves 8/142 [OE *wǣg*]
wax(e), wexe(n) *v.* (**wax, wex** *pa.*; **waxen** *pp.*) grow, become; rise (of colour) 15/444 [OE *waxan*]
we *pron. pl.* we; **ous** *acc. & dat.* us 5/167, 427; **ure** *poss. adj.* our 1/55, 3/32, 4/87 [OE *wē* etc.]
we *interj.* alas 5/176, expressing surprise 14/61 [OE *wǣ*]
wedde *see* **legge**
wede *n.* clothes 10/96; *pl.* clothes, armour [OE *wǣd*]
weder *n.* weather 5/269 [OE *weder*]
wedy *v.* weed 7b/66 [OE *wēodian*]
weet *adj.* wet 16a/253 [OE *wǣt*]
wegge *n.* wedge 14/242; *pl.* 14/235 [OE *wecg*]
weghe *n.* man 10/96; **wehes** *pl.* 10/73 [OE *wiga*]
weylawei *see* **wai**
weis, weyes *n. gen.* in *nanes* ~ not at all 4/16, *noon other* ~ in no other way 15/654 [OE *weg*]
welde *v.* (**walt** *pa.*) wield 9/270, occupy 8/464, 9/485, possess 8/16, 9/231, control 8/322, rule 10/161 [OE **weldan*]
welder *n.* controller 8/129 [from prec.]
wele *n.* riches 9/7, 10/233, joy 8/262, 9/50, 485 [OE *wela*]
wel(e) *adv.* very; much 5/464, 6/186, 8/114, fully 5/183, 350, almost 2/216, easily 1/39, really, indeed 15/7, 12, **wæl** well 1/63 [OE *wel*]
wele-dede *n.* good works 10/301 [OE *weldǣd*]
wel-haled *ppl. adj.* pulled up tight 9/157 [OE *wel* + OF *haler*]
welke *pa.* walked 15/297 [OE *wealcan*]
welkyn *n.* sky 8/207 [OE *weolcen*]
welle *n.* source 15/62, 129, spring 15/211, 215 [OE *wella*]
wel(l)e *adj.* good 13c/8, 12, 15, 14/104 [OE *wel*]
welle-spring *n.* spring 13c/21 [OE *wella* + *spring*]
well-stremes *n. pl.* streams from a spring 15/187 [OE *wella* + *strēam*]
welneȝ(e), -negh, -nyh *adv.* nearly 2/44, 9/7, 10/119, 12/45 [OE *wel-nēh*]
welt *pa.* rolled around 8/115 [ON *velta*]
welþe *n.* well-being 12/97, bliss 14/59 [OE *wela* + *-th*]
welwed *pp.* shrivelled 8/475 [OE *wealwian*]
wemles *adj.* spotless 10/85 [OE *wamm* + *-lēas*]
wende *v.* (**wende** *pa.*) go 2/288, 7b/4, 8/339, 11/176, come 5/427, turn 13g/22, alter 1/71, change 13j/41; ~ *of* turn from 8/403 [OE *wendan*]
wene *v.* (**wenst, wenest** *2 sg.*; **wenestu** *2 sg. + pron.*; **wende(n)** *pa.*) think, believe; suppose 2/303, 371, know 9/270, intend 16a/451; *I* ~ (tag) indeed 13k/4 [OE *wēnan*]

wenyng *n.* belief 8/115 [from prec.]
weole *n.* happiness 13h/35 [OE *wela*]
weorien *v.* defend 3/90; **wered** *pa.* protected 8/486 [OE *werian*]
weorkes *see* **werk**
wepe *n.* weeping 5/195, 234 [from next]
wepe *pa. pl.* wept 5/591 [OE *wēpan*]
wer *see* **wer(re)**
werbles *n. pl.* trillings 9/119 [OF *werble*]
werdis *n. gen.* world's 13o/1 [OE *weorold*]
wered, ywerd *pp.* worn 5/241, 7a/81, 16a/449 [OE *werian*]
wered *see* **weorien**
werk *n.* activity 5/317, 6/1, workmanship 5/374; **weorkes, werkez** *pl.* buildings 1/71, designs 9/164, 216 [OE *we(o)rc*]
wern *see* **be(n)**
werne *v.* refuse 12/224 [OE *wernan*]
werpe *see* **warpeð**
wer(re) *n.* war 5/5, 9/16, 10/215, 12/65 [AN *werre*]
wers(e), wurs *comp. adj. as n.* worse 8/48; *adv.* in *þe* ~ any the worse 2/303, *me is þe* ~ it is the worse for me 2/34 [OE *wyrsa*]
wertes *n. pl.* plants 8/478 [OE *wyrt*]
wes *see* **be(n)**
wesche *pa. pl.* washed 10/333 [OE *wæscan*]
weste *v.* sink in the west 15/266 [from OE *west*]
wete *n.* moisture 10/321 [OE *wǣt*]
wex(en) *see* **wax(e)**
what, wat, whet, quat *adj. & pron.* what; whatever 5/467, 12/258; ~ . . . *so* whatever 9/384, **whatso, quatso** 8/243, 9/255 [OE *hwæt*, *swā-hwæt-swā*]
when, hwen, quen, wan, won *conj.* when 2/324, 4/18, 10/57, 13l/8 [OE *hwanne*, *hwænne*]
wheras *conj.* where 16b/121, 143 [OE *hwǣr* + *ealswā*]
where, quere *adv. & conj.* where, **war** 3/31, 133, **wær** 3/147; **where** wherever 9/100, 15/172 [OE *hwǣr*]
whereso *see* **warsæ**
wherof *adv.* about which 12/37 [OE *hwǣr* + *of*]
whet *see* **what**
whi, wi, hwi, quy *adv.* why 2/218, 268, 4/86, 10/186 [OE *hwī*]
whider *adv.* to where; ~ *so* wherever 5/340 [OE *hwider*]
whil(e), wile *adv.* formerly 2/202, 5/8, 13j/57, for a while 13g/35; *conj.* while 1/35, **quil** 10/215 [OE adv. *hwīle*, conj. *þā-hwīle-þe*]
whylen *adv.* formerly 13j/44, **whilom** once upon a time 16a/201 [OE *hwīl*, dat. pl. *hwīlum*]
whiles *n.* in *þe* ~ in the meantime 7b/6 [OE *hwīl*]
whilke *see* **whoche**
whittore *comp. adj.* whiter 13g/28 [from OE *hwīt*]
who, wo, qwo *pron.* who; ~ *that* whoever 12/256; **wham, hwam** *acc. & dat.* whom 5/128, 13j/8; ~ *se* anyone who 4/38 [OE *hwā* etc.]
whoche *pron.* which 11/15, **whilke** 14/292 [OE *hwylc*, *hwilc*]
whonene *adv.* whence 2/138 [OE *hwonan*]
whoso *pron.* whoever 15/410 [OE *swā hwā swā*]
wi *see* **whi**
wycked *adj.* vicious 13j/24 [? from OE *wicca*, 'wizard']
wyddered *pp.* withered 8/468 [? cf. OE *-widerian*]
wide *adv.* far off 2/288, far and wide 2/300 [OE *wīde*]
wydwe *n.* widow 16b/50 [OE *widewe*]
wyght *see* **wyht**
wigleð *pr. 3 sg.* staggers 4/61 [cf. MLG *wiggelen*]
wyȝe *n.* man, knight, (in address) sir; being 8/111, 206, anyone 8/356 [OE *wiga*]
wyȝt, wight *adj.* loud 9/119, strong, powerful 10/69, 14/199, 279; **wihtere** *gen. pl.* bold 3/125; **wighter** *comp.* stronger 14/201; **wyȝtest** *superl.* bravest 9/261 [ON *vígt*]
wyȝtly *adv.* vigorously 7b/18 [from prec.]
wyht, wight *n.* person 12/176, 15/221, 16a/83; **wiȝte** *pl.* creatures 2/87, 204 [OE *wiht*]
wyht *adv.* at once 13h/36 [ON *vígt*]
wykke *adj.* wicked 8/69 [? from OE *wicca* 'wizard']
wyl, wille *adj.* wandering 8/473; ~ *of* unsuccessful in 14/205 [ON *villr*]
wyldren *n.* desolate region 8/297 [? from OE *wild-dēor*]
wyle *n.*[1] cunning scheme 12/229, guile 13p/13, trick 16a/193; **wiles** *pl.* 12/190 [? AN **wile*]
wile *n.*[2] time 13p/16; *one* ~ for a while 2/199 [OE *hwīl*]
wile *see* **while**
wilful *adv.* deliberately 15/429 [cf. OE *wilful-līce*]
wille *n.* vigour 13h/15; *at* ~ in his power 8/130 [OE *willa*]
wille, wol(e), wulle(n) *pr. 1 & 3 sg.* (**ichil, ichulle** *1 sg.* + *pron.*; **wilte, wolt** *2 sg.*; **wiltow** *2 sg.* + *pron.*; **wule** *3 sg.*; **willen** *pl.*; **wolde** *pa.*; **walden** *pa. pl.*) will, shall; wish 8/83, 9/271, intend to 11/17 [OE *willan*]
wilnable *adj.* capable of being willed 6/52 [from OE *wilnian*]
wind(e) *n.* air 4/1, breath 14/204 [OE *wind*]

winde(n) *v.* approach furtively 3/98, embrace 15/671; **wounden** *pp.* bound around 9/215 [OE *windan*]
winiærd *n.* vineyard 1/71 [OE *wīngeard*]
wynke *pr. 1 sg.* sleep 15/7, 482 [OE *wincian*]
wyn(ne) *n.* joy 9/15, 130/1 [OE *wynn*]
wynne *v.* (**wan** *pa.*; **wonnen** *pa. pl.*; **wonnen, ywon** *pp.*) win 7b/105, 9/70, 13q/18, get 1/68, 13j/40, gain 10/301, produce 7b/18, stock up 7b/343, win over 12/194, reach 8/237, come 9/461; ~ *owy* win back 5/561, ~ *me* find my way 9/402 [OE *gewinnan*]
wintre *n. pl.* years 1/35, 55, 56 [OE *winter*]
wyrche *see* **wurche(n)**
wyrde *n.* fate 8/247 [OE *wyrd*]
wyrk *see* **wurche(n)**
wyse *n.* way, manner; fashion 7b/56, 10/77; *in none* ~ by no means 7b/328, *alle maner* ~ in every way 12/57, *any* ~ in any way 15/457 [OE *wīse*]
wisly *adv.* surely 15/117 [OE *wislīce*]
wysse *v.* instruct 8/60; **wissede** *pa.* directed 7b/162 [OE *wissian*]
wiste *see* **wit(e)**
wyt, wytte *n.* mind 8/74, wisdom 8/129, understanding 7b/59, 15/146, intelligence 11/55, 106, 149, advice 7b/55, clever talk 16a/47 [OE *wit*]
wit *pron.* we two 3/151, 152 [OE *wē*, dual *wit*]
wit *prep.* with 2/287, 301, against 2/56, 57 [OE *wiþ*]
wit(e), witte *v.*[1] (**wot, woet** *pr. 1 & 3 sg.*; **ichot** *1 sg. + pron.*; **wost** *2 sg.*; **wostu** *2 sg. + pron.*; **wite** *imp.* 12/52; **wiste, wuste(n)** *pa.*) know, learn; possess 2/195 [OE *witan*]
wite *v.*[2] keep 5/206; **wat** *pr. 3 sg.* defends 3/96 [OE *-wītian*]
wyter *adj.* wise 13g/26 [ON *vitr*]
witere *imp.* inform 10/185 [ON *vitra*]
wyterly, witterly *adv.* for certain 7a/37, 8/330, 10/183 [from ON *vitr*]
wiþ *prep.* with; by 5/538; ~ *þat* then 10/69 [OE *wiþ*]
wiþal *adv.* with that 12/51; *prep.* with 14/240 [OE *wiþ* + OE *eall*]
wyþer *v.* in ~ *wyth* resist 8/48 [OE *wiþerian*]
wyþerly *adv.* rebelliously 8/74 [from OE *wiþer*]
withoute(n), witute *prep.* without 2/183, 264, outside 13r/10; *adv.* 15/244 [OE *wiþūtan*]
withsitte *v.* oppose 7b/202 [OE *wiþ* + *sittan*]
wiðstonden *v.* resist 4/93 [OE *wiþstandan*]
witnesse *n.* testimony 12/161 [OE *witnes*]
wytte *see* **wyt**
witterly *see* **wyterly**
witute *see* **withoute(n)**
wleoteð *pr. pl.* gleam 3/109 [OE *wlitigian*]
wlyteþ *pr. pl.* warble 13h/11 [? cf. OE *writian*]
wlonk *adj.* luxuriant 8/486 [OE *wlonc*]
wo *n.* sorrow 8/256, 13h/8; *me is* ~ unhappy am I 5/331 [OE *wā*]
wo *see* **who**
wode *n.* woad 2/76 [OE *wād*]
wode, wood(e) *adj.* mad 5/394, 14/63, furious 6/12, 8/142; **wodder** *comp.* 8/162 [OE *wōd*]
wode-gore *n.* cover of the wood 13j/62 [OE *wudu* + *gāra*]
woderove *n.* woodruff (woodland plant) 13h/9 [OE *wudu-rofe*]
wodschip *n.* fury 8/403 [OE *wōdscipe*]
woet *see* **wit(e)**
woȝe *n.* evil 2/164, 198 [OE *wōh*]
wol *adv.* very 13m/6 [OE *wel*]
wol(e), wolde *see* **wille**
wolle *n.* wool 7b/12 [OE *wull*]
wombe *n.* belly, stomach [OE *womb*]
won *n.* place 8/69, dwelling 8/464, 9/257; **wones** *pl.* halls 5/365 [from OE *wunian* 'dwell']
won *see* **when, won(ne)**
wonder, wondir *n.* marvel 9/16, awful fact 14/130 [OE *wundor*]
wonder *adj.* marvellous 11/123; **wonder, wondir, wounder** *adv.* very, extraordinarily 5/104, 356, 401, extremely 13h/32, wonderfully 12/91, terribly 14/207 [from prec.]
wonderly(ch) *adv.* amazingly 8/384, absurdly 11/72 [OE *wundorlīce*]
wondres *pr. pl.* in *opon* ~ wonder at 10/125 [OE *wundrian*]
wone, wony, wunie *v.* (**wonyes** *pr. 2 sg.*; **wonez, wonnes** *3 sg.*; **woned(e)** *pa.*; **woned, wont** *pp.*) dwell 3/170, 10/279, 11/167, 13l/2, remain 6/180, 9/257, live 7a/1, 8/462, 9/50, exist 9/17; *pp.* accustomed 7b/164 [OE *wunian*]
wonges *n. pl.* cheeks 13g/23 [OE *wong*]
woning *n.* lamentation 2/311 [OE *wānung*]
won(ne) *adj.* dark 8/141, pale 13g/23 [OE *wonn*]
wonnen *see* **wynne**
wontreaðe *n.* misery 4/42 [ON *vandræði*]
wood(e) *see* **wode**
woot(t)e *see* **wotte**
worche *see* **wurche(n)**
worching *n.* activity 6/83, operation 15/5 [from OE *wyrcan*]
word(e) *n. pl.* words 2/180, 182, 4/31 [OE *word*]
worded *pp.* said 8/421 [from OE *word*]
wordynge *n.* words 7b/90 [from prec.]
wore *see* **be(n)**
worltlich *adj.* worldly 4/1 [OE *woroldlic*]
worp *see* **warpeð**

wors(c)hip(p)e *n.* honour [OE *weorþscipe*]
worshipe *v.* honour 16b/59 [from prec.]
worthe, wurðen *v.* (**worth** *pr. 3 sg.*; **worþed, warth** *pa.*; **worthyn** *pp.*) be; become 10/330, will be (pr. in fut. sense) 7b/160, befall 7a/98, come 8/360, come to pass 9/485; ~ *him* become for him 4/53, ~ *of* happen to 8/243 [OE *weorþan*]
worthily, worþilych, worþelych *adj.* worthy 7b/9, honoured 9/343, lovely 8/475; **worþloker** *comp.* finer 8/464; **worþyly** *adv.* with decorum 9/72, attractively 9/144 [from OE *weorþlic*, *weorþlīce*]
wost, wostu *see* **wit(e)**
wot *see* **wit(e), wotte**
woþe *n.* danger 9/222, 10/233 [ON *váði*]
wotte *v.* know 14/130; **wot(te)** *pr. pl.* 10/185, 14/261, **woot(t)e** 14/3, 157 [from OE *witan*, pa. *wāt* etc.]
wounden *see* **winden**
wounder *see* **wonder**
wowes *pr. pl.* woo 13h/19; **woweþ** 13h/31 [OE *wōgian*]
wowyng *n.* wooing 13g/31 [from prec.]
wræken *pr. pl. subj.* avenge 3/35, **wreken** 3/36 [OE *wrecan*]
wrake *n.* distress 9/16 [OE *wracu*]
wrakeful *adj.* vengeful 10/215 [from prec.]
wrang(e) *adj.* wrong 14/26, 182 [OE *wrang* from ON]
wrast *pr. pl.* tear 8/80 [OE *wrǣstan*]
wrastel *pr. pl.* wrestle 8/141 [OE **wrǣstlian*]
wrastelynge *vbl. n.* wrestling 15/165 [from prec.]
wrath *v.* be angry 8/431, 518; *refl.* in ~ *hym* become angry 7b/149; **wrathed** *pa.* 8/74 [cf. OE *wrǣþan*]
wreaðfule *adj. as n.* wrathful man 4/28 [from OE *wrǣþþu*]
wreccehed *n.* misery, poverty 1/43 [from next]
wrecc(h)e, wrech *adj.* miserable 2/335, poor, wretched 1/15, 34, 8/258 [OE *wrecca*]
wreken *see* **wræken**
wreker *n.* avenger 15/361 [from OE *wrecan*]
wrenche *n.* trickery 2/247 [OE *wrenc*]
wrenche *v.* twist 4/13; **wrencheð** *pr. 3 sg.* 4/20, 21 [OE *wrencan*]
wrie *v.* turn, go 14/182 [OE *wrīgian*]
write *v.* write; **wroot** *pa.* 16b/131; **write** *pp.* written 12/60, 15/19, **ywrite** 5/1, 11/32, **wretyn** 6/41, 106 [OE *wrītan*]
writelinge *n.* trilling, warbling 2/48 [from OE *writian*]
wriþ *pr. 3 sg.* covers 5/244 [OE *wrēon*]
wryþe *pr. pl.* torture 8/80; **wrythen** *pa. pl.* twisted 1/23 [OE *wrīþan*]
wroche *n.* wretch 5/333 [OE *wrecca*]
wroght(yn), wroȝt, wrohte *see* **wurche(n)**
wronge *pa.* wrung 7b/172 [OE *wringan*]
wroot *see* **write**
wrote *v.* grub in earth 5/255; **wrot** *pa.* dug 8/467 [OE *wrōtan*]
wroþ(e) *adj.* angry; **wroþer** *comp.* 8/162 [OE *wrāþ*]
wroþely *adv.* angrily 8/132; **wroþeloker** *comp.* 8/132 [OE *wrāþlīce*]
wrought, wrouȝt, wrouhte, wrouthte *see* **wurche(n)**
wule, wulle(n) *see* **wille**
wunder *n.* a marvel 2/361; **wunder** *pl.* atrocities 1/34 [OE *wundor*]
wunder *adv.* in ~ *ane* wondrously 3/131, 165 [from prec.]
wunderlice *adj.* wonderful 1/81; **wunderliche** *adv.* gloriously 3/35 [OE *wundorlīce*]
wundri *pr. 1 sg.* in ~ *þarof* wonder at that 2/228 [OE *wundrian*]
wunie *see* **wone**
wunne *adj.* blissful 13h/35 [from OE *wynn*]
wurche(n), worch(e), wyrche, wyrk *v.* (**worching** *pr. p.*; **wroȝt(en), wroghtyn, wrouhte(n), wrohte, wrouthte, wurhte** *pa.*; **iworht, wrouȝt, wro(u)ght, ywro(w)ght** *pp.*) perform, carry out 4/74, 6/1, 8/136, 9/3, 12/215, make 3/15, 5/13, 8/206, 9/399, cause 13q/2, do 9/238, 10/301, 12/217, 14/261, act 14/34, work, be active 6/5, 45, 7a/23, 7b/80, work at 7b/6, do (building) work 1/59, fashion 15/305 [OE *wyrcan*, *wircan*]
wurs *see* **wers(e)**
wurðen *see* **worthe**
wurtscipe *n.* ceremony 1/61 [OE *weorþscipe*]
wuste(n) *see* **wit(e)**

yaf(e) *see* **ȝive**
ye *adv.* yea, yes indeed [OE *gē*]
yerde *n.* in *under youre* ~ subject to you 15/640 [OE *gerd*]
yerne *adv.* rapidly 15/3; eagerly 15/21 [OE *georne*]
yet *adv.* still 16b/188 [OE *gēt*]
yeve *see* **ȝive**
yexeth *pr. 3 sg.* belches 16a/297 [OE *geocsian*]
yo(o)re *adv.* (for) a long time 15/17, 476; *ful* ~ very long ago 16a/43, for a very long time 16a/376 [OE *geāra*]